THE MEANING OF DIFFERENCE

THE MEANING OF DIFFERENCE

American Constructions of Race, Sex and Gender, Social Class, Sexual Orientation, and Disability

Fifth Edition

Karen E. Rosenblum
George Mason University

Toni-Michelle C. Travis
George Mason University

Boston   Burr Ridge, IL   Dubuque, IA   Madison, WI   New York   San Francisco   St. Louis
Bangkok   Bogotá   Caracas   Kuala Lumpur   Lisbon   London   Madrid   Mexico City
Milan   Montreal   New Delhi   Santiago   Seoul   Singapore   Sydney   Taipei   Toronto

Mc Graw Hill **Higher Education**

Published by McGraw-Hill, an imprint of The McGraw-Hill Companies, Inc., 1221 Avenue of the Americas, New York, NY 10020. Copyright © 2008, 2006, 2003, 2000, 1996. All rights reserved. No part of this publication may be reproduced or distributed in any form or by any means, or stored in a database or retrieval system, without the prior written consent of The McGraw-Hill Companies, Inc., including, but not limited to, in any network or other electronic storage or transmission, or broadcast for distance learning.

This book is printed on acid-free paper.

1 2 3 4 5 6 7 8 9 0 DOC / DOC 0 9 8

ISBN: 978-0-07-338005-6
MHID: 0-07-338005-9

Editor in Chief: *Michael Ryan*
Publisher: *Frank Mortimer*
Sponsoring Editor: *Gina Boedeker*
Marketing Manager: *Leslie Oberhuber*
Project Manager: *Paul Wells*
Production Service: *Scratchgravel Publishing Services*
Manuscript Editor: *Tricia Lawrence*
Design Manager: *Margarite Reynolds*
Text Designer: *Kay Lieberherr*
Cover Designer: *Margarite Reynolds*
Photo Research: *Sonia Brown*
Production Supervisor: *Richard DeVitto*
Composition: *International Typesetting and Composition, Inc.*
Printing: *45# New Era Matte Plus, R. R. Donnelley & Sons/Crawfordsville, IN*

Cover: © 1997 Artville, LLC

Library of Congress Cataloging-in-Publication Data
The meaning of difference : American constructions of race, sex and gender, social class, sexual
    orientation, and disability / Karen Rosenblum, Toni-Michelle Travis [editors].—5th ed.
        p. cm.
    Includes index.
    ISBN-13: 978-0-07-338005-6 (alk. paper)
    ISBN-10: 0-07-338005-9 (alk. paper)
    1. United States—Social conditions—1980- 2. Pluralism (Social sciences)—United States.
I. Rosenblum, Karen Elaine. II. Travis, Toni-Michelle, 1947-
HN59.2.M44 2008
306.0973—dc22
                                                                        2007050974

The Internet addresses listed in the text were accurate at the time of publication. The inclusion of a Web site does not indicate an endorsement by the authors or McGraw-Hill, and McGraw-Hill does not guarantee the accuracy of the information presented at these sites.

www.mhhe.com

ABOUT THE AUTHORS

KAREN E. ROSENBLUM is associate professor of sociology at George Mason University in Fairfax, Virginia. She has served as the university's Vice President for University Life and as director of the Women's Studies Program. In addition, she was a Fulbright Lecturer in Japan. Professor Rosenblum received her Ph.D. in sociology from the University of Colorado, Boulder. Her areas of research and teaching include sex and gender, language, and deviance.

TONI-MICHELLE C. TRAVIS is associate professor of government and politics at George Mason University in Fairfax, Virginia. She is a faculty member in Women's Studies and African American Studies. Professor Travis received her Ph.D. in political science from the University of Chicago. Her areas of research and teaching include race and gender dimensions of political participation, urban politics, and American government. She has served as the president of the National Capital Area Political Science Association and the Women's Caucus of the American Political Science Association. A political analyst, she is a frequent commentator on Virginia and national politics.

CONTENTS

SECTION II—EXPERIENCING DIFFERENCE

SECTION III—THE MEANING OF DIFFERENCE

PREFACE

The Meaning of Difference is an effort to understand how *difference* is constructed in contemporary American culture: How do categories of people come to be seen as "different"? How does being "different" affect people's lives? What does difference mean at the level of the individual, social institution, or society? What difference does "difference" make? Focusing on the most significant categories of difference in America—race, sex/gender, sexual orientation, social class, and disability—what is *shared* across these categories? What can be learned from their commonalities? That *The Meaning of Difference* is now in its fifth edition makes us hopeful that this comparative approach can be useful in understanding American conceptions and constructions of difference.

ORGANIZATION AND CONCEPTUAL FRAMEWORK

The Meaning of Difference is divided into four sections. Each section includes an opening Framework Essay and a set of readings, with the Framework Essay providing the conceptual structure by which to understand the readings. Thus, the Framework Essays are not simply introductions to the readings; they are the "text" portion of this **text/reader.**

The first section's Framework Essay and readings describe how categories of difference are *created;* the second considers the *experience* of difference; the third examines the intersections of difference and the *meanings* that are assigned to difference by law, public policy, the economy, and language; and the fourth describes what people can do to *challenge and change these constructions* of difference.

Each of the readings included in the volume has been selected by virtue of its applicability to multiple categories of difference. For example, F. James Davis's conclusions about the construction of race (Reading 2), could be applied to a discussion of sexual identity or disability. How much of "x" does it take to locate someone as gay or straight, disabled or nondisabled? Beverly Daniel Tatum's discussion of the development of racial identity (Reading 25) inevitably makes us think about the development of all the other identities so important to people's lives. Similarly, Suzanne Kessler and Wendy McKenna's exploration of the persistence of gender categories (Reading 11) could easily be extended to a consideration of race and ethnic categories. In all, our aim has been to select readings that help identify both what is unique and what is shared across our experiences of difference.

DISTINGUISHING FEATURES

Five features make *The Meaning of Difference* distinctive:

- First, it offers a conceptual framework by which to understand the commonalities among these categories of difference. This encompassing conceptual approach makes *The Meaning of Difference* unique.
- Second, no other book provides an accessible and historically grounded discussion of the Supreme Court decisions critical to the creation of these differences.
- Third, *The Meaning of Difference* has been designed with an eye toward the pedagogic difficulties that often accompany this subject matter. Our experience has been that when the topic is *simultaneously* race, sex and gender, social class, sexual orientation, and disability no one group can be easily cast as victim or victimizer.
- Fourth, no other volume includes a detailed discussion and set of readings on how to challenge and change the constructions of difference.
- Finally, *The Meaning of Difference* is the first book of its kind to incorporate disability as a master status functioning in ways analogous to the operation of race and ethnicity, sex, sexual orientation, and social class.

CHANGES IN THE FIFTH EDITION

The fifth edition includes thirty-one new readings, four new personal accounts, and a section devoted to intersectionality. This edition incorporates disability throughout.
   Many new and important topics are covered in the readings, including:

- The impact of immigration on America's race and ethnic categories (Reading 7)
- Changing American color lines (Reading 7)
- The relationship between disability and diversity (Reading 22)
- What Hurricane Katrina revealed about American racial stereotypes (Reading 29)
- The widening American income gap and its repercussions for health and mortality (Readings 14 and 37)
- The evolving experience of those of Middle Eastern descent (Readings 26 and 32)
- The changing nature of the closet for people who are gay and lesbian (Reading 33)
- The experience of transracial adoption (Reading 28)
- New understandings of women's sexuality and sexual orientation (Readings 18 and 34)

- Intersectionality (Readings 43, 44, and 48)
- How people talk about race as a way to bridge boundaries (Reading 57)
- Whether it is time for all sexual identity categories to disappear (Reading 19)
- The Cold War impetus behind America's minority rights revolution (Reading 50)
- The 2003 Supreme Court decision on disabled people's access to public buildings (Reading 49)
- Life as a low-wage worker (Reading 36)
- How those with privilege and power can be allies to those facing discrimination (Readings 58, 59, 60, 61, and 62)
- The nature and consequences of the myth of Asian Americans as the model minority (Reading 52)
- The impact of race on Latino identities (Readings 24 and 47)
- Determining who is "really" a Native American (Reading 4)
- How to pursue everyday activism (Readings 58 and 59)
- Racial identity development in adolescence (Reading 25)
- Trying to get around if you are disabled: cabs and mass transit experiences (Reading 40)

HIGHLIGHTS IN THE FIFTH EDITION

Several readings from the previous edition have been retained not only because of their wide popularity among students and faculty, but also because they have become classics in the field. Foremost in this category is F. James Davis's, "Who Is Black? One Nation's Definition." "Whiteness as an 'Unmarked' Cultural Category" by Ruth Frankenberg, "Disability Definitions" by Michael Oliver, and "Can You See the Rainbow?" by Sally French hold this rank as well.

Among readings new to this edition, several are unequivocal classics. These include "White Privilege: Unpacking the Invisible Knapsack" by Peggy McIntosh, "It's All in the Family: Intersections of Gender, Race, and Nation" by Patricia Hill Collins, "'Race' and the Construction of Human Identity" by Audrey Smedley, and "The Heterosexual Questionnaire" by Martin Rochlin.

Certainly, John Larew's "Why Are Droves of Unqualified, Unprepared Kids Getting into Our Top Colleges?" has been eye-opening for students trying to understand affirmative action policies. We expect that Brian Fitzgerald's, "The Opportunity for a College Education," will be equally educational about the impact of social class on college attendance. Laurel Richardson accomplishes the same for gender in her article, "Gender Stereotyping in the English Language."

Every section of this edition also includes new readings, and some sections have been entirely revised. There are several new readings that we think have the potential to become classics: "'We Are All Americans': The Latin Americanization of Race Relations in the United States" by Eduardo Bonilla-Silva and Karen Glover, "Who Put the 'Trans' in Transgender?" by Suzanne Kessler and Wendy McKenna, authors of the landmark volume *Gender: An Ethnomethodological Approach* (1978), and "The Pressure to Cover" by Yale law professor Kenji Yoshino.

SUPPLEMENTS

Instructor's Manual/Test Bank

Jamey Piland, a colleague at Trinity College in Washington, D.C., has used *The Meaning of Difference* in several interdisciplinary courses and, from that experience, has produced an Instructor's Manual that focuses especially on how to teach this material. Few instructors have had the experience of teaching *all* of these topics—let alone all of them in a single course—as Professor Piland has.

The Test Bank, developed by Susan Weldon of Eastern Michigan University, includes multiple-choice and true-false questions for the Framework Essays and each of the readings.

Jonathan M. Bullinger at California State University Northridge did an excellent job revising both Jamey Piland's and Susan Weldon's work for this new edition.

ACKNOWLEDGMENTS

Many colleagues and friends have helped us clarify the ideas we present here. David Haines has been unfailing in his willingness to help Karen think through conceptual, technical, and ethical dilemmas. She could not imagine a colleague more supportive or wise. Theodore W. Travis provided insight on Supreme Court decisions, their relationship to social values, and their impact on American society. As always, this edition has benefited enormously from the comments of our colleagues at George Mason. Since this project first emerged over a decade ago, Victoria Rader has been generous in sharing her insights as a teacher and writer. Her wisdom especially guided our development of the "Bridging Differences" section. We are especially grateful to our colleague and friend Beth Omansky for helping us understand the critical relationship of disability to our work. This edition—with disability as a core topic—is the product of a journey that she helped us make. Two other colleagues—Rose Pascarell and Jamey Piland—are owed special thanks both for their feedback and the good work they accomplish with students. As a friend and friendly editor, none could be better than Sheila Barrows. Finally, we owe thanks to our students at George Mason University for sharing their experiences with us and to Jennifer Flynn-Gollob for her assistance in preparation of the manuscript.

For this edition, we again convey our appreciation to Joan Lester and the Equity Institute of Emeryville, California, for their understanding of the progress that can be made through a holistic analysis.

Gina Boedeker of McGraw-Hill shepherded this volume to completion. As in previous editions, McGraw-Hill proved itself committed to a thorough review process by putting together a panel of accomplished scholars with broad expertise. All offered detailed, insightful, and invaluable critiques, and we are much in their debt:

Denise Dalaimo, California State University, San Marcos

Diana Hayes, Georgetown University

Simona Hill, Susquehanna University

Roberto Ibarra, University of New Mexico, Albuquerque

Ime Kerlee, University of New Mexico, Albuquerque
Robert Lophovsky, Asheville-Buncombe Technical Community College
Marcus J. Maier, Chapman University
Mecktihid Nagel, State University of New York, Cortland
Sarah Shia, Washington University, St. Louis

Karen Rosenblum
Toni-Michelle Travis
George Mason University

THE MEANING OF DIFFERENCE

CONSTRUCTING CATEGORIES OF DIFFERENCE

FRAMEWORK ESSAY

This book considers how *difference* is constructed in contemporary American society. It explores how categories of people are seen as significantly different from one another and how people's lives are affected by these conceptions of difference. The four sections of this book have been organized around what we consider to be the key questions about difference: how it is constructed, how it is experienced by individuals, how meaning is attributed to difference, and how differences can be bridged.

We believe that race, sex, social class, sexual orientation, and disability are currently the primary axes of difference in American society—they are also what social scientists would call *master statuses*. In common usage, the term *status* means prestige or esteem. But for social scientists, the term describes positions in a social structure. In this sense, statuses are like empty slots (or positions) that individuals fill. The most obvious kinds of statuses are kinship and occupational; for example, uncle, mother-in-law, cousin, office manager, paramedic, disk jockey. At any point in time, an individual holds multiple statuses—kinship, occupational, religious—as well as race, sex, social class, sexual orientation, and disability statuses.

This latter set of statuses—the ones we focus on in this book—are significantly more powerful than most other social statuses. Social scientists refer to these as *master* statuses because they so profoundly affect a person's life. The *Oxford Dictionary of Sociology* defines *master statuses* as those that "in most or all social situations will overpower or dominate all other statuses. . . . Master status influences every other aspect of life, including personal identity" (Marshall, 1994:315). This does not mean, however, that people always understand the impact of the master statuses they occupy—indeed much of this book is about recognizing that impact.

This text will explore similarities in the operation of these master statuses. While there are certainly differences of history, experience, and impact, we believe that similar processes are at work when we "see" differences of color, sex and gender, social class, sexual orientation, and disability, and we believe that there are similarities in the consequences of these master statuses for individuals' lives.

In preparing this volume, we noticed that talk about racism, sexism, homophobia,[1] and class status seemed to be everywhere—film, music, news reports, talk shows, sermons, and scholarly publications—and that the topics carried considerable intensity. These are controversial subjects; thus, readers may have strong reactions to these issues. Two perspectives—essentialism and constructionism—are core to this book and should help you understand your own reaction to the material.

---

[1]The term *homophobia* was coined in 1971 by psychologist George Weinberg to describe an irrational fear of, or anger toward, homosexuals. While the psychological application has disappeared, the word remains in common use to describe a strong opposition to or rejection of same-sex relationships. Two alternative words are emerging: *antigay* and *heterosexism*. Heterosexism is the presumption that all people are heterosexual and that heterosexuality is the only acceptable form of sexual expression.

The Essentialist and Constructionist Orientations

The difference between the *constructionist* and *essentialist* orientations is illustrated in the tale of the three umpires, first apparently told by social psychologist Hadley Cantril:

> Hadley Cantril relates the story of three baseball umpires discussing their profession. The first umpire said, "Some are balls and some are strikes, and I call them as they are." The second replied, "Some's balls and some's strikes, and I call 'em as I sees 'em." The third thought about it and said, "Some's balls and some's strikes, but they ain't nothing 'till I calls 'em." (Henshel and Silverman, 1975:26)

The first umpire in the story can be described as an essentialist. In arguing that "I call them as they are," he indicates his assumption that balls and strikes are entities that exist in the world independently of his perception of them. For this umpire, balls and strikes are easily identified, and he is merely a neutral observer of them. This umpire "regards knowledge as objective and independent of mind, and himself as the impartial reporter of things 'as they are'" (Pfuhl, 1986:5). For this essentialist umpire, balls and strikes exist in the world; he simply observes their presence.

Thus, the essentialist orientation presumes that items in a category all share some "essential" quality, their "ball-ness" or "strike-ness." For essentialists, the categories of *race, sex, sexual orientation,* and *social class* identify significant, empirically verifiable differences among people. From the essentialist perspective, racial categories exist apart from any social processes; they are objective categories of real difference among people.

The second umpire is somewhat removed from pure essentialism. His statement, "I call 'em as I sees 'em," conveys the belief that while an independent, objective reality exists, it is subject to interpretation. For him the world contains balls and strikes, but individuals may have different perceptions about which is which.

The third umpire, who says "they ain't nothing 'till I calls 'em," is a constructionist. He operates from the belief that "conceptions such as 'strikes' and 'balls' have no meaning except that given them by the observer" (Pfuhl, 1986:5). For this constructionist umpire, reality cannot be separated from the way a culture makes sense of it; strikes and balls do not exist until they are constructed through social processes. From this perspective, difference is created rather than intrinsic to a phenomenon. Social processes, such as those in political, legal, economic, scientific, and religious institutions, create differences, determine that some differences are more important than others, and assign particular meanings to those differences. From this perspective, the way a society defines difference among its members tells us more about that society than the people so classified. *The Meaning of Difference* operates from the constructionist perspective, since it examines how we have arrived at our race, sex, disability, sexual orientation, and social class categories.

Few of us have grown up as constructionists. More likely, we are essentialists who believe that master statuses such as race or sex entail clear-cut, unchanging, and in some way meaningful differences. Still, not everyone is an essentialist. Those from mixed racial or religious backgrounds are familiar with the ways in which identity is not clear-cut. They grow up understanding how definitions of self vary with the context; how others try to define one as belonging in a particular category; and how, in many ways, one's very presence calls prevailing classification systems into question. For example, the experience Jelita McLeod describes in Reading 27 of being asked "What are you?" is a common experience for biracial people. Such experiences make evident the social constructedness of racial identity.

Most of us are unlikely to be exclusively essentialist or constructionist. As authors we take the constructionist perspective, but we have still relied on essentialist terms we find problematic. The irony of questioning the idea of race but still talking about "blacks," "whites," and "Asians," or of rejecting a dualistic approach to sexual identity while still using the terms *gay* and *straight,* has not escaped us. Indeed, throughout our discussion we have used the currently favored essentialist phrase *sexual orientation* over the more constructionist *sexual preference.*[2]

Further, there is a serious risk that a text such as this falsely identifies people on the basis of *either* their sex, race, sexual orientation, disability, or social class, despite the fact that master statuses are not parts of a person that can be broken off from one another like the segments of a Tootsie Roll (Spelman, 1988). All of us are always *simultaneously* all of our master statuses, an idea encompassed by the concept of *intersectionality,* which highlights the fact that these statuses inevitably interact with one another. As Patricia Hills Collins describes it in Reading 43, "As opposed to examining gender, race, class, and nation, as separate systems of oppression, intersectionality explores how these systems mutually construct one another, . . . [how] certain ideas and practices surface repeatedly across multiple systems of oppression." Thus, while the readings in this section may make it seem as if these were separable statuses, they are not. Indeed, even the concept of master status could mislead us into thinking that there could be only one dominating status in one's life.

Both constructionism and essentialism can be found in the social sciences. Indeed, essentialism has been the basis of probability theory and statistics (Hilts, 1973), and it forms the bedrock for most social scientific research. Both perspectives also are evident in social movements, and those movements sometimes shift from one perspective to the other over time. For example, some feminists and most of those opposed to feminism have held the essentialist belief that women and men are inherently different. The constructionist view that sexual identity is chosen dominated the gay rights movement of the 1970s (Faderman, 1991), but today most members of that movement take the essentialist approach that sexual identity is something one is born with. By contrast, some of those opposed to gay relationships now take the constructionist view that it is chosen. In this case, language often signals which perspective is being used. For example, sexual *preference* conveys active, human decision making with the possibility of change (constructionism), while sexual *orientation* implies something fixed and inherent to a person (essentialism). As evidence that an essentialist approach to sexual identity is becoming more prevalent, Gallup polls show that an increasing percentage of Americans believe homosexuality is a genetic

---

[2]The term *sexual identity* seems now to be replacing *sexual orientation.* It could be used in either an essentialist or a constructionist way.

trait. In 1977, 13 percent indicated they believed that to be the case; in 2004, 37 percent agreed with that statement (Moore, 2004).

This example from journalist Darryl Rist shows the appeal essentialist explanations might have for gay rights activists:

> [Chris Yates's parents were] Pentecostal ministers who had tortured his adolescence with Christian cures for sexual perversity. Shock and aversion therapies under born-again doctors and gruesome exorcisms of sexual demons by spirit-filled preachers had culminated in a plan to have him castrated by a Mexican surgeon who touted the procedure as a way to make the boy, if not straight, at least sexless. Only then had the terrified son rebelled.
>
> Then, in the summer of 1991, the journal *Science* reported anatomical differences between the brains of homosexual and heterosexual men. . . . The euphoric media—those great purveyors of cultural myths—drove the story wildly. Every major paper in the country headlined the discovery smack on the front page. . . . Like many others, I suspect, Chris Yates's family saw in this newly reported sexual science a way out of its wrenching impasse. After years of virtual silence between them and their son, Chris's parents drove several hundred miles to visit him and ask for reconciliation. Whatever faded guilt they might have felt for the family's faulty genes was nothing next to the reassurance that neither by a perverse upbringing nor by his own iniquity was Chris or the family culpable for his urges and actions. "We could never have condoned this if you could do something to change it. But when we finally understood that you were *born* that way, we knew we'd been wrong. We had to ask your forgiveness." (Rist, 1992:425–26)

Understandably, those under attack would find essentialist orientations appealing, just as the expansiveness of constructionist approaches would be appealing in more tolerant eras. Still, either perspective can be used to justify discrimination, since people can be persecuted for the choices they make as well as for their genetic inheritance.

Our discussion of disability as a social construction may generate an intense reaction—many will want to argue that disability is about physical, sensory, or cognitive differences, not social constructs. However, we are working from what is called the "social model" of disability (Oliver, 1990, 1996; Higgins, 1992; Linton, 1999; Barnes and Mercer, 2003), which contends that disability is created by social, political, and environmental obstructions—that social processes make people's impairments into "disabilities." For example, John Hockenberry (Reading 40) and Charles Wilson (Reading 54) describe how mass transit systems that are inaccessible to wheelchair users "disable" them by making it difficult or impossible to work, attend school, or manage basic sociability. Beyond that, however, disability is also constructed through cultural stereotypes and everyday interactions in which difference is defined as undesirable. We once heard a student with spina bifida tell a story addressing this point: In her first day at school, other students kept asking what was "wrong" with her. As she put it, she had always known she was different, but she hadn't thought she was "wrong."

Not only can disability be understood as the result of disabling environments and cultural stereotypes, but the categories of impairment and disability are also themselves socially constructed through medical and legal processes. "Epilepsy, illness, disease, and disability are not 'givens' in nature . . . but rather *socially constructed* categories that emerge from the interpretive activities of people acting together in social situations" (Schneider, 1988:65). Learning disabilities are an example of this process.

> Before the late 1800s when observers began to write about "word blindness," learning disability (whatever its name) did not exist, although the human variation to which it ambiguously refers did—sort of! People who today might be known as learning disabled may have formerly been known as "slow," "retarded," or "odd." But mostly they would not have been known as unusual at all. The learning difficulties experienced today by learning disabled youth have not been experienced by most youth throughout history. For example, most youth have not been asked to learn to read. Thus, they could not experience any reading difficulties, the most common learning disability. As we have expected youth to learn to read and have tried to teach them to do so, many youth have experienced difficulty. However, until the mid-1960s we typically did not understand those difficulties as the consequences of a learning disability. (Higgins, 1992:53)

The social model of disability first emerged out of the disabled people's movement in the 1970s in opposition to the "medical model," which approached disability as a matter of individual deficiencies or defects, rather than societal responses. From the perspective of the medical model, individuals have problems that need to be treated by medical specialists; from that of the social model, individual problems are the result of social structures that need to be changed. Thus, for adherents of the social model the important questions are about civil rights such as equal access. The survey questions posed by Mike Oliver in Reading 21 show how the world is perceived differently from these two perspectives.

Why have we spent so much time describing the essentialist and constructionist perspectives? Discussions about race, sex, disability, sexual orientation, and social class generate great intensity partly because they involve the clash of essentialist and constructionist assumptions. Essentialists are likely to view categories of people as "essentially" different in some important way; constructionists are likely to see these differences as socially created and arbitrary. An essentialist asks what causes people to be different; a constructionist asks about the origin and consequence of the categorization system itself. While arguments about the nature and cause of racism, sexism, homophobia, and poverty are disputes about power and justice, from the perspectives of essentialism and constructionism they are also disputes about what differences in color, sexuality, and social class *mean.*

The constructionist approach has one clear advantage, however. It is from that perspective that one understands that all this talk has a profound significance. Such talk is not simply *about* difference; it is itself the *creation* of difference. In the sections that follow, we examine how categories of people are named, dichotomized, and stigmatized—all toward the construction of difference.

Naming

Difference is constructed first by naming categories of people. Therefore, constructionists pay special attention to the names people use to refer to themselves and others—the times at which new names are asserted, the negotiations that surround the use of particular names, and those occasions when people are grouped together or separated out.

Asserting a Name   Both individuals and categories of people face similar issues in the assertion of a name. A change of name involves, to some extent, the claim of a new identity. For example, one of our colleagues wanted to be called by her full first name rather than by its shortened version because that had come to seem childish to her. It took a few times to remind people that this was her new name, and with most that was adequate. One colleague, however, argued that he could not adapt to the new name; she would just have to tolerate his continued use of the nickname. This was a small but public battle about who had the power to name whom. Did she have the power to enforce her own naming, or did he have the power to name her despite her wishes? Eventually, she prevailed.

A more disturbing example was a young woman who wanted to keep her "maiden" name after she married. Her fiancé agreed with her decision, recognizing that he would be reluctant to give up his name were the tables turned. When his mother heard of this possibility, however, she was outraged. In her mind, a rejection of her family's name was a rejection of her family. She urged her son to reconsider getting married.

Thus, asserting a name can create social conflict. On both a personal and societal level, naming can involve the claim of a particular identity and the rejection of others' power to impose a name. For example, is one Native American, American Indian, or Sioux; African American or black; girl or woman; Asian, Asian American, Korean, or Korean American; gay or homosexual; Chicano, Mexican American, Mexican, Latino, or Hispanic? And

> [j]ust who is Hispanic? The answer depends on whom you ask.
>
> The label was actually coined in the mid-1970s by federal bureaucrats working under President Richard M. Nixon. They came up with it in response to concerns that the government was wrongly applying "Chicano" to people who were not of Mexican descent, and otherwise misidentifying and underserving segments of the population by generally classifying those with ancestral ties to the Spanish cultural diaspora as either Chicano, Cuban, or Puerto Rican.
>
> Nearly three decades later, the debate continues to surround the term Hispanic and its definition. Although mainly applied to people from Latin American countries with linguistic and cultural ties to Spain, it also is used by the U.S. government to refer to Spaniards themselves, as well as people from Portuguese-speaking Brazil.
>
> Especially on college campuses, a sizable and growing minority of people prefer "Latino," which does not have the same association with Spanish imperialism. That term is controversial as well, however, mainly because it stems from the term Latin America and wrongly implies ties to ancient Rome. (Schmidt, 2003)

Deciding what name to use for a category of people is not easy. It is unlikely that all members of the category use the same name; the name members use for one another may not be acceptable for outsiders to use; nor is it always advisable to ask what name a person prefers. We once saw an old friend become quite angry when asked whether he preferred the term *black* or *African American*. "Either one is fine with me," he replied, "*I* know what *I* am." To him, the question meant that he was being seen as a member of a category, not as an individual.

Because naming may involve a redefinition of self, an assertion of power, and a rejection of others' ability to impose an identity, social change movements often claim a new name, while opponents may express opposition by continuing to use the old name. For example, *black* emerged in opposition to *Negro* as the Black Power movement sought to distinguish itself from the Martin Luther King–led moderate wing of the civil rights movement. The term *Negro* had itself been put forward by influential leaders such as W. E. B. Du Bois and Booker T. Washington as a rejection of the term *colored* that had dominated the mid- to late 19th century. "[D]espite its association with racial epithets, 'Negro' was defined to stand for a new way of thinking about Blacks" (Smith, 1992:497–98). Similarly, in 1988 Ramona H. Edelin, president of the National Urban Coalition, proposed that *African American* be substituted for *black*. Now both terms are about equally in use (Smith, 1992; Gallup, 2003).[3] Ironically, *colored people* used to be a derogatory reference to African Americans, but *people of color* is now a common reference to all nonwhites.

Each of these name changes—from *Negro* to *black* to *African American*—was first promoted by activists as a way to demonstrate their commitment to a new order. A similar theme is reflected in the history of the terms *Chicano* and *Chicanismo*. Although the origin of the terms is unclear, the principle was the same. As reporter Ruben Salazar wrote in the 1960s, "a Chicano is a Mexican-American with a non-Anglo image of himself" (Shorris, 1992:101). (*Anglo* is a colloquialism for *white* used in the southwestern and western United States.)

Similarly, the term *homosexual* was first coined in 1896 by a Hungarian physician hoping to decriminalize same-sex relations between men. It was incorporated into the medical and psychological literature of the time, which depicted nonprocreative sex as pathological. Sixty years later, activists rejected the pathological characterization and the name associated with it and began substituting *gay* for *homosexual*. Presently *gay* is used both as a generic term encompassing men and women and as a specific reference to men.[4] The 1990s activist group, Queer Nation, may have started a rejection of the word, however, with its name and slogan: "We're here. We're queer. Get used to it." Once an epithet, *queer* now seems to be on its way toward acceptability, if only as demonstrated in the success of the cable television show, *Queer Eye for the Straight Guy*.

Just as each of these social movements has involved a public renaming that proclaims pride, the women's movement has asserted *woman* as a replacement for *girl*. A student who described a running feud with her roommate illustrates the significance of these two terms. The student preferred the word *woman*, arguing that the word *girl* when applied to females past adolescence was insulting. Her female roommate just

---

[3]Thus, one can find Black Studies, Afro-American Studies, and African American Studies programs in universities across the country.
[4]In the 17th century, *gay* became associated with an addiction to social pleasure, dissipation, and loose morality, and was used to refer to female prostitutes (e.g., *gay girl*). The term was apparently first used in reference to homosexuality in 1925 in Australia. "It may have been both the connotations of femininity and those of immorality that led American homosexuals to adopt the title 'gay' with some self-irony in the 1920s. The slogan 'Glad to Be Gay,' adopted by both female and male homosexuals, and the naming of the Gay Liberation Front, which was born from the Stonewall resistance riots following police raids on homosexual bars in New York in 1969, bear witness to a greater self-confidence" (Mills, 1989:102).

as strongly preferred the term *girl* and regularly applied it to the females she knew. Each of them had such strong feelings on the matter that it was apparent they would not last as roommates.

How could these two words destroy their relationship? It appears that English speakers use the terms *girl* and *woman* to refer to quite different qualities. *Woman,* like *man,* is understood to convey adulthood, power, and sexuality; *girl,* like *boy,* connotes youth, powerlessness, and irresponsibility (Richardson, 1988). Thus, the two roommates were asserting quite different places for themselves in the world. One claimed adulthood; the other saw herself as not having achieved that yet. This is the explanation offered by many females: It is not so much that they like being *girls,* as that they value youth and/or do not yet feel justified in calling themselves women. Yet this is precisely the identity the women's movement has asserted: "We cannot be girls anymore, we must be women."

As each of these cases shows, different categories of people may claim a wide range of names for themselves. A name may reflect the analysis and aspirations of a unified social movement, or it may be the battleground for competing conceptions of the world. The name invoked by movement activists may have no immediate bearing on what people in the streets say, or everyday language may come to be shaped by policymakers external to the social movement. Sometimes, a variety of names may be in use—each with a constituency that feels strongly that only some words are appropriate.

Of all the master statuses we are considering in this book, the naming of those with disabilities is perhaps the least settled, as Simi Linton discusses in Reading 56. The term *handicapped,* which predominated in the period following World War II, shifted to *disabled* with the emergence of the disability rights movement in the 1970s. Theorists from the social model draw a distinction between *impairment,* referring to the "the physical, cognitive, emotional or sensory condition within the person as diagnosed by medical professionals," and *disability,* which is reserved for the social processes that disable a person (Omansky, 2006:27)—but the U.S. disability rights movement uses *disability* to cover both of these features. The style guide for the American Psychological Association urges a "people first" approach, as in "people with disabilities" rather than "disabled people," and "people first" terminology has been formally authorized by some state and local governments. By contrast, one of the founders of the British disability rights movement—Mike Oliver—argued that *disabled people* is ultimately more appropriate:

> It is sometimes argued, often by [nondisabled] professionals and some disabled people, that 'people with disabilities' is the preferred term, for it asserts the value of the person first and the disability then becomes an appendage. This liberal and humanist view flies in the face of reality as it is experienced by disabled people themselves who argue that far from being an appendage, disability is an essential part of the self. In this view, it is nonsensical to talk about the person and the disability separately and consequently disabled people are demanding acceptance as they are, disabled people. (Oliver, 1990:xiii)

In all, the names that we call ourselves and others are rarely a matter of indifference; they are often carefully chosen to reflect worldview and aspirations, and they can also materially shape our lives.

Creating Categories of People   While individuals and groups may assert names for themselves, governments also have the power to create categories of people. The history of the race and ethnicity questions asked in the U.S. census illustrates this process.

Every census since the first one in 1790 has included a question about race. By 1970, the options for race were *white, Negro or black, American Indian* (with a request to print the name of the enrolled or principal tribe), *Japanese, Chinese, Filipino, Hawaiian, Korean,* and *Other* with the option of specifying. The 1970 census began the practice of allowing the head of the household to identify the race of household members: before that, the census taker had made that decision based on the appearance of the family. Thus, the Census Bureau began treating race as primarily a matter of *self*-identification. Still, it was assumed that a person could only be a member of *one* racial group, so respondents were allowed only one option for each household member.

The 1970 census also posed the first ethnicity question, asking whether the individual was of Hispanic or non-Hispanic ancestry. (Ethnicity, which generally refers to national ancestry, is a subject we will return to shortly.) The Hispanic/non-Hispanic question was added at the recommendation of the Census Bureau's Hispanic Advisory Committee as a way to correct for the *differential undercount* of the Hispanic population. A differential undercount means that more people are undercounted in one category than in another; for example, the census yields a larger undercount of those who rent their homes than of those who own them. Undercounting primarily affects the data on low-income residents of inner cities. This is the case because the poor often move and are thus difficult to contact, are more likely to be illiterate or non-English speakers (there was no Spanish-language census form until 1990), and are more likely to be illegal immigrants afraid to respond to a government questionnaire. (The Constitution requires a count of *all* the people in the United States, not just those who are citizens or legal residents.) Because census data affect the distribution of billions of dollars of federal aid, as well as voting rights and civil rights enforcement, undercounting has a significant impact. Indeed, the bureau's Census 2000 FAQ Web page notes that $182 billion will be distributed annually to state, local, and tribal governments based on formulas using Census 2000 data.

Census data have always been critical to the functioning of American government: the apportionment of seats in the U.S. House of Representatives and the distribution of federal funding to states and localities are based on census data. However, by the 1970s information on race was increasingly needed to document and eliminate discrimination. Such data, the newly formed U.S. Commission on Civil Rights argued, was necessary to monitor equal access in housing, education, and employment.

There were the civil rights movement and its offshoots such as the Mexican-American Brown Power movement. In addition, the federal government initiated the War Against Poverty and the Great Society programs. These movements and programs stated clearly that poor minority groups had a legitimate claim to better conditions in cities. Several of the social welfare programs of President Johnson's Great Society distributed dollars by means of statistically driven grant-in-aid formulas. The proliferation of federal grants programs and the cities' increasing dependence upon them tended to heighten the political salience of census statistics. Such formulas often incorporated population size, as measured or estimated by the Census Bureau, as a major factor. By 1978 there were more than one hundred such programs, covering a wide range of concerns, from preschool education (Headstart) to urban mass transportation. . . . [T]he single most commonly used data source was the decennial census. (Choldin, 1994:27–8)

In all, the census offers an important source of information for the courts, Congress, and local entities to gauge the extent of discrimination and monitor civil rights enforcement. Data on race allowed the monitoring of the Voting Rights Act, equal employment opportunity programs, and racial disparities in health, birth, and death rates.

To improve the collection of race data, in the 1970s the Commission on Civil Rights reviewed the race categorization practices of federal agencies and concluded that while "the designations do not refer strictly to race, color, national or ethnic origin," the categories were nonetheless what the general public understood to be *minority groups* (U.S. Commission on Civil Rights, 1973:39). "The federal emphasis was clearly on minority status in a legal sense. Minority group status did not derive from a specific race or ethnicity *per se*, but on the treatment of race and ethnicity to confer a privileged, disadvantaged, or equitable status and to gauge representation and under-representation" (Tamayo Lott, 1998:37). The aim of data collection was to pinpoint the extent of discrimination, not to identify all population categories.

Thus, in 1977 on the recommendation of the Civil Rights Commission, the Office of Management and Budget (OMB) issued Statistical Directive No. 15, "Race and Ethnic Standards for Federal Statistics and Administrative Reporting," which established standard categories and definitions for all federal agencies, including the Bureau of the Census. Directive No. 15 defined four racial and one ethnic category: American Indian or Alaskan Native, Asian or Pacific Islander, Negro or Black, White, and Hispanic.

> The choice of four racial categories and one ethnic category [Hispanic] redefined the United States beyond a White and non-White classification and even beyond a White and Black classification. The new classification facilitated the enumeration of a multiracial and multicultural population. . . . The particular status of Hispanics was recognized in two ways. Hispanic was the only choice for the ethnic category. Furthermore . . . Black and White Hispanics were enumerated as Hispanics. To avoid duplicated counts, the Black and White categories excluded Hispanics. (Tamayo Lott, 1998:54)

The racial and ethnic diversity of the United States is more complex now than it was in the 1970s. Certainly, the most notable change in the 2000 census was its recognition that a person may identify himself or herself as being a member of more than one racial group. For the first time in its 210-year history, the census provided for the identification of mixed lineage—though it did not offer a category called *multiracial.* This change was one outcome of a comprehensive review and revision of OMB's Directive No. 15 that included public hearings, sample surveys of targeted populations, and collaboration among the more than 30 federal agencies that collect and use data on race and ethnicity. While this change was spurred by activists who identified themselves as mixed-race, the bureau's pretesting also indicated that less than 2 percent of respondents would mark more than one race for themselves, and thus the historical continuity with previous censuses would not be compromised. The bureau's expectation was close to the mark—2.4 percent of the population, almost 7 million people, marked two or more races for themselves in the 2000 census.

One change that was not made in the 2000 census, however, was inclusion of an ethnic category called *Arab* or *Middle Eastern* because public comment did not indicate agreement on a definition for this category. Thus, in the 2000 census Arab or Middle Eastern peoples continue to be categorized as *white.*

As in previous censuses, undercounting remains an important fiscal and political issue, given the disproportionate undercounting of people of color. Still, gay couples may well be the most undercounted population. Since the 1990 census, the form has provided *unmarried partner* as a possible answer to the question of how the people in the household are related to one another. The number of gay couples (not gay people) increased more than 300 percent between the 1990 and 2000 censuses, to 594,391 couples, but that number is probably less than a complete count because of respondents' reluctance to report (Cohn, 2001). Indeed, an analysis of data from the 2005 American Community Survey (an annual Census Bureau survey of a sample of U.S. households) found that the number of cohabiting same-sex couples had increased more than 30 percent since 2000—from 600,000 to almost 770,000 (Gates, 2006). An increase this large is most likely attributable to an increased willingness to report.

We end this phase of our discussion with two cautions. On a personal level, many of us find census categorizations objectionable. But as *citizens,* we still seek the benefits and protections of policies based on these data—and as citizens we share the goal of eliminating discriminatory practices.

> [R]eliable racial data are crucial to enforcing our basic laws against intentional racial discrimination, which enjoy broad public support. For example, in order to demonstrate that an employer is engaging in a broad based "pattern or practice" of discrimination in violation of the Civil Rights Act of 1964, a plaintiff must rely on statistical proof that goes beyond the plight of an individual employee. Supreme Court precedent in such cases requires plaintiffs to show a statistically significant disparity between the proportion of qualified minorities in the local labor market and the proportion within the employer's work force. A disparity of more than two standard deviations creates a legal presumption that intentional discrimination is occurring, since a disparity of that magnitude almost never occurs by accident.
>
> Demographic information, in other words, provides the "big picture" that places individual incidents in context. Voting rights cases require similar proof, as do many housing discrimination cases and suits challenging the discriminatory use of federal funds. Without reliable racial statistics, it would be virtually impossible for courts or agencies to detect institutional bias, and antidiscrimination laws would go unenforced. More fundamentally, we simply cannot know as a society how far we've come in conquering racial discrimination and inequality without accurate information about the health, progress and opportunities available to communities of different races. (Jenkins, 1999:15–16)

Still, when considering official counts of the population, we must be careful not to assume that what is counted is real. While census data contribute to the essentialist view that the world is populated by distinct, scientifically defined categories of people, this brief history demonstrates that not even those who collect the data make that assumption. As the Office of Management and the Budget (OMB) warns,

The racial and ethnic categories set forth in the standards should not be interpreted as being primarily biological or genetic in reference. Race and ethnicity may be thought of in terms of social and cultural characteristics as well as ancestry. (Office of Management and Budget, 1997:2)

There are no clear, unambiguous, objective, generally agreed-upon definitions of the terms "race" and "ethnicity." Cognitive research shows that respondents are not always clear on the differences between race and ethnicity. There are differences in terminology, group boundaries, attributes and dimensions of race and ethnicity. . . .

[The Directive No. 15 categories] do not represent objective "truth" but rather are ambiguous social constructs and involve subjective and attitudinal issues. (Office of Management and Budget, 1995:44680)

Aggregating and Disaggregating

The federal identification policies we have been describing collapsed nonwhite Americans into four categories: Hispanics, Native Americans, Blacks, and Asian or Pacific Islanders. This process *aggregated* categories of people; that is, it combined, or "lumped together," different groups. In the census, Puerto Ricans, Mexicans, Cubans, and others from Central and South America all became "Hispanic" in some sense. While *Latino* and *Hispanic* remain commonly used aggregate terms, the diversity of this population has increased dramatically. Data from the 2000 census show that the number of respondents identifying themselves as "Other Spanish/ Hispanic/Latino"—that is, who do not classify themselves as Mexican, Mexican American, Chicano, Puerto Rican, or Cuban—doubled since the 1990 census. "Other Spanish/Hispanic/Latino" is now the fastest growing group in the Spanish/ Hispanic/Latino category (Population Reference Bureau, 2001).

The groups that are lumped together in these categories have historically regarded one another as different, and thus in people's everyday lives the aggregate category is likely to *disaggregate*, or fragment, into its constituent national-origin elements. For example, one might think that *Latino* or *Asian American* are terms used for self-identification, but this is rarely the case. In the United States, "Mexicans, Puerto Ricans, and Cubans have little interaction with each other, most do not recognize that they have much in common culturally, and they do not profess strong affection for each other" (de la Garza et al., 1992:14). Thus, it is not surprising that a survey of the Latino population concludes that "respondents do not primarily identify as members of an Hispanic or Latino community. . . . [Rather, they] overwhelmingly prefer to identify by national origin . . . " (de la Garza et al., 1992:13).

The difficulty with determining who counts as Hispanic is that Hispanics do not appear to share any properties in common. Linguistic, racial, religious, political, territorial, cultural, economic, educational, social class, and genetic criteria fail to identify Hispanics in all places and times. . . .

[Nonetheless], we are treated as a homogeneous group by European Americans and African Americans; and even though Hispanics do not in fact constitute a homogeneous group, we are easily contrasted with European Americans and African Americans because we do not share many of the features commonly associated with these groups. (Gracia, 2000:204–205)

In short, the category *Latino/Hispanic* exists primarily, but not exclusively, from the perspective of non-Latinos.

Like all the differences masked by the terms *Latino* and *Hispanic,* among those in the category *Asian Pacific American* or *Asian American* are groups with different languages, cultures, and religions and sometimes centuries of mutual hostility. Like *Hispanic/Latino,* the category *Asian American* is based more on geography than on any cultural, racial, linguistic, or religious commonalities. "Asian Americans are those who come from a region of the world that *the rest of the world* has defined as Asia" (Hu-Dehart, 1994).[5]

Aggregate classifications such as *Latino* or *Asian American* were not simply the result of federal classifications, however. Student activists inspired by the Black Power and civil rights movements first proposed the terms. As Yen Le Espiritu describes in Reading 5, college students coined the identifier *Asian American* in response to "the similarity of [their] experiences and treatment." *Asian American, Hispanic,* and *Latino* are examples of *panethnic* terms, that is, classifications that span national-origin identities. Panethnicity is "the development of bridging organizations and solidarities among subgroups of ethnic collectivities that are often seen as homogeneous by outsiders. . . . Those . . . groups that, from an outsider's point of view, are most racially homogeneous are also the groups with the greatest panethnic development" (Lopez and Espiritu, 1990:219–20).

The concept of panethnicity is useful but unstable in practice. "The elites representing such groups find it advantageous to make political demands by using the numbers and resources panethnic formations can mobilize. The state, in turn, can more easily manage claims by recognizing and responding to large blocs as opposed to dealing with the specific claims of a plethora of ethnically defined interest groups" (Omi, 1996:180). At the same time, competition and historic antagonisms make such alliances unstable. "At times it is advantageous to be in a panethnic bloc, and at times it is desirable to mobilize along particular ethnic lines" (Omi, 1996:181).

The disability movement is similar to panethnic movements in that it has brought together people with all types of impairments. This approach was a historic "first"—running counter both to the tradition of organizing around specific impairments and to the fact that the needs of people with different impairments are sometimes in conflict. For example, some of the curb cuts that make wheelchair

---

[5]In census classification, the category *Asian* includes Asian Indian, Chinese, Filipino, Japanese, Korean, Vietnamese; *Other Asian* includes Bangladeshi, Bhutanese, Burmese, Cambodian, Hmong, Indo-Chinese, Indonesian, Iwo Jiman, Laotian, Malaysian, Maldivian, Mongolian, Nepalese, Okinawan, Pakistani, Singaporean, Sri Lankan, Thai, and Taiwanese. The category *Pacific Islander* includes Native Hawaiian, Guamanian or Chamorro, Samoan; *Other Pacific Islander* includes Carolinian, Chuukese, Fijian, Kirabati, Kosraean, Mariana Islander, Marshallese, Melanesian, Micronesian, New Hebridian, Palauan, Papua New Guinean, Pohnpeian, Polynesian, Saipanese, Solomon Islander, Tahitian, Tokelauan, Tongan, and Yapese (U.S. Census Bureau, 2001).

In 1980, Asian Indians successfully lobbied to change their census classification from *white* to *Asian American* by reminding Congress that historically immigrants from India had been classed as *Asian.* With other Asians, those from India had been barred from immigration by the 1917 Immigration Act, prohibited from becoming naturalized citizens until 1946, and denied the right to own land by the 1920 Alien Land Law. Indeed, in 1923 the U.S. Supreme Court (in *Thind*) ruled that Asian Indians were nonwhite, and could therefore have their U.S. citizenship nullified (Espiritu, 1992:124–25). Thus, for most of their history in the United States, Asian Indians had been classed as *Asian.*

access possible can make walking more difficult for blind people who need to be able to feel the edges of a sidewalk with their canes. The aggregating of disabled people that began with the disability rights movement was reinforced in the 1990 Americans with Disabilities Act (ADA).

The terms *Native American* and *African American* are also aggregate classifications, but in this case they are the result of conquest and enslavement.

> The "Indian," like the European, is an idea. The notion of "Indians" was invented to distinguish the indigenous peoples of the New World from Europeans. The "Indian" is the person on shore, outside of the boat. . . . There [were] hundreds of cultures, languages, ways of living in Native America. The place was a model of diversity at the time of Columbus's arrival. Yet Europeans did not see this diversity. They created the concept of the "Indian" to give what they did see some kind of unification, to make it a single entity they could deal with, because they could not cope with the reality of 400 different cultures. (Mohawk, 1992:440)[6]

Conquest made "Indians" out of a heterogeneity of tribes and nations that had been distinctive on linguistic, religious, and economic grounds. It was not only that Europeans had the unifying concept of *Indian* in mind—after all, they were sufficiently aware of cultural differences to generate an extensive body of specific treaties with individual tribes. It was also that conquest itself—encompassing as it did the appropriation of land, the forging and violation of treaties, and policies of forced relocation—structured the lives of Native Americans along common lines. While contemporary Native Americans still identify themselves by tribal ancestry, just as those called *Asian American* and *Latino* identify themselves by national origin, their shared experience of conquest also forged the common identity reflected in the collective name, *Native American.*

Similarly, the capture, purchase, and forced relocation of Africans, and their experience of forcibly being moved from place to place as personal property, created the category now called *African American.* This experience forged a single people out of a culturally diverse group; it produced an "oppositional racial consciousness," that is, a unity-in-opposition (Omi and Winant, 1994). "Just as the conquest created the 'native' where once there had been Pequot, Iroquois, or Tutelo, so too it created the 'black' where once there had been Asante or Ovimbundu, Yoruba or Bakongo" (Omi and Winant, 1994:66).

Even the categories of *gay and straight, male and female,* and *poor and middle class* are aggregations that presume a commonality by virtue of shared master status. For example, the category *gay and lesbian* assumes that sharing a sexual orientation binds people together despite all the issues that might divide them as men and women, people of different colors, or people of different social classes. And, just as

---

[6]The idea of *Europe* and the *European* is also a constructed, aggregate category. "Physically, Europe is not a continent. Where is the water separating Europe from Asia? It is culture that separates Europe from Asia. Western Europe roughly comprises the countries that in the Middle Ages were Latin Christendom, and Eastern Europe consists of those countries that in the Middle Ages were Eastern Orthodox Christendom. It was about A.D. 1257 when the Pope claimed hegemony over the secular emperors in Western Europe and formulated the idea that Europeans, that Christians, were a unified ethnicity even though they spoke many different languages" (Mohawk, 1992:439–40).

in the cases we have previously discussed, alliances between gays and lesbians will depend on the circumstances and specific issues.

Still, our analysis has so far ignored one category of people. From whose perspective do the categories of *Native American, Asian American, African American,* and *Latino/Hispanic* exist? Since "difference" is always "difference *from*," from whose perspective is "difference" determined? Who has the power to define "difference"? If "we" are in the boat looking at "them," who precisely are "we"?

Every perspective on the social world emerges from a particular vantage point, a particular social location. Ignoring who is in the boat treats that place as if it were just the view "anyone" would take. Historically, the people in the boat were European; contemporarily, they are white Americans. As Ruth Frankenberg frames it in Reading 6, in America "whites are the nondefined definers of other people," "the unmarked marker of others' differentness." Failing to identify the "us" in the boat means that "white culture [becomes] the unspoken norm," a category that is powerful enough to define others while itself remaining invisible and unnamed. Indeed, Frankenberg argues that those with the most power in a society are best positioned to have their own identities left unnamed, thus masking their power.

The term *androcentrism* describes the world as seen from a male-centered perspective. For example, if we define a good employee as one who is willing to work extensive overtime, we are thinking from a male-centered perspective, since women's child-care responsibilities often preclude extra work commitments. By analogy, we may also describe *Eurocentric, heterocentric,* and *"physicalist"* (Russell, 1994) perspectives, that is, viewpoints that assume everyone is of European origin, heterosexual, and physically agile. Naming these perspectives helps us to see them as particular social locations, like the other master statuses we have considered. Indeed, it is possible to argue that, no matter what their master statuses, all Americans operate from these biases since they are built into the basic fabric of our culture.

Dichotomizing

Many forces promote the construction of aggregate categories of people. Frequently, these aggregates emerge as *dichotomies*. To dichotomize is not only to divide something into two parts; it is also to see those parts as mutually exclusive and in opposition. Dichotomization encourages the sense that there are only two categories, that everyone fits easily in one or the other, and that the categories stand in opposition to each other. In contemporary American culture, we appear to treat the master statuses of race, sex, class, sexual orientation, and disability as if each embodied "us" and "them"—as if for each master status people could be easily sorted into two mutually exclusive, opposed groupings.[7]

---

[7]Springer and Deutsch (1981) coined the term *dichotomania* to describe the belief that there are male and female sides of the brain. We think that term also fits our discussion.

Dichotomizing Race   While three racial categories—*white, Negro,* and *Indian*— were identified throughout the 19th century, all were located within a white/nonwhite dichotomy. In 1854, the California Supreme Court in *People v. Hall* held that blacks, mulattos, Native Americans, and Chinese were "not white" and therefore could not testify for or against a white man in court (Takaki, 1993:205–6). (Hall, a white man, had been convicted of killing a Chinese man on the testimony of one white and three Chinese witnesses; the Supreme Court overturned the conviction.)

Mexican residents of the southwest territories ceded to the United States in the 1848 Treaty of Guadalupe Hidalgo, however, "were defined as a white population and accorded the political-legal status of 'free white persons'" (Omi and Winant, 1994). European immigrants such as the Irish were initially treated as nonwhite, or at least not-yet-white. In turn, they lobbied for their own inclusion in American society on the basis of the white/nonwhite distinction.

> [Immigrants struggled to] equate whiteness with Americanism in order to turn arguments over immigration from the question of who was foreign to the question of who was white. . . . Immigrants could not win on the question of who was foreign. . . . But if the issue somehow became defending "white man's jobs" or "white man's government" . . . [they] could gain space by deflecting debate from nativity, a hopeless issue, to race, an ambiguous one. . . . After the Civil War, the new-coming Irish would help lead the movement to bar the relatively established Chinese from California, with their agitation for a "white man's government," serving to make race, and not nativity, the center of the debate and to prove the Irish white. (Roediger, 1994:189–90)

Historically, *American* has meant *white,* as many Americans of Asian ancestry learn when they are complimented on their English—a compliment that presumes that someone who is Asian could not be a native-born American.[8] A story from the 1998 Winter Olympics illustrates the same point. At the conclusion of the figure skating competition, MSNBC posted a headline that read "American Beats Out Kwan for Women's Figure Skating Title." The reference was to Michelle Kwan, who won the silver medal, losing the gold to Tara Lapinsky. But both Kwan and Lapinsky are Americans. While Kwan's parents immigrated from Hong Kong, she was born and raised in the United States, is a U.S. citizen, and was a member of the U.S. team. The network attributed the mistake to overworked staff and apologized. But for Asian American activists, this was an example of how people of Asian descent have remained perpetual foreigners in American society.

African American novelist Toni Morrison would describe this as a story about "how *American* means *white*":

> Deep within the word "American" is its association with race. To identify someone as South African is to say very little; we need the adjective "white" or "black" or "colored" to make our meaning clear. In this country it is quite the reverse. American means white, and Africanist people struggle to make the term applicable to themselves with . . . hyphen after hyphen after hyphen. (Morrison, 1992:47)

---

[8]Since the historic American ban on Asian immigration remained in place until 1965, it is the case that a high proportion of Asian Americans are foreign-born, although there is considerable variation within that category. For example, most Japanese Americans are native-born.

Because *American* means *white,* those who are not white are presumed to be recent arrivals and often told to go "back where they came from." Thus, we appear to operate within the dichotomized *racial* categories of *American/non-American*—these are racial categories, because they effectively mean *white/nonwhite.*

Perhaps the clearest example of the contemporary dichotomiziation of race is provided by the "one-drop rule," which is described by F. James Davies in Reading 2. This "rule" began as law but now operates as an informal social practice, holding that a person with any traceable African heritage should classify themselves as *black.* The rule, which grew out of the efforts of Southern whites to enforce segregation after the Civil War, came to be endorsed by *both* blacks and whites. Thus, as Jennifer Lee and Frank Bean note in Reading 7, only about 4 percent of black Americans identify themselves as having ancestry from more than one race, even though a much larger percentage would have Native American and/or white ancestry. Similarly, only a little over 2 percent of whites identify themselves that way. These figures are in considerable contrast to the rates at which members of other census groups identify themselves as having more than one racial ancestry: American Indian and Alaska Natives (36 percent), Native Hawaiian or other Pacific Islanders (45 percent), Latinos (16 percent), and Asian Americans (12 percent).

In determining the future strength and significance of the one-drop rule, at least three important points bear consideration. First, there is a higher rate of multiracial identification among recent Asian and Latino immigrants to the United States than among those who are native-born, which might serve to weaken traditional American practices. Although in other cultures people of multiracial ancestry might have the option to define themselves as multiracial, U.S. culture has not historically supported that, especially for black Americans.

Second, an increase in intermarriage and the birth of children who grow up to describe themselves as multiracial might be an indicator that America is moving away from the dichotomization of race. This is precisely the topic that Lee and Bean, in Reading 7, investigate. Their analysis is that the racial boundaries between Latinos, Asian Americans, and whites are becoming more fluid, but that American blacks do not appear to be included in that racial blurring.

Third, as Eduardo Bonilla-Silva and Karen Glover argue in Reading 8, a reduction in the strength of the one-drop rule would not necessarily mean that race had less of an impact on individuals. Rather, it might mean that America was moving to the tri-racial system—white, honorary white, and collective black—characteristic of Latin American countries.

But what exactly *is* race? First, we need to distinguish *race* from *ethnicity.* Social scientists define *ethnic groups* as categories of people who are distinctive on the basis of national origin or heritage, language, or cultural practices. "Members of an ethnic group hold a set of common memories that make them feel that their customs, culture, and outlook are distinctive" (Blauner, 1992). Thus, racial categories encompass different ethnic groups.

For example, in the early 1900s the American racial category *white* included ethnic groups such as Irish, Italian, Mexican, and Polish Americans. Now it includes Afghan, Kurd, Pakistani, Cuban, and Salvadoran Americans.

The concept of ethnicity attempts to capture people's actual practices, which do not always operate consistently or logically. For some, ethnic identity has waned over time; being an Italian American in the 1920s involved much more intensity of feeling, interaction, and political organization than it does now. For others, ethnic identity may retain its strength, but has been transformed over time. For example, Jews may be adherents of a religion and/or members of an ethnic group, since many who do not practice the religion still have a strong sense of being part of a people. Or, in recognizing that ethnic identity may involve some choice between national origin and religion, consider that a survey of Bosnian refugees in the United States found people identifying their ethnicity as Bosnian, Bosnian Muslim, and Muslim, with many others refusing to answer the question at all as it raised the specter of the ethnic cleansing that had made them refugees (Haines, 2007).

While in many ways, ethnic group identification is more important to people than race, it is often obscured by race. For example, focusing only on race would hide the important differences between African Americans and Haitians, Somalis, Ethiopians, or Jamaicans—all black American ethnic groups. Similarly, many Americans with Middle Eastern heritage (who are classified as *white* in the census) are often misdescribed as *Arabs*, even though that term covers only those from Arabic-speaking countries. A scene in the movie *Crash* made this point: in vandalizing the store of an Iranian grocer, the looters left behind graffiti about "Arabs," but Iranians are Persian, speak Farsi, and do not generally consider themselves Arabic. Like the panethnic aggregations *Latino* or *Asian American*, beneath panethnic terms like *Middle Eastern* or *Arab American*, one will probably find stronger ethnic attachments based on national origin or religion.

The term *race* first appeared in the Romance languages of Europe in the Middle Ages to refer to breeding stock (Smedley, 1993). A "race" of horses described common ancestry and a distinctive appearance or behavior. *Race* appears to have been first applied to New World peoples by the Spanish in the 16th century. Later it was adopted by the English, again in reference to people of the New World, and generally came to mean *people, nation,* or *variety.* By the late 18th century, "when scholars became more actively engaged in investigations, classifications, and definitions of human populations, the term 'race' was elevated as the one major symbol and mode of human group differentiation employed extensively for non-European groups and even those in Europe who varied in some way from the subjective norm" (Smedley, 1993:39).

Though elevated to the level of science, the concept of race continued to reflect its origins in animal breeding. Farmers and herders had used the concept to describe stock bred for particular qualities; scholars used it to suggest that human behaviors could also be inherited. "Unlike other terms for classifying people . . . the term 'race' places emphasis on innateness, on the inbred nature of whatever is being judged" (Smedley, 1993:39). Like animal breeders, scholars also presumed that appearance revealed something about potential behavior. Just as the selective breeding of animals entailed the ranking of stock by some criteria, scholarly use of the concept of race involved the ranking of humans. Differences in skin color, hair texture, and the shape of head, eyes, nose, lips, and body were developed into an elaborate hierarchy of merit and potential for "civilization."

As described by Audrey Smedley in Reading 1, the idea of race emerged among all the European colonial powers, although their conceptions of it varied. However, only the British in colonizing North America and South Africa constructed a system of rigid, exclusive racial categories and a social order *based on race,* a "racialized social structure" (Omi and Winant, 1994). "[S]kin color variations in many regions of the world and in many societies have been imbued with some degree of social value or significance, but color prejudice or preferences do not of themselves amount to a fully evolved racial worldview" (Smedley, 1993:25).

This racialized social structure—which in America produced a race-based system of slavery and subsequently a race-based distribution of political, legal, and social rights—was a historical first. "Expansion, conquest, exploitation, and enslavement have characterized much of human history over the past five thousand years or so, but none of these events before the modern era resulted in the development of ideologies or social systems based on race" (Smedley, 1993:15, 25). While differences of color had long been noted, societies had never before been built on those differences.

As scientists assumed that race differences involved more than simply skin color or hair texture, they sought the biological distinctiveness of racial categories—but with little success. In the early 20th century, anthropologists looked to physical features such as height, stature, and head shape to distinguish the races, only to learn that these are affected by environment and nutrition. More recently, the search has turned to genetics, only to find that those cannot be correlated with conventional racial classifications either. Even efforts to reach a consensus about how many races exist or what specific features distinguish one from another are problematic.

> If our eyes could perceive more than the superficial, we might find race in chromosome 11: there lies the gene for hemoglobin. If you divide humankind by which of two forms of the gene each person has, then equatorial Africans, Italians and Greeks fall into the "sickle-cell race"; Swedes and South Africa's Xhosas (Nelson Mandela's ethnic group) are in the healthy hemoglobin race. Or do you prefer to group people by whether they have epicanthic eye folds, which produce the "Asian" eye? Then the !Kung San (Bushmen) belong with the Japanese and Chinese. . . . [D]epending on which traits you pick, you can form very surprising races. Take the scooped-out shape of the back of the front teeth, a standard "Asian" trait. Native Americans and Swedes have these shovel-shaped incisors, too, and so would fall in the same race. Is biochemistry better? Norwegians, Arabians, north Indians and the Fulani of northern Nigeria . . . fall into the "lactase race" (the lactase enzyme digests milk sugar). Everyone else—other Africans, Japanese, Native Americans—form the "lactase-deprived race" (their ancestors did not drink milk from cows or goats and hence never evolved the lactase gene). How about blood types, the familiar A, B, and O groups? Then Germans and New Guineans, populations that have the same percentages of each type, are in one race; Estonians and Japanese comprise a separate one for the same reason. . . . The dark skin of Somalis and Ghanaians, for instance, indicates that they evolved under the same selective force (a sunny climate). But that's all it shows. It does *not* show that they are any more closely related in the sense of sharing more genes than either is to Greeks. Calling Somalis and Ghanaians "black" therefore sheds no further light on their evolutionary history and implies—wrongly—that they are more closely related to each other than either is to someone of a different "race." (Begley, 1995:67, 68)

As one anthropologist has put it, "Classifying people by color is very much like classifying cars by color. Those in the same classification look alike . . . but the classification tells you nothing about the hidden details of construction or about how the cars or people will perform" (Cohen, 1998:12). A "no-race" theory is now widely accepted in physical anthropology and human genetics. This perspective argues that "(1) Biological variability exists but this variability does not conform to the discrete packages labeled races. (2) So-called racial characteristics are not transmitted as complexes. (3) Races do not exist because isolation of groups has been infrequent; populations have always interbred" (Lieberman, 1968:128). Still, few scholars outside of anthropology seem to take this perspective into account.

> [I]t does not appear that this debate [about the existence of race] has had widespread impact on professionals in the fields of medicine, psychology, sociology, history, or political science. . . . [I]t will suffice to point out that virtually all scholars who write about "race and intelligence" assume that the "races" which they study are distinguished on the basis of biologically relevant criteria. So accepted is this fact that most scholars engaged in such research never consider it necessary to justify their assignment of individuals to this or that "race." . . . [Thus], the layman who reads the literature on race and racial groupings is justified in assuming that the existent typologies have been derived through the application of theories and methods current in disciplines concerned with the biological study of human variation. Since the scientific racial classifications which a layman finds in the literature are not too different from popular ones, he can be expected to feel justified in the maintenance of his views on race. (Marshall, 1993:117, 121)

The complexities of incorporating a "no race" position into social science research is highlighted by the difference between anthropology and sociology's treatment of the concept of race on the Web pages of their professional associations. The American Anthropological Association's (AAA) home page (www .aaanet.org) includes a 1998 "Statement on 'Race'" with reference to its ongoing Understanding Race and Human Variation public-education project funded by the National Science Foundation and the Ford Foundation (www.understandingrace .org). The AAA statement is unambiguous: "Racial beliefs constitute myths about the diversity in the human species and about the abilities and behavior of people homogenized into 'racial' categories." For the American Sociological Association (www.asanet.org), however, that does not mean we should stop collecting data on race: its 2002 statement, "The Importance of Collecting Data and Doing Social Scientific Research on Race," urges the continued study of race as a *social* phenomenon because it affects major aspects of social life—including employment, housing, education, and health.

Thus, even though sociologists view race as social, not biological, their work could be interpreted to mean that race must refer to real biological differences. Reports on medical research also sometimes promote the same misconceptions. For example, in 2004 there was much fanfare about BiDil, the first American drug approved for use by a specific race or ethnic population. BiDil was found to be effective for black patients with advanced heart disease. If race were not "real," why would the drug have this effect? There are at least three explanations: First, it remains unclear whether the claims for the drug have been validated—the drug's most extensive tests have been on black Americans, not the comparison of black and nonblack patients (Kimberly, 2005; Wade, 2005). Second, developments like BiDil make it seem as if some genes only appear in a single "race" group, which is not the

…5, Icelandic researchers described a version of a gene that increased the …t attack. They found the gene among Icelanders and about 6 percent of …ericans and theorized that "the active version of the inflammatory gene …passed from Europeans into African-Americans only a few generations …rt a time for development of genes that protect against heart attack" …5). Finally, treating race as real and as based on "real" genetic markers …mission to ignore the *social* factors that affect the quality and length of …s.

By looking at what's in the blood, [geneticists] avoid the messy stuff that happens when humans interact with each other. It's easier to look inside the body because genes, proteins, and SNP patterns are far more measurable than the complex dynamics of society. . . .

When you're talking about genetic diseases, there's usually something in the environment that triggers their onset. Shouldn't we be talking about the trigger?

Take the case of black men and prostate cancer. African-American males have twice the prostate cancer rate that whites do. Right now, the National Cancer Institute is searching for cancer genes among black men. They're not asking, How come black men in the Caribbean and in sub-Saharan Africa have much lower prostate cancer rates than all American men?

A balanced approach might involve asking, Is there something in the American environment triggering these high rates? Is it diet, stress or what? (Dreifus, 2005, interview with Troy Duster, author of *Backdoor to Eugenics,* 2003)

Particularly on medical matters, some anthropologists contend that we would be better off to think about "lineage" than race because then we would recognize the multiplicity of each of our individual inheritances and of the medically relevant genetic inheritances. More important, however, "race implies dividing people into groups, lineage implies *connecting people through lines* (of descent)" (Thompson, 2006:3).

In all, "race is a biological fiction, but a social fact" (Rubio, 2001:xiv). Its primary significance is as a *social* concept. We "see" race, we expect it to tell us something significant about a person, and we organize social policy, law, and the distribution of wealth, power, and prestige around it. From the essentialist position, race is assumed to exist independently of our perception of it; it is assumed to significantly distinguish one group of people from another. From the constructionist perspective, race exists because we have created it as a meaningful category of difference among people.

Dichotomizing Sexual Orientation   Many similarities exist in the construction of race and sexual orientation categories. First, both are often dichotomized—into black/white, white/nonwhite, or gay/straight—and individuals are expected to fit easily into one category or the other. While the term *bisexual* has become increasingly common, and one of the readings included here declares the end of *both* gay and straight identities (Bert Archer in Reading 19), we believe the assumption that people are either gay or straight is still culturally dominant.

For example, scientists continue to seek biological differences between gay and straight people just as they have looked for such differences between the "races." Usually the search is for what causes same-sex attraction, not for what causes heterosexuality—the point made by Martin Rochlin's Heterosexual Questionnaire

(Reading 20). But as with investigations of race difference, here as well the research is intrinsically suspect, since we are unlikely to find any biological structure or process that *all* gay people share but *no* straight people have (Sherman Heyl, 1989). Still, the conviction that such differences must exist propels the search and leads to the popularization of questionable findings.

> Dean Hamer first published his findings about the relationship of genes to sexuality in *Science* and, a little later, in a popular book called *The Science of Desire*. In both report and book, Hamer made clear that he did not figure he'd found a gay gene. He'd found a conspicuous concurrence of a specific genetic marker among self-declared homosexuals. The findings were statistically significant, but the relationship of the genetic marker to the behavior was as yet undetermined. None of which stopped the newspapers from using the euphonic "gay gene" in their headlines, nor other interested parties from citing this fantastic discovery as further proof of the firmly rooted, unchangeable nature of homosexuality. (Archer, 2002:135)

As with race, sexual orientation appears more straightforward than it really is. Because sexuality encompasses physical, social, and emotional attraction, as well as fantasies, self-identity, and actual sexual behavior over a lifetime (Klein, 1978), determining one's sexual orientation may involve emphasizing one of these features over the others. Just as the system of racial classification asks people to pick *one* race, the sexual orientation system requires that all the different aspects of sexuality be distilled into two possible choices.

For example, an acquaintance described the process by which he came to self-identify as gay. In high school and college he had dated and been sexually active with women, but his relations with men had always been more important to him. He looked to men for emotional and social gratification, as well as for relief from the "gender games" he felt required to play with women. He had been engaged to be married, but when that ended, he spent his time exclusively with other men. Eventually he established a sexual relationship with another man and came to identify himself as gay. His experience reflects the varied dimensions of sexuality and shows the resolution of those differences by choosing a single sexual identity. Rather than say "I used to be straight but I am now gay," he described himself as always "really" having been gay.

Alfred Kinsey's landmark survey of American sexual practices showed that same-sex experience was more common than had been assumed, and that sexual practices could change over the lifespan. He suggested that instead of thinking about *homosexuals* and *heterosexuals* as if these were two discrete categories of people, we should recognize that sexual behavior exists along a continuum from those who are exclusively heterosexual to those who are exclusively gay. Letitia Anne Peplau and Linda D. Garnets, in Reading 18 provide an interesting update to this approach by identifying the fluidity of women's sexuality across age and social contexts.

Further, there is no necessary correspondence between identity and sexual behavior (which Esther Rothblum explores for women in Reading 34). Someone who self-identifies as gay is still likely to have had some heterosexual experience; someone who self-identifies as straight may have had some same-sex experience; and even those who have had *no* sexual experience may lay claim to being gay or straight. Identity is not always directly tied to behavior. Indeed, a person who self-identifies as gay may have had *more* heterosexual experience than someone who self-identifies as straight. This distinction between identity and experience was underscored by the results of a 1994 survey, the most comprehensive American sex survey since Kinsey's. Only 2.8 percent of the men and 1.4 percent of the women identified themselves as gay, but an additional 7.3 percent and 7.2 percent, respectively, reported a same-sex experience or attraction (Michael, 1994).

One last analogy between the construction of race and sexual orientation bears discussion. Most Americans would not question the logic of this sentence: "Tom has been married for 30 years and has a dozen children, but I think he's *really* gay." In a real-life illustration of the same logic, a young man and woman were often seen kissing on our campus. When this became the subject of a class discussion, a suggestive ripple of laughter went through the room: Everyone "knew" that the young man was really gay.

How could they "know" that? For such conclusions to make sense, we must believe that someone could be gay irrespective of his or her actual behavior. Just as it is possible in this culture for one to be "black" even if one looks "white," apparently one may be gay despite acting straight. Just as "black" can be established by any African heritage, "gay" is apparently established by displaying any behavior thought to be associated with gays. Indeed, "gay" can be "established" by reputation alone, by a failure to demonstrate heterosexuality, or even by the demonstration of an overly aggressive heterosexuality. Therefore, "gay" can be assigned no matter what one actually does. In this sense, gay can function as an *essential identity* (Katz, 1975), that is, an identity assigned to an individual *irrespective of his or her actual behavior,* as in "I know she's a genius even though she's flunking all her courses." Because no behavior can ever conclusively prove one is *not* gay, this label is an extremely effective mechanism of social control.

In all, several parallels exist between race and sexual orientation classifications. With both, we assume there are a limited number of possibilities—usually two, but no more than three—and we assume individuals can easily fit into one or the other option. We treat both race and sexual orientation categories as encompassing populations that are internally homogeneous and profoundly dissimilar from each other. For both, this presumption of difference has prompted a wide-ranging search for the biological distinctiveness of the categories. Different races or sexual orientations are judged superior and inferior to one another, and members of each category historically have been granted unequal legal and social rights. Finally, we assume that sexual orientation, like skin color, tells us something meaningful about a person.

Dichotomizing Class   Any discussion of social class in the United States must begin with the understanding that Americans "almost never speak of themselves or their society in class terms. In other words, class is not a central category of cultural discourse in America" (Ortner, 1991:169). Indeed, considering the time and attention Americans devote to sexual orientation, sex/gender, or race, it is hard not to conclude that social class is a taboo subject in our culture (Fussell, 1983). Because social class is so seldom discussed, the vocabulary for talking about it is not well developed.

Yet despite its relative invisibility, as Michael Zweig notes in Reading 12, social class operates in ways quite similar to race and sex. That is, just as American culture offers interpretations of what differences in color or sex mean, it also provides interpretations about what differences in income, wealth, or occupation might mean. As is the case with the other master status categories, social class is also often dichotomized, usually into those called *poor* and those called *middle class*. This social class dichotomization is particularly interesting in that it reflects an actual polarization of income and wealth among Americans, although not one accurately captured by "poor and middle class."

Since 1970 the distribution of wealth and income among Americans has become much more unequal, with an increasing gap between rich and poor and a declining number of families in the middle class (Wiefek, 2003). So the real social class division would appear to between rich and poor. Reading 13, from *The Economist*, describes it this way: "If all Americans were set on a ladder with ten rungs, the gap between the wages of those on the ninth rung and those on the first has risen by a third since 1980," with the highest 1 percent of income earners having doubled their share of aggregate income to 16 percent since 1980. Nonetheless, Americans are more likely to assume the country is divided between the poor and the middle class, as if those in the highest brackets were "just like the rest of us."

Further, Americans often approach class standing as if it reflected an individual's merit as a person. More often than people of other nationalities, Americans explain success and failure in terms of *individual merit* rather than economic or social forces (Morris and Williamson, 1982)—we even sometimes forget the inherited wealth behind "self-made" billionaires, as Dusty Horwitt describes in Reading 16.

But Americans have not always thought this way. In the early part of the 20th century, those who were poor were more likely to be considered hardworking, economically productive, constrained by artificial barriers, and probably in the majority. Today, however, "many of the least well off are not regarded as productive in any respect" (Arrow, Bowles, and Durlauf, 2000:x), and both popular opinion and social science research explains social class standing in terms of individual attributes and values rather than economic changes or discrimination (Kahlenberg, 1997; Mincey, 1994).

Now Americans are prone to think that those who succeed financially do so on the basis of their own merit, and that those who don't succeed have failed because they *lack* merit. Indeed many talk about social class as if it were just the result of personal values or attitudes. Surveys indicate that over half of the American public believe "that lack of effort by the poor was the principal reason for poverty, or a reason at least equal to any that was beyond a person's control. . . . Popular majorities did not consider any other factor to be a very important cause of poverty—not low wages, or a scarcity of jobs, or discrimination, or even sickness" (Schwarz and Volgy, 1992:11).

This attribution of poverty and wealth to individual merit hides the complex reality of American social class. It ignores the 5 percent of people in the labor force who are "working poor," that is, who work but do not earn enough to rise above the poverty line. In 2003, three out of five people classified as working poor usually worked full time (U.S. Department of Labor, 2005). Although Americans are aware of a broad range of social class differences, the widespread conviction that one's station in life reflects one's ability and effort in many ways overshadows this awareness. In all, social class standing is taken to reveal one's core worth—a strikingly essentialist formulation.

Dichotomizing Sex   First, to clarify the terms *sex* and *gender,* most work in the social sciences has used *sex* to refer to females and males—that is, to chromosomal, hormonal, anatomical, and physiological differences—and *gender* to describe the socially constructed roles associated with each sex. Over the last 20 years or so, however, newspapers and magazines have increasingly used *gender* to cover both biological differences and social behavior. For example, it is now common to see descriptions of male and female voting patterns as "gender differences." In popular culture generally, *sex* seems now to refer almost exclusively to sexual intercourse, while *gender* applies to the participants. Adding to the confusion, many scholars, such as Suzanne Kessler and Wendy McKenna in Reading 11, deliberately refer to biological sex as *gender* to underscore that it is socially constructed much as masculinity and femininity is. In these Framework Essays, we have maintained the traditional social science sex/gender distinction because we find it clearer.

Although the approach can be unsettling, biological sex can be understood as a socially created dichotomy much like race, sexual orientation, and gender. Reading 9 by developmental geneticist Anne Fausto-Sterling describes the belief in Western culture that there are two, and only two, sexes and that all individuals can be clearly identified as one or the other (Kessler and McKenna, 1978). But like sexual orientation, sex refers to a complex set of attributes—anatomical, chromosomal, hormonal, physiological—that may sometimes be inconsistent with one another or with individuals' sense of their own identity. This situation is illustrated by a Spanish athlete who is anatomically female, but in a pregame genetic test was classified as male. On the basis of that test, she was excluded from the 1985 World University Games. She was then reclassified as female in 1991, when the governing body for track-and-field contests abandoned genetic testing and returned to physical inspection. As the gynecologist for the sports federation noted, "about 1 in 20,000 people has genes that conflict with his or her apparent gender" (Lemonick, 1992).

Just as with race and sexual orientation, people are assigned to the categories of male or female irrespective of inconsistent or ambiguous evidence. In order to achieve consistency between the physical and psychological, some people undergo sex change surgery as they seek to produce a body consistent with their self-identities. Others will pursue psychotherapy to find an identity consistent with their bodies. In either case, it makes more sense to some people to use surgery and/or therapy to create consistency than to accept inconsistency: a man who feels like a woman must become a woman rather than just being a man who feels like a woman.

In Reading 11, "Who Put the 'Trans' in Transgender," Suzanne Kessler and Wendy McKenna pose the question that is most basic to the study of sex and gender: whether it is possible to escape the binaries of male/female and masculine/feminine. While transsexuals may change their sex to fit their gender and transgendered people may produce a gender that is different from their sex, neither moves beyond the world of two and only two sex/genders. As Kessler and McKenna conclude, "theorizing about gender has in many ways unsettled the meaning of gender, but it has done no damage to the gender dichotomy."

Dichotomization and Disability Our discussion of race, sexual orientation, sex and gender, and social class has emphasized that each of these categories encompasses a continuum of behavior and characteristics rather than a finite set of discrete or easily separated groupings. It has also stressed that difference is a social creation—that differences of color or sex, for example, have no meaning other than what is attributed to them.

Can the same be said about disability? It is often assumed that people are easily classed as disabled or nondisabled, but that is no more true in this case than it is for the other master statuses. The comments of sociologist Irving Zola show how our use of statistics contributes to this misconception.

> The way we report statistics vis-à-vis disability and disease is generally misleading. If we speak of ratio figures for a particular disease as 1 in 8, 1 in 14, etc., we perpetuate what Rene Dubos (1961) once called "The Mirage of Health." For these numbers convey that if 1 person in 10 does get a particular disease, that 9 out of 10 do not. This means, however, only that those 9 people do not get that particular disease. It does not mean that they are disease-free, nor are they likely to be so. . . .
>
> Similarly deceptive is the now-popular figure of "43 million people with a disability". . . for it implies that there are over 200 million Americans without a disability. . . . But the metaphor of being but a banana-peel slip away from disability is inappropriate. The issue of disability for individuals . . . is not *whether* but *when,* not so much *which one* but *how many* and *in what combination.* (Zola, 1993:18)

Apart even from how we count the disabled, how do we determine the disability of any particular person, on any particular day? Irving Zola describes his experience of being able to work longer hours than others on an assembly line because his torso was in a brace (Zola, 1993); although he was "disabled," on the line he was also less disabled than others. This situation, where impairment is relative, is more the rule than the exception and thus undermines notions about fixed distinctions between disability and nondisability.

Constructing the "Other"

We have seen how the complexity of a population may be reduced to aggregates and then to a simplistic dichotomy. Aggregation assumes that those who share a master status are alike in "essential" ways. It ignores the multiple and conflicting statuses an individual inevitably occupies. Dichotomization especially promotes the image of a mythical "other" who is not at all like "us." Whether in race, sex, sexual orientation, social class, or disability, dichotomization yields a vision of "them" as profoundly different. Ultimately, dichotomization results in stigmatizing those who are less powerful. It provides the grounds for whole categories of people to become the objects of contempt.

Constructing "Others" as Profoundly Different The expectation that "others" are profoundly different can be seen most clearly in the significance that has been attached to sex differences. In this case, biological differences between males and females have been the grounds from which to infer an extensive range of nonbiological differences. Women and men are assumed to differ from each other in behavior, perception, and personality, and such differences are used to argue for different legal, social, and economic roles and rights. The expectation that men and women are not at all alike is so widespread that we often talk about them as members of the "opposite" sex; indeed, it is not unusual to talk about the "war" between the sexes.

While this assumption of difference undergirds everyday life, few significant differences in behavior, personality, or even physical ability have been found between men and women of any age. Indeed, there are more differences *within* each sex than *between* the sexes. Susan Basow illustrates this point in the following:

> The all-or-none categorizing of gender traits is misleading. People just are not so simple that they either possess all of a trait or none of it. This is even more true when trait dispositions for groups of people are examined. Part a of Figure 1 illustrates what such an all-or-none distribution of the trait "strength" would look like: all males would be strong, all females weak. The fact is, most psychological and physical traits are distributed according to the pattern shown in Part b of Figure 1 with most people possessing an average amount of that trait and fewer people having either very much or very little of that trait.
>
> To the extent that females and males may differ in the average amount of the trait they possess (which needs to be determined empirically), the distribution can be characterized by *overlapping normal curves*, as shown in Part c of Figure 1. Thus, although most men are stronger than most women, the shaded area indicates that some men are weaker than some women and vice versa. The amount of overlap of the curves generally is considerable. Another attribute related to overlapping normal curves is that differences within one group are usually greater than the differences between the two groups. Thus, more variation in strength occurs within a group of men than between the average male and the average female. (Basow, 1992:8)

The lack of difference between women and men is especially striking given the degree to which we are all socialized to produce such differences. Thus, while boys and girls, and men and women, are often socialized to be different as well as being treated differently, this does not mean they inevitably *become* different. Even though decades of research have confirmed few sex differences, the search for difference continues and some suggest may even have been intensified by the failure to find many differences.

The same expectation that the "other" differs in personality or behavior emerges in race, class, and sexual orientation classifications. Race differences are expected to involve more than just differences of color, those who are "gay" or "straight" are expected to differ in more ways than just their sexual orientation, and the poor and middle class are expected to differ in more than just economic standing. In each case, scientific research is often directed toward finding such differences.

Sanctioning Those Who Associate with the "Other"   There are also similarities in the sanctions against those who cross race, sex, class, or sexual orientation boundaries. Parents sometimes disown children who marry outside of their racial or social class group, just as they often sever connections with children who are gay. Those who associate with the "other" are also in danger of being labeled a member of that category.

For example, during the Reconstruction period following the Civil War, the fear of invisible black ancestry was pervasive among southern whites, because

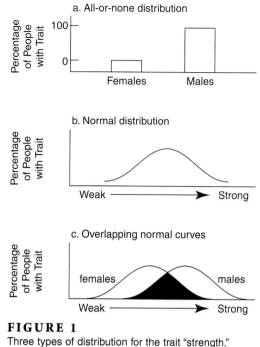

FIGURE 1

Three types of distribution for the trait "strength."
(Basow, 1992:8)

that heritage would subject them to a restricted life based on de jure segregation. "Concern about people passing as white became so great that even behaving like blacks or willingly associating with them were often treated as more important than any proof of actual black ancestry" (Davis, 1991:56). Thus, southern whites who associated with blacks ran the risk of being defined as black.

A contemporary parallel can be found in gay/straight relations. Those who associate with gays and lesbians or defend gay rights are often presumed—by gays and straights alike—to be gay. Many men report that when they object to homophobic remarks, they simply become the target of them. Indeed, the prestige of young men in fraternities and other all-male groups often rests on a willingness to disparage women and gays (Sanday, 1990).

Similarly, few contemporary reactions are as strongly negative as that against men who appear feminine. Because acting like a woman is so disparaged, boys learn at an early age to control their behavior or suffer public humiliation. This ridicule has its greatest effect on young men; the power and prestige usually available to older men reduces their susceptibility to such accusations. There is a long list of behavior young men must avoid for fear of being called feminine or gay: don't be too emotional, watch how you sit, don't move your hips when you walk, take long strides, don't put your hands on your hips, don't talk too much, don't let your voice show emotion, don't be too compliant or eager to please, etc.

Because men who exhibit such traits are often assumed to be gay, they become targets for verbal and physical abuse. Indeed, as Laura Sessions Stepp describes in Reading 35, even elementary school boys are subject to this abuse. The popular linkage of effeminate behavior with a gay sexual orientation is so strong that it may be the primary criterion most Americans use to decide who is gay: A "masculine" man must be straight; a "feminine" man must be gay. But gender and sexual orientation are *separate* phenomena. Knowing that someone is a masculine man or a feminine woman does not tell us what that person's sexual orientation is—indeed, our guesses are most likely to be "false negatives"; that is, we are most likely to falsely identify someone as straight. Because we do not know who among us is gay, we cannot accurately judge how gay people behave.

In the world of mutual "othering," being labeled one of "them" is a remarkably effective social control mechanism. Boys and men control their behavior so that they are not called gay. Members of racial and ethnic groups maintain distance from one another to avoid the criticism that might be leveled by members of their own and other groups. These social controls are effective because all parties continue to enforce them.

Stigma

In the extreme, those depicted as "other" may be said to be *stigmatized*. Whole categories of people have been stigmatized as a result of the outcome of large-scale social and historical processes.

The term *stigma* comes from ancient Greece, where it meant a "bodily sign designed to expose something unusual and bad about the moral status of [an individual]." Such signs were "cut or burnt into the body to advertise that the bearer was a slave, a criminal, or a blemished person, ritually polluted, to be avoided, especially in public places" (Goffman, 1963:1). Stigmatized people are those "marked" as bad, unworthy, and polluted because of the category they belong to, for example, because of their disability, or their race, sex, sexual orientation, or social class category. The core assumption behind stigma is that internal merit is revealed through external features—for the Greeks, that a brand or a cut showed the moral worth of the person. This is not an unusual linkage; for example, physically attractive people are often assumed to possess a variety of positive attributes (Adams, 1982). We assume that people who look good must *be* good.

Judgments of worth based on membership in certain categories have a self-fulfilling potential. Those who are judged superior by virtue of their membership in some category are given more opportunity to prove themselves; those who are judged less worthy by virtue of membership in a stigmatized category have difficulty establishing their merit no matter what they do. For example, social psychology data indicate that many whites perceive blacks as incompetent, regardless of evidence to the contrary: white subjects were "reluctant or unable to recognize that a black person is higher or equal in intelligence compared to themselves" (Gaertner and Dovidio, 1986:75). This would explain why many whites react negatively to affirmative action programs. If they cannot conceive of black applicants as being *more* qualified than whites, they will see such programs as only mandates to hire the less qualified.

Stigma involves objectification as well as devaluation. *Objectification* means treating people as if they were objects, members of a category rather than possessors of individual characteristics. In objectification, the "living, breathing, complex individual" ceases to be seen or valued (Allport, 1958:175). In its extreme, those who are objectified are "viewed as having no other noteworthy status or identity. When that point is reached a person becomes *nothing* but 'a delinquent,' 'a cripple,' 'a homosexual,' 'a black,' 'a woman.' The indefinite article 'a' underlines the depersonalized nature of such response" (Schur, 1984:30–31).

Examples of Stigmatized Master Statuses: Women, Poor People, and Disabled People   Sociologist Edwin Schur argues that because women are subject to both objectification and devaluation, they are discredited, that is, stigmatized. First, considering objectification, Schur argues that women are seen

> as all alike, and therefore substitutable for one another; as innately passive and objectlike; as easily ignored, dismissed, trivialized, treated as childlike, and even as a non-person; as having a social standing only through their attachments to men (or other non-stigmatized groups); and as a group which can be easily victimized through harassment, violence, and discrimination. (Schur, 1984:33)

Objectification occurs when women are thought of as generally indistinguishable from one another; for example, when someone says, "Let's get the woman's angle on this story." It also occurs when women are treated as nothing more than their body parts, for example, when young girls are assumed to be sexually promiscuous because they are big-breasted: they are nothing more than their cup size; they are objects.

African Americans, Latinos, Asian Americans, and gay/lesbian people are often similarly treated as indistinguishable from one another. Indeed, hate crimes have been defined by this quality of interchangeability, such as an attack on any black family that moves into a neighborhood or the assault of any woman or man who looks gay. Hate crimes are also marked by excessive brutality and personal violence rather than property destruction—all of which indicate that the victims have been objectified (Levin and McDevitt, 1993).

Some members of stigmatized categories objectify themselves in the same ways that they are objectified by others. Thus, women may evaluate their own worth in terms of their physical appearance. In the process of self-objectification, a woman "joins the spectators of herself"; that is, she views herself as if from the outside, as if she were nothing more than what she looked like (Berger, 1963:50). This sense of making an object of oneself was captured several years ago in a cereal commercial where a bikini-clad woman posed before a mirror. She had lost weight for an upcoming vacation and was imagining herself as a stranger on the beach might see her. Thus, she succeeded in making an object of herself. While physical appearance is also valued for men, it rarely takes precedence over all other qualities. Rather, men are more likely to be objectified in terms of wealth and power.

In addition to being objectified, there is a strong case that American women as a category remain devalued, a conclusion drawn from the characteristics most frequently attributed to men and women. Research conducted over the last 40 years has documented a remarkable consistency in those attributes. Both sexes are described as possessing valued qualities, but the characteristics attributed to men are more valued in the culture as a whole. For example, the female-valued characteristics include being talkative, gentle, religious, aware of the feelings of others, security oriented, and attentive to personal appearance. Male-valued traits include being aggressive, independent, unemotional, objective, dominant, active, competitive, logical, adventurous, and direct (Basow, 1992; Baron and Byrne, 2004).[9] (Remember that these attributes are only people's *beliefs* about sex differences.)

In many ways, the characteristics attributed to women are inconsistent with core American values. While American culture values achievement, individualism, and action—all understood as male attributes—women are expected to subordinate their personal interests to the family and to be passive and patient (Richardson, 1977). Therefore, "women are asked to become the kind of people that this culture does not value" (Richardson, 1977:11). Thus, it is more acceptable for women to display masculine traits, since these are culturally valued, than it is for men to display less-valued feminine characteristics. Men who are talkative, gentle, religious, aware of the feelings of others, security oriented, and attentive to personal appearance are much maligned. In contrast, women may be independent, unemotional, objective, dominant, active, competitive, logical, adventurous, and direct with fewer negative consequences. The characteristics we attribute to women are not valued for everyone, unlike the characteristics attributed to men.

Much of what we have described about the stigmatization of women applies to the poor as well. Indeed, being poor is a much more obviously shameful status than being female. The category *poor* is intrinsically devalued. At least in contemporary American culture, it is presumed there is little commendable to be said about poor people; "they" are primarily constructed as a "problem." Poor people are also objectified; they are described as "*the* poor," as if they were all alike, substitutable for and interchangeable with one another.

> Most of the writing about poor people, even by sympathetic observers, tells us that they are different, truly strangers in our midst: Poor people think, feel, and act in ways unlike middle-class Americans. . . .
>
> We can think about poor people as "them" or as "us." For the most part, Americans have talked about "them." Even in the language of social science, as well as in ordinary conversation and political rhetoric, poor people usually remain outsiders, strangers to be pitied or despised, helped or punished, ignored or studied, but rarely full citizens, members of a larger community on the same terms as the rest of us. They are . . . "those people," objects of curiosity, analysis, prurience, or compassion, not subjects who construct their own lives and history. Poor people seem

---

[9]"Compared with White women, Black women are viewed as less passive, dependent, status conscious, emotional and concerned about their appearance. . . . Hispanic women tend to be viewed as more 'feminine' than White women in terms of submissiveness and dependence. . . . [A] similar stereotype holds for Asian women, but with the addition of exotic sexuality. . . . Native-American women typically are stereotyped as faceless . . . drudges without any personality. . . . Jewish women are stereotyped as either pushy, vain 'princesses' or overprotective, manipulative 'Jewish mothers' . . . working-class women are stereotyped as more hostile, confused, inconsiderate and irresponsible than middle-class women . . . and lesbians are stereotyped as possessing masculine traits" (Basow, 1992:4).

cardboard cutouts, figures in single dimension, members of inferior categories, rarely complex, multifaceted, even contradictory in the manner of other persons. (M. Katz, 1989:6, 126)

And, like women, poor people are not expected to display attributes valued in the culture as a whole.

Everything that we have described about stigma applies directly to the experience of disabled people. The concept of stigma was initially developed by sociologist Erving Goffman with disabled people in mind, and there are so many ways that the term applies that it is difficult to select a single focus. From assumptions that one is pitiable, sick, unhappy, incompetent, dependent, childlike, unattractive, and sexually undesirable, to notions that disability is a punishment for sin, disabled people are cast as essentially unworthy.

In addition to the stigma, those who are disabled—like many others in stigmatized categories—must also manage the paternalism of those who are not disabled. Taken from the position of a father toward his children, paternalism is the automatic assumption of superiority.

Paternalism is often subtle in that it casts the oppressor as benign, as protector. . . . Paternalism often must transform its subjects into children or people with childlike qualities. . . . Paternalism is experienced as the bystander grabs the arm of a blind person and, without asking, 'helps' the person across the street. . . . It is most of all, however, the assumption that people with disabilities are intrinsically inferior and unable to take responsibility for their own lives. (Charlton, 2000:53)

For those of us outside the stigmatized group, a paternalistic attitude is dangerous because it keeps us from actually seeing the person in front of us: "A person who cannot see or is using a wheelchair for mobility may be a happy, prosperous, well-adjusted person, but most people encountering him or her immediately feel pity" (Charlton, 2000:55).

Stereotypes about People in Stigmatized Master Statuses　　Finally, in an effort to capture the general features of what "we" say about "them," let us consider five common stereotypes about individuals in stigmatized master statuses.

First, they are presumed to lack the values the culture holds dear. Neither women nor those who are poor, disabled, gay, black, Asian American, or Latino are expected to be independent, unemotional, objective, dominant, active, competitive, logical, adventurous, or direct. Stigmatized people are presumed to lack precisely those values that nonstigmatized people are expected to possess.

Second, stigmatized people are likely to be seen as a problem (Adam, 1978; Wilson and Gutierrez, 1985). Certainly black, Latino, and Native American men and women, gay and lesbian people of all colors, white women, all disabled people, and people living in poverty are constructed as *having* problems and *being* problems. Often the implication is that they are also responsible for many of our national problems. While public celebrations often highlight the historic contributions of such groups to the culture, little in the public discourse lauds their current contributions. Indeed, those in stigmatized categories are often constructed as *nothing but a problem*, as if they did not exist apart from those problems. This was once illustrated by a black student who described her shock at hearing white students describe her middle-class neighborhood as a "ghetto."

Ironically, this depiction of stigmatized people as nothing but a problem is often accompanied by the trivialization of those problems. For example, a 2002 Gallup poll showed 34 percent of men very satisfied with the way women are treated in society, compared to only 18 percent of women (Brooks, 2004). Similarly, despite the participation of thousands of people in annual Gay Pride marches throughout the country, television footage typically trivializes that population by focusing on the small number in drag. Whites' opinion that blacks prefer welfare to supporting themselves similarly trivializes the experience of poverty (Thornton and Whitman, 1992). Thus, the problems that stigmatized categories of people create for those in privileged statuses are highlighted, while the problems they experience are discounted.

Third, people in stigmatized master statuses are often stereotyped as lacking self-control; they are characterized as being lustful, immoral, and carriers of disease (Gilman, 1985, 1991). Currently, such accusations hold center stage in the depictions of gay men, but historically such charges have been leveled at African American, Latino, and Asian American men (e.g., Chinese immigrants in the late 19th century). Poor women and women of color have been and continue to be depicted as promiscuous, while poor men and women are presumed to be morally irresponsible.

Fourth, people in stigmatized categories are often marked as having too much or too little intelligence, and in either case as tending to deception or criminality. Many stigmatized categories of people have been assumed to use their "excessive" intelligence to unfair advantage. This was historically the charge against Jews, and now appears to be a characterization of Asian Americans.

> [T]he educational achievement of Asian American students was, and continues to be, followed by a wave of reaction. The image of Asian Americans as diligent super-students has often kindled resentment in other students. Sometimes called "damned curve raisers," a term applied first to Jewish students at elite East Coast colleges during the 1920s and 1930s, Asian American students have increasingly found themselves taking the brunt of campus racial jokes. (Takagi, 1992:60)

Fifth, people in stigmatized categories are depicted as both childlike and savagely brutal. Historically, characterizations of Native Americans, enslaved Africans, and Chinese immigrants reflected these conceptions. Currently, the same is true for the poor in their representation as both pervasively violent and irresponsible. A related depiction of women as both "virgins and whores" has been well documented in scholarship over time.

Perhaps because people in stigmatized master statuses are stereotyped as deviant, it appears that those who commit violence against them are unlikely to be punished. For example, "most murders in the USA are intra-racial, that is, the alleged perpetrator and the victim are of the same race. . . . Yet of the 845 prisoners executed between 17 January 1977 and 10 April 2003, 53 percent were whites convicted of killing whites and 10 percent were blacks convicted of killing blacks" (Amnesty International, 2003). While a number of factors are operating here, one conclusion is that stigmatized minority victims are valued less than white victims. The same conclusion could be reached in terms of the punishment meted out to those accused of sexual assault. "Major offenses *against* women, which we *profess* to consider deviant, in practice have been responded to with much ambivalence" (Schur, 1984:7). Indeed, some have argued that one way to recognize a stigmatized category of people is that the violence directed at them is not treated seriously (Schur, 1984).

Overall, individuals in stigmatized master statuses are represented as not only physically distinctive but also the antithesis of the culture's desired behaviors and attributes. They are seen as not operating from cultural values. They are problems; they are immoral and disease ridden; their intelligence is questionable; they are childlike and savage. Such characterizations serve to dismiss claims of discrimination and unfair treatment, affirming that those in stigmatized categories deserve such treatment, that they are themselves responsible for their plight. Indeed, many of these stereotypes are also applied to teenagers, whom the media depict as violent, reckless, hypersexed, ignorant, out of control, and the cause of society's problems (Males, 1994).

A Final Comment

It is disheartening to think of oneself as a member of a stigmatized group, just as it is disheartening to think of oneself as thoughtlessly perpetuating stigma. Still, there are at least two important points of hopefulness here. First, the characteristics attributed to stigmatized groups are similar across a great variety of master statuses. Thus, there is the relief of impersonality because the stigmatized characteristics are not tied to the actual characteristics of any particular group. Second, people who are stigmatized have often formed alliances with those who are not stigmatized to successfully lobby against these attributions.

As we said at the outset of this essay, our hope is to provide you with a framework by which to make sense of what sex, disability, race, social class, and sexual orientation mean in contemporary American society. Clearly, these categorizations are complex; they are tied to emotionally intense issues that are uniquely American; and they have consequences that are both mundane and dramatic. From naming, to aggregating, to dichotomizing, and ultimately to stigmatizing, difference has a meaning for us. The readings in Section I explore the construction of these categorizations; the readings in Section II examine how we experience them; the readings in Section III address the meaning that is attributed to difference; and the readings in Section IV describe how we can bridge these differences.

KEY CONCEPTS

aggregate To combine or lump together (verb); something composed of different elements (noun). (pages 13–16)

-centrism or -centric Suffix meaning centered around, focused around, taking the perspective of. Thus, **androcentric** means focused around or taking the perspective of men; **heterocentric** means taking the perspective of heterosexuals; and **eurocentric** means having a European focus. (page 16)

constructionism The view that reality cannot be separated from the way a culture makes sense of it— that meaning is "constructed" through social, political, legal, scientific, and other practices. From this perspective, differences among people are created through social processes. (pages 3–6)

dichotomize To divide into two parts and to see those parts as mutually exclusive. (pages 16–27) of Asian ancestry found it necessary to disassociate themselves from other Asian groups.

The development of a pan-Asian consciousness and constituency reflected broader societal developments and demographic changes as well as the group's political agenda. Before World War II, pan-Asian unity was not feasible because the predominantly foreign-born Asian population did not share a common language. During the postwar years, owing to immigration restrictions and the growing dominance of the second and even third generations, U.S.-born Asians outnumbered immigrants. By 1960 approximately two-thirds of the Asian population in California had been born in the United States (Ong 1989, 5–8). With English as the common language, persons from different Asian backgrounds were able to communicate with one another (Ling 1984, 73) and in so doing to create a common identity associated with the United States. Also, the breakdown of economic and residential barriers during the postwar period provided the first opportunity for an unprecedented number of Asian Americans to come into intimate, sustained contact with the larger society—and with one another. Formerly homogeneous, the Asian ethnic enclaves started to house mixed-Asian communities, as well as non-Asian groups. Multigroup suburban centers also emerged. Paul Wong (1972, 34) reported that since the early 1960s Asian Americans of diverse national origins had moved into the suburbs outside the major Asian communities such as Berkeley and San Mateo, California. Although a small proportion of the local population, these Asian Americans tended to congregate in pockets; consequently, in some residential blocks a majority of the residents were Asian Americans.

Although broader social struggles and internal demographic changes provided the impetus for the Asian American movement, it was the Asian Americans' politics—explicitly radical, confrontational, and pan-Asian—that shaped the movement's content. Inspired by anticolonial revolutions in Asia and by black and Chicano revolutionary nationalism, college students of Asian ancestry sought to transcend inter-Asian ethnic divisions and to ally themselves with other "Third World" minorities (Blauner 1972,

ch. 2; Omatsu 1994). Through pan-Asian organizations, publications, and Asian American studies programs, Asian American activists forged a pan-Asian consciousness by highlighting their shared resistance to Western imperialism and to U.S. racism. The pan-Asian concept enabled diverse Asian American groups to understand their "unequal circumstances and histories as being related" (Lowe 1991, 30). By the mid-1970s, "Asian American" had become a familiar term (Lott 1976, 30). Although first coined by college activists, the pan-Asian concept began to be used extensively by professional and community spokespersons to lobby for the health and welfare of Americans of Asian descent. Commenting on the "literally scores of pan-Asian organizations" in the mid-1970s, William Liu (1976, 6) asserted that "the idea of pan-Asian cooperation [was] viable and ripe for development."

The advent of state-sponsored affirmative action programs provided another material reason for Asian American subgroups to consolidate their efforts. Because the welfare state bureaucracy often treats all Asian Americans as a single administrative unit in distributing economic and political resources, it imposes a pan-Asian structure on persons and communities dependent on government support. As dealings with government bureaucracies increased, political organization along a pan-Asian line became necessary, not only because numbers confer power but also because the pan-Asian category is the institutionally relevant category in the political and legal system. Administratively treated as a homogeneous group, Asian Americans found it necessary—and even advantageous—to respond as a group. The pan-Asian strategy has led to some political victories. For example, Asian American legislators, community leaders, and organizations united to fight the Census Bureau's proposal to collapse all Asian racial codes into one summary category for the 1980 and 1990 censuses. Partly in response to the strength of their political lobbying, the Census Bureau finally conceded to the coalition's demand for a detailed enumeration of Asian subgroups.[2] Indeed, the emergence of the pan-Asian entity may be one of the most significant political developments in Asian American affairs. . . .

differential undercount In the census, undercounting more of one group than of another. (pages 10–13)

disaggregate To separate something into its constituent elements. (pages 13–16)

essential identity An identity that is treated as core to a person. Essential identities can be attributed to people even when they are inconsistent with actual behavior. (page 24)

essentialism The view that reality exists independently of our perception of it, that we perceive the meaning of the world rather than construct that meaning. From this perspective, there are real and important (essential) differences among categories of people. (pages 3–6)

ethnic group, ethnicity Those who share a sense of being a "people," usually based on national origin, language, or religion. (page 18)

gender Masculinity and femininity; the acting out of the behaviors thought to be appropriate for a particular sex. (page 26)

heterosexism The presumption that all people are heterosexual (in this sense, synonymous with heterocentric); the presumption that heterosexuality is the only acceptable form of sexual expression. (page 2)

intersectionality Consideration of the ways that master statuses interact and mutually construct one another. (page 4)

master status A status that has a profound effect on one's life, that dominates or overwhelms the other statuses one occupies. (page 2)

objectification Treating people as if they were objects, as if they were nothing more than the attributes they display. (page 31)

Other A usage designed to refer to those considered profoundly unlike oneself. (page 27)

panethnic A classification that spans ethnic identities. (page 14)

race The conception that people can be classified into groups based on skin color, hair texture, shape of head, eyes, nose, and lips. (pages 17–22)

sex The categories of male and female. (page 26)

status A position in society. Individuals occupy multiple statuses simultaneously, such as occupational, kinship, and educational statuses. (page 2)

stigma An attribute for which someone is considered bad, unworthy, or deeply discredited. (pages 30–35)

REFERENCES

Adam, Barry. 1978. *The Survival of Domination.* New York: Elsevier.

Adams, Gerald R. 1982. Physical Attractiveness. *In the Eye of the Beholder: Contemporary Issues in Stereotyping,* edited by A. G. Miller, 253–304. New York: Praeger.

Allport, Gordon. 1958. *The Nature of Prejudice.* Garden City, NY: Doubleday Anchor.

Amnesty International. 2003. Death by Discrimination: The Continuing Role of Race in Capital Cases. http://web.amnesty.org/library/print/ENGAMR510462003.

Archer, Bert. 2002. *The End of Gay (and the Death of Heterosexuality).* New York: Thunder's Mouth Press.

Arrow, Kenneth, Samuel Bowles, and Steven Durlauf. 2000. Introduction. *Meritocracy and Economic Inequality,* edited by Kenneth Arrow, Samuel Bowles, and Steven Durlauf, ix–xv. Princeton, NJ: Princeton University Press.

Barnes, Colin, and Geof Mercer. 2003. *Disability.* Cambridge, UK: Polity Press.

Baron, Robert A., and Donn Byrne. 2004. *Social Psychology.* Boston: Pearson.

Basow, Susan A. 1992. *Gender: Stereotypes and Roles.* 3d ed. Pacific Grove, CA: Brooks/Cole Publishing.

Begley, Sharon. 1995. Three Is Not Enough. *Newsweek,* February 13, 67–69.

Berger, Peter L. 1963. *Invitation to Sociology: A Humanistic Perspective.* Garden City, NY: Doubleday Anchor.

Blauner, Robert. 1992. Talking Past Each Other: Black and White Languages of Race. *The American Prospect,* 10.

Brooks, Deborah Jordan. 2004. Job Equality Views: Gender Gap Still Wide. *Gallup Poll News Service.* August 27.

Charlton, James. 2000. *Nothing About Us Without Us: Disability Oppression and Empowerment.* Los Angeles, CA: University of California Press.

Choldin, Harvey M. 1986. Statistics and Politics: The "Hispanic Issue" in the 1980 Census. *Demography,* 23:403–18.

———. 1994. *Looking for the Last Percent: The Controversy over Census Undercounts.* New Brunswick, NJ: Rutgers University Press.

Cohen, G. 1995. *Self, Ownership, Freedom, and Equality.* Cambridge: Cambridge University Press.

Cohen, Mark Nathan. 1998. *Culture of Intolerance: Chauvinism, Class, and Racism in the United States.* New Haven, CT: Yale University Press.

Cohn, D'Vera. 2001. Counting of Gay Couples Up 300%. *Washington Post,* August 22, A.

Coles, Gerald. 1987. *The Learning Mystique: A Critical Look at "Learning Disabilities."* New York: Pantheon.

Conrad, Peter, and Joseph W. Schneider. 1980. *Deviance and Medicalization: From Badness to Sickness.* Philadelphia: Temple University Press.

Davis, F. James. 1991. *Who Is Black? One Nation's Rule.* University Park, PA: Pennsylvania State University Press.

de la Garza, Rudolfo O., Louis DeSipio, F. Chris Garcia, John Garcia, and Angelo Falcon. 1992. *Latino Voices: Mexican, Puerto Rican, and Cuban Perspectives on American Politics.* Boulder, CO: Westview Press.

Dreifus, Claudia. 2005. A Sociologist Confronts "The Messy Stuff": A Conversation with Troy Duster. *The New York Times,* October 18, Science Times.

Dubos, Rene. 1961. *Mirage of Health.* Garden City, NY: Anchor Books.

Espiritu, Yen Le. 1992. *Asian American Panethnicity: Bridging Institutions and Identities.* Philadelphia: Temple University Press.

Faderman, Lillian. 1991. *Odd Girls and Twilight Lovers: A History of Lesbian Life in Twentieth-Century America.* New York: Penguin Books.

Fussell, Paul. 1983. *Class.* New York: Ballentine Books.

Gaertner, Samuel L., and John F. Dovidio. 1986. The Aversive Form of Racism. *Prejudice, Discrimination, and Racism,* edited by John F. Dovidio and Samuel L. Gaertner, 61–89. Orlando, FL: Academic Press.

Gallup Organization, Gallup Poll News Service. 2003. Q&A: Black-White Relations in the U.S.

Gates, Gary J. 2006. *Same-Sex Couples and the Gay, Lesbian, Bisexual Population: New Estimates from the American Community Survey.* The Williams Institute on Sexual Orientation Law and Public Policy, UCLA School of Law.

Gilman, Sander. 1985. *Difference and Pathology: Stereotypes of Sexuality, Race, and Madness.* Ithaca, NY: Cornell University Press.

———. 1991. *The Jew's Body.* New York: Routledge.

Goffman, Erving. 1963. *Stigma: Notes on the Management of Spoiled Identity.* Englewood Cliffs, NJ: Prentice-Hall.

Gordon, Margaret T., and *Female Fear.* New York:

Gracia, Jorge J. E. 2000. A Yes and No. *Hispanics/L Ethnicity, Race, and Righ* and Pablo De Greiff, 20

Haines, David W. 2007. F Religion, and Nationali among Recent United States Arrivals. *Identities. Global Studies in Culture and Power,* 14:1–28.

Henshel, Richard L., and Robert A. Silverman. 1975. *Perceptions in Criminology.* New York: Columbia University Press.

Higgins, Paul C. 1992. *Making Disability: Exploring the Social Transformation of Human Variation.* Springfield, IL: Charles C. Thomas.

Hilts, V. 1973. Statistics and Social Science. *Foundations of Scientific Method in the Nineteenth Century,* edited by R. Giere and R. Westfall, 206–33. Bloomington, IN: Indiana University Press.

Hu-Dehart, Evelyn. 1994. Asian/Pacific American Issues in American Education. Presentation at the 7th Annual National Conference on Race and Ethnicity in American Higher Education, Atlanta, sponsored by The Southwest Center for Human Relations Studies, University of Oklahoma, College of Continuing Education.

Jenkins, Alan. 1999. See No Evil. *The Nation,* June 28:15–19.

Kahlenberg, Richard D. 1997. *The Remedy: Class, Race, and Affirmative Action.* New York: Basic Books.

Katz, Jack. 1975. Essences as Moral Identities: Verifiability and Responsibility in Imputations of Deviance and Charisma. *American Journal of Sociology,* 80:1369–90.

Katz, Michael B. 1989. *The Undeserving Poor: From the War on Poverty to the War on Welfare.* New York: Pantheon Books.

Kessler, Suzanne J., and Wendy McKenna. 1978. *Gender: An Ethnomethodological Approach.* New York: John Wiley & Sons.

Kimberly, Margaret. 2005. A Bitter Pill for Black Hearts. *AlterNet.* http://www.alternet.org/story/23185 (accessed June 28, 2005).

Kinsey, Alfred, Wardell Pomeroy, and Clyde Martin. 1948. *Sexual Behavior in the Human Male.* Philadelphia: W. B. Saunders.

Klein, Fritz. 1978. *The Bisexual Option.* New York: Arbor House.

chael. 1992. Genetic Tests under Fire.
ruary 24, 65.

mon. 1991. A Difference in Hypothalmic
ucture between Heterosexual and Homosexual
Men. Science, 253:1034–37.

Levin, Jack, and Jack McDevitt. 1993. *Hate Crimes.*
New York: Plenum Press.

Lieberman, Leonard. 1968. A Debate over Race: A Study
in the Sociology of Knowledge. *Phylon,* 29:127–41.

Linton, Simi. 1999. *Claiming Disability: Knowledge and
Identity.* New York: New York University Press.

Lopez, David, and Yen Espiritu. 1990. Panethnicity in
the United States: A Theoretical Framework. *Ethnic
and Racial Studies,* 13:198–224.

Males, Mike. 1994. Bashing Youth: Media Myths about
Teenagers. *Extra!* March/April, 8–11.

Marshall, Gloria. 1993. Racial Classifications: Popular
and Scientific. *The "Racial" Economy of Science:
Toward a Democratic Future,* edited by Sandra
Harding, 116–27. Bloomington, IN: Indiana University
Press (Originally published 1968).

Marshall, Gordon. 1994. *The Concise Oxford Dictionary
of Sociology.* Oxford: Oxford University Press.

Michael, Robert T. 1994. *Sex in America: A Definitive
Survey.* Boston: Little, Brown.

Mills, Jane. 1989. *Womanwords: A Dictionary of Words
about Women.* New York: Henry Holt.

Mincey, Ronald B. 1994. *Confronting Poverty: Prescriptions
for Change.* Cambridge: Harvard University Press.

Mohawk, John. 1992. Looking for Columbus: Thoughts
on the Past, Present and Future of Humanity. *The
State of Native America: Genocide, Colonization, and
Resistance,* edited by M. Annette Jaimes, 439–44.
Boston: South End Press.

Moore, David W. 2004. Modest Rebound in Public
Acceptance of Homosexuals. *Gallup Poll News
Service,* May 20.

Morris, Michael, and John B. Williamson. 1982.
Stereotypes and Social Class: A Focus on Poverty.
In the Eye of the Beholder, edited by Arthur G. Miller,
411–65. New York: Praeger.

Morrison, Toni. 1992. *Playing in the Dark.* New York:
Vintage.

Office of Management and Budget. 1995. Standards
for the Classification of Federal Data on Race and
Ethnicity Notice. *Federal Register* 60:44674–693.

———. October 1997. *Revisions to the Standards for the
Classification of Federal Data on Race and Ethnicity.*
Washington, DC: U.S. Government Printing Office.

Oliver, Michael. 1990. *The Politics of Disablement.*
London: Macmillan.

———. 1996. *Understanding Disability.* New York:
Palgrave.

Omansky, Beth. 2006. *Not Blind Enough: Living in
the Borderland Called Legal Blindness.* Ph.D. Thesis,
University of Queensland.

Omi, Michael. 1996. Racialization in the Post–Civil
Rights Era. *Mapping Multiculturalism,* edited by
A. Gordon and C. Newfield, 178–85. Minneapolis:
University of Minnesota Press.

———, and Howard Winant. 1994. *Racial Formation in
the United States.* New York: Routledge.

Ortner, Sherry B. 1991. Reading America. Preliminary
Notes on Class and Culture. *Recapturing Anthropology:
Working in the Present,* edited by Richard G. Fox, 163–89.
Santa Fe, NM: School of American Research Press.

Pfuhl, Erdwin H. 1986. *The Deviance Process.* 2d ed.
Belmont, CA: Wadsworth.

Population Reference Bureau. 2001. Increasing Diversity
in the U.S. Hispanic Population. www.prb.org.

Richardson, Laurel. 1977. *The Dynamics of Sex and
Gender: A Sociological Perspective.* New York: Harper
and Row.

———. 1988. *The Dynamics of Sex and Gender:
A Sociological Perspective.* 3d ed. New York: Harper
and Row.

Rist, Darrell Yates. 1992. Are Homosexuals Born That
Way? *The Nation,* 255:424–29.

Roediger, David. 1994. *Towards the Abolition of
Whiteness.* London: Verso.

Rubio, Philip F. 2001. *A History of Affirmative Action:
1619–2000.* Jackson: University of Mississippi Press.

Russell, Marta. 1994. Malcolm Teaches Us Too. *The
Ragged Edge: The Disability Experience from the Pages
of the First Fifteen Years of the Disability Rag,* edited by.
Barrett Shaw, 11–14. Louisville, KY: Avocado Press.

Sanday, Peggy Reeves. 1990. *Fraternity Gang Rape.*
New York: New York University Press.

Schmidt, Peter. 2003. The Label "Hispanic" Irks Some,
but Also Unites. *The Chronicle of Higher Education,*
November 23, A9.

Schneider, Joseph W. 1988. Disability as Moral
Experience: Epilepsy and Self in Routine
Relationships. *Journal of Social Issues,* 44:63–78.

Schur, Edwin. 1984. *Labeling Women Deviant: Gender,
Stigma, and Social Control.* New York: Random House.

Schwarz, John E., and Thomas J. Volgy. 1992. *The
Forgotten Americans.* New York: W. W. Norton.

Sherman Heyl, Barbara. 1989. Homosexuality: A Social Phenomenon. *Human Sexuality: The Societal and Interpersonal Context,* edited by Kathleen McKinney and Susan Sprecher, 321–349. Norwood, NJ: Ablex.

Shipman, Pat. 1994. *The Evolution of Racism: Human Differences and the Use and Abuse of Science.* New York: Simon and Schuster.

Shorris, Earl. 1992. *Latinos: A Biography of the People.* New York: W. W. Norton.

Smedley, Audrey. 1993. *Race in North America: Origin and Evolution of a Worldview.* Boulder, CO: Westview Press.

Smith, Tom W. 1992. Changing Racial Labels: From "Colored" to "Negro" to "Black" to "African American." *Public Opinion Quarterly,* 56:496–514.

Spelman, Elizabeth. 1988. *Inessential Woman.* Boston: Beacon Press.

Springer, S. P., and G. Deutsch. 1981. *Left Brain, Right Brain.* San Francisco: Freeman.

Steinberg, Stephen. 1989. *The Ethnic Myth: Race, Ethnicity, and Class in America.* Boston: Beacon Press.

Takagi, Dana Y. 1992. *The Retreat from Race: Asian-American Admission and Racial Politics.* New Brunswick, NJ: Rutgers University Press.

Takaki, Ronald. 1990. *Iron Cages: Race and Culture in 19th-Century America.* New York: Oxford University Press.

———. 1993. *A Different Mirror.* Boston: Little Brown.

Tamayo Lott, Juanita. 1998. *Asian Americans: From Racial Category to Multiple Identities.* Walnut Creek, CA: Altamira Press.

Thompson, Eric C. 2006. The Problem of "Race" as a Social Construct. *Anthropology News* 47(2): 6–7.

Thornton, Jeannye, and David Whitman. 1992. Whites' Myths about Blacks. *U.S. News and World Report,* November 9:41–44.

U.S. Census Bureau. 2001. *Census 2000 Summary File 2, Technical Documentation:* September 2001, SF2/01: G39–G41.

U.S. Commission on Civil Rights. 1973. *To Know or Not to Know: Collection and Use of Racial and Ethnic Data in Federal Assistance Programs.* Washington, DC: U.S. Government Printing Office.

U.S. Department of Commerce. 2001. People Who Reported Two or More Races Are Young and Tend to Live in the West. *United States Department of Commerce News,* November 29.

U.S. Department of Education, 1990. *To Assure the Free Appropriate Public Education of All Handicapped Children: Twelfth Annual Report to Congress on the Implementation of the Education of the Handicapped Act.* Washington, DC: U.S. Government Printing Office.

U.S. Department of Labor. 2005. A Profile of the Working Poor, 2003. Report 983. U.S. Bureau of Labor Statistics.

Wade, Nicholas. 2005. "Genetic Find Stirs Debate on Race-Based Medicine." *The New York Times, Science Times,* November 11.

Weinberg, George. 1973. *Society and the Healthy Homosexual.* Garden City, NY: Anchor.

Wiefek, Nancy. 2003. *The Impact of Economic Anxiety in Postindustrial America.* Westport, CT: Praeger.

Wilson, Clint, II, and Felix Gutierrez. 1985. *Minorities and the Media.* Beverly Hills, CA: Sage.

Zola, Irving K. 1993. Disability Statistics, What We Count and What It Tells Us: A Personal and Political Analysis. *Journal of Disability Policy Studies,* 4:10–37.

WHAT IS RACE? WHAT IS ETHNICITY?

"Race" and the Construction of Human Identity

Audrey Smedley

HISTORICAL CONSTRUCTIONS OF IDENTITY

Historical records, including the Old and New Testaments of the Bible, evince scenarios of inter-ethnic interaction that suggest some very different principles in operation throughout much of human history.[1] Ethnic groups have always existed in the sense that clusters of people living in demarcated areas develop lifestyles and language features that distinguish them from others and they perceive themselves as being separate societies with distinct social histories. Although some conflicts among different groups have been characteristic from the earliest recorded histories, hostilities were usually neither constant nor the basis on which long-term relationships were established.

One factor separates many in the contemporary world, at least some of our understandings of it, from earlier conceptions of human identity. That is that "ethnic" identity was not perceived as ineluctably set in stone. Individuals and groups of individuals often moved to new areas or changed their identities by acquiring membership in a different group. People of the ancient world seemed to have understood that cultural characteristics were external and acquired forms of behavior, and that "barbarians" could learn to speak the language of the Romans or the Greeks and become participants in those cultures, and even citizens of these states. Languages were indeed avenues to new social

Audrey Smedley is professor emeritus of anthropology at Virginia Commonwealth University.

identities, and ethnic identity itself was fluid and malleable.

Until the rise of market capitalism, wage labor, the Protestant Ethic, private property, and possessive individualism, kinship connections also operated as major indices that gave all peoples a sense of who they were. Even in the technologically and politically most advanced societies of the ancient world such as in Rome, kinship was the important diacritic of connectedness to the social system. In all of the mostly patrilineal societies of the Middle East. Africa, and the Mediterranean, the normal person was identified by who his or her father was. The long list of names of who begat whom in the Old Testament (Book of Genesis) attests to the importance, especially at the tribal and chiefdom levels, of genealogical identity.

Another important diagnostic of identity was occupation. Whether one was a farmer, carpenter, fisherman, tanner, brass worker, herdsman, philosopher, government official, senator, poet, healer, warrior, or harlot, was significantly salient in the eyes of the ancient world to require the label. Occupations determined to some extent how people were viewed and treated, as well as underscored their contribution to the society.

Throughout much of the period of the early imperial states, numerous groups were in contact with one another, and individuals often traveled from one region to another as traders, warriors, craftsmen, travelers, geographers, teachers, and so forth. From one end of the Mediterranean to another, in spite of the lack of modern forms of transportation, many men and women were interacting in an interethnic melange that included a wide range of cultures and peoples. From time to time, a conquest state would expand outward and incorporate some or most of this great variety. Populations did not necessarily lose any form of ethnic identity, but change was clearly understood as virtually inevitable as each society learned something new from the cultures of others. . . .

When Alexander conquered peoples and lands all the way to the Indus Valley in India, interacting with "civilized" populations, nomadic pastoralists, settled villagers, and a variety of hunting and fishing peoples, he exhorted his warriors to intermarry with the peoples they conquered in order to learn their languages and cultures. Garrisons of military men were stationed all over the Roman world, from Brittany to the Danube and the Black Sea, from Gibraltar to the Tigris/Euphrates valley and the Indian Ocean, and soldiers often took local women as wives. When the armies of the Moroccan king brought down the Songhai empire in 1591, his soldiers stayed on the Western Sudan frontier area and intermarried with the local people. Most of northern Africa, including Egypt of the Delta, has been periodically invaded and ruled by outsiders for the last three thousand years or so. Hittites and Hyksos from the mountainous areas of Turkey, Assyrians, Persians, Syrians, Phoenicians, Greeks, Babylonians, Romans, and various more recent Turkish and Arabian groups have settled in the towns of the coasts and interacted with the indigenous Berbers and other peoples like the Libyan groups, the Garamantes, the Carthaginians, Syngambrians, and many others. Less well known is the fact that both the Greeks and the Romans used mercenaries from inner Africa (Nubians, Ethiopians, Kushites, among others) in conflicts such as the Persian and Peloponnesian wars (Herodotus, in Godolphin 1942).[2]

Peoples of different cultures coexisted for the most part without strife, with alien segments often functioning in distinct roles in the larger cities. One-third of the population of Athens were foreigners as early as the Classical period, five hundred years before the Christian era (Boardman et al. 1986:222). And the city of Alexandria was (and still is) a heterogeneous, sophisticated, and complex community under the Greeks, Romans, Christians, and Arabs. Carthage was founded in North Africa by Phoenicians, but peoples from all over the Mediterranean world and other parts of Africa made their residence, or served as slaves, in this great trading city. Moreover, men and women of different ethnic groups intermarried frequently, largely because marriage was often used as a political or economic strategy. Men gave their daughters

and sisters to other men, the historians tell us, because they desired political and/or economic alliances with powerful and wealthy men, without regard to ethnic origins. Timotheus was the son of a Jewish mother and a Greek father. Samson married a Philistine woman; Moses married an Ethiopian woman; and many leaders, and lesser men, of the Greeks and Romans married women not from their own societies.

Different societies and localized segments of larger societies were known either by their ethnic name for themselves or by the region, town, or village of their origins. That identities of this type were fluid is indicated by the depictions of individual lives. Paul of Tarsus traveled and preached extensively throughout much of the known Mediterranean world during the early Christian era and encountered individuals of different ethnic backgrounds. He even identified himself as a Roman on occasion when it was useful to do so. There are other examples of individuals in ancient writings who changed their ethnic identities for personal or private reasons.

Scholars who have studied African societies, especially African history, have also been aware of the malleability of ethnic identity on that continent. New ethnic groups have emerged out of the colonial period, and individuals have been known to transform themselves according to their ethnic or religious milieus. One may be a Christian in one context, and a Muslim in another, with no sense of ambivalence or deception. I have encountered this phenomenon myself. Most Africans spoke several different languages, and this facilitated the molding of multiple ethnicities by providing immediate access to cultural knowledge. In situations of potential or real conflict, allegiances could be firmly established without denial of the extrinsic nature of social/ethnic identities (Connah 1987; Davidson 1991).

In addition to identities that are predicated on place of birth, membership in kin groups, or descent in the male or female line from known ancestors, language spoken, and lifestyle to which individuals have been conditioned, another feature critical to individual identity in the state systems was social position. Aristocrats seemed to have been recognized even beyond the boundaries of their immediate societies. And certain men were widely famed for their specialized skills or crafts that set them above others. Every society had its large body of commoners and usually a great number of slaves captured in war or traded in when this enterprise became a common regional feature. Slaves were usually outsiders, but slavery was not considered by law and custom a permanent condition as slaves could be manumitted, redeemed by kinspeople, or could purchase their own freedom (Smedley [1993]1999: ch. 6). While enslavement was considered an unfortunate circumstance and most slaves did the menial and onerous tasks of society, the roles of slaves varied widely. There are numerous examples of slaves rising to political power in the ancient states of the Mediterranean and in the Muslim world. Often they held positions as generals who led armies of conquest and were frequently rewarded for their successes. Whole slave dynasties like the Mamluks in Egypt reigned in various areas of the Muslim world (Hitti 1953).

With the appearance of the proselytizing universal religions, Christianity and later Islam, that became competitors with one another for the souls of all human groups, a new focus of identity was gradually and increasingly placed on membership in a religious community. During the Middle Ages of Europe, Christians and Muslims were competing not only for land and souls, but for political power and influence. And various sects that developed within each large religious community complicated matters by fostering internal dissension and even warfare inter alia. Whether one was Sunni or Shiite, Protestant or Catholic, was a critical determinant of one's identity locally and in the wider world. As with other aspects of ethnicity and ethnic differences, individuals often changed their religious affiliation under circumstances prompted by self-interest, or self-preservation, as in the case of the 300,000 or more Jews who were forced to convert to Catholicism in Medieval Spain during the Inquisition (Castro 1971). Yet Christians, Jews, and Muslims had lived together in relative amity, and

even intermarried, for several hundred years after the Muslim conquests and before the rise of the Christian kingdoms to challenge Muslim power.

What was absent from these different forms of human identity is what we today would perceive as classifications into "racial" groups, that is, the organization of all peoples into a limited number of unequal or ranked categories theoretically based on differences in their biophysical traits. There are no "racial" designations in the literature of the ancients and few references even to such human features as skin color. Frank Snowden has demonstrated that ever since at least the second millennium B.C. the peoples of the Mediterranean world have interacted with other groups having a variety of physical traits that differed from the Italians and Greeks. Artistic depictions of Africans of clear "negroid" features have been found, and numerous statues and paintings throughout the classical era show that physical variations in different populations were recognized and accurately depicted (Snowden 1983).

Except for indigenous Americans, members of all three of the large geographic areas that came to be categorized as "races" in the nineteenth and twentieth centuries (Mongoloid, Negroid, and Caucasoid) interacted in the ancient world. Chinese porcelain vases have been found widely distributed in the East African coastal trading cities, indicating trade between these peoples at least two thousand years old. The peoples of the Malagasy Republic represent a mixture of African and Asian (Indonesian) ancestry dating back several thousand years. Greek sailors sailed down the Red Sea into the Indian Ocean and met East Africans long before the Christian era. The peoples of the Mediterranean regularly traded with dark-skinned peoples of the upper Nile valley (and all those in between) northwest Africa, and the contrasting lighter-skinned peoples of Northern Europe. Various states of the Mediterranean called upon and used Ethiopian warriors as mercenaries in their armies, as we have seen. Some of the more desired slaves were very fair-skinned Slaves (from whom the term *slave* was derived) who were traded down the Danube by German tribesmen. Northern European slaves were shipped as far away as Egypt, Syria, Saudi Arabia, and the Muslim capital at Baghdad (Davis 1966).

What seems strange to us today is that the biological variations among human groups were not given significant social meaning. Only occasionally do ancient writers ever even remark on the physical characteristics of a given person or people. Herodotus, in discussing the habits, customs, and origins of different groups and noting variations in skin color, specifically tells us that this hardly matters. The Colchians are of Egyptian origin, he wrote, because they have black skins and wooly hair "which amounts to but little, since several other nations are so too."[3] Most writers explained such differences as due to natural environmental factors such as the hot sun causing people to be dark skinned. No structuring of inequality, whether social, moral, intellectual, cultural or otherwise, was associated with people *because of their skin color,* although all "barbarians" varied in some ways from the somatic norm of the Mediterranean world. But barbarians were not irredeemably so, and, as we have seen, nothing in the values of the public life denied the transformability of even the most backward of barbarians.

We in the contemporary Western world have often found it difficult to understand this phenomenon and assume that differences in skin color must have had some important meaning. Historians have tried to discover "racial" meanings in the literature of the ancients, assuming that these writers had the same attitudes and beliefs about human differences found in nineteenth- and twentieth-century North America. The reason for our myopia has to do with our deeply entrenched conditioning to the racial worldview (Smedley 1993, 1998). When "race" appeared in human history, it brought about a subtle but powerful transformation in the world's perceptions of human differences. It imposed social meanings on physical variations among human groups that served as the basis for the structuring of the total society. Since that time many people in the West have continued to link human identity to external physical features. We have been socialized to an ideology about the meaning of these differences

based on a notion of heredity and permanence that was unknown in the ancient world and in the Middle Ages.

RACE: THE MODERN CONCEPTION OF HUMAN DIFFERENCES AND HUMAN IDENTITY

In the eighteenth century this new mode of structuring inequality in human societies evolved in the American colonies and soon was present throughout the overseas territories of the colonizing countries of Western Europe. "Race" was a form of social identification and stratification that was seemingly grounded in the physical differences of populations interacting with one another in the New World, but whose real meaning rested in social and political realities. The term *race* had been used to refer to humans occasionally since the sixteenth century in the English language but was rarely used to refer to populations in the slave trade. It was a mere classificatory term like *kind, type,* or even *breed,* or *stock,* and it had no clear meaning until the eighteenth century. During this time, the English began to have wider experiences with varied populations and gradually developed attitudes and beliefs that had not appeared before in Western history and which reflected a new kind of understanding and interpretation of human differences. Understanding the foundations of race ideology is critical to our analysis.

English settlers in North America failed to assimilate the peoples whom they conquered; indeed they generally kept them at great length and social distance from themselves (Morgan 1975; Nash 1982). Indigenous Indians were different in both cultural and biological features, but this was not the necessary and sufficient reason for the English habits and policies of separateness. They had had a long history of enmity with earlier peoples, especially the Irish, on their very borders and had generated out of their hostility with the Irish an image of "savagery" that became institutionalized as a major part of public consciousness about "the other." The policies and practices of the English in

Ireland functioned to keep those Irish who refused to accept English domination segregated from themselves. Failing to even attempt an understanding of Irish customs and institutions, the English expressed an abiding contempt and hatred for both Irish culture and people that reached a crescendo during the sixteenth and seventeenth centuries when the English were also settling in the New World. It was an extreme form of ethnocentrism or ethnic chauvinism that some historians believe came close to being racial (Allen 1994; Canny 1973; Liggio 1976).

"Savagery" was an image about human differences that became deeply embedded in English life and thought and provided a foil against which they constructed their own identity as "civilized" Englishmen. They brought this image of what savagery was all about with them to the New World where it was soon imposed on the native populations when they, too, began to resist English encroachment. Savagery carried with it an enormous burden of negative and stereotypic characteristics grotesquely counterposed against the vision that the English had of themselves as a civilized people. Every new experience, along with a growing technological superiority, widened the differences and denigrated all other peoples who were not part of the civilized world. The concept of "civilized" polities in contrast to savagery and barbarism was beginning to take hold in much of Western Europe, and in this sense Englishmen were not much different from the rest of the Western world. But English notions of their own superiority were enhanced by their technological, material, and political successes, by their earlier successful split from the Catholic realm, by the early rise of merchant capitalism, the development of new forms of wealth, notions about individual freedom, property rights, and self-sufficiency, and by a growing sense of their own uniqueness even among other Europeans. This was summed up in the myth of Anglo-Saxonism (Horsman 1981).

"Race" emerged as a social classification that reflected this greatly expanded sense of human separateness and differences. Theodore Allen (1997) argues that the "invention" of the white race took place after an early, but unsuccessful, colonial revolt of servants and poor freedmen known as Bacon's Rebellion in 1676. Colonial leaders subsequently decided it would be useful to establish a division among the masses of poor to prevent their further collaboration against the governmental authorities. As African servants were vulnerable to policies that kept them in servitude indefinitely, and European servants had the protection of English law, colonial leaders developed a policy backed by new laws that separated African servants and freedmen from those of European background. Over the next half century, they passed numerous laws that provided resources and benefits to poor, white freedmen and other laws that restricted the rights of "Africans," "mulattoes," and "Indians."

Calling upon the model of the Chain of Being, and using natural differences in physical features, they created a new form of social identity. "Race" developed in the minds of some Europeans as a way to rationalize the conquest and brutal treatment of Native American populations, and especially the retention and perpetuation of slavery for imported Africans. As an ideology structuring social, economic, and political inequality, "race" contradicted developing trends in England and in Western European societies that promoted freedom, democracy, equality, and human rights. Europeans justified this attitude toward human differences by focusing on the physical features of the New World populations, magnifying and exaggerating their differences, and concluding that the Africans and Indians and their descendants were lesser forms of human beings, and that their inferiority was natural and/or God-given.

The creation of "race" and racial ideology imposed on the conquered and enslaved peoples an identity as the lowest status groups in society. Myths about their inferior moral, intellectual, and behavioral features had begun to develop and these facilitated proscription of any competition with Europeans. By the mid-eighteenth century, Negroes had been segregated from poor whites in the laws of most colonies and transformed into property as slaves in a state of permanent bondage.

Edmund Morgan (1975) also interpreted the actions of the early colonists in the process of establishing "racial" identities as stemming from the propertied colonists' fear of poor whites and possibly slaves engaging in rebellions together. Colonial leaders consciously formulated policies that would separate poor whites from Indians, blacks, and mulattoes and proceeded to provide the white poor, whom they had hitherto treated with contempt and hatred, with some privileges and special advantages.[4] In time, class divisions diminished in the minds of poor whites and they saw themselves as having something in common with the propertied class, symbolized by their light skins and common origins in Europe. With laws progressively continuing to reduce the rights of blacks and Indians, it was not long before the various European groups coalesced into a white "racial" category whose high-status identity gave them access to wealth, power, opportunity, and privilege.[5]

By the mid-nineteenth century virtually all Americans had been conditioned to this arbitrary ranking of the American peoples, and racial ideology had diffused around much of the world, including to the colonized peoples of the Third World and among Europeans themselves.

"RACE" AS IDENTITY

In the United States the biophysical features of different populations, which had become markers of social status, were internalized as sources of individual and group identities. After the Civil War, although slavery ended, race and racial ideology remained and were strengthened. African Americans particularly had to grapple with the reality of being defined as the lowest status group in American society and with the associated stereotyping that became increasingly part of the barriers to their integration into American society (Conrad 1969). And Native Americans had to try to reinvent their identities, whether in towns or isolated on remote reservations where traditional lifestyles were no longer possible. American society had made "race" (and the physical features

connected to it) equivalent to, and the dominant source of, human identity, superseding all other aspects of identity.

The problems that this has entailed, especially for the low-status "races," have been enormous, immensely complex, and almost intractable. Constant and unrelenting portrayals of their inferiority conditioned them to a self-imagery of being culturally backward, primitive, intellectually stunted, prone to violence, morally corrupt, undeserving of the benefits of civilization, insensitive to the finer arts, and (in the case of Africans) aesthetically ugly and animal-like. Because of the cultural imperative of race ideology, all Americans were compelled to the view that a racial status, symbolized by biophysical attributes, was the premier determinant of their identity. "Race" identity took priority over religion, ethnic origin, education and training, socioeconomic class, occupation, language, values, beliefs, morals, lifestyles, geographical location, and all other human attributes that hitherto provided all groups and individuals with a sense of who they were. The dilemma for the low-status races was, and still is, how to construct a positive identity for themselves in the light of the "racial" identity imposed on them by the dominant society.

In recent decades, one response to this dilemma on the part of some African Americans has been Afrocentrism (which is not the same as an older version of "Negritude" that black intellectuals had developed earlier in this century). And for some Indians a new form of "Nativism" has emerged, harkening back to a Native American lifestyle. Afrocentrism seeks to reidentify with the peoples and cultures of Africa and to elevate Africans to a position of esteem by emphasizing valuable aspects of African cultures. Some Afrocentrists also make assertions about the positive qualities of African people and seek to recognize and objectify Africanisms in the behavior of African-descended peoples who have been scattered all over the New World. Many assume or operate on the premise that all peoples who descended from Africans during the diaspora maintain certain behaviorisms that mark them off from other peoples. Their arguments seem similar to that of the biological determinists in the dominant society, but most would probably not go so far as to assert a genetic basis to certain "African"-originated behaviors. Those who take the position asserting a common African personality or behavior reflect the degree to which the ideology of "race" has been implanted in them. Like most Americans, they find it difficult to think beyond the racial worldview and draw upon the same strategies as white racists in claiming superior features for "African" people. At the same time, there are many Afrocentrists who are very conscious of the fact that theirs is a political position and that they are using the same biological arguments as racists, the people whom they theoretically oppose. They fail to realize that operating within the racial worldview, accepting its premises that biologically distinct races exist, each with unique cultural/behavioral features, and simply denying inferiority while asserting African superiority does nothing to change the racism in our society.

However, we also must understand that what Afrocentrism is really intended to do is to restore a sense of pride and dignity to ordinary African Americans, regardless of how whites and others regard their positions. By looking to the "real" Africa, studying her history, learning about and being involved in certain rituals and festivals that focus on African arts, dance, dress, music, and so on, some activists feel that they are engendering this pride and helping to remove the contempt and denigration that has accompanied our ideas about Africa in the past. They understand that for too long African Americans have been conditioned to the same negative beliefs about Africa and Africans as have whites and others and that there is a need to eliminate the self-depreciation and self-hatred that black Americans have experienced with regard to their African ancestry. . . .

THE NON-PROBLEM OF "MIXED-RACE" PEOPLE

One of the more tragic aspects of the racial worldview has been the seeming dilemma of people whose parents are identifiably of different "races."

Historically, "race" was grounded in the myth of biologically separate, exclusive, and distinct populations. No social ingredient in our race ideology allowed for an identity of "mixed-races." Indeed over the past century and a half, the American public was conditioned to the belief that "mixed-race" people (especially of black and white ancestry) were abnormal products of the unnatural mating of two species, besides being socially unacceptable in the normal scheme of things. The tragedy for "mixed" people is that powerful social lie, the assumption at the heart of "race," that a presumed biological essence is the basis of one's true identity. Identity is biology, racial ideology tells us, and it is permanent and immutable. The emphasis on and significance given to "race" precludes any possibility for establishing our premier identities on the basis of other characteristics. In this sense it may be argued that the myth of "race" has been a barrier to true human identities.

The unfortunate consequence of race ideology is that many of the people with this "mixed-race" background have also been conditioned to the belief in the biological salience of "race." Their efforts to establish a "Mixed-Race" category in the American census forms show a total misunderstanding of what "race" is all about, and this is, of course, a major part of the tragedy. Their arguments imply a feeling of having no identity at all because they do not exist formally (that is, socially) as a "biological" category.

The fact is that from the standpoint of biology, there have been "mixed" people in North America ever since Europeans first encountered indigenous Americans and the first Africans were brought to the English colonies in the 1620s. The average African American has about one-quarter of his or her genes from non-African (nonblack) ancestors, although most estimates are likely to be conservative (cf. Marks 1995; Reed 1969). There is a greater range of skin colors, hair textures, body sizes, nose shapes, and other physical features among black Americans than almost any other people identified as a distinct population. Virtually all of them could identify as of "mixed-race." But the physical markers of race status are always open to interpretation by others. "Race" as social status is in the eye of the beholder. "Mixed" people will still be treated as black if their phenotypes cause them to be so perceived by others. Insistence on being in a separate classification will not change that perception or the reaction of people to them.

What compounds and complicates matters is another lie that is one of the basic tenets, or constituent components, of the racial worldview: the myth that biology has some intrinsic connection to culture. Some advocates of a new "mixed-race" category have argued that they want to recognize the "culture" of their other parent. For example, in a black/white mixed marriage, a black parent presumably has "black" culture, and the white parent has "white" culture. These advocates fail to realize what anthropologists have long known, that there is no relationship between one's culture or lifestyle and one's genes or biological features. All native-born Americans share some basic cultural similarities, and the ancestors of modern African Americans have been "American" longer than the ancestors of most European Americans.[6] It is the ideological myths of the racial worldview that prevent us from seeing how very much alike culturally black and white Americans are. (This is not to suggest that there are not differences in the way blacks and whites experience our culture and lifestyle variations that reflect social-class differences and the isolation of inner-city populations.)

On the other hand, if one parent did come from a very different cultural background (e.g., recently emigrated from Asia), a child does not automatically have that culture because of the biology of the parent. Humans acquire culture; it is learned behavior. In order for Tiger Woods (a golfing star) to have Thai culture, he would have to *learn* the language and the elements of Thai culture. One can learn these without having a single gene from a Thai parent. Moreover, there is no reason why one should learn the cultures of ancestors merely because of some genetic or genealogical connections. None of us have the cultures of any of our ancestors two centuries ago because all cultures,

including American culture, have changed, some of them drastically, during that time. Cultures constantly change without any corresponding changes in biological features.

Americans should understand clearly that humans learn cultural features from one another all the time because that has been one of the most profound experiences of human, and especially American, history. What prevents us from understanding this is that component in the ideology of "race," as we have seen, that holds that each race has separate, biologically determined patterns of cultural behavior. The racial worldview, with its emphasis on assumptions of innateness and immutability, makes it possible to interpret all forms of human behavior as hereditary. In fact, it almost mandates such a perspective because of powerful forces within our culture that preserve and promote hereditarian ideas. The belief in racially determined cultural behavior, despite all evidence to the contrary, is perpetuated in American society by the popular media and as a part of folk wisdom about human differences. Witness the inordinate attention to and sales of Herrnstein and Murray's *The Bell Curve* (1994). This belief has been a necessary component of the ideology of "race," because it helps to perpetuate the notion that major differences between "races" exist.

People who consider themselves of "mixed race" and experience some form of psychic stress because they feel they have no identity in American society, perhaps more than most, need to have understanding of this history. . . .

TRANSCENDING THE RESTRICTIONS OF "RACIAL" IDENTITY

Today scholars are beginning to realize that "race" is nothing more and nothing less than a social invention. It has nothing to do with the intrinsic, or potential, qualities of the physically differing populations, but much to do with the allocation of power, privilege, and wealth among them. *This conceptual separation of actual physical variations within the species from the socially invented characterizations of them represents a major paradigm shift in how many scholars now think about the human experience.* Anthropologists and biologists no longer see "races" as discrete populations defined by blood-group patterns or "types" defined by averages of statistical measurements. Biophysical variations are seen as continuous and gradual, overlapping population boundaries, fluid, and subject to evolutionary changes. In like manner, scholars honestly examining the history of American attitudes toward human differences have concluded that "race" was a social invention of the eighteenth century that took advantage of the superficial physical differences among the American population and the social roles that these peoples played, and transposed these into a new form of social stratification. The symbols of race identity became the substance.

Recognizing the reality of the racial worldview and how it developed as a sociocultural reality requires a whole new way of looking at human diversity in all of its many forms. It means that (1) we can better recognize and comprehend accurately and objectively the natural causes of human physical variations around the world without attempting to homogenize people into limited "racial" categories; (2) we can liberate ourselves from the need to utilize physical differences in apprehending human identities; (3) freed from the myths of racial determinism, we can now improve our understanding of the true nature of culture and cultural differences and begin to view the processes of cultural change in a more accurate light; and (4) we can begin to understand the real nature of "race" as a social construct and to deal with the problems that racial identities have imposed on people.

For example, using this new perspective, we would be able to avoid the problems encountered when scholars examine the African Diaspora and attempt to determine which peoples are legitimately black products of this massive process of displacement. Several years ago, two Asian students who had recently immigrated to the United States came to me confidentially after class with a puzzle. They wanted to know why were people like Hazel O'Leary (just appointed as U.S. Secretary of Energy)

and Thurgood Marshall, Justice of the United States Supreme Court, identified as "black" in American society when it was obvious that they were not. I explained some of the history of the idea of "race" and the interactions among peoples in the New World. I also pointed out that there is a great deal more to the identification of African Americans than similarities in physical traits, that in fact, biological variations have little to do with the social categories of race. Indeed the people of the African Diaspora are a biogenetically diverse category of people who have an identity derived from common experiences of exploitation and racism. It is far more accurate and more fruitful to scholarship, and possibly to the future of humankind, to define African American people by their sense of *community, consciousness,* and *commitment* than by some mystical "racial" essence. It is the Community into which they were born and reared, a Consciousness of the historical realities and shared experiences of their ancestors, and a Commitment to the perspectives of their "blackness" and to the diminishing of racism that is critical to the identities of the Thurgood Marshalls and Hazel O'Learys of our society. The social categories of "race" have always encompassed more than mere physical similarities and differences. Theodore Allen tells us in the acknowledgements to his two-volume excoriation of white racism that he has learned to say, "I am not white" (1994).

Even without all of the intermixtures of peoples, some Americans have already experienced a high level of uncertainty about the "racial" status of individuals with whom they have had some interaction. Many peoples in the world, from Morocco to the Persian Gulf, to the islands in the South Pacific Ocean, have physical features that cause them to be "mistaken" for black Americans. In that broad band of the earth called the tropics we find indigenous peoples with tan to brown to dark brown skins, and hair that may be frizzly, kinky, curly, or straight. As more and more of these peoples either travel to the United States or are encountered by Americans on missions abroad, Americans must deal with their perceptions of these peoples. Some time ago, in the space of about eight months, I met a Samoan, a person from the New

Guinea area, and a number of Arabs who in the course of conversations have indicated that they have been "mistaken" for blacks.[7] Many peoples from the southern regions of Saudi Arabia look very much like their neighboring Africans across the Red Sea, having evolved in the same climate and latitude (and having intermingled over eons of time). To try to maintain racial categories based on physical features in the face of the real world of human biological diversity, I suspect, will be increasingly difficult.

There is another option, one that we have not yet claimed in the establishing and referencing of our human identities. We cannot ignore the fact that since the fifteenth century, what has happened in the Americas, and to varying degrees in many parts of the Third World, has been the fusion of genetic materials from all of the great continents. So-called "racial" mixture has occurred extensively in Latin America, and to a lesser extent in North America, so that most people are descendants of ancestors from Europe, Africa, and the Americas, and in many places like the Caribbean, from Asia also (Graham 1990: Morner 1967). Throughout the colonial world, complex genetic mixtures among various peoples have taken place: and increasingly Europeans at home are participants in, and products of, new genetic combinations with individuals absorbed into their societies from distant lands.

In addition to the increasing genetic heterogeneity of individuals and groups, there is the obvious fact that cultural features have traveled all over the world independently of the spread of genetic material. In the midst of the Sahara desert, signs proclaim "Coca-Cola," everyone from the Siberian tundra to the Melanesian forests wears "jeans," African clothing and designs are found from Paris to Sydney, Australia, and Americans eat more pizzas and tacos (burritos, tortillas, etc.) than almost any other people outside of Italy and Mexico. White boys wear dreadlocks, and Chinese and other Asian, and increasingly African, ethnic restaurants are found around the world. Fast foods, music, dance, dress, Hollywood films, whole industrial complexes (including the world of computers), and a wide range of political, religious, and social beliefs have diffused around the world. Few cultures have not experienced the impact of such massive infusion of new traits.

The peoples who have resulted from all this continuous blending of genetic features and cultural traits are truly "universal" human beings, regardless of what languages they speak or cultures they participate in. The concept of "universal" human beings might very well in time obviate racial categories (but not ethnic identities) and may help to bring about the elimination of all such designations. Many persons will come to recognize themselves as "universal" human beings, and there should be perhaps an early census category that proclaims this reality. What anthropologists must do is to make sure that the ideas of "ethnicity" and "ethnic identity" do not become perceived as hereditary, permanent, and unalterable, but remain fluid forms of identity that will make us all "multicultural."

DISCUSSION QUESTIONS

1. Why was the social classification of race invented?
2. Is Afrocentrism a response to racism?
3. What does the term "mixed race" tell us about biology and culture?

NOTES

1. Reference materials for this section were taken largely from the following: Boardman et al. (1986), Godolphin (1942), and Snowden (1983). But I have read widely in ancient history and am aware that such materials are not generally considered part of the anthropological repertoire. We need to realize that historical materials are widely available to all, and we should encourage students to avail themselves of them, especially since American students have been shown to be woefully ignorant of history and geography.
2. Herodotus lists more than two dozen different nations that fought on the different sides in the Persian wars: Arabians, Ethiopians, Armenians, Thracians, Libyans, and many others.
3. The Persian Wars, Book II, p. 130, in Godolphin (1942).
4. Morgan claims that the Virginia Assembly "deliberately did what it could to foster the contempt of whites for blacks and Indians" (1975:331).
5. For insightful analysis of this process, see also Allen (1994, 1997).

6. Bohannan and Curtin (1995:13) have observed that half the ancestors of African Americans were already here in the United States by 1780 while the median date for the arrival of European ancestors was "remarkably late, 1890s." We need more of this kind of honesty in recognizing historical realities on the part of scholars in all disciplines.

7. See Morsy (1994). When Arabs began to migrate to the Detroit area several generations ago, many were frequently mistaken for blacks. This became an acute problem in the area around Dearborn, Michigan, where many of them settled. There had long been a law in Dearborn that prohibited blacks from being in the city after sundown. The Dearborn police, among others, were often very confused.

REFERENCES

Allen, Theodore W. [1994]1997 *The Invention of the White Race*, vols. 1 and 2, London: Verso.

Boardman, John, J. Griffin, and O. Murray, eds. 1986 *The Oxford History of the Classical World*. Oxford: Oxford University Press.

Canny, Nicholas P. 1973 The Ideology of English Colonization: From Ireland to America. *William and Mary Quarterly* (3rd ser.) 30:575–598.

Castro, Americo 1971 *The Spaniards*. Berkeley: University of California Press.

Connah, Graham 1987 *African Civilizations*. New York: Cambridge University Press.

Conrad, Earl 1969 *The Invention of the Negro*. New York: Paul S. Erikson.

Davidson, Basil 1991 *African Civilization Revisited*. Trenton, NJ: African World Press.

Davis, David Brion 1966 *The Problem of Slavery in Western Culture*. Middlesex, England: Penguin.

Godolphin, Francis R. B., ed. 1942 *The Greek Historians*, vols. 1 and 2. New York: Random House.

Graham, Richard, ed. 1990 *The Idea of Race in Latin America, 1870–1940*. Austin: University of Texas Press.

Hitti, Phillip 1953 *History of the Arabs*. London: Macmillan Publishing Co.

Horsman, Reginald 1981 *Race and Manifest Destiny*. Cambridge, MA: Harvard University Press.

Liggio, Leonard P. 1976 English Origins of Early American Racism. *Radical History Review* 3(1):1–26.

Marks, Jonathan 1995 *Human Biodiversity: Genes, Race, and History*. New York: Aldine de Gruyter.

Morgan, Edmund S. 1975 *American Slavery: American Freedom*. New York: W. W. Norton and Co.

Mörner, Magnus 1967 *Race Mixture in the History of Latin America*. Boston: Little, Brown.

Morsy, Soheir 1994 Beyond the Honorary "White" Classification of Egyptians: Societal Identity in Historical Context. In *Race*. S. Gregory and R. Sanjek, eds. Pp. 175–198. New Brunswick, NJ: Rutgers University Press.

Nash, Gary 1982 *Red, White, and Black: The Peoples of Early America*. Englewood Cliffs, NJ: Prentice Hall.

Reed, T.E. 1969 Caucasian Genes in American Negroes. *Science* 165 (3,895): 762–768.

Smedley, Audrey [1993]1999 *Race in North America: Origin and Evolution of a Worldview*. 2nd edition, revised and enlarged. Boulder, CO: Westview Press.

Snowden, Frank M., Jr. 1983 *Before Color Prejudice*. Revised edition. Cambridge, MA: Harvard University Press.

READING 2

Who Is Black? One Nation's Definition

F. James Davis

In a taped interview conducted by a blind, black anthropologist, a black man nearly ninety years old said: "Now you must understand that this is just a name we have. I am not black and you are not black either, if you go by the evidence of your eyes. . . . Anyway, black people are all colors. White people don't look all the same way, but there are more different kinds of us than there are of them. Then too, there is a certain stage [at] which you cannot tell who is white and who is black. Many of the people I see who are thought of as black could just as well be white in their appearance. Many of the white people I see are black as far as I can tell by the way they look. Now, that's it for looks. Looks don't mean much. The things that makes us different is how we think. What we believe is important, the ways we look at life" (Gwaltney, 1980:96).

How does a person get defined as a black, both socially and legally, in the United States? What is the nation's rule for who is black, and how did it come to be? And so what? Don't we all know who is black, and isn't the most important issue what opportunities the group has? Let us start with

F. James Davis is professor emeritus of sociology at Illinois State University.

some experiences of three well-known American blacks—actress and beauty pageant winner Vanessa Williams, U.S. Representative Adam Clayton Powell, Jr., and entertainer Lena Horne.

For three decades after the first Miss America Pageant in 1921, black women were barred from competing. The first black winner was Vanessa Williams of Millwood, New York, crowned Miss America in 1984. In the same year the first runner-up—Suzette Charles of Mays Landing, New Jersey—was also black. The viewing public was charmed by the television images and magazine pictures of the beautiful and musically talented Williams, but many people were also puzzled. Why was she being called black when she appeared to be white? Suzette Charles, whose ancestry appeared to be more European than African, at least looked like many of the "lighter blacks." Notoriety followed when Vanessa Williams resigned because of the impending publication of some nude photographs of her taken before the pageant, and Suzette Charles became Miss America for the balance of 1984. Beyond the troubling question of whether these young women could have won if they had looked "more black," the publicity dramatized the nation's definition of a black person.

Some blacks complained that the Rev. Adam Clayton Powell, Jr., was so light that he was a stranger in their midst. In the words of Roi Ottley, "He was white to all appearances, having blue eyes, an aquiline nose, and light, almost blond, hair" (1943:220), yet he became a bold, effective black leader—first as minister of the Abyssinian Baptist Church of Harlem, then as a New York city councilman, and finally as a U.S. congressman from the state of New York. Early in his activist career he led 6,000 blacks in a march on New York City Hall. He used his power in Congress to fight for civil rights legislation and other black causes. In 1966, in Washington, D.C., he convened the first black power conference.

In his autobiography, Powell recounts some experiences with racial classification in his youth that left a lasting impression on him. During Powell's freshman year at Colgate University, his roommate did not know that he was a black until his father, Adam Clayton Powell, Sr., was invited to give a chapel talk on Negro rights and problems, after which the roommate announced that because Adam was a Negro they could no longer be roommates or friends.

Another experience that affected Powell deeply occurred one summer during his Colgate years. He was working as a bellhop at a summer resort in Manchester, Vermont, when Abraham Lincoln's aging son Robert was a guest there. Robert Lincoln disliked blacks so much that he refused to let them wait on him or touch his luggage, car, or any of his possessions. Blacks who did got their knuckles whacked with his cane. To the great amusement of the other bellhops, Lincoln took young Powell for a white man and accepted his services (Powell, 1971:31–33).

Lena Horne's parents were both very light in color and came from black upper-middle-class families in Brooklyn (Horne and Schickel, 1965; Buckley, 1986). Lena lived with her father's parents until she was about seven years old. Her grandfather was very light and blue-eyed. Her fair-skinned grandmother was the daughter of a slave woman and her white owner, from the family of John C. Calhoun, well-known defender of slavery. One of her father's great-grandmothers was a Blackfoot Indian, to whom Lena Horne has attributed her somewhat coppery skin color. One of her mother's grandmothers was a French-speaking black woman from Senegal and never a slave. Her mother's father was a "Portuguese Negro," and two women in his family had passed as white and become entertainers.

Lena Horne's parents had separated, and when she was seven her entertainer mother began placing her in a succession of homes in different states. Her favorite place was in the home of her Uncle Frank, her father's brother, a red-haired, blue-eyed teacher in a black school in Georgia. The black children in that community asked her why she was so light and called her a "yellow bastard." She learned that when satisfactory evidence of respectable black parents is lacking, being light-skinned implies illegitimacy and having an underclass white parent and is thus a disgrace in the black community. When her mother married a white Cuban, Lena also learned that blacks can be very hostile to the white spouse, especially when the "black" mate is very light. At this time she began to blame the confused color line for her childhood troubles. She later endured much hostility from blacks and whites alike when her own second marriage, to white composer-arranger Lennie Hayton, was finally made public in 1950 after three years of keeping it secret.

Early in Lena Horne's career there were complaints that she did not fit the desired image of a black entertainer for white audiences, either physically or in her style. She sang white love songs, not the blues. Noting her brunette-white beauty, one white agent tried to get her to take a Spanish name, learn some Spanish songs, and pass as a Latin white, but she had learned to have a horror of passing and never considered it, although Hollywood blacks accused her of trying to pass after she played her first bit part in a film. After she failed her first screen test because she looked like a white girl trying to play black-face, the directors tried making her up with a shade called "Light Egyptian" to make her look darker. The whole procedure embarrassed and hurt her deeply. . . .

Other light mulatto entertainers have also had painful experiences because of their light skin and other caucasoid features. Starting an acting career is never easy, but actress Jane White's difficulties in the 1940s were compounded by her lightness. Her father was NAACP leader Walter White. Even with dark makeup on her ivory skin, she did not look like a black person on the stage, but she was not allowed to try out for white roles because blacks were barred from playing them. When she auditioned for the part of a young girl from India, the director was enthusiastic, although her skin color was too light, but higher management decreed that it was unthinkable for a Negro to play the part of an Asian Indian (White, 1948:338). Only after great perseverance did Jane White make her debut as the educated mulatto maid Nonnie in the stage version of Lillian Smith's *Strange Fruit* (1944). . . .

THE ONE-DROP RULE DEFINED

As the above cases illustrate, to be considered black in the United States not even half of one's ancestry must be African black. But will one-fourth do, or one-eighth, or less? The nation's answer to the question "Who is black?" has long been that a black is any person with *any* known African black ancestry (Myrdal, 1944:113–18; Berry and Tischler, 1978:97–98; Williamson, 1980:1–2). This definition reflects the long experience with slavery and later with Jim Crow segregation. In the South it became known as the "one-drop rule," meaning that a single drop of "black blood" makes a person a black. It is also known as the "one black ancestor rule," some courts have called it the "traceable amount rule," and anthropologists call it the "hypo-descent rule," meaning that racially mixed persons are assigned the status of the subordinate group (Harris, 1964:56). This definition emerged from the American South to become the nation's definition, generally accepted by whites and blacks alike (Bahr, Chadwick, and Stauss, 1979:27–28). Blacks had no other choice. This American cultural definition of blacks is taken for granted as readily by judges, affirmative action officers, and black protesters as it is by Ku Klux Klansmen.

Let us not be confused by terminology. At present the usual statement of the one-drop rule is in terms of "black blood" or black ancestry, while not so long ago it referred to "Negro blood" or ancestry. The term "black" rapidly replaced "Negro" in general usage in the United States as the black power movement peaked at the end of the 1960s, but the black and Negro populations are the same. The term "black" is used [here] for persons with any black African lineage, not just for unmixed members of populations from sub-Saharan Africa. The term "Negro," which is used in certain historical contexts, means the same thing. Terms such as "African black," "unmixed Negro," and "all black" are used here to refer to unmixed blacks descended from African populations.

We must also pay attention to the terms "mulatto" and "colored." The term "mulatto" was originally used to mean the offspring of a "pure African Negro" and a "pure white." Although the root meaning of mulatto, in Spanish, is "hybrid," "mulatto" came to include the children of unions between whites and so-called "mixed Negroes." For example, Booker T. Washington and Frederick Douglass, with slave mothers and white fathers, were referred to as mulattoes (Bennett, 1962:255). To whatever extent their mothers were part white, these men were more than half white. Douglass was evidently part Indian as well, and he looked it (Preston, 1980:9–10). Washington had reddish hair and gray eyes. At the time of the American Revolution, many of the founding fathers had some very light slaves, including some who appeared to be white. The term "colored" seemed for a time to refer only to mulattoes, especially lighter ones, but later it became a euphemism for darker Negroes, even including unmixed blacks. With widespread racial mixture, "Negro" came to mean any slave or descendant of a slave, no matter how much mixed. Eventually in the United States, the terms mulatto, colored, Negro, black, and African American all came to mean people with any known black African ancestry. Mulattoes are racially mixed, to whatever degree, while the terms black, Negro, African American, and colored include both mulattoes and unmixed blacks. These terms have quite different meanings in other countries.

Whites in the United States need some help envisioning the American black experience with ancestral fractions. At the beginning of miscegenation between two populations presumed to be racially pure, quadroons appear in the second generation of continuing mixing with whites, and octoroons in the third. A quadroon is one-fourth African black and thus easily classed as black in the United States, yet three of this person's four grandparents are white. An octoroon has seven white great-grandparents out of eight and usually looks white or almost so. Most parents of black American children in recent decades have themselves been racially mixed, but often the fractions get complicated because the earlier details of the mixing were obscured generations ago. Like so many white Americans, black people are forced to speculate about some of the fractions—one-eighth this, three-sixteenths that, and so on. . . .

PLESSY, PHIPPS, AND OTHER CHALLENGES IN THE COURTS

Homer Plessy was the plaintiff in the 1896 precedent-setting "separate-but-equal" case of *Plessy v. Ferguson*

(163 U.S. 537). This case challenged the Jim Crow statute that required racially segregated seating on trains in interstate commerce in the state of Louisiana. The U.S. Supreme Court quickly dispensed with Plessy's contention that because he was only one-eighth Negro and could pass as white he was entitled to ride in the seats reserved for whites. Without ruling directly on the definition of a Negro, the Supreme Court briefly took what is called "judicial notice" of what it assumed to be common knowledge: that a Negro or black is any person with any black ancestry. (Judges often take explicit "judicial notice" not only of scientific or scholarly conclusions, or of opinion surveys or other systematic investigations, but also of something they just assume to be so, including customary practices or common knowledge.) This has consistently been the ruling in the federal courts, and often when the black ancestry was even less than one-eighth. The federal courts have thus taken judicial notice of the customary boundary between two sociocultural groups that differ, on the average, in physical traits, not between two discrete genetic categories. In the absence of proof of a specific black ancestor, merely being known as a black in the community has usually been accepted by the courts as evidence of black ancestry. The separate-but-equal doctrine established in the Plessy case is no longer the law, as a result of the judicial and legislative successes of the civil rights movement, but the nation's legal definition of who is black remains unchanged.

State courts have generally upheld the one-drop rule. For instance, in a 1948 Mississippi case a young man, Davis Knight, was sentenced to five years in jail for violating the antimiscegenation statute. Less than one-sixteenth black, Knight said he was not aware that he had any black lineage, but the state proved his great-grandmother was a slave girl. In some states the operating definition of black has been limited by statute to particular fractions, yet the social definition—the one-drop rule—has generally prevailed in case of doubt. Mississippi, Missouri, and five other states have had the criterion of one-eighth. Virginia changed from one-fourth to one-eighth in 1910, then in 1930 forbade white intermarriage with a person with any black ancestry. Persons in Virginia who are one-fourth or more Indian and less than one-sixteenth African black are defined as Indians while on the reservation but as blacks when they leave (Berry, 1965:26). While some states have had general race classification statutes, at least for a time, others have legislated a definition of black only for particular purposes, such as marriage or education. In a few states there have even been varying definitions for different situations (Mangum, 1940:38–48). All states require a designation of race on birth certificates, but there are no clear guidelines to help physicians and midwives do the classifying.

Louisiana's latest race classification statute became highly controversial and was finally repealed in 1983 (Trillin, 1986:77). Until 1970, a Louisiana statute had embraced the one-drop rule, defining a Negro as anyone with a "trace of black ancestry." This law was challenged in court a number of times from the 1920s on, including an unsuccessful attempt in 1957 by boxer Ralph Dupas, who asked to be declared white so that a law banning "interracial sports" (since repealed) would not prevent him from boxing in the state. In 1970 a lawsuit was brought on behalf of a child whose ancestry was allegedly only one two-hundred-fifty-sixth black, and the legislature revised its law. The 1970 Louisiana statute defined a black as someone whose ancestry is more than one thirty-second black (La. Rev. Stat. 42:267). Adverse publicity about this law was widely disseminated during the Phipps trial in 1983 (discussed below), filed as *Jane Doe v. State of Louisiana*. This case was decided in a district court in May 1983, and in June the legislature abolished its one thirty-second statute and gave parents the right to designate the race of newborns, and even to change classifications on birth certificates if they can prove the child is white by a "preponderance of the evidence." However, the new statute in 1983 did not abolish the "traceable amount rule" (the one-drop rule), as demonstrated by the outcomes when the Phipps decision was appealed to higher courts in 1985 and 1986.

The history in the Phipps (Jane Doe) case goes as far back as 1770, when a French planter named Jean Gregoire Guillory took his wife's slave, Margarita, as his mistress (Model, 1983:3–4). More than two centuries and two decades later, their great-great-great-great-granddaughter, Susie Guillory Phipps, asked the Louisiana courts to change the classification on her deceased parents' birth certificates to "white" so she and her brothers and sisters could be designated white. They all looked white, and some were blue-eyed blonds. Mrs. Susie Phipps had been denied a passport because she had checked "white" on her application although her birth certificate designated her race as "colored." This designation was based on information supplied by a midwife, who presumably relied on the parents or on the family's status in the community. Mrs. Phipps claimed that this classification came as a shock, since she had always thought she was white, had lived as white, and had twice married as white. Some of her relatives, however, gave depositions saying they considered themselves "colored," and the lawyers for the state claimed to have proof that Mrs. Phipps is three thirty-seconds black (Trillin, 1986:62–63, 71–74). That was more than enough "blackness" for the district court in 1983 to declare her parents, and thus Mrs. Phipps and her siblings, to be legally black.

In October and again in December 1985, the state's Fourth Circuit Court of Appeals upheld the district court's decision, saying that no one can change the racial designation of his or her parents or anyone else's (479 So. 2d 369). Said the majority of the court in its opinion: "That appellants might today describe themselves as white does not prove error in a document which designates their parents as colored" (479 So. 2d 371). Of course, if the parents' designation as "colored" cannot be disturbed, their descendants must be defined as black by the "traceable amount rule." The court also concluded that the preponderance of the evidence clearly showed that the Guillory parents were "colored." Although noting expert testimony to the effect that the race of an individual cannot be determined with scientific accuracy, the court said the law of racial designation is not based on science, that "individual race designations are purely social and cultural perceptions and the evidence conclusively proves those subjective perspectives were correctly recorded at the time the appellants' birth certificates were recorded" (479 So. 2d 372). At the rehearing in December 1985, the appellate court also affirmed the necessity of designating race on birth certificates for public health, affirmative action, and other important public programs and held that equal protection of the law has not been denied so long as the designation is treated as confidential.

When this case was appealed to the Louisiana Supreme Court in 1986, that court declined to review the decision, saying only that the court "concurs in the denial for the reasons assigned by the court of appeals on rehearing" (485 So. 2d 60). In December 1986 the U.S. Supreme Court was equally brief in stating its reason for refusing to review the decision: "The appeal is dismissed for want of a substantial federal question" (107 Sup. Ct. Reporter, interim ed. 638). Thus, both the final court of appeals in Louisiana and the highest court of the United States saw no reason to disturb the application of the one-drop rule in the lawsuit brought by Susie Guillory Phipps and her siblings.

CENSUS ENUMERATION OF BLACKS

When the U.S. Bureau of the Census enumerates blacks (always counted as Negroes until 1980), it does not use a scientific definition, but rather the one accepted by the general public and by the courts. The Census Bureau counts what the nation wants counted. Although various operational instructions have been tried, the definition of black used by the Census Bureau has been the nation's cultural and legal definition: all persons with any known black ancestry. Other nations define and count blacks differently, so international comparisons of census data on blacks can be extremely misleading. For example, Latin American countries generally count as black only unmixed African blacks, those only slightly mixed, and the very poorest mulattoes. If they used the U.S. definition, they would count far more blacks

than they do, and if Americans used their definition, millions in the black community in the United States would be counted either as white or as "coloreds" of different descriptions, not as black.

Instructions to our census enumerators in 1840, 1850, and 1860 provided "mulatto" as a category but did not define the term. In 1870 and 1880, mulattoes were officially defined to include "quadroons, octoroons, and all persons having any perceptible trace of African blood." In 1890 enumerators were told to record the *exact* proportion of the "African blood," again relying on visibility. In 1900 the Census Bureau specified that "pure Negroes" be counted separately from mulattoes, the latter to mean "all persons with some trace of black blood." In 1920 the mulatto category was dropped, and black was defined to mean any person with any black ancestry, as it has been ever since.

In 1960 the practice of self-definition began, with the head of household indicating the race of its members. This did not seem to introduce any noticeable fluctuation in the number of blacks, thus indicating that black Americans generally apply the one-drop rule to themselves. One exception is that Spanish-speaking Americans who have black ancestry but were considered white, or some designation other than black, in their place of origin generally reject the one-drop rule if they can. American Indians with some black ancestry also generally try to avoid the rule, but those who leave the reservation are often treated as black. At any rate, the 1980 census count showed that self-designated blacks made up about 12 percent of the population of the United States.

No other ethnic population in the nation, including those with visibly non-caucasoid features, is defined and counted according to a one-drop rule. For example, persons whose ancestry is one-fourth or less American Indian are not generally defined as Indian unless they want to be, and they are considered assimilating Americans who may even be proud of having some Indian ancestry. The same implicit rule appears to apply to Japanese Americans, Filipinos, or other peoples from East Asian nations and also to Mexican Americans who have Central

American Indian ancestry, as a large majority do. For instance, a person whose ancestry is one-eighth Chinese is not defined as just Chinese, or East Asian, or a member of the mongoloid race. The United States certainly does not apply a one-drop rule to its white ethnic populations either, which include both national and religious groups. Ethnicity has often been confused with racial biology and not just in Nazi Germany. Americans do not insist that an American with a small fraction of Polish ancestry be classified as a Pole, or that someone with a single remote Greek ancestor be designated Greek, or that someone with any trace of Jewish lineage is a Jew and nothing else.

It is interesting that, in *The Passing of the Great Race* (1916), Madison Grant maintained that the one-drop rule should be applied not only to blacks but also to all the other ethnic groups he considered biologically inferior "races," such as Hindus, Asians in general, Jews, Italians, and other Southern and Eastern European peoples. Grant's book went through four editions, and he and others succeeded in getting Congress to pass the national origins quota laws of the early 1920s. This racist quota legislation sharply curtailed immigration from everywhere in the world except Northern and Western Europe and the Western Hemisphere, until it was repealed in 1965. Grant and other believers in the racial superiority of their own group have confused race with ethnicity. They consider miscegenation with any "inferior" people to be the ultimate danger to the survival of their own group and have often seen the one-drop rule as a crucial component in their line of defense. Americans in general, however, while finding other ways to discriminate against immigrant groups, have rejected the application of the drastic one-drop rule to all groups but blacks.

UNIQUENESS OF THE ONE-DROP RULE

Not only does the one-drop rule apply to no other group than American blacks, but apparently the rule is unique in that it is found only in the United States and not in any other nation in the world.

In fact, definitions of who is black vary quite sharply from country to country, and for this reason people in other countries often express consternation about our definition. James Baldwin relates a revealing incident that occurred in 1956 at the Conference of Negro-African Writers and Artists held in Paris. The head of the delegation of writers and artists from the United States was John Davis. The French chairperson introduced Davis and then asked him why he considered himself Negro, since he certainly did not look like one. Baldwin wrote, "He *is* a Negro, of course, from the remarkable legal point of view which obtains in the United States, but more importantly, as he tried to make clear to his interlocutor, he was a Negro by choice and by depth of involvement—by experience, in fact" (1962:19).

The phenomenon known as "passing as white" is difficult to explain in other countries or to foreign students. Typical questions are: "Shouldn't Americans say that a person who is passing as white is white, or nearly all white, and has previously been passing as black?" or "To be consistent, shouldn't you say that someone who is one-eighth white is passing as black?" or "Why is there so much concern, since the so-called blacks who pass take so little negroid ancestry with them?" Those who ask such questions need to realize that "passing" is so much more a social phenomenon than a biological one, reflecting the nation's unique definition of what makes a person black. The concept of "passing" rests on the one-drop rule and on folk beliefs about race and miscegenation, not on biological or historical fact.

The black experience with passing as white in the United States contrasts with the experience of other ethnic minorities that have features that are clearly non-caucasoid. The concept of passing applies only to blacks—consistent with the nation's unique definition of the group. A person who is one-fourth or less American Indian or Korean or Filipino is not regarded as passing if he or she intermarries and joins fully the life of the dominant community, so the minority ancestry need not be hidden. It is often suggested that the key reason for this is that the physical differences between these other groups and whites are less pronounced than the physical differences between African blacks and whites, and therefore are less threatening to whites. However, keep in mind that the one-drop rule and anxiety about passing originated during slavery and later received powerful reinforcement under the Jim Crow system.

For the physically visible groups other than blacks, miscegenation promotes assimilation, despite barriers of prejudice and discrimination during two or more generations of racial mixing. As noted above, when ancestry in one of these racial minority groups does not exceed one-fourth, a person is not defined solely as a member of that group. Masses of white European immigrants have climbed the class ladder not only through education but also with the help of close personal relationships in the dominant community, intermarriage, and ultimately full cultural and social assimilation. Young people tend to marry people they meet in the same informal social circles (Gordon, 1964:70–81). For visibly non-caucasoid minorities other than blacks in the United States, this entire route to full assimilation is slow but possible.

For all persons of any known black lineage, however, assimilation is blocked and is not promoted by miscegenation. Barriers to full opportunity and participation for blacks are still formidable, and a fractionally black person cannot escape these obstacles without passing as white and cutting off all ties to the black family and community. The pain of this separation, and condemnation by the black family and community, are major reasons why many or most of those who could pass as white choose not to. Loss of security within the minority community, and fear and distrust of the white world are also factors.

It should now be apparent that the definition of a black person as one with any trace at all of black African ancestry is inextricably woven into the history of the United States. It incorporates beliefs once used to justify slavery and later used to buttress the castelike Jim Crow system of segregation. Developed in the South, the definition of "Negro" (now black) spread and became the nation's social and legal definition. Because blacks are defined according to the one-drop rule, they are a socially constructed category in which there is wide variation in racial traits and therefore not a race group in the scientific sense. However, because that category has a definite status position in the society it has become a self-conscious social group with an ethnic identity.

The one-drop rule has long been taken for granted throughout the United States by whites and blacks alike, and the federal courts have taken "judicial notice" of it as being a matter of common knowledge. State courts have generally upheld the one-drop rule, but some have limited the definition to one thirty-second or one-sixteenth or one-eighth black ancestry, or made other limited exceptions for persons with both Indian and black ancestry. Most Americans seem unaware that this definition of blacks is extremely unusual in other countries, perhaps even unique to the United States, and that Americans define no other minority group in a similar way. . . .

DISCUSSION QUESTIONS

1. Is black a color category or a status?
2. Do you think passing still occurs?

REFERENCES

Bahr, Howard M., Bruce A. Chadwick, and Joseph H. Stauss. 1979. *American Ethnicity.* Lexington, MA: D.C. Heath & Co.

Baldwin, James. 1962. *Nobody Knows My Name.* New York: Dell Publishing Co.

Bennett, Lerone, Jr. 1962. *Before the Mayflower: A History of the Negro in America 1619–1962.* Chicago: Johnson Publishing Co.

Berry, Brewton. 1965. *Race and Ethnic Relations.* 3rd ed. Boston: Houghton Mifflin Co.

Berry, Brewton, and Henry L. Tischler. 1978. *Race and Ethnic Relations.* 4th ed. Boston: Houghton Mifflin Co.

Buckley, Gail Lumet. 1986. *The Hornes: An American Family.* New York: Alfred A. Knopf.

Gordon, Milton M. 1964. *Assimilation in American Life.* New York: Oxford University Press.

Grant, Madison. 1916. *The Passing of the Great Race.* New York: Scribner.

Gwaltney, John Langston. 1980. *Drylongso: A Self-Portrait of Black America.* New York: Vintage Books.

Harris, Melvin. 1964. *Patterns of Race in the Americas.* New York: W. W. Norton.

Horne, Lena, and Richard Schickel. 1965. *Lena.* Garden City, NY: Doubleday & Co.

Mangum, Charles Staples, Jr. 1940. *The Legal Status of the Negro in the United States.* Chapel Hill: University of North Carolina Press.

Model, F. Peter, ed. 1983. "Apartheid in the Bayou." *Perspectives: The Civil Rights Quarterly 15* (Winter–Spring), 3–4.

Myrdal, Gunnar, assisted by Richard Sterner and Arnold M. Rose. 1944. *An American Dilemma.* New York: Harper & Bros.

Ottley, Roi. 1943. *New World A-Coming.* Cleveland: World Publishing Co.

Powell, Adam Clayton, Jr. 1971. *Adam by Adam: The Autobiography of Adam Clayton Powell, Jr.* New York: Dial Press.

Preston, Dickson J. 1980. *Young Frederick Douglass: The Maryland Years.* Baltimore: Johns Hopkins University Press.

Trillin, Calvin. 1986. "American Chronicles: Black or White." *New Yorker,* April 14, 1986, pp. 62–78.

White, Walter. 1948. *A Man Called White: The Autobiography of Walter White.* New York: Viking Press.

Williamson, Joel. 1980. *New People: Miscegenation and Mulattoes in the United States.* New York: The Free Press.

READING 3

The Evolution of Identity

Washington Post

Decade to decade, the U.S. census has changed its classifications of race and ethnicity. Partially, this reflects the growing diversity of the country. It also reveals the nation's evolving politics and social mores. When the first census was taken in 1790, enumerators classified free residents as white or "other," while slaves were counted separately. By 1860, residents were classified as white, black or mulatto. Hispanic origin first became a category in 1970. Here are the categories used in the decennial counts from 1860 to 2000, as presented by AmeriStat (www.ameristat.org).

1860	1870	1880	1890¹	1900²	1910	1920	1930	1940	1950	1960	1970	1980	1990	2000
White	White	White	White	White	White	White	White	White	White	White	White	White	White	White
Black	Black	Black	Black	Black (Negro descent)	Black	Black	Black	Black	Negro	Negro	Negro or Black	Black or Negro	Black or Negro	Black, African American or Negro
Mulatto	Mulatto	Mulatto	Mulatto		Mulatto	Mulatto								
	Chinese	Chinese	Chinese	Chinese	Chinese	Chinese	Chinese	Chinese	Chinese	Chinese	Chinese	Chinese	Chinese	Chinese
	Indian	Indian	Indian	Indian	Indian	Indian	Indian	Indian	Amer. Indian	Amer. Indian	Indian (Amer.)	Indian	Indian (Amer.)	Amer. Indian or Alaska Native
			Quadroon											
			Octoroon											
			Japanese	Japanese	Japanese	Japanese	Japanese	Japanese	Japanese	Japanese	Japanese	Japanese	Japanese	Japanese
						Filipino	Filipino	Filipino	Filipino	Filipino	Filipino	Filipino	Filipino	Filipino
						Hindu	Hindu	Hindu						
						Korean	Korean	Korean			Korean	Korean	Korean	Korean
												Asian Indian	Asian Indian	Asian Indian
							Mexican							
										Aleut		Aleut	Aleut	
										Eskimo		Eskimo	Eskimo	
										Hawaiian	Hawaiian	Hawaiian	Hawaiian	Native Hawaiian
										Part Hawaiian				
												Vietnamese	Vietnamese	Vietnamese
												Guamanian	Guamanian	Guamanian or Chamorro
												Samoan	Samoan	Samoan
														Other Asian
													Other Asian Pacific Islander	**Other Pacific Islander**
					Other	Other	Other	Other	Other	Other	Other	Other	Other race	Some other race

ETHNICITY

1970	1980	1990	2000
Mexican	Mexican, Mexican Amer. **Chicano** Puerto Rican	Mexican, Mexican Amer. Chicano Puerto Rican	Mexican, Mexican Amer. Chicano Puerto Rican
Puerto Rican			
Central/So. American			
Cuban	Cuban Other Spanish/ Hispanic Not Spanish/ Hispanic	Cuban Other Spanish/ Hispanic Not Spanish/ Hispanic	Cuban Other Spanish/ Hispanic/Latino Not Spanish/ Hispanic/Latino
Other Spanish			
(None of these)			

---

1 In 1890, mulatto was defined as a person who was three-eighths to five-eighths black. A quadroon was one-quarter black and an octoroon one-eighth black.

2 American Indians have been asked to specify their tribe since the 1900 Census.

Bold letters indicate first usage since 1860.

NOTE: Before the 1970 Census, enumerators wrote in the race of individuals using the designated categories. In subsequent censuses, respondents or enumerators filled in circles next to the categories with which the respondent identified. Also beginning with the 1970 Census, people choosing American Indian, other Asian, other race, or for the Hispanic question, other Hispanic categories, were asked to write in a specific tribe or group. Hispanic ethnicity was asked of a sample of Americans in 1970 and of all Americans beginning with the 1980 Census.

Sources: AmeriStat, "200 Years of U.S. Census Taking: Population and Housing Questions 1790–1990," U.S. Census Bureau. FROM: *The Washington Post*, Federal Page, August 13, 2001.

59

READING 4

Real Indians: Identity and the Survival of Native America

Eva Marie Garroutte

The most common tribal requirement for determining citizenship concerns "blood quantum," or degree of Indian ancestry. . . . About two-thirds of all federally recognized tribes of the coterminous United States specify a minimum blood quantum in their legal citizenship criteria, with one-quarter blood degree being the most frequent minimum requirement.[1] (In the simplest instance, an individual has a one-quarter blood quantum if any one of her four grandparents is of exclusively Indian ancestry and the other three are non-Indian.) The remaining one-third of Indian tribes specify *no* minimum blood quantum. They often simply require that any new enrollee be a lineal (direct) descendant of another tribal member. . . .

Legal definitions of tribal membership regulate the rights to vote in tribal elections, to hold tribal office, and generally to participate in the political, and sometimes also the cultural, life of the tribe. One's ability to satisfy legal definitions of identification may also determine one's right to share in certain tribal revenues (such as income generated by tribally controlled businesses). Perhaps most significantly, it may determine the right to live on a reservation or to inherit land interests there.

The tribes' power to determine citizenship allows them to delimit the distribution of certain important resources, such as reservation land, tribal monies, and political privileges. But this is hardly the end of the story of legal definitions of identity. The federal government has many purposes for which it, too, must distinguish Indians from non-Indians, and it uses its own, separate legal definition for doing so. More precisely, it uses a whole array of legal definitions.

Since the U.S. Constitution uses the word "Indian" in two places but defines it nowhere, Congress has made its own definitions on an ad hoc basis.[2] A 1978 congressional survey discovered no less than *thirty-three* separate definitions of Indians in use in different pieces of federal legislation.[3] These may or may not correspond with those any given tribe uses to determine its citizenship.

Most federal legal definitions of Indian identity specify a minimum blood quantum—frequently one-quarter but sometimes one-half—but others do not. Some require or accept tribal citizenship as a criterion of federal identification, and others do not. Some require reservation residency, or ownership of land held in trust by the government, and others do not. Other laws affecting Indians specify *no* definition of identity, such that the courts must determine to whom the laws apply.[4] Because of these wide variations in legal identity definitions and their frequent departure from the various tribal ones, many individuals who are recognized by their tribes as citizens are nevertheless considered non-Indian for some or all federal purposes. The converse can be true as well.[5]

There are a variety of contexts in which one or more federal legal definitions of identity become important. The matter of economic resource distribution—access to various social services, monetary awards, and opportunities—probably comes immediately to the minds of many readers. The legal situation of Indian people, and its attendant opportunities and responsibilities, are the result of historic negotiations between tribes and the federal government. In these, the government agreed to compensate tribes in various ways for the large amounts of land and other resources that the tribes had surrendered, often by force.[6] Benefits available to those who can satisfy federal definitions of Indian identity are administered through a variety of agencies, including the Bureau of Indian Affairs, the Indian Health Service, the Department of Agriculture, the Office of Elementary and Secondary Education, and the Department of Labor, to name a few.[7]

Legal definitions also affect specific economic rights deriving from treaties or agreements that

---

Eva Marie Garroutte is a professor of sociology at Boston College.

some (not all) tribes made with the federal government. These may include such rights as the use of particular geographic areas for hunting, harvesting, fishing, or trapping. Those legally defined as Indians are also sometimes exempted from certain requirements related to state licensure and state (but not federal) income and property taxation.[8] . . .

"IF HE GETS A NOSEBLEED, HE'LL TURN INTO A WHITE MAN"

North American Indians who successfully negotiate the rigors of legal definitions of identity at the federal level can achieve what some consider the dubious distinction of being a "card-carrying Indian." That is, their federal government can issue them a laminated document (in the United States, a CDIB; in Canada an Indian status card) that certifies them as possessing a certain "degree of Indian blood."

. . . Canadian-born country music singer Shania Twain has what it takes to be a card-carrying Indian: she is formally recognized as an Anishnabe (Ojibwe) Indian with band membership in the Temagami Bear Island First Nation (Ontario, Canada). More specifically, she is legally on record as possessing one-half degree Indian blood. Given this information, one might conclude that Twain's identity as an Indian person is more or less unassailable. It's not.

Controversy has engulfed this celebrity because of an anonymous phone call to a Canadian newspaper a few years ago that led to the disclosure of another name by which Shania was once known: Eileen Regina Edwards. Eileen/Shania was adopted by a stepfather in early childhood and took the surname of Twain at that time. So far well and good—except for one thing. Both sides of her *biological* family describe themselves not as Indian but as white. It is only Jerry Twain, her late stepfather, who was Indian.

As the adopted child of an Anishnabe man, Shania Twain occupies an unusual status. Though the U.S. government allows for the assignment of blood quantum only to biological descendants of Indian people, Canada allows for the naturalization of non-Native children through adoption.[9]

Although Twain has stated that her white mother (now deceased) had told her, in childhood, that her biological father (also deceased) had some Indian heritage, his family denies the suggestion entirely. They say they are French and Irish. Ms. Twain explains: "I don't know how much Indian blood I actually have in me, but as the adopted daughter of my father Jerry, I became legally registered as 50-percent North American Indian. Being raised by a full-blooded Indian and being part of his family and their culture from such a young age is all I've ever known. That heritage is in my heart and my soul, and I'm proud of it."[10]

Twain has been sharply criticized, in both the United States and Canada, for not making the full details of her racial background clearer, especially to awards-granting agencies such as the First Americans in the Arts (FAITA), which honored her in February 1996 as a Native performer. FAITA itself has made no such complaint. The group states that it is satisfied that "Ms. Twain has not intentionally misrepresented herself." And more importantly, her adopted family defends her. An aunt observes: "She was raised by us. She was accepted by our band. If my brother were alive, he'd be very upset. He raised her as his own daughter. My parents, her grandparents, took her into the bush and taught her the [Native] traditions."[11]

Twain's case shows with uncommon clarity that legal and biological definitions are conceptually distinct. . . .

In their modern American construction, at least, biological definitions of identity assume the centrality of an individual's genetic relationship to other tribal members. Not just any degree of relationship will do, however. Typically, the degree of closeness is also important. And this is the starting point for much of the controversy that swirls around issues of biological Indianness. . . .

Sociologist Eugeen Roosens summarizes such common conceptions about the importance of blood quantum for determining Indian identity:

> There is . . . [a] principle about which the whites and the Indians are in agreement. . . . People with more Indian blood . . . also have more rights to inherit what

their ancestors, the former Indians, have left behind. In addition, full blood Indians are more authentic than half-breeds. By *being* pure, they have more right to respect. They *are,* in all aspects of their being, more *integral.*[12]

Biological ancestry can take on such tremendous significance in tribal contexts that it overwhelms all other considerations of identity, especially when it is constructed as "pure." As Cherokee legal scholar G. William Rice points out, "Most [people] would recognize the full-blood Indian who was enrolled in a federally recognized tribe as an Indian, even if the individual was adopted at birth by a non-Indian family and had never set foot in Indian country nor met another Indian."[13] Mixed-race individuals, by contrast, find their identity claims considerably complicated. Even if such an individual can demonstrate conclusively that he has *some* Native ancestry, the question will still be raised: Is the *amount* of ancestry he possesses "enough"? Is his "Indian blood" sufficient to distinguish him from the mixed-blood individual spotlighted by an old quip: "If he got a nosebleed, he'd turn into a white man"?

Members of various tribes complain of factionalism between these two major groups—full bloods and mixed bloods—and they suggest that the division arose historically because of mixed bloods' greater access to the social resources of the dominant society and their enhanced ability to impose values and ideas upon others.[14] As Julie M., a citizen of the United Keetowah Band of Cherokee Indians, says: "For the Cherokee people, there's been this mixed blood/full blood kind of dynamic going from before the removal [in 1838, also known as the Trail of Tears]. . . . It's kind of like us-and-them. . . . It's almost been like a *war* in some cases. . . . It's a 'who's-really-going-to-be-in-control-of-the-tribe?' kind of thing." Many historians have similarly found it logical that political allegiances would tend to shift for those Indian people who formed alliances, through intermarriage, with members of the dominant society, and that this has made the division between full bloods and mixed bloods politically important.[15]

Modern biological definitions of identity, however, are much more complicated than this historical explanation can account for. This complexity did not originate in the ideas and experiences of Indian tribes. Instead, they closely reflect nineteenth- and early-twentieth-century theories of race introduced by Euro-Americans. These theories (of which there were a great many) viewed biology as definitive, but they did not distinguish it from culture. Thus, blood became quite literally the vehicle for the transmission of cultural characteristics. "'Half-breeds' by this logic could be expected to behave in 'half-civilized,' i.e., partially assimilated, ways while retaining one half of their traditional culture, accounting for their marginal status in both societies."[16]

These turn-of-the-century theories of race found a very precise way to talk about *amount* of ancestry in the idea of blood quantum, or degree of blood. The notion of blood quantum as a standard of Indianness emerged with force in the nineteenth century. Its most significant early usage as a standard of identification was in the General Allotment (Dawes) Act of 1887, which led to the creation of the Dawes Rolls [the "base roll" or written record of tribal membership in a specific year]. It has been part of the popular—and legal and academic—lore about Indians ever since.

Given this standard of identification, full bloods tend to be seen as the "really real," the quintessential Indians, while others are viewed as Indians in diminishing degrees. The original, stated intention of blood quantum distinctions was to determine the point at which the various responsibilities of the dominant society to Indian peoples ended. The ultimate and explicit federal intention was to use the blood quantum standard as a means to liquidate tribal lands and to eliminate government trust responsibility to tribes, along with entitlement programs, treaty rights, and reservations. Through intermarriage and application of a biological definition of identity Indians would eventually become citizens indistinguishable from all other citizens.[17]

Degree of blood is calculated, with reference to biological definitions, on the basis of the immediacy of one's genetic relationship to those whose bloodlines are (supposedly) unmixed. As in the case with legal definitions, the initial calculation for most tribes' biological definitions begins with a base roll, a listing of tribal membership and blood quanta in some particular year. These base rolls make possible very elaborate definitions of identity. For instance, they allow one to reckon that the offspring of, say, a full-blood Navajo mother and a white father is one-half Navajo. If that half-Navajo child, in turn, produces children with a Hopi person of one-quarter blood degree, those progeny will be judged one-quarter Navajo and one-eighth Hopi. Alternatively, they can be said to have three-eighths general Indian blood.

As even this rather simple example shows, over time such calculations can become infinitesimally precise, with people's ancestry being parsed into so many thirty-secondths, sixty-fourths, one-hundred-twenty-eighths, and so on. . . .

For those of us who have grown up and lived with the peculiar precision of calculating blood quantum, it sometimes requires a perspective less influenced by the vagaries of American history to remind us just how far from common sense the concepts underlying biological definitions of identity are. I recall responding to an inquiry from a Southeast Asian friend about what blood quantum was and how it was calculated. In mid-explanation, I noticed his expression of complete amazement. "That's the dumbest thing I ever heard," he burst out. "Who ever thought of *that?*"

The logic that underlies the biological definition of racial identity becomes even more curious and complicated when one considers the striking difference in the way that American definitions assign individuals to the racial category of "Indian," as opposed to the racial category "black." As a variety of researchers have observed, social attributions of black identity have focused (at least since the end of the Civil War) on the "one-drop rule," or rule of hypodescent.[18] . . .

Far from being held to a one-drop rule, Indians are generally required—both by law and by popular opinion—to establish rather *high* blood quanta in order for their claims to racial identity to be accepted as meaningful, the individual's own opinion notwithstanding. Although people must have only the slightest trace of "black blood" to be *forced* into the category "African American," modern American Indians must (1) formally produce (2) strong evidence of (3) often rather substantial amounts of "Indian blood" to be *allowed* entry into the corresponding racial category. The regnant biological definitions applied to Indians are simply quite different than those that have applied (and continue to apply) to blacks. Modern Americans, as Native American Studies professor Jack Forbes (Powhatan/Lenape/Saponi) puts the matter, "are *always finding 'blacks'* (even if they look rather un-African), and . . . *are always losing 'Indians.'*"[19]

BIOLOGICAL DEFINITIONS: CONTEXTS AND CONSEQUENCES

Biological definitions of Indian identity operate, in short, in some curious and inconsistent ways. They are nevertheless significant in a variety of contexts. And they have clear relationships, both direct and indirect, to legal definitions. The federal government has historically used a minimum blood quantum standard to determine who was eligible to receive treaty rights, or to sell property and manage his or her own financial affairs.[20] Blood quantum is *one* of the criteria that determines eligibility for citizenship in many tribes; it therefore indirectly influences the claimant's relationship to the same kinds of rights, privileges, and responsibilities that legal definitions allow.[21]

But biological definitions of identity affect personal interactions as well as governmental decisions. Indian people with high blood quanta frequently have recognizable physical characteristics. As Cherokee Nation principal tribal chief Chad Smith observes, some people are easily recognizable as Indians because they pass "a brown paper bag test," meaning that their skin is "darker than a #10 paper sack." It is these individuals who are often most closely associated with negative racial stereotypes in the larger society. Native American Studies professor Devon Mihesuah makes a point about Indian women that is really applicable to either gender: "Appearance is the most visible aspect of one's race;

it determines how Indian women define themselves and how others define and treat them. Their appearance, whether Caucasian, Indian, African, or mixed, either limits or broadens Indian women's choices of ethnic identity and ability to interact with non-Indians and other Indians."[22]

Every day, identifiably Indian people are turned away from restaurants, refused the use of public rest rooms, ranked as unintelligent by the education system, and categorized by the personnel of medical, social service, and other vital public agencies as "problems"—all strictly on the basis of their appearance. As Keetoowah Band Cherokee full-blood Donald G. notes, a recognizably Indian appearance can be a serious detriment to one's professional and personal aspirations: "It seems the darker you are, the less important you are, in some ways, to the employer. . . . To some, it would be discouraging. But I am four-fourths [i.e., full-blood] Cherokee, and it doesn't matter what someone says about me. . . . I feel for the person who doesn't like my skin color, you know?"

There are circumstances, however, in which it is difficult for the victims of negative racial stereotyping to maintain an attitude as philosophical as this. In one interview, a Mohawk friend, June L., illustrated the potential consequences of public judgments based on skin color. She reminded me of a terrifying episode that had once unfolded while I was visiting at her house. Our conversation was interrupted by a phone call informing this mother of five that her college-student son, who had spent the summer day working on a roof, had suddenly become ill while driving home. Feeling faint, he had pulled up to a local convenience store and made his way inside, asking for a drink of water. The clerk refused. Dangerously dehydrated, the young man collapsed on the floor from sunstroke. "The worst thing about it," June recalled, "was that I have to keep wondering: What was the reason for that? Did that clerk refuse to help my son because she was just a mean person? Or was it because she saw him stumble into the store and thought, 'Well, it's just some drunken Indian'?" Anxiety about social judgments of this kind are a fact of daily life for parents of children whose physical appearance makes their Indian ancestry clearly evident.

At the same time, June's remarks showed the opposite side to the coin of physical appearance. In some contexts, not conforming to the usual notions of "what Indians look like" can also be a liability:

> My aunt was assistant dean at a large Ivy League university. One day she called me on the phone. She had one scholarship to give out to an Indian student. One of the students being considered was blonde-haired and blue-eyed. The other one was black-haired and dark-skinned, and she looked Indian. The blonde girl's grades were a little better. My aunt didn't know what to do. She said to me, "Both these girls are tribal members. Both of them are qualified [for the scholarship]. They're sitting outside my office. What would *you* do?" I told her that, as an Indian person, there was only one thing I *could* say. Which was to give the money to the one with the dark skin. As Indian people, we *do* want to have Indian people that *look* like they're Indian to represent us.

Readers may be surprised by such a candid statement. But June's pragmatic reasoning takes account of certain historical realities. As she explained further, "We like people to *know* who's doing those accomplishments, like getting scholarships. We want them to know this is an Indian person doing this. Because I come from a background where if you looked Indian, you were put in special education because the schools said you couldn't learn. And it wasn't true. We need Indian people today who look Indian to show everyone the things we can do."

A physical appearance that is judged insufficiently "Indian" can also act as a barrier to participation in certain cultural activities. Bill T., a Wichita and Seneca minister in his midfifties, recalls that, in his youth, he witnessed light-skinned individuals who attempted to participate in powwow dances being evicted from the arena. "That kind of thing is still happening today," he added sadly, and other respondents readily confirmed this observation. A more unusual instance of the relevance of physical appearance to cultural participation was volunteered by Frank D., a Hopi respondent. His tribe's ceremonial dances feature the appearance of powerful spirit beings called kachinas, which are embodied by masked Hopi men. Ideally, the everyday, human identity of the dancers remains unknown to observers. Frank commented on the subject of tribal members whose skin tone is noticeably either lighter or darker than the norm:

Frank D.: Say, for instance, if a Hopi marries a black person . . . [and] you get a male child . . . it's gonna be darker skinned. It might even be black. A black kachina just wouldn't fit out here [at Hopi]. You see, everybody'd know who it is. He'd be very visible [in the ceremonial dances]. . . . It'd be very hard on that individual. Kids don't work the other way, too—if they're real light. . . . Kachinas gotta be *brown.*

Author: So there are certain ceremonial roles that people could not fill because of their appearance?

Frank D.: Well, they *could,* but it would be awful tough. A lot of these [ceremonial] things are done with secrecy. No one knows who the kachinas are. Or at least, the kids don't. And then, say you get somebody who really stands out, then everybody knows who that [dancer] is, and it's not good. For the ceremony—because everybody knows who that person is. And so the kids will start asking questions—"How come that kachina's so dark, so black?" or "How come that kachina's white?" They start asking questions and it's really hard. So I think, if you're thinking about kids, it's really better if kachinas are brown.

Finally, the physical appearance borne by mixed bloods may not only create barriers to tribal cultural participation; it may also offer an occasion for outrightly shaming them. Cornelia S. remembers her days at the Eufala Indian School:

You *had* to be Indian to be [allowed admission] there. . . . But . . . if [certain students] . . . didn't look as Indian as we did, or if they looked like they were white, they were kind of looked down upon, like treated differently because [people would say] "oh, that's just a white person." . . . They just [would] tease 'em and stuff. Say "oh, whatcha doin' white boy" or "white girl"—just stuff like that.

Nor is the social disapproval of light-skinned mixed bloods strictly the stuff of schoolyard teasing. The same respondent added that even adults confront questions of blood quantum with dead seriousness:

Us Indians, whenever we see someone else who is saying that they're Indian . . . or trying to be around us Indians, and act like us, and they don't look like they're Indian and we know that they're not as much Indian as *we* are, yeah, we look at them like they're not Indian and, ya know, don't really like why they're acting like that. . . . But you know, I'm not *that* far off . . . into judging other people and what color [they are].

The late author Michael Dorris, a member of the Modoc tribe (California), has written that humiliations related to his appearance were part of his daily experience. He describes (in his account of his family's struggle with his son's fetal alcohol syndrome, *The Broken Cord*) an encounter with a hospital admissions staff, to whom he had just identified himself and his son as Indians. "They surveyed my appearance with curiosity. It was an expression I recognized, a reaction, familiar to most people of mixed-blood ancestry, that said, 'You don't *look* like an Indian.' No matter how often it happened, no matter how frequently I was blamed by strangers for not resembling their image of some Hollywood Sitting Bull, I was still defensive and vulnerable. 'I'm part Indian,' I explained."[23]

Even his tragic death has not safeguarded Dorris from insinuations about inadequate blood quantum. Shortly after his 1997 suicide, a story on his life and death in *New York* magazine reported that the author's fair complexion had always caused some observers to wonder about his racial identity and archly repeated a rumor: "It is said he . . . [eventually] discovered tanning booths."[24]

In short, many Indian people, both individually and collectively, continue to embrace the assumption that close biological connections to other Indian people—and the distinctive physical appearance that may accompany those connections—imply a stronger claim on identity than do more distant ones. As Potawatomi scholar of Native American Studies Terry Wilson summarizes, "Few, if any, Native Americans, regardless of upbringing in rural, reservation, or urban setting, ignore their own and other Indians' blood quantum in everyday life. Those whose physical appearances render their Indian identities suspect are subject to suspicious scrutiny until precise cultural explanations, especially blood quantum, are offered or discovered."[25]

DISCUSSION QUESTIONS

1. As Garroutte describes them, what are the various ways that one might be defined as a "real" Indian? When might these different definitions of "Indianness" conflict?

2. Thinking about June's description of her son being refused a drink of water and her advice about who should receive the Indian scholarship, do you see any consistencies or inconsistencies in her approach?

3. Garroutte notes that turn-of-the century race theorists treated blood as the "vehicle for the transmission of cultural characteristics." Can you give some specific examples of what this might mean? Do you think contemporary American social practices operate from the same premise?

NOTES

1. Thornton surveyed 302 of the 317 tribes in the lower forty-eight states that enjoyed federal acknowledgment in 1997. He found that 204 tribes had some minimum blood quantum requirement, while the remaining 98 had none. Russell Thornton, "Tribal Membership Requirements and the Demography of 'Old' and 'New' Native Americans," *Population Research and Policy Review* 16 (1997): 37.

2. The two mentions of "Indians" in the Constitution appear in passages regarding the regulation of commerce and the taking of a federal census. The word "tribe" also appears once in the Constitution, in the Commerce Clause.

3. Sharon O'Brien, "Tribes and Indians: With Whom Does the United States Maintain a Relationship?" *Notre Dame Law Review* 66 (1991): 1481.

4. One particularly important law that provides no definition of "Indian" is the Major Crimes Act of 1885 (23 Stat. 385, U.S.C. Sec. 1153). It subjects reservation Indians to federal prosecution for certain offenses for which non-Indians would face only state prosecution.

5. For a detailed discussion of legal cases bearing on the definition of "Indian," see Felix S. Cohen, *Handbook of Federal Indian Law* (Charlottesville, Va.: Michie/Bobbs-Merrill, 1982).

6. Wilcomb E. Washburn, *Red Man's Land/White Man's Law: A Study of the Past and Present States of the American Indian* (New York: Charles Scribner's Sons, 1971).

7. These agencies administer resources and programs in areas such as education, health, social services, tribal governance and administration, law enforcement, nutrition, resource management, tribal economic development, employment, and the like. The most recently published source describing various programs and the requirements for participation is Roger Walk, *Federal Assistance to Native Americans: A Report Prepared for the Senate Select Committee on Indian Affairs of the US Senate* (Washington, D.C.: Government Printing Office, 1991). In fiscal year 2001, recognized tribes and their members had access to approximately four billion dollars of federal funding for various social programs. U.S. Government Accounting Office, *Indian Issues: Improvements Needed in Tribal Recognition Process*, Report to Congressional Requesters, Washington D.C.: Government Printing Office, November 2001.

8. Non-Indian students in my classes sometimes tell me that Indians also regularly receive such windfalls as free cars and monthly checks from the government strictly because of their race. It is my sad duty to puncture this fantasy; there is no truth in it. The common belief that Indians receive "free money" from the government probably stems from the fact that the government holds land in trust for certain tribes. As part of its trust responsibility, it may then lease that land, collect the revenue, and distribute it to the tribal members. Thus, some Indians do receive government checks, but these do not represent some kind of manna from heaven; they are simply the profits derived from lands which they own. For details on the special, political-economic relationship of Indians to the federal government in relation to taxation and licensure, see Gary D. Sandefur, "Economic Development and Employment Opportunities for American Indians," in *American Indians: Social Justice and Public Policy,* ed. Donald E. Green and Thomas V. Tonneson, Ethnicity and Public Policy Series, vol. 9 (Milwaukee: University of Wisconsin System Institute on Race and Ethnicity, 1991), 208–22.

9. Aside from the issue of adopted children, the legal requirements for establishing legal status as Indian in Canada have been even more complicated and peculiar than the U.S. ones, and the tensions related to them even more severe. Until 1985, a Canadian Indian woman who married a legally non-Indian man lost her legal status as an Indian, and her children (who might have a blood quantum of one-half) could never be recognized

as Indian under Canadian law. A non-Indian woman who married an Indian man, however, gained Indian status for herself and her children. Men could neither gain nor lose Indian status through marriage. When a 1985 bill amended the Indian Act, which governed such matters, the issue of "real Indianness" came to a head. Many Canadian Indian women and children sought and received Indian legal status, but when they attempted to return to the reservations, they often got a chilly welcome from Indian communities already overburdened with financial obligations to their existing population. Like their American counterparts, Canadian Indian bands continue to struggle with the issue of how to conceive the boundaries of their membership. For a good discussion of Canadian Indian identification policies, see Eugeen Roosens, *Creating Ethnicity: The Process of Ethnogenesis* (Newbury Park, Calif.: Sage, 1989).

10. Shania Twain quoted in Jackie Bissley, "Country Star Shania Twain's Candor Is Challenged," *Indian Country Today,* 9–16 April 1996.

11. Quoted in Jackie Bissley, "Country Singer Says Stories Robbing Her of Her Native Roots," *Indian Country Today,* 16–23 April 1996. Even Twain's unusual situation does not exhaust the intricate aspects of the Canadian legal system as it struggles with matters of Indian identity. Roosens describes other fine points of Indian identity in force north of the border over a period of several decades:

Since 1951, to be registered as an Indian one has to be the legitimate child of an Indian father. The ethnic origin of the mother is irrelevant. . . . Furthermore, if the grandmother on the Indian side of a mixed marriage (the father's mother) is a non-Indian by descent, then the grandchild loses his or her status at the age of 21. Thus, one can be officially born an Indian and lose this status at the age of maturity. (Roosens, *Creating Ethnicity,* 24)

12. Roosens, *Creating Ethnicity,* 41–42. Roosens is discussing the situation of Canadian Indians, but the same remarks apply to American Indians.

13. G. William Rice, "There and Back Again—An Indian Hobbit's Holiday: Indians Teaching Indian Law," *New Mexico Law Review* 26, no. 2 (1996): 176.

14. Melissa L. Meyer, "American Indian Blood Quantum Requirements: Blood Is Thicker than Family," in *Over the Edge: Remapping the American West,* ed. Valerie J. Matsumoto and Blake Allmendiger (Berkeley: University of California Press, 1999).

15. Historians such as Grace Steele Woodward and Marion Starkey have made this argument. But see also Julia Coates, "None of Us Is Supposed to Be Here" (Ph.D. diss., University of New Mexico, 2002) for a revisionist understanding of Cherokee history.

16. C. Matthew Snipp, "Who Are American Indians? Some Observations about the Perils and Pitfalls of Data for Race and Ethnicity," *Population Research and Policy Review* 5 (1986): 249. For excellent and intriguing discussions of the evolution of ideas about blood relationships among European and Euro-American peoples over several centuries, and transference of these ideas into American Indian tribal populations, see Meyer, "Blood Quantum Requirements," and Circe Sturm, *Blood Politics: Race, Culture, and Identity in the Cherokee Nation of Oklahoma* (Berkeley: University of California Press, 2002). See further Peggy Pascoe, "Miscegenation Law, Court Cases, and Ideologies of 'Race' in Twentieth Century America," *Journal of American History* 83, no. 1 (June 1996): 44–69. For the processes by which some of these theories were rejected by scientists, see Elazar Barkan, *Retreat of Scientific Racism: Changing Concepts of Race in Britain and the United States between the World Wars* (Cambridge: Cambridge University Press, 1992).

17. Thomas Biolsi, "The Birth of the Reservation: Making the Modern Individual among the Lakota," *American Ethnologist* 22, no. 1 (February 1995): 28–49; Patrick Limerick, *The Legacy of Conquest: The Unbroken Past of the American West* (New York: W. W. Norton, 1988).

18. Naomi Zack, "Mixed Black and White Race and Public Policy," *Hypatia* 10, 1 (1995): 120–32; Ariela J. Gross, "Litigating Whiteness: Trials of Racial Determination in the Nineteenth-Century South," *Yale Law Journal* 108 (1998): 109–88.

19. Jack D. Forbes, "The Manipulation of Race, Caste, and Identity: Classifying AfroAmericans, Native Americans and Red-Black People," *Journal of Ethnic Studies* 17, no. 4 (1990): 24; original emphasis. Indians are "lost," in Forbes' sense, both to black *and* to white racial classifications, but at differing rates. Popular conventions of racial classification in America tend to prevent individuals with any discernible black ancestry from identifying themselves as Indians. As an interview respondent quoted by anthropologist Circe Sturm observes, "This is America, where being to any degree Black is the same thing as being to any degree pregnant." Sturm, *Blood Politics,* 188.

By contrast, individuals with discernible white ancestry are *sometimes* allowed by others to identify as Indian. In their case the legitimacy of their assertion is likely to be evaluated with reference to the *amount* of white ancestry, and with beliefs about whether that amount is enough to merely *dilute* or to entirely *compromise* Indian identity. Other factors, such as culture and upbringing, may also be taken into account. People of partial white ancestry, in other words, are typically somewhat more free (although not entirely free) to negotiate a legitimate identity as Indian than are people of partial black ancestry.

20. For further details on the historical impact of blood quantum on individuals' legal rights, see Felix S. Cohen, *Cohen's Handbook of Federal Indian Law* (Charlottesville, Va.: Michie/Bobbs-Merrill, 1982).

21. For a listing of the blood quantum requirements that different tribes require for tribal citizenship, see Edgar Lister, "Tribal Membership Rates and Requirements," unpublished table (Washington, D.C.: Indian Health Service, 1987). An edited version of the table appears in C. Matthew Snipp, *American Indians: The First of This Land* (New York: Russell Sage Foundation, 1989), appendix.

22. Devon A. Mihesuah, "Commonality of Difference: American Indian Women and History," in *Natives and Academics: Researching and Writing about American Indians*, ed. Devon A. Mihesuah (Lincoln: University of Nebraska Press, 1998), 42. For a fascinating and detailed discussion of the significance of appearance among contemporary Cherokees in Oklahoma, see Sturm, *Blood Politics*, 108–15.

23. Michael Dorris, *The Broken Cord* (New York: Harper Perennial, 1990), 22.

24. Eric Konigsberg, "Michael Dorris's Troubled Sleep," *New York Magazine*, 16 June 1997, 33. For a related article, see Jerry Reynolds, "Indian Writers: The Good, the Bad, and the Could Be, Part 2: Indian Writers: Real or Imagined," *Indian Country Today*, 15 September 1993.

25. Terry P. Wilson, "Blood Quantum: Native American Mixed Bloods," in *Racially Mixed People in America*, ed. Maria P. P. Root (Newbury Park, Calif.: Sage, 1992), 109.

READING 5

Asian American Panethnicity: Contemporary National and Transnational Possibilities

Yen Le Espiritu

In an article published in *Gidra*, an activist Asian American news magazine, Naomi Iwasaki (1999, under "Asian American or Not") writes, "You know, the hardest thing about pan-Asian solidarity is the 'pan' part. It forces us all to step outside of our comfort zones, whether they be constructed by ethnicity, class, home city, identity, whatever." Iwasaki's statement calls attention to the social constructedness

Yen Le Espiritu is a professor of ethnic studies at the University of California, San Diego.

of panethnicity—panethnic identities are self-conscious products of political choice and actions, not of inherited phenotypes, bloodlines, or cultural traditions. In my 1992 publication *Asian American Panethnicity: Bridging Institutions and Identities*, I identify the twin roots of Asian American panethnicity—in the racialization of Asian national groups by dominant groups and in Asian Americans' responses to those constructions. Employing a racial formation perspective (Omi and Winant 1986), I argue that the racialist constructions of Asians as homogeneous and interchangeable spawn important alliances and affiliations among ethnic and immigrant groups of Asian origin. Adopting the dominant group's categorization of them, Asian Americans have institutionalized pan-Asianism as their political instrument, thereby enlarging their own capacities to challenge and transform the existing structure of power. In other words, Asian Americans did not just adopt the pan-Asian concept but also transformed it to conform to their political, economic, and ideological needs.

Though powerful, pan-Asianism is not unproblematic: it can mask salient divisions, subsume non-dominant groups, and create marginalities, all of which threatens the legitimacy and effectiveness of pan-Asianism and bolsters (however inadvertently) the racist discourses and practices that construct Asians as homogeneous. In the three decades since the emergence of the pan-Asian concept in the late 1960s, Asian American communities have changed in dramatic ways. No longer constrained by race-based exclusion laws, Asian immigrants began arriving in much larger numbers than before. Many of the post-1965 immigrants have little direct experience with the Asian American movement and little reason to think of themselves as Asian American rather than as immigrants, as low-wage workers, or as members of different national and ethnic groups (Espiritu et al. 2000, 131). Moreover, recent immigration has further diversified Asian Americans along cultural, generational, economic, and political lines—all of which have compounded the difficulties of forging pan-Asian identities and institutions.

This ... review [of] the history of Asian American panethnicity in the United States *then to now* [pays] particular attention to the ways in which pan-Asian identities and institutions have been transformed by the post-1965 immigration and by changes in the global economy. The first section documents the social, political, and demographic factors that led to the emergence of pan-Asianism in the late 1960s and early 1970s. The second details how the post-1965 immigration has diversified the Asian American population and made it more difficult for groups to imagine shared origins and destinies. The third establishes that the construction of Asian American identities not only is a response to conditions in the United States but also is deeply bound to U.S. colonial and imperialist practices that propel the contemporary migration of Asians to the United States in the first place. The fourth discusses the political importance of cross-group affiliation, not only among Asians but also with other groups across class, ethnic, racial, and national lines. Of the four sections, the third conveys the central argument: pan-Asianism in the United States has been determined not exclusively by events and population changes in the United States but also by U.S. colonialism and imperialism in Asia. Much of the published work in the field of U.S. immigration studies has remained "America-centric," focusing on the immigrants' "modes of incorporation" and the process of their "becoming American." In contrast, this [reading] takes a *critical transnational approach* to the study of Asian Americans, calling attention to the deep historical entanglements of immigration and imperialism.[1]

COMING TOGETHER: THE EMERGENCE OF PAN-ASIANISM

Arriving in the United States, nineteenth-century immigrants from Asian countries did not think of themselves as "Asians." Coming from specific districts and provinces in different nations, Asian immigrant groups did not even think of themselves as Chinese, Japanese, Korean, and so forth, but rather as people from Toishan, Hoiping, or some other

district in Guandong Province in China or from Hiroshima, Yamaguchi, or some other prefecture in Japan. Members of each group considered themselves culturally and politically distinct. Historical enmities between their countries of origin further separated the groups even before their arrival in the United States. However, non-Asians had little understanding or appreciation of these distinctions. For the most part, outsiders accorded to people from Asia certain common characteristics and traits that were essentially supranational. Indeed, the exclusion acts and quotas limiting Asian immigration to the United States relied on racialist constructions of Asians as homogeneous (Lowe 1991, 28).

The development of panethnicity among Asian Americans has a short history. It was not until the late 1960s, with the advent of the Asian American movement, that a pan-Asian consciousness and constituency were first formed. Before the 1960s, Asians in the United States frequently practiced ethnic disidentification: distancing one's group from another group so as not to be mistaken for a member of that group and to avoid suffering the blame for its presumed misdeeds (Hayano 1981, 161, 162; Daniels 1988, 113). For example, in the late nineteenth century, aware of Chinese exclusion, Japanese immigrant leaders did everything possible to distinguish themselves from the Chinese immigrants (Ichioka 1988, 250). In the end Japanese attempts at disidentification failed. With the passage of the 1924 Immigration Act, the Japanese joined the Chinese as a people deemed unworthy of becoming Americans. Less than two decades later, after the bombing of Pearl Harbor, it was the turn of the Chinese to disassociate themselves from the Japanese. Fearful that they would be targets of anti-Japanese activities, many Chinese immigrants took to wearing buttons that proclaimed positively, "I'm Chinese." Some Chinese immigrants—and also Korean and Filipino migrants—even joined the white persecution with buttons that added, "I hate Japs worse than you do" (Daniels 1988, 205; Takaki 1989, 370–71). These two examples are instructive not only as evidence of ethnic disidentification but also as documentation of the pervasiveness of racial lumping. Precisely because of racial lumping, persons

America's newcomers are simply crossing over the color line rather than helping to eradicate it (Alba 1999, Bean & Stevens 2003, Gans 1999, Gitlin 1995, Hollinger 1995, Lee & Bean 2003, Rodriguez 2000, Sanjek 1994, Skrentny 2001, Waters 1999). In this review, we attempt to address the question about the placement and strength of America's color lines by examining the extant theories and recent findings concerning immigrant incorporation, intermarriage, and multiracial identification in the United States, focusing specifically on intergroup differences among whites, blacks, Latinos, and Asians. After carefully reviewing the literature, we assess the implications of these findings for America's changing color lines. . . .

CHANGING RACIAL/ETHNIC BOUNDARIES

. . . Today, social scientists generally agree that race is a social rather than biological category and have documented the processes by which ethnic and racial boundaries have changed throughout our nation's history. For instance, previously "nonwhite" immigrant ethnic groups such as Irish, Italians, and eastern European Jews became "white," often by deliberately distinguishing themselves from blacks (Alba 1999, Brodkin 1998, Foner 2000, Gerstle 1999, Ignatiev 1995, Jacobson 1998, Perlmann & Waldinger 1997, Roediger 1991). Historians such as Ignatiev (1995) and Jacobson (1998) describe how white ethnics went to extreme measures to distance themselves from black Americans to achieve whiteness. Another critical factor that helped to change the status of Irish, Italians, and Jews from nonwhite to white was the end of large-scale European immigration in the 1920s. The cessation of massive immigration not only diminished fears about an overflow of allegedly racial inferiors, but also facilitated the economic incorporation of European immigrants, especially during the golden years following World War II (Foner 2000). In addition to the successful incorporation of white ethnics into the nation's economic and social structure, black migration patterns within the United States influenced the nation's

color lines, redrawing the racial configuration along a stark binary black/white divide in which Irish, Italians, and Jews fell on the white side of the color line (Jacobson 1998).

However, many social scientists caution that the very fact that Irish, Italians, and Jews were not subject to the same type of systematic legal discrimination as African Americans illustrates that they were on a different plane from blacks to begin with, a standing that facilitated their eventual racial treatment as whites (Alba 1985, Foner 2000, Lieberson 1980). Moreover, the disappearance of national origin differences among European ethnics and the discontinuation of tendencies to view such differences not only in racial terms but in fact in rigid black/white terms contributed to the development of the idea that, for many European immigrants, race was an achieved rather than an ascribed status (Alba 1990, Gans 1979, Perlmann & Waldinger 1997, Waters 1990). But this in all likelihood was because such persons were viewed as nonwhite rather than black. In that time period's rigidly compartmentalized black/white world governed by the "one-drop" rule (which emphasized pure whiteness versus everything else), not being white did not necessarily involve actually being black, but it was like being black. Thus, it is not surprising that these national origin groups were treated as black. Perhaps because in fact they were not black, their status was eventually allowed to change, thus hastening the evolution and acceptance of the idea that at least some racial categories—maybe all except black—could in fact be changed.

White ethnics such as Italians, Irish, and eastern European Jews are not the only groups to have changed their status from nonwhite to white. Asian ethnic groups such as the Chinese in Mississippi and Japanese Americans also changed their racial status from almost black to almost white. Loewen (1971), for example, documents how Chinese Americans in the Mississippi Delta made conscious efforts to change their lowly racial status by achieving economic mobility, emulating the cultural practices of whites, intentionally distancing themselves from blacks, and rejecting fellow ethnics who married

ETHNIC DIVERSIFICATION

Before the post-1965 immigration surge, the Asian American population was composed mainly of three ethnic groups: Japanese, Chinese, and Filipino. In 1970 Japanese Americans constituted the single largest group (41 percent of the Asian American population), followed by Chinese Americans (30 percent) and Filipino Americans (24 percent). Members of other national origins groups (mostly Koreans) represented less than 5 percent of the Asian American population total (Zhou and Gatewood 2000, 13). Coming of age in the 1960s, U.S.-born Japanese and Chinese Americans formed the core force of the Asian American movement on West Coast college campuses and in the Northeast (Espiritu 1992). In contrast, in 2000 the U.S. census recorded twenty-four national origins groups, and no single group accounted for more than one-quarter of the Asian American population. Although Japan has sent very few immigrants to the United States, the Philippines, China and Taiwan, Korea, India, and Vietnam have been on the list of the top ten sending countries since 1980 (USINS 1997). Reflecting these changing immigration patterns, in 2000 the Japanese American share of the Asian American population fell to only 8 percent, and the five largest Asian American groups were Chinese and Taiwanese (24 percent), Filipino (18 percent), Asian Indian (17 percent), Korean (11 percent), and Vietnamese (11 percent) (Barnes and Bennett 2002).[3] The new Asian American demographics have complicated the delicate pan-Asian alignments created in the 1960s and 1970s among the then-largest Asian American groups: Japanese, Chinese, and, to a lesser extent, Filipino Americans.

Generational Diversification

Between the 1940s and 1960s, when immigration from Asia was restricted, U.S.-born Asian Americans dominated the Asian American population. By the 1970s the foreign-born reemerged as a large majority. In 2000, 7.2 million Asian Pacific Americans—approximately 70 percent of the total Asian American population—were foreign-born (U.S. Department of Commerce 2002). The foreign-born component dominated all Asian American groups except for Japanese Americans; over 60 percent of Filipinos and nearly 80 percent of Vietnamese and other Asians were foreign-born (Zhou and Gatewood 2000, 14). Because of legal exclusion in the past, it is only among the two oldest immigrant groups—the Japanese and Chinese Americans—that a sizable third or fourth generation exists. Among Asian American children under eighteen years of age, more than 90 percent are either foreign-born or children of foreign-born parents (Zhou and Gatewood 2000, 23). Paul Ong and Suzanne Hee (1993) have predicted that the foreign-born segment will still be a majority in the year 2020.

Class Diversification

Post-1965 immigration has also increased the economic diversity of Asian Americans. In contrast to the largely unskilled immigrant population of the pre–World War II period, the new arrivals include not only low-wage service-sector workers but also significant numbers of white-collar professionals. According to the 1990 U.S. census, more than 60 percent of immigrants (age twenty-five or older) from India and Taiwan reported having attained a college degree (three times the proportion of average Americans), but fewer than 5 percent of those from Cambodia and Laos made such a report. Among the employed workers, about 45 percent of immigrants from India and Taiwan held managerial or professional occupations, more than twice the proportion of average American workers, but fewer than 5 percent of those from Laos and only about 10 percent of those from Cambodia had held such a position. Further, immigrants from India, the Philippines, and Taiwan reported a median household income of about $45,000, compared to $30,000 for average American households; those from Cambodia and highland Laos reported a median household income below $20,000. . . .

Implications for Panethnicity in Contemporary Asian America

By most accounts, the expanding diversity of Asian Americans has brought into question the very definition of Asian America—and along with it, the feasibility and appropriateness of pan-Asian identities and practices. In a major public policy report on the state of Asian America, editor Paul Ong (2000) suggests that the pan-Asian identity is "fragile," citing as evidence the group's ethnic and economic diversity as well as the growing population of bi- and multiracial Asian Americans who want to acknowledge their combined racial heritage.[4] Similarly, in the introduction to their substantial multidisciplinary reader on contemporary Asian America, editors Min Zhou and James Gatewood (2000, 27) caution that "differences in class background among the immigrant generation and divergent modes of incorporation of that generation can deter the formation of panethnicity." Comparing the experiences of affluent Chinese immigrants and Cambodian refugees, Aihwa Ong (1996, 751) concludes that the category "Asian American" "must confront the contradictions and instabilities within the imposed solidarity, brought about by the group's internal class, ethnic, and racial stratifications." In Asian American studies, many scholars have critically pointed to the field's privileging of East Asians (the "old" Asian Americans) over South and Southeast Asians (the "new" Asian Americans)—a clear indictment of the suppression of diverse histories, epistemologies, and voices within the pan-Asian framework. For example, in an edited volume on South Asians in Asian America aptly titled *A Part, Yet Apart,* Rajiv Shankar (1998, x) laments that South Asians "find themselves so unnoticed as an entity that they feel as if they are merely a crypto-group, often included but easily marginalized within the house of Asian America."

A CRITICAL TRANSNATIONAL APPROACH TO PAN-ASIAN ETHNICITY

Elsewhere (Espiritu and Ong 1994; Espiritu 1992, 1996), I have discussed at length one of the challenges facing the contemporary Asian American community: how do Asian Americans build pan-Asian solidarity amid increasing diversities? Like other Asian American scholars and activists, I have suggested that

if Asian Americans are to build a self-consciously pan-Asian solidarity, they need to take seriously the heterogeneities among their ranks and overcome the narrow dominance of the professional class and that of the two oldest Asian American groups. I still subscribe to this view—that Asian Americans need to tend to the social, political, and economic inequalities that exist within their communities. At the same time, I am concerned that this view narrowly locates the "problems" of pan-Asian ethnicity *not* in the political and economic oppression or violence that produced massive displacements and migrations of Asians in the first place, but in the internal workings of the Asian American community itself. Thus told, the internal diversities within Asian America become "interiorized," and the focus is shifted away from global politics and power and toward identity politics within Asian America. . . .

Certainly, ethnic, generational, and class diversity pose new obstacles for pan-Asian mobilization. But to begin and stop the analysis here would be to engage in an "America-centric" approach to the question of the relation between race, ethnicity, nation, and migration. From this perspective, the analysis of pan-Asian ethnicity begins when the immigrants arrive on U.S. soil. Thus told, intra-Asian differences—along ethnic, class, and generational lines—become naturalized, unmediated by global politics and power. Departing from this perspective, I resituate the discussion of pan-Asian relations within a critical transnational framework, one that is attentive to global relations, which set the context for immigration and immigrant life. That is, instead of just asking how the massive influx of immigrants from Asia—and the resultant diversification of the population along class, generational, and ethnic lines—has reshaped pan-Asian identities and practices, we also need to ask how the influx of immigrants from Asia—with its specific configurations—came into being in the first place. As I argue later, pan-Asian American "racial formation" has been determined not exclusively by events in the United States but also by U.S. geopolitical interests in Asia and needs for different types and sources of labor—all of which have produced the particular ethnic, generational, and class configurations that have rendered the term "Asian American" problematic for the post-1965 community.

In the United States public discussion on immigration is fundamentally about people who cross borders. The media, elected officials, and the general public often represent border crossers as desperate individuals migrating in search of the "land of opportunity." This representation makes invisible other important border crossers: U.S. colonizers, military, and corporations that invade and forcefully deplete the economic and cultural resources of less-powerful countries. Calling attention to global structures of inequality, recent social theorists have linked migration processes with the global penetration of Western economic systems, technological infrastructures, and popular cultures in non-Western countries (Burawoy 1976; Petras 1978; Portes 1978; Zolberg 1986). Although details vary, these works posit that the internalization of a capitalistic economic system in "Third World" countries has produced imbalances in their internal social and economic structures and subsequently spurred emigration. As Saskia Sassen (1992, 15) argues, "U.S. efforts to open its own and other countries to the flow of capital, goods, services, and information created the conditions that mobilized people for migration." Indeed, all of the nation-states from which the largest number of U.S. immigrants originate—Mexico, China (including Taiwan and Hong Kong), the Philippines, El Salvador, the Dominican Republic, South Korea, Guatemala, Vietnam, Laos, and Cambodia—have had sustained and sometimes intimate social, political, and economic relations with the United States.

A transnational approach that stresses the global structures of inequality is critical for understanding Asian immigration and Asian American lives in the United States. Linking global economic development with global histories of colonialism, Edna Bonacich and Lucie Cheng (1984) argue that the pre–World War II immigration of Asians to the United States has to be understood within the context of the development of capitalism in Europe and the United States and the emergence of imperialism, especially in relation to Asia. From World War II onward, as the world economy became much more globally integrated, Asia was the site for U.S. expansion. As a result, contemporary immigrants from the Philippines, South Vietnam, South Korea, Cambodia, and Laos come from countries that have been deeply disrupted by U.S. colonialism, war, and neocolonial capitalism (Lowe 1996). The "transnational porosity between the United States and Asia" (Kang 1997, 408) means that "there has been an important continuity between the considerable distortion of social relations in Asian countries affected by U.S. imperialist war and occupation and the emigration of Asian labor to the United States" (Lowe 1996, 7).

The history of U.S. imperialism in Asia suggests that Asian American "racial formation" has never been exclusively shaped by events in the United States but has also been influenced by U.S. colonialism, neocolonialism, and militarism in Asia. However, the process of Asian American racial formation has been neither singular nor unified. Owing to the multiple contexts of colonialism and its various extensions within the development of global capitalism, Asians in the United States have experienced different processes of racialization specific to each group's historical and material conditions. It is these historical and material conditions—rather than intrinsic intra-Asian differences—that we need to investigate to understand the uneven formation of panethnicity among Asian Americans. . . . I confine my analysis to the experiences of Filipino immigrants and Vietnamese refugees—two groups with very different socioeconomic profiles—to illustrate the importance of a global conceptual framework in the theorizing of Asian American panethnicity.

Filipinos: Colonized Immigrant

In the twenty years following passage of the 1965 Immigration Act, about 40 percent of the documented immigration to the United States has come from Asia. The Philippines has been the largest source, with Filipinos comprising nearly one-quarter of the total Asian immigration. In the 1961 to 1965 period, fewer than 16,000 Filipinos immigrated to the United States, compared to more than 210,000 in the 1981 to 1985 period. Since 1979 over 40,000 Filipinos have been admitted annually, making the Philippines the second-largest source of all immigration, surpassed only by Mexico. Overall, the post-1965 Filipino immigrants constitute a relatively affluent group: in 1990 more than half joined the ranks of managers and professionals; their median household income exceeded that of all Americans and even that of whites; and the percentage of Filipino college graduates was twice that of all Americans. As Zhou and Gatewood (2000) report, many Filipino immigrants to the United States are college graduates with transferable job skills.

Unlike European or other Asian groups, Filipinos come from a homeland that was once a U.S. colony. Therefore, the Filipino American history of immigration and settlement can best the understood within the context of the colonial and postcolonial association between the Philippines and the United States. Since the 1960s the Philippines has sent the largest number of professional immigrants to the United States, the majority of whom are physicians, nurses, and other health-related practitioners (Rumbaut 1991). The overrepresentation of health professionals among contemporary Filipino immigrants is not accidental; it is the result of a U.S.-built economic infrastructure in the Philippines that proved to be ill suited to the needs of the local populace. During the 1960s, responding to the needs of the United States in its ongoing war effort in Vietnam, the Philippines (over)developed medical and nursing programs to provide personnel to care for the military and civilian casualties in Vietnam. This health professional educational infrastructure remained in place after the Vietnam War had ended and has continued to produce a surplus of physicians and nurses, many of whom migrate to the United States (Liu and Cheng 1994). The migration of Filipino health professionals was also a direct response to deliberate recruitment by U.S. hospitals, nursing homes, and health organizations seeking to address their perennial shortage of medical personnel.

In particular, the Philippines has become the major source of foreign-trained nurses in the United States, with at least 25,000 Filipino nurses arriving between 1996 and 1985. In fact, many women in the Philippines study nursing in the hope of securing employment abroad, and many of the nursing programs in the Philippines accordingly orient themselves toward supplying the U.S. market (Ong and Azores 1994). . . . By the 1960s Filipina nurses entered the United States through two major avenues: the Exchange Visitor Program and the new occupational preference categories of the Immigration Act of 1965.

Vietnamese: The Refugees

Unlike Filipino and most other contemporary immigrants, the Vietnamese were pushed out of their country and forced to leave without adequate preparation and with little control over their final destinations. Because refugees are less likely to be a self-selected labor force than economic migrants, their numbers include many unemployables: young children, the elderly, religious and political leaders, and people in poor mental and physical condition (Portes and Rumbaut 1990). They are also less likely to have acquired readily transferable skills and are more likely to have made investments (in training and education) specific to the country of origin. For example, significant numbers of Southeast Asian military personnel possess skills for which there is no longer a market in the United States. In a discussion of the economic diversity within Asian America, Evelyn Hu-DeHart (1999, 17) refers to Vietnamese and other Southeast Asian Americans as "the Other Asian America": "'traumatized' immigrants who do not arrive with families intact, and do not come armed with social skills and human capital that can be readily adapted to modern American society." Zhou and Gatewood (2000, 16) concur: "Southeast Asian refugees . . . were pushed out of their homelands by force and suffer tremendous postwar trauma and social displacement, compounded by a lack of education and professional skills, which negatively affects their resettlement."

The Vietnamese are the largest of the refugee groups to have settled in the United States since the mid-1970s. Their arrival is primarily the result of U.S. military intervention in Southeast Asia. I will not rehearse here the violent history of U.S. engagement in the Vietnam War, except to point out that the U.S. desire to contain the spread of communism in Southeast Asia rendered Vietnam completely dependent on U.S. financial and material assistance for its military, its administration, and its economy (Viviani 1984, 13). Soon after the withdrawal of U.S. troops from Vietnam in April 1975, the North Vietnamese took over South Vietnam, triggering an exodus of refugees who fled the country by sea, land, and air. Influenced by the pervasive American presence in their countries in the decade before 1975, some 135,000 Southeast Asian refugees—95 percent of whom were Vietnamese—fled to the United States that year. The number of refugees dropped to 15,000 in 1976 and 7,000 in 1977. Starting in 1978, a more heterogeneous second wave of refugees—the "boat people"—started streaming into the United States. Annual arrivals jumped from 20,574 in 1978 to 76,521 in 1979, to 163,799 in 1980. Their exodus was triggered by continued conflict, natural disasters, and deteriorating economic conditions in Vietnam and also by the legacy of thirty years of warfare, which "demolished cities, destroyed farmland, denuded forests, poisoned water sources, and left countless unexploded mines" (Chan 1991, 157). By 1990 Vietnamese Americans numbered over 615,000, constituting almost 10 percent of the nation's Asian American population.

The Vietnam War (as well as the Korean War) was a major direct and indirect contributor to the supply of working-class Asian immigrants. With the exception of the relatively small elite group who left at the fall of Saigon, most of the refugees lacked education, job skills, and measurable economic resources (Zhou 2001). In addition, the post-1978 refugees had suffered terrible tragedies under the new Communist regimes, survived brutal journeys to neighboring countries, and endured prolonged stays in refugee camps where they received little education and/or job training prior to their resettlement in the United States. Once in the United States, almost all of the refugees started out on public assistance (Zhou 2001, 188). Although their economic situation has improved over the years, the Vietnamese are still heavily concentrated in minimum-wage jobs and still disproportionately rely on public assistance to survive. By 1990 the poverty rate of the Vietnamese stood at 25 percent, down from 28 percent in 1980 but still substantially higher than the national average (Zhou 2001).

Using the Filipino and Vietnamese cases as examples, I argue that different circumstances of exit—the product of different types of U.S. engagement in their respective countries—have shaped the size and timing of migration and the socioeconomic composition of different Asian groups and thus have profoundly affected the process of group formation and differentiation in the United States. Given their divergent migration histories and disparate economic backgrounds, Asian groups from different ends of the class spectrum—such as Filipino Americans and Vietnamese Americans—have few material reasons to come together under the pan-Asian umbrella. Moreover, existing evidence indicates that pan-Asian organizations often reproduce these national and ethnic hierarchies as class and organizational hierarchies. . . .

PAN-ASIAN NATIONAL AND TRANSNATIONAL POSSIBILITIES

As we begin the twenty-first century, the Asian American community is at a crossroads: how is it to build pan-Asian solidarity amid increasing internal diversities and amid an increasingly racially polarized U.S. society? As I have argued here, Asian American panethnicity is a socially constructed identity that emerged in large part from the violence of racism and imperialism to contest and disrupt these structures of inequality and domination. But it is also a contested category, encompassing not only cultural differences but also social, political, and economic inequalities. In the past two decades underrepresented groups within the pan-Asian coalition have decried the dangers of an Asian American cultural and political agenda that erases differences or tokenizes and patronizes its less dominant members (Strobel 1996; Misir 1996; Nguyen 2002). But pan-Asian possibilities also abound. Since panethnic identities are self-conscious products of political choice and actions, I provide here examples of instances where Asian Americans have made conscious choices to organize politically across difference.

The growing population of bi- and multiracial Asian Americans poses an immediate challenge to pan-Asianism. On the other hand, some existing evidence suggests that the growth in the population of multiracial Asians need not spell the end of pan-Asianism. For example, in their analyses of Asian American intermarriages from 1980 and 1990 census data, Larry Hajime Shinagawa and Gin Yong Pang (1996, 140–41) report a prominent counter-trend toward pan-Asian interethnic marriages, regardless of gender, nativity, region, and generation: "For a span of ten years (1980 to 1990), nationally and for California, the number of Asian interethnic marriages approaches or now exceeds interracial marriages. Meanwhile, interethnic marriages for Asian Pacific men increased from 21.1 percent in 1980 to 64 percent in 1990, and for women from 10.8 percent to 45.5 percent." They attribute this rise to a combination of factors, including the large population increases and concentrations of Asian Americans, their growing similarities in socioeconomic attainment and middle-class orientation, and their growing racial consciousness in an increasingly racially stratified U.S. society.

But what of the multiracial children? According to the 2000 U.S. census, approximately 850,000 people reported that they were Asian and white, and 360,000 reported that they were two or more Asian groups (Barnes and Bennett 2002, table 4). While there exist no comprehensive data on the racial identification of multiracial Asians, the close contact with Asian American advocacy groups maintained by the Hapa Issues Forum (HIF)—a national multiracial Asian American organization—suggests that multiracial Asian and pan-Asian identities need not be mutually exclusive. From its inception, HIF has pursued a double political mission: pushing for recognition of multiracial Asians as well as for the civil rights agendas of existing Asian American groups. . . .

Asian American activists have also engaged in *proactive* efforts to draw together Asian Americans of different classes to organize against anti-Asian racism, defined not as random attacks against Asians but as a product of structural oppression and everyday encounters (Kurashige 2000, 15). The activities of the Asian Americans United, a panethnic community-based organization in Philadelphia, provide an example (Kurashige 2000). When large numbers of Southeast Asian immigrants began experiencing problems in Philadelphia with racist violence, educational inequality, and poor housing, a small group of educated East and South Asian American activists responded. Modeling themselves after the militant Yellow Seeds organization in the 1970s, group members insisted on anti-imperialist politics, a critique of racism as institutional and structural, and a focus on activist organizing and politics. They organized a successful rent strike and were part of a victorious legal campaign to institute bilingual education in the local schools. Most important, they sought to build relationships with working-class Southeast Asian communities by creating a youth leadership training program organized around a pan-Asian identity and radical politics. When a violent attack on Southeast Asian youths in that city by a group of white youths led to a fight that left one of the white attackers dead, city police and prosecutors portrayed the attackers as victims and laid the responsibility for the violence at the hands of the Southeast Asians. Although unable to secure full justice in the court cases that ensued, Asian Americans United seized on the incident as a means of educating its constituency about institutionalized racism. The group succeeded in mobilizing parts of the Asian American community around these efforts, and its success enabled it to move from panethnic to interethnic affiliation through an alliance with a Puerto Rican youth group also plagued by hate crimes, police brutality, and prosecutorial racism (Espiritu et al. 2000, 132).

This example suggests that class need not be a source of cleavage among Asian Americans, and that the concerns of working-class Asian Americans *can* unite people at the grassroots level with class-conscious members of the intellectual and professional strata (Kurashige 2000).

Given our globalizing world and the resultant demographic changes, the construction of an Asian American identity is no longer situated—if indeed it ever was—only within Asian America but also through relations and struggles with other communities of color. Today working-class immigrants of diverse backgrounds coexist with African American and U.S.-born Latinos in urban communities across the country. This "social geography of race" has produced new social subjects and new coalitions. For example, young Laotian women in northern California joined Chinese and Japanese Americans in panethnic struggles against anti-Asian racism and also against the "neighborhood race effects" of underfunded schools, polluted air and water, and low-wage jobs that they and their families share with their African American, Latino, Arab American, and poor white neighbors (Espiritu et al. 2000; Shah 2002). In the same way, recognizing their common histories of political fragmentation and disfranchisement, Japanese, Chinese, and Mexicans in the San Gabriel Valley of Los Angeles County formed political alliances to work together on the redistricting and reapportionment process in the Valley (Saito 1998, 10).

Finally, given the internationalization and feminization of the labor force in recent decades, some Asian women in the United States *and* in Asia have begun to conceive of themselves as similarly situated racial, gendered, and classed subjects. The dominance of women in contemporary immigration reflects the growth of female-intensive industries in the United States, particularly in services, health care, microelectronics, and apparel manufacturing. To escape the tightening labor market, employers in the United States have opted either to shift labor-intensive processes to less-developed countries or to import migrant labor, especially female, to fill low-wage, insecure assembly and service-sector jobs (Lim 1983; Hossfeld 1994). Women thus have become a rapidly growing segment of the world's migratory and international workforce (Sacks and Scheper-Hughes 1987).

For post-1965 immigrant women from Asia, their politically insecure status as "alien" and their limited English proficiency have interacted with geographical segregation, racist and sexist hiring practices, and institutional barriers to recertification by U.S. professional boards to narrow greatly their occupational choices. Consequently, many Asian immigrant women, instead of gaining access to a better, more modern, and more liberated life in the United States, have been confined to low-paying service jobs and factory assembly-line work, especially in the garment and microelectronics industries. The similarities in the labor conditions for Asian women here and in Asia, brought about by global capitalism, constitute the "situating grounds for a strategic transnational affiliation" (Kang 1997, 415). . . . The racialized feminization of labor gives rise to a "common context of struggle" among Asian women within, outside, and across the borders of the United States and has resulted in the establishment of numerous cross-border and transnational women's organizations, such as Gabriela, the support committee for Maquiladora workers, and Asian Immigrant Women Advocates (Lowe 1996).

These cross-racial and cross-border alliances and the radical mobilization around gender issues underscore the centrality of "unlikely coalitions" in contemporary political organizing. As Angela Davis (1997, 322) points out, we can accomplish important things in the struggle for social justice if we focus on the creation of "unpredictable or unlikely coalitions grounded in political projects." A complex world requires a complex set of alliances. These unlikely coalitions, including pan-Asian coalitions, along with the antiglobal organizations that are seeking to impose workplace and environmental restraints on multinational corporations and capital, could prove a potent force for social change at both the national and global levels.

PERSONAL ACCOUNT

I Thought My Race Was Invisible

In a conversation with a close friend, I noticed that I am, to her, a representative of my entire racial category. To put things in perspective, my friend Janet and I have been friends for eight years. During this period, it has come up that I am a third-generation Japanese-American who has no ties to being Japanese other than a couple of sushi dishes I learned how to make from my grandmother. Nonetheless, whenever a question regarding "Asians" comes up, she comes to me as if I can provide the definitive answer to every Asian mystery.

Yesterday Janet asked me if there is a cultural reason why Asians "always drive so slow." Not having noticed that Asians drive slowly (in fact, I have noticed a number of Asians who actually exceed the speed limit), I commented that perhaps they are law-abiding citizens. She said that must explain it: "They are used to following the law." I thought, "Am I one of 'they'?" but didn't comment further. Before we switched subjects, she noted that she "knew there had to be a cultural reason" for their driving.

Janet then told me about a Vietnamese woman at the Hair Cuttery who cut her husband's hair. As is normal, her husband talked to the woman as she worked on his hair; he asked her what she did before working at the Hair Cuttery. She said that she used to work in the fields in California (i.e., she was a field hand). Janet told me of the healthy respect that she and her husband had for a woman who worked in the fields, put herself through cosmetology school, moved East, and became a professional hairstylist. She commented that "Blacks" should follow her example and work instead of complaining of their lot in life.

This conversation was interesting and a bit startling. Janet is a good friend who shares many interests with me. What I realized from this conversation, and in remembering others that were similar, is that she feels that I am a representative of the whole Asian race. Not only is this unrealistic, but it is surprising that she would imagine I could answer for my race given my lack of real cultural exposure. In relaying the story of the Vietnamese woman, I had a sense that she was complimenting me, and my race, for the industriousness "we" demonstrate. It seems to me that she approved of the "typically" Asian way of working (quietly, so as not to insult or offend), even though this woman was probably underpaid and overworked in her field hand job. While she approved of her reticence, Janet did not approve of "Black" complaints.

I realize that to Janet, I will always be Asian. I had not really thought about it before, but I never think of Janet as White; her race is invisible to me. I had thought that my race was invisible too; however, I realize now that I will always be the "marked" friend. This saddens me a bit, but I accept it with the knowledge that she is a close friend. Nonetheless, it is unfortunate to think that even between friends, race is an issue.

Sherri H. Pereira

CONCLUSION

Since the pan-Asian concept was forged in the late 1960s, the Asian American population has become much more variegated. The post-1965 immigration surge from Asia has fragmented Asian America more clearly than in the past along ethnic, generational, and class lines. This increasing diversity has brought into question the very feasibility and appropriateness of pan-Asian identities and practices, challenging Asian Americans to take seriously the social, political, and economic inequalities that exist within their communities. My main contention in this [reading] is that we cannot examine Asian American panethnicity solely in terms of racial politics within the framework of the U.S. nation-state. While important, this framework narrowly focuses on identity politics within Asian America, not on the global politics and power that produced massive displacements and migrations of Asians in the first place. Calling for a critical transnational perspective on the study of panethnicity, I argue instead that different circumstances of exit—the product of different types of U.S. engagement in different Asian countries—have shaped the size and timing of migration and the socioeconomic profile of different Asian groups and thus have profoundly affected their group formation and differentiation in the United States. This approach expands the discussion on pan-Asian ethnicity by viewing it as an integral part not only of Asian American studies or American studies but also of international and transnational studies. In all, the examples cited in this chapter confirm the plural and ambivalent nature of panethnicity: it is a highly contested terrain on which Asian Americans merge and clash over terms of inclusion but also an effective site from which to forge crucial alliances with other groups both within and across the borders of the United States in their ongoing efforts to effect larger social transformation.

Acknowledgments

I would like to thank Richard Delgado, Jean Stefancic, Nancy Foner, Josh DeWind, and the participants in the "Immigration, Race, and Ethnicity: Then and Now" workshops for their helpful comments on earlier versions of this chapter.

DISCUSSION QUESTIONS

1. What are the shortcomings of Asian American panethnicty?
2. How do ethnic, generational, and class diversity present obstacles for mobilization among Asian immigrants?
3. How has U.S. imperialism affected Asian American racial formation?

NOTES

1. For an extended discussion of the critical transnational approach to immigration, see Espiritu (2003). Certainly, I am not the first scholar to apply a critical transnational framework to the study of Asian Americans. Oscar Campomanes (1997), Sucheta Mazumdar (1990), Shirley Hune (1989), and others have written persuasively on the importance of conducting Asian American studies through an "international" frame.
2. For a detailed account of the disputes over the classification of Asian Americans in the 1980 and 1990 censuses, please see Espiritu (1992, ch. 5).
3. In 1990 the Japanese American share of the Asian American population was 12 percent, and the five largest Asian American groups were Chinese (23 percent), Filipino (19 percent), Asian Indian (11 percent), Korean (11 percent), and Vietnamese (8 percent).

4. According to the 2000 U.S. census, approximately 850,000 people reported that they were Asian and white, and 360,000 reported that they were two or more Asian groups (Barnes and Bennett 2002, table 4). The debate over the classification of multiracials in the 2000 census often posed the interests of multiracial Asian Americans—the right to claim their full heritage—in opposition to the civil rights needs of pan-Asian America—the possible loss of political clout that is tied to numbers (see Espiritu 2001, 31). Refusing this "splitting," Asian American multiracial organizations rejected the "stand-alone multiracial" category and endorsed the "check more than one" format because the latter would allow them to identify as multiracial *and* "still be counted with their Asian American brethren and sisters" (King 2000, 202). This stance suggests that multiracial Asian and pan-Asian identities need not be mutually exclusive.

REFERENCES

Barnes, Jessica, and Claudette E. Bennett. 2002. *The Asian Population 2000.* Washington: U.S. Department of Commerce.

Blauner, Robert. 1972. *Racial Oppression in America.* New York: Harper & Row.

Bonacich, Edna, and Lucie Cheng. 1984. "Introduction: A Theoretical Orientation to International Labor Migration." In *Labor Immigration Under Capitalism: Asian Workers in the United States Before World War II,* edited by Lucie Cheng and Edna Bonacich. Berkeley: University of California Press.

Burawoy, Michael. 1976. "The Functions and Reproduction of Migrant Labor: Comparative Material from Southern Africa and the United States." *American Journal of Sociology* 81(5, March): 1050–87.

Campomanes, Oscar. 1997. "New Formations of Asian American Studies and the Questions of U.S. Imperialism." *Positions* 5(2): 523–50.

Chan, Sucheng. 1991. *Asian Americans: An Interpretive History.* Boston: Twayne.

Daniels, Roger, 1988. *Asian America: Chinese and Japanese in the United States Since 1850.* Seattle: University of Washington Press.

Davis, Angela. 1997. "Interview with Lisa Lowe—Angela Davis: Reflections on Race, Class, and Gender in the USA." In *The Politics of Culture in the Shadow of Capital,* edited by Lisa Lowe and David Lloyd. Durham, N.C.: Duke University Press.

Espiritu, Yen Le. 1992. *Asian American Panethnicity: Bridging Institutions and Identities.* Philadelphia: Temple University Press.

———. 1995. *Filipino American Lives.* Philadelphia: Temple University Press.

———. 1996. "Crossroads and Possibilities: Asian Americans on the Eve of the Twenty-first Century." *Amerasia Journal* 22(2): vii–xii.

———. 2001. "Possibilities of a Multiracial Asian America." In *The Sum of Our Parts: Mixed Heritage Asian Americans,* edited by Teresa Williams-Leon and Cynthia L. Nakashima. Philadelphia. Temple University Press.

———. 2003. *Home Bound: Filipino American Lives Across Cultures, Communities, and Countries.* Berkeley: University of California Press.

Espiritu, Yen Le, and Paul Ong. 1994. "Class Constraints on Racial Solidarity Among Asian Americans." In *The New Asian Immigration in Los Angeles and Global Restructuring,* edited by Paul Ong, Edna Bonacich, and Lucie Cheng. Philadelphia: Temple University Press.

Espiritu, Yen Le, Dorothy Fujita Rony, Nazli Kibria, and George Lipsitz. 2000. "The Role of Race and Its Articulations for Asian Pacific Americans." *Journal of Asian American Studies* 3(2): 127–37.

Hayano, David. 1981. "Ethnic Identification and Disidentification: Japanese-American Views of Chinese Americans." *Ethnic Groups* 3(2): 157–71.

Hossfeld, Karen. 1994. "Hiring Immigrant Women: Silicon Valley's 'Simple Formula.'" In *Women of Color in U.S. Society,* edited by Maxine Baca Zinn and Bonnie Thornton Dill. Philadelphia: Temple University Press.

Hu-DeHart, Evelyn. 1999. "Introduction: Asian American Formations in the Age of Globalization." In *Across the Pacific: Asian Americans and Globalization,* edited by Evelyn Hu-DeHart. Philadelphia: Temple University Press.

Hune, Shirley. 1989. "Expanding the International Dimension of Asian American Studies." *Amerasia Journal* 15(2): xix–xxiv.

Ichioka, Yuji. 1988. *The Issei: The World of the First Generation Japanese Americans, 1885–1924.* New York: Free Press.

Iwasaki, Naomi. 1999. "Pan-Asian What?" *Asian American Revolutionay Movement Ezine,* http://www.aamovement. net/narratives/panasian.html (accessed December 4, 2003).

Kang, Laura Hyun Yi. 1997. "Si(gh)ting Asian/American Women as Transnational Labor." *Positions* 5(2): 403–37.

King, Rebecca Chiyoko. 2000. "Racialization, Recognition, and Rights: Lumping and Splitting Multiracial Asian Americans in the 2000 Census." *Journal of Asian American Studies* 3(2): 191–217.

Kurashige, Scott. 2000. "Panethnicity and Community Organizing: Asian Americans United's Campaign Against Anti-Asian Violence." *Journal of Asian American Studies* 3(2): 163–90.

Ling, Susie Hsiuhan. 1984. "The Mountain Movers: Asian American Women's Movement in Los Angeles." M.A. thesis, University of California at Los Angeles.

Lim, Linda Y. C. 1983. "Capitalism, Imperialism, and Patriarchy: The Dilemma of Third-World Women Workers in Multinational Factories." In *Women, Men, and the International Division of Labor,* edited by June Nash and Maria Patricia Fernandez-Kelly. Albany: State University of New York Press.

Liu, John, and Lucie Cheng. 1994. "Pacific Rim Development and the Duality of Post-1965 Asian Immigration to the United States." In *The New Asian Immigration in Los Angeles and Global Restructuring,* edited by Paul Ong, Edna Bonacich, and Lucie Cheng. Philadelphia: Temple University Press.

Liu, William. 1976. "Asian American Research: Views of a Sociologist." *Asian Studies Occasional Report* 2: whole issue.

Lott, Juanita. 1976. "The Asian American Concept: In Quest of Identity." *Bridge* (November): 30–34.

Lowe, Lisa. 1991. "Heterogeneity, Hybridity, Multiplicity: Marking Asian American Differences." *Diaspora* 1(1, Spring): 25–44.

———. 1996. *Immigrant Acts: On Asian American Cultural Politics.* Durham, N.C.: Duke University Press.

Mazumdar, Sucheta. 1990. "Asian American Studies and Asian Studies: Rethinking Roots." In *Asian Americans: Comparative and Global Perspectives,* edited by Shirley Hune et al. Pullman: Washington State University Press.

Misir, Deborah N. 1996. "The Murder of Navroze Mody: Race, Violence, and the Search for Order." *Amerasia Journal* 22(2): 55–76.

Nguyen, Viet Thanh. 2002. *Race and Resistance: Literature and Politics in Asian America.* New York: Oxford University Press.

Omatsu, Glenn. 1994. "'The Four Prisons and the Movements of Liberation: Asian American Activism from the 1960s to the 1990s." In *The State of Asian America: Activism and Resistance in the 1990s,* edited by Karin Aguilar-San Juan. Boston: South End.

Omi, Michael. 1993. "Out of the Melting Pot and into the Fire: Race Relations Policy." In *The State of Asian Pacific Americans: Policy Issues to the Year 2000.* Los Angeles: LEAP Asian Pacific American Public Policy Institute and UCLA Asian American Studies Center.

Omi, Michael, and Howard Winant. 1986. *Racial Formation in the United States: From the 1960s to the 1980s.* New York: Routledge & Kegan Paul.

Ong, Aihwa. 1996. "Citizenship as Subject Making: New Immigrants Negotiate Racial and Ethnic Boundaries." *Current Anthropology* 25(5): 737–62.

Ong, Paul, 1989. "California's Asian Population: Past Trends and Projections for the Year 2000." Los Angeles: Graduate School of Architecture and Urban Planning.

———. 2000. "The Asian Pacific American Challenge to Race Relations." In *The State of Asian Pacific Americans: Transforming Race Relations,* edited by Paul Ong. Los Angeles: LEAP Asian Pacific American Public Policy Institute and UCLA Asian American Studies Center.

Ong, Paul, and Tania Azores. 1994. "The Migration and Incorporation of Filipino Nurses." In *The New Asian Immigration in Los Angeles and Global Restructuring,* edited by Paul Ong, Edna Bonacich, and Lucie Cheng. Philadelphia: Temple University Press.

Ong, Paul, and Suzanne J. Hee. 1993. "The Growth of the Asian Pacific American Population. In *The State of Asian Pacific Americans: Policy Issues to the Year 2000.* Los Angeles: LEAP Asian Pacific American Public Policy Institute and UCLA Asian American Studies Center.

Petras, James. 1978. *Critical Perspectives of Imperialism and Social Class in the Third World.* New York: Monthly Review Press.

Portes, Alejandro. 1978. "Migration and Underdevelopment." *Politics and Society* 8: 1–48.

Portes, Alejandro, and Rubén Rumbaut. 1990. *Immigrant America: A Portrait.* Berkeley: University of California Press.

Rumbaut, Rubén. 1991. "Passages to America: Perspectives on the New Immigration." In *America at Century's End,* edited by Alan Wolfe. Berkeley and Los Angeles: University of California Press.

Sacks, Karen, and Nancy Scheper-Hughes. 1987. "Introduction." *Women's Studies* 13(3): 175–82.

Saito, Leland. 1998. *Race and Politics: Asian Americans, Latinos, and Whites in a Los Angeles Suburb.* Urbana and Chicago: University of Illinois Press.

Sassen, Saskia. 1992. "Why Migration." *Report on the Americas* 26(1, July): whole issue.

Shah, Bindi. 2002. "Making the 'American' Subject: Culture, Gender, Ethnicity, and the Politics of Citizenship in the Lives of Second-Generation Laotian Girls." Ph.D. diss., University of California at Davis.

Shankar, Rajiv. 1998. "Foreword: South Asian Identity in Asian America." In *A Part, Yet Apart: South Asians in Asian America,* edited by Lavina Dhingra Shankar and Rajini Srikanth. Philadelphia: Temple University Press.

Shinagawa, Larry Hajime, and Gin Yong Pang. 1996. "Asian American Panethnicity and Intermarriage." *Amerasia Journal* 22(2): 127–52.

Strobel, Leny Mendoza. 1996. "'Born-Again Filipino': Filipino American Identity and Asian American Panethnicity." *Amerasia Journal* 22(2): 31–54.

Takaki, Ronald. 1989. *Strangers from a Different Shore: A History of Asian Americans.* Boston: Little, Brown.

U.S. Department of Commerce. U.S. Census Bureau. 2002. "Coming to America: A Profile of the Nation's Foreign Born (2000 Update)." *Census Briefs: Current Population Survey, February 2002.* Washington: U.S. Census Bureau.

U.S. Immigration and Naturalization Service (USINS). 1997. *Statistical Yearbook of the Immigration and Naturalization Service, 1995.* Washington: U.S. Government Printing Office.

Viviani, Nancy. 1984. *The Long Journey: Vietnamese Migration and Settlement in Australia.* Carlton, Victoria: Melbourne University Press.

Wong, Paul. 1972. "The Emergence of the Asian-American Movement." *Bridge* 2(1): 33–39.

Zhou, Min. 2001. "Straddling Different Worlds: The Acculturation of Vietnamese Refugee Children." In *Ethnicities: Children of Immigrants in America,* edited by Rubén G.

Rumbaut and Alejandro Portes. Berkeley: University of California Press.

Zhou, Min, and James V. Gatewood. 2000. "Introduction: Revisiting Contemporary Asian America." In *Contemporary Asian America: A Multidisciplinary Reader,* edited by Min Zhou and James V. Gatewood. New York: New York University Press.

Zolberg, Aristide. 1986. "International Factors in the Formation of Refugee Movement." *International Migration Review* 20(2, Summer): 151–69.

READING 6

Whiteness as an "Unmarked" Cultural Category

Ruth Frankenberg

America's supposed to be the melting pot. I know that I've got a huge number of nationalities in my blood, but how do I—what do I call myself? And hating this country as I do, I don't like to say I'm an American. Even though it is what I am. I hate identifying myself as only an American, because I have so much objections to Americans' place in the world. I don't know how I felt about that when I was growing up, but I never—I didn't like to pledge allegiance to the flag. . . . Still, at this point in my life, I wonder what it is that somebody with all this melting pot blood can call their own. . . .

Especially growing up in the sixties, when people *did* say "I'm proud to be Black," "I'm proud to be Hispanic," you know, and it became very popular to be proud of your ethnicity. And even feminists, you know, you could say, "I'm a woman," and be proud of it. But there's still a majority of the country that can't say they are proud of anything!

Suzie Roberts's words powerfully illustrate the key themes . . . that stirred the women I interviewed* as they examined their own identities: what had

---

Ruth Frankenberg is living and working in Bangalore, India.
*Between 1984 and 1986 I interviewed 30 white women, diverse in age, class, region of origin, sexuality, family situation and political orientation, all living in California at the time of the interviews.

formed them, what they counted as (their own or others') cultural practice(s), and what constituted identities of which they could be proud. This [discussion] explores perceptions of whiteness as a location of culture and identity, focusing mainly on white feminist . . . women's views and contrasting their voices with those of more politically conservative women. . . .

[M]any of the women I interviewed, including even some of the conservative ones, appeared to be self-conscious about white power and racial inequality. In part because of their sense of the links and parallels between white racial dominance in the United States and U.S. domination on a global scale, there was a complex interweaving of questions about race and nation—whiteness and Americanness—in these women's thoughts about white culture. Similarly, conceptions of racial, national, and cultural belonging frequently leaked into one another.

On the one hand, then, these women's views of white culture seemed to be distinctively modern. But at the same time, their words drew on much earlier historical moments and participated in long-established modes of cultural description. In the broadest sense, Western colonial discourses on the white self, the nonwhite Other, and the white Other too, were very much in evidence. These discourses produced dualistic conceptualizations of whiteness versus other cultural forms. The women thus often spoke about culture in ways that reworked, and yet remained tied to, "older" forms of racism.

For a significant number of young white women, being white felt like being cultureless. Cathy Thomas, in the following description of whiteness, raised many of the themes alluded to by other feminist and race-cognizant women. She described what she saw as a lack of form and substance:

> . . . the formlessness of being white. Now if I was a middle western girl, or a New Yorker, if I had a fixed regional identity that was something palpable, then I'd be a white New Yorker, no doubt, but I'd still be a New Yorker. . . . Being a Californian, I'm sure it has its hallmarks, but to me they were invisible. . . . If I had an ethnic base to identify from, if I was even Irish American, that would have been something formed,

> if I was a working-class woman, that would have been something formed. But to be a Heinz 57 American, a white, class-confused American, land of the Kleenex type American, is so formless in and of itself. It only takes shape in relation to other people.

Whiteness as a cultural space is represented here as amorphous and indescribable, in contrast with a range of other identities marked by race, ethnicity, region, and class. Further, white culture is viewed here as "bad" culture. In fact, the extent to which identities can be named seems to show an inverse relationship to power in the U.S. social structure. The elisions, parallels, and differences between characterizations of white people, Americans, people of color, and so-called white ethnic groups will be explored [here].

Cathy's own cultural positioning seemed to her impossible to grasp, shapeless and unnameable. It was easier to know others and to know, with certainty, what one was *not*. Providing a clue to one of the mechanisms operating here is the fact that, while Cathy viewed New Yorkers and midwesterners as having a cultural shape or identity, women from the East Coast and the Midwest also described or mourned their own seeming lack of culture. The self, where it is part of a dominant cultural group, does not have to name itself. In this regard, Chris Patterson hit the nail on the head, linking the power of white culture with the privilege not to be named:

> I'm probably at the stage where I'm beginning to see that you can come up with a definition of white. Before, I didn't know that you could turn it around and say, "Well what *does* white mean?" One thing is, it's taken for granted. . . . [To be white means to] have some sort of advantage or privilege, even if it's something as simple as not having a definition.

The notion of "turning it around" indicates Chris's realization that, most often, whites are the nondefined definers of other people. Or, to put it another way, whiteness comes to be an unmarked or neutral category, whereas other cultures are specifically marked "cultural."

Many of the women shared the habit of turning to elements of white culture as the unspoken norm. This assumption of a white norm was so prevalent that even Sandy Alvarez and Louise Glebocki, who were acutely aware of racial inequality as well as being members of racially mixed families, referred to "Mexican" music versus "regular" music, and regular meant "white."

Similarly, discussions of race difference and cultural diversity at times revealed a view in which people of color actually embodied difference and whites stood for sameness. Hence, Margaret Phillips said of her Jamaican daughter-in-law that: "She *really* comes with diversity." In spite of its brevity, and because of its curious structure, this short statement says a great deal. It implicitly designates whiteness as norm, and Jamaicans as having or bearing with them "differentness." At the risk of being crass, one might say that in this view, diversity is to the daughter-in-law as "the works" is to a hamburger—added on, adding color and flavor, but not exactly essential. Whiteness, seen by many of these women as boring, but nonetheless definitive, could also follow this analogy. This mode of thinking about "difference" expresses clearly the double-edged sword of a color- and power-evasive repertoire, apparently valorizing cultural difference but doing so in a way that leaves racial and cultural hierarchies intact.

For a seemingly formless entity, then, white culture had a great deal of power, difficult to dislodge from its place in white consciousness as a point of reference for the measuring of others. Whiteness served simultaneously to eclipse and marginalize others (two modes of making the other inessential). Helen Standish's description of her growing-up years in a small New England town captured these processes well. Since the community was all white, the differences at issue were differences between whites. (This also enables an assessment of the links between white and nonwhite "marked" cultures.) Asked about her own cultural identity, Helen explained that "it didn't seem like a culture because everyone else was the same." She had, however, previously mentioned Italian Americans in the town, so I asked about their status. She responded as follows, adopting at first the voice of childhood:

They are different, but I'm the same as everybody else. They speak Italian, but everybody else in the U.S. speaks English. They eat strange, different food, but I eat the same kind of food as everybody else in the U.S. . . . The way I was brought up was to think that everybody who was the same as me were "Americans," and the other people were of "such and such descent."

Viewing the Italian Americans as different and oneself as "same" serves, first, to marginalize, to push from the center, the former group. At the same time, claiming to be the same as everyone else makes other cultural groups invisible or eclipses them. Finally, there is a marginalizing of all those who are not like Helen's own family, leaving a residual, core or normative group who are the true Americans. The category of "American" represents simultaneously the normative and the residual, the dominant culture and a nonculture.

Although Helen talked here about whites, it is safe to guess that people of color would not have counted among the "same" group but among the communities of "such and such descent" (Mexican American, for example). Whites, within this discursive repertoire, became conceptually the real Americans, and only certain kinds of whites actually qualified. Whiteness and Americanness both stood as normative and exclusive categories in relation to which other cultures were identified and marginalized. And this clarifies that there are two kinds of whites, just as there are two kinds of Americans: those who are truly or only white, and those who are white but also something more—or is it something less?

In sum, whiteness often stood as an unmarked marker of others' differentness—whiteness not so much void or formlessness as norm. I associate this construction with colonialism and with the more recent assymetrical dualisms of liberal humanist views of culture, race, and identity. For the most part, this construction views nonwhite cultures as lesser, deviant, or pathological. However, another trajectory has been the inverse: conceptualizations of the cultures of peoples of color as somehow better than the dominant culture, perhaps more natural or more spiritual. These are positive evaluations of a sort, but they are equally dualistic. Many of the women I interviewed saw white culture as less appealing and found the cultures of the "different" people more interesting. As Helen Standish put it:

> [We had] Wonder bread, white bread. I'm more interested in, you know, "What's a bagel?" in other people's cultures rather than my own.

The claim that whiteness lacks form and content says more about the definitions of culture being used than it does about the content of whiteness. However, I would suggest that in describing themselves as cultureless these women are in fact identifying specific kinds of unwanted absences or presences in their own culture(s) as a generalized lack or nonexistence. It thus becomes important to look at what they *did* say about the cultural content of whiteness.

Descriptions of the content of white culture were thin, to say the least. But despite the paucity of signifiers, there was a great deal of consistency across the narratives. First, there was naming based on color, the linking of white culture with white objects—the clichéd white bread and mayonnaise, for example. Freida Kazen's identification of whiteness as "bland," together with Helen Standish's "blah," also signified paleness or neutrality. The images connote several things—color itself (although exaggerated, and besides, bagels are usually white inside, too), lack of vitality (Wonder bread is highly processed), and homogeneity. However, these images are perched on a slippery slope, at once suggesting "white" identified as a color (though an unappealing one) and as an absence of color, that is, white as the unmarked marker.

Whiteness was often signified in these narratives by commodities and brands: Wonder bread, Kleenex, Heinz 57. In this identification whiteness came to be seen as spoiled by capitalism, and as being linked with capitalism in a way that other cultures supposedly are not. Another set of signifiers that constructed whiteness as uniquely tainted by capitalism had to do with the "modern condition": Dot Humphrey described white neighborhoods as "more privatized," and Cathy Thomas used "alienated" to describe her cultural condition.

Clare Traverso added to this theme, mourning her own feeling of lack of identity, in contrast with images of her husband's Italian American background (and here, Clare is again talking about perceived differences between whites):

> Food, old country, mama. Stories about a grandmother who can't speak English. . . . Candles, adobe houses, arts, music. [It] has emotion, feeling, belongingness that to me is unique.

In linking whiteness to capitalism and viewing nonwhite cultures as untainted by it, these women were again drawing on a colonial discourse in which progress and industrialization were seen as synonymous with Westernization, while the rest of the world is seen as caught up in tradition and "culture." In addition, one can identify, in white women's mourning over whiteness, elements of what Raymond Williams has called "pastoralism," or nostalgia for a golden era now gone by (but in fact, says Williams, one that never existed).[1]

The image of whiteness as corrupted and impoverished by capitalism is but one of a series of ways in which white culture was seen as impure or tainted. White culture was also seen as tainted by its relationship to power. For example, Clare Traverso clearly counterposed white culture and white power, finding it difficult to value the former because of the overwhelming weight of the latter:

> The good things about whites are to do with folk arts, music. Because other things have power associated with them.

For many race-cognizant white women, white culture was also made impure by its very efforts to maintain race purity. Dot Humphrey, for example, characterized white neighborhoods as places in which people were segregated by choice. For her, this was a good reason to avoid living in them.

The link between whiteness and domination, however, was frequently made in ways that both artificially isolated culture from other factors and obscured economics. For at times, the traits the women envied in Other cultures were in fact at least in part the product of poverty or other dimensions of oppression. Lack of money, for example, often means lack of privacy or space, and it can be valorized as "more street life, less alienation." Cathy Thomas's notion of Chicanas' relationship to the kitchen ("the hearth of the home") as a cultural "good" might be an idealized one that disregards the reality of intensive labor.

Another link between class and culture emerged in Louise Glebocki's reference to the working-class Chicanos she met as a child as less pretentious, "closer to the truth," more "down to earth." And Marjorie Hoffman spoke of the "earthy humor" of Black people, which she interpreted as, in the words of Langston Hughes, a means of "laughing to keep from crying." On the one hand, as has been pointed out especially by Black scholars and activists, the positions of people of color at the bottom of a social and economic hierarchy create the potential for a critique of the system as a whole and consciousness of the need to resist.[2] From the standpoint of race privilege, the system of racism is thus made structurally invisible. On the other hand, descriptions of this kind leave in place a troubling dichotomy that can be appropriated as easily by the right as by the left. For example, there is an inadvertent affinity between the image of Black people as "earthy" and the conservative racist view that African American culture leaves African American people ill equipped for advancement in the modern age. Here, echoing essentialist racism, both Chicanos and African Americans are placed on the borders of "nature" and "culture."

By the same token, often what was criticized as "white" was as much the product of middle-class status as of whiteness as such. Louise Glebocki's image of her fate had she married a white man was an image of a white-collar, nuclear family:

> Him saying, "I'm home, dear," and me with an apron on—ugh!

The intersections of class, race, and culture were obscured in other ways. Patricia Bowen was angry with some of her white feminist friends who, she felt, embraced as "cultural" certain aspects of African American, Chicano, and Native American cultures (including, for example, artwork or dance performances) but would reject as "tacky" (her term) those aspects of daily life that communities of color shared with working-class whites, such as the stores and supermarkets of poor neighborhoods. This, she felt, was tantamount to a selective expansion of middle-class aesthetic horizons, but not to true antiracism or to comprehension of the cultures of people of color. Having herself grown up in a white working-class family, Pat also felt that middle-class white feminists were able to use selective engagement to avoid addressing their class privilege.

I have already indicated some of the problems inherent in this kind of conceptualization, suggesting that it tends to keep in place dichotomous constructions of "white" versus Other cultures, to separate "culture" from other dimensions of daily life, and to reify or strip of history *all* cultural forms. There are, then, a range of issues that need to be disentangled if we are to understand the location of "whiteness" in the terrain of culture. It is, I believe, useful to approach this question by means of a reconceptualization of the concept of culture itself. A culture, in the sense of the set of rules and practices by means of which a group organizes itself and its values, manners, and worldview—in other words, culture as "a field articulating the life-world of subjects . . . and the structures created by human activity"[3]—is an indispensable precondition to any individual's existence in the world. It is nonsensical in terms of this kind of definition to suggest that anyone could actually have "no culture." But this is not, as I have suggested, the mode of thinking about culture that these women are employing.

Whiteness emerges here as inextricably tied to domination partly as an effect of a discursive "draining process" applied to both whiteness and Americanness. In this process, any cultural practice engaged in by a white person that is not identical to the dominant culture is automatically counted as either "not really white"—and, for that matter, not really American, either—(but rather of such and such descent), or as "not really cultural" (but rather "economic"). There is a slipperiness to whiteness here: it shifts from "no culture" to "normal culture" to "bad culture" and back again. Simultaneously, a range of marginal or, in Trinh T. Minh-ha's terminology, "bounded" cultures are generated. These are viewed as enviable spaces, separate and untainted by relations of dominance or by linkage to other structures or systems. By contrast, whiteness is conceived as axiomatically tied to dominance, to economics, to political structures. In this process, both whiteness and nonwhiteness are reified, made into objects rather than processes, and robbed of historical context and human agency. As long as the discussion remains couched in these terms, a critique of whiteness remains a double-edged sword: for one thing, whiteness remains normative because there is no way to name the cultural practices associated with it *as* cultural. Moreover, as I have suggested, whether whiteness is viewed as artificial and dominating (and therefore "bad") or civilized (and therefore "good"), whiteness and all varieties of nonwhiteness continue to be viewed as ontologically different from one another.

A genuine sadness and frustration about the meaning of whiteness at this moment in history motivated these women to decry white culture. It becomes important, then, to recognize the grains of truth in their views of white culture. It is important to acknowledge their anger and frustration about the meaning of whiteness as we reach toward a politicized analysis of culture that is freer of colonial and pastoral legacies.

The terms "white" and "American" as these women used them signified domination in international and domestic terms. This link is both accurate and inaccurate. While it is true that, by and large, those in power in the United States are white, it is also true that not all those who are white are in power. Nor is the axiomatic linkage between Americanness and power accurate, because not all Americans have the same access to power. At the same time, the link between whiteness, Americanness, and power *are* accurate because, as we have seen, the terms "white" and "American" both function discursively to exclude people from normativity—including white people "of such and such descent." But here we need to distinguish

between the fates of people of color and those of white people. Notwithstanding a complicated history, the boundaries of Americanness and whiteness have been much more fluid for "white ethnic" groups than for people of color.

There have been border skirmishes over the meaning of whiteness and Americanness since the inception of those terms. For white people, however, those skirmishes have been resolved through processes of assimilation, not exclusion. The late nineteenth and early twentieth centuries in the United States saw a systematic push toward the cultural homogenization of whites carried out through social reform movements and the schools. This push took place alongside the expansion of industrial capitalism, giving rise to the sense that whiteness signifies the production and consumption of commodities under capitalism.[4] But recognition of this history should not be translated into an assertion that whites were stripped of culture (for to do that would be to continue to adhere to a colonial view of "culture"). Instead one must argue that certain cultural practices replaced others. Were one to undertake a history of this "generic" white culture, it would fragment into a thousand tributary elements, culturally specific religious observances, and class survival mechanisms as well as mass-produced commodities and mass media.

There are a number of dangers inherent in continuing to view white culture as no culture. Whiteness appeared in the narratives to function as both norm or core, that against which everything else is measured, and as residue, that which is left after everything else has been named. A far-reaching danger of whiteness coded as "no culture" is that it leaves in place whiteness as defining a set of normative cultural practices against which all are measured and into which all are expected to fit. This normativity has underwritten oppression from the beginning of colonial expansion and has had impact in multiple ways: from the American pioneers' assumption of a norm of private property used to justify appropriation of land that within their worldview did not have an owner, and the ideological construction of nations like Britain as white,[5] to Western feminism's Eurocentric shaping of its movements and institutions. It is important for white feminists not to continue to participate in these processes.

And if whiteness has a history, so do the cultures of people of color, which are worked on, crafted, and created, rather than just "there." For peoples of color in the United States, this work has gone on as much in the context of relationships to imperialism and capitalism as has the production of whiteness, though it has been premised on exclusion and resistance to exclusion more than on assimilation. Although not always or only forged in resistance, the visibility and recognition of the cultures of U.S. peoples of color in recent times *is* the product of individual and collective struggle. Only a short time has elapsed since those struggles made possible the introduction into public discourse of celebration and valorization of their cultural forms. In short, it is important not to reify any culture by failing to acknowledge its createdness, and not to view it as always having been there in unchanging form.

Rather than feeling "cultureless," white women need to become conscious of the histories and specificities of our cultural positions, and of the political, economic, and creative fusions that form all cultures. The purpose of such an exercise is not, of course, to reinvert the dualisms and valorize whiteness so much as to develop a clearer sense of where and who we are.

DISCUSSION QUESTIONS

1. Why is whiteness considered to be lacking diversity?
2. How would you describe the cultural content of whiteness?
3. Why do some people feel "cultureless"?

NOTES

1. Raymond Williams, *The Country and the City* (New York: Oxford University Press, 1978).
2. The classic statement of this position is W. E. B. Du Bois's concept of the "double consciousness" of Americans of African descent. Two recent feminist statements of similar positions are Patricia Hill Collins, *Black Feminist*

Thought: Knowledge, Consciousness, and the Politics of Empowerment (Boston: Unwin Hyman, 1990); and Aida Hurtado, "Relating to Privilege: Seduction and Rejection in the Subordination of White Women and Women of Color," *Signs* 14, no. 4:833–55.

3. Paul Gilroy, *There Ain't No Black in the Union Jack.* London: Hutchinson, 1987.
4. See, for example, Winthrop Talbot, ed., *Americanization* (New York: H. W. Wilson, 1917), esp. Sophonisba P. Breckinridge, "The Immigrant Family," 251–52, Olivia Howard Dunbar, "Teaching the Immigrant Woman," 252–56, and North American Civic League for Immigrants, "Domestic Education among Immigrants," 256–58; and Kathie Friedman Kasaba, "'To Become a Person': The Experience of Gender, Ethnicity and Work in the Lives of Immigrant Women, New York City, 1870–1940," doctoral dissertation, Department of Sociology, State University of New York, Binghamton, 1991. I am indebted to Katie Friedman Kasaba for these references and for her discussions with me about working-class European immigrants to the United States at the turn of this century.
5. Gilroy, *There Ain't No Black in the Union Jack.*

READING 7

America's Changing Color Lines: Immigration, Race/Ethnicity, and Multiracial Identification

Jennifer Lee

Frank D. Bean

INTRODUCTION

By the year 2002, the number of foreign-born people living in the United States exceeded 34.2 million, with the size of the U.S.-born second generation about 31.5 million, so that immigrants and their children accounted for almost 66 million people, or about 23% of the U.S. population (Fix et al. 2003, U.S. Bureau of Census 2002). Unlike the immigrants who arrived at the turn of the twentieth

Jennifer Lee is a professor of sociology at the University of California, Irvine. Frank D. Bean is a professor of sociology at the University of California, Irvine.

century, today's immigrants are notable because they are mainly non-European. By the 1980s, only 12% of legal immigrants originated in Europe or Canada, whereas nearly 85% reported origins in Asia, Latin America, or the Caribbean (U.S. Immigration and Naturalization Service 2002, Waldinger & Lee 2001). According to National Research Council projections, by the year 2050, America's Latino and Asian populations are expected to triple, constituting about 25% and 8% of the U.S. population, respectively (Smith & Edmonston 1997). Once a largely biracial society with a large white majority and relatively small black minority—and a relatively impenetrable color line dividing these groups—the United States is now a society composed of multiple racial and ethnic groups. America's newcomers have undeniably altered the nation's racial and ethnic landscape.

At the same time that immigration has increased racial and ethic diversity in the United States, rises in rates of racial/ethnic intermarriage have also occurred. Over the past four decades—a time coinciding with the rise of the new immigration–intermarriage between whites and Asians and whites and Latinos have increased substantially, whether assessed on an individual or married-couple basis. For example, the percentages of Asian or Latino husbands or wives having spouses of another race or ethnicity exceeded 30% by the late 1990s, with the vast majority married to a white partner (Bean & Stevens 2003, p. 195). Similarly, the percentages of Asian or Latino marriages during the 1990s (defined as those with at least one spouse being a member of the race or ethnic group in question) that included a white spouse exceeded 50% in the third generation (Jacoby 2001, Waters 1999). Such rises in intermarriage have, in turn, led to a sizeable and growing multiracial population. Currently, 1 in 40 persons identifies himself or herself as multiracial, and this figure is twice as high for those under the age of 18 (Bean & Lee 2002, Grieco & Cassidy 2001). By the year 2050, as many as 1 in 5 Americans could claim a multiracial background (Farley 2001, Smith & Edmonston 1997).

It is not at all clear that today's immigrants see themselves, or for that matter that others see the immigrants, as either black or white. In short, most late-twentieth-century immigrants may be people of color, but the degree to which they view themselves and are viewed by others as closer to black or white is highly ambiguous. Today's immigration thus may be moving the nation far beyond the traditional and relatively persistent black/white color line that has long divided the country, a demarcation reflecting the practice of slavery, its legacy of discrimination, and a history of black social and economic disadvantage (Bobo 1997; Clark 1965; Drake & Cayton 1993; Farley & Allen 1987; Massey & Denton 1993; Myrdal 1944; Patterson 1998a,b; Smelser et al. 2001; Wilson 1980, 1987). This fault line, of course, was famously forecast in 1903 by the prominent African American social theorist W.E.B. Du Bois when he prophesied that the "problem of the twentieth-century is the problem of the color line" (1997, p. 45). However, even in 1903, during a time of substantial immigration, it seems unlikely that Du Bois could have anticipated that America's racial and ethnic makeup would be so drastically changed by the late-twentieth-century immigration.

The arrival of unprecedented numbers of Asians and Latinos thus complicates the black/white portrait of America and calls into question where today's immigrants fit along its bipolar divide. If a black/white color line no longer characterizes the nature of racial/ethnic relations in the United States, and a new line is emerging, where will the line be redrawn? Although the birth of a new divide is certainly one possible scenario, another prospect is a shift toward unconditional boundary crossing and the fading of racial boundaries altogether. The rising rates of intermarriage combined with a growing multiracial population may indicate that boundaries are weakening overall, providing evidence of a declining significance of race for all groups.

Which of these scenarios more accurately depicts today's demographic scene and the changing nature of America's color lines is a question fraught with theoretical and social significance. Social scientists are beginning to wrestle with the question of whether today's immigrants are helping to blur racial boundaries generally or whether

blacks, as well as their Chinese-black multiracial children. Spickard (1989) notes a similar process of change among Japanese Americans who were once at the bottom of the ethnic ladder along with blacks at the beginning of the twentieth century, but whose status improved dramatically just three-quarters of a century later.

The change in racial classification among ethnic groups from nonwhite to white or almost white vividly illustrates that race is a cultural rather than a biological category that has expanded over time to incorporate new immigrant groups. As Gerstle (1999, p. 289) explains, whiteness as a category "has survived by stretching its boundaries to include Americans—the Irish, eastern and southern Europeans—who had been deemed nonwhite. Contemporary evidence suggests that the boundaries are again being stretched as Latinos and Asians pursue whiteness much as the Irish, Italians, and Poles did before them." There are two points to underscore here: first, changes in ethnic and racial boundaries are a fundamental part of the immigrant incorporation experience; and second, racial and ethnic boundaries have stretched in the past and will undoubtedly continue to change. Although boundary changes may be a given, uncertainties remain about where the racial and ethnic divides will fade, where they will persist, and where today's newest immigrants will fall along these divides. It is impossible to predict exactly where the racial boundaries will be redrawn, but based on trends in immigrant incorporation, intermarriage, and multiracial identification, we can obtain a sense of the direction of these changes. . . .

INTERMARRIAGE IN THE UNITED STATES

At the beginning of the twentieth century, intermarriage between white ethnics was rare and nearly caste-like, especially between "old" white ethnics and newer arrivals from eastern and southern Europe (Pagnini & Morgan 1990). Today, white ethnics intermarry at such high rates that only one-fifth of whites has a spouse with an identical ethnic background, reflecting the virtual disappearance of boundaries among

white ethnic groups (Alba 1990; Lieberson & Waters 1988, 1993; Waters 1990). By contrast, marriage across racial groups, while on the rise, is still relatively uncommon between some groups, and all groups continue to intermarry at rates lower than would be predicted at random (Moran 2001). For example, more than 93% of white and black marriages are endogamous, whereas only about 70% of Asian and Hispanic and 33% of American Indian marriages are (Harrison & Bennett 1995, Waters 2000b).

In one sense, that interracial marriage is not as common as white interethnic marriage should come as little surprise given that it was illegal in 16 states as recently as 1967, when the Supreme Court ruling Loving v. Commonwealth of Virginia overturned the last remaining antimiscegenation laws. The ruling had an enormous impact on the rise in interracial marriage, which increased tenfold within a 30-year period from 150,000 in 1960 to 1.6 million in 1990 (Jacoby 2001, Waters 2000b), far beyond what would be predicted by population growth alone. Trends in exogamy are significant because social scientists conceive of racial/ethnic intermarriage as a measure of decreasing social distance, declining racial/ethnic prejudice, and changing racial/ethnic group boundaries (Davis 1941, Fu 2001, Gilbertson et al. 1996, Gordon 1964, Kalmijn 1993, Lee & Fernandez 1998, Lieberson & Waters 1988, Merton 1941, Rosenfeld 2002, Tucker & Mitchell-Kernan 1990). Given its theoretical significance, we review recent findings on intermarriage between whites and nonwhites and explore their implications for America's color lines.

Today, about 13% of American marriages involve persons of different races, a considerable increase over the past three and a half decades (Bean & Stevens 2003, Lee & Bean 2003). Although the rise in interracial marriage might initially suggest that racial boundaries are eroding, recent findings indicate that not all racial/ethnic groups are equal partners in this growth. For instance, about 30% of married native-born Asians and Latinos have a spouse of a different racial background, mostly white. Among young (25- to 34-year-old) U.S.-born Asians and Latinos, the intermarriage figures are even higher; nearly two-thirds of married Asians and two-fifths of Latinos out-marry, again mostly with whites (Qian 1997). By contrast, only one-tenth of young blacks marry someone of a different racial background (Perlmann 2000).

Although the rate of intermarriage increased for all groups since 1970, on the whole the intermarriage rate for whites and blacks remains relatively low (Kalmijn 1993). In the late 1990s, among married whites and married blacks only 5.8% and 10.2% involved a member of another racial group, respectively (Bean & Stevens 2003). The intermarriage rates for Asians and Latinos are nearly three times as high as that of blacks and more than five times the rate of whites. Among married Asians and Latinos, 27.2% and 28.4% of marriages involve a member of another racial group, typically whites (Bean & Stevens 2003, Lee & Bean 2003). The comparatively higher rates of intermarriage among native-born Asians and Latinos indicate that as these groups incorporate into the United States, they not only become receptive to intermarriage but also are perceived by whites as suitable marriage partners (Moran 2001).

In sum, there appear to be three distinct trends in interracial marriage in the United States. First, intermarriage for all racial groups has increased dramatically over the past 35 years and will probably continue to rise. Second, intermarriage is not uncommon in the cases of newer immigrant groups such as Asians and Latinos (particularly among the young, native-born populations). Third, compared with Asians, Latinos, and American Indians, intermarriage is still relatively uncommon among blacks (Perlmann 2000).

The differential rates of intermarriage among nonwhite racial groups suggest that racial/ethnic boundaries are more prominent for some groups than for others. The significantly higher rates of intermarriage among Asians and Latinos indicate that racial/ethnic boundaries are more fluid and flexible, and racial/ethnic prejudice less salient for these groups. By contrast, the lower rates of intermarriage among blacks suggest that racial boundaries are more prominent, and the black/white divide more salient than the Asian/white or

Latino/white divides. Hence, although boundaries are fading, boundary crossing among racial groups is not unconditional, and race is not declining in significance at the same pace for all groups.

THE MULTIRACIAL POPULATION IN THE UNITED STATES

The rise in interracial marriage has resulted in the growth of the multiracial population in the United States. This population became especially visible when, for the first time in the nation's history, the 2000 Census allowed Americans to select "one or more races" to indicate their racial identification. Brought about by a small but highly influential multiracial movement, this landmark change in the way the United States measures racial identification reflects the view that race is no longer conceived as a bounded category (DaCosta 2000; Farley 2001, 2002; Hirschman et al. 2000; Morning 2000; Waters 2000a; Williams 2001). In 2000, 6.8 million persons, or 2.4% of Americans, identified themselves as multiracial—about 1 in every 40 people. Although these figures may not appear large, a recent National Academy of Science study noted that the multiracial population could rise to 21% by the year 2050 when—because of rising patterns in intermarriage—as many as 35% of Asians and 45% of Hispanics might claim a multiracial background (Smith & Edmonston 1997). The growth of the multiracial population provides a new reflection on the nation's changing racial boundaries.

Although it has been apparent for some time that the multiracial population will continue to grow, the phenomenon has been relatively understudied in social science research. For example, only a handful of studies have examined the question of how interracial couples identify their multiracial children (Eschbach 1995, McKenney & Bennett 1994, Saenz et al. 1995, Xie & Goyette 1997, Waters 2000b), revealing that about 50% of American Indian/white and Asian/white intermarried couples report a white racial identity for their children. A somewhat larger but still not sizeable number of studies have examined the ways in which multiracial individuals self-identify, often based on small samples generating conflicting findings (Dalmage 2000; Harris & Sim 2002; Johnson et al. 1997; Korgen 1998; Root 1992, 1996; Salgado de Snyder et al. 1982; Spickard 1989; Stephan & Stephan 1989; Tizard & Phoenix 1993; Zack 1993). For example, Salgado de Snyder et al. (1982) find that 70% of multiracial children in California with one Mexican origin parent identify as Mexican, a rate much higher than Stephan & Stephan (1989) find for multiracial Hispanic college students in New Mexico, where only 44% adopt a Hispanic identity.

Previous research indicates that there are several important variables that affect the choice of racial identification among children of interracial unions, such as generational status, bilingualism, and proximity to a nonwhite community. For instance, in their studies of biracial children with one Asian parent, Saenz et al. (1995) and Xie & Goyette (1997) find that nativity and generational status matter. First-generation biracial Asian children are most likely to be identified as Asian compared with subsequent generations. However, the third-generation is more likely to be identified as Asian compared with their second-generation counterparts. Although this finding appears to contradict the classic assimilation model—which predicts fading ethnic identification with each successive generation—Xie & Goyette (1997) argue that choosing to identify one's child as Asian does not necessarily signify a stronger sense of racial identification. Rather, they posit that the racial identification of multiracial Asian children is largely optional, likening it to the ethnic options available for whites. Providing further support for this claim, Harris & Sim (2002) find in their study of multiracial youth that when asked to choose a single race, Asian/white youth are equally likely to identify as Asian or white, demonstrating that the racial identification of Asian/white multiracials is largely a matter of choice.

A second consistent finding is that speaking a language other than English at home significantly increases the likelihood that biracial children will adopt a nonwhite identity, supporting the thesis that language maintenance is critical in ethnic identity formation (Saenz et al. 1995; see also Portes & Rumbaut 2001, Zhou & Bankston 1998). A third finding is that neighborhood context matters, and exposure to the minority parent's culture increases the likelihood that biracial children will adopt a nonwhite identity (Harris & Sim 2002, Korgen 1998, Saenz et al. 1995, Stephan & Stephan 1989, Xie & Goyette 1997). For example, living among a large coethnic community or residing in a public use micro area (PUMA) that is greater than 20% Asian positively affects the degree to which interracially married Asians and whites identify their multiracial children as Asian (Saenz et al. 1995, Xie & Goyette 1997). Furthermore, Stephan & Stephan (1989) posit that the higher rates of multiracial identification of the Japanese in Hawaii (73%) compared with the Hispanics in New Mexico (44%) reflects the greater multicultural milieu in Hawaii, including a multiplicity of locally available labels for the multiracial/multiethnic population. Eschbach (1995) too discovers vast regional differences in the choice of an American Indian identity for American Indian/white multiracials—ranging from 33% to 73%.

Patterns of Multiracial Identification

. . . Mirroring trends in intermarriage, there appear to be three distinct patterns in multiracial identification. First, the multiracial population seems likely to continue to grow in the foreseeable future because of increasing intermarriage. Second, multiracial identification is not uncommon among the members of new immigrant groups such as Asians and Latinos (particularly for those under the age of 18). Third, at only 4.2%, multiracial identification remains relatively uncommon among blacks compared with Asians and Latinos. Why blacks are far less likely to report a multiracial background is particularly noteworthy considering that the U.S. Census Bureau estimates that at least three-quarters of the black population in the United States is ancestrally multiracial (Davis 1991, Spencer 1997). In other words, while at least 75% of black Americans have some alternative ancestry (mostly white) and thus could claim multiracial identities on that basis,

PERSONAL ACCOUNT

The Best of Both Worlds

It was the fall of 1988, November 30 to be exact. I had just given birth to a beautiful baby girl six weeks prior. I was getting ready to visit the doctor for a checkup and asked my best friend if she could baby-sit my daughter while I went for my visit to the doctor's office. She was delighted and previously had been begging me to let her watch the baby.

My fiancé was stationed in Saudi Arabia with the U.S. Army. He was a commander in his unit and was a Green Beret. He stayed in Saudi Arabia for seven years during and after the Persian Gulf War.

I guess I need to mention that I am Hispanic, and my daughter is half Hispanic and half African American, which then makes her "biracial" in our country. I had about 45 minutes to get my daughter and the diaper bag ready and make it to my appointment. I was getting nervous on both accounts, leaving my little bundle of joy with my friend and also to go and get a complete physical from the gynecologist.

I heard the phone ring, and I contemplated not answering it in order to save a little time, but I grabbed it. On the other side of the phone, all I could hear was sobbing and gasps of air, and I finally said, "Hello? Who is this?" Then it came: It was my best friend crying her eyes out and confessing that she could not watch my daughter this evening. I asked her "Why?" and much to my surprise, she answered me that her mother would not allow her to watch my daughter because she was half African American and that her mother did not want my daughter in her house.

I stayed on the phone speechless, actually numb. I can't even explain how I felt. All I could do was tell her it was okay, and all she could do was apologize over and over. I knew it wasn't her fault. I cried for hours and canceled my appointment and realized that it had begun. I had been told on every occasion that I would be facing this the minute my little angel came into this world. I denied it but now knew it to be true. How could anyone discriminate against an infant? It was prejudice, ignorance, and just plain unnecessary.

We have both come a long way since that cold, cold autumn day in 1988. My daughter is now 16, a beautiful caramel-colored, young lady with so much to offer the world. She is fluent in English and Spanish and has been in a gifted and talented program since the second grade. She loves the theater and the arts and has read numerous books by famous authors. She has been dancing since she was three and competes in tap and jazz.

Not a day goes by that I don't tell her that she has the best of both worlds and that it will be up to her to utilize it and embrace it. She knows discrimination, and it will be a fight she will have to endure for years to come, but she is ready. She is definitely ready!

Mindy Peral

---

just over 4% choose to do so, although recent studies reveal that younger black/white multiracials feel less constrained to adopt a black monoracial identity. For example, Korgen's (1998) study of 40 black/white adults reveals that only one-third of her sample under the age of 30 exclusively identifies as black. Moreover, Harris & Sim's (2002) study of multiracial youth shows that 17.1% of black/white adolescents choose white as the single race that best describes them.

Although younger blacks are less likely to report a black monoracial identity than older black cohorts, blacks overall are still far less likely to report multiracial backgrounds compared with Asians and Latinos.

The tendency of black Americans to be less likely to report multiracial identifications undoubtedly is due to the legacy of slavery, including lasting discrimination and the formerly de jure and now de facto invocation of the "one-drop rule" of hypodescent (Davis 1991, Haney Lopez 1996, Nobles 2000). For no other racial or ethnic group in the United States and in no other country does the one-drop rule so tightly circumscribe a group's identity choices (Harris et al. 1993). Unlike the one-drop rule of hypodescent that has historically constrained racial identity options for multiracial blacks, the absence of such a traditional practice of labeling among multiracial Asians, Latinos, and American Indians leaves room for exercising discretion in the selection of racial/ethnic identities (Bean & Stevens 2003, Eschbach 1995, Harris & Sim 2002, Lee & Bean 2003, Stephan & Stephan 1989, Xie & Goyette 1997). The higher rates of multiracial reporting among Latinos and Asians, both as a proportion of the total Latino and Asian populations, and vis-à-vis blacks, indicate that racial boundaries are less constraining for these groups compared with blacks. Although boundary crossing may be more common for all groups, it appears that the legacy of institutional racism in the country, as exemplified in such practices as the informal rule of hypodescent, more forcefully constrains the identity options for blacks compared with other nonwhite groups.

In addition, because a significant proportion of Latinos and Asians in the United States are either immigrants or the children of immigrants, their understanding of race, racial boundaries, and the black/white color divide is shaped by a different set of circumstances than those of African Americans. Most importantly, what sets Latinos and Asians apart is that their experiences are not rooted in the same historical legacy of slavery with its systematic and persistent patterns of legal and institutional discrimination and inequality from which the tenacious black/white divide was born and cemented. Unlike African Americans who were forcefully brought to this country as slaves, today's Latino and Asian newcomers are voluntary migrants, and consequently their experiences are distinct from those of African Americans. The unique history and experience of black Americans in this country make the black/white racial gap qualitatively and quantitatively different from the Latino/white or Asian/white racial divides. For these reasons, racial/ethnic boundaries appear more fluid for the newest immigrants than for native-born blacks, consequently providing multiracial Asians and Latinos more racial options than their black counterparts.

In fact, some research even indicates that the racial boundaries among Latinos, Asians, and American Indians more generally are beginning to assume the fluidity and mutability of ethnicity. For instance, in their longitudinal study of high school students,

Eschbach & Gomez (1998) note that only 68% of the more than 6500 students interviewed within a two-year period (1980 and 1982) consistently identified as Hispanic. They suggest that the change in racial/ethnic identification points to a process of transformation from ascribed to optional ethnicity. Similarly, Eschbach et al. (1998) note that the American Indian population grew from 827,000 in 1970 to 1.96 million in 1990–an increase far in excess of natural population growth. They posit that the change in racial identification from white to American Indian signifies the flexibility of racial boundaries for this group. Furthermore, as social scientists have documented, the racial identification for Asians has changed over time from "almost black" to "almost white," pointing to the mutability of boundaries for at least some Asian ethnic groups (Loewen 1971, Spickard 1989; see also Spickard & Fong 1995). Thus, recent findings suggest that at least for some Asians, Latinos, and American Indians, race is adopting the optional and symbolic character of white ethnicity. . . .

Acknowledgments

We thank the Russell Sage Foundation and the Center for Immigration, Population and Public Policy at the University of California, Irvine, for supporting the research on which this paper is based. This paper was partially completed while Jennifer Lee was a Fellow at the Center for Advanced Study in the Behavioral Sciences, with generous financial support provided by the William and Flora Hewlett Foundation, Grant #2000-5633, and while Frank D. Bean was a Visiting Scholar at the Russell Sage Foundation.

The Annual Review of Sociology is online at http://mutex.gmu.edu:3415.

DISCUSSION QUESTIONS

1. Where do new immigrants stand along the black/white color line?

2. How did race change from a biological to a cultural category?

3. In an interracial union, what are some of the factors that affect the choice of racial identification of children?

READING 7: America's Changing Color Lines **95**

REFERENCES

Alba RD. 1985. *Italian Americans: Into the Twilight of Ethnicity.* Engelwood. Cliffs, NJ: Prentice Hall.

Alba RD. 1990. *Ethnic Identity: The Transformation of White America.* New Haven, CT: Yale Univ. Press.

Alba RD. 1999. Immigration and the American realities of assimilation and multiculturalism. *Sociol. Forum* 14(1): 3–25.

Bean FD, Lee J. 2002. America's changing color lines: Immigration, racial/ethnic diversity, and multiracial identification. Presented at the Center for the Comparative Study of Race and Ethnicity, Stanford Univ.

Bean FD, Stevens G. 2003. *America's Newcomers and the Dynamics of Diversity.* New York: Russell Sage Found.

Bobo L. 1997. The color line, the dilemma, and the dream: Race relations in America at the close of the twentieth century. In *Civil Rights and Social Wrongs,* ed. J Higham, pp. 31–55. University Park: Penn. State Univ. Press.

Brodkin K. 1998. *How Jews Became White Folks and What That Says about Race in America.* New Brunswick, NJ: Rutgers Univ. Press.

Clark K. 1965. *Dark Ghetto: Dilemmas of Social Power.* New York: Harper and Row.

DaCosta K. 2000. Remaking the Color Line: Social Bases and Implications of the Multiracial Movement. Doc. Diss., Univ. Calif., Berkeley.

Dalmage HM. 2000. *Tripping on the Color Line: Black–White Multiracial Families in a Racially Divided World.* New Brunswick, NJ: Rutgers Univ. Press.

Davis FJ. 1991. *Who Is Black? One Nation's Definition.* University Park: Penn. State Univ. Press.

Davis K. 1941. Intermarriage in caste societies. *Am Anthropol.* 43:388–95.

Drake SC, Cayton HR. 1993 (1945). *Black Metropolis: A Study of Negro Life in a Northern City.* Chicago, IL: Univ. Chicago Press.

Du Bois WEB. 1997 (1903). *The Souls of Black Folk.* Boston, MA: Bedford Books.

Eschbach K. 1995. The enduring and vanishing American Indian: American Indian population growth and intermarriage in 1980. *Ethn. Racial. Stud.* 18(1): 89–108.

Eschbach K, Gomez C. 1998. Choosing Hispanic identity: Ethnic identity switching among respondents to high school and beyond. *Soc. Sci. Q.* 79(1): 74–90.

Eschbach K, Supple K, Snipp CM. 1998. Changes in racial identification and the educational attainment of American Indians, 1970–1990. *Demography* 35(1): 35–43.

Farley R. 2001. Identifying with multiple races. Rep. 01-491. Popul. Stud. Cent., Ann Arbor, MI: Univ. Mich.

Farley R. 2002. Racial identities in 2000: The response to the multiple-race response option. In *The New Race Question: How the Census Counts Multiracial Individuals,* ed. J Perlmann, MC Waters, pp. 33–61. New York: Russell Sage Found.

Farley R, Allen WR. 1987. *The Color Line and the Quality of Life in America.* New York: Russell Sage Found.

Fix M, Passel J, Sucher K. 2003. *Trends in Naturalization.* Washington, DC: Urban Inst.

Foner N. 2000. *From Ellis Island to JFK: New York's Two Great Waves of Immigration.* New Haven, CT/New York: Yale Univ. Press/Russell Sage Found.

Fu V. 2001. Racial intermarriage pairing. *Demography* 38(2): 147–60.

Gans HJ. 1979. Symbolic ethnicity: The future of ethnic groups and cultures in America. *Ethn. Racial Stud.* 2: 1–20.

Gans HJ. 1999. The possibility of a new racial hierarchy in the twenty-first century United States. In *The Cultural Territories of Race,* ed. M Lamont, pp. 371–90. Chicago, IL/New York: Univ. Chicago Press/Russell Sage Found.

Gerstle G. 1999. Liberty, coercion, and the making of Americans. In *The Handbook of International Migration,* ed. C Hirschman, P Kasinitz, J DeWind, pp. 275–93. New York: Russell Sage Found.

Gilbertson G, Fitzpatrick JF, Yang L. 1996. Hispanic intermarriage in New York City: New evidence from 1991. *Int. Migr. Rev.* 30: 445–59.

Gitlin T. 1995. *The Twilight of Common Dreams.* New York: Metropolitan.

Gordon M. 1964. *Assimilation in American Life.* New York: Oxford Univ. Press.

Grieco EM, Cassidy RC. 2001. Overview of race and Hispanic origin. Census 2000 Brief. U.S. Dep. Commer., Econ. Stat. Admin. U.S. Census Bur.

Haney Lopez IF. 1996. *White by Law: The Legal Construction of Race.* New York: New York Univ. Press.

Harris DR, Sim JJ. 2002. Who is multiracial? Assessing the complexity of lived race. *Am. Sociol. Rev.* 67(4): 614–27.

Harris M, Consorte JG, Lang J, Byrne B. 1993. Who are the whites? Imposed census categories and the racial demography of Brazil. *Soc. Forces* 72(2): 451–62.

Harrison R, Bennett C. 1995. Racial and ethnic diversity. In *State of the Union: America in the 1990s,* Vol. 2: *Social Trends,* ed. R Farley. New York: Russell Sage Found.

Hirschman C, Alba R, Farley R. 2000. The meaning and measurement of race in the U.S. Census: Glimpses into the future. *Demography* 37: 381–93.

Hollinger DA. 1995. *Postethnic America: Beyond Multiculturalism.* New York: Basic Books.

Ignatiev N. 1995. *How the Irish Became White.* New York: Routledge.

Jacobson MF. 1998. *Whiteness of a Different Color: European Immigrants and the Alchemy of Race.* Cambridge, MA: Harvard Univ. Press.

Jacoby T. 2001. An end to counting race? *Commentary* 111 (6): 37–40.

Johnson TP, Jobe JB, O'Rourke D, Sudman S, Warnecke RB, et al. 1997. Dimensions of self-identification among multiracial and multiethnic respondents in survey interviews. *Eval. Rev.* 21(6):671–87.

Kalmijn M. 1993. Patterns in black/white intermarriage. *Soc. Forces* 72(1): 119–46.

Korgen KO. 1998. *From Black to Biracial: Transforming Racial Identity Among Americans.* Westport, CT: Praeger.

Lee J, Bean FD. 2003. Beyond black and white: Remaking race in America. *Contexts* 2(3): 26–33.

Lee SM, Fernandez M. 1998. Patterns in Asian American racial/ethnic intermarriage: A comparison of 1980 and 1990 census data. *Sociol. Perspect.* 41(2): 323–42.

Lieberson S. 1980. *A Piece of the Pie: Blacks and White Immigrants since 1880.* Berkeley: Univ. Calif. Press.

Lieberson S, Waters MC. 1988. *From Many Strands: Ethnic and Racial Groups in Contemporary America.* New York: Russell Sage Found.

Lieberson S, Waters MC. 1993. The ethnic responses of whites: What causes their instability, simplification, and inconsistency? *Soc. Forces* 72(2): 421–50.

Loewen J. 1971. *The Mississippi Chinese: Between Black and White.* Cambridge, MA: Harvard Univ. Press.

Massey DS, Denton NA. 1993. *American Apartheid: Segregation and the Making of the Underclass.* Cambridge, MA: Harvard Univ. Press.

McKenney NR, Bennett CE. 1994. Issues regarding data on race and ethnicity: The Census Bureau experience. *Public Health Rep.* 109(1): 16–25.

Merton RK. 1941. Intermarriage and the social structure: fact and theory. *Psychiatry* 4:361–74.

Moran RF. 2001. *Interracial Intimacy: The Regulation of Race and Romance.* Chicago IL: Univ. Chicago Press.

Morning A. 2000. Counting on the color line. Presented at the Annu. Meet. Popul. Assoc. Am., Los Angeles, CA, March.

Myrdal G. 1944. *An American Dilemma: The Negro Problem and Modern Democracy.* New York: Harper.

Nobles M. 2000. *Shades of Citizenship: Race and the Census in Modern Politics.* Stanford, CA: Stanford Univ. Press.

Pagnini DL, Morgan SP. 1990. Intermarriage and social distance among U.S. immigrants at the turn of the century. *Am. J. Sociol.* 96(2): 405–32.

Patterson O. 1998a. *The Ordeal of Integration.* Washington, DC: Civitas.

Patterson O. 1998b. *Rituals of Blood.* Washington, DC: Civitas.

Perlmann J. 2000. Reflecting the changing face of America: Multiracials, racial classification, and American intermarriage. In *Interracialism: Black-White Intermarriage in American History, Literature, and Law,* ed. W. Sollars, pp. 506–33. New York: Oxford Univ. Press.

Perlmann J, Waldinger R. 1997. Second generation decline? Children of immigrants, past and present—a reconsideration. *Int. Migr. Rev.* 31(4): 893–922.

Portes A, Rumbaut RG. 2001. *Legacies: The Story of the Immigrant Second Generation.* Berkeley: Univ. Calif. Press.

Qian Z. 1997. Breaking the racial barriers: Variations in interracial marriage between 1980 and 1990. *Demography* 34(2): 263–76.

Rodriguez CE. 2000. *Changing Race: Latinos, the Census, and the History of Ethnicity in the United States.* New York: NY Univ. Press.

Roediger DR. 1991. *The Wages of Whiteness.* New York: Verso.

Root MPP, ed. 1992. *Racially Mixed People in America.* Newbury Park, CA: Sage.

Root MPP, ed. 1996. *The Multiracial Experience: Racial Borders as the New Frontier.* Thousand Oaks, CA: Sage.

Rosenfeld MJ. 2002. Measures of assimilation in the marriage market: Mexican Americans 1970–1990. *J. Marriage Fam.* 64:152–62.

Saenz R, Hwang S, Aguirre BE, Anderson RN. 1995. Persistence and change in Asian identity among children of intermarried couples. *Sociol. Perspect.* 38(2): 175–94.

Salgado de Snyder N, Lopez CM, Padilla AM. 1982. Ethnic identity and cultural awareness among the offspring of Mexican interethnic marriages. *J. Early Adolesc.* 2:277–82.

Sanjek R. 1994. Intermarriage and the future of the races. In *Race,* ed. S Gregory, R Sanjek, pp. 103–30. New Brunswick, NJ: Rutgers Univ. Press.

Skrentny JD, ed. 2001. *Color Lines: Affirmative Action, Immigration, and Civil Rights Options for America.* Chicago, IL: Univ. Chicago Press.

Smelser NJ, Wilson WJ, Mitchell F, eds. 2001. *America Becoming: Racial Trends and their Consequences.* Washington, DC: Natl. Acad. Press.

Smith JP, Edmonston B. 1997. *The New Americans.* Washington, DC: Natl. Acad. Press.

Spencer JM. 1997. *The New Colored People: The Mixed-Race Movement in America.* New York: New York Univ. Press.

Spickard PR. 1989. *Mixed Blood.* Madison: Univ. Wis. Press.

Spickard PR, Fong R. 1995. Pacific Islander Americans and multiethnicity: A vision of America's future? *Soc. Forces* 73(4): 1365–83.

Stephan CW, Stephan WG. 1989. After intermarriage: Ethnic identity among mixed-heritage Japanese-Americans and Hispanics. *J. Marriage Fam.* 51: 507–19.

Tizard B, Phoenix A. 1993. *Black, White or Mixed Race? Race and Racism in the Lives of Young People of Mixed Parentage.* New York: Routledge.

Tucker MB, Mitchell-Kernan C. 1990. New patterns in Black American interracial marriage: The social structural context. *J. Marriage Fam.* 52: 209–18.

U.S. Bur. Census. 2002. Current Population Survey: Monthly Demographic File, March (Computer file). Washington, DC: U.S. Dep. Commer.

U.S. Immigr. Nat. Serv. 2002. *2000 INS Statistical Yearbook.* Washington, DC: USGPO.

Waldinger R, Lee J. 2001. New immigrants in urban America. In *Strangers at the Gates,* ed. R Waldinger, pp. 30–79. Berkeley: Univ. Calif. Press.

Waters MC. 1990. *Ethnic Options: Choosing Identities in America.* Berkeley: Univ. Calif. Press.

Waters MC. 1999. *Black Identities: West Indian Immigrant Dreams and American Realities.* Cambridge, MA: Harvard Univ. Press.

Waters MC. 2000a. Immigration, intermarriage, and the challenges of measuring racial/ethnic identities. *Am. J Public Health* 90:1735–37.

Waters MC. 2000b. Multiple ethnicities and identity in the United States. In *We Are a People,* ed. P Spikard, WJ Burroughs, pp. 23–40. Philadelphia, PA: Temple Univ. Press.

Williams K. 2001. Boxed In: The United States Multiracial Movement. Unpubl. Diss., Cornell Univ.

Wilson WJ. 1980. *The Declining Significance of Race.* Chicago, IL: Univ. Chicago Press. 2nd ed.

Wilson WJ. 1987. *The Truly Disadvantaged: The Inner City, the Underclass, and Public Policy.* Chicago, IL: Univ. Chicago Press.

Xie Y, Goyette K. 1997. The racial identification of biracial children with one Asian parent: Evidence from the 1990 Census. *Soc. Forces* 76:547–70.

Zack N. 1993. *Race and Mixed Race.* Philadelphia, PA: Temple Univ. Press.

Zhou M, Bankston CL III. 1998. *Growing Up American: How Vietnamese Children Adapt to Life in the United* States. New York: Russell Sage Found.

READING 8

"We Are All Americans": The Latin Americanization of Race Relations in the United States

Eduardo Bonilla-Silva

Karen S. Glover

We need to speak about the impossible because we know too much about the possible.

Silvio Rodríguez
Cuban New Song Movement
Singer and Composer

"*We are all Americans!*" This, we contend, will be the racial mantra of the United States in years

Eduardo Bonilla-Silva is a professor of sociology at Duke University. Karen S. Glover is a graduate student in sociology at Texas A&M University.

to come. Although for many analysts, because of this country's deep history of racial divisions, this prospect seems implausible, nationalist statements denying the salience of race are the norm throughout the world.[1] Countries such as Malaysia and Indonesia, Trinidad and Belize, and, more significantly for our discussion, Iberian countries such as Puerto Rico, Cuba, Brazil, and Mexico, all exhibit this ostrichlike approach to racial matters. That is, they all stick their heads deep into the social ground and say, "We don't have races here. We don't have racism here. Races and racism exist in the United States and South Africa. We are all Mexicans (Cubans, Brazilians, or Puerto Ricans)!"

Despite these claims, racial minorities in these self-styled racial democracies tend to be worse off, comparatively speaking, than racial minorities in Western nations. In Brazil, for example, blacks and "pardos" (tan or brown) earn 40 to 45 percent as much as whites. In the United States blacks earn 55 to 60 percent as much as whites. In Brazil blacks are half as likely as blacks in the United States to be employed in professional jobs, and about one-third as less likely to attend college; they have a life expectancy, controlling for education and income, between five and six years shorter than that of white Brazilians. This last statistic is similar in size to the black-white difference in the United States (Andrews 1991; Silva do Valle 1985; Hasenbalg 1985; Lovell and Wood 1998; Telles 1999; Hasenbalg and Silva 1999; do Nascimento and Larkin-Nascimento 2001).

[We] contend that racial stratification and the rules of racial (re)cognition in the United States are becoming Latin America–like. We suggest that the biracial system typical of the United States, which was the exception in the world racial system, is becoming the "norm" (for the racialization of the world system, see Balibar and Wallerstein 1991; Goldberg 1993, 2002; Mills 1997; Winant 2001). That is, the U.S. system is evolving into a complex racial stratification system.[2] Specifically, we argue that the United States is developing a tri-racial system with "whites" at the top, an intermediary group of "honorary whites" (similar to the coloreds in South Africa during formal apartheid), and a nonwhite group or the "collective black" at the bottom.[3] We predict that the "white" group will include "traditional" whites, new "white" immigrants, and, in the near future, assimilated Latinos, some (light-skinned) multiracials, and other subgroups. The intermediate racial group, or "honorary whites," will comprise most light-skinned Latinos (most Cubans, for instance, and segments of the Mexican and Puerto Rican communities; Rodríguez 1998), Japanese Americans, Korean Americans, Asian Indians, Chinese Americans, the bulk of multiracials (Rockquemore and Arend, forthcoming), and most Middle Eastern Americans.[4] Finally, the "collective black" will include blacks, dark-skinned Latinos, Vietnamese, Cambodians, Laotians, and maybe Filipinos.

PRELIMINARY MAP OF TRI-RACIAL SYSTEM IN THE UNITED STATES

"Whites"

- Whites
- New whites (Russians, Albanians, and so on)
- Assimilated white Latinos
- Some (white-looking) multiracials
- Assimilated (urban) Native Americans
- A few Asian-origin people

"Honorary Whites"

- Light-skinned Latinos
- Japanese Americans
- Korean Americans
- Asian Indians
- Chinese Americans
- Middle Eastern Americans
- Most multiracials

"Collective Black"

- Filipinos
- Vietnamese
- Hmong
- Laotians
- Dark-skinned Latinos
- Blacks
- New West Indian and African immigrants
- Reservation-bound Native Americans

This map is heuristic, however, rather than definitive. It is included as a guide for how we think various ethnic groups will line up in the new emerging racial order. We acknowledge several caveats: the position of some groups may change (for example, Chinese Americans, Asian Indians, or Arab Americans); the map does not include all groups in the United States (Samoans and Micronesians, for instance, do not appear). . . . More significantly, if our Latin Americanization thesis is accurate, the categories will be porous and a "pigmentocracy" will make the map useful for group-level rather than individual-level predictions. (By porous we mean that individual members of a racial stratum can move up [or down] the stratification system, as might happen when a light-skinned middle-class black person marries a white woman and moves to the "honorary white" stratum. Pigmentocracy refers to the rank ordering of groups and members of groups according to phenotype and cultural characteristics, such as may happen when Filipinos move to the top of the "collective black" stratum because of their high level of education and income and a high rate of interracial marriage with whites.). . .

[W]e have four aims. First, we draw on research on race in Latin American and Caribbean societies to provide insight into the key features of their racial stratification systems. Second, we outline five reasons why Latin Americanization will occur at this historical juncture in the United States. Third, we examine various objective (income, education, occupation), subjective (racial views and racial self-classification), and social interaction indicators (residential preferences and interracial marriage) to assess whether the data point in the direction predicted by the Latin Americanization thesis. Finally, we discuss the likely implications of Latin Americanization for the future of race relations in the United States.

HOW RACE WORKS
IN THE AMERICAS

To advocate transculturation without attempting to change the systems and institutions that breed the power differential would simply help to perpetuate the utopian vision that constructs Latin America . . . as the continent of hope.

Lourdes Martínez-Echazabal (1998, 32)

One of the authors has argued elsewhere that racial stratification systems operate in most societies without races being officially acknowledged (Bonilla-Silva 1999). For example, although racial inequality is more pronounced in Latin America than in the United States, racial data in Latin America are gathered inconsistently or not at all. Yet most Latin Americans, including those most affected by racial stratification, do not recognize the inequality between "whites" and "nonwhites" in their countries as racial. "Prejudice" (Latin Americans do not talk about "racism") is viewed as a legacy from slavery and colonialism, and inequality is regarded as the product of class dynamics (Wagley 1952; for a critique, see Skidmore 1990). . . .

Miscegenation or "Mestizaje"

Latin American nation-states, with the exceptions of Argentina, Chile, Uruguay, and Costa Rica, are thoroughly racially mixed. This mixture has led many observers to follow the historian Gilberto Freyre (1959, 7)—who described Brazil as having "almost perfect equality of opportunity for all men regardless of race and color"—and label them "racial democracies." However, all contacts between Europeans and the various peoples of the world have involved racial mixing. The important difference is that the mixing in Latin America led to a socially and sometimes legally recognized intermediate racial stratum of mestizos, browns, or "trigueños."[5]

However, racial mixing in no way challenged white supremacy in colonial or postcolonial Latin America. Four pieces of evidence support this claim: the mixing was between white men and Indian or black women, thus maintaining the race-gender order; the men were fundamentally poor or working-class, which helped maintain the race-class order; the mixing followed a racially hierarchical pattern in which "whitening" was the goal; and marriages among people in the three main racial groups were (and still are) mostly homogamous (Hoetink 1967, 1971; Morner 1967; Martínez-Alier 1974; for Puerto Ricans, see Fitzpatrick 1971). The last point requires qualification: although most marriages have been within-stratum, they have produced phenotypical variation because members of all racial strata have variations in phenotype. This means that members of any stratum can try to "marry up" by choosing a light-skinned partner *within* their stratum.

The Tri-racial Stratification System

Although Portuguese and Spanish colonial states wanted to create "two societies," the demographic realities of colonial life superseded their wishes.[6] Because most colonial outposts were scarcely populated by Europeans, all these societies developed an intermediate group of "browns," "pardos," or "mestizos" who buffered sociopolitical conflicts. Even though this group did not achieve the status of "white," it nonetheless had a better status than the Indian or black masses and therefore developed its own distinct interest. As many commentators have observed, without this intermediate group, Latin American countries would have followed the path of Haiti (us versus them). The similarities between a tri-racial stratification system and a complex class stratification system are clear: whereas class *polarization* leads to rebellion, a *multiplicity* of classes and strata leads to diffused social conflict (for an early summary on classes in modern industrial societies, see Bottomore 1968).

Colorism or Pigmentocracy

There is yet another layer of complexity in Latin American racial stratification systems: the three racial strata are also internally stratified by "color." By color we mean skin tone, but also phenotype, hair texture, eye color, culture and education, and class. All of these features matter in the Latin American system of racial stratification, and this further stratification by "color" is referred to as pigmentocracy or colorism (Kinsbrunner 1996). Pigmentocracy has been central to the maintenance of white power in Latin America because it has fostered: (1) divisions among all those in secondary racial strata, (2) divisions *within* racial strata that limit the likelihood of *within*-strata unity; (3) the view that mobility is *individual* and conditional on "whitening"; and (4) the belief that white elites should be regarded as legitimate representatives of the "nation" even though they do not look like the average member of the nation.[7]

Blanqueamiento: Whitening as Ideology and Practice

"Blanqueamiento" (whitening) has been treated in research on Latin America as an ideology (Degler 1986). However, blanqueamiento is not simply an ideology; it is an economic, political, and personal process. It is a "dynamic that involves culture, identity and values" (Wade 1997, 341). At the personal level members of families can be color-divided or even racially divided and treat their dark-skinned members differently (Kasper 2000). The material origin of "whitening" was the 1783 Cédulas de Gracias al Sacar (petitions to "cleanse" persons of "impure origins"), which allowed mulattoes to buy certificates that officially declared them to be white (Guerra 1998). With this certificate, they were allowed to work in the military and colonial administrative posts. It was also a ticket to mobility for their offspring (Kinsbrunner 1996).

As a social practice, whitening "is not just neutral mixture but hierarchical movement . . . and the most valuable movement is upward" (Wade 1997, 342). Thus, whitening does not reveal a Latin American racial flexibility but instead demonstrates the effectiveness of the logic of white supremacy. This practice also works in apparently homogeneous societies such as Haiti (Trouillot 1990) and even Japan (Weiner 1997), where slight variations in skin tone (lighter shade) and cultural affectations

(being more French in Haiti or Western-oriented in Japan) are regarded as valuable assets in the marriage market.

The National Ideology of Mestizaje

National independence in Latin America meant, among other things, the silencing of discussions about race and the forging of a myth of national unity (Morner 1993; Marx 1998). . . .

"We Are All Latinoamericanos": Race as Nationality and Culture

Most Latin Americans, even those who are obviously "black" or "Indian," refuse to identify themselves in racial terms. Instead, they prefer to use national (or cultural) descriptors, such as "I am Puerto Rican" or "I am Brazilian."[8] This behavior has been the subject of much confusion and described as an example of the fluidity of race in Latin America (for examples, see the otherwise superb work of Clara Rodríguez [1991, 2000]). However, defining the nation and the "people" as the "fusion of cultures" (even though the fusion is viewed in a Eurocentric manner) is the logical outcome of all of the factors mentioned here. Rather than evidence of nonracialism, nationalist statements such as "We are all Puerto Ricans" are a direct manifestation of the racial stratification peculiar to Latin America. . . .

WHY LATIN AMERICANIZATION NOW?

Why are race relations in the United States becoming Latin America–like at this point in our history? The reasons are multiple. First, the demography of the nation is changing. Racial minorities make up 30 percent of the population today. Population projections suggest that minorities as a group may become a numeric majority in the year 2050 (U.S. Department of Commerce 1996). More recent data from the census of 2000 suggest that these projections may be an underestimate, since the Latino population exceeded expectations and the proportion white was lower than expected (Grieco and Cassidy 2001).

The rapid darkening of America is creating a situation similar to that of Puerto Rico, Cuba, and Venezuela in the sixteenth and seventeenth centuries, or Argentina, Chile, and Uruguay in the late eighteenth and early nineteenth centuries. In both historical periods, the elites realized that their countries were becoming "black" (or "nonwhite"), and they devised a number of strategies (unsuccessful in the former and successful in the latter) to whiten their population (Helg 1990). Although whitening the population through immigration or by classifying many newcomers as white (Gans 1999; Warren and Twine 1997) is one possible outcome of the new American demography for reasons discussed later . . . we do not think it is likely that these strategies will be implemented. Rather, we argue that a more plausible response to the new racial reality will be to (1) create an intermediate racial group to buffer racial conflict; (2) allow some newcomers into the white racial stratum; and (3) incorporate most immigrants into the collective black stratum.

The second reason we believe Latin Americanization will occur now is because of the tremendous reorganization that has transpired in America in the post–civil rights era. Specifically, a kinder and gentler white supremacy has emerged. Elsewhere, Bonilla-Silva has labeled this the "new racism" (Bonilla-Silva and Lewis 1999; Bonilla-Silva 2001; see also Smith 1995). In post–civil rights America, systemic white privilege is maintained socially, economically, and politically through institutional, covert, and apparently nonracial practices. Whether in banks or universities, in stores or housing markets, "smiling discrimination" (Brooks 1990) tends to be the order of the day. This new white supremacy has produced the accompanying Latin America–like ideology: color-blind racism. . . .

A third reason for Latin Americanization is that race relations have become globalized (Lusane 1997). The once almost all-white Western nations have now "interiorized the other" (Miles 1993). The new world systemic need for capital accumulation has led to the incorporation of "dark" foreigners as "guest workers" and even as permanent workers

(Schoenbaum and Pond 1996). Thus, European nations today have in their midst racial minorities who are progressively becoming an underclass (Castles and Miller 1993; Cohen 1997; Spoonley 1996). . . .

A fourth reason for the emergence of Latin Americanization in the United States is the convergence of the political and ideological actions of the Republican Party, conservative commentators and activists, and the so-called multiracial movement (Rockquemore and Brunsma 2002). This has created the space for a radical transformation of the way in which racial data are gathered in America. One possible outcome of the Census Bureau's changes in racial and ethnic classifications is either the dilution of racial data or the elimination of race as an official category. . . .

A LOOK AT THE DATA

To recapitulate, we contend that because of a number of important demographic, sociopolitical, and international changes, the United States is developing a more complex system of racial stratification. This system resembles those typical of Latin American societies. We suggest that three racial strata will develop: whites, honorary whites, and the collective black. . . .

Objective Standing of "Whites," "Honorary Whites," and "Blacks"

If Latin Americanization is happening in the United States, gaps in income, poverty rates, education, and occupational standing between whites, honorary whites, and the collective black should be evident. The available data suggest this is the case. In terms of income, as table 1 shows, "white" Latinos (Argentines, Chileans, Costa Ricans, and Cubans) are doing much better than dark-skinned Latinos (Mexicans, Puerto Ricans). The apparent exceptions in table 1—Bolivians and Panamanians—are examples of the effect of self-selection among these immigrant groups.[9] Table 1 also shows that Asians exhibit a pattern similar to that of Latinos. Hence, a severe income gap exists between honorary white

TABLE 1

MEAN PER CAPITA INCOME OF SELECTED ASIAN AND LATINO ETHNIC GROUPS, 2000

Latinos	Mean Income (U.S. Dollars)	Asian Americans	Mean Income (U.S. Dollars)
Mexicans	9,467.30	Chinese	20,728.54
Puerto Ricans	11,314.95	Japanese	23,786.13
Cubans	16,741.89	Koreans	16,976.19
Guatemalans	11,178.60	Asian Indians	25,682.15
Salvadorans	11,371.92	Filipinos	19,051.53
Costa Ricans	14,226.92	Taiwanese	22,998.05
Panamanians	16,181.20	Hmong	5,175.34
Argentines	23,589.99	Vietnamese	14,306.74
Chileans	18,272.04	Cambodians	8,680.48
Bolivians	16,322.53	Laotians	10,375.57
Whites	17,968.87	Whites	17,968.87
Blacks	11,366.74	Blacks	11,366.74

Source: 2000 Public Use Microdata Sample, 5 Percent Sample.
Note: We use per capita income because family income distorts the status of some groups (particularly Asians and whites), since some groups have more people in the household who are contributing toward the family income.

TABLE 2

MEDIAN YEARS OF SCHOOLING OF SELECTED ASIAN AND LATINO ETHNIC GROUPS, 2000

Latinos	Median Years of Education	Asian Americans	Median Years of Education
Mexicans	9.00	Chinese	12.00
Puerto Ricans	11.00	Japanese	14.00
Cubans	12.00	Koreans	12.00
Guatemalans	7.50	Asian Indians	14.00
Salvadorans	9.00	Filipinos	14.00
Costa Ricans	12.00	Taiwanese	14.00
Panamanians	12.00	Hmong	5.50
Argentines	12.00	Vietnamese	11.00
Chileans	12.00	Cambodians	9.00
Bolivians	12.00	Laotians	10.00
Whites	12.00	Whites	12.00
Blacks	12.00	Blacks	12.00

Source: 2000 Public Use Microdata Sample, 5 Percent Sample.

Asians (Japanese, Koreans, Filipinos, and Chinese) and those Asians we contend belong to the collective black (Vietnamese, Cambodian, Hmong, and Laotians).

Table 2 exhibits similar patterns in terms of education. Table 2 shows that light-skinned Latinos have between three and four years of educational advantage over dark-skinned Latinos. The same table indicates that elite Asians have up to eight years more education than most of the Asian groups we classify as belonging to the collective black. A more significant fact, given that the American job market is becoming bifurcated such that good jobs go to the educated and bad jobs to the undereducated, is that the proportion of white Latinos with "some college" is equal to or higher than the proportion of the white population with the same level of education. . . .

Substantial group differences are also evident in occupational status. The light-skinned Latino

TABLE 3

OCCUPATIONAL STATUS OF SELECTED LATINO GROUPS, 2000

Ethnic Groups	Managers and Professional Related Occupations	Sales and Office	Services	Construction, Extraction, and Maintenance	Production, Transportation, and Materials Moving	Farming, Forestry, and Fishing
Mexicans	13.18%	20.62%	22.49%	14.41%	23.76%	5.54%
Puerto Ricans	21.14	29.46	21.40	8.34	19.01	0.66
Cubans	27.84	28.65	16.09	10.21	16.68	0.53
Guatemalans	9.49	16.13	29.73	14.59	27.55	2.51
Salvadorans	8.96	17.29	32.11	15.44	24.84	1.37
Costa Ricans	23.35	22.76	25.46	11.61	16.27	0.55
Panamanians	31.07	32.82	20.27	5.61	9.94	0.29
Argentines	39.77	24.68	14.84	9.24	10.96	0.51
Chileans	32.12	23.92	20.05	10.32	13.13	0.46
Bolivians	27.20	25.80	23.85	11.19	11.73	0.23
Whites	32.07	27.03	15.02	10.12	14.77	1.00
Blacks	21.48	26.48	23.96	7.57	19.84	0.65

Source: 2000 Public Use Microdata Sample, 5 Percent Sample.

groups have achieved parity with whites in their proportional representation in the top jobs in the economy. Thus, the share of Argentines, Chileans, and Cubans in the top two occupational categories ("managers and professional related occupations" and "sales and office") is 55 percent or higher, a figure similar to whites' 59 percent (see table 3). In contrast, dark-skinned Latino groups such as Mexicans, Puerto Ricans, and Central Americans are concentrated in the four lower occupational categories.[10] Along the same lines, the Asian groups we classify as "honorary whites" are more likely to be well represented in the top occupational categories than those we classify as the "collective black." For instance, whereas 61 percent of Taiwanese and 56 percent of Asian Indians are in the top occupational category, only 15 percent of Hmong, 13 percent of Laotians, 17 percent of Cambodians, and 25 percent of Vietnamese are in that category (see table 4)[11]

Subjective Standing of Whites, Honorary Whites, and the Collective Black

Social psychologists have demonstrated that it takes very little for groups to form, to develop a common view, and to create status positions based on nominal characteristics (Tajfel 1970; Ridgeway 1991).

Thus, it should not be surprising if gaps in income, occupational status, and education contribute to group formation and consciousness. That is, honorary whites may classify themselves as "white" and believe they are different (better) than those in the collective black category. If this is happening, this group should also be in the process of developing whitelike racial attitudes befitting their new social position and also differentiating themselves from the collective black.

In line with our thesis, we also expect whites to make distinctions between honorary whites and the collective black by exhibiting a more positive outlook toward honorary whites than toward members of the collective black. Finally, if Latin Americanization is occurring, we speculate that the collective black should exhibit a diffused and contradictory racial consciousness similar to what occurs among blacks and Indians throughout Latin America and the Caribbean (Hanchard 1994). The following sections examine these possibilities.

Social Identity of Honorary Whites

Self-Reports on Race: Latinos Historically, most Latinos have classified themselves as "white," but the proportion who do so varies tremendously

TABLE 4

OCCUPATIONAL STATUS OF SELECTED ASIAN ETHNIC GROUPS, 2000

Ethnic Groups	Managers and Professional Related Occupations	Sales and Office	Services	Construction, Extraction, and Maintenance	Production, Transportation, and Materials Moving	Farming Forestry, and Fishing
Chinese	47.79%	22.83%	15.04%	2.77%	11.42%	0.15%
Japanese	46.90	28.05	13.24	4.50	6.70	0.60
Koreans	36.51	31.26	15.65	3.97	12.38	0.23
Asian Indians	55.89	23.39	8.07	2.25	10.03	0.37
Filipinos	34.87	28.70	18.49	4.62	12.35	0.98
Taiwanese	60.95	24.78	8.44	1.34	4.43	0.06
Hmong	14.67	24.14	17.33	4.51	38.57	0.77
Vietnamese	25.21	19.92	19.64	6.02	28.50	0.71
Cambodians	16.66	25.37	17.26	5.45	34.67	0.59
Laotians	12.55	20.60	15.02	6.07	44.96	0.81
Whites	32.07	27.03	15.02	10.12	14.77	1.00
Blacks	21.48	26.48	23.96	7.57	19.84	0.65

Source: 2000 Public Use Microdata Sample, 5 Percent Sample.

by group. As table 5 shows, whereas 60 percent or more of the members of the Latino honorary white groups classify themselves as "white," about 50 percent—or fewer—of the members of the groups we regard as belonging to the collective black do so. As a case in point, Mexicans, Dominicans, and Central Americans are very likely to report "other" as their preferred racial classification, while most Costa Ricans, Cubans, Chileans, and Argentines choose the "white" descriptor. The 2000 census data mirror the results of the 1988 Latino National Political Survey (de la Garza et al. 1992).[12]

"Racial" Distinctions Among Asians Although on political matters Asians tend to vote panethnically (Espiritu 1992), distinctions between native-born and foreign-born (for example, American-born Chinese and foreign-born Chinese) and between

TABLE 5

RACIAL SELF-CLASSIFICATION BY SELECTED LATIN AMERICA–ORIGIN LATINO ETHNIC GROUPS, 2000

Ethnic Groups	White	Black	Other	Native American	Asian
Dominicans	28.21%	10.93%	59.21%	1.07%	0.57%
Salvadorans	41.01	0.82	56.95	0.81	0.41
Guatemalans	42.95	1.24	53.43	2.09	0.28
Hondurans	48.51	6.56	43.41	1.24	0.29
Mexicans	50.47	0.92	46.73	1.42	0.45
Puerto Ricans	52.42	7.32	38.85	0.64	0.77
Costa Ricans	64.83	5.91	28.18	0.56	0.53
Bolivians	65.52	0.32	32.79	1.32	0.05
Colombians	69.01	1.53	28.54	0.49	0.44
Venezuelans	75.89	2.58	20.56	0.36	0.60
Chileans	77.04	0.68	21.27	0.44	0.56
Cubans	88.26	4.02	7.26	0.17	0.29
Argentines	88.70	0.33	10.54	0.08	0.35

Source: 2000 Public Use Microdata Sample, 5 Percent Sample.

economically successful and unsuccessful Asians are developing. In fact, many analysts have argued that, given the tremendous diversity of experiences among Asian Americans, "all talk of Asian pan-ethnicity should now be abandoned as useless speculation" (San Juan 2000, 10). . . .

To be sure, Asian Americans have engaged in coalition politics and, in various locations, in concerted efforts to elect Asian American candidates (Saito 1998). However, we argue that it is also important to bear in mind that the group labeled "Asian Americans" is profoundly divided along many axes. We further suggest that many of those already existing divisions will be racialized by whites. . . .

Social Interaction among Members of the Three Racial Strata

If Latin Americanization is happening in the United States, we would expect to see more social contact (such as friendships and associations as neighbors) and intimate contact (marriage, for instance) between whites and honorary whites than between whites and members of the collective black. A cursory analysis of the data support this expectation.

Interracial Marriage   Although most marriages in America are still intraracial, the rates vary substantially by group. Whereas 93 percent of whites and blacks marry within-group, 70 percent of Latinos and Asians do so, and only 33 percent of Native Americans marry other Native Americans (Moran 2001, 103). More significantly, when we disentangle the generic terms "Asian" and "Latino," the data fit even more closely the Latin Americanization thesis. For example, Latinos, Cubans, Mexicans, Central Americans, and South Americans have higher rates of out-marriage than Puerto Ricans and Dominicans (Gilbertson, Fitzpatrick, and Yang 1996). Although interpreting the Asian American out-marriage pattern is very complex (groups such as Filipinos and Vietnamese have higher than expected rates owing in part to the Vietnam War and the military bases in the Philippines), it is worth pointing out that the highest rate belongs

to Japanese Americans and Chinese (Kitano and Daniels 1995) and the lowest to Southeast Asians.

Furthermore, racial assimilation through marriage ("whitening") is significantly more likely for the children of Asian-white and Latino-white unions than for those of black-white unions, a fact that bolsters our Latin Americanization thesis. Hence, whereas only 22 percent of the children of black fathers and white mothers are classified as white, the children of similar unions among Asians are twice as likely to be classified as white (Waters 1999). For Latinos, the data fit the thesis even more closely: Latinos of Cuban, Mexican, and South American origin have high rates of exogamy compared to Puerto Ricans and Dominicans (Gilbertson et al. 1996). We concur with Rachel Moran's (2001) speculation that the high percentage of dark-skinned Puerto Ricans and Dominicans (see table 5) results in restricted chances for out-marriage to whites in a highly racialized marriage market.

Residential Segregation among Racial Strata
An imperfect measure of interracial interaction is the level of neighborhood "integration" (for some of the limitations of this index, see Bonilla-Silva and Baiocchi 2001). Nevertheless, the various segregation indices devised by demographers allow us to gauge in general terms the level of interracial contact in various cities. In this section, we focus on the segregation of Latinos and Asians, since the extreme segregation of blacks is well known (Massey and Denton 1993; Yinger 1995).

Latinos are less segregated from and more exposed to whites than blacks (Massey and Denton 1987; Charles 2003). Yet it is also true that dark-skinned Latinos experience blacklike rates of residential segregation from whites. Early research on Latino immigrant settlement patterns in Chicago, for example, showed that Mexicans and Puerto Ricans were relegated to spaces largely occupied by blacks, in part because of skin color discrimination (Betancur 1996). More contemporary studies also demonstrate the race effect on Latino residential segregation patterns. Latinos who identify as white, primarily Cubans and South Americans, are considerably more likely to reside in areas with non-Latino whites than are Latinos who identify as black, mainly Dominicans and Puerto Ricans (Logan 2001; Alba and Logan 1993; Massey and Bitterman 1985).

Asian Americans are the least segregated of all the minority groups. However, they have experienced an increase in residential segregation in recent years (Frey and Farley 1996; White, Biddlecom, and Guo 1993). In a recent review, Camille Charles (2003) finds that from 1980 to 2000 the index of dissimilarity for Asians had increased three points (from 37 to 40) while the exposure to whites had declined sixteen points (from 88 to 62).[13] Part of the increase in segregation (and the concomitant decrease in exposure) may be the result of the arrival of newer immigrants from Southeast Asia (Vietnam, Cambodia, and Laos) over the last two decades (Frey and Farley 1996). For example the Vietnamese—who, we theorize, will be considered part of the collective black during the Latin Americanization process—have almost doubled their U.S. presence during the 1990 to 2000 period (Logan 2001). The majority of residential segregation studies are based on black-Latino-Asian proximity to whites and thus limit an examination of intragroup differences among Asians (and Latinos). Nevertheless, the totality of the lower dissimilarity indexes and higher exposure indexes for Asians to whites vis-à-vis Latinos—and particularly blacks—to whites tends to fit our prediction that the bulk of Asians belong to the honorary white category. Phenotype research on blacks, Latinos, and Asians, based on subgroup research within each category, is needed in order for studies on the effect of skin color to fully develop.

CONCLUSION

We have presented a broad and bold thesis about the future of racial stratification in the United States.[14] However, at this early stage of the analysis, and given the serious limitations of the data on "Latinos" and "Asians" (the data are not generally parceled out by subgroups and little is separated by skin tone)

it is hard to make a conclusive case. It is possible that factors such as nativity or socioeconomic characteristics explain some of the patterns we documented.[15] Nevertheless, almost all of the objective, subjective, and social interaction indicators we reviewed go in the direction of Latin Americanization. For example, the objective data clearly show substantial gaps between the groups we labeled "white," "honorary white," and "collective black." In terms of income and education, whites tend to be slightly better off than honorary whites, who are in turn significantly better off than the collective black. Not surprisingly a variety of subjective indicators signal the emergence of *internal* stratification among racial minorities. For example, whereas some Latinos (such as Cubans, Argentines, and Chileans) are very likely to self-classify as whites, others do not (for example, Dominicans and Puerto Ricans living in the United States). This has resulted in a racial attitudinal profile—at least in terms of subscription to stereotypical views about groups—similar to that of whites. Finally, the objective and subjective indicators have a behavioral correlate. Data on interracial marriage and residential segregation show that whites are significantly more likely to live near and intermarry with honorary whites than with members of the collective black.

If our predictions are right, what will be the consequences of Latin Americanization for race relations in the United States? First, racial politics will change dramatically. The "us-versus-them" racial dynamic will lessen as honorary whites grow in size and social importance. They are likely to buffer racial conflict—or derail it—as intermediate groups do in many Latin American countries. Second, the ideology of color-blind racism will become even more salient among whites and honorary whites and will also have an impact on members of the collective black. Color-blind racism (Bonilla-Silva 2001), similar to the ideology prevalent in Latin American societies, will help glue the new social system and further buffer racial conflict.

Third, if the state decides to stop gathering racial statistics, the struggle to document the impact of race in a variety of social venues will become monumental. More significantly, because state actions always have an impact on civil society, if the state decides to erase race from above, the *social* recognition of "races" in the polity may become harder. We may develop a Latin American–like "disgust" for even mentioning anything that is race-related.

Fourth, the deep history of black-white divisions in the United States has been such that the centrality of the black identity will not dissipate. Even the research on the "black elite" shows that this group exhibits racial attitudes in line with their racial group (Dawson 1994). That identity, as we argue, . . . may be taken up by dark-skinned Latinos, as it is being rapidly taken up by most West Indians. For example, Al, a fifty-three-year-old Jamaican engineer interviewed by Milton Vickerman (1999, 199), stated:

> I have nothing against Haitians; I have nothing against black Americans. . . . If you're a nigger, you're a nigger, regardless of whether you are from Timbuktu. . . . There isn't the unity that one would like to see. . . . Blacks have to appreciate blacks, no matter where they are from. Just look at it the way I look at it: That you're the same.

However, even among blacks, we predict some important changes. Namely blacks' racial consciousness will become more diffused. For example, blacks will be more likely to accept many stereotypes about themselves (for example, "We are lazier than whites") and to have a "blunted oppositional consciousness" (see Bonilla-Silva 2001, ch. 6). Furthermore, the external pressure of "multiracials" in white contexts (Rockquemore and Brunsma 2002) and the internal pressure of "ethnic" blacks may change the notion of "blackness" and even the position of some "blacks" in the system. Colorism may become an even more important factor as a way of making social distinctions among "blacks" (Keith and Herring 1991).

Fifth, the new racial stratification system will be more effective in maintaining "white supremacy" (Mills 1997). Whites will still be at the top of the social structure but will face fewer race-based challenges. As an aside, to avoid confusion about our claim about "honorary whites," it is important to note that their standing and status will be subject to whites' wishes and practices. "Honorary" means that they will remain secondary, will still face discrimination, and will not receive equal treatment in society. For example, although Arab Americans should be regarded as honorary whites, their treatment in the post–September 11 era suggests that their status as "white" and "American" is very tenuous.

Although some analysts and commentators may welcome Latin Americanization as a positive trend in American race relations, those at the bottom of the racial hierarchy will discover that behind the statement, "We are all Americans," hides a deeper, hegemonic way of maintaining white supremacy. As a Latin America–*like* society, the United States will become a society with more rather than less racial inequality, but with a reduced forum for racial contestation.[16] The apparent blessing of "not seeing race" will become a curse for those struggling for racial justice in the years to come. We may become "all Americans," as television commercials in recent times suggest. But to paraphrase George Orwell, "some will be more American than others."

DISCUSSION QUESTIONS

1. What are the indications of the development of a tri-racial stratification system?
2. What are the potential consequences of Latin Americanization in the United States?
3. How accurate is the term "honorary white"?

NOTES

1. Since September 11, 2001, the United States has embarked on what we regard as temporary "social peace." Hence, in post–September 11 America the motto "We are all Americans" is commonplace. This new attitude can be seen in pronouncements by politicians and television commercials parading the multiracial nature of the country. Notably, however, there are no commercials presenting interracial unions, which suggests that we may all be Americans, but we still have our own subnational or primary racial associations. Moreover, this new attitude has not changed the status differences between minorities and whites, between men and women, or between workers and capitalists. Lastly, this new nationalism excludes "foreigners," dark people, those

who are not Christian, and those with unfashionable accents (German and French accents are acceptable). In short, this new Americanism, like the old Americanism, is a *herrenvolk* nationalism (Lipsitz 1998; Winant 1994).

2. To be clear, our contention is not that the black-white dynamic has ordained race relations throughout the United States, but that at the national macro level, race relations have been organized along a white-nonwhite divide. This large divide, depending on context, has included various racial groups (whites, blacks, and Indians or whites, Mexicans, Indians, and blacks or other combinations). However, under the white-nonwhite racial order, "whites" have often been treated as superior and "nonwhites" as inferior. For a few exceptions to this pattern, see Reginald Daniel's (2002) discussion of "tri-racial isolates."

3. We are adapting Antonio Negri's (1984) idea of the "collective worker" to the situation of all those at the bottom of the racial stratification system.

4. Kerry Ann Rockquemore and Patricia Arend (forthcoming) have predicted, based on data from a mixed-race (one black parent and one white parent) student sample, that most mixed-race people will be honorary whites, a significant component will belong to the collective black, and a few will move into the white strata.

5. A middle racial stratum emerged in the United States in South Carolina and Louisiana and in eighteenth- and nineteenth-century South Africa (Fredrickson 1981). However, in both cases the status of the intermediate stratum later changed because of political necessities (South Africa) or because it was a peculiar situation that could not affect the larger, national pattern (United States). In South Africa the "colored" group was reintroduced at a later point, and in South Carolina and Louisiana those in the intermediate stratum to this day maintain a sense of *difference* from their black brethren.

6. This challenges the romantic view that Latin American states and societies were more pluralist than Great Britain or France because of their Catholic religion or their supposedly less prejudicial attitudes toward Africans; see Marx (1998) and Morner (1993).

7. Few Latin Americans object to the fact that most politicians in their societies are "white" (by Latin American standards). Yet it is interesting to point out that Latin American elites always object to the few "minority" politicians on *racial* grounds. Two recent cases are the racist opposition in the Dominican Republic to the election of the black candidate José Peña Gómez (Howard 2001) and the opposition by the business elite to the mulatto president Hugo Cesar Chávez in Venezuela.

8. When pushed to choose a racial descriptor, many Latin Americans self-describe as white or highlight their white heritage, regardless of how remote or minimal it is. For example, according to a recent study in a community in Brazil, one-third of the Afro-Brazilians were registered as whites, and a large proportion of the remainder were registered as pardos (Twine 1998, 114). For a similar discussion on Puerto Ricans see Torres (1998).

9. Specifically, whereas the Bolivian census of 2001 reports that 71 percent of Bolivians self-identify as Indian, fewer than 20 percent have more than a high school diploma, and 58.6 percent live below the poverty line. By contrast, 66 percent of Bolivians in the United States self-identify as white, 64 percent have twelve or more years of education, and they enjoy a per capita income comparable to that of whites (Censo Nacional de Población y Vivienda 2002). In short, Bolivians in the United States do not represent Bolivians in Bolivia. Instead, they are a self-selected group.

10. The concentration of Puerto Ricans in the lower occupational categories is slightly below 50 percent. However, looking specifically at the category "sales and office," where 20.46 percent of Puerto Ricans are located, Puerto Ricans are more likely to be in the lower-paying jobs within this broad category.

11. It is important to point out that occupational representation in a category does not mean equality. The work of Sucheng Chan (1991) shows that many Asians are pushed into self-employment after suffering occupational sedimentation in professional jobs; see also Takaki (1993).

12. Survey experiments have shown that if the question on Hispanic origin is asked first, the proportion of Latinos who report being white increases from 25 to 39 percent (Martin, Demaio, and Campanelli 1990). The same research also shows that when Latinos report belonging to the "other" category, they are not mistaken. That is, they do want to signify that they are neither black nor white. Unfortunately, we do not have results by national groups. Are Cubans more likely to claim to be white if the order of the questions is changed? Or is the finding symmetrical for all groups? However these questions may be answered, we think this finding does not alter the direction of the overall findings on the self-identification of various Latino groups.

13. The dissimilarity index expresses the percentage of a minority population that would have to move to result in a perfectly even distribution of the population across census tracts. This index runs from 0 (no segregation) to 100 (total segregation), and it is symmetrical (not affected by population size). The exposure index measures the degree of potential contact between two populations (majority and minority) and expresses the probability of a member of a minority group meeting a member of the majority group. Like the dissimilarity index, it runs from 1 to 100, but unlike that index, it is asymmetrical (it is affected by the population size).

14. We are not alone in making this kind of prediction. Arthur K. Spears (1999), Suzanne Oboler (2000), Gary Okihiro (1994), and Mari Matsuda (1996) have made similar claims recently.

15. An important matter to disentangle empirically is whether it is color, nativity, education, or class that determines where groups fit in our scheme. A powerful alternative explanation for many of our preliminary findings is that the groups we label "honorary whites" come with high levels of human capital *before* they achieve honorary white status in the United States. That is, they fit this intermediate position not because of their color or race but because of their class background. Although this is a plausible alternative explanation that we hope to examine in the future, some available data suggest that race-color has something to do with the success of immigrants in the United States. For example, the experience of West Indians—who come to the United States with class advantages (educational and otherwise) and yet "fade to black" in a few generations—suggests that the "racial" status of the group has an independent effect in the process (Model 1991; Kasinitz, Battle, and Miyares 2001). It is also important to point out that even when some of these groups do well objectively, an examination of their returns to their characteristics, such as the monetary "return" on their education investment, when compared to whites, reveals how little they get for what they bring (Butcher 1994). And as Mary Waters and Karl Eschbach (1995, 442) stated in a review of the literature on immigration, "the evidence indicates that direct discrimination is still an important factor for all minority subgroups except very highly educated Asians." Even highly educated and acculturated Asians, such as Filipinos, report high levels of racial discrimination in the labor market. Not surprisingly, second- and third-generation Filipinos self-identity as Filipino American rather than as white or "American" (Espiritu and Wolf 2001). For a similar finding on Vietnamese, see Zhou (2001), and for a discussion of the indeterminate relation between education and income among many other groups, see Portes and Rumbaut (1990).

16. "Latin America–like" does not mean exactly "like Latin America." The four-hundred-year history of American "racial formation" (Omi and Winant 1994) has stained the racial stratification order forever. Thus, we expect some important differences in this new American racial stratification system compared to that of Latin American societies. First, "shade discrimination" (Kinsbrunner 1996) will not work perfectly. Hence, for example, although Asian Indians are dark-skinned, they will still be higher in the stratification system than, for example, Mexican American mestizos. Second, Arabs, Asian Indians, and other non-Christian groups will not be allowed complete upward mobility. Third, because of the three hundred years of dramatic racialization and group formation, most members of the nonwhite group will maintain ethnic (Puerto Ricans) or racial (blacks) claims and demand group-based rights.

REFERENCES

Alba, Richard D., and John R. Logan. 1993. "Minority Proximity to Whites in Suburbs: An Individual-Level Analysis of Segregation." *American Journal of Sociology* 98(6): 1388–1427.

Andrews, George R. 1991. *Blacks and Whites in São Paulo, Brazil, 1888–1988.* Madison: University of Wisconsin Press.

Balibar, Etienne, and Immanuel Wallerstein. 1991. *Race, Nation, and Class: Ambiguous Identities.* London: Verso.

Betancur, John J. 1996. "The Settlement Experience of Latinos in Chicago: Segregation, Speculation, and the Ecology Model." *Social Forces* 74(4): 1299–1324.

Bonilla-Silva, Eduardo. 1999. "The Essential Social Fact of Race: A Reply to Loveman. *American Sociological Review* 64(6): 899–906.

———. 2001 *White Supremacy and Racism in the Post Civil Rights Era.* Boulder, Colo.: Lynne Rienner.

Bonilla-Silva, Eduardo, and Gianpaolo Baiocchi, 2001. "Anything but Racism: How Sociologists Limit the Significance of Racism." *Race and Society* 4(2001): 117–31.

Bonilla-Silva, Eduardo, and Amanda E. Lewis. 1999. "The New Racism: Toward an Analysis of the U.S. Racial Structure, 1960s to 1990s." In *Race, Nation, and Citizenship,* edited by Paul Wong. Boulder, Colo.: Westview Press.

Bottomore, Thomas B. 1968. *Classes in Modern Society.* New York: Vintage Books.

Brooks, Roy L. 1990. *Rethinking the American Race Problem.* Berkeley: University of California Press.

Butcher, Kristin F. 1994. "Black Immigrants in the United States: A Comparison with Native Blacks and Other Immigrants." *Industrial and Labor Relations Review* 47: 265–84.

Castles, Stephen, and Mark Miller. 1993. *The Age of Migration: International Population Movements in the Modern World.* Hong Kong: Macmillan.

Censo Nacional de Población y Vivienda. 2002. *Bolivia: Caraterísticas de la Población.* Serie Resultados, vol. 4. La Paz: Ministerio de Hacienda.

Chan, Sucheng. 1991. *Asian Americans: An Interpretive History.* Boston: Twayne.

Charles, Camille Zubrinsky. 2003. "The Dynamics of Racial Residential Segregation." *Annual Review of Sociology* 29: 167–207.

Cohen, Robin. 1997. *Global Diasporas: An Introduction.* Seattle: University of Washington Press.

Daniels, Reginald G. 2002. *More Than Black? Multiracial Identity and the New Racial Order.* Philadelphia: Temple University Press.

Dawson, Michael C. 1994. *Behind the Mule. Race and Class in African American Politics.* Princeton, N.J.: Princeton University Press.

———. 2000. "Slowly Coming to Grips with the Effects of the American Racial Order on American Policy Preferences." In *Racialized Politics,* edited by David O. Sears, Jim Sidanius, and Lawrence Bobo. Chicago: University of Chicago Press.

Degler, Carl N. 1986. *Neither Black nor White: Slavery and Race Relations in Brazil and the United States.* Madison: University of Wisconsin Press.

De la Fuente, Alejandro. 2001. *A Nation for All Race Inequality, and Politics in Twentieth-Century Cuba.* Chapel Hill: University of North Carolina Press.

De la Garza, Rodolfo O., Louis DeSipio, F. Chris Garcia, John Garcia, and Angelo Falcon, eds. 1992. *Latino Voices: Mexican, Puerto Rican, and Cuban Perspectives on American Politics.* Boulder, Colo.: Westview Press.

Do Nascimento, Abdias, and Elisa Larkin-Nascimento. 2001. "Dance of Deception: A Reading of Race Relations in Brazil." In *Beyond Racism,* edited by Charles Hamilton et al. Boulder: Lynne Rienner.

Espiritu, Yen Le. 1992. *Asian American Pan-ethnicity: Bridging Institutions and Identities.* Philadelphia: Temple University Press.

Espiritu, Yen Le, and Diane L. Wolf. 2001. "The Paradox of Assimilation: Children of Filipino Immigrants in San Diego." In *Ethnicities: Children of Immigrants in America,* edited by Rubén G. Rumbaut and Alejandro Portes, Berkeley: University of California Press.

Fitzpatrick, Joseph. 1971. *Puerto Rican Americans.* Englewood Cliffs, N.J. Prentice-Hall.

Fredrickson, George M. 1981. *White Supremacy.* Oxford: Oxford University Press.

Frey, William H., and Reynolds Farley. 1996. "Latino, Asian, and Black Segregation in U.S. Metropolitan Areas: Are Multi-ethnic Metros Different? *Demography* 33(1): 35–50.

Freyre, Gilberto. 1959. *New World in the Tropics: The Culture of Modern Brazil.* New York: Alfred A. Knopf.

Gans, Herbert J. 1999. *The Possibility of a New Racial Hierarchy in the Twenty-first-Century United States,* edited by Michele Lamont. Chicago: University of Chicago Press.

Gilbertson, Greta A., Joseph P. Fitzpatrick, and Lijun Yang. 1996. "Hispanic Intermarriage in New York City: New Evidence from 1991." *International Migration Review* 30(2): 445–59.

Goldberg, David T. 1993. *Racist Culture: Philosophy and the Politics of Meaning* Cambridge, Mass.: Blackwell.

———. 2002. *The Racial State.* Malden, Mass.: Blackwell.

Grieco, Elizabeth M., and Rachel C. Cassidy. 2001. *Overview of Race and Hispanic Origin 2000.* Washington: U.S. Government Printing Office.

Guerra, Lillian. 1998. *Popular Expression and National Identity in Puerto Rico: The Struggle for Self, Community, and Nation.* Gainesville: University Press of Florida.

Hanchard, Michael. 1994. *Orpheus and Power: The Movimiento Negro of Rio de Janeiro and Sâo Paulo, Brazil, 1945–1988.* Princeton, N.J.: Princeton University Press.

Hasenbalg, Carlos A. 1985. "Race and Socioeconomic Inequalities in Brazil." In *Race, Class, and Power in Brazil,* edited by Pierre-Michel Fontaine. Los Angeles: University of California Press and Center for African American Studies.

Hasenbalg, Carlos A., and Nelson do Valle Silva. 1999. "Notes on Racial and Political Inequality in Brazil." In *Racial Politics in Contemporary Brazil,* edited by Michael George Hanchard. Durham, N.C.: Duke University Press.

Helg, Aline. 1990. "Race in Argentina and Cuba, 1880–1930: Theory, Policies, and Popular Reaction." In *The Idea of Race in Latin America, 1870–1940,* edited by Richard Graham. Austin: University of Texas Press.

Hoetink, Harry. 1967. *The Two Variants in Caribbean Race Relations: A Contribution to the Sociology of Segmented Societies.* Oxford: Oxford University Press.

———. 1971. *Caribbean Race Relations: A Study of Two Variants.* London: Oxford University Press.

Howard, David. 2001. *Coloring the Nation: Race and Ethnicity in the Dominican Republic.* Boulder, Colo.: Lynne Rienner.

Kasinitz, Philip, Juan Battle, and Ines Miyares. 2001. "Fade to Black? The Children of West Indian Immigrants in Southern Florida." In *Ethnicities: Children of Immigrants in America,* edited by Rubén G. Rumbaut and Alejandro Portes. Berkeley: University of California Press.

Kasper, Deana. 2000. "'Y tu abuela donde está' (And your grandmother, where is she?)." Ph.D. diss., Texas A&M University.

Keith, Verna M., and Cedric Herring. 1991. "Skin Tone and Stratification in the Black Community." *American Journal of Sociology* 97(3): 760–78.

Kinsbrunner, Jay. 1996. *Not of Pure Blood: The Free People of Color and Racial Prejudice in Nineteenth-Century Puerto Rico.* Durham, N.C.: Duke University Press.

Kitano, Harry H. L., and Roger Daniels. 1995. *Asian Americans: Emerging Minorities,* 2nd ed. Englewood Cliffs, N.J.: Prentice-Hall.

Lipsitz, George. 1998. *The Possessive Investment in Whiteness: How White People Profit from Identity Politics.* Philadelphia: Temple University Press.

Logan, John R. 2001. *From Many Shores: Asians in Census 2000.* Report by the Lewis Mumford Center for Comparative Urban and Regional Research. Albany, N.Y.: University of Albany.

Lovell, Peggy A., and Charles H. Wood. 1998. "Skin Color, Racial Identity, and Life Chances in Brazil." *Latin American Perspectives* 25(3): 90–109.

Lusane, Clarence. 1997. *Race in the Global Era: African Americans at the Millennium.* Boston: South End Press.

Martin, Elizabeth, Theresa J. Demaio, and Pamela C. Campanelli. 1990. "Context Effects for Census Measures of Race and Hispanic Origin." *Public Opinion Quarterly* 54(4): 551–66.

Martínez-Alier, Verena. 1974. *Marriage, Class and Color in Nineteenth-Century Cuba: A Study of Racial Attitudes and Sexual Values in a Slave Society.* London: Cambridge University Press.

Martínez-Echazabal, Lourdes. 1998. "Mestizaje and the Discourse of National Cultural Identity in Latin America, 1845–1959." *Latin American Perspectives.* 25(3): 21–42.

Marx, Anthony W. 1998. *Making Race and Nation.* Cambridge: Cambridge University Press.

Massey, Douglas S., and Brooks Bitterman. 1985. "Explaining the Paradox of Puerto Rican Segregation." *Social Forces* 64(2): 306–31.

Massey, Douglas S., and Nancy A. Denton. 1987. "Trends in the Residential Segregation of Blacks, Hispanics, and Asians: 1970–1980." *American Sociological Review* 52(6): 802–25.

———. 1993. *American Apartheid.* Cambridge, Mass.: Harvard University Press.

Matsuda, Mari J. 1996. *Where Is Your Body? and Other Essays on Race, Gender, and the Law.* Boston: Beacon Press.

Miles, Robert. 1993. *Racism After Race Relations.* London: Routledge.

Mills, Charles W. 1997. *The Racial Contract.* Ithaca, N.Y.: Cornell University Press.

Model, Suzanne. 1991. "Caribbean Immigrants: A Black Success Story?" *International Migration Review* 25(2): 248–76.

Moran, Rachel. 2001. *Interracial Intimacy: The Regulation of Race and Romance* Chicago: University of Chicago Press.

Morner, Magnus. 1967. *Race Mixture in the History of Latin America.* Boston Little, Brown.

———. 1993. *Region and State in Latin America.* Baltimore: Johns Hopkins University Press.

Negri, Antonio. 1984. *Marx Beyond Marx: Lessons on the Grundrisse,* edited by Jim Fleming. South Hadley, Mass.: Bergin & Garvey.

Oboler, Suzanne. 2000. "It Must Be a Fake!" Racial Ideologies, Identities, and the Question of Rights in Hispanics-Latinos." In *The United States: Ethnicity, Race, and Rights,* edited by Jorge J. E. Gracia and Pablo de Greiff. New York: Routledge.

Okihiro, Gary. 1994. *Margins and Mainstreams: Asians in American History and Culture.* Seattle: University of Washington Press.

Omi, Michael, and Howard Winant. 1994. *Racial Formation in the United States from the 1960s to the 1990s.* New York: Routledge.

Portes, Alejandro, and Rubén Rumbaut. 1990. *Immigrant America: A Portrait.* Berkeley: University of California Press.

Ridgeway, Cecilia L. 1991. "The Social Construction of Status Value: Gender and Other Nominal Characteristics." *Social Forces* 70(2): 367–86.

Rockquemore, Kerry Ann, and Patricia Arend. Forthcoming. Opting for White: Choice, Fluidity, and Black Identity Construction in Post–Civil Rights America." *Race and Society.*

Rockquemore, Kerry Ann, and David L. Brunsma. 2002. *Beyond Black: Biracial Identity in America.* Thousand Oaks, Calif.: Sage Publications.

Rodríguez. Clara E. 1991. *Puerto Ricans Born in the U.S.A.* Boulder, Colo.: Westview Press.

———. 2000. *Changing Race: Latinos, the Census, and the History of Ethnicity in the United States.* New York: New York University Press.

Rodriguez, Victor M. 1998. "Boricuas, African Americans, and Chicanos in the 'Far West': Notes on the Puerto Rican Pro Independence Movement in California, 1960s–1980s." *New Political Science* 20(4, December): 421–39.

Saito, Leland T. 1998. *Race and Politics: Asian Americans, Latinos, and Whites in a Los Angeles Suburb.* Urbana: University of Illinois Press.

San Juan, Epifanio, Jr. 2000. "The Limits of Ethnicity and the Horizon of Historical Materialism." In *Asian American Studies: Identity. Images, Issues Past and Present,* edited by Esther Mikyung Ghymn. New York: Peter Lang.

Schoenbaum, David, and Elizabeth Pond. 1996. *The German Question and Other German Questions.* New York: St. Martin's Press.

Silva do Valle, Nelson. 1985. "Updating the Cost of Not Being White in Brazil." In *Race, Class, and Power in Brazil,* edited by Pierre-Michel Fontaine. Los Angeles: University of California Press and Center for Afro-American Studies.

Skidmore, Thomas E. 1990. "Racial Ideas and Social Policy in Brazil, 1870–1940." In *The Idea of Race in Latin America, 1870–1940,* edited by Richard Graham. Austin: University of Texas Press.

Smith, Robert C. 1995. *Racism in the Post–Civil Rights Era: Now You See It, Now You Don't.* Albany: State University of New York Press.

Spears, Arthur K. 1999. *Race and Ideology: Language, Symbolism, and Popular Culture.* Detroit: Wayne State University Press.

Spoonley, Paul. 1996. "Mahi Awatea? The Racialization of Work in Aotearoa/New Zealand." In *Nga Patai: Racism and Ethnic Relations in Aotearoa/New Zealand,* edited by Paul Spoonley, David Pearson, and Cluny Macpherson. Palmerston North, N.Z.: Dunmore Press.

Tajfel, Henri. 1970. "Experiments in Intergroup Discrimination." *Scientific American* 223: 96–102.

Takaki, Ronald. 1993. *A Different Mirror: A History of Multicultural America.* Boston: Little, Brown.

Telles, Edward E. 1999. "Ethnic Boundaries and Political Mobilization Among African Brazilians: Comparisons with the U.S. Case." In *Racial Politics in Contemporary Brazil,* edited by Michael Hanchard. Durham, N.C.: Duke University Press.

Torres, Arlene. 1998. "La gran familia Puetorriqueña 'El Prieta de Beldá'" (The Great Puerto Rican Family Is Really Really Black). In *Blackness in Latin America and the Caribbean,* vol. 2. Bloomington: Indiana University Press.

Trouillot, Michel-Rolph. 1990. *Haiti, State Against Nation: Origins and Legacy of Duvalierism.* New York: Monthly Review Press.

Twine, France Winddance. 1998. *Racism in a Racial Democracy.* New Brunswick, N.J.: Rutgers University Press.

U.S. Department of Commerce. U.S. Bureau of the Census. 1996. *Population Projections of the United States by Age, Sex, Race, and Hispanic Origin: 1995 to 2050.* Washington: U.S. Government Printing Office.

Vickerman, Milton. 1999. *Crosscurrents: West Indian Immigrants and Race.* New York: Oxford University Press.

Wade, Peter. 1997. *Race and Ethnicity in Latin America.* London: Pluto Press.

Wagley, Charles. 1952. *Race and Class in Rural Brazil.* Paris: UNESCO.

Warren, Jonathan W., and France Winddance Twine. 1997. "White Americans, the New Minority? Nonblacks and the Ever-Expanding Boundaries of Whiteness." *Journal of Black Studies* 28(2): 200–18.

Waters, Mary C. 1999. *Black Identities: West Indian Immigrant Dreams and American Realities.* New York and Cambridge, Mass.: Russell Sage Foundation and Harvard University Press.

Waters, Mary C., and Karl Eschbach. 1995. "Immigration and Ethnic and Racial Inequality in the United States." *Annual Review of Sociology* 21: 419–46.

Weiner, Michael. 1997. *Japan's Minorities: The Illusion of Homogeneity.* London: Routledge.

White, Michael J., Ann E. Biddlecom, and Shenyang Guo. 1993. "Immigration, Naturalization, and Residential Assimilation Among Asian Americans in 1980." *Social Forces* 72(1): 93–117.

Winant, Howard. 1994. *Racial Conditions: Politics, Theory, Comparisons.* Minneapolis: University of Minnesota Press.

———. 2001. *The World Is a Ghetto.* New York: Basic Books.

Yinger, John. 1995. *Closed Doors, Opportunities Lost: The Continuing Costs of Housing Discrimination.* New York: Russell Sage Foundation.

Zhou, Min. 2001. "Straddling Different Worlds: The Acculturation of Vietnamese Refugee Children." In *Ethnicities: Children of Immigrants in America,* edited by Rubén G. Rumbaut and Alejandro Portes. Berkeley: University of California Press.

WHAT IS SEX? WHAT IS GENDER?

READING 9

The Five Sexes, Revisited

Anne Fausto-Sterling

As Cheryl Chase stepped to the front of the packed meeting room in the Sheraton Boston Hotel, nervous coughs made the tension audible. Chase, an activist for intersexual rights, had been invited to address the May 2000 meeting of the Lawson Wilkins Pediatric Endocrine Society (LWPES), the largest organization in the United States for specialists in children's hormones. Her talk would be the grand finale to a four-hour symposium on the treatment of genital ambiguity in newborns, infants born with a mixture of both male and female anatomy, or genitals that appear to differ from their

chromosomal sex. The topic was hardly a novel one to the assembled physicians.

Yet Chase's appearance before the group was remarkable. Three and a half years earlier, the American Academy of Pediatrics had refused her request for a chance to present the patients' viewpoint on the treatment of genital ambiguity, dismissing Chase and her supporters as "zealots." About two dozen intersex people had responded by throwing up a picket line. The Intersex Society of North America (ISNA) even issued a press release: "Hermaphrodites Target Kiddie Docs."

It had done my 1960s street-activist heart good. In the short run, I said to Chase at the time, the picketing would make people angry. But eventually, I assured her, the doors then closed would open. Now, as Chase began to address the physicians at their own convention, that prediction was coming true. Her talk, titled "Sexual Ambiguity: The Patient-Centered Approach," was a measured critique of the near-universal practice of performing immediate, "corrective" surgery on thousands of infants born each year with ambiguous

---

Anne Fausto-Sterling is a professor of biology and gender studies at Brown University.

genitalia. Chase herself lives with the consequences of such surgery. Yet her audience, the very endocrinologists and surgeons Chase was accusing of reacting with "surgery and shame," received her with respect. Even more remarkably, many of the speakers who preceded her at the session had already spoken of the need to scrap current practices in favor of treatments more centered on psychological counseling.

What led to such a dramatic reversal of fortune? Certainly, Chase's talk at the LWPES symposium was a vindication of her persistence in seeking attention for her cause. But her invitation to speak was also a watershed in the evolving discussion about how to treat children with ambiguous genitalia. And that discussion, in turn, is the tip of a bicultural iceberg—the gender iceberg—that continues to rock both medicine and our culture at large.

Chase made her first national appearance in 1993, . . . announcing the formation of ISNA in a letter responding to an essay I had written for *The Sciences,* titled "The Five Sexes" [March/April 1993]. In that article I argued that the two-sex system embedded in our society is not adequate to encompass the full spectrum of human sexuality. In its place, I suggested a five-sex system. In addition to males and females, I included "herms" (named after true hermaphrodites, people born with both a testis and an ovary); "merms" (male pseudohermaphrodites, who are born with testes and some aspect of female genitalia); and "ferms" (female pseudohermaphrodites, who have ovaries combined with some aspect of male genitalia).

I had intended to be provocative, but I had also written with tongue firmly in cheek. So I was surprised by the extent of the controversy the article unleashed. Right-wing Christians were outraged, and connected my idea of five sexes with the United Nations–sponsored Fourth World Conference on Women, held in Beijing in September 1995. At the same time, the article delighted others who felt constrained by the current sex and gender system.

Clearly, I had struck a nerve. The fact that so many people could get riled up by my proposal to revamp our sex and gender system suggested that change—as well as resistance to it—might be in the

offing. Indeed, a lot has changed since 1993, and I like to think that my article was an important stimulus. As if from nowhere, intersexuals are materializing before our very eyes. Like Chase, many have become political organizers, who lobby physicians and politicians to change current treatment practices. But more generally, though perhaps no less provocatively, the boundaries separating masculine and feminine seem harder than ever to define.

Some find the changes under way deeply disturbing. Others find them liberating.

Who is an intersexual—and how many intersexuals are there? The concept of intersexuality is rooted in the very ideas of male and female. In the idealized, Platonic, biological world, human beings are divided into two kinds: a perfectly dimorphic species. Males have an X and a Y chromosome, testes, a penis and all of the appropriate internal plumbing for delivering urine and semen to the outside world. They also have well-known secondary sexual characteristics, including a muscular build and facial hair. Women have two X chromosomes, ovaries, all of the internal plumbing to transport urine and ova to the outside world, a system to support pregnancy and fetal development, as well as a variety of recognizable secondary sexual characteristics.

That idealized story papers over many obvious caveats: some women have facial hair, some men have none; some women speak with deep voices, some men veritably squeak. Less well known is the fact that, on close inspection, absolute dimorphism disintegrates even at the level of basic biology. Chromosomes, hormones, the internal sex structures, the gonads and the external genitalia all vary more than most people realize. Those born outside of the Platonic dimorphic mold are called intersexuals.

In "The Five Sexes" I reported an estimate by a psychologist expert in the treatment of intersexuals, suggesting that some 4 percent of all live births are intersexual. Then, together with a group of Brown University undergraduates, I set out to conduct the first systematic assessment of the available data on intersexual birthrates. We scoured the medical literature for estimates of the frequency of various categories of intersexuality, from additional chromosomes to mixed gonads, hormones and genitalia. For some conditions we could find only anecdotal evidence; for most, however, numbers exist. On the basis of that evidence, we calculated that for every 1,000 children born, seventeen are intersexual in some form. That number—1.7 percent—is a ballpark estimate, not a precise count, though we believe it is more accurate than the 4 percent I reported.

Our figure represents all chromosomal, anatomical and hormonal exceptions to the dimorphic ideal; the number of intersexuals who might, potentially, be subject to surgery as infants is smaller—probably between one in 1,000 and one in 2,000 live births. Furthermore, because some populations possess the relevant genes at high frequency, the intersexual birthrate is not uniform throughout the world.

Consider, for instance, the gene for congenital adrenal hyperplasia (CAH). When the CAH gene is inherited from both parents, it leads to a baby with masculinized external genitalia who possesses two X chromosomes and the internal reproductive organs of a potentially fertile woman. The frequency of the gene varies widely around the world: in New Zealand it occurs in only forty-three children per million; among the Yupik Eskimo of southwestern Alaska, its frequency is 3,500 per million.

Intersexuality has always been to some extent a matter of definition. And in the past century physicians have been the ones who defined children as intersexual—and provided the remedies. When only the chromosomes are unusual, but the external genitalia and gonads clearly indicate either a male or a female, physicians do not advocate intervention. Indeed, it is not clear what kind of intervention could be advocated in such cases. But the story is quite different when infants are born with mixed genitalia, or with external genitals that seem at odds with the baby's gonads. Most clinics now specializing in the treatment of intersex babies rely on case-management principles developed in the 1950s by the psychologist John Money and the psychiatrists Joan G. Hampson and John L. Hampson, all of Johns Hopkins University in Baltimore, Maryland. Money believed that gender identity is completely malleable for about eighteen months after birth. Thus, he argued, when a treatment team

is presented with an infant who has ambiguous genitalia, the team could make a gender assignment solely on the basis of what made the best surgical sense. The physicians could then simply encourage the parents to raise the child according to the surgically assigned gender. Following that course, most physicians maintained, would eliminate psychological distress for both the patient and the parents. Indeed, treatment teams were never to use such words as "intersex" or "hermaphrodite"; instead, they were to tell parents that nature intended the baby to be the boy or the girl that the physicians had determined it was. Through surgery, the physicians were merely completing nature's intention.

Although Money and the Hampsons published detailed case studies of intersex children who they said had adjusted well to their gender assignments, Money thought one case in particular proved his theory. It was a dramatic example, inasmuch as it did not involve intersexuality at all: one of a pair of identical twin boys lost his penis as a result of a circumcision accident. Money recommended that "John" (as he came to be known in a later case study) be surgically turned into "Joan" and raised as a girl. In time, Joan grew to love wearing dresses and having her hair done. Money proudly proclaimed the sex reassignment a success.

But as recently chronicled by John Colapinto, in his book *As Nature Made Him*, Joan—now known to be an adult male named David Reimer—eventually rejected his female assignment. Even without a functioning penis and testes (which had been removed as part of the reassignment) John/Joan sought masculinizing medication, and married a woman with children (whom he adopted).

Since the full conclusion to the John/Joan story came to light, other individuals who were reassigned as males or females shortly after birth but who later rejected their early assignments have come forward. So, too, have cases in which the reassignment has worked—at least into the subject's mid-twenties. But even then the aftermath of the surgery can be problematic. Genital surgery often leaves scars that reduce sexual sensitivity. Chase herself had a complete clitoridectomy, a procedure that is less frequently performed on intersexuals today. But the newer surgeries, which reduce the size of the clitoral shaft, still greatly reduce sensitivity.

The revelation of cases of failed reassignments and the emergence of intersex activism have led an increasing number of pediatric endocrinologists, urologists and psychologists to reexamine the wisdom of early genital surgery. For example, in a talk that preceded Chase's at the LWPES meeting, the medical ethicist Laurence B. McCullough of the Center for Medical Ethics and Health Policy at Baylor College of Medicine in Houston, Texas, introduced an ethical framework for the treatment of children with ambiguous genitalia. Because sex phenotype (the manifestation of genetically and embryologically determined sexual characteristics) and gender presentation (the sex role projected by the individual in society) are highly variable, McCullough argues, the various forms of intersexuality should be defined as normal. All of them fall within the statistically expected variability of sex and gender. Furthermore, though certain disease states may accompany some forms of intersexuality, and may require medical intervention, intersexual conditions are not themselves diseases.

McCullough also contends that in the process of assigning gender, physicians should minimize what he calls irreversible assignments: taking steps such as the surgical removal or modification of gonads or genitalia that the patient may one day want to have reversed. Finally, McCullough urges physicians to abandon their practice of treating the birth of a child with genital ambiguity as a medical or social emergency. Instead, they should take the time to perform a thorough medical workup and should disclose everything to the parents, including the uncertainties about the final outcome. The treatment mantra, in other words, should be therapy, not surgery.

I believe a new treatment protocol for intersex infants, similar to the one outlined by McCullough, is close at hand. Treatment should combine some basic medical and ethical principles with a practical but less drastic approach to the birth of a mixed-sex child. As a first step, surgery on infants should be performed only to save the child's life or to substantially improve the child's physical well-being. Physicians may assign a sex—male or female—to

an intersex infant on the basis of the probability that the child's particular condition will lead to the formation of a particular gender identity. At the same time, though, practitioners ought to be humble enough to recognize that as the child grows, he or she may reject the assignment—and they should be wise enough to listen to what the child has to say. Most important, parents should have access to the full range of information and options available to them.

Sex assignments made shortly after birth are only the beginning of a long journey. Consider, for instance, the life of Max Beck: Born intersexual, Max was surgically assigned as a female and consistently raised as such. Had her medical team followed her into her early twenties, they would have deemed her assignment a success because she was married to a man. (It should be noted that success in gender assignment has traditionally been defined as living in that gender as a heterosexual.) Within a few years, however, Beck had come out as a butch lesbian; now in her mid-thirties, Beck has become a man and married his lesbian partner, who (through the miracles of modern reproductive technology) recently gave birth to a girl.

Transsexuals, people who have an emotional gender at odds with their physical sex, once described themselves in terms of dimorphic absolutes—males trapped in female bodies, or vice versa. As such, they sought psychological relief through surgery. Although many still do, some so-called transgendered people today are content to inhabit a more ambiguous zone. A male-to-female transsexual, for instance, may come out as a lesbian. Jane, born a physiological male, is now in her late thirties and living with her wife, whom she married when her name was still John. Jane takes hormones to feminize herself, but they have not yet interfered with her ability to engage in intercourse as a man. In her mind Jane has a lesbian relationship with her wife, though she views their intimate moments as a cross between lesbian and heterosexual sex.

It might seem natural to regard intersexuals and transgendered people as living midway between the poles of male and female. But male and female, masculine and feminine, cannot be parsed as some kind of continuum. Rather, sex and gender are best conceptualized as points in a multidimensional space. For some time, experts on gender development have distinguished between sex at the genetic level and at the cellular level (sex-specific gene expression, X and Y chromosomes); at the hormonal level (in the fetus, during childhood and after puberty); and at the anatomical level (genitals and secondary sexual characteristics). Gender identity presumably emerges from all of those corporeal aspects via some poorly understood interaction with environment and experience. What has become increasingly clear is that one can find levels of masculinity and femininity in almost every possible permutation. A chromosomal, hormonal and genital male (or female) may emerge with a female (or male) gender identity. Or a chromosomal female with male fetal hormones and masculinized genitalia—but with female pubertal hormones—may develop a female gender identity.

The medical and scientific communities have yet to adopt a language that is capable of describing such diversity. In her book *Hermaphrodites and the Medical Invention of Sex,* the historian and medical ethicist Alice Domurat Dreger of Michigan State University in East Lansing documents the emergence of current medical systems for classifying gender ambiguity. The current usage remains rooted in the Victorian approach to sex. The logical structure of the commonly used terms "true hermaphrodite," "male pseudohermaphrodite" and "female pseudohermaphrodite" indicates that only the so-called true hermaphrodite is a genuine mix of male and female. The others, no matter how confusing their body parts, are really hidden males or females. Because true hermaphrodites are rare—possibly only one in 100,000—such a classification system supports the idea that human beings are an absolutely dimorphic species.

At the dawn of the twenty-first century, when the variability of gender seems so visible, such a position is hard to maintain. And here, too, the old medical consensus has begun to crumble. Last fall the pediatric urologist Ian A. Aaronson of the Medical University of South Carolina in Charleston organized the North American Task Force on Intersexuality (NATFI) to review the clinical responses to genital ambiguity in infants. Key medical associations, such as the American Academy

of Pediatrics, have endorsed NATFI. Specialists in surgery, endocrinology, psychology, ethics, psychiatry, genetics and public health, as well as intersex patient-advocate groups, have joined its ranks.

One of the goals of NATFI is to establish a new sex nomenclature. One proposal under consideration replaces the current system with emotionally neutral terminology that emphasizes developmental processes rather than preconceived gender categories. For example, Type I intersexes develop out of anomalous virilizing influences; Type II result from some interruption of virilization; and in Type III intersexes the gonads themselves may not have developed in the expected fashion.

What is clear that since 1993, modern society has moved beyond five sexes to a recognition that gender variation is normal and, for some people, an arena for playful exploration. Discussing my "five sexes" proposal in her book *Lessons from the Intersexed,* the psychologist Suzanne J. Kessler of the State University of New York at Purchase drives this point home with great effect:

> The limitation with Fausto-Sterling's proposal is that . . . [it] still gives genitals . . . primary signifying status and ignores the fact that in the everyday world gender attributions are made without access to genital inspection. . . . What has primacy in everyday life is the gender that is performed, regardless of the flesh's configuration under the clothes.

I now agree with Kessler's assessment. It would be better for intersexuals and their supporters to turn everyone's focus away from genitals. Instead, as she suggests, one should acknowledge that people come in an even wider assortment of sexual identities and characteristics than mere genitals can distinguish. Some women may have "large clitorises or fused labia," whereas some men may have "small penises or misshapen scrota," as Kessler puts it, "phenotypes with no particular clinical or identity meaning."

As clearheaded as Kessler's program is—and despite the progress made in the 1990s—our society is still far from that ideal. The intersexual or transgendered person who projects a social gender—what Kessler calls "cultural genitals"—that conflicts with his or her physical genitals still may die for the transgression. Hence legal protection for people whose cultural and physical genitals do not match is needed during the current transition to a more gender-diverse world. One easy step would be to eliminate the category of "gender" from official documents, such as driver's licenses and passports. Surely attributes both more visible (such as height, build and eye color) and less visible (fingerprints and genetic profiles) would be more expedient.

A more far-ranging agenda is presented in the International Bill of Gender Rights, adopted in 1995 at the fourth annual International Conference on Transgender Law and Employment Policy in Houston, Texas. In lists ten "gender rights," including the right to define one's own gender, the right to change one's physical gender if one so chooses and the right to marry whomever one wishes. The legal bases for such rights are being hammered out in the courts as I write and, most recently, through the establishment, in the state of Vermont, of legal same-sex domestic partnerships.

No one could have foreseen such changes in 1993. And the idea that I played some role, however small, in reducing the pressure—from the medical community as well as from society at large—to flatten the diversity of human sexes into two diametrically opposed camps gives me pleasure.

Sometimes people suggest to me, with not a little horror, that I am arguing for a pastel world in which androgyny reigns and men and women are boringly the same. In my vision, however, strong colors coexist with pastels. There are and will continue to be highly masculine people out there; it's just that some of them are women. And some of the most feminine people I know happen to be men.

DISCUSSION QUESTIONS

1. To what extent is Dr. Money's view that gender identity is completely malleable accurate?
2. What are the potential problems of physicians making sexual assignments immediately after birth?
3. What are some of the problems with the current sex terminology?

READING 10

The Gendered Society

Michael S. Kimmel

In no country has such constant care been taken as in America to trace two clearly distinct lines of action for the two sexes, and to make them keep pace with the other, but in two pathways which are always different.

Alexis de Tocqueville
Democracy in America (1835)

Daily, we hear how men and women are different. They tell that we come from different planets. They say we have different brain chemistries, different brain organization, different hormones. They say our different anatomies lead to different destinies. They say we have different ways of knowing, listen to different moral voices, have different ways of speaking and hearing each other.

You'd think we were different species, like, say lobsters and giraffes, or Martians and Venutians. In his best-selling book, pop psychologist John Gray informs us that not only do women and men communicate differently, but they also "think, feel, perceive, react, respond, love, need, and appreciate differently."[1] It's a miracle of cosmic proportions that we ever understand one another!

Yet, despite these alleged interplanetary differences, we're all together in the same workplaces, where we are evaluated by the same criteria for raises, promotions, bonuses, and tenure. We sit in the same classrooms, eat in the same dining halls, read the same books, and are subject to the same criteria for grading. We live in the same houses, prepare and eat the same meals, read the same newspapers, and tune into the same television programs.

What I have come to call this "interplanetary" theory of complete and universal *gender difference* is also typically the way we explain another

Michael S. Kimmel is a professor of sociology at the State University of New York at Stony Brook.

universal phenomenon: *gender inequality*. Gender is not simply a system of classification, by which biological males and biological females are sorted, separated, and socialized into equivalent sex roles. Gender also expresses the universal inequality between women and men. When we speak about gender we also speak about hierarchy, power, and inequality, not simply difference.

So the two tasks of any study of gender, it seems to me, are to explain both difference and inequality, or, to be alliterative, *difference* and *dominance*. Every general explanation of gender must address two central questions, and their ancillary derivative questions.

First: *Why is it that virtually every single society differentiates people on the basis of gender?* Why are women and men perceived as different in every known society? What are the differences that are perceived? Why is gender at least one—if not the central—basis for the division of labor?

Second: *Why is it that virtually every known society is also based on male dominance?* Why does virtually every society divide social, political, and economic resources unequally between the genders? And why is it that men always get more? Why is a gendered division of labor also an unequal division of labor? Why are women's tasks and men's tasks valued differently?

It is clear . . . that there are dramatic differences among societies regarding the type of gender differences, the levels of gender inequality, and the amount of violence (implied or real) that is necessary to maintain both systems of difference and domination. But the basic facts remain: *Virtually every society known to us is founded upon assumptions of gender difference and the politics of gender inequality.*

On these axiomatic questions, two basic schools of thought prevail: biological determinism and differential socialization. We know them as "nature" and "nurture," and the question of which is dominant has been debated for a century in classrooms, at dinner parties, by political adversaries, and among friends and families. Are men and women different because they are "hardwired" to be different, or are they different because they've

been taught to be? Is biology destiny, or is it that human beings are more flexible, and thus subject to change?

Most of the arguments about gender difference begin . . . with biology. . . . Women and men *are* biologically different, after all. Our reproductive anatomies are different, and so are our reproductive destinies. Our brain structures differ, our brain chemistries differ. Our musculature is different. Different levels of different hormones circulate through our different bodies. Surely, these add up to fundamental, intractable, and universal differences, and these differences provide the foundation for male domination, don't they?

The answer is an unequivocal maybe. Or, perhaps more accurately, yes and no. There are very few people who would suggest that there are no differences between males and females. At least, I wouldn't suggest it. What social scientists call *sex differences* refer precisely to that catalog of anatomical, hormonal, chemical, and physical differences between women and men. But even here, as we shall see, there are enormous ranges of femaleness and male-ness. Though our musculature differs, plenty of women are physically stronger than plenty of men. Though on average our chemistries are different, it's not an all-or-nothing proposition—women do have varying levels of androgens, and men have varying levels of estrogen in their systems. And though our brain structure may be differently lateralized, males and females both do tend to use both sides of their brain. And it is far from clear that these biological differences automatically and inevitably lead men to dominate women. Could we not imagine, as some writers already have, a culture in which women's biological abilities to bear and nurse children might be seen as the expression of such ineffable power—the ability to create life—that strong men wilt in impotent envy?

In fact, in order to underscore this issue, most social and behavioral scientists now use the term *gender* in a different way than we use the word *sex*. Sex refers to the biological apparatus, the male and the female—our chromosomal, chemical, anatomical organization. Gender refers to the meanings that are attached to those differences within a culture. Sex is male and female; gender is masculinity and femininity—what it means to be a man or a woman. . . . And while biological sex varies very little, gender varies enormously. What it means to possess the anatomical configuration of male or female means very different things depending on where you are, who you are, and when you are living. . . .

The other reigning school of thought that explains both gender difference and gender domination is *differential socialization*—the "nurture" side of the equation. Men and women are different because we are taught to be different. From the moment of birth, males and females are treated differently. Gradually we acquire the traits, behaviors, and attitudes that our culture defines as "masculine" or "feminine." We are not necessarily born different; we become different through this process of socialization.

Nor are we born biologically predisposed toward gender inequality. Domination is not a trait carried on the Y chromosome; it is the outcome of the different cultural valuing of men's and women's experiences. Thus, the adoption of masculinity and femininity implies the adoption of "political" ideas that what women do is not as culturally important as what men do.

Developmental psychologists have also examined the ways in which the meanings of masculinity and femininity change over the course of a person's life. The issues confronting a man about proving himself and feeling successful will change, as will the social institutions in which he will attempt to enact those experiences. The meanings of femininity are subject to parallel changes, for example, among prepubescent women, women in childbearing years, and postmenopausal women, as they are different for women entering the labor market and those retiring from it.

Although we typically cast the debate in terms of *either* biological determinism *or* differential socialization—nature versus nurture—it may be useful to pause for a moment to observe what characteristics they have in common. Both schools of thought share two fundamental assumptions. First, both "nature lovers" and "nurturers" see women and men as markedly different from each other—truly, deeply, and irreversibly different. (Nurture does allow for some possibility of change, but they still argue that the process of socialization is a process of making males and females different from each other—differences that are normative, culturally necessary, and "natural.") And both schools of thought assume that the differences *between* women and men are far greater and more decisive (and worthy of analysis) than the differences that might be observed *among* men or *among* women. Thus, both "nature lovers" and "nurturers" subscribe to some version of the interplanetary theory of gender.

Second, both schools of thought assume that gender domination is the inevitable outcome of gender difference, that difference causes domination. To the biologists, it may be because pregnancy and lactation make women more vulnerable and in need of protection, or because male musculature makes them more adept hunters, or that testosterone makes them more aggressive with other men and with women too. Or it may be that men have to dominate women in order to maximize their chances to pass on their genes. Psychologists of "gender roles" tell us that, among other things, men and women are taught to devalue women's experiences, perceptions, and abilities, and to overvalue men's.

I argue . . . that both of these propositions are false. First, . . . the differences between women and men are not . . . nearly as great as are the differences among women or among men. Many perceived differences turn out to be differences based less on gender than on the social positions people occupy. Second, I . . . argue that gender difference is the product of gender inequality, and not the other way around. In fact, gender difference is the chief outcome of gender inequality, because it is through the idea of difference that inequality is legitimated. As one sociologist recently put it, "The very creation of difference is the foundation on which inequality rests."[2]

Using what social scientists have come to call a "social constructionist" approach, . . . I make the case that neither gender difference nor gender inequality is inevitable in the nature of things, nor, more specifically, in the nature of our bodies. Neither are difference and domination explainable solely by reference to differential socialization of boys and girls into sex roles typical of men and women.

When proponents of both nature and nurture positions assert that gender inequality is the inevitable outcome of gender difference, they take, perhaps inadvertently, a political position that assumes that inequality may be lessened, or that its most negative effects may be ameliorated, but that it cannot be eliminated—precisely because it is based upon intractable differences. On the other hand, to assert, as I do, that the exaggerated gender differences that we see are not as great as they appear and that they are the result of inequality allows a far greater political latitude. By eliminating gender inequality, we will remove the foundation upon which the entire edifice of gender difference is built.

What will remain, I believe is not some non-gendered androgynous gruel, in which differences between women and men are blended and everyone acts and thinks in exactly the same way. Quite the contrary, I believe that as gender inequality decreases, the differences among people—differences grounded in race, class, ethnicity, age, sexuality *as well as* gender—will emerge in a context in which each of us can be appreciated for our individual uniqueness as well as our commonality.

MAKING GENDER VISIBLE FOR BOTH WOMEN AND MEN

. . . A dramatic transformation in thinking about gender . . . has occurred over the past thirty years. In particular, three decades of pioneering work by feminist scholars, both in traditional disciplines and in women's studies, has made us aware of the centrality of gender in shaping social life. We now know that gender is one of the central organizing principles around which social life revolves. Until the 1970s, social scientists would have listed only class and race as the master statuses that defined and proscribed social life. If you wanted to study

gender in the 1960s in social science, for example, you would have found but one course designed to address your needs—"Marriage and the Family"—which was sort of the "Ladies Auxiliary" of the social sciences. There were no courses on gender. But today, gender has joined race and class in our understanding of the foundations of an individual's identity. Gender, we now know, is one of the axes around which social life is organized and through which we understand our own experiences.

In the past thirty years, feminist scholars properly focused most of their attention on women—on what Catharine Stimpson has called the "omissions, distortions, and trivializations" of women's experiences—and the spheres to which women have historically been consigned, such as private life and the family.[3] Women's history sought to rescue from obscurity the lives of significant women who had been ignored or whose work has been minimized by traditional androcentric scholarship, and to examine the everyday lives of women in the past—the efforts, for example, of laundresses, factory workers, pioneer homesteaders, or housewives to carve out lives of meaning and dignity in a world controlled by men. Whether the focus has been on the exemplary or the ordinary, though, feminist scholarship has made it clear that gender is a central axis in women's lives. . . .

But when we study men, we study them as political leaders, military heroes, scientists, writers, artists. Men, themselves, are invisible *as men.* Rarely, if ever, do we see a course that examines the lives of men as men. What is the impact of gender on the lives of these famous men? How does masculinity play a part in the lives of great artists, writers, presidents, etc. How does masculinity play out in the lives of "ordinary" men—in factories and on farms, in union halls and large corporations? On this score, the traditional curriculum suddenly draws a big blank. Everywhere one turns there are courses about men, but virtually no information on masculinity.

Several years ago, this yawning gap inspired me to undertake a cultural history of the idea of masculinity in America, to trace the development and shifts in what it has meant to be a man over the course of our history.[4] What I found is that American men have been very articulate in describing what it means to be a man, and in seeing whatever they have done as a way to prove their manhood, but that we haven't known how to hear them.

Integrating gender into our courses is a way to fulfill the promise of women's studies—by understanding men as gendered as well. In my university, for example, the course on nineteenth-century British literature includes a deeply "gendered" reading of the Brontës, that discusses their feelings about femininity, marriage, and relations between the sexes. Yet not a word is spoken about Dickens and masculinity, especially about his feelings about fatherhood and the family. Dickens is understood as a "social problem" novelist, and his issue was class relations—this despite the fact that so many of Dickens's most celebrated characters are young boys without fathers, and who are searching for authentic families. And there's not a word about Thomas Hardy's ambivalent ideas about masculinity and marriage in, say, *Jude the Obscure*. Hardy's grappling with premodernist conceptions of an apathetic universe is what we discuss. And my wife tells me that in her nineteenth-century American literature class at Princeton, gender was the main topic of conversation when the subject was Edith Wharton, but the word was never spoken when they discussed Henry James, in whose work gendered anxiety erupts variously as chivalric contempt, misogynist rage, and sexual ambivalence. James, we're told, is "about" the form of the novel, narrative technique, the stylistic powers of description and characterization. Certainly not about gender.

So we continue to act as if gender applied only to women. Surely the time has come to make gender visible to men. As the Chinese proverb has it, the fish are the last to discover the ocean. . . .

THE CURRENT DEBATE

I believe that we are, at this moment, having a national debate about masculinity in this country—but that we don't know it. For example, what

gender comes to mind when I invoke the following current American problems: "teen violence," "gang violence," "suburban violence," "drug violence," "violence in the schools?" And what gender comes to mind when I say the words "suicide bomber" or "terrorist hijacker"?

Of course, you've imagined men. And not just any men—but younger men, in their teens and twenties, and relatively poorer men, from the working class or lower middle class.

But how do our social commentators discuss these problems? Do they note that the problem of youth and violence is really a problem of young *men* and violence? Do they ever mention that everywhere ethnic nationalism sets up shop, it is young men who are the shopkeepers? Do they ever mention masculinity at all?

No. Listen, for example, to the voice of one expert, asked to comment on the brutal murder of Matthew Shepard, a gay twenty-one-year-old college student at the University of Wyoming. After being reminded that young men account for 80 percent to 90 percent of people arrested for "gay bashing" crimes, the reporter quoted a sociologist as saying that "[t]his youth variable tells us they are working out identity issues, making the transition away from home into adulthood."[5] This "*youth variable*"? What had been a variable about age and gender had been transformed into a variable about age. Gender had disappeared. That is the sound of silence, what invisibility looks like.

Now, imagine that these were all women—all the ethnic nationalists, the militias, the gay bashers. Would that not be *the* story, the *only* story? Would not a gender analysis be at the center of every single story? Would we not hear from experts on female socialization, frustration, anger, PMS, and everything else under the sun? But the fact that these are men earns nary a word.

Take one final example. What if it had been young girls who opened fire on their classmates in West Paducah, Kentucky, in Pearl, Mississippi, in Jonesboro, Arkansas, or in Springfield, Oregon? And what if nearly all the children who died were boys? Do you think that the social outcry would demand that we investigate the "inherent violence" of Southern culture, or simply express dismay that young "people" have too much access to guns? I doubt it. And yet no one seemed to mention that the young boys who actually committed those crimes were simply doing—albeit in dramatic form at a younger age—what American men have been taught to do for centuries when they are upset and angry. Men don't get mad; they get even. . . .

I believe that until we make gender visible for both women and for men we will not, as a culture, adequately know how to address these issues. That's not to say that all we have to do is address masculinity. These issues are complex, requiring analyses of the political economy of global economic integration, of the transformation of social classes, of urban poverty and hopelessness, of racism. But if we ignore masculinity—if we let it remain invisible—we will never completely understand them, let alone resolve them.

THE PLURAL AND THE POWERFUL

When I use the term *gender,* then, it is with the explicit intention of discussing both masculinity and femininity. But even these terms are inaccurate because they imply that there is one simple definition of masculinity and one definition of femininity. One of the important elements of a social constructionist approach—especially if we intend to dislodge the notion that gender differences alone are decisive—is to explore the differences *among* men and *among* women, since, as it turns out, these are often more decisive than the differences between women and men.

Within any one society at any one moment, several meanings of masculinity and femininity coexist. Simply put, not all American men and women are the same. Our experiences are also structured by class, race, ethnicity, age, sexuality, region. Each of these axes modifies the others. Just because we make gender visible doesn't mean that we make these other organizing principles of social life invisible. Imagine, for example, an older, black, gay man in Chicago and a young, white, heterosexual farm boy in Iowa. Wouldn't they have different definitions of masculinity? Or imagine a twenty-two-year-old wealthy Asian American heterosexual woman in San Francisco and a poor white Irish Catholic lesbian in Boston. Wouldn't their ideas about what it means to be a woman be somewhat different?

If gender varies across cultures, over historical time, among men and women within any one culture, and over the life course, can we really speak of masculinity or femininity as though they were constant, universal essences, common to all women and to all men? If not, gender must be seen as an ever-changing fluid assemblage of meanings and behaviors. In that sense, we must speak of *masculinities* and *femininities,* and thus recognize the different definitions of masculinity and femininity that we construct. By pluralizing the terms, we acknowledge that masculinity and femininity mean different things to different groups of people at different times.

At the same time, we can't forget that all masculinities and femininities are not created equal. American men and women must also contend with a particular definition that is held up as the model against which we are expected to measure ourselves. We thus come to know what it means to be a man or a woman in our culture by setting our definitions in opposition to a set of "others"—racial minorities, sexual minorities. For men, the classic "other" is, of course, women. It feels imperative to most men that they make it clear—eternally, compulsively, decidedly—that they are unlike women.

For most men, this is the "hegemonic" definition—the one that is held up as the model for all of us. It is as Virginia Woolf wrote in 1938, "the quintessence of virility, the perfect type of which all the others are imperfect adumbrations."[6] The hegemonic definition of masculinity is "constructed in relation to various subordinated masculinities as well as in relation to women," writes sociologist R. W. Connell. The sociologist Erving Goffman once described this hegemonic definition of masculinity like this:

> In an important sense there is only one complete unblushing male in America: a young, married, white,

urban, northern, heterosexual, Protestant, father, of college education, fully employed, of good complexion, weight, and height, and a recent record in sports. . . . Any male who fails to qualify in any one of these ways is likely to view himself—during moments at least—as unworthy, incomplete, and inferior.[7]

Women contend with an equally exaggerated ideal of femininity, which Connell calls "emphasized femininity." Emphasized femininity is organized around compliance with gender inequality, and is "oriented to accommodating the interests and desires of men." One sees emphasized femininity in "the display of sociability rather than technical competence, fragility in mating scenes, compliance with men's desire for titillation and ego-stroking in office relationships, acceptance of marriage and childcare as a response to labor-market discrimination against women."[8] Emphasized femininity exaggerates gender difference as a strategy of "adaptation to men's power" stressing empathy and nurturance; "real" womanhood is described as "fascinating" and women are advised that they can wrap men around their fingers by knowing and playing by the "rules." In one research study, an eight-year-old boy captured this emphasized femininity eloquently in a poem he wrote:

If I were a girl, I'd have to attract a guy
  wear makeup; sometimes.

Wear the latest style of clothes and try to be
  likable.

I probably wouldn't play any physical sports like
  football or soccer.

I don't think I would enjoy myself around men
  in fear of rejection

or under the pressure of attracting them.[9]

GENDER DIFFERENCE AS "DECEPTIVE DISTINCTIONS"

The existence of multiple masculinities and femininities dramatically undercuts the idea that the gender differences we observe are due solely to differently gendered people occupying gender-neutral positions.

Moreover, that these masculinities and femininities are arrayed along a hierarchy, and measured against one another, buttresses the argument that domination creates and exaggerates difference.

The interplanetary theory of gender assumes, whether through biology or socialization, that women act like women, no matter where they are, and that men act like men no matter where they are. Psychologist Carol Tavris argues that such binary thinking leads to what philosophers call the "law of the excluded middle," which, as she reminds us, "is where most men and women fall in terms of their psychological qualities, beliefs, abilities, traits and values."[10] It turns out that many of the differences between women and men that we observe in our everyday lives are actually not *gender* differences at all, but differences that are the result of being in different positions or in different arenas. It's not that gendered individuals occupy these ungendered positions, but that the positions themselves elicit the behaviors we see as gendered. The sociologist Cynthia Fuchs Epstein calls these "deceptive distinctions" because, while they appear to be based on gender, they are actually based on something else.[11]

Take, for example, the well-known differences in communication patterns observed by Deborah Tannen in her best-selling book *You Just Don't Understand*. Tannen argues that women and men communicate with the languages of their respective planets—men employ the competitive language of hierarchy and domination to get ahead; women create webs of inclusion with softer, more embracing language that ensures that everyone feels O.K. At home, men are the strong silent types, grunting monosyllabically to their wives, who want to use conversation to create intimacy.[12]

But it turns out that those very same monosyllabic men are very verbal at work, where they are in positions of dependency and powerlessness, and need to use conversation to maintain a relationship with their superiors at work; and their wives are just as capable of using language competitively to maximize their position in a corporate hierarchy. When he examined the recorded transcripts of women's and men's testimony in trials, anthropologist William O'Barr concluded that the witnesses' occupation was a more accurate predictor of their use of language than was gender. "So-called women's language is neither characteristic of all women, nor limited only to women," O'Barr writes. If women use "powerless" language, it may be due "to the greater tendency of women to occupy relatively powerless social positions" in society.[13] Communication differences turn out to be "deceptive distinctions" because rarely do we observe the communication patterns of dependent men and executive women. . . .

What about those enormous gender differences that some observers have found in the workplace? . . . Men, we hear, are competitive social climbers who seek advancement at every opportunity; women are cooperative team builders who shun competition and may even suffer from a "fear of success." But the pioneering study by Rosabeth Moss Kanter, reported in *Men and Women of the Corporation,* indicated that gender mattered far less than opportunity. When women had the same opportunities, networks, mentors, and possibilities for advancement, they behaved just as the men did. Women were not successful because they lacked opportunities, not because they feared success; when men lacked opportunities, they behaved in stereotypically "feminine" ways.[14]

Finally, take our experiences in the family. . . . Here, again, we assume that women are socialized to be nurturing and maternal, men to be strong and silent, relatively emotionally inexpressive arbiters of justice—that is, we assume that women do the work of "mothering" because they are socialized to do so. And again, sociological research suggests that our behavior in the family has somewhat less to do with gender socialization than with the family situations in which we find ourselves.

Research by sociologist Kathleen Gerson, for example, found that gender socialization was not very helpful in predicting women's family experiences. Only slightly more than half the women who were primarily interested in full-time motherhood were, in fact, full-time mothers; and only slightly

more than half the women who were primarily interested in full-time careers had them. It turned out that marital stability, husbands' income, women's workplace experiences, and support networks were far more important than gender socialization in determining which women ended up full-time mothers and which did not.[15]

On the other side of the ledger, research by sociologist Barbara Risman found that despite a gender socialization that downplays emotional responsiveness and nurturing, most single fathers are perfectly capable of "mothering." Single fathers do not hire female workers to do the typically female tasks around the house; they do those tasks themselves. In fact, Risman found few differences between single fathers and mothers (single or married) when it came to what they did around the house, how they acted with their children, or even in their children's emotional and intellectual development. Men's parenting styles were virtually indistinguishable from women's, a finding that led Risman to argue that "men can mother and that children are not necessarily better nurtured by women than by men."[16] . . .

Based on all this research, you might conclude, as does Risman, that "if women and men were to experience identical structural conditions and role expectations, empirically observable gender differences would dissipate."[17] I am not fully convinced. There *are* some differences between women and men, after all. Perhaps, as this research suggests, those differences are not as great, decisive, or as impervious to social change as we once thought. . . .

THE MEANING OF MEAN DIFFERENCES

Few of the differences between women and men are hardwired into all males to the exclusion of all females, or vice versa. Although we can readily observe differences between women and men in rates of aggression, physical strength, math or verbal achievement, caring and nurturing, or emotional expressiveness, it is not true that all males and no females are aggressive, physically strong,

PERSONAL ACCOUNT

Basketball

I frequently watch my boyfriend play basketball at an outdoor court with many other males in pick-up games. One time when I was there, there was a new face among the others waiting to play—a female face, and she was not sitting with the rest of the women who were watching. She was dressed and ready to play. I had never seen her in all the time I'd been there before, nor had I ever seen another woman there try to play.

For several games, she did not play. The guys formed teams and she was not asked to join. It was almost like there was a purposeful avoidance of her, with no one even acknowledging that she was there. Finally, she made a noticeable effort, and with some reluctance she was included in the next team waiting to play the winner of the current game. There were whispers and snickers among the guys, and I think it had a lot to do with the perception that she was challenging their masculinity. A "girl" was intruding into their area. My guess is that they were also somewhat nervous about the fact that she really might be good and embarrass some of them.

Anyway, the first couple of times up and down the court she was not given the ball despite the fact that she was wide open. The other guys on the team forced bad

shots and tried super hard in what seemed like an effort to prove that she was not needed. The guy who was supposed to guard her on defense really didn't pay her much attention, and that same guy who she was guarding at the other end made sure he drove around her and scored on two occasions.

Finally, one time down the court she called for the ball and sank a shot from at least 16 feet. A huge feeling of relief and satisfaction came over me. Being a basketball player myself, I figured she was probably good or would not be there in the first place, but being a woman I was also happy to see her *first* shot go in. I found out later she had played basketball for a university and she had a great outside shot.

Even after she made one more shot off a rebound that ended up in her hands, she was not given the ball again. I suppose after some of the loud comments from some of the guys on the sidelines, that she was beating the male players out there, she wasn't going to get the ball again. I was kind of shocked that she wasn't *more* accepted even after she showed she was talented. I haven't seen her there since.

Andrea M. Busch

and adept at math and science, and all females and no males are caring and nurturing, verbally adept, or emotionally expressive. What we mean when we speak of gender differences are mean differences, differences in the average scores obtained by women and men.

These mean scores tell us something about the differences between the two groups, but they tell us nothing about the distributions themselves, the differences *among* men or *among* women. Sometimes these distributions can be enormous: There are large numbers of caring or emotionally expressive men, and of aggressive and physically strong women. (See figure 1.) In fact, in virtually all the research that has been done on the attributes associated with masculinity or femininity,

FIGURE 1

Schematic rendering of the overlapping distributions of traits, attitudes, and behaviors by gender. Although mean differences might obtain on many characteristics, these distributions suggest far greater similarity between women and men, and far greater variability among men and among women.

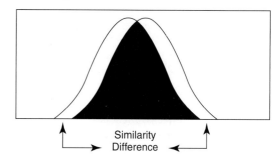

the differences among women and among men are far greater than the mean differences between women and men. We tend to focus on the mean differences, but they may tell us far less than we think they do.

What we think they tell us, of course, is that women and men are different, from different planets. This is what I . . . call the interplanetary theory of gender difference—that the observed mean differences between women and men are decisive and that they come from the fact that women and men are biologically so physically different.

For example, even the idea that we are from different planets, that our differences are deep and intractable, has a political dimension: To call the "other" sex the "opposite" sex obscures the many ways we are alike. As the anthropologist Gayle Rubin points out:

> Men and women are, of course, different. But they are not as different as day and night, earth and sky, yin and yang, life and death. In fact from the standpoint of nature, men and women are closer to each other than either is to anything else—for instance mountains, kangaroos, or coconut palms. . . . Far from being an expression of natural differences, exclusive gender identity is the suppression of natural similarities.[18]

The interplanetary theory of gender difference is important not because it's right—in fact, it is wrong far more often than it is right—but because, as a culture, we seem desperately to *want* it to be true. That is, the real sociological question about gender is not the sociology of gender differences—explaining the physiological origins of gender difference—but the sociology of knowledge question that explores why gender difference is so important to us, why we cling to the idea of gender difference so tenaciously, why, I suppose, we shell out millions of dollars for books that "reveal" the deep differences between women and men, but will probably never buy a book that says, "Hey, we're all Earthlings!"

That, however, is [my] message. . . . Virtually all available research from the social and behavioral sciences suggests that women and men are not from Venus and Mars, but are both from planet Earth. We're not opposite sexes, but neighboring sexes—we have far more in common with each other than we have differences. We pretty much have the same abilities, and pretty much want the same things in our lives.

DISCUSSION QUESTIONS

1. What do you understand Kimmel to mean when he says that gender inequality produces gender difference? Can you give an example?
2. What is your reaction to Kimmel's position that we are engaged in a national debate about masculinity?
3. In your own words, explain the "deceptive distinctions" aspect of gender.

NOTES

1. John Gray, *Men Are from Mars, Women Are from Venus* (New York: HarperCollins, 1992), 5.
2. Barbara Risman, *Gender Vertigo* (New Haven: Yale University Press, 1998), 25. See also Judith Lorber, *Paradoxes of Gender* (New Haven: Yale University Press, 1994).
3. Catharine Stimpson, *Where the Meanings Are* (New York: Methuen, 1988).
4. See Michael Kimmel, *Manhood in America: A Cultural History* (New York: The Free Press, 1996).
5. Cited in James Brooke, "Men Held in Beatings Lived on the Fringes," *New York Times*, October 16, 1998, A16. Valerie Jenness, the sociologist who was quoted in the story, told me that she was *mis*quoted, and that of course she had mentioned gender as well as age—which suggests that the media's myopia matches that of the larger society.
6. Virginia Woolf, *Three Guineas* [1938] (New York: Harcourt, 1966), 142.
7. R. W. Connell, *Gender and Power* (Stanford: Stanford University Press, 1987), 183; Erving Goffman, *Stigma* (Englewood Cliffs, NJ: Prentice-Hall, 1963), 128.
8. Connell, *Gender and Power*, 183, 188, 187.
9. Cited in Risman, *Gender Vertigo*, 141.
10. Carol Tavris, "The Mismeasure of Woman," *Feminism and Psychology* (1993):153.
11. Cynthia Fuchs Epstein, *Deceptive Distinctions* (New Haven: Yale University Press, 1988).
12. Deborah Tannen, *You Just Don't Understand* (New York: William Morrow, 1991).
13. William O'Barr and Jean F. O'Barr, *Linguistic Evidence: Language, Power and Strategy—The Courtroom* (San Diego: Academic Press, 1995); see also Alfie Kohn, "Girl Talk, Guy Talk," *Psychology Today*, February 1988, 66.

14. Rosabeth M. Kanter, *Men and Women of the Corporation* (New York: Harper and Row, 1977).

15. Kathleen Gerson, *Hard Choices* (Berkeley: University of California Press, 1985); *No Man's Land* (New York: Basic Books, 1993).

16. Risman, *Gender Vertigo,* 70.

17. Risman, *Gender Vertigo,* 21.

18. Gayle Rubin, "The Traffic in Women," in *Toward an Anthropology of Women,* ed. R. R. Reiter, 179–80 (New York: Monthly Review Press, 1975).

READING 11

Who Put the "Trans" in Transgender?[1] Gender Theory and Everyday Life

Suzanne Kessler

Wendy McKenna

The prefix "trans" has 3 different meanings. Trans means change, as in the word "transform." In this first sense transgendered people change their bodies to fit the gender they feel they always were. They change from male to female or vice versa. Transgender in this sense is synonymous with what is typically meant by the term "transsexual." Trans means across as in the word "transcontinental." In this second sense a transgendered person is one who moves across genders (or maybe aspects of the person cross genders). This meaning does not imply being essentially or permanently committed to one or the other gender and therefore has a more social-constructionist connotation. Nevertheless, the transgendered person in this meaning does not leave the realm of two genders. Persons who assert that although they are "really"

Suzanne Kessler is a professor of psychology at Purchase College. Wendy McKenna is an instructor and family services coordinator at the Oregon State University Child Development Center.

the other gender they do not need to change their genitals, are transgendered in this sense of "trans." The emphasis is on the crossing and not on any surgical transformation accompanying it. Such a person might say, "I want people to attribute the gender "female" to me, but I'm not going to get my genitals changed. I don't mind having my penis." This type of identity is relatively recent as an open, public identity, but it does not seem to be an identity separate from male and female. It is more like a previously unthinkable combination of male and female. But even a combination of male and female reflexively gives credence to these categories. There are still two genders. The third meaning of "trans" is beyond or through as in the word "transcutaneous." In this third sense a transgendered person is one who has gotten through gender, beyond gender. No clear gender attribution can be made, or is allowed to be made. Gender ceases to exist, both for this person and those with whom they interact. This third meaning is the most radical and the one of greatest importance to gender theorists like us who are interested in the possibility, both theoretical and real, of eliminating gender.

THE SOCIAL CONSTRUCTION OF GENDER: TRANSSEXUALS

Over 20 years ago we wrote a book asserting that all aspects of gender, including the physical/biological aspects, which people refer to as "sex," are socially constructed.[2] Our point was that the male/female dichotomy is not essentially given in nature. In developing our argument, we analyzed the natural attitude toward gender.[3] These taken-for-granted beliefs of the culture include:

1. There are two and only two genders. Apparent violations are not really violations. If you look long enough, ask enough questions, or do enough medical tests, the "real" gender will be revealed.
2. Gender exists as a biological "fact" independently of anyone's ideas about gender.
3. A person's gender never changes.

4. Genitals are the essential defining feature of gender. That is, if you do not have the right organ between your legs, you cannot be what you say you are. You are not the "genuine article," even if you have everything else. (That is why transsexuals, at least historically, were not really the gender they claimed until they had surgery, and that is why intersexed infants are required to have genital "reconstructive" surgery.)

By the mid-1970's most people, in and out of academia, were beginning to accept that roles, appearances, and characteristics (what they called "gender") were socially defined and culturally varied. However, biological features (what they called "sex") were considered to be given in nature. We argued that the biological is as much a construction as the social is. Although hormones, chromosomes, gonads, and genitals, are real parts of the body, seeing them as dichotomous and essential to being a female or male is a social construction. That is why we believed (and continue to believe) that in discussions of this topic it is critical to only use "gender" and never use "sex" (in the conventional meanings). If anything is primary, it is not some biological sign, but what we called "gender attribution"—the decision one makes in every concrete case that someone is either a male or a female. Virtually all of the time, gender attribution is made with no direct knowledge of the genitals or any other biological "sex marker."

It seemed to us in the mid-1970's that transsexuals exemplified the social construction of gender. We talked to as many as we could about what their experience was with gender attributions made to them and how they insured that "mistakes" were not made. As we pondered our conversations with them, we were struck by how the immediate and interactive presentation of gender is impossible to ignore. In a social setting we do not see one another's chromosomes, genitals, or gender history. In fact, once we make a gender attribution, we are able to discount or reinterpret chromosomes, genitals, or gender history that does not "match" the gender attribution. If you are "obviously" a man and then you tell new acquaintances that you were given a female gender assignment at birth and do not have a penis, they have an adjustment to make, but that will probably not mean that they will change their minds about whether you are a man. We asserted that the primacy of gender attribution benefits transsexuals—if they make an initial credible gender presentation—because other people will interpret contradictory information (like the gender on a driver's license) as a clerical error rather than as evidence of the person's intent to deceive. What we did not consider 25 years ago was the possibility that someone might not want to make a credible gender presentation—might not want to be seen as clearly either male or female. In addition, although we advocated that because of the primacy of gender attribution, persons could be whatever gender they wanted without costly and dangerous surgery, it did not seem to us that this would happen for a very long time, if ever. It did not even occur to us that within 20 years there would be some people who would want to confront others with the contradiction between their gender presentation and other "facts" such as their genitals or gender history. In other words, we did not address what has come to be called "transgender." Transgender was neither a concept nor a term 25 years ago. Transsexual was radical enough.

TRANSGENDER: TRANSFORMATION, TRANSFER, OR TRANSCENDENCE?

Recently, we did a Web search for "transgender," using the Google search engine and found over 3300 matches for that term. Clearly "it" exists, but what is "it"? And what is the meaning of "gender" now? Realizing that we needed more information about this, especially from younger people, in the Fall of 1999 we gave a questionnaire to 83 students in a human sexuality class at a college with a reputation for attracting and reasonably tolerating all types of genders and sexualities. The students' answers to our questions are some indication of what is different now and what is the same, at least among young, liberal and presumably gender-progressive people. Our first two questions, "What is the meaning of the category gender?" and "How do you know someone's gender?" were treated as reasonable questions—not nonsensical ones. In 1975 we suspect most people would have been mystified as to why we were asking questions like that. It would have been like asking "How can you tell if someone is dead or alive?" a question about a simple, objective fact. The students still believe there are two genders, but they seem to have more of a sense that gender is a complex, not a simple, dichotomy; yet it is still a dichotomy. There is the acknowledgment by some that gender characteristics can be mixed. (Perhaps we have Jerry Springer and other purveyors of the atypical to thank for this.) The answers to "how do you know" in any given case were those things that we had described as important in gender attribution like breasts, Adam's apples, body shape, and voice.

Although students rarely wrote that they use genitals to decide a person's gender, they did write that genitals are the essential defining feature of what it means to be a gender. Men have penises and women have vaginas, even if later on in the questionnaire they said that other combinations are possible like men with vaginas and women with penises. The equation gender = genitals is no different from what we found 25 years ago. However, there has been a significant change regarding genitals. In our original work we provided evidence that the penis was the only socially real genital. People held the often unstated belief that males had penises and females had no penises. In this recent questionnaire though, the vagina was mentioned almost as often as the penis. It appears that the vagina and vulva have become more socially real. How and why has this happened, and what that implies are intriguing areas for further inquiry.

Although these students may consider gender extremely complex and allow for the possibility that it is not that important to categorize people by gender, in everyday life not knowing a person's gender still makes them very uncomfortable. They try to find out what the person "really" is. Gender continues to be real and dichotomous, even if an ambiguous presentation is tolerated.

The students said that what has changed in the way their generation thinks about gender compared to their parents is awareness and acceptance of alternatives (mainly homosexuality) and more flexibility/inclusion in expectations for women. Whatever changes in expectations there have been for men, this was not acknowledged by the students. Why has the "trans" formation only gone in one direction?

In light of the question "Who put the "trans" in transgender?" of particular interest is the students' answers to the question, "What does transgendered mean?" Almost none of the students indicated that they knew what it meant. A few who did, said that it referred to someone who changes gender, and then they described what most people mean by "transsexual." One person said the term referred to someone being "torn between a physical existence and a mental existence," but only one or two referred to a person who feels comfortable with physical aspects of both genders, e.g., having breasts and a penis. Only four of the students said they knew a transgendered person. However, there were others who understood that their belief that they did not know transgendered people only meant that "as far as they knew" they did not, but they might. We think that in 1975 basically everyone would have believed that they would know if a person was not "all man or all woman." Judging from this one sample, as well as observations and discussion with others, we could conclude that in the last 25 years the absolute either/or aspect of biological gender has been reduced, at least for some people. But just because more people acknowledge that gender features can be mixed together or that a person can move more easily between categories, this has not led to an expansion of or transcendence of the gender categories. There are still two and only two genders, even if some of the women have penises and some of the men have vaginas. Twenty-five years ago we thought that because transsexualism seemed to violate the rule that you can not change gender, it had revolutionary potential. Now what seems radical are those who identify as "transgender" and reject "transsexual" as too restrictive and too diagnostic. But even if there are transgendered people for whom the gender dichotomy ceases to exist, of what import is that if transgendered people live in a world of two conventional genders? Could a person with a transgendered identity translate it into a public transgendered attribution, where the attributor would say "That's neither a woman nor a man," rather than "I can't tell if that's a woman or a man"?

To cultivate such an attribution in this third sense of transgender (beyond or through) is extraordinarily difficult and might be impossible.

Transgendered people (even those who are publicly "out" on stage, in print, or among trustworthy others) know that unless they do what it takes to get a male or female gender attribution, their physical safety may be in jeopardy. How do we reconcile the desire to radically transform gender (which some transgenderists and theorists share) with the practical need to transform the publicly visible body in gender dichotomous ways? People with a public transgender identity still have one of the standard gender attributions made about them by the casual passerby, even if the passerby has questions. This is because the gender attribution process is an interactive one, grounded in the attributors' unshakable belief that everyone can and must be classified as female or male. In everyday life even gender theorists do not treat the gender dichotomy as problematic.

Twenty-five years of our and others' theorizing about gender has in many ways unsettled the meaning of gender, but it has done no damage to the gender dichotomy. The next challenge is understanding why.

DISCUSSION QUESTIONS

1. What does *transgendered* mean to you?
2. Do you agree with Kessler and McKenna that transsexual and transgendered people reaffirm rather than challenge the gender dichotomy?
3. Is American society now at a point where some people would be able to say of a transgendered person, "That's neither a woman nor a man," rather than "I can't tell if that's a woman or a man"?

NOTES

1. Virginia Prince should probably be credited as having introduced the term "transgender." Because she needed a term to describe her decision to become a woman without changing her genitals (what she would call her "sex") the term "transsexual" would not do. C.F. Prince, Virginia. 1979. "Charles to Virginia: Sex Research as a Personal Experience." In The Frontiers of Sex Research. ed. Vern Bullough, 167–175. Buffalo, NY: Prometheus Books.
2. Kessler, Suzanne, and Wendy McKenna. 1978. Gender: An Ethnomethodological Approach. New York: Wiley.
3. This analysis was based on Harold Garfinkel's description of the natural attitude toward gender. Garfinkel, Harold. 1967. Studies in Ethnomethodology. Englewood Cliffs, N.J.: Prentice Hall.

WHAT IS SOCIAL CLASS?

READING 12

What's Class Got to Do with It?

Michael Zweig

Whether in regard to the economy or issues of war and peace, class is central to our everyday lives. Yet class has not been as visible as race or gender, not nearly as much a part of our conversations and sense of ourselves as these and other "identities." We are of course all individuals, but our individuality and personal life chances are shaped—limited or enhanced—by the economic and social class in which we have grown up and in which we exist as adults.

Even though "class" is an abstract category of social analysis, class is real. Since social abstractions can seem far removed from real life, it may help to consider two other abstractions that have important consequences for flesh-and-blood individuals: race and gender. Suppose you knew there were men and women because you could see the difference, but you didn't know about the socially constructed concept of "gender." You would be missing something vitally important about the people you see. You would have only a surface appreciation of their lives. If, based only on direct observation of skin color, you knew there were white people and black people, but you didn't know about "race" in modern society, you would be ignorant of one of the most important determinants of the experience of those white and black people. Gender and race are abstractions, yet they are powerful, concrete influences in everyone's lives. They carry significant meaning despite wide differences in experience within the populations of men, women, whites, blacks.

Similarly, suppose that based on your observation of work sites and labor markets you knew there were workers and employers, but you didn't recognize the existence of class. You would be blind

Michael Zweig is a professor of economics at the State University of New York, Stony Brook.

to a most important characteristic of the individual workers and employers you were observing, something that has tremendous influence in their lives. Despite the wide variety of experiences and identities among individual workers, capitalists, and middle class people, it still makes sense to acknowledge the existence and importance of class in modern society. In fact, without a class analysis we would have only the most superficial knowledge of our own lives and the experiences of others we observe in economic and political activity. . . .

When people in the United States talk about class, it is often in ways that hide its most important parts. We tend to think about class in terms of income, or the lifestyles that income can buy. . . . [But class can be better understood] as mainly a question of economic and political power. . . . Power doesn't exist alone within an individual or a group. Power exists as a relationship between and among different people or groups. This means that we cannot talk about one class of people alone, without looking at relationships between that class and others.

The working class is made up of people who, when they go to work or when they act as citizens, have comparatively little power or authority. They are the people who do their jobs under more or less close supervision, who have little control over the pace or the content of their work, who aren't the boss of anyone. They are blue-collar people like construction and factory workers, and white-collar workers like bank tellers and writers of routine computer code. They work to produce and distribute goods, or in service industries or government agencies. They are skilled and unskilled, engaged in over five hundred different occupations tracked by the U.S. Department of Labor: agricultural laborers, baggage handlers, cashiers, flight attendants, home health care aides, machinists, secretaries, short order cooks, sound technicians, truck drivers. In the United States, working class people are by far the majority of the population. Over eighty-eight million people were in working class occupations in 2002, comprising 62 percent of the labor force.[1]

On the other side of the basic power relation in a capitalist society is the capitalist class, those most senior executives who direct and control the corporations that employ the private-sector working class. These are the "captains of industry" and finance, CEOs, chief financial officers, chief operating officers, members of boards of directors, those whose decisions dominate the workplace and the economy, and whose economic power often translates into dominant power in the realms of politics, culture, the media, and even religion. Capitalists comprise about 2 percent of the U.S. labor force.

There are big differences among capitalists in the degree of power they wield, particularly in the geographic extent of that power. The CEO of a business employing one hundred people in a city of fifty thousand might well be an important figure on the local scene, but not necessarily in state or regional affairs. On the national scale, power is principally in the hands of those who control the largest corporations, those employing over five hundred people. Of the over twenty-one million business enterprises in the United States, only sixteen thousand employ that many. They are controlled by around two hundred thousand people, fewer than two-tenths of 1 percent of the labor force.

Even among the powerful, power is concentrated at the top. It's one thing to control a single large corporation, another to sit on multiple corporate boards and be in a position to coordinate strategies across corporations. In fact, if we count only those people who sit on multiple boards, so-called interlocking directors, they could all fit into Yankee Stadium. They and the top political leaders in all branches of the federal government constitute a U.S. "ruling class" at the pinnacle of national power.

Capitalists are rich, of course. But when vice-president Dick Cheney invited a select few to help him formulate the country's energy policy shortly after the new Bush administration came into office in 2001, he didn't invite "rich people." He invited people who were leaders in the energy industry, capitalists. The fact that they were also rich was incidental. Capitalists are rich people who control far more than their personal wealth. They control the wealth of the nation, concentrated as it is in the largest few thousand corporations. There is no lobby in Washington representing "rich people." Lobbyists represent various industries or associations of industries that sometimes coordinate their efforts on behalf of industry in general. They represent the interests that capitalists bring to legislative and regulatory matters.

Something similar operates for the working class. Over thirteen million people are in unions in the United States. Most of these unions—like the United Auto Workers (UAW); the American Federation of State, County, and Municipal Employees (AFSCME); the Carpenters; and the International Brotherhood of Teamsters (IBT)—maintain offices in Washington and in major and even smaller cities where their members work. In addition to engaging in collective bargaining at the workplace, these unions lobby for their members and occasionally coordinate their efforts to lobby for broader working class interests. Sixty-eight unions have joined under the umbrella of the American Federation of Labor, Congress of Industrial Organizations (AFL-CIO) to pool resources and try to advance the interests of working people in general. These organizations represent workers, not "the poor" or "middle-income people," even though some workers are poor and some have an income equal to that of some in the middle class.[2]

In between the capitalist and the working classes is the middle class. The "middle class" gets a lot of attention in the media and political commentary in the United States, but this term is almost always used to describe people in the middle of the income distribution. People sometimes talk about "middle class workers," referring to people who work for a wage but live comfortable if modest lives. Especially in goods-producing industries, unionized workers have been able to win wages that allow home ownership, paid vacations, nice cars, home entertainment centers, and other consumer amenities.

When class is understood in terms of income or lifestyle, these workers are sometimes called "middle class." Even leaders of the workers' unions use the term to emphasize the gains unions have been able to win for working people. "Middle class workers" are supposed to be "most people," those with stable jobs and solid values based in the work ethic, as opposed to poor people—those on welfare or the "underclass"—on one side, and "the rich" on the other. When people think about classes in terms of "rich, middle, and poor," almost everyone ends up in the middle.

Understanding class in terms of power throws a different light on the subject. In this view, middle class people are in the middle of the power grid that has workers and capitalists at its poles. The middle class includes professional people like doctors, lawyers, accountants, and university professors. Most people in the "professional middle class" are not self-employed. They work for private companies or public agencies, receive salaries, and answer to supervisors. In these ways they are like workers.

But if we compare professional middle class people with well-paid workers, we see important differences. A unionized auto assembly worker doing a lot of overtime makes enough money to live the lifestyle of a "middle class worker," even more money than some professors or lawyers. But a well-paid unionized machinist or electrician or autoworker is still part of the working class. Professors and lawyers have a degree of autonomy and control at work that autoworkers don't have. The difference is a question of class.

It is also misleading to equate the working class as a whole with its best-paid unionized members. Only 9 percent of private sector workers belong to unions, and millions of them are low-paid service employees. The relatively well-paid manufacturing industries are not typical of American business, and they are shrinking as a proportion of the total economy.

The middle class also includes supervisors in the business world, ranging from line foremen to senior managers below the top decision-making executives. As with the professional middle class, some people in the supervisory middle class are close to working people in income and lifestyle. We see this mostly at the lower levels of supervision, as with line foremen

or other first-level supervisors. They often are promoted from the ranks of workers, continue to live in working class areas, and socialize with working class friends. But a foreman is not a worker when it comes to the power grid. The foreman is on the floor to represent the owner, to execute orders in the management chain of command. The foreman is in the middle—between the workers and the owners. When a worker becomes a supervisor, he or she enters the middle class. But just as the well-paid "middle class worker" is atypical, so "working class bosses" make up a small fraction of supervisory and managerial personnel in the U.S. economy.

We see something similar with small business owners, the third component of the middle class. Some come out of the working class and continue to have personal and cultural ties to their roots. But these connections do not change the fact that workers aspire to have their own business to escape the regimentation of working class jobs, seeking instead the freedom to "be my own boss." That freedom, regardless of how much it might be limited by competitive pressures in the marketplace and how many hours the owner must work to make a go of it, puts the small business owner in a different class from workers.

At the other end of the business scale, senior managers and high-level corporate attorneys and accountants share quite a bit with the capitalists they serve. They have considerable authority, make a lot of money, and revolve in the same social circles. But they are not the final decision makers. They are at a qualitatively different level in the power grid from those they serve, who pay them well for their service but retain ultimate authority. They, too, are in the middle class.

In all three sections of the middle class—professionals, supervisors, and small business owners—there are fuzzy borders with the working class and with the capitalists. Yet the differences in power, independence, and life circumstances among these classes support the idea of a separate middle class. The middle class is about 36 percent of the labor force in the United States—sizable, but far from the majority, far from the "typical" American.

Lucky Americans

I identify myself as a biracial, middle/working-class female. My earliest memory of feeling that I was privileged was when I was about six years old, when I first moved to Arlington, Virginia. My parents had just reconciled after being separated, and my siblings and I moved back to Virginia from California. Because my dad had been living on his own, all we had to go back to was a one-bedroom apartment in a moderately rough neighborhood. Many people there were minorities, a large number were immigrants, and many of my peers came from broken homes.

My family and I were not in a better financial situation than other people in the neighborhood, but we were privileged because both my parents had at least a high school education, spoke English, and worked. Others in our neighborhood considered us "lucky," or they thought that we believed we were better than them. Ironically, these feelings often came from people who had fewer children and lived in bigger apartments (there were six of us living in a one bedroom). I realized I was in a "privileged" class because my mom and I often had to translate for our neighbors. We were the Americans "who had it all." I was privileged because I came from a family of natural-born American citizens.

It felt good to know that we had some advantages rather than disadvantages growing up, but I didn't like feeling that our neighbors thought we couldn't relate to them or didn't understand their struggle. My family and I were struggling too, although in a different way. True, we didn't have a language barrier, but my parents were young, with really no trade skills, and on top of that we had no money. I talked to our neighbors but often felt their jealousy and resentment, so I didn't usually feel like being around them.

LeiLani Page

Like the working class and the capitalists, the middle class is represented in the political process by professional associations and small business groups. There is no "middle-income" lobby, but there are, for example, the Trial Lawyers Association, the American Medical Association, the American Association of University Professors, the National Association of Realtors.

Clearly, classes are not monolithic collections of socially identical people. We have seen that each class contains quite a bit of variation. Rather than sharp dividing lines, the borders between them are porous and ambiguous—important areas to study and better understand. Also, beyond the differences in occupations and relative power within classes, which lead to differences in incomes, wealth, and lifestyles, each class contains men and women of every race, nationality, and creed. Yet, despite these rich internal variations and ambiguous borders, a qualitative difference remains between the life experience of the working class compared with that of the professional and managerial middle class, to say nothing of differences both of these have with the capitalists.

DISCUSSION QUESTIONS

1. How is social class like and also different from race, sex, gender, and sexual orientation?
2. Would you agree with Zweig that "without a class analysis, we would have only the most superficial knowledge of our own lives and the experience of others"?
3. In your own mind, what are the key criteria or concepts Zweig is using to define social class? What is your opinion of his definition of social class?

NOTES

1. For a detailed discussion of the class composition of the United States, on which these and the following findings are based, see Michael Zweig, *The Working Class Majority: America's Best Kept Secret* (Ithaca, NY: Cornell University Press, 2000), chap. 1.
2. Some middle class people are represented by unions, such as university professors in the American Federation of Teachers (AFT) and legal aid attorneys in the UAW. Most union members are in the working class.

The Rich, the Poor, and the Growing Gap between Them— Inequality in America

The Economist

Americans do not go in for envy. The gap between rich and poor is bigger than in any other advanced country, but most people are unconcerned. Whereas Europeans fret about the way the economic pie is divided, Americans want to join the rich, not soak them. Eight out of ten, more than anywhere else, believe that though you may start poor, if you work hard, you can make pots of money. It is a central part of the American Dream.

The political consensus, therefore, has sought to pursue economic growth rather than the redistribution of income, in keeping with John Kennedy's adage that "a rising tide lifts all boats." The tide has been rising fast recently. Thanks to a jump in productivity growth after 1995, America's economy has outpaced other rich countries' for a decade. Its workers now produce over 30% more each hour they work than ten years ago. In the late 1990s everybody shared in this boom. Though incomes were rising fastest at the top, all workers' wages far outpaced inflation.

But after 2000 something changed. The pace of productivity growth has been rising again, but now it seems to be lifting fewer boats. After you adjust for inflation, the wages of the typical American worker—the one at the very middle of the income distribution—have risen less than 1% since 2000. In the previous five years, they rose over 6%. If you take into account the value of employee benefits, such as health care, the contrast is a little less stark. But, whatever the measure, it seems clear that only the most skilled workers have seen their pay packets swell much in the current economic expansion. The fruits of productivity gains have been skewed towards the highest earners, and towards companies, whose profits have reached record levels as a share of GDP. . . .

. . . The statistics suggest that the economic boom may fade. Americans still head to the shops with gusto, but it is falling savings rates and rising debts (made possible by high house prices), not real income growth, that keep their wallets open. A bust of some kind could lead to widespread political disaffection. Eventually, the country's social fabric could stretch. "If things carry on like this for long enough," muses one insider, "we are going to end up like Brazil"—a country notorious for the concentration of its income and wealth.

America is nowhere near Brazil yet. Despite a quarter century during which incomes have drifted ever farther apart, the distribution of wealth has remained remarkably stable. The richest Americans now earn as big a share of overall income as they did a century ago (see chart 1), but their share of overall wealth is much lower. Indeed, it has barely budged in the few past decades.

The elites in the early years of the 20th century were living off the income generated by their accumulated fortunes. Today's rich, by and large, are earning their money. In 1916 the richest 1% got only a fifth of their income from paid work, whereas the figure in 2004 was over 60%.

CHART 1
Rich pickings. *Source:* Emmanuel Saez et al.

Income share in US, excluding capital gains, %

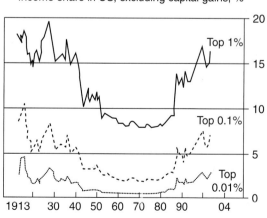

THE NOT-SO-IDLE RICH

The rise of the working rich reinforces America's self-image as the land of opportunity. But, by some measures, that image is an illusion. Several new studies,* show parental income to be a better predictor of whether someone will be rich or poor in America than in Canada or much of Europe. In America about half of the income disparities in one generation are reflected in the next. In Canada and the Nordic countries that proportion is about a fifth.

It is not clear whether this sclerosis is increasing: the evidence is mixed. Many studies suggest that mobility between generations has stayed roughly the same in recent decades, and some suggest it is decreasing. Even so, ordinary Americans seem to believe that theirs is still a land of opportunity. The proportion who think you can start poor and end up rich has risen 20 percentage points since 1980.

That helps explain why voters who grumble about the economy have nonetheless failed to respond to class politics. John Edwards, the Democrats' vice-presidential candidate in 2004, made little headway with his tale of "Two Americas," one for the rich and one for the rest. Over 70% of Americans support the abolition of the estate tax (inheritance tax), even though only one household in 100 pays it.

Americans tend to blame their woes not on rich compatriots but on poor foreigners. More than six out of ten are sceptical of free trade. A new poll in *Foreign Affairs* suggests that almost nine out of ten worry about their jobs going offshore. Congressmen reflect their concerns. Though the economy grows, many have become vociferous protectionists.

Other rich countries are watching America's experience closely. For many Europeans, America's brand of capitalism is already far too unequal. Such sceptics will be sure to make much of any sign that the broad middle-class reaps scant benefit from the current productivity boom, setting back the course of European reform even further.

---

*The papers mentioned in this article can be found at www.economist.com/inequality.

The conventional tale is that the changes of the past few years are simply more steps along paths that began to diverge for rich and poor in the Reagan era. During the 1950s and 1960s, the halcyon days for America's middle class, productivity boomed and its benefits were broadly shared. The gap between the lowest and highest earners narrowed. After the 1973 oil shocks, productivity growth suddenly slowed. A few years later, at the start of the 1980s, the gap between rich and poor began to widen.

The exact size of that gap depends on how you measure it. Look at wages, the main source of income of most people, and you understate the importance of health care and other benefits. Look at household income and you need to take into account that the typical household has fallen in size in recent decades, thanks to the growth in single-parent families. Look at statistics on spending and you find that the gaps between top and bottom have widened less than for income. But every measure shows that, over the past quarter century, those at the top have done better than those in the middle, who in turn have out-paced those at the bottom. The gains of productivity growth have become increasingly skewed.

If all Americans were set on a ladder with ten rungs, the gap between the wages of those on the ninth rung and those on the first has risen by a third since 1980. Put another way, the typical worker earns only 10% more in real terms than his counterpart 25 years ago, even though overall productivity has risen much faster. Economists have long debated why America's income disparities suddenly widened after 1980. The consensus is that the main cause was technology, which increased the demand for skilled workers relative to their supply, with freer trade reinforcing the effect. Some evidence suggests that institutional changes, particularly the weakening of unions, made the going harder for people at the bottom.

Whether these shifts were good or bad depends on your political persuasion. Those on the left lament the gaps, often forgetting that the greater income disparities have created bigger incentives to get an education, which has led to a better trained, more productive workforce. The share of American workers with a college degree, 20% in 1980, is over 30% today.

THE EXCLUDED MIDDLE

In their haste to applaud or lament this tale, both sides of the debate tend to overlook some nuances. First, America's rising inequality has not, in fact, been continuous. The gap between the bottom and the middle—whether in terms of skills, age, job experience or income—did widen sharply in the 1980s. High-school dropouts earned 12% less in an average week in 1990 than in 1980; those with only a high-school education earned 6% less. But during the 1990s, particularly towards the end of the decade, that gap stabilised and, by some measures, even narrowed. Real wages rose faster for the bottom quarter of workers than for those in the middle.

After 2000 most people lost ground, but, by many measures, those in the middle of the skills and education ladder have been hit relatively harder than those at the bottom. People who had some college experience, but no degree, fared worse than high-school dropouts. Some statistics suggest that the annual income of Americans with a college degree has fallen relative to that of high-school graduates for the first time in decades. So, whereas the 1980s were hardest on the lowest skilled, the 1990s and this decade have squeezed people in the middle.

The one truly continuous trend over the past 25 years has been towards greater concentration of income at the very top. The scale of this shift is not visible from most popular measures of income or wages, as they do not break the distribution down finely enough. But several recent studies have dissected tax records to investigate what goes on at the very top.

The figures are startling. According to Emmanuel Saez of the University of California, Berkeley, and Thomas Piketty of the Ecole Normale Superieure in Paris, the share of aggregate income going to the highest-earning 1% of Americans has doubled from 8% in 1980 to over 16% in 2004. That going to the top tenth of 1% has tripled from 2% in 1980 to 7% today. And that going to the top one-hundredth of 1%—the 14,000 taxpayers at the very top of the income ladder—has quadrupled from 0.65% in 1980 to 2.87% in 2004.

Put these pieces together and you do not have a picture of ever-widening inequality but of what

Lawrence Katz of Harvard University, David Autor of the Massachusetts Institute of Technology and Melissa Kearney of the Brookings Institution call a polarisation of the labour market. The bottom is no longer falling behind, the top is soaring ahead and the middle is under pressure.

SUPERSTARS AND SUPER-SQUEEZED

Can changes in technology explain this revised picture? Up to a point. Computers and the internet have reduced the demand for routine jobs that demand only moderate skills, such as the work of bank clerks, while increasing the productivity of the highest-skilled. Studies in Britain and Germany as well as America show that the pace of job growth since the early 1990s has been slower in occupations that are easy to computerise.

For the most talented and skilled, technology has increased the potential market and thus their productivity. Top entertainers or sportsmen, for instance, now perform for a global audience. Some economists believe that technology also explains the soaring pay of chief executives. One argument is that information technology has made top managers more mobile, since it no longer takes years to master the intricacies of any one industry. As a result, the market for chief executives is bigger and their pay is bid up. Global firms plainly do compete globally for talent: Alcoa's boss is a Brazilian; Sony's chief executive is American (and Welsh).

But the scale of America's income concentration at the top, and the fact that no other country has seen such extreme shifts, has sent people searching for other causes. The typical American chief executive now earns 300 times the average wage, up tenfold from the 1970s. Continental Europe's bosses have seen nothing similar. This discrepancy has fostered the "fat cat" theory of inequality: greedy businessmen sanction huge salaries for each other at the expense of shareholders.

Whichever explanation you choose for the signs of growing inequality, none of the changes seems transitory. The middle rungs of America's labour market are likely to become ever more squeezed. And that squeeze feels worse thanks to another change that has hit the middle class most: greater fluctuations in people's incomes.

The overall economy has become more stable over the past quarter century. America has had only two recessions in the past 20 years, in 1990–91 and 2001, both of which were mild by historical standards. But life has become more turbulent for firms and people's income now fluctuates much more from one year to the next than it did a generation ago. Some evidence suggests that the trends in short-term income volatility mirror the underlying wage shifts and may now be hitting the middle class most.

What of the future? It is possible that the benign pattern of the late 1990s will return. The disappointing performance of the Bush era may simply reflect a job market that is weaker than it appears. Although unemployment is low, at 4.6%, other signals, such as the proportion of people working, seem inconsistent with a booming economy.

More likely, the structural changes in America's job market that began in the 1990s are now being reinforced by big changes in the global economy. The integration of China's low-skilled millions and the increased offshoring of services to India and other countries has expanded the global supply of workers. This has reduced the relative price of labour and raised the returns to capital. That reinforces the income concentration at the top, since most stocks and shares are held by richer people. More important, globalisation may further fracture the traditional link between skills and wages.

As Frank Levy of MIT points out, offshoring and technology work in tandem, since both dampen the demand for jobs that can be reduced to a set of rules or scripts, whether those jobs are for bookkeepers or call-centre workers. Alan Blinder of Princeton, by contrast, says that the demand for skills depends on whether they must be used in person: X-rays taken in Boston may be read by Indians in Bangalore, but offices cannot be cleaned at long distance. So who will be squeezed and who will not is hard to predict.

The number of American service jobs that have shifted offshore is small, some 1 [million] at the most.

And most of those demand few skills, such as operating telephones. Mr Levy points out that only 15 radiologists in India are now reading American X-rays. But nine out of ten Americans worry about offshoring. That fear may be enough to hold down the wages of college graduates in service industries.

All in all, American's income distribution is likely to continue the trends of the recent past. While those at the top will go on drawing huge salaries, those in the broad middle of the middle class will see their incomes churned. The political consequences will depend on the pace of change and the economy's general health. With luck, the offshoring of services will happen gradually, allowing time for workers to adapt their skills while strong growth will keep employment high. But if the economy slows, Americans' scepticism of globalisation is sure to rise. And even their famous tolerance of inequality may reach a limit.

DISCUSSION QUESTIONS

1. Why don't Americans complain about the rich?
2. Is technology the main cause of the widening income inequality?
3. Why will those in the middle class continue to get squeezed?

READING 14

Framing Class: Media Representations of Wealth and Poverty in America

Diana Kendall

"The Simple Life 2"—the second season of the reality show, on which the celebutante Paris Hilton and her Best Friend Forever, the professional pop-star-daughter Nicole Richie, are set on a cross-country road trip—*once again takes the heaviest of topics and makes them as weightless as a social X-ray.*[1]

Diana Kendall is a professor of sociology at Baylor University.

This statement by television critic Choire Sicha in her review of FOX TV's reality-based entertainment show *The Simple Life,* sums up a recurring theme. . . . The media typically take "the heaviest of topics," such as class and social inequality, and trivialize it. Rather than providing a meaningful analysis of inequality and showing realistic portrayals of life in various social classes, the media either play class differences for laughs or sweep the issue of class under the rug so that important distinctions are rendered invisible. By ignoring class or trivializing it, the media involve themselves in a social construction of reality that rewards the affluent and penalizes the working class and the poor. In real life, Paris Hilton and Nicole Richie are among the richest young women in the world; however, in the world of *The Simple Life,* they can routinely show up somewhere in the city or the country, pretend they are needy, and rely on the kindness of strangers who have few economic resources. . . .

MEDIA FRAMING AND THE PERFORMANCE OF CLASS IN EVERYDAY LIFE

In a mass-mediated culture such as ours, the media do not simply mirror society; rather, they help to shape it and to create cultural perceptions.[2] The blurring between what is real and what is not real encourages people to emulate the upper classes and shun the working class and the poor. Television shows, magazines, and newspapers sell the idea that the only way to get ahead is to identify with the rich and powerful and to live vicariously through them. From sitcoms to reality shows, the media encourage ordinary people to believe that they may rise to fame and fortune; they too can be the next American Idol. Constantly bombarded by stories about the lifestyles of the rich and famous, viewers feel a sense of intimacy with elites, with whom they have little or no contact in their daily lives.[3] According to the social critic bell hooks, we overidentify with the wealthy, because the media socialize us to believe that people in the upper classes are better than we are. The media also suggest that we need have no allegiance to people in our own class or to those who are less fortunate.[4]

Vicarious living—watching how other individuals live rather than experiencing life for ourselves—through media representations of wealth and success is reflected in many people's reading and viewing habits and in their patterns of consumption. According to hooks, television promotes hedonistic consumerism:

> Largely through marketing and advertising, television promoted the myth of the classless society, offering on one hand images of an American dream fulfilled wherein any and everyone can become rich and on the other suggesting that the lived experience of this lack of class hierarchy was expressed by our *equal right to purchase anything we could afford.*[5]

As hooks suggests, equality does not exist in contemporary society, but media audiences are encouraged to view themselves as having an "equal right" to purchase items that somehow will make them equal to people above them in the social class hierarchy. However, the catch is that we must actually be able to afford these purchases. Manufactures and the media have dealt with this problem by offering relatively cheap products marketed by wealthy celebrities. Paris Hilton, an heir to the Hilton Hotel fortune, has made millions of dollars by marketing products that give her fans a small "slice" of the good life she enjoys. Middle- and working-class people can purchase jewelry from the Paris Hilton Collection—sterling silver and Swarovski crystal jewelry ranging in price from fifteen to a hundred dollars—and have something that is "like Paris wears." For less than twenty dollars per item, admirers can purchase the Paris Hilton Wall Calendar; a "Paris the Heiress" Paper Doll Book; Hilton's autobiography, *Confessions of an Heiress;* and even her dog's story. *The Tinkerbell Hilton Diaries: My Life Tailing Paris Hilton.* But Hilton is only one of thousands of celebrities who make money by encouraging unnecessary consumerism among people who are inspired by media portrayals of the luxurious and supposedly happy lives of rich celebrities. The title of Hilton's television show, *The Simple Life,* appropriates the image of simple people, such as the working class and poor, who might live happy, meaningful lives, and transfers this image to women whose lives are anything but simple as they flaunt designer clothing and spend collectively millions of dollars on entertainment, travel, and luxuries that can be afforded only by the very wealthy.[6]

How the media frame stories about class *does* make a difference in what we think about other people and how we spend our money. Media frames constitute a mental shortcut (schema) that helps us formulate our thoughts.

The Upper Classes: Affluence and Consumerism for All

Although some media frames show the rich and famous in a negative manner, they still glorify the material possessions and lifestyles of the upper classes. Research has found that people who extensively watch television have exaggerated views of how wealthy most Americans are and what material possessions they own. Studies have also found that extensive television viewing leads to higher rates of spending and to lower savings, presumably because television stimulates consumer desires.[7]

For many years, most media framing of stories about the upper classes has been positive, ranging from *consensus framing* that depicts members of the upper class as being like everyone else, to *admiration framing* that portrays them as generous, caring individuals. The frame most closely associated with rampant consumerism is *emulation framing*, which suggests that people in all classes should reward themselves with a few of the perks of the wealthy, such as buying a piece of Paris's line of jewelry. The writers of television shows such as ABC's *Life of Luxury*, E!'s *It's Good to Be . . .* [a wealthy celebrity, such as Nicole Kidman], and VH1's *The Fabulous Life* rely heavily on admiration and price-tag framing, by which the worth of a person is measured by what he or she owns and how many assistants constantly cater to that person's whims. On programs like FOX's *The O.C.* and *North Shore* and NBC's *Las Vegas,* the people with the most expensive limousines, yachts, and

jet aircraft are declared the winners in life. Reality shows like *American Idol, The Billionaire, For Love or Money,* and *The Apprentice* suggest that anyone can move up the class ladder and live like the rich if he or she displays the best looks, greatest talent, or sharpest entrepreneurial skills. It is no wonder that the economist Juliet B. Schor finds that the overriding goal of children age ten to thirteen is to get rich. In response to the statement "I want to make a lot of money when I grow up," 63 percent of the children in Schor's study agreed, whereas only 7 percent disagreed.[8]

Many adults who hope to live the good life simply plunge farther into debt. Many reports show that middle- and working-class American consumers are incurring massive consumer debts as they purchase larger houses, more expensive vehicles, and many other items that are beyond their means. According to one analyst, media portrayals of excessive consumer spending and a bombardment of advertisements by credit-card companies encourage people to load up on debt.[9] With the average U.S. household now spending 13 percent of its after-tax income to *service* debts (not pay off the principal!), people with average incomes who continue to aspire to lives of luxury like those of the upper classes instead may find themselves spending their way into the "poor house" with members of the poverty class.

The Poor and Homeless: "Not Me!"— Negative Role Models in the Media

The sharpest contrasts in media portrayals are between depictions of people in the upper classes and depictions of people at the bottom of the class structure. At best, the poor and homeless are portrayed as deserving of our sympathy on holidays or when disaster strikes. In these situations, those in the bottom classes are depicted as being temporarily down on their luck or as working hard to get out of their current situation but in need of public assistance. At worst, however, the poor are blamed for their own problems; stereotypes of the homeless as bums, alcoholics, and drug addicts, caught in a hopeless downward spiral because of their *individual* pathological behavior, are omnipresent in the media.

For the most part, people at the bottom of the class structure remain out of sight and out of mind for most media audiences. *Thematic framing* depicts the poor and homeless as "faceless" statistics in reports on poverty. *Episodic framing* highlights some problems of the poor but typically does not link their personal situations concerns to such larger societal problems as limited educational opportunities, high rates of unemployment, and jobs that pay depressingly low wages.

The poor do not fare well on television entertainment shows, where writers typically represent them with one-dimensional, bedraggled characters standing on a street corner holding cardboard signs that read "Need money for food." When television writers tackle the issue of homelessness, they often portray the lead characters (who usually are white and relatively affluent) as helpful people, while the poor and homeless are depicted as deviants who might harm themselves or others. Hospital and crime dramas like *E.R., C.S.I.,* and *Law & Order* frequently portray the poor and homeless as "crazy," inebriated in public, or incompetent to provide key information to officials. Television reality shows like *Cops* go so far as to advertise that they provide "footage of debris from the bottom tiers of the urban social order."[10] Statements such as this say a lot about the extent to which television producers, directors, and writers view (or would have us view) the lower classes.

From a sociological perspective, framing of stories about the poor and homeless stands in stark contrast to framing of stories about those in the upper classes, and it suggests that we should distance ourselves from "those people." We are encouraged to view the poor and homeless as the *Other,* the outsider; in the media we find little commonality between our lives and the experiences of people at the bottom of the class hierarchy. As a result, it is easy for us to buy into the dominant ideological construction that views poverty as a problem of individuals, not of the society as a whole, and we may feel justified in our rejection of such people.[11]

The Working Class: Historical Relics and Jokes

As we have seen, the working class and the working poor do not fare much better than the poor and homeless in media representations. The working class is described as "labor," and people in this class are usually nothing more than faces in a crowd on television shows. The media portray people who *produce* goods and services as much less interesting than those who *excessively consume* them, and this problem can only grow worse as more of the workers who produce the products are thousands of miles away from us, in nations like China, very remote from the typical American consumer.[12]

Contemporary media coverage carries little information about the working class or its problems. Low wages, lack of benefits, and hazardous working conditions are considered boring and uninteresting topics, except on the public broadcasting networks or an occasional television "news show" such as *60 Minutes* or *20/20,* when some major case of worker abuse has recently been revealed. The most popular portrayal of the working class is *caricature framing,* which depicts people in negative ways, such as being dumb, white trash, buffoons, bigots, or slobs. Many television shows featuring working-class characters play on the idea that the clothing, manners, and speech patterns of the working class are not as good as those of the middle or upper classes. For example, working-class characters (such as Roseanne, the animated Homer Simpson, and *The King of Queens'* Doug) may compare themselves to the middle and upper classes by saying that they are not as "fancy as the rich people." Situation comedy writers have perpetuated working-class stereotypes, and now a number of reality shows, such as *The Swan* and *Extreme Makeover,* try to take "ordinary" working-class people and "improve" them through cosmetic surgery, new clothing, and different hairstyles.

Like their upper-class celebrity counterparts, so-called working-class comedians like Jeff Foxworthy have ridiculed the blue-collar lifestyle. They also have marketed products that make fun of the working class. Foxworthy's website, for example,

WHAT IS DISABILITY?

Disability Definitions:
The Politics of Meaning

Michael Oliver

THE IMPORTANCE
OF DEFINITIONS

The social world differs from the natural world in (at least) one fundamental respect; that is, human beings give meanings to objects in the social world and subsequently orientate their behavior towards these objects in terms of the meanings given to them. W. I. Thomas (1966) succinctly puts it thus: "if men define situations as real, they are real in their consequences." As far as disability is concerned, if it is seen as a tragedy, then disabled people will be treated as if they are the victims of some tragic happening or circumstance. This treatment will occur not just in everyday interactions but will also be translated into social policies which will attempt to compensate these victims for the tragedies that have befallen them.

Alternatively, it logically follows that if disability is defined as social oppression, then disabled people will be seen as the collective victims of an uncaring or unknowing society rather than as individual victims of circumstance. Such a view will be translated into social policies geared towards alleviating oppression rather than compensating individuals. It almost goes without saying that at present, the individual and tragic view of disability dominates both social interactions and social policies.

A second reason why definitions are important historically centres on the need to identify and classify the growing numbers of the urban poor in

Michael Oliver is a professor of disability studies at the University of Greenwich in the United Kingdom.

modern industrial societies. In this process of identification and classification, disability has always been an important category, in that it offers a legitimate social status to those who can be defined as unable to work as opposed to those who may be classified as unwilling to do so (Stone, 1985). Throughout the twentieth century this process has become ever more sophisticated, requiring access to expert knowledge, usually residing in the ever-burgeoning medical and paramedical professions. Hence the simple dichotomy of the nineteenth century has given way to a whole new range of definitions based upon clinical criteria or functional limitation.

A third reason why definitions are important stems from what might be called "the politics of minority groups." From the 1950s onwards, though earlier in the case of alcoholics, there was a growing realisation that if particular social problems were to be resolved, or at least ameliorated, then nothing more or less than a fundamental redefinition of the problem was necessary. Thus a number of groups including women, black people and homosexuals, set about challenging the prevailing definitions of what constituted these problems by attacking the sexist and racist biases in the language used to underpin these dominant definitions. They did this by creating, substituting or taking over terminology to provide more positive imagery (e.g., gay is good, black is beautiful, etc.). Disabled people too have realised that dominant definitions of disability pose problems for individual and group identity and have begun to challenge the use of disablist language. Whether it be offensive (cripple, spastic, mongol, etc.) or merely depersonalising (the handicapped, the blind, the deaf, and so on), such terminology has been attacked, and organisations of disabled people have fostered a growing group consciousness and identity.

There is one final reason why this issue of definitions is important. From the late fifties onwards there was an upswing in the economy and an increasing concern to provide more services for disabled people out of an ever-growing national cake. But clearly, no government (of whatever includes figurines ("little statues for *inside* the house"), redneck cookbooks, Games Rednecks Play, and calendars that make fun of the working class generally. Although some people see these items as humorous ("where's yore sense of humor?"), the real message is that people in the lower classes lack good taste, socially acceptable manners, and above all, middle-class values. If you purchase "redneck" merchandise, you too can make fun of the working class and clearly distance yourself from it.

MIDDLE-CLASS FRAMING AND KIDDY-CONSUMERISM

Media framing of stories about the middle class tells us that this economic group is the value center and backbone of the nation. *Middle-class values framing* focuses on the values of this class and suggests that they hold the nation together. Early television writers were aware that their shows needed to appeal to middle-class audiences, who were the targeted consumers for the advertisers' products, and middle-class values of honesty, integrity, and hard work were integral ingredients of early sitcoms. However, some contemporary television writers spoof the middle class and poke fun at values supposedly associated with people in this category. The writers of FOX's *Malcolm in the Middle* and *Arrested Development*, for example, focus on the dysfunctions in a fictional middle-class family, including conflicts between husband and wife, between parents and children, and between members of the family and outsiders.

Why do these shows make fun of the middle class? Because corporations that pay for the advertisements want to capture the attention of males between ages eighteen and thirty-nine, and individuals in this category are believed to enjoy laughing at the uptight customs of conventional middle-class families. In other shows, as well, advertisers realize the influence that their programs have on families. That is why they are happy to spend billions of dollars on product placements (such as a Diet Coke can sitting on a person's desk) in the shows and on ads during commercial breaks. In recent research, Schor examined why very young children buy into the consumerism culture and concluded that extensive media exposure to products was a key reason. According to Schor, "More children [in the United States] than anywhere else believe that their clothes and brands describe who they are and define their social status. American kids display more brand affinity than their counterparts anywhere else in the world; indeed, experts describe then as increasingly 'bonded to brands.'"[13]

Part of this bonding occurs through constant television watching and Internet use, as a steady stream of ads targets children and young people. Schor concludes that we face a greater problem than just excessive consumerism. A child's well-being is undermined by the consumer culture: "High consumer involvement is a significant cause of depression, anxiety, low self-esteem, and psychosomatic complaints."[14] Although no similar studies have been conducted to determine the effects of the media's emphasis on wealth and excessive consumerism among adults, it is likely that today's children will take these values with them into adulthood if our society does not first reach the breaking point with respect to consumer debt.

The issue of class in the United States is portrayed in the media not through a realistic assessment of wealth, poverty, or inequality but instead through its patterns of rampant consumerism. The general message remains, one article stated, "We pledge allegiance to the mall."[15]

DISCUSSION QUESTIONS

1. What is your favorite television show? Is it consistent with Diana Kendall's analysis of the media framing of social class?
2. Does Kendall's discussion of consumerism remind you of any of your own recent purchases?
3. Do you think your view of social class has been influenced by the media as much as Kendall would argue?

NOTES

1. Choire Sicha, "They'll Always Have Paris," *New York Times,* June 13, 2004, AR31 [emphasis added].
2. Tim Delaney and Allene Wilcox, "Sports and the Role of the Media," in *Values, Society and Evolution,* ed. Harry Birx and Tim Delaney, 199–215 (Auburn, N.Y.: Legend, 2002).
3. bell hooks [Gloria Watkins], *Where We Stand: Class Matters* (New York: Routledge, 2000), 73.

4. hooks, *Where We Stand,* 77.
5. hooks, *Where We Stand,* 71 [emphasis added].
6. hooks, *Where We Stand,* 72.
7. Juliet B. Schor, *Born to Buy: The Commercialized Child and the New Consumer Culture* (New York: Scribner, 2004).
8. Schor, *Born to Buy.*
9. Joseph Nocera, *A Piece of the Action: How the Middle Class Joined the Money Class* (New York: Simon and Schuster, 1994).
10. Karen De Coster and Brad Edmonds, "TV Nation: The Killing of American Brain Cells," Lewrockwell.com, 2004, www.lewrockwell.com/decoster/decoster78.html (accessed July 7, 2004).
11. Judith Butler ("Performative Acts and Gender Constitution: An Essay in Phenomenology and Feminist Theory," in *Performing Feminisms: Feminist Critical Theory and Theatre,* ed. Sue-Ellen Case [Baltimore: Johns Hopkins University Press. 1990], 270) has described gender identity as performative, noted that social reality is not a given but is continually created as an illusion "through language, gesture, and all manner of symbolic social sign." In this sense, class might also be seen as performative, in that people act out their perceived class location not only in terms of their own class-related identity but in regard to how they treat other people, based on their perceived class position.
12. See Thomas Ginsberg, "Union Hopes to Win Over Starbucks Shop Workers," *Austin American-Statesman.* July 2, 2004, D6.
13. Schor, *Born to Buy,* 13.
14. Schor, *Born to Buy,* 167.
15. Louis Uchitelle, "We Pledge Allegiance to the Mall," *New York Times,* December 6, 2004, C12.

READING 15

Middle-Class Social Reproduction: The Activation and Negotiation of Structural Advantages

Peter Kaufman

. . . Within the study of social mobility, one body of work focuses on the process through which social-class standing is reproduced from one generation

Peter Kaufman is a professor of sociology at SUNY New Paltz.

to the next: social reproduction theory (Althusser, 1972; Bourdieu and Passeron, 1990; Bowles and Gintis, 1976; Willis, 1977). Research on social reproduction rejects the premise of widespread social mobility and attempts instead to explain the persistence of social-class positions. . . .

Some studies of working-class social reproduction suggest that middle-class social reproduction is largely attributable to a structurally advantageous social position. Middle-class social reproduction is not always recognized as an active process of negotiation and construction—much less contestation. Both Willis (1977:1) and MacLeod (1995:214) allude to the structurally determined nature of middle-class reproduction by suggesting that middle-class students reproduce because of the actions of others toward them and not because of their own actions. This argument implies that middle-class social reproduction is a process that does not require much human agency. This perspective is notably different from the constructionist explanations of working-class reproduction, in which individuals actively (re)produce their social positions, and some even resist, contest, and reject structural impositions. Although middle-class students engaged in social reproduction may not exhibit such overt strategies of resistance and rejection, they still must engage in the negotiation and construction of their social reality. As Lareau notes, middle-class individuals must actively utilize their structural resources if they hope to reproduce their social-class standing: "Possession of high status cultural resources does not therefore *automatically* lead to a social investment. Rather, these cultural resources must be effectively activated by individuals, in and through their own actions and decisions" (Lareau, 2000:178). . . .

THE ACTIVE AND CONSTRUCTED PROCESS OF MIDDLE-CLASS SOCIAL REPRODUCTION

When reviewing the literature on working-class social reproduction, three themes emerge that largely explain the inter-generational transfer of social class: acts of resistance and contestation; the importance of the peer group; and the structural location of the family. In the following analysis [of interviews with forty-one college seniors], I explore the extent to which these themes characterize middle-class social reproduction.

Resistance, Rejection, and Contestation

Since Willis's (1977) study detailed the process through which blue-collar youth oppose the dominant school ideology, the themes of resistance, rejection, and contestation have often been used to explain working-class social reproduction. Theorists working from this perspective suggest that working-class individuals reject the interpersonal strategies and institutional affiliations that characterize middle-class life. The lads in Willis's study, the Hallway Hangers that McLeod (1995) observed, and the antischool culture of the girls in McRobbie's (1978) research all reject the prevailing achievement ideology and subsequently disqualify themselves from anything but working-class jobs. Similarly, Foley's (1990) discussion of the "dehumanizing expressive practices" characteristic of capitalism that working-class *vatos* explicitly resist is yet another example of how working-class social reproduction occurs through rejection. All of these studies provide important insight into the interpersonal process through which working-class reproduction transpires. But do middle-class individuals also engage in resistance and contestation? If so, what form does it take, and how does it affect the inter-generational transfer of their social class?

The most prominent example of resistance and contestation to middle-class social reproduction would be students who reject their structural advantages and refuse to strive toward a middle-class lifestyle. . . . Some middle-class individuals engaged in acts of resistance and rejection, although the form of this process and its consequences differ from those of their working-class peers. The middle-class students I studied, generally manifested rejection in two ways: Rejecting parental direction and rejecting nonprofessional occupations. In both processes, the rejection that occurred fostered middle-class social reproduction.

Rejecting Parental Direction   Middle-class students, like many of their peers, are not averse to rejecting the path their parents have mapped out for them. A good example of this process comes from AJ, whose parents were very clear about what he should do: they expected him to become a doctor. Initially, AJ did attend a college that accepted him into a special, 7-year BA/MD program. But after a year, he burned out, "blew up" at his parents, and rejected the medical career they had planned for him. His parents, who were both surprised and distraught, refused to talk to AJ for a month. The reaction of AJ's parents, while extreme, reflects the extent to which "the task of recreating the middle-class is a total preoccupation" for some parents, who stake "much of their own sense of success on the lives of their children" (Newman, 1993:92). When the lines of communication were finally re-opened between AJ and his parents, they kept up the pressure:

> So they were asking me what's the option? Obviously if I was making such a grand, earth-shattering change I should have a plan. Obviously I didn't, because I didn't know anything else; I hadn't had time to think of anything else. So I told them. "I don't know," and unfortunately [that was] not what they were waiting to hear, so they were like, "Well, don't expect us to pay $30,000 a year for you to go to _____ University and figure out what you are going to do. God knows, you could come out and become a theater major." So they told me to choose a state school.

Upon enrolling at a public university, AJ took a broad spectrum of liberal arts courses and finally settled on majoring in history—a choice his parents would rather not have heard:

> I quote from my father, "AJ, do you know what kind of people major in history?" And I was fully expecting a derogatory answer, "People who can't cut it in any other major." It was an answer that I expected, but after a while they've gotten used to it, and I'm doing very well. Then I decided to go to law school, and this is something that I really want to do, and thank God it's something that they approve of.

A similar process of rejection is illustrated by the case of Amy, who expects to create a much different middle-class lifestyle than the one her parents expect of her. Amy's parents are both well educated and working in professional managerial occupations. Her father is an environmental conservationist for the government, and her mother is a nurse supervisor. Although they are solidly middle class, Amy's parents do not live the type of well-polished, professional lifestyle that Amy desires:

> My mother says, "I hope you are kidding when you say that," because I'm always saying, "It's all about the outfit, mom." Whatever's going to give me the outfit, that's what I'm going to do. She is very concerned about me doing something socially conscious. I am concerned about the overall perception of my lifestyle, which is something that I probably wasn't raised to do. I've been to Washington, D.C., and I could just so see myself there. All those people in suits, and I don't like martinis, but, you know, the whole martini bar kind of thing. I could see myself doing that for a while. And the wine and cheese parties, and driving the Lexus, that's what I could see myself doing.

Amy, like AJ, is negotiating a different path of social reproduction than what her parents had hoped. But unlike AJ, who is constructing an identity more consistent with his parent's desires, Amy is engaged in constructing an identity that, while it will ensure her social reproduction (and maybe even produce upward mobility), will also result in a considerable change in lifestyle. Amy's orientation is an example of what Emirbayer and Mische (1998) refer to as the "protective element" of agency, whereby she is creatively reconfiguring the structural resources that her middle-class upbringing have granted her.

In addition to illustrating the variations of middle-class lifestyles and the need for individuals to actively choose the path they will take, the examples of AJ and Amy also reflect some of the ways in which class intersects with race and gender. In both examples, desired social class outcomes are refracted through the lens of race and gender. AJ was partially aware of these effects when he noted how difficult it was to contest his parents' expectations, given his racial-ethnic background: "It's somewhat stereotypical and somewhat it's not. You know, it's Asian American parents, only male child,

both of my parents were extreme overachievers just in everything they've done." In this sense, AJ's occupational choice allows him to reproduce his parents' social class and achieve the stereotypical gender script for an Asian American male (Hirschman and Wong, 1986). Similarly, Amy alludes to the intersection of gender, race, and class by emphasizing her dress as the driving force behind the form she hopes her social reproduction will take (Davis, 1992). She even references Sigourney Weaver's character in the movie *Working Girl* as the type of high-powered female executive she hopes to emulate. Amy is not only striving to reproduce (or transcend) her parents' middle-class status, she is more generally striving for a white, upper-middle-class female ideal.

Not all students in the sample rejected parental direction, but those that did followed patterns similar to those of AJ and Amy. The ability to reject parental direction and still embark on a solid path of social reproduction suggests the intersection between structural advantages and individual action. . . . Middle-class reproducers like AJ and Amy do have the structural resources to reject a particular middle-class path, knowing full well that their acts of resistance do not necessarily disqualify them from remaining middle class.

Rejecting Nonprofessional Occupations A second form of rejection exhibited by nearly all of the respondents was their disapproval of nonprofessional careers. Unlike some of their working-class peers, who resist the achievement ideology and disqualify themselves from professional, middle-class jobs, the respondents in my sample did not contest the notion that a middle-class lifestyle was within their reach. Instead, they explicitly rejected the idea of pursuing a nonprofessional career track. In essence, they reject the idea of rejection and embrace reproduction. That they do not leave school and renounce the professional lifestyle for which they are groomed is an important example of the way they exert their agency within a context of structural privileges. The advantages of growing up middle class play a significant role in getting them primed to reproduce their class standing, but they still must actively pursue a course of action that will ensure their success. In large measure, this course of action involves embracing an orientation toward a professional occupation and rejecting nonprofessional careers. What makes this process especially significant is that the respondents' rejection of working-class occupations arose, in part, from actually working these jobs. Their experiences reinforced the idea that they were capable, both individually and structurally, of doing something more rewarded by society. Consider Maurice's response when I asked him why he would not want to continue working in retail. In particular, notice how his answer reflects Kohn's (1977) distinction between middle-class self-direction and working-class conformity to rules: "Retail, I really don't think you are very, like you really can't make that many decisions; everything is told to you. You have to put this sign here and that sign there and this many things here, and I'm really not into that." Dave, who will graduate with a music degree, is also dismissive of the jobs that he has been doing during his education:

> I've been working at a golf course for five years, a landscaper for two years. You know, it's labor, man, I don't want to do that labor. I would rather finish college and say I got a degree, and this proves I can do something in music. I could teach music lessons, teach general music. I could use my head instead of just my arms and not be a muscle man and laboring and breaking my back. I don't want to do that.

This notion of occupational worth was articulated further by a number of students who focused particularly on the distinction between a job and a career. Felix, who while in high school and college worked his way up to manager at a discount department store, refers to this distinction when asked if he would consider staying in this position full time: "No, not at all. It was just a job for me so that I would have spending cash. It never crossed my mind as being a career. It was just a job." Mary, who has worked as a retail clerk in a large department store and more recently as a bank teller, discusses this distinction more fully when asked why she would not want to be a teller for her whole life:

I guess it's not something I would consider a career. If I went into banking, and I worked as a representative of the bank, then that's something different. But I wouldn't consider, I don't want to sound kind of snobby, but I don't consider retail or being a sales clerk or being a teller a career. It's a career, but it's more of a job that you do. I guess I consider a career something you have to work for, you have to go to school for. Being a teller you don't have to go to school [college]. . . .

Because of their structural location, middle-class reproducers may be adept at recognizing and articulating the distinction between jobs and careers. Relatives may have told them about the difference between jobs and careers, and they may have gained insight from working in their part-time and temporary nonprofessional jobs. More important, their structural location may shape their outlook in that they believe they can aim higher because most of their parents and family members work in professional careers; therefore, there is no reason to believe they will do any differently. Maurice is insightful on this matter: "Yes, I see myself as a white-collar worker. Basically that's the only business I've known. I go to work, and all my managers are wearing shirts and ties, business attire. My father, growing up I've seen him in business attire. I haven't seen many blue-collar workers around." . . .

In rejecting nonprofessional jobs, the respondents are also implicitly rejecting the possibility of downward mobility. In essence, there was no "fear of falling" expressed by any of the students. Although several social scientists have indicated that middle-class status has become increasingly precarious (Childress, 2001; Ehrenreich, 1989; Newman, 1988), no respondents voiced such concerns. All of the students expected to graduate from college and then embark on professional career tracks that would establish and reproduce their middle-class standing. This finding is particularly interesting, given that a handful of respondents did have parents who had experienced or were experiencing a downward shift due to job loss. Despite this stark reality for some, the respondents were unwavering in their confidence and optimism that they would be successful. . . .

The Importance of the Peer Group

A second common theme in the literature on working-class social reproduction is the importance of the peer group. Most adolescent peer groups share a strong sense of belonging in which the group largely shapes individual behavior, values, and attitudes through social comparisons and reflected appraisals (Rosenberg, 1986). Because the members of the peer group share such a strong solidarity, the idea of leaving the group and attempting to succeed on one's own is not really an option. The ethos of the group is to stick together and act as one (MacLeod, 1995). The peer group is particularly important in the context of social reproduction for two reasons. First, because of patterns of social-class segregation in the United States, the peer group often reflects parental social class. For many kids, their friendship pool comprises mostly kids from similar race and class backgrounds. This point was illustrated clearly by Albert: "Almost all of my friends from high school lived in comparable communities. Almost all of the people I was friendly with lived in houses about the same as mine. Almost [all] of the people that I was friendly with, that I identified with, also lived the same type of lifestyle that I did." The second and related reason why the peer group is relevant to social reproduction is that many of the peer-related attributes formed in this period of later adolescence stay with the individual and contribute to the formation of his or her adult identity (Harter, 1990; Harris, 1995, 1998). Consequently, students who grew up middle class and make middle-class friends tend to engage in individual actions and social interactions that largely mirror such middle-class orientations.

Peer group loyalty is not specific to working-class youth. Middle-class youth are similarly influenced by the interactions with their friends. In fact, for the majority of the respondents, the peer group was the first answer given when I asked why they decided to attend college. The following explanation [was] typical:

> I wasn't really enthusiastic about it. I just kind of figured I'd go. You know, I was only 17, and I didn't know what else I was going to do anyway. And pretty much all my friends ended up in college, so I guess it was just kind of the thing to do (Eddie). I guess the end of my junior year in high school. I heard everyone getting excited that they were graduating and what they plan on doing, and I wanted to go away to school like them. I just wanted to see what it was like. At that time my sister was in college, and, being her younger brother, I always hung out with her and her friends, and I thought it [college] was really exciting, and I said I wanted to go away to school instead of being home (Ted).

. . . In addition to influencing the decision to pursue higher education, the peer group of the middle-class reproducers was also instrumental in shaping other values and behaviors that are equally important to successful social reproduction. For instance, Meredith talks about how her goal of being a teacher was largely influenced by her friends: "I want to get settled and start a career. I think there's a lot of pressure because all of my friends are graduating and are going to be doing something, so I don't want to be the only one who is doing nothing. I have to have a career and be a big girl. That's just where I want to be." Similarly, Ngozi identifies her friends as being the main influence on her professional career aspirations. Although she does not expect a career in the health sector like some of her friends, Ngozi does expect a middle-class career: "All of my friends want to do things. A lot of them here are in biology and stuff. They want to be doctors and stuff. Some of my friends back home pretty much the same thing. They want to be physical therapists and stuff like that. I expect that stuff for me too."

The case of Larry offers a more developed example of how peer group solidarity shapes the values and orientations that are necessary for middle-class social reproduction. After 2 years of college, Larry dropped out to pursue a career in retail sales. After some time working in this field, Larry began to re-evaluate his decision and realized that the lifestyle that he enjoyed with his middle-class childhood friends would not be possible much longer. While his friends were completing college and embarking on professional careers, Larry was feeling stuck in a dead-end job:

Well, in the retail jobs I saw people in their forties working these jobs, but I looked at myself at 40 and I realized I don't want to be working all of these weird hours at 40 years old for minimum money, $30,000–35,000 year. I want to have a family and at $30,000–$35,000 per year unless I'm in a steel town in Pennsylvania, it's not going to cut it. I knew I had to go back to have the things I wanted, the life I wanted. I knew I couldn't keep up with my friends or do the things we used to do. They graduated college and were starting above that, right out of college. I knew the lifestyle I was used to I could never do working for the local retail chain making enough money to live but not enough to do the things I was used [to]. I knew the only way to do that was to get my butt back in college, get a real job, along with the possibility of going somewhere with it and eventually getting my Master's degree and so on and so forth.

The lifestyle that Larry desired, that he hoped to enact, was a direct product of the structural advantages of his upbringing. He knew about the good life primarily because he experienced it first hand. Larry's experiences in the real world showed him that he could not achieve this lifestyle by relying solely on his privileged structural conditions; rather, he needed to engage in direct action to achieve his goal. He needed to play a more active role in accumulating resources and adhering to specific requirements, such as completing college, gaining a degree, and embarking on a professional career, that would allow him to join his friends, reproduce his social-class standing, and assume the position of male breadwinner. Without purposive action to activate his structural resources, Larry would probably not be a middle-class reproducer.

The preceding examples all suggest a process of attachment whereby the individual strives to reinforce the bond with the peer group. However, the peer group may also influence social reproduction by encouraging individuals to separate themselves from certain members of the group. Such associational distancing occurs when some members feel the need to disassociate from others who do not exhibit the same orientations and aspirations as the group (Snow and Anderson, 1987). By detaching themselves from those peer group members with whom they no longer want to associate, these individuals further reinforce the bond with those group members they find most similar. What is particularly noteworthy about this process for middle-class reproducers is that the acquaintances from whom they were distancing themselves were not middle class. Although they may primarily associate with kids from similar backgrounds, middle-class kids do not necessarily grow up in homogenous social-class environments; rather, they may work temporarily in low-skill service jobs, and they may socialize with kids from other social classes in school. Working-class kids like the lads and the Hallway Hangers divorced themselves from anyone and anything middle class, and the individuals in my study engaged in similar interpersonal strategies to sever ties with peers they deemed dissimilar. A typical example of this process of peer disassociation comes from Gary:

> I had a set of close friends in high school, and they got in a little bit of trouble, and we have disbanded and no longer see each other. They got into things that I wasn't into, mainly drugs, and we just kind of drifted apart. Most of these guys did not go to college; some went to the military. Half of these guys I split with during high school, and the other half I split with after high school. I hang out with people I met a work and school, and most of them are current or graduate college students. We don't go out and do a lot of outrageous things because I guess we are all mature; I don't know what a good word is, we are all responsible, maybe that's good word.

The fear of being cast out by the peer group seems quite real because some of these middle-class reproducers have actually ended friendships in order to maintain their commitment to middle-class success. These examples reflect the effort that middle-class individuals expend to sustain the identities and interactions that will keep them on a middle-class path. Disassociating from others is an active and calculated choice that people make to achieve a desired end. Susan, an aspiring respiratory therapist, experienced the painful process of closing out some of her childhood friends:

> It was my summer [before senior year of college] when I had taken anatomy, plus I had taken physics and then later on in the summer microbiology, so I

was really busy, and they would call me up, and one in particular who I felt very close was like, "Oh, you stink, you can't come out," and I really felt like that wasn't what I needed to hear. I needed to hear support, and "I admire you for doing this," and I didn't get this often enough. I felt like her priorities were just in the wrong area, and we've just really grown apart, and I really regret cutting ties with them, but I really felt like I grew apart from them.

Whether it serves to bring individuals together and strengthen preexisting ties or pull them apart and orient them toward alternative possibilities, the peer group plays an important role in social reproduction. Indeed, structured social relations such as those in the peer group are what give rise to social behavior (Emirbayer and Goodwin, 1994). The peer group processes discussed in this section reveal some of the social actions that middle-class individuals must engage in if they are to successfully reproduce their class positions. In this sense, middle-class reproduction transpires in much the same fashion as working-class reproduction. Individuals must exert their agency and decide which friends they will follow and emulate, and which ones they will reject and discredit. In neither case does social reproduction occur automatically; rather, the actions of individuals embedded in a structural location lead to the inter-generational transfer of social class.

Familial Advantages

Implicit in the preceding analyses about rejection and resistance and the importance of the peer group is the significant role played by the family. The entire premise of social reproduction revolves around the intergenerational transmission of the family's social class standing. In essence, social reproduction is a familial process. The family provides individuals with the structural resources (or lack thereof) that enable (or impede) the process of social reproduction. . . .

When discussing the influence of their families, many of the respondents were keenly aware of the significant effect the family had on goals and aspirations, most notably when they were asked why they decided to attend college. If the peer group was not mentioned first, then the family was identified as the main reason for going to college. Students credited their parents with providing them both the structural resources and the direction to make college a priority. Some respondents mentioned their parent's encouragement to attend college fairs, enroll in test preparation courses, and visit college campus. A more general type of guidance was also quite typical, as illustrated by Neena's explanation for attending college: "I never thought about not going to college. I was just set. Ever since we were little, our parents just pushed us to study. My sister went to college, I was next, and my brother was next. We just knew. If you wanted to excel you would go to college. It was in our mind set. Our parents never talked about not going to college, so basically it was just known that we had to go to college." . . .

In addition to providing the foundation for attending college, middle-class students enjoyed other family-based structural resources that were potentially instrumental in their social reproduction. For some, such resources were as basic as being offered spending money, as in the case of Christopher. "They [his parents] wanted us all to be, what did they say, pencil pushers. Whenever I would mention even to get a job for a little extra money, like a dishwashing job, they would say, 'Nah, you can't do that, we'll give you extra cash if you need it.'" For others, the parental resources more directly reflected Bourdieu's notion of cultural capital. Consider Helene's comments on eating out and attending cultural events with her family:

A lot of Indian, I love Indian restaurants. Japanese. Not so much Chinese. Italian of course because my mom is Italian. A lot of Kosher delis because my dad is Jewish. Never fast food, or diners, or anything like that. We only went to *nice* places. [Also,] my parents, um, any opportunity to learn about any program on T.V.—like we would watch a lot of PBS, so if there was a show about African tribes or something, we would watch it. Or if the Met was putting on an exhibition about Indian art, we would go.

Through these leisure experiences, Helene acquired cultural resources that allowed her to navigate

PERSONAL ACCOUNT

I Am a Pakistani Woman

I am a Pakistani woman, raised in the U.S. and Canada, and often at odds with the Western standard of beauty.

As a child in Nova Scotia and later growing up in New York and Indiana, I was proud of my uniqueness. On traditional Pakistani and Muslim holidays, I got to wear bright, fun clothes from my country and colorful jewelry. I had a whole rich tradition of my own to celebrate in addition to Christmas and Easter. However, as I started school, I somehow came to realize that being different wasn't so great—that in other people's viewpoint, I looked strange and acted funny. I learned the importance of fitting in and behaving like the other girls. This involved dressing well, giggling a lot, and having a superior, but flirtatious attitude toward boys. I was very outgoing and had very good grades, so outwardly I was able to "assimilate" with some success. But my sister, who was quiet and reticent, often took the brunt of other children's cruelty. I realize how proud and ashamed I was of my heritage when I look at my relationship with my family.

A lesson I learned early on in the U.S. was that being beautiful took a lot of money. It is painful, as an adult, for me to consider the inexorable, never-ending pressure that my father was under to embody the dominant, middle-class cultural expressions of masculinity, as in success at one's job, making a big salary, and owning status symbols. I resented him so much then for being a poor, untenured professor and freelance writer. I wanted designer clothes, dining out at nice restaurants, and a big allowance. Instead, I had a deeply spiritual thinker, writer, and theologian for a dad. I love(d) him and am so very grateful for what he's taught me, but as a child I didn't think of him as a success.

The prettiest girls in school all had a seemingly endless array of outfits, lots of makeup and perfume, and everything by the "right" designers. I hated my mom for making many of my clothes and buying things on sale (and my mom was a great seamstress). I hungrily read about Brooke Shields's seemingly perfect life, with her excursions to expensive restaurants and appointments with personal trainers at exclusive spas. I felt a sense of hopelessness that I could never have the resources or opportunities necessary to compete, to be beautiful.

Instead I found safety in conformity. When I was in high school, the WASPy, preppy look was hot; it represented the epitome of success and privilege in America. I worked hard to purchase a wardrobe of clothes with a polo-horse insignia, by many hours at an after-school job. I tried to hide my exotic look behind Khakis, boat shoes, hair barrettes, and pearl studs. There was comfort in conformity. I saw the class "sex symbol" denigrated for wearing tight dresses and having a very well-developed body for a sixteen-year-old, and the more unique dressers dismissed as frivolous, trendy, and more than a little eccentric. You couldn't be too pretty, too ugly, too different—you had to just blend in.

Though I did it well, I perpetually felt like an imposter. This rigidly controlled, well-dressed preppy going through school with good grades in advanced placement classes in no way represented what I felt to be my true essence.

Hoorie I. Siddique

certain social circles. However, Helene's cultural capital is largely irrelevant unless she decides to activate the cultural benefits her upbringing has furnished, and this holds for the rest of the sample as well. Parental encouragement to study hard and attend college, much less the cultivation of an appreciation for fine art and non-Western culture, will only go as far as the student embracing and adopting such orientations takes them. If the student rejects the achievement ideology, then the benefits of these class-based resources will be undermined and unfulfilled. . . .

The case of Sheryl further illustrates the extent to which middle-class social reproduction requires people to take purposive action in order to activate their familial privileges. Sheryl and her older brother grew up in a solid middle-class family (their father was an executive of a telecommunications company). They both enjoyed the benefits that such an upbringing provides, but Sheryl utilized these resources, while her brother did not. Sheryl's brother made it through a year of college, dropped out, and then found a manual labor job with the phone company. Interestingly, he acquired this job through his father's contacts, suggesting that middle-class structural resources may even benefit those who reject reproduction. Her brother is now working as a foreman, but he hates his job. Sheryl, on the other hand, is preparing to attend law school. Sheryl is not only aware of her privileges, but she has taken advantage of them by embracing the exhortations and resources that her family has offered. In the following except, Sheryl relates how her father has prepared her to reproduce her social class and transform her gender status:

> I had opportunities other people didn't. I have opportunities to get jobs and things because of whom my parents knew and that whole networking thing: "When you finish school, Sheryl, give us a call, and I'll get you a job." And it was usually a white-collar, middle-class job. Nepotism, that's the word I was trying to think of. It's hard for my brother to adjust to the working-class atmosphere that he must deal with at work. He identifies more with the managers than with the crew he supervises. . . . I have a cousin who is a lawyer, and I talk with him a lot. I want to do contract law like my cousin or advocacy law. . . . My father raised me very independent. He always took the "you can do anything you want to" approach. Don't let being a woman hold you back. . . .

There is no denying the importance of the family in the process of social reproduction. For all social classes, the family provides both the model and the resources that set individuals on the path of emulating their parents' social standing. But when discussing the role of the family, it is crucial to remember that social reproduction does not occur involuntarily. Familial dispositions need to be activated by the individual. Cultural capital, social networks, and professional orientations do not necessarily translate into social profits. Moreover, although parental cultural resources are important within the framework of social reproduction, they may be independent of and less salient than the individual's own actions and experiences (Aschaffenburg and Maas, 1997). Thus, the advantages bestowed upon the middle-class students in this sample are made real by their conscious efforts to benefit from these resources. If they rejected the resources afforded

to them by their parents, then there would be no guarantee that social reproduction would occur. By choosing to activate the structural advantages provided by their parents, they are actively striving to replicate their parents' middle-class status.

CONCLUSION AND DISCUSSION

. . . As I have demonstrated in this [study], the process of remaining middle class requires both external advantages and individual exertions. This perspective suggests the need to consider the interaction between social structure and human agency. We should recognize the capabilities of individuals (not only their intentions), given their social structural location, and then consider their ongoing social exertions in the face of these structural realities (Archer, 1988; Fine, 1992; Giddens, 1984; Hays, 1994; Sewell, 1992; Sztompka, 1981; Young, 1999). . . .

Although a person may construct an identity that does not reflect his or her social-class background, engaging in social transformation instead of social reproduction (Granfield, 1991; Kaufman, 2003), to do so requires considerable effort and potential risk at both the individual and structural level. Individually, one must risk being ostracized by peers and/or family for constructing an identity that deviates from the social-class norm. Then, the person must be able to ensure that this identity can be fully realized. Structurally, rules may have to be altered or established, and resources may have to be reallocated or restricted. Given the unlikelihood that both the individual and the structural changes will occur simultaneously, it is not surprising that social-class mobility in the United States has remained relatively stable, and there are even signs of "stagnating opportunities" for some (Gilbert, 1998).

Acknowledgments

I am grateful to Robert Max Jackson, editor of *Sociological Forum,* Kenneth A. Feldman, and the four anonymous reviewers for their helpful comments on earlier drafts of this paper.

DISCUSSION QUESTIONS

1. What distinction do you make between a job and a career?
2. What are the steps in replicating a parent's middle-class status?
3. How do middle-class reproduction and working-class social reproduction differ?

REFERENCES

Aschaffenburg, Karen, and Ineke Maas. 1997. "Cultural and educational careers: The dynamics of social reproduction." *American Review of Sociology* 62: 573–587.

Althusser, L. 1972. "Ideology and ideological state apparatuses." In B. R. Cosin (ed.), *Education: Structure and Society:* 242–280. London: Open University Press.

Archer, Margaret. 1988. *Culture and Agency: The Place of Culture in Social Theory.* Cambridge, UK: Cambridge University Press.

Bourdieu, Pierre, and Jean-Claude Passeron. 1990. *Reproduction in Education, Society and Culture.* London: Sage.

Bowles, Samuel, and Herbert Gintis. 1976. *Schooling in Capitalist America.* New York: Basic Books.

Childress, Caroline. 2001. "Downward Mobility 101: Learning to be 'flexible' in an age of uncertainly." In Eric Margolis (ed.). *The Hidden Curriculum in Higher Education:* 115–134. New York: Routledge.

Davis, Fred. 1992. *Fashion, Culture, and Identity.* Chicago: University of Chicago Press.

Ehrenreich, Barbara. 1989. *Fear of Falling: The Inner Life of the Middle Class.* New York: Pantheon.

Emirbayer, Mustafa, and Ann Mische. 1998. "What is agency?" *American Journal of Sociology* 103(4): 962–1023.

Emirbayer, Mustafa, and Jeff Goodwin. 1994. "Network analysis, culture, and the problem of agency. *American Journal of Sociology* 99(6): 1411–1454.

Fine, Gary Alan. 1992. "Agency, structure and comparative contexts: Toward a synthetic interaction." *Symbolic Interaction* 15(1): 87–107.

Foley, Douglas E. 1990. *Learning Capitalist Culture.* Philadelphia, PA: University of Pennsylvania Press.

Giddens, Anthony. 1984. *The Constitution of Society: Outline of the Theory of Structuration.* Berkeley and Los Angeles: University of California Press.

Gilbert, Dennis. 1998. *The American Class Structure in an Age of Growing Inequality.* Belmont, CA: Wadsworth.

Granfield, Mark. 1991. "Making it by faking it: Working-class students in an elite academic environment." *Journal of Contemporary Ethnography* 20(3): 331–351.

Harris, Judith Rich. 1995. "Where is the child's environment: A group socialization theory of development." *Psychological Review* 102(3): 458–489.

———. 1998. *The Nurture Assumption: Why Children Turn Out the Way They Do.* New York: The Free Press.

Harter, Susan. 1990. "Self and identity development." In S. Shirley Feldman and Glen R. Elliott (eds.), *At the Threshold: The Developing Adolescent:* 352–87. Cambridge, MA: Harvard University Press.

Hays, Sharon. 1994. "Structure and agency and the sticky problem of culture." *Sociological Theory.* 12(1): 57–72.

Hirschman, Charles, and Morrison G. Wong. 1986. "The extraordinary educational attainment of Asian-Americans: A search for historical evidence and explanations," *Social Forces* 65(1): 1–27.

Kaufman, Peter. 2003. "Learning to not labor: How working-class individuals construct middle-class identities." *The Sociological Quarterly* 44(3): 481–504.

Lareau, Annette. 2000. *Home Advantage: Social Class and Parental Intervention in Elementary Education.* Lanham, MD: Rowman & Littlefield.

MacLeod, Jay. 1995. *Ain't No Makin' It.* Boulder, CO: Westview Press.

McRobbie, Angela. 1978. "Working-class girls and the culture of femininity. "In Women's Study Group (eds.), *Women Take Issue:* 96–108. London: Hutchinson.

Newman, Katherine. 1988. *Falling from Grace: The Experience of Downward Mobility in the American Middle Class.* New York: Free Press.

———. 1993. *Declining Fortunes: The Withering of the American Dream.* New York: Basic Books.

Rosenberg, Morris. 1986. *Conceiving the Self.* Malabar, FL: Robert E. Krieger Publishing.

Sewell Jr., William. 1992. "A theory of structure: Duality, agency, and transformation." *American Journal of Sociology* 98(1):1–29.

Snow, David A., and Leon Anderson. 1987. "Identity work among the homeless: The verbal construction and avowal of personal identities." *American Journal of Sociology* 92: 1336–71.

Sztompka, Piotr. 1991. *Society in Action: The Theory of Social Becoming.* Chicago: University of Chicago Press.

Willis, Paul. 1977. *Learning to Labor.* New York: Columbia University Press.

Young Jr., Alford A. 1999. "The (non)accumulation of capital: Explicating the relationship of structure and agency in the lives of poor black men." *Sociological Theory* 17(2): 201–227.

This Hard-Earned Money Comes Stuffed in Their Genes

Dusty Horwitt

In every age and every nation, the rich and powerful employ new myths to preserve their privileged status. In the 17th and 18th centuries, European monarchs justified their rule through "the divine right of kings," perhaps most famously articulated by Bishop Jacques-Benigne Bossuet, a tutor to Louis XIV's son. "God establishes Kings as his ministers, and reigns through them over the people," Bossuet wrote in a document published posthumously in 1709. . . .

[Similarly,] many wealthy Americans and their political allies have fueled the popular myth that we earn all of our money through individual effort. After all, if our money is fully "hard-earned," the argument goes, it's unfair for the government to take it away—and especially unfair to provide it to the less affluent among us who didn't "earn" their way as we did.

But like the divine right of kings, there is more myth than truth in the phrase "hard-earned" money.

Exhibit A is *Forbes* magazine's list of the 400 wealthiest Americans, which tells the story of a massive redistribution of wealth based more on birth than on hard work.

Among the 100 wealthiest Americans on this year's list, *Forbes* reports that 46, or almost half, owe at least a chunk of their fortunes to inheritance. They include real estate mogul Donald Trump (net worth $2.5 billion), media baron Rupert Murdoch (net worth $7.2 billion) and five heirs to the Wal-Mart fortune Alice, Helen, Jim, John and Robson Walton who are worth $20.5 billion each.

While some people who inherit money work as hard and competently as some who haven't inherited

---

Dusty Horwitt is a lawyer who works for a nonprofit environmental organization in Washington, DC.

piles of cash, inherited money is not the product of the heir's hard work. Neither is the wealth created by inherited investments.

And inherited money is only one form of unearned wealth. Other types include the businesses, jobs and even access to universities that millions of Americans inherit, at least in part.

Take the case of Fidelity Investments Chairman and CEO Edward C. Johnson III (net worth $4.9 billion) who is described by *Forbes* as "self-made." The magazine doesn't mention that Johnson III took over Fidelity from his father, Fidelity founder Edward C. Johnson II. *Forbes* does note, however, that "self-made" Viacom CEO Sumner Redstone (net worth $9.7 billion) got his start by taking charge of his father's drive-in theater business and that "self-made" financier Charles Bartlett Johnson (net worth $2 billion) and his brother got started by seizing the reins of their father's mutual fund business.

The nation's leading NASCAR dad, Bill France Jr. (net worth $1.2 billion, according to an article in [the *Washington Post*] in 2001), chairman of NASCAR's board of directors, is the son of Bill France Sr., NASCAR's founder. France Jr. has also appointed to NASCAR's board his brother Jim (net worth $1.2 billion), son Brian and daughter Lesa France Kennedy.

The Bush administration has found places for several well-connected offspring including Vice President Cheney's daughter Elizabeth, who until recently was a deputy assistant secretary of state; Supreme Court Justice Antonin Scalia's son Eugene, who formerly served as solicitor of the Labor Department; and Secretary of State Colin Powell's son, Michael, the chairman of the Federal Communications Commission.

Then there are the colleges and universities that give special preferences in the admissions process to children of alumni. Many of the top schools, including Harvard, Princeton, Stanford and the University of Pennsylvania, admit so-called legacies at a rate two to four times that of their overall applicant pool, the *Wall Street Journal* reported [in 2003].

Adam Bellow, author of the recent book *In Praise of Nepotism: A Natural History,* freely acknowledges that he got his publishing job through the connections of his famous father, novelist Saul Bellow. The younger Bellow notes that nepotism benefits Americans of every class, profession and political persuasion—from middle-income firefighters to fantastically wealthy movies stars such as Gwyneth Paltrow to presidential candidates such as Al Gore. (Of course there's a big difference in wealth between landing a job at the fire station and one as a Hollywood star.) As with inherited money, those who receive family help landing a job or a seat at an elite college may be just as hardworking and talented as those who don't. But getting the position in the first place is undeniably a step toward success that is not fully earned.

So what about people like Bill Gates (net worth $46 billion) or Warren Buffett (net worth $36 billion), who seem to have succeeded without significant family help or inheritance? Didn't they earn all of their money? Not according to Buffett.

As the billionaire investor wrote in [the *Washington Post* in 2003], he too, owes much of his wealth to forces outside his control. Buffet explained that he was financially "luckier" than his receptionist of relatively modest means because "I came wired at birth with a talent for capital allocation—a valuable ability to have had in this country during the past half-century. Credit America with most of this value, not me. If the receptionist and I had both been born in, say, Bangladesh, the story would have been far different. There, the market value of our respective talents would not have varied greatly." The same could be said about Bill Gates's lucky mix of talent and timing in the computer world.

Perhaps more obvious is the role of such luck in sports. Michael Jordan undoubtedly worked hard. But he owes much of his wealth to his largely unearned 6-foot-6-inch height and world-class leaping ability (this skill can be modestly improved through effort), not to mention his advertising-friendly good looks and the fact that he came of age at a time of inflated sports salaries. If you don't think timing influences salary, just ask home-run king Hank Aaron who never earned more than $240,000 a season, the same amount that current star, Alex Rodriguez, earns in two games.

Even our hard work itself is not always the result of individual effort. Take the case of Louisiana's boy wonder, Bobby Jindal. Son of Indian immigrants. Rhodes Scholar. Louisiana's secretary for Health and Hospitals at age 24 and near-miss candidate for governor at age 32. Jindal seems like the quintessential Horatio Alger. But like most, if not all, "self-made" individuals, a look beneath the surface reveals a more complex story.

"My dad is from one of those families where if you brought home a grade—a 90—he'd always ask what happened to the other 10 points," [the *Washington Post*] quoted Jindal as saying. Growing up in a family like that, it's fair to say that Jindal's success was not only a product of his hard work or even of his own choice. His parents pushed him to succeed, just as millions of caring parents, including my own, encouraged or required success for their own children.

Would things have turned out less rosy for Jindal or me if we had been born to less worthy parents? Probably. For example, 47 percent of inmates in state prisons have a parent or other close relative who has also been incarcerated, according to the Bureau of Justice Statistics, as reported in the *New York Times*. In addition, half of all juveniles in custody have a father, mother or other close relative who has been in jail or prison. Maybe I'm going out on a limb, but I'm guessing that if these juveniles brought home a grade of 90, their parents didn't ask about the other 10 points.

When you add up the overwhelming influence of inheritance, family connections, God-given talents, timing, government investments, the benefit or burden of being born to a particular set of parents (or maybe just one parent), as well as all the other twists and turns we experience, it's clear that only a portion of our money is hard-earned and probably not the majority of it. After all, most of us work hard but only 10 percent of Americans control 70 percent of our wealth, while more than 43 million Americans lack something as basic as health insurance. Differences in individual effort cannot explain these disparities. The notion of "hard-earned money" is simplistic at best. What we are given is at least as important to our success as what we earn.

DISCUSSION QUESTIONS

1. Is the belief that we earn all our money by our own effort better described as a myth or an ideology?
2. Do you agree that Warren Buffett and Bill Gates owe their wealth to forces outside their control?

Wouldn't they have succeeded anywhere, example, in Bangladesh?

3. Thinking about the jobs you have held, what portion of your earnings would you attribute to your own "hard-earned effort" versus your connections, timing, government investments, God-given talents, and parental efforts?

WHAT IS SEXUAL ORIENTATION?

READING 17

Is Homosexual a Noun?

Paul R. Abramson

Steven D. Pinkerton

The question that interests us is not whether biology or the environment is the greater contributor to sexual orientation, but how these influences interact in different people to produce the variability in sexual object "choice" evident throughout history, both within and across cultures. The cross-cultural study of sexuality clearly demonstrates that homosexuality is not a unitary phenomenon. . . .

There are at least four distinct conceptualizations to consider: existentialism (homosexuality as a state of being), behaviorism (homosexual acts), self-identification (sexual identity), and sexual orientation (desire, fantasy, etc., as distinct from overt behavior). The question of the relationship among these various aspects is critical to understanding just what it is that should be explained by a biological theory of homosexuality.

To begin with, we need to decide whether *homosexual* is a concrete entity (noun), or merely a descriptor (adjective).[1] In other words, is homosexuality simply a behavior in which certain people

Paul R. Abramson is a professor of psychology at the University of California, Los Angeles. Steven D. Pinkerton is a professor of psychiatry and behavioral medicine at the Medical College of Wisconsin.

occasionally (or consistently) engage, or does it constitute a fundamental characteristic of the self—that of *being* a homosexual? Would we even bother to recognize (or heatedly argue about) homosexuality if society did not pathologize it? In a different context, might it be merely curious, or perhaps even trivially commonplace? And if so, why do we consider it to be a unifying theme of identity? Imagine, that society had instead decided to classify people by the beer that they drink. Such a classification scheme would obviously be trivial because the resulting identities would be based upon an inessential characteristic that reveals little of substance.[2] Similarly, perhaps homosexuality is a biological nonentity that arises as a descriptor merely because society has maligned nonprocreative sex too severely. That is, by making *homosexual behavior* taboo, society may have created *homosexuality* as a cultural entity.

Evidence that this is so may be found in the recent historical record. In the Middle Ages, homosexual acts were condemned by Christians and Jews alike as an "abomination" and a "sin against nature,"[3] yet the performance of a homosexual act did not, in and of itself, brand the sinner as a distinct category of being. Having sex with a same-sex partner no more made one a "homosexual" than coveting a neighbor's wife made one a "coveter."[4] However, with the rise of science, and the psychiatric profession in particular, in the late eighteenth and early nineteenth centuries, homosexual behaviors became pathologized, and those who practiced them became deviants, degenerates, "inverts,"—in other words, "homosexuals."[5] As John De Cecco suggests:

CCOUNT
_____

isibly

For me, coming out is a Sisyphean task. Because of my invisible differences, I constantly have to reveal different parts of my identity. It's not an easy task, either. When I come out as a lesbian/queer woman, people are often surprised because I don't "look" queer. I can count on one hand the number of times I have been recognized by a stranger as part of the LGBT "family." Some people are also surprised to learn that I'm half Taiwanese. I am also half-white, and often assumed to be white, making my race another invisible identity. Because of this, there have been times when people have made racist jokes—either about Asians or other groups—because they thought I was white, and thus thought that these were "acceptable" jokes to tell in my presence.

Invisible identities work differently from other differences. I am lucky not to be harassed on the street because of my race, and since I don't appear queer to your average passerby, I don't usually get harassed for that. I benefit from the privilege of passing as a straight and white, but most days I wish that I could give up that privilege. It is extremely difficult to live your life where some of the most important things about you are hidden. For example, I never know when it is appropriate to come out as queer in class, and almost feel guilty if I never do, even though it may not always be necessary or appropriate. Because I am invisible, I bear the burden of disclosure. When someone assumes that I'm heterosexual, I have to correct her or him (my mother still doesn't believe that I'm queer). When someone assumes that I'm white, I do the same. Regardless, I come out all the time to new people in my life, and each time I do, I hope that they will be able to handle the information with care and respect.

Most people respond well when I come out to them, and I can breathe another sigh of relief when my peers accept me. College, especially, has been a (mostly) safe space for me to be out and proud about my race and sexuality. Living with my multiple invisible identities has taught me to be more assertive in all areas of my life, and I have learned to take risks. I know quite well how privilege works, and how that privilege can be taken away in an instant. I am also proud of all of my identities. The difficulty of coming out is well worth the satisfaction and pride I have of living my life the way that I have always wanted to.

Tara S. Ellison

It was nineteenth-century psychiatry that made homosexual behavior a mental "condition"—either love-sick or gender-sick or both—that enveloped the personality and became its core. The psychiatric name of this mythical state has endlessly changed as new variations arrived at the doctors' consulting room doors, from the original pederasty, contrary sexual feeling, psychic hermaphroditism, sexual inversion, and the lovely Italian *l'amore invertito,* to the less blatant but still pernicious sexual orientation disturbance and egodystonic homosexuality.[6]

Indeed, it was not until 1869 that the German term *homosexualität* was coined for this "condition."[7] In that year, Karl Maria Kertbeny described a "homosexual urge" that "creates in advance a direct horror of the opposite sex, and the victim of this passion finds it impossible to suppress the feeling which individuals of his own sex exercise upon him."[8] Even then, however, homosexuality was typically characterized as predominantly an inversion of gender (masculinity/femininity) rather than of sexual orientation or behavior. This heightened interest in what had hitherto been a stigmatized and often criminalized behavior, but not a defining characteristic of an individual, dovetailed nicely (and certainly not coincidentally) with the nascent social purity movement, which sought to ban prostitution as a means of shoring up the family. In a review of this historical period, John Marshall observes, "the emphasis throughout (and the reason for the link between homosexuality and prostitution) is upon the regulation of male lust and the channeling of sexuality into an institutionalized pattern of 'normal' heterosexual monogamy."[9] The resultant scientific and social scrutiny to which homosexual behaviors and those who practiced them were subjected, in turn, may very well have created the modern homosexual.

All of this illustrates just how complex the issues surrounding homosexuality and sexual orientation really are. There are obviously wide variations in sexual expression, both between individuals and between cultures. Even within an individual there may be discordance between *preference,* which tends to exist as an enduring facet of one's personality (though not always), and *behavior,* which is often situationally determined. Many macho American boys, who grow into macho American men, engage in clandestine homosexual activities as adolescents. And many other men and women suddenly "discover" their "true" homosexual proclivities after years of being happily and heterosexually married:

> Confessions of a false lesbian: I was married to a man when I first came out, and when I fell in love with a woman I searched my past hard and long for evidence that I had "really" "always" been a lesbian. Much more eager to prove to myself that I was a lesbian than to find evidence that I wasn't, I just couldn't say to myself, "I choose to be a lesbian." I was afraid I'd have to be straight unless I could prove I wasn't.[10]

Furthermore, the manner in which people express their sexuality is not necessarily discrete, but is instead embedded in a larger network of cultural meanings. American men who want to try something different rarely engage in same-sex relations, preferring instead to widen their heterosexual repertoires. In America, homosexual diversions are deemed inconsistent with both machismo and, in some interpretations, maleness itself.

… The Sambia warriors of Papua New Guinea provide an especially striking example of the transience of "homosexuality."[11] Survival in the forbidding landscape of the New Guinea highlands necessitates that Sambia men be as strong and courageous as possible. To the Sambia, the essence of male masculinity and strength (*jerungdu*) is semen; the more semen, the more macho the man. However, because the "semen organ" is initially "solid and dry" (i.e., incapable of ejaculation), semen is thought to be absent in boys. To masculinize the boys requires some means of infusing them with semen. The Sambia solution is for young "bachelors" to act as donors, providing semen to the preadolescent boys through fellatio. In time, by swallowing adult semen, the boys become men.[12] They can then act as donors themselves, becoming fellatees rather than fellators. Eventually, each Sambia youth finds a wife and begins raising a family (following marriage is a period of bisexual behavior that ends with the arrival of the couple's first child—all homosexual activities cease when a man becomes a father). Thus, *all* boys—who ultimately become husbands, fathers, and fierce warriors—go through a period of exclusive homosexual behavior as a necessary step on the road to manhood.

In stark contrast to the American mythology, the Sambia believe that adolescent homosexuality, and the ingestion of older men's semen, is essential to masculine development and toughness. Both boys (receptive) and men (insertive) participate in these homosexual activities, yet seldom does either have any trouble shifting to his eventual heterosexual role. The homosexual behavior of adolescence and bachelorhood is rarely continued into "adulthood" (i.e., after a man's first child is born). When it is, it typically takes the form of bisexuality, in that the sexual alliances with boys supplement heterosexual contacts with a wife and a full family life. Rarely does a man profess an exclusive preference for boys, for to do so is to invite the scorn of the entire community, and to admit weakness and a lack of *jerungdu*, making one a "rubbish man."[13]

Age-structured homosexuality also challenges a cherished American myth, that of the exclusive homosexual identity. According to this myth, a person either is or isn't a homosexual, and whatever one is, he or she is for life. In America, the alleged incongruence between having a heterosexual identity and participating in homosexual behaviors leads to the further assumption that *any* homosexual activity is, ipso facto, evidence of a homosexual identity. To Americans, it would appear, "you are *who* you do." …

The question is, which of the many "homosexualities" are biologists trying to explain? It clearly isn't the situational homosexuality of the prisoner serving a life sentence. It might not even be the life-long homosexuality of the Freudian prototype, unable to disentangle himself from his mother's apron strings. In fact, the targets of biological explanations of sexual orientation—and especially homosexuality—are seldom specified. This uncertainty in the phenomenon being described, it seems to us, casts aspersions on the whole enterprise.

DISCUSSION QUESTIONS

1. What would the authors say were the key factors that turned homosexuality from an adjective to a noun, at least in Western society?
2. Do you envision the possibility of homosexuality becoming an adjective again? Why or why not?

NOTES

1. See also De Cecco (1990), Richardson (1984), and Weinberg (1978).
2. For whatever it's worth, we prefer *Samuel Adam's Boston Lager* (S.P.) and *Mackeson's Stout* (P.A.).
3. The basis of the Judeo-Christian condemnation of (male) homosexual behaviors is God's commandment to Moses, "thou shalt not lie with mankind, as with womankind: It is abomination" (Leviticus 18:22).
4. Boswell (1980).
5. See Foucault (1990); Weeks (1977).
6. De Cecco (1990).
7. Halperin (1989); Herzer (1985).
8. Quoted in Bullough (1967), p. 637.
9. Marshall (1981), p. 139.
10. Whisman (1993), p. 54.
11. Herdt (1981, 1987).
12. The Sambia belief that masculinity can be passed from man to boy through the former's semen bears certain similarities to the Greek pederastic tradition in which sex was "supposed to transmit manly virtues of mind and body from nobleman to young lover" (Karlen, 1980, p. 79).
13. Stoller and Herdt (1985) describe one instance of a "rubbish man." See also Herdt (1987).

REFERENCES

Boswell, J. (1980). *Christianity, Social Tolerance, and Homosexuality.* Chicago: University of Chicago Press.

Bullough, V. L. (1967). *Sexual Variance in Society and History.* New York: Wiley.

De Cecco, J. P. (1990). Confusing the actor with the act: Muddled notions about homosexuality. *Archives of Sexual Behavior, 19,* 409–412.

Foucault, M. (1990). *The History of Sexuality.* New York: Vintage.

Halperin, D. M. (1989). *One Hundred Years of Homosexuality and Other Essays on Greek Love.* New York: Routledge.

Herdt, G. H. (1981). *Guardians of the Flute.* New York: McGraw-Hill.

Herdt, G. H. (1987). *The Sambia: Ritual and Gender in New Guinea.* New York: Holt, Rinehart & Winston.

Herzer, M. (1985). Kertbenny and the nameless love. *Journal of Homosexuality, 12,* 1–26.

Karlen, A. (1980). Homosexuality in history. In J. Marmor (ed.), *Homosexual Behavior: A Modern Reappraisal.* New York: Basic Books.

Marshall, J. (1981). Pansies, perverts and macho men: Changing conceptions of homosexuality. In K. Plummer (ed.), *The Making of the Modern Homosexual.* Totowa, NJ: Barnes & Noble.

Richardson, D. (1984). The dilemma of essentiality in homosexual theory. *Journal of Homosexuality, 9,* 79–90.

Stoller, R. J. & Herdt, G. H. (1985). Theories of origins of male homosexuality. *Archives of General Psychiatry, 42,* 399–404.

Weeks, J. (1977). *Coming Out: Homosexual Politics in Britain from the Nineteenth Century to the Present.* London: Quartet Books.

Weinberg, T. S. (1978). On "doing" and "being" gay: Sexual behavior and homosexual male self-identity. *Journal of Homosexuality, 4,* 143–156.

Whisman, V. (1993). Identity crisis: Who is a lesbian anyway? In A. Stein (ed.), *Sisters, Sexperts, Queers.* New York: Penguin.

READING 18

A New Paradigm for Understanding Women's Sexuality and Sexual Orientation

Letitia Anne Peplau

Linda D. Garnets

Scientific research on women's sexuality and sexual orientation is still a young endeavor. Nonetheless, several basic findings have been supported consistently

Letitia Anne Peplau is a professor of social psychology at University of California, Los Angeles. Linda D. Garnets is a professor of psychology and women studies at the University of California, Los Angeles.

by empirical research. Taken together, these findings highlight the need to reject old models of women's sexual orientation and to develop a new paradigm that is grounded in scientific research and sensitive to the realities of women's lives. Too often, old theories have taken male experience as the norm for human experience. Yet there appear to be important differences in the sexualities of women and men that emerge when women's lives are the central focus of investigation. Consequently, we believe that a necessary research strategy will be to develop separate analyses of women's and men's sexualities, each based on a careful examination of the nature and antecedents of sexual orientation for that half of humankind. Whether or not generalizations and unified theories applicable to both sexes will eventually emerge remains to be seen.

We begin by summarizing well established empirical findings about women's sexualities. . . . As relevant, we note differences between women and men to underline the importance of research and theory that put women center stage. We then identify key ingredients in a new paradigm for understanding women's sexual orientation.

MENTAL HEALTH AND SEXUAL ORIENTATION: REJECTING THE ILLNESS MODEL

Implicit in many discussions of sexual orientation is the assumption that heterosexuals are normal and mentally healthy but homosexuals are abnormal and impaired in their psychological functioning (see review by Bullough & Bullough, 1997). This illness model has influenced theories about the causes of women's sexual orientation, as seen in the idea that lesbians have arrested psychosexual development. It has led to stereotypes of sexual-minority individuals as unhappy, maladjusted, and unable to form satisfying intimate relationships. A growing body of empirical work has refuted the illness model. Based on scientific evidence, the consensus among psychiatrists and psychologists is that homosexuality is not a form of pathology nor is it associated with mental illness or poor psychological functioning. On standardized

measures of personal adjustment and psychological well-being, gay and lesbian individuals (Gonsiorek, 1991), couples (Peplau & Spalding, 2000), and parents (Patterson & Redding, 1996) are comparable to their heterosexual counterparts. Although research about bisexuals is limited, Fox (1996) found no evidence of psychopathology in nonclinical samples of bisexual women and men.

In summary, the illness model of sexual orientation is no longer scientifically viable. One implication is that scientific researchers should avoid taking heterosexuality as the norm for mental health (see Herek, Kimmel, Amaro, & Melton, 1991, for research guidelines).

GENDER AND WOMEN'S SEXUAL ORIENTATION: REJECTING THE INVERSION MODEL

Early-20th-century sex experts such as Havelock Ellis (1928) and Krafft-Ebing (1908/1950) proposed an inversion model of homosexuality, suggesting that sexual orientation is closely tied to gender. Normal heterosexual women are feminine in their physiology, personality, and attractions to men. Lesbians are sexual inverts, women who are masculine in aspects of their physiology, personality, and attraction to women. The cumulative record of research on women's sexual orientation has repeatedly disconfirmed this model (see review by Peplau, Spalding, Conley, & Veniegas, 1999). There is no inherent link between heterosexuality and femininity in women or between homosexuality and masculinity in women. Biological models based on inversion premises, most notably the proposal that prenatal hormones "masculinize" the brains of females destined to be lesbians, have not been confirmed by scientific research.

Research . . . has demonstrated, instead, that there are consistent similarities among women, regardless of sexual orientation. Research on the centrality of intimacy and relationships to women's sexuality is illustrative. In addition, studies of bisexual women raise important questions about gender and sexual attractions (see Rust, 2000). Compared to other women, bisexual women appear to be less constrained by gender in their sexual and affectional attractions (Firestein, 1996). Bisexuals emphasize individual characteristics rather than gender in selecting a partner (Fox, 1996).

In summary, although the inversion model of sexual orientation remains popular, it lacks scientific support. There is no intrinsic association between gender conformity and women's sexual orientation; masculinity and femininity are linked to sexual orientation in some social contexts but not in others.

BIOLOGY AND WOMEN'S SEXUAL ORIENTATION: CHALLENGING BIOLOGICAL MODELS

Empirical research has failed to demonstrate that biological factors are a major influence in the development of women's sexual orientation. (In addition to the review by Veniegas and Conley, 2000, see also Bailey, 1995; Peplau et al., 1999.) Lesbian and heterosexual women are indistinguishable in their body build (A. Ellis, 1963). Researchers generally agree that there is no causal relationship between adult sex hormone levels and sexual orientation (Byne, 1995). Studies of the impact of prenatal sex hormones on human development show that the great majority of women exposed to atypical levels of sex hormones before birth are heterosexual in their attractions and behavior. According to one leading expert, "the main bone of contention is whether variations in the prenatal hormonal milieu have any effect at all and, if they do, are [they] of any practical significance" (Zucker, Bradley, & Lowry Sullivan, 1992, p. 93). Investigations of sexual orientation and brain structure in women have never been conducted.

Currently, the most promising biological research on women's sexual orientation focuses on genetics (Bailey & Pillard, 1995). Research has found that lesbians are more likely than heterosexual women to report having homosexual relatives. Studies of twins reared together find greater concordance (similarity) between the sexual orientation of monozygotic ("identical") twins than between dizygotic twins or adoptive sisters. Proponents of genetic perspectives

see these findings as encouraging. In contrast, skeptics emphasize possible limitations of the studies (e.g., McGuire, 1995) and the need for studies of twins reared apart. The one study that attempted to identify a genetic marker for homosexuality in women was unsuccessful (Hu et al., 1995). A definitive understanding of possible genetic influences on women's sexual orientation must await future research.

In summary, there is little evidence that biological factors are a major determinant of women's sexual orientation. In a recent review, Baumeister (2000, p. 356) acknowledged gaps in the available evidence, but nonetheless concluded, "the currently available data offer the best guess that male homosexuality is more strongly linked to innate or genetic determinants while female homosexuality remains more subject to personal choice and social influence." Although additional research will fill in gaps in our knowledge, there is no reason to expect that biological factors play anything other than a minor and probably indirect role in women's sexual orientation.

THE FLUIDITY OF WOMEN'S SEXUALITY

Scholars from many disciplines have noted that women's sexuality tends to be fluid, malleable, and capable of change over time. This point is often made in comparison to men, whose sexuality and sexual orientation are viewed as less flexible and more automatic. Recently social psychologist Roy Baumeister (2000) systematically reviewed empirical research on gender differences in erotic plasticity. Baumeister defined *plasticity* as the degree to which a person's sex drive can be shaped and altered by cultural, social, and situational pressures. By contrast, a lack of plasticity would indicate that a person's sexuality is more rigidly patterned early in life, as a result of biological and/or childhood influences.

The concept of sexual fluidity is the cornerstone of a new paradigm for understanding women's sexuality and sexual orientation. If women's sexuality is not primarily determined by biological programming but is instead responsive to social contexts, then theories about women's experiences must be social psychological in focus. To make the case for this core idea, we next review evidence from Baumeister and others that supports three specific predictions concerning the fluidity of female sexuality.

Influence of the Social Environment

A first prediction is that to the extent that sexuality is plastic and malleable, it can be shaped by a range of social and situational influences. Baumeister (2000) marshaled considerable evidence showing that such factors as education, religion, and acculturation have greater impact on aspects of women's sexuality than on men's. Consider the link between education and sexual orientation. The National Health and Social Life Survey (Laumann, Gagnon, Michael, & Michaels, 1994, p. 305) found that completing college doubled the likelihood that a man identified as gay or bisexual but was associated with a 900% increase in the percentage of women identifying as lesbian/bisexual (from 0.4% of women high school graduates to 3.6% of college graduates). Similarly, the association between religious conservatism and a heterosexual identity was stronger among women than men. Also consistent with the plasticity hypothesis is evidence that active involvement in the 1970s feminist movement led some women to turn away from sexual relations with men and to establish relationships with women (e.g., Kitzinger, 1987; Rosenbluth, 1997; Whisman, 1996). Pearlman (1987) explained that "many of the new, previously heterosexual, radical lesbians had based their choice as much on politics as on sexual interest in other women" (p. 318).

Within-Person Variation or Change Over Time

A second prediction by Baumeister (2000) is that some degree of erotic plasticity would make it possible for an individual to have nonexclusive attractions toward both women and men. In addition, plasticity would permit a woman to change aspects of her sexuality or sexual orientation across the lifespan. There is considerable evidence that both nonexclusive attractions and change over time do characterize the experiences of some women (see Rust, 2000). American women who are not exclusively heterosexual are more likely to be bisexual rather than exclusively homosexual in their attractions and relationships (e.g., Laumann et al., 1994; Weinberg, Williams, & Pyror, 1994). For example, a recent study of 6,935 self-identified lesbians from all 50 states found that 77% of lesbians had had one or more male sexual partners during their lifetime (Diamant, Schuster, McGuigan, & Lever, 1999). The study's authors cautioned health care providers and others not to "assume that a woman who identifies herself as a lesbian has not had any sexual contact with men, or that such contact was only in the distant past" (p. 2734). Baumeister documented that this pattern of bisexual attraction and behavior is significantly more common among women than men.

Further, both women's identification as lesbian, bisexual, or heterosexual and women's actual behavior can vary over time. In an early study of bisexuality in women, Blumstein and Schwartz (1976) interviewed women who had a long-term heterosexual relationship followed by a long-term lesbian relationship. Some of these women subsequently returned to relationships with men. Other researchers have also documented the experiences of married women who switch course and start a new life with a female partner (e.g., Kitzinger & Wilkinson, 1995). The reverse pattern also occurs: Women who identified as lesbians may begin sexual relationships with men (e.g., Bart, 1993; Rust, 1992).

Claims about the potential erotic plasticity of women do *not* mean that most women will actually exhibit change over time. At a young age, many women adopt patterns of heterosexuality that are stable across their lifetime. Some women adopt enduring patterns of same-sex attractions and relationships. To the extent that the social influences acting on a woman remain constant, there is little reason to expect change based on the sexual plasticity hypothesis. The key point is that at least some women are capable of variation and change, and that such plasticity appears to be more characteristic of women than men (cf. Diamond, 2000). . . .

Attitude-Behavior Consistency

A third issue relevant to sexual fluidity concerns the consistency among an individual's sexual attitudes, desires, and behavior. Baumeister (2000) argued that "if women's behavior is more malleable by situational forces than men's, then women will be more likely than men to do things contrary to their general attitudes" (p. 359). In the area of sexual orientation, the plasticity hypothesis would challenge the popular belief that sexual desires, behavior, and identity are invariably interconnected. To be sure, many individuals do report complete consistency: A woman might identify as lesbian, be attracted exclusively to women, and have sex with women partners only. But exceptions to this pattern of consistency are common. For example, a woman who identifies as lesbian might develop a strong attraction to a man. A woman may have strong attractions to both men and women but not identify as bisexual. A heterosexual woman may employ homoerotic fantasies when having sex with her male partner. . . .

CHILDHOOD INFLUENCES ON WOMEN'S SEXUAL ORIENTATION

It is often believed that childhood experiences in the family and with peers are formative in shaping many aspects of adult personality, attitudes, and behavior. From this perspective, one would expect that sexual orientation is strongly influenced by childhood experiences. Yet empirical research has so far failed to identify events or activities that predictably point a girl in our culture on the path toward lesbian or bisexual attractions (Bohan, 1996).

Efforts to test psychoanalytic theories about the family history antecedents of sexual orientation have failed (e.g., Bell, Weinberg, & Hammersmith, 1981; Downey & Friedman, 1998). Furthermore, the sexual orientation of parents appears to have limited impact on the sexual orientation of their children: most lesbians were raised by heterosexual parents and most

children raised by gay or lesbian parents become heterosexual adults (e.g., Bailey & Dawood, 1998; Patterson, 1997). There is some suggestive evidence that gender nonconformity in childhood may be correlated with adult sexual orientation (e.g., Bailey & Zucker, 1995). Based on retrospective reports, lesbians are more likely than heterosexual women to remember having been a tomboy as a child. Such studies are inconclusive, however, because memories of childhood may be colored by adult experiences. Equally important, most tomboys grow up to be heterosexuals.

Two issues concerning childhood influences on women's sexual orientation are noteworthy. First, according to the sexual plasticity hypothesis, we might expect women's sexuality to be more strongly influenced by childhood events than men's sexuality. Baumeister (2000) considered and rejected this possibility on empirical grounds. His review of research on childhood gender nonconformity, sexual dysfunction, and paraphilias suggested the opposite: that childhood experiences have stronger and more lasting effects on male than female sexuality. So, for example, the correlation between adult sexual orientation and retrospective reports of childhood gender nonconformity is significantly higher among men than among women (Bailey & Zucker, 1995). To explain this apparent contradiction, Baumeister (p. 368) proposed that "male sexuality may undergo a childhood phase (akin to imprinting in animals) during which social and environmental influences can have a major influence." In contrast, females may have no such critical period and so exhibit greater sexual fluidity across the lifecycle. This speculation needs empirical investigation (cf. Weinrich, 1987).

Second, it is possible that important early antecedents of women's sexual orientation have simply been overlooked by researchers and could be identified with further effort. For instance, in a society that is hostile to homosexuality, lesbians may be women who are willing to challenge convention and take social risks. Researchers have not investigated whether the development of personality characteristics such as risk taking or independence affects adult sexual orientation in women. Longitudinal studies charting the development of sexual orientation in women over time would be valuable.

SOCIOCULTURAL INFLUENCES ON WOMEN'S SEXUAL ORIENTATION

Identity

Sexual identity can be defined as "an individual's enduring sense of self as a sexual being that fits a culturally created category and accounts for one's sexual fantasies, attractions, and behavior" (Savin-Williams, 1995, p. 166). Historical changes in cultural interpretations of women's romantic relationships illustrate how cultural categories shape identity. The romantic friendships between women that flourished in the 18th and 19th centuries were socially acceptable and had no implications for a woman's identity (Faderman, 1981). As the 20th century unfolded, however, the identity of "lesbian" emerged, and social attitudes about these relationships changed. Faderman (1991, p. 303) explained that

> love between women, especially those of the middle class, was dramatically metamorphosed from romantic friendships [into] "lesbianism" once the sexologists formulated the concept, economic factors made it possible for large numbers of women to live independently of men, and mobility allowed many women to travel to places where they might meet others who accepted the lesbian label.

Historians contend that the creation of "homo-sexual" and "heterosexual" as defining identities is a relatively recent development (e.g., Katz, 1995). As Rust (2000) has discussed, these sexual identities then set the stage for the emergence of a new social identity, that of the bisexual person.

Institutions

Another way in which cultures influence sexual orientation is through the creation of social institutions that provide both opportunities for and constraints on women's sexuality and relationships. As Blumstein and Schwartz (1990, p. 310) observed, these social arrangements can "be as concrete as a woman being unable to have heterosexual experience because her interactions with men are always chaperoned, or as subtle as her being unable to have sexual relations outside of her marriage because she is a suburban housewife who . . . never finds herself in the company of men."

As another example, living in same-sex institutions also tends to increase the likelihood of romantic and erotic relationships between women. In the 1920s, Katharine Davis (1929) surveyed more than 2,000 graduates of women's colleges. Fully 42% of the sample reported that they had had an intense emotional relationship with another woman in college; 1 woman in 5 reported having a sexual relationship with a best friend in college. Same-sex relationships are also common among prison populations and appear to be more prevalent among women than men in prison (see review in Baumeister, 2000; Rust, 2000): In both cases, institutions created for nonsexual purposes—education and incarceration—provide settings that foster same-sex bonds between women.

An important implication of cross-cultural and historical findings is that researchers cannot assume that the experiences of contemporary American women are universal or even typical of the full range of women's erotic attractions and relationships. More broadly, the phenomena of sexual orientation are not fixed and universal, but rather highly variable across time and place. Researchers interested in understanding the general nature of female sexuality must look beyond their immediate cultural and historical context.

Sexual Prejudice

The experiences of contemporary lesbian and bisexual women must be understood in the context of widespread prejudice against sexual minorities in our society (see Herek, 2000). Indeed, bisexual women may encounter negative attitudes not only from heterosexuals but from lesbians as well (Rust, 1993).

Similarly, individuals who are both ethnic and sexual minorities may encounter sexual prejudice from both mainstream society and from their own racial/ethnic communities (Rust, 1996; Savin-Williams, 1996).

Sexual prejudice is closely linked to attitudes about gender and women's sexuality. Lesbians and gay men are disliked in part because they are perceived to violate traditional gender roles (Storms, 1978). Gender nonconformity is a central theme in antigay stereotypes, which depict lesbians as masculine or unfeminine and gay men as effeminate or unmasculine (Herek, 1984, Kite & Deaux, 1987). Furthermore, antigay prejudice is stronger among heterosexuals who endorse traditional, restrictive attitudes about gender and family roles and who reject equality between the sexes (Herek, 1984).

All people are affected by sexual prejudice and discrimination. Women who identify as lesbian or bisexual must navigate through hostile social environments and may experience difficult dilemmas about when to conceal versus reveal their sexual orientation and intimate relationships. Women who are uncertain about their sexual orientation may be discouraged from considering sexual-minority options. Sexual prejudice also touches the lives of heterosexuals. Fear of being labeled gay is a powerful socialization influence (see Hyde & Jaffee, 2000). Regardless of their sexual orientation, girls and women who appear to be masculine in their appearance or interests, who dress in nontraditional clothes or resist a man's sexual advances, who work in nontraditional occupations or appear assertive risk being called lesbians (Kite, 1994). As a result, heterosexuals may experience social pressure to conform to traditional gender roles in order to avoid the stigmatizing label of homosexuality. For example, varsity women athletes often wear dresses, makeup, jewelry or long hair to avoid being considered lesbian (Blinde & Taub, 1992).

In summary, cultural and historical research documents the varied patterns of women's sexuality and erotic relationships. These findings add support to characterization of women's sexuality as potentially fluid and influenced by social forces.

THE IMPORTANCE OF RELATIONSHIPS FOR WOMEN'S SEXUALITY AND SEXUAL ORIENTATION

For many theorists, especially those taking male experiences as their model, sexuality and sexual orientation are first and foremost about sexual behavior. Increasingly, however, researchers with diverse theoretical orientations have suggested that love and intimacy are more important for understanding women's sexuality than for understanding men's sexuality (e.g., Golden, 1996; Weinrich, 1987). For example, Regan and Berscheid (1996, p. 116) asked young heterosexual adults, "What is sexual desire?" These comments are illustrative:

> *Man:* Sexual desire is wanting someone . . . in a physical manner. No strings attached. Just for uninhibited *sexual intercourse.* (italics in original)
> *Woman:* Sexual desire is the longing to be emotionally intimate and to express love for another person.

Regan and Berscheid concluded that men were more likely to "sexualize" and women to "romanticize" the experience of sexual desire. Similarly, based on their study of bisexuals, Weinberg and colleagues (1994, p. 7) concluded: "For men it was easier to have sex with other men than to fall in love with them. For women it was easier to fall in love with other women than to have sex with them." We are not suggesting that eroticism is unimportant in women's lives or irrelevant to their sexual orientation. Rather, we think it is crucial to acknowledge and analyze the central role emotional intimacy often has for women's sexual experiences. Similarly, we do not propose that emotional intimacy is unimportant to men's lives or their sexual orientation.

Gender differences in sexuality have been widely discussed (e.g., Sprecher & McKinney, 1993). In general, women have been characterized as having a relational or partner-centered orientation to sexuality and men as having a recreational or body-centered orientation (e.g., Baldwin & Baldwin, 1997; DeLamater, 1987). Both biological and social explanations have been proposed for these differences.

Oliver and Hyde (1993) reviewed five theoretical perspectives—sociobiology, neoanalytic, social learning, social roles, and script theory—all of which predict sex differences in sexuality—for instance, that compared to males, females will have a smaller number of sex partners and hold more negative attitudes toward premarital sex. Several lines of research provide empirical support for these generalizations and suggest that they may apply regardless of sexual orientation. . . .

Multiple Pathways

The emerging view of scholars is that sexual orientation is multiply determined by many influences. No single factor reliably predicts whether a woman embarks on a path toward heterosexuality, homosexuality, bisexuality, or some other pattern. Further, there are multiple developmental pathways leading to common outcomes (see Diamond & Savin-Williams, 2000). In contemporary society, a woman's assertion that she is heterosexual or lesbian may be based on quite diverse and nonlinear developmental trajectories. Women may be drawn to a particular lifestyle for differing reasons. Knowing that a woman labels herself as heterosexual, lesbian, or bisexual does not necessarily inform us about the pattern of her life experiences or the nature of her current erotic thoughts and feelings. Indeed, Pattatucci (1998) criticized research on sexual orientation for concentrating on "end states" (i.e., self-identification as lesbian) and ignoring how individuals reach that point. Demo and Allen (1996, p. 426) urged researchers to focus on the "multiple trajectories and social contexts . . . shaping individual lives; . . . the transitions and turning-points lesbians and gay men experience form their families of origin through the families they form and maintain as adults." . . .

DISCUSSION QUESTIONS

1. What appear to be the differences between the sexualities of men and women?
2. How is the fluidity of women's sexuality manifested?
3. What common assumptions and prejudices about sexuality are being undermined by the research summarized in this article?

REFERENCES

Bailey, J.M. (1995). Biological perspectives on sexual orientation. In A. R. D'Augelli & C. J. Patterson (Eds.), *Lesbian, gay and bisexual identities over the lifespan* (pp. 104–135). New York: Oxford University Press.

Bailey, J. M., & Dawood, K. (1998). Behavioral genetics, sexual orientation, and the family. In C. J. Patterson & A. R. D'Augelli (Eds.), *Lesbian, gay, and bisexual identities in families* (pp. 3–18). New York: Oxford University Press.

Bailey, J. M., & Pillard, R. C. (1995). Genetics of human sexual orientation. In R. C. Rosen (Ed.), *Annual Review of Sex Research* (Vol. 6, pp. 136–150). Mason City, IA: Society for the Scientific Study of Sexuality.

Bailey, J. M., & Zucker, K. J. (1995). Childhood sex-typed behavior and sexual orientation: A conceptual analysis and quantitative review. *Developmental Psychology, 31,* 43–55.

Baldwin, J. D., & Baldwin, J. I. (1997). Gender differences in sexual interest. *Archives of Sexual Behavior, 26*(2), 181–210.

Bart, P. (1993). Protean women: The liquidity of female sexuality and the tenaciousness of lesbian identity. In S. Wilkinson & C. Kitzinger (Eds.), *Heterosexuality: Feminism and psychology reader* (pp. 246–252). London: Sage.

Baumeister, R. F. (2000). Gender differences in erotic plasticity: The female sex drive as socially flexible and responsive. *Psychological Bulletin, 126,* 347–374.

Bell, A. P., Weinberg, M. S., & Hammersmith, S. K. (1981). *Sexual preference.* Bloomington: Indiana University Press.

Blinde, E. M., & Taub, D. E. (1992). Women athletes as falsely accused deviants: Managing the lesbian stigma. *Sociological Quarterly, 33,* 521–533.

Blumstein, P. W., & Schwartz, P. (1976). Bisexuality in women. *Archives of Sexual Behavior, 5*(2), 171–181.

Blumstein, P. W., & Schwartz, P. (1990). Intimate relationships and the creation of sexuality. In D. M. McWhirter, S. A. Sanders, & J. M. Reinisch (Eds.). *Homosexuality/ heterosexuality* (pp. 307–320). New York: Oxford.

Bohan, J. S. (1996). *Psychology and sexual orientation.* New York: Routledge.

Bullough, V. L., & Bullough, B. (1997). The history of the science of sexual orientation 1880–1980. *Journal of Psychology and Human Sexuality, 9*(2), 1–16.

Byne, W. (1995). Science and belief: Psychobiological research on sexual orientation. *Journal of Homosexuality, 28*(3/4), 303–344.

Davis, K. B. (1929). *Factors in the sex life of twenty-two hundred women.* New York: Harper

DeLamater, J. (1987). Gender differences in sexual scenarios. In K. Kelley (Ed.), *Females, males and sexuality: Theories and research* (pp. 127–129). Albany: State University of New York Press.

Demo, D. H., & Allen, K. R. (1996). Diversity within lesbian and gay families: Challenges and implications for family theory and research. *Journal of Social and Personal Relationships, 13*(3), 415–434.

Diamant, A. L., Schuster, M. A., McGuigan, K., & Lever, J. (1999). Lesbians' sexual history with men. *Archives of Internal Medicine, 159,* 2730–2736.

Diamond, L. M. (2000). Sexual identity, attractions and behavior among young sexual-minority women over a two-year period. *Developmental Psychology, 36,* 241–250.

Diamond, L. M. & Savin-Williams, R. C. (2000). Explaining diversity in the development of same-sex sexuality among young women. *Journal of Social Issues, 56*(2), 297–313.

Downey, J. I., & Friedman, R. C. (1998). Female homosexuality: Classical psychoanalytic theory reconsidered. *Journal of the American Psychoanalytic Association, 46*(2), 471–506.

Ellis, A. (1963). Constitutional factors in homosexuality. In H. G. Beigel (Ed.), *Advances in sex research* (pp. 161–186). New York: Harper and Row.

Ellis, H. (1928). *Studies in the psychology of sex. Vol. II: Sexual inversion.* Philadelphia: F. A. Davis.

Faderman, L. (1981). *Surpassing the love of men.* New York: Morrow.

Faderman, L. (1991). *Odd girls and twilight lovers.* New York: Columbia University Press.

Firestein, B. A. (1996). Bisexuality as a paradigm shift: Transforming our disciplines. In B. Firestein (Ed.), *Bisexuality: The psychology and politics of an invisible minority* (pp. 263–291). Thousand Oaks, CA: Sage.

Fox, R. (1996). Bisexuality in perspective: A review of theory and research. In B. Firestein (Ed.), *Bisexuality: The psychology and politics of an invisible minority* (pp. 3–50). Thousand Oaks, CA: Sage.

Golden, C. (1996). What's in a name? Sexual self-identification among women. In R. C. Savin-Williams & K. M. Cohen (Eds.), *The lives of lesbians, gays and bisexuals* (pp. 229–247). New York: Harcourt Brace.

Gonsiorek, J. (1991). The empirical basis for the demise of the illness model of homosexuality. In J. Gonsiorek & J. Weinrich (Eds.), *Homosexuality: Research implications for public policy* (pp. 115–136). Newbury Park, CA: Sage.

Herek, G. M. (1984). Beyond homophobia: A social psychological perspective on attitudes toward lesbians and gay men. *Journal of Homosexuality, 10*(1/2), 1–21.

Herek, G. M. (2000). The psychology of sexual prejudice. *Current Directions in Psychological Science, 9,* 19–22.

Herek, G. M., Kimmel, D. C., Amaro, H., & Melton, G. B. (1991). Avoiding heterosexual bias in psychological research. *American Psychologist 46,* 957–963.

Hu, S., Pattatucci, A. M., Patterson, C., Li, L., Fulker, D. W., Cherny, S. S., Kruglyak, L., & Hamer, D. (1995). Linkage between sexual orientation and chromosome Xq28 in males but not in females. *Nature Genetics, 11,* 248–256.

Hyde, J. S. & Jaffee, S. R. (2000). Becoming a heterosexual adult: The experiences of young women. *Journal of Social Issues, 56*(2), 283–296.

Katz, J. N. (1995). *The invention of heterosexuality.* New York: Dutton.

Kite, M. E. (1994). When perceptions meet reality: Individual differences in reactions to gay men and lesbians. In B. Greene & G. Herek (Eds.), *Lesbian and gay psychology: Theory, research, and clinical applications* (pp. 25–53). Thousand Oaks, CA: Sage.

Kite, M. E. & Deaux, K. (1987). Gender belief systems: Homosexuality and the implicit inversion theory. *Psychology of Women Quarterly, 11,* 83–96.

Kitzinger, C. (1987). *The social construction of lesbianism.* London: Sage.

Kitzinger, C., & Wilkinson, S. (1995). Transitions from heterosexuality to lesbianism. *Developmental Psychology, 31,* 95–104.

Krafft-Ebing, R. (1950). *Psychopathia sexualis* (F. J. Rebman, Trans.). Brooklyn, NY: Physicians and Surgeons Book Co. (Original work published 1908)

Laumann, E. O., Gagnon, J. H., Michael, R. T., & Michaels, S. (1994). *The social organization of sexuality: Sexual practices in the United States.* Chicago, IL: University of Chicago Press.

McGuire, T. R. (1995). Is homosexuality genetic? A critical review and some suggestions. *Journal of Homosexuality, 28*(1/2), 115–145.

Oliver, M. B., & Hyde, J. S. (1993). Gender differences in sexuality: A meta-analysis. *Psychological Bulletin, 114*(1), 29–51.

Pattatucci, A. M. L. (1998). Biopsychosocial interactions and the development of sexual orientation. In C. J. Patterson & A. R. D'Augelli (Eds.), *Lesbian, gay and bisexual identities in families* (pp. 19–39). New York: Oxford University Press.

Patterson, C. J. (1997). Children of lesbian and gay parents. In T. H. Ollendick & R. J. Prinz (Eds.), *Advances in clinical child psychology* (Vol. 19, pp. 235–282). New York: Plenum Press.

Patterson, C. J., & Redding, R. E. (1996). Lesbian and gay parents and their children: Legal and public policy implications of social science research. *Journal of Social Issues, 52,* 29–50.

Pearlman, S. F. (1987). The saga of continuing clash in lesbian community, or will an army of ex-lovers fail? In Boston Lesbian Psychologies Collective (Ed.), *Lesbian psychologies* (pp. 313–326). Urbana, IL: University of Illinois Press.

Peplau, L. A., & Spalding, L. R. (2000). The close relationships of lesbians, gay men, and bisexuals. In C. Hendrick & S. S. Hendrick (Eds.), *Close relationships: A sourcebook* (pp. 111–124). Thousand Oaks, CA: Sage.

Peplau, L. A., Spalding, L. R., Conley, T. D., & Veniegas, R. C. (1999). The development of sexual orientation in women. *Annual Review of Sex Research, 10,* 70–99.

Regan, P. C., & Berscheid, E. (1996). Beliefs about the state, goals, and objects of sexual desire. *Journal of Sex and Marital Therapy, 22,* 110–120.

Rosenbluth, S. (1997). Is sexual orientation a matter of choice? *Psychology of Women Quarterly, 21,* 595–610.

Rust, P. C. (1992). The politics of sexual identity: Sexual attraction and behavior among lesbian and bisexual women. *Social Problems, 39*(4), 366–386.

Rust, P. C. (1993). Neutralizing the political threat of the marginal woman: Lesbians' beliefs about bisexual women. *Journal of Sex Research, 30*(3), 214–228.

Rust, P. C. (1996). Managing multiple identities: Diversity among bisexual men and women. In B. Firestein (Ed.), *Bisexuality: The psychology and politics of an invisible minority* (pp. 53–83). Thousand Oaks, CA: Sage.

Rust, P. C. (2000). Bisexuality: A contemporary paradox for women. *Journal of Social Issues, 56*(2), 205–221.

Savin-Williams, R. C. (1995). Lesbian, gay male, and bisexual adolescents. In A. R. D'Augelli & C. J. Patterson (Eds.), *Lesbian, gay and bisexual identities over the lifespan* (pp. 165–189). New York: Oxford University Press.

Savin-Williams, R. C. (1996). Ethnic-minority and sexual-minority youths. In R. C. Savin-Williams & K. M. Cohen (Eds.), *The lives of lesbians, gays and bisexuals* (pp. 152–165). New York: Harcourt Brace.

Sprecher, S., & McKinney, K. (1993). *Sexuality.* Newbury Park, CA: Sage.

Storms, M. D. (1978). Attitudes toward homosexuality and femininity in men. *Journal of Homosexuality. 3*(3), 257–263.

Veniegas, R. C. & Conley, T. D. (2000). Biological research on women's sexual orientations: Evaluating the scientific evidence. *Journal of Social Issues, 56*(2), 267–282.

Weinberg, M. S., Williams, C. J., & Pryor, D. W. (1994). *Dual attraction: Understanding bisexuality.* New York: Oxford.

Weinrich, J. D. (1987). *Sexual landscapes.* New York: Scribner.

Whisman, V. (1996). *Queer by choice.* New York: Routledge.

Zucker, K. J., Bradley, S. U., & Lowry Sullivan, C. B. (1992). Gender identity disorder in children. *Annual Review of Sex Research, 3,* 73–120.

READING 19

The End of Gay (and the Death of Heterosexuality)

Bert Archer

Gay ended for me on a late afternoon in March of 1991 in a men's residence in a small Catholic college in Toronto. It was an inauspicious ending

Bert Archer is a columnist for *fab*, and a regular reviewer for *Publishers Weekly* and the *New York Blade.* His writing has also appeared in several national and international newspapers and magazines including *The Globe and Mail, The Toronto Star, The Georgia Straight, POZ Magazine,* and *Xtra.*

to something that had begun so nobly the century before, that had earned its stripes so bravely on that June New York night in 1969 in front of a little tavern on Christopher Street called Stonewall, and not only survived but flourished through a decade of a plague that any reasonable Bible-literalist could only assume was heaven-sent. Who would have guessed it could be snuffed so easily by some big Italian guy named Vince.

The common room was populated on that day, as it usually was, almost entirely by suburban men in their first and second undergraduate years, sitting around in front of the television flipping through the channels and newspapers, casually meandering in and out of conversations, like the one that was going on around one of the tables about Madonna's "Justify My Love" video, which was getting a lot of play on talk shows and in the news. MTV had refused to run it, and *Entertainment Tonight, Saturday Night Live,* CNN's *Showbiz Today, The Howard Stern Show* and *Nightline* all decided to air it and discuss it and make sure everyone was talking about it.[1] The video was filled with gender-blending images of men kissing women kissing women humping men licking other men, against the backdrop of some breathily erotic throb-pop music. . . .

Madonna was at the height of her celebrity and she had chosen to make a big fat same-sex statement. I remember thinking it was all sorta sexy, the attention and mostly tacit approbation a sign, for sure, of the gaying of the Western Madonna-loving world. I even continued thinking that for a little while after Vince, a first-generation Calabrese-Canadian friend of mine, said, "Y'know, I could see myself doin' a guy. I mean, I'm not a fag or nuthin', but y'know, if I was totally horned up, sure." There were general nods and murmurs from two others (also Italo-Canadesi) around the table, and shocked and guarded silence from the fourth. When I realised it wasn't some sort of entrapment ploy to flush me out (a constant concern of mine at the time), my first thought was, "Whoa, Vince is like this total closet case. Cool." . . .

I was a bit of an outsider in a lot of those common room and dining hall discussions. By this time

I'd been sexually and more or less romantically involved with a guy in residence, Mark, for about four years. We'd met in first year, had separate rooms on the same floor of the same residence, and we'd known each other about six months by the time we took a long walk, I think drunken, late one night and he told me that he might not be entirely heterosexual, and wondered about me.

I'd wondered about me too. For the few years leading up to college, and the first months in it, I'd been pretty excited about the whole boy thing. And like many others, I hadn't ever bothered to think of myself as gay because of it. Less, I think, out of any internal homophobia than out of a sense that gays were essentially girls in boys' clothing, readily identifiable creatures that I didn't feel my own fascination with Jon Griffin's chest in grade eight or Bill Dawson's stomach in grade eleven had much at all to do with. Round about age twelve or thirteen, I started figuring girls' tits were pretty cool, and I had the good fortune to have access to a couple of nice ones, belonging to a sixteen-year-old named Shelley. A couple of years later, in grade eleven and twelve, I had a girlfriend. Pretty in a luscious sort of way, but frustratingly intransigent on the whole sex thing. A familiar story—she was about a year younger, liked the idea of being coyly sexual, but wasn't sure about actually having sex. Not as sure as I was, anyway. Front seats, back seats, ocean-front piers and waterbeds all resulted in bits of exposed flesh, a finger here, a tongue there, tussle, try, tickle, poke, pout, give up, go home.

It was only later, once I'd started something up with Mark, that I looked back and figured that they were anything other than standard, frustrating, exciting, confusing teenage relationships. . . .

By the time of the Vince Incident . . . I was . . . convinced I was gay, though maybe not a fag: I had a boyfriend whom I found sexually interesting and with whom I was thoroughly in love, and had pretty much eliminated women from both my social scene and my sexual prospects. The process had been slow, and since Mark and I had the courage to go to a gay bar precisely once, it had all been pretty petri dish, too.

So I hadn't reached the Doc Martens and slogan T-shirt stage yet (that'd come later), and I did, when I cared to think back, remember more early crushes on girls. But as time went on, I was more and more sure they had been sisterly sorts of things, social attractions to something safe and away from what must have been my more disturbing feelings for boys. Things seemed, in my twenty-second year, pretty much settled, my impression being that girls who had sex with girls and guys who had sex with guys were gay. The ones who did and didn't think they were, were closet cases. Simple. Satisfying.

Then what was up with Vince? I'd never encountered this sort of thing before, never had any of that adolescent sex with otherwise straight boys that might have immunised me against the shock of what Vince said. Sure, I'd heard all about the pubescent sex-play that went on, but I'd obviously been in the wrong scout troop. And I guess I always figured that all the participants, whatever their public identification, were really gay. But as I thought more about it in the days and weeks after the Vince Incident, it became clear that he, for one, wasn't gay. At least not by my working definition. He'd clearly rather have sex with women. But he seemed to have a notion of a sort of interzone I couldn't quite get my head around. It bothered me. . . .

My first reaction, to assume that Vince was gay, was a result of my belief in the binary nature of sexuality. Though there had been times when bisexuality was considered a viable third option, too many of those who ended up gay had gone through a self-professed bisexual period as a way of easing themselves into gay for that to be taken too seriously. But when I realised that whatever sexual possibilities Vince entertained, he was simply not gay, his statement did more for me than imply that straight boys could waver. It eventually resulted in the ungaying of me.

Vince's wasn't a new way of thinking. It was in fact a very old way of thinking, a way of thinking that hadn't been too affected by all the sexual progress made in the name of gay in the almost two decades since my housemates had been born. It was a way of thinking that was once again becoming workable in a North American and Western European context. Madonna had done an end-run around gay, lifted up her dress and flashed everybody in a characteristically rowdy version of what the ancient Greeks called *anasyrma* [a ritual exposing of one's genitals usually associated with religion or art]. And so, though it was odd to encounter these attitudes in a young North American like Vince, it was precisely that (and similar notions and feelings that remained dormant in others of the same generation), when mixed with a sexual culture steeped in fifties bohemianism, soaked in sixties softening, dripping with seventies glam and abandon, and shot through with cold eighties realism culminating in a nineties present represented by Madonna—and Prince and Morrissey and Rufus Wainwright and Sandra Bernhard and Michael Stipe—that allowed for the beginning of the end of gay and the death of heterosexuality. A process of cultural benediction had begun, and desires, tendencies, ideas that had lain dormant at least since the seventies and eighties were beginning to poke their heads up and find they weren't being instantly lopped off.

I received an alumni newsletter a couple of years ago with a little note in their happy-news column about Vince's marriage. I never had any notion that he'd go off after that table talk and start boffing girls and boys left and right. I even doubted, as I began thinking about him and thinking about using his offhand observation for this book, that he'd remember the afternoon in question, or even recognise his comments in the context I've put them in here. That talk around the table in that upper room was more signifier than signified. It's what alerted me to what was going on, both around me and within me.

It gave me the first hint as to what to think about and what to look for. And as I said, I continued to think about gay and straight and sexual identity in much the same ways that I had for some time, but something had shifted. I realised that Vince and I were on different paths, though they were paths I came to figure would ultimately converge. . . .

I was meanwhile becoming a lot more sexually adventurous. I'd only ever had sex with Mark, and figured it was about time to start using my twenties the way I figured one's twenties ought to be used. And as I started meeting other guys and having sex with a few of them, I started noticing two things. First, that sex could be a lot of fun in all sorts of different ways. And second, that I was having sex with a remarkable number of straight guys.

Now, I'm fully aware of the unreconstructed lust a lot of gay men feel for the mere fact of straightness. All you've got to do is take a look through the personals, or listen in on a cruiseline for a few minutes, and you'll see and hear the deluge of "straight-acting, straight-lookings" and mostly (upon closer inspection) fantastical "straight man looking for same or bi for first-time encounters." And then there's that sub-subgenre of picture books with titles like *Straight Boys*. I do admit to a certain general attraction to that which ought to be, or is at least considered, unattainable. But, being the coy boy I was, in none of these straight-guy incidents did I even come close to initiating things. They all knew I had sex with boys and did the maths themselves. The first time it happened, I figured I was helping some poor soul out of the closet (and felt quite evangelical about it all, frankly). The second time, too. By the third, I started to wonder—two of the three continued to be completely happy, practising straight guys. And by the fourth, when fully half the men I'd had some form of sexual intercourse with identified as straight, I simply had no idea what was going on. . . .

Current common sense would indicate that there was a good deal of repression going on, a good deal of denial, of cognitive dissonance—"I'm doing it, but I'm not that way."

That Way. That Sort. The whole modern gay movement, from mid- to late-Mattachine[2]-style homophilia to Gay Is Good to Queer Nation and OutRage! to *Ellen, Queer as Folk* and beyond, has been a struggle first to define, then to justify and/or celebrate and/or revel in, then to normalise what was still thought of by many as being That Way. And there have been wild successes, genuine victories resulting in real progress being made in very short spans of time in thinking and acting on sexuality and human relationships. But there's a forgotten, ignored, or perhaps never acknowledged baby splashing about in all that bath water the Movement's been sumping: the possibility of a sexual attraction that is neither primarily nor exclusively based in anatomy nor especially relevant to your sense of self. It's an idea that lesbian communities have been dealing with for some time, something about which they have a lot to teach the rest of us.

It's also precisely this idea that was eventually brought home to me by Vince and friends in a what's-old-is-new-again sort of way.

So in my own drawn-out process of trying to figure out what sex was all about, I added [other encounters] to what I'd stored away from the Vince Incident and came up with . . . not much. Just a lot of confusion that I was happy to set aside for the time being as I tried to find some sex, and maybe a boyfriend.

What I found instead was my first girlfriend since high school.

I had been thinking about all this stuff, somewhere in the back of my head where most of my really entertaining thinking goes on, and then this woman appeared who was so thoroughly bright and attractive and funny and *interested*. I hesitated briefly, and then dove in. Well, I suppose waded would be an apter metaphor. I liked her, and I liked it (the relationship, the sex, the social possibilities), though I was always at a remove or two when I was with her. Should I be doing this? I wondered as I kissed her. I'm gay, I'd say to myself as I unhooked her bra. Man, I'm fucked up, I'd tentatively conclude as my tongue slid down her stomach.

The relationship didn't last long. And it probably would have been even shorter had she not lived in another city, allowing me to put off what I was quickly concluding was the inevitable. I liked her, I could even foresee loving her, but I figured I was fooling myself, and her. The sex was . . . distant, and I guessed it probably wouldn't get any better. I was gay and she wasn't a guy.

About three months after I ended it I was reading a book—*A Suitable Boy*, I think it was—when it struck me. I lowered the book to my lap and said out loud, "Man, that was stupid," and then raised it again and continued reading. What had struck me fully formed and in a flash was that it didn't matter. Girl, boy—it just didn't matter. The sex wasn't bad because she was a girl, it was bad because I couldn't stop thinking about it, chastising myself for it.[3] Though I hadn't gone looking for it, and though I was not instantly turned on by her the way I was instantly turned on by any number of bike couriers zipping past on any given day, I had been genuinely interested in her physically once we got down to it. Though it seemed counter-intuitive at the time, I really dug the whole vagina thing and got totally turned on by mucking around with it. It was, I discovered, innately sexual, just like a cock, just like an anus (we have just got to find a better word for that). I enjoyed the different ways we positioned ourselves for different aspects of sex, enjoyed how different they were from the ones I used when I was with guys. I noticed some real engineering advantages.

A major factor in my decision to break it off was the reaction of my gay male friends when I told them about her. Without exception (I think I told three or four of them), the first look I got was guarded, the second vaguely angry or frustrated, and the third tutelary.

'You sure you wanna be doing that?' I'd get from one. 'You *are* still gay, right?' from another. 'Man, are you fucked up or what?' from a third. 'You trying to run back into the closet or something? C'mon—are you trying to tell me you're as turned on by her as you are by'—zip—'him? You know as well as I do the pressures that come to bear on us from all corners, and the temptation to recidivism is . . .' (you get the idea).

There'd be supportive, even curious noises in there too from time to time ('So . . . um . . . what's it . . . like?'), and even, as I brought the subject up in more general terms with others, the occasional 'Oh, yeah, I've done that. It was fine,' but they were always underpinned by a barely contained mixture of offence and defensiveness. In our early twenties many of us were still too close to the then common high-school cover-date experience, that smothering feeling of being forced to date a member of the opposite sex, to pull a pretty comprehensive and usually long-term scam on your date, your peers, and your family to belay fears and suspicions of sexual difference. The whole late eighties and early nineties . . . come-out-come-out-wherever-you-are movement was a reaction against that very thing. We'd all read it, and we were all, to a greater or lesser extent, living it. We certainly all believed it. We were in the middle of a stridently and necessarily monolithic time in the creation of the basic modern homosexual, and challenges to that monolith were met, from within ourselves and without, with condescending and evangelical anger usually reserved for free thinkers during times of war. I didn't, significantly, take these questions and problems to any of my straight friends (whose numbers were on the wane). I saw myself as a member of a group that had definite image problems it was vigorously trying to resolve, and dissension among the ranks could only vindicate the homophobic presuppositions of the mainstream. One of the most insidious was that gay was a phase in the young, a case of arrested development in the old, and I did not want to give any straight person the impression that I was wavering, that I was coming to the end of my gay phase, which I never really figured I was.

Another question I was asked by most I mentioned this girlfriend quandary to was, did she mean I was bisexual? I assured them I wasn't, as immediately as I'd said I was the first time Mark asked me if I thought I might be gay. I wondered from time to time whether I'd have to reconfigure all this lavish identity construction I'd done over the past couple of years and start looking for a bisexual community to become a part of. New friends, new vocab, a confusing club scene—way too much to handle so soon after such major personal upheavals. And besides, the more I thought about it, the more I was pretty certain that, empirical evidence to the contrary, I wasn't bisexual. I had liked my girlfriend, I was attracted to her on any number of levels—and I liked the sex and in retrospect figured I would have liked it even more as time went on, if I let it (which is how it happens with most of my sex). But I was still gay. I still paid

way more attention to Hugh Grant's butt and lips than I did to Elizabeth Hurley's. I still knew Ryan Phillippe's filmography by heart. I still bought underwear for the pretty pictures on the box.

All this of course caused some fissures in my understanding of the terms involved, but I figured I had more important things to worry about and banished them to the back of my head. Well, almost to the back. Those couple of years when I could unabashedly declare myself to be gay were over. I still told people I was, but there was now a nagging little pull inside that kept prompting me to add, 'Well, actually, to be perfectly honest . . . ,' but there was no word for it as far as I could tell, and it would only come out sounding like I was embarrassed to be gay, which wasn't it at all. So I shut that nagging little pulling part of me up; the offending relationship was over and done with, and I doubted, given all the agitation it caused me, that it would be repeated. So I continued having a mostly gay old time. . . .

And then, after I'd finished with the magazine job and begun to think and write on my own full time, when I started really grilling my friends (whose numbers by this time turned to a roughly 70-30 straight-gay split), I found that they, especially the straight women, were right on-side, that it had, in fact, been something a lot of them had thought about but never talked about—not with a guy, anyway. I found many of them either had had some sort of adult sex with another woman or looked forward to someday doing it or didn't rule out the possibility if the right girl and the right circumstances were to present themselves. It was another case of that Starbucks-tramway syndrome. But this time, I just walked right in and ordered a latte to stay. . . .

SEXUAL IDENTITY

Sexual identity—like gender, race, and class—is generally spoken of in either exceedingly measured or exceedingly strident tones; either in academic, theoretical journals and treatises or through megaphones from makeshift podiums in front of government buildings and crowds of unusually dressed (or worse yet, self-consciously normally dressed) people. As a result, and entirely reasonably as far as I'm concerned, most people just tend to turn off when the term comes up. Sexual identity, oppression, rights, blahblahblah—anything else on?

Never has something so big been talked about by so many, so often, to such little intellectual effect. Listen in any local gay café or restaurant and you'll hear, in the background noise, the words 'sex', 'gay', 'out', 'sexuality', 'orientation', 'Ricky Martin and Enrique Iglesias', all indications of conversations on the subject of themselves, of this defining aspect of themselves. But as has been the case with many of the transsexuals I've spoken to, despite the fact of their self-definition, little progress has been made in the understanding of the issues around which they've centred their lives.

But also like gender, race, and class, sexual identity, and our understanding of it, has a lot to do with our everyday lives and how much happiness we can squeeze out of them. You'd just never know it to listen to the people who tend to talk the most about it.

Dropping sexual identity from our collective psychic wardrobe might at first seem like a big, complicated thing. It certainly seemed that way to many of the sex radicals of the sixties and seventies who figured it was one part of an inexorable path to socialism, or anarchy . . . as it did to the queer theorists who stumbled on the notion again in the eighties. . . . But these days dropping it seems a lot more straightforward. Though it can be explained and bolstered with the use of any number of philosophical and theoretical exoskeletons, when it comes right down to it, it's a simple and—apologies to the poststructuralists—natural thing. Leaving sexual identity behind is simply what happens when our natural instincts to love and to fuck come together with a culture that has brought sexuality in general, not just homosexuality, out of the closet, that has taken it out from under the ever-frowning gaze of religion and removed it from its place as a grim, grey cornerstone of the social order in the formalised shape of marriage.

In a society that has pretty successfully separated sex from reproduction and even, to a large extent,

from its role as a stable basis of social propagation, the door's been left open for sex to be a lot more fun than it has been in millennia.

It's in the name of fun that I want to talk about sexuality. And it's tough to talk about sexuality without starting out with gay. Just as there is no nationalism without at least one nation feeling impinged upon by another, no notion of race without at least two races, there is no sexual identity without one group identifying itself as sexually different, making itself heard, and thereby impinging on the rest of us, throwing up this notion that is every bit as amorphous and every bit as enervating as nationalism and race.

Before people came up with the notion that there was such a thing as gay, people were seen, and saw themselves, as pretty much of a piece. And as a result they were. Despite what the nascent gay studies departments tell us, Edward II wasn't gay; he was just a man who seems to have loved Piers more than Isabella. And neither were Michelangelo, Goethe, nor, for that matter, Oscar Wilde. For most of the Christian era in Western Europe and North America, there were those who got married and those who entered religious life. And in both categories, men fell in love with and had sex with men, and women with women, and this said not a thing about what sorts of people they were.

It's pretty clear by now though that sexual identity is a reality. Every time you rebuff a potentially sexual advance by someone of the same sex by saying 'Sorry, I'm not gay' instead of 'Sorry, not interested', you are negatively defining yourself as straight, just as every time you rebuff a potentially sexual advance by someone of the opposite sex by saying 'Sorry, I'm gay' or 'You got a sister?', you're positively identifying as gay. Every time you see a movie on gay themes and think to yourself, 'Well, that's all well and good, but it's not really got much to do with *my* life', you're just as implicated in sexual identity as the person who goes to see that movie expressly because it's about gayness. Gay, in this not so roundabout way, far from involving the 10 percent of us we usually figure (or, if we believe the more recent and no more reliable studies,

1 to 2 percent), actually affects approximately 100 percent of us.

So we're all implicated. So what?

It all comes down to identity, that thing we carry around with us tucked away somewhere near the middle of our brains that enables us to distinguish ourselves from other people. It's part of the same mechanism, the same way we have of understanding ourselves, that allows us to read headlines like 'Crazed Killer on the Loose' and understand it to mean that there are people in this world who are crazed killers and then there are people like us, allowing us in the process a certain degree of comfort in the knowledge that no matter how poorly things go at work, no matter how loudly that sweet little child screams at us about the mess she's made in her diaper, we will not use this knife gleaming up at us from the counter to do anything about either. It allows us, in short, to imagine there's a connection between action and identity, to imagine an equal sign between the verb 'kill' and the noun 'killer'.

Sexual identity is a new addition to the identity portfolio, and we can see in recent history, and to a large extent even within living memory, the process of its accretion. That's just plain interesting, I think, like being able to watch a pearl form in front of our eyes. Why not take a look, since we're able. It can't help but give us a better, perhaps even a more profound, view of ourselves.

But I'd say it's most important because sexual identity, like that equal sign between verb and noun, is in the end a house built on sand, the living in which makes us, through omission rather than commission, more anxious, less happy people than we might otherwise be. . . .

EX-GAYS

. . . I was once myself convinced that I was utterly unattracted to members of the opposite sex, and further, that I never had been. I remembered my prepubescent relationships with Stacey and Corinne and Kimberly and Susan as being essentially sisterly, or at least lacking the urgency of my equally early relationships with Scott and Michael

and Richard and Brent. It was only when I decided that this part of me was worth investigation that I realised, consciously attempting to remove the retrospective filter of a gay identity, that the relationships were pretty much the same; it was only then that I remembered I played prepubescent sex games with Brenda (which I found just as naughtily alluring as learning about erections—in theory—from Kenny), that I had a just-presexual crush on Monica, and that I never played sex games with boys, nor even thought of it. And though I can hear explanations like I must have felt safer playing sex games with girls, in whom I wasn't really interested, than I did with boys, who I thought might be too incriminating, I've heard the opposite reasoning put to work far too often to explain same-sex sex games to put much faith in either scenario. And when, in grade six and seven, I first started feeling those more visceral rumblings sitting beside certain people and not others, even though that dreamy set of Calgarian twins named Christian and Richard were the first to set things in motion, the buxom-before-her-time Jennifer ran a close second. Before I sat down to write this, I had completely forgotten about Jennifer, and about Brenda and Monica.

But enough about me. Let's talk about you.

I think it would be fairly uncontroversial to suggest that your own attractions have changed over time. Perhaps you were once attracted to girls in kilts? Or skaters? Maybe Kurt Cobain or Helena Bonham Carter once did it for you. And now, though you may either retain vestigial attractions for these or have developed a distinct dislike for them, you are perhaps attracted to the lawyer type, or the matronly sort, or maybe you've just moved from Kurt or Helena over to, say, Ewan McGregor or Gwyneth Paltrow. It seems to me that throughout our lives we are continually adding and subtracting attractions as a result of our experiences, of our changes in circumstance, of our aging. Very rarely, I think, do those initial pubescent attractions—to Mister Rogers or Wonder Woman—stick around in anything other than nostalgic or ironic form. All sorts of barriers are crossed in the development of our attractions—when once we were attracted to teenagers we become attracted to adults, when once we were attracted to people because of how they looked we become attracted to them because of how they think. Not everyone undergoes drastic shifts, but we all suffer alterations in the nature of our attractions. ('What did I ever see in her?' is a pretty common sort of thing to ask yourself.) True, sometimes these shifts may be seen as a honing, from Wonder Woman to S/M, from Mister Rogers to daddy types, but the change remains the same. And most people, I'd guess, see this and take it as self-evident that since we don't do this with the sex of those we're attracted to, it's in a different category from, say, superhero outfits. Very few people, they'd say, go from being attracted to women to being attracted to men.

But since attraction is overdetermined, and since not only aging and financial advancement but also societal pressures and cultural norms all play a role in its development, and since fluidity in the choice of the sex of the sexual object has not been permissible, it has not been an option.

But things have changed, and continue to change. Unrestricted sexual choice, which was once common but unspoken, became less common and more spoken about, then even less common and even more loudly talked about, and is now more universally shouted about than ever and becoming more common once again. In the few years since it has become acceptable to create reasonable portrayals of same-sex attraction in the American and northern European mass media, those who are young enough, independent enough, or sexually introspective enough have started—just started, mind you—to accrete a little less seamlessly. As it becomes obvious through public representation that there are no particular types of people who are either straight or gay, that there are very straight-seeming people who have sex with members of the same sex and very gay-seeming people who have sex with members of the opposite sex,[4] and all sorts of stuff in between and beyond, the connection between act and essence is becoming weaker in people's minds. Echoing my own de-revision (or re-envisioning) of the development of my attractions, Edmund White,

one of the most prominent creators of English-language gay literature of the eighties and nineties, said in a review of Marjorie Garber's book on sexuality that reading it had made him realise that he had 'denied the authenticity of my earlier heterosexual feelings in the light of my later homosexual identity'. The same cultural markers that led Garber to write her book and me to write mine are allowing people younger than the fifty-something White to avoid some levels of those original denials and revisions-on-the-run. It's by no means a universal, or even remarkably common, thing for teens and young adults to completely ignore sexual identity and follow less walled-off paths of attraction and relationships. Not yet. But the common teen habit of sexual experimentation, on this far side of gay rights and cultural sexual discourse, has come to mean different things. Experiences that were once singular, or at least confined within age boundaries, are becoming less so. . . .

DISCUSSION QUESTIONS

1. Do you agree with Archer that people born since the 1980s are less committed to sexual identity categories? What evidence would you offer for your position?
2. Is Archer really just bisexual?

NOTES

1. *Showbiz Today* got its highest rating of the week running 112 seconds of it, *Saturday Night Live* got its highest rating of the season for the 90-second excerpt it ran, *Nightline* ran it uncensored and got its highest ratings of the year, and *The Howard Stern Show*, which ran it with minor censoring, got its highest rating ever.
2. The Mattachine Society was an early, secretive homosexual rights organisation, founded in 1951 in Los Angeles, a rough equivalent in many ways to other early groups, like the Homophile Association of London, Ontario. Though its founder, Harry Hay, was a devoted Communist, the organisation soon became thoroughly conservative (and Hay left). See Hay's *Radically Gay: Gay Liberation in the Words of its Founder*, edited by Will Roscoe (Boston: Beacon Press, 1996) for the best account I've found of Mattachine and this era in US gay activist thought.

3. Perhaps an opportune moment to point out that I'm a firm subscriber to the Woody Allen School of Qualitative Sexuality—bad sex is a highly relative term in my books, akin to filthy lucre.

4. See, for instance, 'Trials of a Gay-seeming Straight Male' by Leif Ueland on nerve.com, posted 12 June 1998, in which Ueland writes: 'Maybe what my people need is a new definition, a nice user-friendly label. Something that says, "not gay, but not straight in the way to which you're accustomed, and maybe not even willing to rule out the possibility of being gay in the future".'

READING 20

The Heterosexual Questionnaire

Martin Rochlin

This Heterosexual Questionnaire reverses the questions that are very often asked of gays and lesbians by straight people. By having to answer this type of question, the heterosexual person will get some intellectual and emotional insight into how oppressive and discriminatory a "straight" frame of reference can be to lesbians and gays.

1. What do you think caused your heterosexuality?
2. When and how did you first decide you were a heterosexual?
3. Is it possible that your heterosexuality is just a phase you may grow out of?
4. Is it possible that your heterosexuality stems from a neurotic fear of others of the same sex?
5. If you've never slept with a person of the same sex, is it possible that all you need is a good gay lover?

6. To whom have you disclosed you[r] tendencies?
7. Why do you heterosexuals feel [?] seduce others into your lifestyle?
8. Why do you insist on flaunting your heterosexuality? Can't you just be what you are and keep it quiet?
9. Would you want your children to be heterosexual, knowing the problem they'd face?
10. A disproportionate majority of child molesters are heterosexuals. Do you consider it safe to expose your children to heterosexual teachers?
11. Even with all the societal support marriage receives, the divorce rate is spiraling. Why are there so few stable relationships among heterosexuals?
12. Why do heterosexuals place so much emphasis on sex?
13. Considering the menace of overpopulation, how could the human race survive if everyone were heterosexual like you?
14. Could you trust a heterosexual therapist to be objective? Don't you fear that the therapist might be inclined to influence you in the direction of his or her own leanings?
15. How can you become a whole person if you limit yourself to compulsive, exclusive heterosexuality and fail to develop your natural, healthy homosexual potential?
16. There seem to be very few happy heterosexuals. Techniques have been developed that might enable you to change if you really want to. Have you considered trying aversion therapy?

DISCUSSION QUESTIONS

1. What is your reaction to the Heterosexual Questionnaire?
2. Do you think these questions mirror the kinds of questions that gay and lesbian people are asked?
3. What are the assumptions behind these questions?

Martin Rochlin (1928–2003) was one of the founders of the Association of Gay Psychologists and a leader in the campaign that led to removing homosexuality from the list of mental disorders in the *Diagnostic and Statistical Manual of Mental Disorders*.

persuasion) was going to commit itself to a whole range of services without some idea of what the financial consequences of such a commitment might be. Thus, after some pilot work, the Office of Population Censuses and Surveys (OPCS) was commissioned in the late sixties to carry out a national survey in Britain which was published in 1971 (Harris, 1971). Subsequent work in the international context (Wood, 1981) and more recently a further survey in this country, which has recently been published (Martin, Meltzer and Elliot, 1988), built on and extended this work. However, this work has proceeded isolated from the direct experience of disability as experienced by disabled people themselves, and this has led to a number of wide-ranging and fundamental criticisms of it. . . .

THE POLITICS OF MEANING

It could be argued that in polarising the tragic and oppressive views of disability, a conflict is being created where none necessarily exists. Disability has both individual and social dimensions and that is what official definitions from Harris (1971) through to WHO [World Health Organization] (Wood, 1981) have sought to recognize and to operationalize. The problem with this, is that these schemes, while acknowledging that there are social dimensions to disability, do not see disability as arising from social causes. . . .

This view of disability can and does have oppressive consequences for disabled people and can be quite clearly shown in the methodology adopted by the OPCS survey in Britain (Martin et al., 1988). [Table 1 presents] a list of questions drawn from the face-to-face interview schedule of this survey.

These questions clearly ultimately reduce the problems that disabled people face to their own personal inadequacies or functional limitations. It would have been perfectly possible to reformulate these questions to locate the ultimate causes of disability as within the physical and social environments [as they are in Table 2].

This reformulation is not only about methodology or semantics, it is also about oppression. In

TABLE 1

SURVEY OF DISABLED ADULTS—OPCS, 1986

Can you tell me what is wrong with you?

What complaint causes your difficulty in holding, gripping or turning things?

Are your difficulties in understanding people mainly due to a hearing problem?

Do you have a scar, blemish or deformity which limits your daily activities?

Have you attended a special school because of a long-term health problem or disability?

Does your health problem/disability mean that you need to live with relatives or someone else who can help look after you?

Did you move here because of your health problem/disability?

How difficult is it for you to get about your immediate neighborhood on your own?

Does your health problem/disability prevent you from going out as often or as far as you would like?

Does your health problem/disability make it difficult for you to travel by bus?

Does your health problem/disability affect your work in any way at present?

order to understand this, it is necessary to understand that, according to OPCS's own figures, 2231 disabled people were given face-to-face interviews (Martin et al., 1988, Table 5.2). In these interviews, the interviewer visits the disabled person at home and asks many structured questions in a structured way. It is in the nature of the interview process that the interviewer presents as expert and the disabled person as an isolated individual inexperienced in research, and thus unable to reformulate the questions in a more appropriate way. It is hardly surprising that, given the nature of the questions and their direction that, by the end of the interview, the disabled person has come to believe that his or her problems are caused by their own health/disability problems rather than by the organization of society. It is in this sense that the process of the interview is oppressive, reinforcing on to isolated, individual disabled people the idea that the problems they experience in everyday living are a direct result of their own personal inadequacies or functional limitations. . . .

TABLE 2

ALTERNATIVE QUESTIONS

Can you tell me what is wrong with society?

What defects in the design of everyday equipment like jars, bottles and tins causes you difficulty in holding, gripping or turning them?

Are your difficulties in understanding people mainly due to their inabilities to communicate with you?

Do other people's reactions to any scar, blemish or deformity you may have, limit your daily activities?

Have you attended a special school because of your education authority's policy of sending people with your health problem or disability to such places?

Are community services so poor that you need to rely on relatives or someone else to provide you with the right level of personal assistance?

What inadequacies in your housing caused you to move here?

What are the environmental constraints which make it difficult for you to get about in your immediate neighborhood?

Are there any transport or financial problems which prevent you from going out as often or as far as you would like?

Do poorly designed buses make it difficult for someone with your health problem/disability to use them?

Do you have problems at work because of the physical environment or the attitudes of others?

IMPAIRMENT: A STRUCTURED ACCOUNT

Recently it has been estimated that there are some 500 million severely impaired people in the world today, approximately one in ten of the population (Shirley, 1983). These impairments are not randomly distributed throughout the world but are culturally produced.

> The societies men live in determine their chances of health, sickness and death. To the extent that they have the means to master their economic and social environments, they have the means to determine their life chances. (Susser and Watson, 1971, p. 45)

Hence in some countries impairments are likely to stem from infectious diseases, poverty, ignorance and the failure to ensure that existing medical treatments reach the population at risk (Shirley, 1983). In others, impairments resulting from infectious diseases are declining, only to be replaced by those stemming from the aging of the population, accidents at work, on the road or in the home, the very success of some medical technologies in ensuring the survival of some severely impaired children and adults and so on (Taylor, 1977). To put the matter simply, impairments such as blindness and deafness are likely to be more common in the Third World, whereas heart conditions, spina bifida, spinal injuries and so on, are likely to be more common in industrial societies.

Again, the distribution of these impairments is not a matter of chance, either across different societies or within a single society, for

> Social and economic forces cause disorder directly; they redistribute the proportion of people at high or low risk of being affected; and they create new pathways for the transmission of disorders of all kinds through travel, migration and the rapid diffusion of information and behaviour by the mass communication media. Finally, social forces affect the conceptualisation, recognition and visibility of disorders. A disorder in one place and at one time is not seen as such in another; these social perceptions and definitions influence both the provision of care, the demands of those being cared for, and the size of any count of health needs. (Susser and Watson, 1971, p. 35)

Social class is an important factor here both in terms of the causes of impairments or what Doyal (1979) calls degenerative diseases, and in terms of outcomes, what Le Grand (1978) refers to as long-standing illnesses.

Just as we know that poverty is not randomly distributed internationally or nationally (Cole and Miles, 1984; Townsend, 1979), neither is impairment, for in the Third World at least

> Not only does disability usually guarantee the poverty of the victim but, most importantly, poverty is itself a major cause of disability. (Doyal, 1983, p. 7)

There is a similar relation in the industrial countries. . . . Hence, if poverty is not randomly distributed and there is an intrinsic link between poverty and impairment, then neither is impairment randomly distributed.

Even a structured account of impairment cannot, however, be reduced to counting the numbers of impaired people in any one country, locality, class or social group, for

> Beliefs about sickness, the behaviours exhibited by sick persons, and the ways in which sick persons are responded to by family and practitioners are all aspects of social reality. They, like the health care system itself, are cultural constructions, shaped distinctly in different societies and in different social structural settings within those societies. (Kleinman, 1980, p. 38)

The discovery of an isolated tribe in West Africa where many of the population were born with only two toes illustrates this point, for this made no difference to those with only two toes or indeed the rest of the population (Barrett and McCann, 1979). Such differences would be regarded as pathological in our society, and the people so afflicted subjected to medical intervention.

In discussing impairment, it was not intended to provide a comprehensive discussion of the nature of impairment but to show that it occurs in a structured way. However

> such a view does not deny the significance of germs, genes and trauma, but rather points out that their effects are only ever apparent in a real social and historical context, whose nature is determined by a complex interaction of material and nonmaterial factors. (Abberley, 1987, p. 12)

This account of impairment challenges the notion underpinning personal tragedy theory, that impairments are events happening to unfortunate individuals. . . .

DISCUSSION QUESTIONS

1. Can you list some words that have changed meaning over time?
2. Why must minority groups continue to challenge definitions?

REFERENCES

Abberley, P. (1987). "The Concept of Oppression and the Development of a Social Theory of Disability," *Disability, Handicap and Society,* Vol. 2, no. 1, 5–19.

Barrett, D., and McCann, E. (1979). "Discovered: Two Toed Man," *Sunday Times Colour Supplement,* n.d.

Cole, S., and Miles, I. (1984). *Worlds Apart* (Brighton: Wheatsheaf).

Doyal, L. (1979). *The Political Economy of Health* (London: Pluto Press).

Doyal L. (1983). "The Crippling Effects of Underdevelopment" in Shirley, O. (ed.).

Harris, A. (1971). *Handicapped and Impaired in Great Britain* (London: HMSO).

Le Grand, J. (1978). "The Distribution of Public Expenditure: the Case of Health Care," *Economica,* Vol. 45.

Martin, J., Meltzer, H., and Elliot, D. (1988). *The Prevalence of Disability Amongst Adults* (London: HMSO).

Shirley, O. (ed.) (1983). *A Cry for Health: Poverty and Disability in the Third World* (Frome: Third World Group and ARHTAG).

Stone, D. (1985). *The Disabled State* (London: Macmillan).

Susser, M., and Watson, W. (2nd ed.) (1971). *Sociology in Medicine* (London: Oxford University Press).

Taylor, D. (1977). *Physical Impairment—Social Handicap* (London: Office of Health Economics).

Thomas, W. I. (1966). In Janowitz, M. (ed.), *Organization and Social Personality: Selected Papers* (Chicago: University of Chicago Press).

Townsend, P. (1979). *Poverty in the United Kingdom* (Harmondsworth: Penguin).

Wood, P. (1981). *International Classification of Impairments, Disabilities and Handicaps* (Geneva: World Health Organization).

READING 22

What Do Disabilities Have to Do with Diversity?

Pat McCune

It all starated when Rachel Arfa came into my office with a challenging question: Are students with disabilities part of diversity at the University of

Pat McCune is director of the Office of Graduate Student Success, Horace H. Rackham School of Graduate Studies, University of Michigan.

Michigan? This was in February 1999, when I was administering the university's campuswide theme semester—Diversity: Theories and Practices. The semester was in full swing, with over one hundred courses in fourteen of our schools and colleges, special events, and research funding for faculty and students. There was also funding for the Capstone Week, which would take place at the end of March and feature activities intended to highlight the project as the semester drew to a close. Rachel had seen a notice for the funding available for Capstone student projects. She told me that she wanted to organize a video event that would pose a central question: Are disabilities part of diversity?

I can't remember what I told her. I probably blinked for a moment or two, then smiled professionally and said something like, "I don't see why not, but the final decision is up to the funding committee." I *can* remember what I felt. I was anxious and uncomfortable, certain that I would offend her somehow, because Rachel has a hearing impairment, and at that first meeting I had difficulty understanding her. And like many people, I was too embarrassed to say so. This meant that I was missing about a third of what she said, between her unfamiliar speech patterns and my racing thoughts—racing because I was intrigued. *Were* disabled students a component in the diversity that the University of Michigan valued and in fact had been defending in the courts its right to value? [See the discussion of the Michigan Cases: *Gratz v. Bollinger et al.* (2003) and *Grutter v. Bollinger et al.* (2003) in Reading 49.]

I am the program coordinator for Dialogues on Diversity, a campuswide initiative that, as the mission statement says, promotes "opportunities for the open exchange of views about the value of diversity." Our objective is to "enrich campus discussion and facilitate honest dialogue concerning the broad range of topics relating to diversity." I've held this position since the initiative began in January 1998—just a few months after the lawsuits were filed by unsuccessful applicants to the University of Michigan. Jennifer Gratz, Patrick Hamacher, and Barbara Grutter thought they were unjustly denied

a place at the University of Michigan and challenged the use of affirmative action in the admissions process at the College of Literature, Science and the Arts and at the law school. Since 1998 I've developed a variety of programs, focusing primarily on racial and ethnic minorities and occasionally on women and religion, but never on the disabled. I think this is because, historically, people with disabilities either have been categorized by the type of disability and thus been thought to have nothing in common with people who have other disabilities or, worse yet, have not even been acknowledged as participating members of our society. . . .

I have to admit that I was making arguments to support [Rachel's video] project not only to my executive committee but also to myself. I was concerned that other minority groups or administrators would challenge me, that I might be accused of deflecting attention from the core issues of diversity in higher education. In talking this through with [colleagues], we saw the parallels between disabled students as a group and other student minority groups. There are many examples. For instance, in the admissions process, students with disabilities, like students of color, are faced with the dilemma of whether and when to reveal this part of their identity. Once here, they might be perceived as special admits who don't deserve to be here and can't do the work. There are formal student services to assist them with special accommodations. Many of the students can be stereotyped by the way they look or sound. Our institution still has facilities and procedures that are impediments in the realities of these students' daily lives. Students with disabilities definitely are an unacknowledged minority here on campus. . . .

[The project ultimately took the form of interviews.] Early on, Rachel and I agreed that the subjects would be self-defining: all students who said they had a disability and wanted to take part would be included. Basically, this meant we'd have to actively seek the participation of those with physical, learning, and psychiatric disabilities. At this point I had no idea what I would ask them or how I could guarantee that the final content pertained to diversity as well as disability. We did know it would never work unless the students with disabilities were central to the production. We did know students would be inclined to become involved if the video might be part of a larger project. Students were less likely to feel their experience was being exploited if participation in the video might lead to positive changes at the university. . . .

The interviewing process solved the script dilemma. Each of the students had met and talked with me in a general, wide-ranging discussion. After that, I realized in going through my notes that they shared common concerns and experiences—though how they reacted to those experiences differed markedly. Then I met again with each for a preinterview session in which I asked the students if the topics I was addressing were important and encouraged them to elaborate on their answer to that question. I became convinced that the program we produced had to be totally subjective, featuring the fifteen students as individuals and allowing them to voice their own experiences with no narrator to structure the audience's reception. There would be no pretense of objectivity and no claim that these students were representative of all with disabilities.

We taped the fifteen interviews in March and April, but it wasn't until I read the transcripts that I realized what we had. The parallels with the experience of other student minorities are striking. Let's begin with the application process. Like many students of color, these disabled students had thought long and hard about making reference to their disabilities at any point in the application; their experience had been, all too often, that it evoked stereotypes subtly used as grounds for exclusion. Perhaps officials would see them as a burden because of all the services they would require or the physical changes that would have to be made in facilities. An inappropriately paternalistic admissions officer might decide they were not up to the challenge or misunderstand the nature of the disease.

Those with physical disabilities are not the only ones who withhold information. Laura Wernick, a graduate student with learning disabilities, had this concern when she applied to the School of Social Work. "Because there's so much stigma around learning disabilities, a lot of misconception about what that's about," she said, "I was afraid to self-disclose my LD during the application process." However, there were students who saw a strategy in disclosure that could work to their advantage. This, too, parallels the approach some students of color can take. Cynthia Overton, for example, knew that the pool of applicants to her program in education contained few people with disabilities and that it was therefore probably to her advantage to include her disability in her personal statement. Carey Larabee has cerebral palsy and began working with the university's Office of Services for Students with Disabilities while he was still in high school in order to optimize his chances for a successful application.

Once here, students with disabilities contend on a daily basis with the pernicious effects of stereotyping. Like students of color, those who can be identified at a glance as physically different experience assumptions about inferior intellectual capacity. Heidi Lengyel sometimes uses a wheelchair and had this to say about her experiences: "I find that people automatically assume that your intelligence level is lower. They sort of talk maybe slower to you or in a patronizing way. . . . They don't speak right at you or act like you know anything. And they're always surprised to find out that I'm a college student. Then they are surprised to find out where I go to school. They think, 'How could you go to U of M?' So sometimes they'll even say that."

The same stereotype is applied to students with learning disabilities. Perhaps we are loath to admit it, but many Americans suspect that a diagnosis of learning disability is somehow a hoax, a trick to secure an extra advantage. And many other stereotypes play into such an assumption. Michael Gonzales, a graduate student in public health at the medical school who is learning-disabled is all too familiar with this "double whammy." "I feel, like, dumb," he said, "because especially if they know that I'm a medical student then they're like, 'Why are you so slow with this?' Then if they know that I'm Mexican on top of that they go, 'Oh, you just got in medical school because you're Mexican, and you're just not smart enough.'"

Students with mental illness similarly face the suspicion that they deceive others in order to secure accommodations with regard to coursework and other responsibilities. As a result, they often hide their suffering or deny their symptoms. For example, a first-year student (who asked to remain anonymous) resisted seeking treatment for fear of what it would mean: "The symptoms are horrible, but I think that the perceived or the actual stigma, or the perceived or the actual judgment that falls upon someone who does have a mental illness can be much harder, especially in a university setting."

The disability that marks students for discrimination also forms a significant component, if not the dominant one, in their identity. Each day, they are required to face the challenge of certain cultural and physical realities. Just as people of color in our country rarely, if ever, are allowed to forget that others consider race their most important feature, so it is with these students. Identity was a topic they considered in complex detail. Tim Kaiser is on the job market this year and has thought carefully about how to present his disability when interviewed. "My abilities are not standard, are not like everyone else's," Tim said, "because of my visual impairment. So I'm going to bring something different to the university, wherever I'm going to end up teaching. I won't do things like the professor next door. It's going to be different. And so that's good, I think."

Rachel feels that from an early age she repeatedly has had to choose whether to be part of hearing society or deaf society, and she has never been comfortable with that either-or attitude. As she explained it, "I spent a lot of time thinking about it; that's not how I am, that's not how I view myself, but that's how I'm going to be viewed in society. And the only way I could change that is to empower myself, to do something about it, to stop hiding myself."

Mary Kay Sisson, a nondegree student preparing to apply to medical school, was keenly aware of the debates about cultural definition and identification in the deaf community, even if she was uncertain where she stood. "I think," she observed, "they form not 'a' minority group. I think they form multiple minority groups. I should say we." To many people, Matt Conaway appears severely impaired by cerebral palsy. Yet his very determination to live the way he chooses has created false expectations and misperceptions about who he really is. "Yeah, they expect me to be a supercripple," he said. "But I'm not a supercripple. I'll be damned if I'll be a supercripple. I mean, I've been there, and I'm not going to do it. You know, and if people think I'm not being independent, well, I don't know what else they want. I live here by myself. I live in this apartment by myself and I run my business by myself. And if that's not being independent then I don't know what is."

Yet for a few, the very characteristic disdained by society at large is intensely valued. Becky Messing had no doubts: "I guess when we look at the definition of disability, my anxiety disorder definitely puts me at a disadvantage, and I've had to fight through many of my own physical limitations to remain here at the university and remain where I'm studying and in my everyday life. But it's something I've dealt with since I was little. It's a part of me. I wouldn't necessarily... I *wouldn't* give it up. It helps drive me to do what I do." Although they focused on the role their particular disability had in shaping their identity, the students all identified with the encompassing label of *disabled*. Cynthia Overton's summary echoes what was said by many of the students I interviewed: "I feel as though all people with disabilities make up some sort of culture. I mean, we share many of the same experiences, many of the same problems and same issues."

How, then, does their sense of belonging to a minority affect their views on the value of diversity in higher education? Carey Larabee had been considering where he fit in on campus when he posed a question: "Do I see myself as part of the university's diversity that they have spent so much time on?" His answer was, "No, I don't think so. I think, you know, the university prides itself so much on diversity and, you know, African Americans, homosexuals, or whatever. But I think the disabled population is kind of . . . I don't want to say 'hidden,' but it's just not noticed as much and really paid attention to as much as some of the other groups on campus."

All the students I interviewed voiced a similar sense that the disabled are rarely acknowledged in all the talk of diversity. Rachel shares this view with Carey. In the course of her activism during her four years on campus, she's given a lot of thought to how we define diversity. "Students with disabilities are not recognized as a minority group, but I think that it's an invisible population," she said. "When we talk about diversity it's usually in color but it's not in . . . what shapes our experience, which is something that disability does."

Jack Bernard is a graduate of our law school, now an attorney in our general counsel's office and a strong supporter of the university's defense of its emphasis on diversity. He admitted that the university wasn't as inclusive as he would like it to be in terms of students with disabilities, pointing out that these students have certainly not been even close to the top of the university's diversity agenda.

Interestingly, although in interviews students expressed views about the admissions lawsuits and affirmative action that spanned the political spectrum, none doubted the value diversity adds to education. Steve Laux, a graduate student in engineering, now paraplegic as the result of an accident, had a very pragmatic approach to the issue: "The U.S. prides itself on being probably the most diversified country. . . . You know, when we enter the jobs and work with teams, then yeah, we're going to need to know how to deal with those people."

Tim Kaiser, whose vision became impaired while he was in graduate school, presented the relationship between disability and diversity in different terms: "It has made me aware also, then, that people who can't hide their disabilities or their skin color or whatever it's going to be are forced to deal with these things on a daily basis."

Although it is true that these students with disabilities voiced experiences that parallel those of other minority students, there was one exception that emerged in the interviews. Most of them had faced blatant discrimination in the classroom. Instructors, perhaps out of ignorance, anxiety, or a misguided sense of fairness, refused to provide accommodations and often humiliated the students by publicly discussing their special needs. (Hearing about these incidents brought back shameful memories of my own responses to disabled students when I was teaching.)

The experience Heidi Lengyel related is not unusual: "Then she told me also that the other students in the class felt uncomfortable with me in the class. At this time, I had a brace on my leg and I was using crutches. But I mean, it could have looked to someone like I had broken my leg. So she said that they were very uncomfortable with me in the class and wanted to know what was wrong with me. Those were the words she used. And she wanted me to get up in front of the class and explain it. I said 'No.' Then I ended up having to go to Services for Students with Disabilities and talking about this."

Often the faculty response was not so overtly cruel but simply thoughtless—and that in itself can be devastating. Becky Messing related the experiences she had had with seeking help from her professors: "I was actually very discouraged, especially by some of the faculty in the College of Engineering that were trying to help. One woman told me, 'Well, maybe chemical engineering is not for you.' And it didn't make any sense to me because I hadn't taken any engineering classes. . . . There's a lack of education about anxiety disorders and mental health and mental illnesses in general. And it was *really* frustrating to get discouragement from people that I looked up to."

Rachel Arfa told of this experience with a professor: "I had this one professor who was very intimidated by having real-time captioning in the classroom. It was a piece of technology; she didn't understand what it was for; she didn't try to learn what it was about. And then bad things started happening because as that affected me, she wasn't making the effort to reach out to me and treat me as a member of the class. She saw me as the girl sitting next to the real-time captioning."

A Time I Didn't Feel Normal

I was tested for Learning Disabilities (LD) when I was in third grade and diagnosed with being ADD and LD because of short-term memory loss and mild dyslexia. I thought nothing of it because I didn't really understand what it meant. All I knew was it got me out of class to go work with a woman on my schoolwork. However, the next year I moved from Ohio to Virginia and discovered that I was different from most of my peers. It got worse when I got to fifth grade because I still had to leave class twice a week to go work with the disabilities counselor with two other kids in my class. I soon realized that people would actually talk down to me in my class because I wasn't really "one of them," that I wasn't as smart. The stereotype, even at such a young age, about being LD was not a good one. The other two kids that were in my LD class were not exactly popular and a little weird. So because I was with them, I became one of them. I would get made fun of and stopped really trying in class because if I messed up people would look at me as though it was expected that I would do things wrong. It got so bad that I told my mom I didn't want to go back to school. I asked her to home school me so that I wouldn't have to deal with the other kids in my class judging me and making me feel like I was stupid. My mom refused to do it, so I did the only other thing I could think of: I forced my way out of the LD program at my school. I don't know how I got them to let me out but I felt that it was the only way for me to be "normal." I continued to struggle throughout my school career but I wasn't treated as differently, I was more socially accepted.

Today, I don't have a problem with telling people about my "disabilities," but back then I would never have admitted it. I have grown to the point where my "disabilities" don't really affect me all that much. I've learned to cope with them and still do well in school. So, I don't feel like an idiot, or stupid, or a lesser student because of my LD anymore. However, back then I would cry because I thought I wasn't as smart as everyone else and that there was something wrong with me that made me different from everyone else. I felt isolated at times and envied my friends who were "normal." My parents did what they could to help me with my homework and in overcoming my difficulties, but no one really stuck up for me at school or seemed to care how I felt, or even notice how upset I was. I am a better person today because of this though; I realize how hard it is for people to be treated as though there is something wrong with them even though there really isn't. Judging people for their "disabilities" is wrong and cruel and people really need to step back and think about how their actions affect others.

Heather Callender

Unfortunately, Rachel's experience is one shared by other students who take advantage of the great advances in technology.

Brent Baribeau, who came to the University of Michigan on a golf scholarship, then suffered a spinal cord injury in an accident, couched these problems with faculty in the most generous terms: "There are instances when I do feel like some of my professors don't really I guess grasp or appreciate what it entails for me just to be a student. I think they tend to overlook the fact that I do deal with more than the average student does on a daily basis. That definitely can be frustrating that I just feel like at times they really miss the bigger picture."

How then can we convey the bigger picture? The call for change I heard repeatedly in my interviews and conversations was matched by the plans these students have. Heidi Lengyel has written a proposal for a peer mentorship program that would ease the transition to college life for students with disabilities. Rachel Arfa has spoken to the administration about the need for a meeting room in the student union designated as a lounge for disabled students. Many, like Steve Laux, saw ignorance as the primary impediment: "I don't like this to define who I am, so I don't necessarily like to associate with only other people in wheelchairs. But at the same time . . . we need to come together and get stuff accomplished as a whole because there's just so much unawareness out there." Jack Bernard sees similarities with earlier political movements that advanced the interests of minority groups: "The more people we have on campus who have disabilities, hidden or otherwise, I think, the better it is for the community. There's a little more sensitivity out there. And that's like with any of the other movements we've had. The best way to improve understanding is to improve interaction."

Among all the competing demands for attention by student minority groups, there is a tendency to think that efforts to level the playing field for one group will somehow interfere with similar efforts for other groups. But why? Haven't we learned that the inclusion of one group does not require the exclusion of another? Over the last two decades we all have seen increasing access to higher education for a growing number of minority groups. What has kept us from including students with disabilities in that access—and from recognizing how they contribute to our community? Let's face it: sometimes we're held back by fear and repulsion, more often by simple embarrassment and ignorance, and sometimes by the desire to spend our allotted funding on another program affecting a greater number of students. We should be encouraged by the parallel experiences between disabled students and other minority groups. It's time to stop telling them who they are or aren't and instead simply listen.

As a society, we are ready. After the experience of making this video, I'm convinced that attitudes about disability really have changed over the past two decades. Rachel's initiating question—whether students with disabilities were part of diversity—has been answered with a resounding yes, at least on our campus. For there was no doubt here at the University of Michigan that students with disabilities contribute to the wealth of experience that so enriches the quality of education we provide. The response to the completed video program, *And You Can Quote Me on That: Students with Disabilities at the University of Michigan,* has been striking and powerful. I had expected an audience of perhaps one hundred at the most for the premiere in September. More than twice that number came that night; every inch of the room was occupied, and people were waiting in the hallway. Following

the screening six of the students who were featured took questions from the audience. For an hour the questions came—questions that focused not on the disabled as some foreign group but as a part of the community unfairly excluded. The next day my e-mail in box was flooded with requests from faculty, students, and staff for copies of the tape. The requests continue to come in, because of the full coverage the premiere received in the student and staff newspapers and the word of mouth that promotes its value.

I don't know what the next step is, but we're ready.

DISCUSSION QUESTIONS

1. In your college experience, has disability been treated as part of campus diversity?
2. What consequences might follow from explicitly including disability as part of a college's discussion of diversity?
3. Comparing the experience of disabled students with students of color and gay and lesbian students, what do you think are the similarities and differences in their college experience?

READING 23

A World of Their Own

Liza Mundy

As her baby begins to emerge after a day of labor, Sharon Duchesneau has a question for the midwife who is attending the birth. Asking it is not the easiest thing, just now. Sharon is deaf, and communicates using American Sign Language, and the combination of intense pain and the position she has sought to ease it—kneeling, resting her weight

---

Liza Mundy is a feature writer for the *Washington Post Magazine.*

on her hands—makes signing somewhat hard. Even so, Sharon manages to sign something to Risa Shaw, a hearing friend who is present to interpret for the birth, which is taking place in a softly lit bedroom of Sharon's North Bethesda home.

"Sharon wants to know what color hair you see," Risa says to the midwife.

The midwife cannot tell because the baby is not—quite—visible. He bulges outward during contractions, then recedes when the contraction fades. But now comes another contraction and a scream from Sharon, and the midwife and her assistant call for Sharon to keep pushing but to keep it steady and controlled. They are accustomed to using their voices as a way of guiding women through this last excruciating phase; since Sharon can't hear them, all they can hope is that she doesn't close her eyes.

"Push through the pain!" shouts the midwife.

"Little bit!" shouts her assistant, as Risa frantically signs.

And suddenly the baby is out. One minute the baby wasn't here and now the baby is, hair brown, eyes blue, face gray with waxy vernix, body pulsing with life and vigor. A boy. "Is he okay?" signs Sharon, and the answer, to all appearances, is a resounding yes. There are the toes, the toenails, the fingers, the hands, the eyes, the eyelashes, the exquisite little-old-man's face, contorted in classic newborn outrage. The midwife lays the baby on Sharon and he bleats and hiccups and nuzzles her skin, the instinct to breast-feed strong.

"Did he cry?" signs Sharon, and the women say no, he cried remarkably little.

"His face looks smushed," Sharon signs, regarding him tenderly.

"It'll straighten out," says the midwife.

Presently the midwife takes the baby and performs the Apgar, the standard test of a newborn's condition, from which he emerges with an impressive score of nine out of a possible 10. "He's very calm," she notes as she weighs him (6 pounds 5 ounces), then lays him out to measure head and chest and length. She bicycles his legs to check the flexibility of his hips; examines his testicles to make sure they are descended; feels his vertebrae for gaps.

All in all, she pronounces the baby splendid. "Look how strong he is!" she says, pulling him gently up from the bed by his arms. Which means that it is, finally, possible to relax and savor his arrival. Everyone takes turns holding him: Sharon; her longtime partner, Candace McCullough, who is also deaf, and will be the boy's adoptive mother; their good friend Jan DeLap, also deaf; Risa Shaw and another hearing friend, Juniper Sussman. Candy and Sharon's five-year-old daughter, Jehanne, is brought in to admire him, but she is fast asleep and comically refuses to awaken, even when laid on the bed and prodded. Amid the oohing and aahing someone puts a cap on the baby; somebody else swaddles him in a blanket; somebody else brings a plate of turkey and stuffing for Sharon, who hasn't eaten on a day that's dedicated to feasting. Conceived by artificial insemination 38 weeks ago, this boy, Gauvin Hughes McCullough, has arrived two weeks ahead of schedule, on Thanksgiving Day.

"A turkey baby," signs Sharon, who is lying back against a bank of pillows, her dark thick hair spread against the light gray pillowcases.

"A turkey baster baby," jokes Candy, lying next to her.

"A perfect baby," says the midwife.

"A perfect baby," says the midwife's assistant.

But there is perfect and there is perfect. There is no way to know, yet, whether Gauvin Hughes McCullough is perfect in the specific way that Sharon and Candy would like him to be. Until he is old enough, two or three months from now, for a sophisticated audiology test, the women cannot be sure whether Gauvin is—as they hope—deaf.

Several months before his birth, Sharon and Candy—both stylish and independent women in their mid-thirties, both college graduates, both holders of graduate degrees from Gallaudet University, both professionals in the mental health field—sat in their kitchen trying to envision life if their son turned out not to be deaf. It was something they had a hard time getting their minds around. When they were looking for a donor to inseminate Sharon, one thing they knew was that they wanted a deaf donor. So they contacted a local sperm bank and asked whether the bank would provide one. The sperm bank said no; congenital deafness is precisely the sort of condition that, in the world of commercial reproductive technology, gets a would-be donor eliminated.

So Sharon and Candy asked a deaf friend to be the donor, and he agreed.

Though they have gone to all this trouble, Candy and Sharon take issue with the suggestion that they are "trying" to have a deaf baby. To put it this way, they worry, implies that they will not love their son if he can hear. And, they insist, they will. As Sharon puts it: "A hearing baby would be a blessing. A deaf baby would be a special blessing."

As Candy puts it: "I would say that we wanted to increase our chances of having a baby who is deaf."

It may seem a shocking undertaking: two parents trying to screen in a quality, deafness, at a time when many parents are using genetic testing to screen out as many disorders as science will permit. Down's syndrome, cystic fibrosis, early-onset Alzheimer's—every day, it seems, there's news of yet another disorder that can be detected before birth and eliminated by abortion, manipulation of the embryo or, in the case of in vitro fertilization, destruction of an embryo. Though most deafness cannot be identified or treated in this way, it seems safe to say that when or if it can, many parents would seek to eliminate a disability that affects one out of 1,000 Americans.

As for actively trying to build a deaf baby. "I think all of us recognize that deaf children can have perfectly wonderful lives," says R. Alta Charo, a professor of law and bioethics at the University of Wisconsin. "The question is whether the parents have violated the sacred duty of parenthood, which is to maximize to some reasonable degree the advantages available to their children. I'm loath to say it, but I think it's a shame to set limits on a child's potential."

In the deaf community, however, the arrival of a deaf baby has never evoked the feelings that it does among the hearing. To be sure, there are many deaf parents who feel their children will have an easier life if they are born hearing. "I know that my parents were disappointed that I was deaf, along with my brother, and I know I felt, just for a fleeting second, bad that my children were deaf," says Nancy Rarus, a staff member at the National Association of the Deaf. Emphasizing that she is speaking personally and not on behalf of the association, she adds, "I'm a social animal, and it's very difficult for me to talk to my neighbors. I wish I could walk up to somebody and ask for information. I've had a lot of arguments in the deaf community about that. People talk about 'The sky's the limit,' but being deaf prevents you from getting there. You don't have as many choices."

"I can't understand," she says, "why anybody would want to bring a disabled child into the world."

Then again, Rarus points out, "there are many, many deaf people who specifically want deaf kids." This is true particularly now, particularly in Washington, home to Gallaudet, the world's only liberal arts university for the deaf, and the lively deaf intelligentsia it has nurtured. Since the 1980s, many members of the deaf community have been galvanized by the idea that deafness is not a medical disability, but a cultural identity. They call themselves Deaf, with a capital D, a community whose defining and unifying quality is American Sign Language (ASL), a fluent, sophisticated language that enables deaf people to communicate fully, essentially liberating them—when they are among signers—from one of the most disabling aspects of being deaf. Sharon and Candy share the fundamental view of this Deaf camp; they see deafness as an identity, not a medical affliction that needs to be fixed. Their effort—to have a baby who belongs to what they see as their minority group—is a natural outcome of the pride and self-acceptance the Deaf movement has brought to so many. It also would seem to put them at odds with the direction of reproductive technology in general, striving as it does for a more perfect normalcy.

But the interesting thing is—if one accepts their worldview, that a deaf baby could be desirable to some parents—Sharon and Candy are squarely part of a broader trend in artificial reproduction. Because, at the same time that many would-be parents are screening out qualities they don't want, many are also selecting for qualities they do want. And in many cases, the aim is to produce not so much a superior baby as a specific baby. A white baby. A black baby. A boy. A girl. Or a baby that's been even more minutely imagined. Would-be parents can go on many fertility clinic Web sites and type in preferences for a sperm donor's weight, height, eye color, race, ancestry, complexion, hair color, even hair texture.

"In most cases." says Sean Tipton, spokesman for the American Society of Reproductive Medicine, "what the couples are interested in is someone who physically looks like them." In this sense Candy and Sharon are like many parents, hoping for a child who will be in their own image.

And yet, while deafness may be a culture, in this country it is also an official disability, recognized under the Americans with Disabilities Act. What about the obligation of parents to see that their child has a better life than they did?

Then again, what does a better life mean? Does it mean choosing a hearing donor so your baby, unlike you, might grow up hearing?

Does it mean giving birth to a deaf child, and raising it in a better environment than the one you experienced?

What if you believe you can be a better parent to a deaf child than to a hearing one?

"It would be nice to have a deaf child who is the same as us. I think that would be a wonderful experience. You know, if we can have that chance, why not take it?"

This is Sharon, seven months pregnant, dressed in black pants and a stretchy black shirt, sitting at their kitchen table on a sunny fall afternoon, Candy beside her. Jehanne, their daughter, who is also deaf, and was conceived with the same donor they've used this time, is at school. The family has been doing a lot of nesting in anticipation of the baby's arrival. The kitchen has been renovated, the backyard landscaped. Soon the women plan to rig a system in which the lights in the house will blink one rhythm if the TTY—the telephonic device that deaf people type into—is ringing; another rhythm when the front doorbell rings; another for the side door. They already have a light in the bedroom that will go on when the baby cries.

In one way, it's hard for Sharon and Candy to articulate why they want to increase their chances of having a deaf child. Because they don't view deafness as a disability, they don't see themselves as bringing a disabled child into the world. Rather, they see themselves as bringing a different sort of normal child into the world. Why not bring a deaf child into the world? What, exactly, is the problem? In their minds, they are no different from parents who try to have a girl. After all, girls can be discriminated against. Same with deaf people. Sharon and Candy have faced obstacles, but they've survived. More than that, they've prevailed to become productive, self-supporting professionals. "Some people look at it like, 'Oh my gosh, you shouldn't have a child who has a disability,'" signs Candy. "But, you know, black people have harder lives. Why shouldn't parents be able to go ahead and pick a black donor if that's what they want? They should have that option. They can feel related to that culture, bonded with that culture."

The words "bond" and "culture" say a lot; in effect, Sharon and Candy are a little like immigrant parents who, with a huge and dominant and somewhat alien culture just outside their door, want to ensure that their children will share their heritage, their culture, their life experience. If they are deaf and have a hearing child, that child will move in a world where the women cannot fully follow. For this reason they believe they can be better parents to a deaf child, if being a better parent means being better able to talk to your child, understand your child's emotions, guide your child's development, pay attention to your child's friendships. "If we have a hearing child and he visits a hearing friend, we'll be like, 'Who is the family?'" says Candy. "In the deaf community, if you don't know a family, you ask around. You get references. But with hearing families, we would have no idea."

They understand that hearing people may find this hard to accept. It would be odd, they agree, if a hearing parent preferred to have a deaf child. And if they themselves—valuing sight—were to have a blind child, well then, Candy acknowledges, they would probably try to have it fixed, if they could, like hearing parents who attempt to restore their child's hearing with cochlear implants. "I want to be the same as my child," says Candy. "I want the baby to enjoy what we enjoy."

Which is not to say that they aren't open to a hearing child. A hearing child would make life rich and interesting. It's just hard, before the fact, to know what it would be like. "He'd be the only hearing member of the family," Sharon points out, laughing. "Other than the cats." . . .

Candy usually signs with both hands, using facial expressions as well as signs. This is all part of ASL, a physical language that encompasses the whole body, from fingers to arms to eyebrows, and is noisy, too: There is lots of clapping and slapping in ASL, and in a really great conversation, it's always possible to knock your own eyeglasses off.

When she drives, though, Candy also signs one-handed, keeping the other hand on the wheel. Chatting with Sharon, she maneuvers her Volvo through Bethesda traffic and onto I-270, making her way north toward Frederick, home to the Maryland School for the Deaf. State residential schools have played a huge role in the development of America's deaf community. Historically, deaf children often left their homes as young as five and grew up in dorms with other deaf kids. This sometimes isolated them from their families but helped to create an intense sense of fellowship among the deaf population, a group that, though geographically spread out, is essentially a tribe, a small town, a family itself.

Now that people are more mobile, families with deaf children often relocate near a residential school for the deaf, where the young children are more likely to be day students. Jehanne is one; today she's waiting for them in a low corridor inside the elementary school building at MSD, petite, elfin, dimpled, with tousled brown hair and light brown, almost amber eyes. Essentially, the baby

Sharon is carrying represents a second effort that they're making because the first was so successful. (Candy tried to have their second child, but a year of efforts didn't take.) At her own infant audiology test, Jehanne was diagnosed as profoundly deaf. In their baby book, under the section marked "first hearing test," Candy wrote, happily, "Oct. 11, 1996—no response at 95 decibels—DEAF!"

This afternoon, Jehanne greets her mothers and begins immediately to sign. She has been signed to since birth and, unlike her mothers, has been educated from the start in sign. At five she is beginning to read English quite well; when they're riding in the car, she'll notice funny shop names, like Food Lion and For Eyes. But she is also fluent in ASL, more fluent even than Sharon.

The women have arrived to visit Jehanne's kindergarten classroom, which in most ways is similar to that of any other Maryland public school; the kids are using flashcards to learn about opposites, conducting experiments to explore concepts like wet and dry, light and heavy. The classes are small, and teachers are mostly deaf, which is something new; years ago, even at MSD, deaf people weren't permitted to teach the young kids, because it was believed that sign would interfere with their learning to read. Now that's all changed. Sign is used to teach them reading. They learn science in sign; they sign while doing puzzles, or gluing and pasting, or coloring, or working in the computer lab.

There is a speech therapy class, but it's optional, and a far cry from the ones that Sharon and Candy remember, where laborious hours were spent blowing on feathers to see the difference between a "b" and a "p." In general, Sharon and Candy have tried not to make what they see as the mistakes their own parents did. Sharon, for example, resents having been made to wear hearing aids and denied the opportunity to learn sign, while Candy—who really wanted to try a hearing aid when she was little—was told by her father that she couldn't because it would be expensive and pointless, anyway. Trying to chart a middle course, they let Jehanne decide for herself whether she wanted to try a hearing aid; she did, one summer when attending camp at Gallaudet. It was hot pink. She wore it about a week. . . .

"Do you think this baby's hearing?" Candy asks Sharon afterward, when they are having lunch in downtown Frederick.

"I don't know," says Sharon. "I can say that I hope the baby's deaf, but to say I feel it's deaf, no."

They are talking about an old saying in the deaf community: If the mother walks into a place with loud music, and the baby moves, the baby is hearing. "If you base it on that, I do think it's deaf," says Sharon.

"I just say to myself that the baby's deaf," Candy says. "I talk as if the baby's deaf. If the baby's hearing, I'll be shocked."

"You better be prepared" Sharon tells her. "With Jehanne, I prepared myself. It could happen." Thinking about it, she speculates: "A hearing child would force us to get out and find out what's out there for hearing children. Maybe that would be nice."

Candy looks at her, amazed.

"It's not that it's my preference," says Sharon. "But I'm trying to think of something positive." . . .

In trying to know how to think about Sharon and Candy's endeavor, there are any number of opinions a person might have. Any number of abstract ideas a person might work through in, say, an ethics course. Are the women being selfish? Are they inflicting too much hardship on the child? How does one think of them compared with, say, a mother who has multiple embryos implanted in the course of fertility treatments, knowing that this raises the likelihood of multiple births and, with it, birth defects in some or all of the babies? Morally, how much difficulty can a parent impose on a child in order to satisfy the desire to have a child, or to have a certain kind of child?

A person can think about this, and think about it, but eventually will run up against the living, breathing fact of the child herself. How much difficulty have Sharon and Candy imposed on Jehanne? They haven't deafened her. They've given life to her. They've enabled her to exist. If they had used a hearing donor, they would have had a different child. That child would exist, but this one wouldn't. Jehanne can only exist as what she is: Jehanne, bright, funny, loving, loved, deaf.

And now what about Gauvin, who, at three months, already resembles his sister? He has the same elfin face shape, the same deep dimples when he smiles. On his head is a light fuzz of hair; bulkier now, alert and cheery, he's wearing gray overalls and groovy red leather sneakers. The question that will be answered this February afternoon, at Children's National Medical Center, is whether Gauvin, like Jehanne, is deaf. Whether the coin has landed on the same side twice. By now, Gauvin has had an initial hearing screening, which he failed. They considered this good news, but not conclusive. From there he was referred to this one, which is more sophisticated. The preliminaries take awhile. Sharon lays Gauvin in a crib and a technician applies conductive paste at points around his head, then attaches electrodes to the paste. He needs to be asleep for the test, in which microphones will be placed in his ears and a clicking noise sent through the wires. Through the electrodes, a machine will monitor the brain response. If the waves are flat, there is no hearing. He stirs and cries, so Sharon breast-feeds him, wires dangling from his head, until he falls asleep. The technician slips the microphone in his ear, turns on the clicking noise—up and up, louder and louder—and the two women look at the computer screen. Even at 95 decibels, a sound so loud that for hearing people it's literally painful, the line for the left ear is flat. But there is a marked difference in the right. For softer sounds the line is flat, but at 75 decibels there is a distinct wave. The technician goes to fetch the doctor, and the mothers contemplate their sleeping son, who, it appears, might be neither deaf nor hearing but somewhere in between.

The doctor, Ira Weiss, bustles in; he is a white-haired, stocky man, jovial and accustomed to all sorts of parents, hearing and deaf, happy and sobbing.

The technician points to the wave and suggests that perhaps it represents some noise that Gauvin himself was making. "No," says the doctor, "I think it's not just noise." Sharon looks up at Candy and lets out a little breath. The doctor disappears to get a printout of the results, then returns, reading it. Gauvin, he says, "has a profound hearing loss in his left ear and at least a severe hearing loss in his right ear.

"It does appear," he adds, "that his right ear has some residual hearing. There might be some usable hearing at this time. Given the mother's history, it will probably get worse over time. If you want to take advantage of it, you should take advantage of it now. Right now it's an ear that could be aided, to give him a head start on spoken English. Obviously, he's going to be a fluent signer."

At this stage, Weiss says later, a hearing parent would probably try a hearing aid, in the hope that with it, that right ear could hear something. Anything. A word, here and there. A loud vowel. Maybe just enough residual sound to help him lipread. Maybe just enough to tell him when to turn his head to watch someone's lips. Hearing parents would do anything—anything—to nudge a child into the hearing world. Anything—anything—to make that child like them. For a similar reason, Sharon and Candy make the opposite choice. If he wants a hearing aid later, they'll let him have a hearing aid later. They won't put one on him now. After all, they point out, Sharon's hearing loss as a child occurred at below 40 decibels, which meant that under certain conditions she could make out voices, unaided. Gauvin's, already, is far more severe than hers. Bundling Gauvin up against the cold, they make their way down the corridor, and into the car, and home, where they will tell Jehanne, and Jan, and friends, and family, a sizable group, really, that wants to know. He is not as profoundly deaf as Jehanne, but he is quite deaf. Deaf enough.

DISCUSSION QUESTIONS

1. What reactions do you have to Sharon and Candy's wish for a deaf child?
2. Would you have wanted them to wish for a child who was not hearing impaired?

EXPERIENCING DIFFERENCE

FRAMEWORK ESSAY

In the first framework essay, we considered the social construction of difference as master statuses were named, aggregated, dichotomized, and stigmatized. Now we turn to *experiencing* these statuses. A story from a friend provides the first illustration of what we mean by this. She and her husband had wanted to see *Men in Black* when it opened in the theaters, but they had not been able to find a babysitter for their eight-year-old daughter. They had watched many movies as a family and thought their daughter had a good understanding of the difference between real and pretend, so they decided it would be all right to take her with them to the show. They were wrong.

> Our perception of the movie was that while there was plenty of action, it was definitely a comedy. The "alien monsters" were ridiculous to us, inspiring laughter or mild disgust like that of a yucky bug you find in your bathroom and flush down the toilet. Jenny, however, found the movie to be scary and gross. It was beyond her ability to laugh away as "pretend." She hid her eyes through 90 percent of the movie and did not agree with us that it was funny. She talked for months about how scary it was and chastised us for letting her see it.

This story holds a small lesson about *experiencing* your social status. What we notice in the world depends in large part on the statuses we occupy; in this way we may be said to *experience* our social status. Jenny thought the movie was scary both because of the unique person she is and because of her age, a master status. Her parents did not see the movie that way for the same reasons. All *experienced* the movie through their unique personalities and as people of certain ages.

Although we do not specifically address age in this book, it operates in ways that are analogous to race, sex, class, sexual orientation, and disability. For example, being young affects the way a person is treated in innumerable ways: at a minimum, restrictions on driving, employment, military enlistment, marriage, abortion, admission to movies, and alcohol and cigarette consumption; higher insurance rates; mandatory school attendance; and "status offenses" (acts that are illegal only for minors). In addition, minors are excluded from voting and exercising other legal rights.

In these ways, those defined as "young" are treated differently from those who are not so defined. Because of that treatment, those who are younger see the world differently from those who are older and no longer operating within these constraints. The young notice things that older people need not notice, because they are not subject to the same rules. Our experiences are tied to the statuses we occupy.

A second example of experiencing one's status comes from the autobiography of one of the first black students in an exclusive white prep school. She recalls what it was like to hear white students say, "It doesn't matter to me if somebody's white or black or green or purple. I mean people are just people." While she appreciates the students' intentions, she also hears her own *real* experience being trivialized by comparison to the Muppets. Her status helps to explain what she noticed in these conversations (Cary, 1991:83–84).

In all, you experience your social statuses; you live through them. They are the filters through which you see and make sense of the world, and in large measure they account for how you are treated and what you notice. In the sections that follow, we will focus on the experiences of privilege and stigma associated with master statuses.

THE EXPERIENCE OF PRIVILEGE

Just as status helps to explain what we notice, it also explains what we *don't* notice. In the following classroom discussion between a black and a white student the white student argues that because she and the black woman are both female, they should be allies. The black woman responds,

> "When you wake up in the morning and look in the mirror what do you see?"
>
> "I see a woman," replied the white woman.
>
> "That's precisely the issue," replied the black woman. "I see a black woman. For me, race is visible every day, because it is how I am *not* privileged in this culture. Race is invisible to you [because it is how you are privileged]." (Kimmel and Messner, 1989:3; emphasis added)

Thus, we are likely to be unaware of the statuses that *privilege* us, that is, provide us with advantage, and acutely aware of those that are the source of trouble—those that yield negative judgments and unfair treatment. Indeed, the mirror metaphor used by the black woman in this conversation emerges frequently among those who are stigmatized: "I looked in the mirror and saw a gay man." These moments of suddenly realizing your social position with all of its life-shaping ramifications are usually about recognizing how some statuses leave you stigmatized and underprivileged, but rarely about how you might be privileged or advantaged by others.

Examples of Privilege

This use of the term *privilege* was first developed by Peggy McIntosh (1988) from her experience teaching women's studies courses. As she describes in Reading 46, McIntosh noticed that while many men were willing to grant that women were disadvantaged (or "underprivileged") because of sexism, it was far more difficult for them to acknowledge that they were themselves advantaged (or "overprivileged") because of it. Extending the analysis to race, she generated an extensive list of the ways in which she, as a white woman, was overprivileged by virtue of racism.

One feature of privilege is that it makes life easier: it is easier to get around, to get what one wants, and to be treated in an acceptable manner. Perhaps the privilege least noticed by nondisabled people is the simple ease of getting around—accessing buildings, restaurants, and movie theaters; accessing print information such as store names, bus stops, and street signs, riding public transportation; using public bathrooms; in short, having fairly uncomplicated access to the world. By contrast, notice the rage and exhaustion that reporter John Hockenberry describes as he tries to hail a cab or use the Brooklyn subway (Reading 40). Or ponder the indignity detailed in *Tennessee v. Lane*, the 2004 Supreme Court case about county court houses that lacked elevators, which meant that paraplegic people had to crawl or be carried up the steps (Reading 49). Thus, one usually unnoticed privilege of not being disabled is the ability to get around. Life is just easier, because everything is designed for your use.

While privilege makes people's lives easier, it also makes their lives safer. For example, many black and Hispanic students describe being closely monitored by security guards for shoplifting when they are in department stores. Indeed, in one class discussion of this, an African American student mentioned that she had the habit of walking through stores with her hands held out, palms open in front of her, to prove that she was not stealing. Thus, an important privilege of being white is the presumption that you are not a criminal, violent, or dangerous to others—which incidentally makes it easier for white people to shoplift because security people are busy watching the black and Latino customers.

More consequentially, if one assumes that a person or group is dangerous, taking preemptive action against them to ward off violence is seen as somehow legitimate. While whites do not generally assume that other whites are a threat, they do assume that of blacks. The percentage appears to be declining, but about half of whites think blacks are aggressive or violent (Smith, 2001). An example of the consequence of this belief is provided by law professor and author Patricia J. Williams:

> My best friend from law school is a woman named C. For months now I have been sending her drafts of this book, filled with many shared experiences, and she sends me back comments and her own associations. Occasionally we speak by telephone. One day, after reading the beginning of this chapter, she calls me up and tells me her abiding recollection of law school. "Actually, it has nothing to do with law school," she says.
>
> "I'll be the judge of that," I respond.
>
> "Well," she continues, "It's about the time I was held at gunpoint by a SWAT team."
>
> It turns out that during one Christmas vacation C. drove to Florida with two friends. Just outside Miami they stopped at a roadside diner. C. ordered a hamburger and a glass of milk. The milk was sour, and C. asked for another. The waitress ignored her. C. asked twice more and was ignored each time. When the waitress finally brought the bill, C. had been charged for the milk and refused to pay for it. The waitress started to shout at her, and a highway patrolman walked over from where he had been sitting and asked what was going on. C. explained that the milk was sour and that she didn't want to pay for it. The highway patrolman ordered her to pay and get out. When C. said he was out of his jurisdiction, the patrolman pulled out his gun and pointed it at her.
>
> ("Don't you think," asks C. when I show her this much of my telling of her story, "that it would help your readers to know that the restaurant was all white and that I'm black?" "Oh, yeah," I say. "And six feet tall.")
>
> Now C. is not easily intimidated and, just to prove it, she put her hand on her hip and invited the police officer to go ahead and shoot her, but before he did so *he* should try to drink the damn glass of milk, and so forth and so on for a few more descriptive rounds. What cut her off was the realization that, suddenly and silently, she and her two friends had been surrounded by eight SWAT team officers, in full guerrilla gear, automatic weapons drawn. Into the pall of her ringed speechlessness, they sent a local black policeman, who offered her twenty dollars and begged her to pay and be gone. C. describes how desperately he was perspiring as he begged and, when she didn't move, how angry he got—how he accused her of being an outside agitator, that she could come from the North and go back to the North, but that there were those of "us" who had to live here and would pay for her activism.
>
> C. says she doesn't remember how she got out of there alive or why they finally let her go; but she supposes that the black man paid for her. But she does remember returning to the car with her two companions and the three of them crying, sobbing, all the way to Miami. "The

damnedest thing about it," C. said, "was that no one was interested in whether or not I was telling the truth. The glass was sitting there in the middle of all this, with the curdle hanging on the side, but nobody would taste it because a black woman's lips had touched it." (Williams, 1991:56–57)

Several front-page cases have shown dramatically how whites' fear of blacks has prompted aggression toward blacks—and then been used after the fact to legitimate the violence.[1] Among the more notorious cases are Bernard Goetz's 1984 New York subway shooting of four unarmed black teenagers (two shot in the back), for which Goetz was found innocent of attempted murder; the 1989 Boston case of Charles Stuart who murdered his pregnant wife but so convinced the police that she had been shot by a black gunman that they failed to pursue an investigation that would have led to the plot hatched by Stuart and his brother; and the 1991 beating of Rodney King by several white Los Angeles police officers, all of whom were acquitted. Thus, African Americans, especially men, must be vigilant about becoming the targets of preemptive violence.

Since the 9/11 attacks on the World Trade Center and the Pentagon, the presumption that a category of people is dangerous and thus appropriately the target of preemptive action has been extended to Middle-Eastern men. Parallels between the experience of African Americans and those who look Middle Eastern are especially evident around the topic of *racial profiling* (Harris, 2002). Racial profiling means singling out members of a particular racial group for heightened police surveillance. Since 1996, as a result of a Supreme Court decision related to the War on Drugs *(Whren et al. v. United States)*, it has been legal for the police to use routine traffic stops as an opportunity for an investigation of drugs or other crimes. Motorists pulled over for traffic violations can be asked if they will consent to a search of their car and person. If, in the course of the traffic stop, the officer finds visual evidence of a crime, a search can proceed without the driver's consent. Because the number of potential traffic violations is almost limitless, virtually any vehicle can be pulled over anytime.

As a result, a considerable public uproar emerged about police departments across the country disproportionately pulling over black drivers. The phrase "driving while black"—or Latino or Indian—became commonplace. Research by several social scientists confirmed that racial targeting was indeed taking place—for example, state police data in Maryland in the 1990s showed that while 17 percent of drivers on Interstate 95 were black, 70 percent of those stopped and searched were black. Since racial profiling operates from the assumption that people of color are likely to be criminal, those stopped by police are themselves often in danger. For example, in 1998 two New Jersey state troopers fired 11 shots into a van carrying black and Latino men from the Bronx to a basketball camp. Three of the men were wounded. At their sentencing in 2002, the troopers "said their supervisors had trained them to focus on black- and brown-skinned drivers because, they were told, they were more likely to be drug traffickers" (Kocieniewski, 2002).

---

[1]Despite whites' fear of violence at the hands of African Americans, crime is predominately *intra*racial.

Not only is profiling dangerous to those who are targeted, it is also bad police work:

> Does racial profiling in fact help us to catch criminals? [Since African Americans and Latinos are disproportionately arrested and jailed for drug-related crime, doesn't racial profiling] actually "up the odds" of police finding bad guys, guns, or drugs when they make traffic stops and conduct searches? . . .
>
> The answer comes in the form of something called the hit rate: the rate at which police actually find criminals, uncover guns, and confiscate drugs when they perform stops and searches. . . . In just the last couple of years, data have become available in a growing number of jurisdictions that allow us to calculate the hit rate, and to do so separately for blacks, whites, and Latinos. In all of these studies, police stop and search whites not because of race, but because they have observed suspicious behavior. Blacks and Latinos, on the other hand, were stopped not only because of suspicious behavior, but also because of race or ethnic appearance. . . . All of the studies in which the data collected allow for the calculation of hit rates have generated strikingly similar results. All of these studies show higher hit rates not for blacks and Latinos, but for whites. In other words, officers "hit" less often when they use race or ethnic appearance to decide which person seems suspicious enough to merit stops and searches than they do when they use suspicious behavior and not race as their way of selecting suspects. When stops and searches are not racialized, they are more productive. (Harris, 2003:77)

In an effort to stop racial profiling, more than a dozen states have passed antiprofiling legislation and hundreds of police departments now collect data on all traffic stops. While the phrase *racial profiling* first became familiar to the public through traffic stops, in reality the practice occurs in any setting in which a category of people are targeted for heightened surveillance or arrest. This would include the surveillance of shoppers mentioned earlier, as well as immigration raids prompted by the ethnic composition of the workforce rather than information about illegal activity. It would also extend to the arrest of Middle Eastern men immediately following the 9/11 attacks, the 2002 National Security Entry/Exit Registration System requiring men from Muslim and Middle Eastern countries[2] and North Korea to report to Immigration and Naturalization Services (INS) for registration and interrogation, and the internment of Japanese Americans during the Second World War.

But the targeting of Arab Americans and Middle Eastern noncitizens is susceptible to the same criticism as profiling at traffic stops. "Profiling is a crude substitute for behavior-based enforcement and . . . invites screeners to take a less vigilant approach to individuals who don't fit the profile, even if they engage in conduct that should cause concern" (Carter, 2002:12). In other words, those of us who do not look Middle Eastern have the privilege of not being treated like terrorists. This could be described as a life-saving privilege.

A different privilege, likely to be invisible to those in single-race families, is the privilege of being recognized as a family. The following account by a mother illustrates how the failure to perceive a family is linked to the expectation of black criminality.

---

[2]Afghanistan, Algeria, Bahrain, Bangladesh, Egypt, Eritrea, Indonesia, Iran, Iraq, Jordan, Kuwait, Libya, Lebanon, Morocco, Oman, Pakistan, Qatar, Saudi Arabia, Somalia, Sudan, Syria, Tunisia, United Arab Emirates, and Yemen.

> When my son was home visiting from college, we met in town one day for lunch. . . . On the way to the car, one of us thought of a game we'd often played when he was younger.
>
> "Race you to the car!"
>
> I passed my large handbag to him, thinking to more equalize the race since he was a twenty-year-old athlete. We raced the few blocks, my heart singing with delight to be talking and playing with my beloved son. As we neared the car, two young white men yelled something at us. I couldn't make it out and paid it no mind. When we arrived at the car, both of us laughing, they walked by and mumbled "Sorry" as they quickly passed, heads down.
>
> I suddenly understood. They hadn't seen a family. They had seen a young Black man with a pocketbook, fleeing a pursuing middle-aged white woman. My heart trembled as I thought of what could have happened if we'd been running by someone with a gun.
>
> Later I mentioned the incident in a three-day diversity seminar I was conducting at a Boston corporation. A participant related it that evening to his son, a police officer, and asked the son what he would have done if he'd observed the scene.
>
> The answer: "Shot out his kneecaps." (Lester, 1994:56–7)

Turning now from privileges of race to privileges of sexual orientation, the most obvious privilege enjoyed by heterosexuals is that they are allowed to be open about their relationships. From idle conversation and public displays of affection, to the legal and religious approval embodied in marriage, heterosexuals are able to declare that they love and are loved. That privilege is not just denied to lesbians and gays; they are actively punished for such expressions by ostracism, physical assault, unemployment, and even loss of child custody and visitation—not so surprising given the lack of legal recognition of gay families.

Even the ability to display a picture of one's partner on a desk at work stands as an invisible privilege of heterosexuality.

> Consider, for example, an employee who keeps a photograph on her desk in which she and her husband smile for the camera and embrace affectionately. . . . [T]he photo implicitly conveys information about her private sexual behavior. [But] most onlookers (if they even notice the photo) do not think of her partner primarily in sexual terms. . . .
>
> [But] if the photograph instead shows the woman in the same pose with a same-sex partner, everyone is likely to notice. As with the first example, the photograph conveys the information that she is in a relationship. But the fact that the partner is a woman overwhelms all other information about her. The *sexual* component of the relationship is not mundane and implicit as with the heterosexual spouse. (Herek, 1992:95–6; emphasis added)

Because heterosexual public affection is so commonplace, it rarely conjures up images of sexual activity. But that is exactly what we may think of when we see a same-sex couple embrace. This is why gay and lesbian people are often accused of "flaunting" their sexuality: *any* display of affection between them is understood by many heterosexuals as virtually a display of the sex act.

In the realm of class privilege, several readings in this text address the considerable differences in health, life span, educational access, and quality of life that accompany American class differences. But these are perhaps the more visible privileges of being middle and upper class. Less apparent is the privilege of being treated as a deserving and competent member of the community. Higher education institutions provide a number of examples of this. One of the boons of the legacy admission system, described by John Larew in Reading 38, is its invisibility. The students admitted to universities this way—who are predominately middle- and upper-class whites—don't have their qualifications questioned by faculty or other students, nor are they likely to agonize about whether they deserved to be admitted.

> Like many children of University of Virginia graduates, Mary Stuart Young of Atlanta, Georgia, wore Cavalier orange and blue long before she took an SAT or mailed an application.
>
> "Coming here just felt right," said Young, 21, who expects to graduate with a religious studies degree in 2004. "This was where I should be."
>
> After all, with two generations of faithful alumni backing her, Young doubled her chances of getting into Thomas Jefferson's university. (Associated Press, 2003)

One of the privileges of being a legacy admission rather than an "affirmative action admit" is that you are treated as a deserving and competent member of the community, rather than someone who is not qualified to be there.

The assumption that students are middle or upper class is pervasive within higher education, so working-class students often find schools oblivious or even antagonistic to their needs. Students are presumed to understand how college works, because it is assumed that their parents are college graduates and can advise them: "In an article on working class students in higher education, one student was paraphrased as saying that college is a very unforgiving place. It is unforgiving not of those who don't know the rules, but rather of those who did not know the rules before arriving on campus" (Tokarczyk, 2004:163). Thus, one of the privileges of being a college student from the middle or upper classes is that you come to the university with a good deal of information about how it works.

"Working class students often have difficulty in their studies partially because colleges and universities—elite and nonelite—refuse to recognize that many students must work" (Tokarczyk, 2004:163). For example, schools that require unpaid internships, off-campus experiences, or study abroad trips may forget not only the costs associated with these requirements but also the fact that working-class students may have to quit their jobs to fulfill the requirement. The same is true of faculty office hours—set as if students could easily arrange their schedules to fit the professor's. If working-class students were seen as deserving and competent members of the community, their needs would be factored in automatically, not as a "special favor."

In all, one of the privileges of being middle or upper class is that higher education—which is absolutely critical to upward mobility—is in sync with your experience. When you go to a college or university, you can expect to have your life experiences and perspective treated as the norm. The institution will be organized around those experiences in ways large and small, from assuming that everyone should live on campus (and bear the expense of room and board) to assuming you will be able to cover the cost of texts or forgo employment to demonstrate commitment to your studies. In these ways, students from the middle or upper classes have the privilege of feeling like they belong.

Beyond that, as Brian Fitzgerald explains in Reading 39, higher education is increasingly becoming available only to those in the middle and upper classes.

Terry Hartle, senior vice president at the American Council on Education, described the current state of affairs this way: "Smart poor kids go to college at the same rate as stupid rich kids" (Kirp, 2003:18).

Overall, two privileges shape the experience of all those in nonstigmatized statuses: the privilege of being "unmarked" and the privilege of being seen as "entitled." *Entitlement* is the belief that one has the right to be respected, acknowledged, protected, and rewarded. This is so much taken for granted by those in nonstigmatized statuses that they are often shocked and angered when it is denied them.

> [After the lecture, whites in the audience] shot their hands up to express how excluded they felt because [the] lecture, while broad in scope, clearly was addressed first and foremost to the women of color in the room. . . . What a remarkable sense of entitlement must drive their willingness to assert their experience of exclusion! If I wanted to raise my hand every time I felt excluded, I would have to glue my wrist to the top of my head. (Ettinger, 1994:51)

Like entitlement, the privilege of occupying an "unmarked" status is shared by most of those in nonstigmatized categories. *Doctor* is an *unmarked* status; *woman doctor* is *marked*. Unmarked categories convey the usual and expected distribution of individuals in social statuses—the distribution that does not require any special comment. Thus, the unmarked category tells us what a society takes for granted.

Theoretically, the unmarked category *doctor* might include anyone, but in truth it refers to white males. How do we know that? Because other occupants of that status are usually marked: woman doctor, black doctor, and so on. While the marking of a status signals infrequency—there are few female astronauts or male nurses—it may also imply inferiority. A "woman doctor" or a "black doctor" may be considered less qualified.

Thus, a privilege of those who are not stigmatized is that their master statuses are not used to discount their accomplishments or imply that they serve only special interests. Someone described as "a politician" is presumed to operate from a universality that someone described as "a white male politician" is not. Because white male politicians are rarely described as such, their anchoring in the reality of their own master statuses is hidden. In this way, those in marked statuses appear to be always operating from an "agenda," or "special interest" (e.g., a black politician is often presumed to represent only black constituents), while those in unmarked statuses can appear to be agenda-free. Being white and male thus becomes invisible, since it is not regularly identified as important. For this reason, some recommend identifying *everyone's* race and sex as a way to recognize that we are all grounded in our master statuses.

Marked and unmarked statuses also operate in classroom interactions. At white-dominated universities, white students are unlikely to be asked what white people think or asked to explain the "white experience." In this way, those who are white, male, heterosexual, and middle class appear to have no race, sex, sexual orientation, or social class, and thus have the privilege of escaping classroom discussions about the problems of "their people."

The Experience of Privilege by Stigmatized People; the Experience of Stigma by Privileged People

We have described some of the privileges enjoyed by those in nonstigmatized statuses. However, those with stigma also have some experience of privilege—it is just less frequent. For example, the Urban Institute investigated racial discrimination in employment by sending pairs of black and white male college students to apply for jobs in Washington, D.C., and Chicago. The students had been coached to present identical personal styles, dialects, educations, and job histories.

> In 20 percent [of the 576 job applications], the white applicant advanced farther in the hiring process [from obtaining a job application, to interview, to hiring] than his black counterpart, and in 15 percent the white applicant was offered a job while his equally qualified black partner was not. Blacks were favored over comparable white applicants in a much smaller share of cases; in 7 percent of the audits the black advanced farther in the hiring process, and in 5 percent only the black received the job offer. (Turner, Fix, and Struyk, 1991:18)

Black and white applicants both had some experience of preferential hiring, but the white applicant had two to three times more. A similar study of job discrimination against Latino males conducted in Chicago and San Diego indicated an even larger gap between the level of privilege experienced by Anglos and Latinos (Cross, Kenney, Mell, and Zimmermann, 1990).

Thus, concerns about "reverse discrimination" often miss the mark. While blacks, Latinos, Asian Americans, or white women are sometimes favored in hiring, they are not favored as *frequently* as white males. Discrimination continues in its historic direction as evidenced also in the constancy of race differences in income. In 1975, black per capita median annual income was 58.5 percent that of whites; in 1997, it was 60.5 percent; in 2003 it was 58.2 percent. In 1975, the same measure for Latinos was 56.1 percent of whites; in 1997, it was 52.7 percent; in 2003, it was 50.3 percent (U.S. Department of Commerce, 1993:454; U.S. Bureau of the Census, 1997; U.S. Bureau of the Census, 2003).[3]

Because the focus is so frequently on how stigma affects those who bear it, it is easy to assume that only the targets of discrimination are affected by it. But that is not the case. Those who are not themselves the targets of discrimination may still be affected by it. For example,

> Think of white slaveowners and their wives: the meaning of the sexual difference between them was constructed in part by the alleged contrast between them as whites and other men and women who were Black; what was supposed to characterize their relationship was not supposed to characterize the relationship between white men and Black women, or white women and Black men. . . . So even though the white men and women were of the same race, and even though they were not the victims of racism, this does not mean that we can understand the relationship between them without reference to their race and to the racism that their lives enacted. (Spelman, 1988:104–5)

---

[3]Income figures exclude "money income received before payments for personal income, taxes, Social Security, union dues, Medicare deductions, food stamps, health benefits, subsidized housing, or rent-free housing and goods produced and consumed on the farm" (U.S. Department of Commerce, 1993:425).

Similarly, interactions between men are affected by sexism, even though the men themselves are not subject to it.

> For example, we can't understand the racism that fueled white men's lynching of Black men without understanding its connection to the sexism that shaped their protective and posses- sive attitudes toward white women. The ideology according to which whites are superior and ought to dominate Blacks is nested with the ideology according to which white men must protect their wives from attack by Black men. . . . That men aren't subject to sexism doesn't mean sexism has no effect on their relationships to each other. (Spelman, 1988:106)

Similar examples apply to sexual orientation, social class, and disability. Certainly, homophobia shapes heterosexual relations, treatment of those who are disabled affects those who are not disabled, and the stereotypes about poor people affect interactions among those in the middle class. Thus, the most obvious privilege of those in nonstigmatized statuses—that they are not affected by stigma—is not as straightforward as one might think.

Because privilege is usually invisible to those who possess it, they may assume that everyone is treated as they are. When they learn about instances of discrimina- tion, they may think that the incident was exceptional rather than routine, that the victim was overreacting or misinterpreting, or that the victim must have provoked the encounter. Such responses do not necessarily deny that the incident took place; rather, they deny that the event carries any negative or special meaning.

Through such dismissals, those operating from positions of privilege can deny the experience of those without privilege. For example, college-age students often describe university administrators as unresponsive until they have their parents call to complain. If the parents later said, "I don't know why *you* had such a problem with those people; they were very nice to *me*. Did you do something to antagonize them?" that would indicate they were oblivious to their privileged status in the uni- versity setting as well as unaware of their student's underprivileged status in it.

Dismissals like these treat the stigmatized person like a child inadequate to judge the world. Often such dismissals are framed in terms of the very stigma about which people are complaining. In this way, what stigmatized people say about their status is discounted precisely because they are stigmatized. The implication is that those who occupy a stigmatized status are somehow the ones *least* able to assess its con- sequence. The effect is to dismiss precisely those who have had the most experience with the problem.

This process, called *looping* or *rereading,* is described by many who have studied the lives of patients in psychiatric hospitals (Rosenhan, 1973; Schur, 1984; Goffman, 1961, 1963). If a patient says, "The staff here are being unfair to me," and the staff respond, "Of course he would think that—he's crazy," they have reread, or looped, his words through his status. His words have been heard in light of his stigma and dismissed for exactly that reason.

These dismissals serve a function. Dismissing another's experience of status- based mistreatment masks the possibility that one has escaped such treatment pre- cisely because of one's privilege. If we do not acknowledge that *their* status affects *their* treatment, we need not acknowledge that *our* status affects *our* treatment.

Thus, we avoid the larger truth that those who are treated well, those who are treated poorly, and all the rest in between are always evaluated both as individuals and as occupants of particular esteemed and disesteemed categories.

Hierarchies of Stigma and Privilege

While it may appear that people can be easily separated into two categories—privileged and stigmatized—every individual occupies several master statuses. The privilege or stigma that might be associated with one status emerges in the context of *all* of one's other statuses. For example, a middle-class, heterosexual Mexican American male may be privileged in terms of class, sex, and sexual orientation, but stigmatized by virtue of being Chicano. Given the invisibility of privilege, he is more likely to notice the ways in which his ethnic status stigmatizes him than to notice the privileges that follow from his other statuses. Nonetheless, he is simultaneously all of his statuses; the privileges and disadvantages of each emerge in the context of all the others. An Anglo male and a Latino male may both be said to experience the privilege of sex, but they do not experience the *same* privilege.

While individuals may experience both privilege and stigma, some stigmas are so strong that they cancel out the privileges that one's other statuses might provide, which is certainly the case for people who are disabled. Describing how use of a wheelchair "canceled out" expectations about her intelligence even though she was in college, one of Pat McCune's informants in Reading 22 mentioned this experience:

> I find that people automatically assume your intelligence level is lower. They sort of talk maybe slower to you or in a patronizing way. . . . They don't speak right at you or act like you know anything. And they're always surprised to find out that I'm a college student. . . . They think "How could you go to U of M?" Sometimes they'll even say that.

There is much evidence that the stigma of being black in America cancels any privileges that might be expected to follow from being middle-class. For example,

> A large body of published research reveals that racial and ethnic minorities experience a lower quality of health services, and are less likely to receive even routine medical procedures than are white Americans. Relative to whites, African Americans—and in some cases, Hispanics—are less likely to receive appropriate cardiac medication or to undergo coronary artery bypass surgery, are less likely to receive hemodialysis and kidney transplantation, and are likely to receive a lower quality of basic clinical services such as intensive care, even when variations in such factors as insurance status, income, age, co-morbid conditions, and symptom expression are taken into account. . . . The majority of studies . . . find that racial and ethnic disparities remain even after adjustment for socioeconomic differences and other healthcare access-related factors. (Institute of Medicine, 2003:1, 2)

> Despite the attention given to lending discrimination over the last decade by lenders, financial regulators, federal officials, secondary mortgage market institutions, and community groups, mortgage loan applications from black and Hispanic households are still much more likely to be denied than are applications from whites. For conventional home purchase loans in 2000, blacks were twice as likely as whites to be turned down for a loan. . . . [Mortgage] loan denial rates are higher for black and Hispanic applicants than for white applicants at all income

levels. Moreover, for blacks, Hispanics, and Asians, the minority/white denial ratio increases steadily with income. This increase is particularly striking for blacks; the denial ratio is only 1.19 in the lowest income category but climbs to 2.48 in the highest category. (Ross and Yinger, 2002:6, 8)

Black families annually earning at least $50,000 were just as [residentially] segregated as those earning less than $2,500. Indeed, Black families annually earning more than $50,000 were more segregated than Hispanic or Asian families earning less than $2,500. In other words, the most affluent Blacks appear to be more segregated than the poorest Hispanics or Asians; and in contrast to the case of Blacks, Hispanic and Asian segregation levels fall steadily as income rises, reaching low or moderate levels at incomes of $50,000 or more. . . . [Contrary to the argument that this residential segregation is self-imposed] most Blacks continue to express strong support for the idea of integration. When asked on opinion polls whether they favor "desegregation, strict segregation, or something in-between," Blacks answer "desegregation" in large numbers. (Massey, 2001:411–412)

[Researcher Devah Pager investigated the effect of having a criminal record on employment.] . . . pairs of young, well-groomed, well-spoken college men with identical résumés [were sent to] apply for 350 advertised entry-level [low-wage] jobs in Milwaukee. The only difference was that one said he had served an 18-month prison sentence for cocaine possession. Two teams were black, two white. For the black testers, the callback rate was 5 percent if they had a criminal record and 14 percent if they did not. For whites, it was 17 percent with a criminal record, and 34 percent without. (Kroeger, 2004) [As researcher Pager notes] both race and criminal record had a huge effect on the likelihood of receiving a callback from employers. Probably the most surprising finding was that a black applicant with no criminal record was no more likely, in fact even slightly less likely, to receive a callback from employers than was a white applicant with a felony conviction. (Pager, 2003)

Research on the effects of other stigmatized racial statuses has not been as thorough, nor are its findings as consistent, but it is clear that for African Americans, middle-class standing provides little protection against racism.

Does the stigma of being an out-of-the-closet gay or lesbian cause one to lose the privilege that comes from being middle class, white, or both? While the proportion of Americans who believe gays should have equal job opportunities has increased—from 56 percent in 1977 to 89 percent in 2004 (Gallup, 2004)—there is still no federal protection barring discrimination against gays in employment, housing, or health care. In 1998, President Clinton issued an executive order barring federal agencies from such discrimination, but the House of Representatives denied funding to carry out the order (Berke, 1998). For this reason, it often seems as though gays are predominately white and at least middle class; in the absence of federal protection, few others can afford to publicly identify themselves as gay (Lester, 1994). While some jurisdictions enact protections, many of those ordinances are later challenged and repealed. At present, it appears that the stigma of being gay still overwhelms the privileges that one's other statuses might afford.

But which status is most important: one's race, sex, disability, sexual orientation, or social class? For the sizable population that occupies multiple stigmatized statuses, it makes little sense to argue which status presents the greatest obstacle since most people live in the *intersection* of their master statuses. That experience is the subject of a set of readings in Section III, as well as the subtext of many other readings throughout this book. While people are often asked to make alliances based on one status being more significant than another, their real experience is rarely so one-dimensional.

Philosopher Elizabeth Spelman (1988), however, suggests a way to assess the relative priority of each of these statuses. If each master status is imagined as a room we will enter, we can consider which sequential ordering of these rooms most accurately reflects our experience. If the first rooms we encounter are labeled black, white, or Asian, we will find ourselves in a room with those who share our "race" but are different in terms of sex, social class, ethnicity, and sexual orientation. If the second set of rooms is labeled male and female, we will find ourselves with people of the same race and sex. Other rooms might be labeled with sexual orientation or social class categorizations.

Many white feminists have presumed that the first rooms we encounter are sex categorizations, thus arguing that the statuses of female and male have priority over race or class designations; that one is discriminated against first by virtue of one's sex and then by race. Latino, black, and some white feminists have countered that the first rooms are race classifications. In this case, it is argued that racism so powerfully affects people that men and women within racial categories have more in common with one another than they do with those of the same sex but of a different race. Alliances of gay and lesbian people by implication assume that the first doors are marked gay and straight, with sex, race, and class following; disability rights activists would argue that status takes precedence over everything else. In addition to the orderings that correspond to the historical experience of categories of people, each of us likely maintains an ordering based on our personal experience of these statuses.

THE EXPERIENCE OF STIGMA

The previous section considered the privileges conferred by some master statuses; now we examine the stigma conferred by other master statuses.

In his classic analysis of stigma, sociologist Erving Goffman (1963) distinguished between the *discredited,* whose stigma is immediately apparent to an observer (for example, race, sex, some disabilities), and the *discreditable,* whose stigma can be hidden (for example, sexual orientation, cognitive disabilities, or social class). Since stigma plays out differently in the lives of the discredited and the discreditable, each will be examined separately.

The Discreditable: "Passing"

The discreditable are those who are *passing,* that is, not publicly acknowledging the stigmatized statuses they occupy. (Were they to acknowledge that status, they would become discredited.) The term *passing* comes from "passing as white," which emerged as a phenomenon after 1875 when southern states reestablished racial segregation through hundreds of "Jim Crow"[4] laws. At that point, some African Americans passed as white as a way to get better paying jobs.

> [S]ome who passed as white on the job lived as black at home. Some lived in the North as white part of the year and as black in the South the rest of the time. More men passed than women . . . the vast majority who could have passed permanently did not do so, owing to the pain of family separation, condemnation by most blacks, their fear of whites, and the loss of the security of the black community. . . . Passing as white probably reached an all-time peak between 1880 and 1925. (Davis, 1991:56–57)

"Passing as white" is now quite rare and strongly condemned by African Americans. We will use the term *passing* here to refer to those who have not made their stigmatized status evident; it is similar to the phrase "being in the closet," which is usually applied to gays. Steven Seidman, in Reading 33, argues that passing was at its peak for lesbian and gay Americans between 1950 and 1980 and plays somewhat less of a role in people's lives now. Still, it remains a significant concern and topic of discussion for both gays and straights.

One may engage in passing by chance as well as by choice. For example, the presumption that everyone is heterosexual can have the effect of putting gay people in the closet even when they had not intended to be. During a series of lectures on the family, one of our faculty colleagues realized that he had been making assignments, lecturing, and encouraging discussion assuming that all of the students in the class had, or wanted to have, heterosexual relationships. Unless his gay and lesbian students specifically countered his assumption, they were effectively passing. His actions forced them to choose between announcing or remaining silent about their status. Had he assumed that students would be involved only with others of the same race, he would have created a similar situation for those in interracial relationships. Thus, assumptions about others' private lives—for example, asking whether someone is married—may have the effect of making them choose between silence or an announcement of something they may consider private.

Since most heterosexuals assume that everyone is heterosexual, many social encounters either put gay people in the closet or require that they announce their status. For example, in the first session of one class, a student opened his remarks by saying, "Well, you all know I am a gay man, and as a gay man I think . . ." The buzz of conversation stopped, other students stared at him, and one asked, "How would we know you were gay?" The student pointed to a pink triangle he had pinned to his book bag and explained that he thought they knew that someone wearing it would be gay. (Pink triangles were assigned to gay men during the Nazi era, black triangles to lesbians and other "unwanted" women. Both have been adopted as badges of pride among gay activists. Still, his logic was questionable: Anyone supportive of gay rights might wear the button.)

---

[4]"Jim Crow" was "a blackface, singing-dancing-comedy characterization portraying black males as childlike, irresponsible, inefficient, lazy, ridiculous in speech, pleasure-seeking, and happy, [and was] a widespread stereotype of blacks during the last decades before emancipation . . ." (Davis, 1991:51). "Jim Crow" laws were laws by which whites imposed segregation following the Civil War.

This announcement—which moved the student from a discreditable to a discredited status—may have been intended to keep his classmates from making overtly antigay comments in his presence. His strategy was designed to counter the negative consequences of passing.

> Every encounter with a new classful of students, to say nothing of a new boss, social worker, loan officer, landlord, doctor, erects new closets [that] . . . exact from at least gay people new surveys, new calculations, new draughts and requisitions of secrecy or disclosure. Even an *out* gay person deals daily with interlocutors about whom she doesn't know whether they know or not [or whether they would care]. . . . The gay closet is not a feature only of the lives of gay people. But for many gay people it is still the fundamental feature of social life; there can be few gay people . . . in whose lives the closet is not a shaping presence. (Sedgwick, 1990:68)

Inadvertent passing is also experienced by those whose racial status is not immediately apparent. An African American acquaintance of ours who looks white is often in settings in which others do not know that she is African American—or in which she does not know if they know. Thus, she must regularly decide how and when to convey that information. This is important to her as a way to discourage racist remarks, since whites sometimes assume it is acceptable to make racist remarks to one another (as men may assume it is acceptable to make sexist remarks to other men, or as straights presume it acceptable to make antigay remarks to those they think are also straight). It is also important to her that others know she is black so that they understand the meaning of her words—so that they will hear her words through her status as an African American woman. Those whose stigma is not apparent must go to some lengths to avoid being in the closet by virtue of others' assumptions.

Those with relatively invisible disabilities also face the tension of inadvertent passing. Beth Omansky, in Reading 42, describes the experiences of those who are legally, rather than totally, blind. Observers who assume the person is fully sighted can react with disbelief or even anger to learn otherwise; others may insist that the person behave as if they were totally blind, to avoid confusing observers. Either way, the person suffers the consequence of inadvertent passing.

But passing may also be an intentional choice. For example, one of our students, who was in the process of deciding that he was gay, had worked for many years at a local library, where he became friends with several of his coworkers. Much of the banter at work, however, involved disparaging gay, or presumably gay, library patrons. As he grappled with a decision about his own sexual identity, his social environment reminded him that being gay is a stigmatized status in American society. This student did not so much face prejudice personally (since he was not "out" to his work friends) as he faced an "unwilling acceptance of himself by individuals who are prejudiced against persons of the kind he can be revealed to be" (Goffman, 1963:42). Thus, he was not the person his friends took him to be. While survey data indicate that those who personally know a gay man hold more positive feelings about gays in general (Herek and Glunt, 1993), the decision to publicly reveal a stigma that others have gone on record as opposing is not made lightly.

Revealing stigma changes one's interactions with "normals," even with those who are not particularly prejudiced. Such revelations are likely to alter important relationships. Parents sometimes disown gay children, just as they do children involved in interracial relationships. Thus, the decision to pass or be "out" is not easily made. For the discreditable, what Goffman euphemistically described as "information management" is at the core of one's life. "To tell or not to tell; to let on or not to let on; to lie or not to lie; and in each case, to whom, how, when, and where" (Goffman, 1963:42). Such choices are faced daily by those who are discreditable—not just those who are gay and lesbian, but also those who are poor, have been imprisoned, attempted suicide, terminated a pregnancy through abortion, are HIV-positive, are drug or alcohol dependent, or have been the victims of incest or rape. By contrast, those who do not occupy stigmatized statuses don't have to invest emotional energy in monitoring information about themselves; they can choose to talk openly about their personal history.

Passing has both positive and negative aspects. On the positive side, passing lets the stigmatized person exert some power over the situation; the person controls the information, the flow of events, and their privacy. By withholding his or her true identity until choosing to reveal it, the person may create a situation in which others' prejudices are challenged. Passing forces one to be judged as an individual rather than be discounted by virtue of a stigma. Passing also limits one's exposure to verbal and physical abuse, allows for the development of otherwise forbidden relationships, and improves employment security by minimizing one's exposure to discrimination.

On the negative side, passing consumes a good deal of time, energy, and emotion in the management of personal information. It introduces deception and secrecy even into close relationships. Passing also denies others the opportunity to prove themselves unprejudiced, and it makes one vulnerable to blackmail by those who do know about one's stigma.

The Discredited: The Problems of Visibility

While the discreditable face problems of invisibility, *visibility* is the problem for those who are discredited. Those who are discredited suffer from undue attention and are subject to being stereotyped.

Being discredited means that one's stigma is immediately apparent to others. As essayist bell hooks describes, those who are discredited often have little patience for those who at least have the option of passing.

> Many of us have been in discussions where a non-white person—a black person—struggles to explain to white folks that while we can acknowledge that gay people of all colors are harassed and suffer exploitation and domination, we also recognize that there is a significant difference that arises because of the visibility of dark skin. . . . While it in no way lessens the severity of such suffering for gay people, or the fear that it causes, it does mean that in a given situation the apparatus of protection and survival may be simply not identifying as gay. In contrast, most people of color have no choice. No one can hide, change, or mask dark skin color. White people, gay and straight, could show greater understanding of the impact of racial oppression on people of color by not attempting to make these oppressions synonymous, but rather by showing the ways they are linked and yet differ. (hooks, 1989:125)

For the discredited, stigma is likely to always shape interaction with those who are not stigmatized. However, its effect does not necessarily play out in ways one can easily determine. For those whose stigma is visible, every situation forces them to decide whether the world is responding to them or their stigma. Florynce Kennedy, a black activist in the civil rights and women's movements, once commented that the problem with being black in America was that you never knew whether what happened to you, good or bad, was because of your talents or because you were black (Kennedy, 1976). This situation was described in 1903 by sociologist W. E. B. Du Bois as the *"double consciousness"* of being black in America. The concept was key to Du Bois's classic, *The Souls of Black Folk,* for which he was rightfully judged "the father of serious black thought as we know it today" (Hare, 1982:xiii). Du Bois described double consciousness this way:

> the Negro . . . [is] gifted with a second-sight in this American world—a world which yields him no true self-consciousness, but only lets him see himself through the revelation of the other world. It is a peculiar sensation, this double consciousness, this sense of always looking at one's self through the eyes of others, of measuring one's soul by the tape of a world that looks on in amused contempt and pity. One ever feels his twoness. . . . (1982:45)

This is the sense of seeing oneself through the eyes of a harshly critical other, and it relates to our discussion of objectification in Framework Essay I. When those who are stigmatized view themselves from the perspective of the nonstigmatized, they have reduced themselves to objects. This theme of double or "fractured" consciousness can also be found in contemporary analyses of women's experience.

The greatest effect of being visibly stigmatized is on one's life chances—literally, one's chances for living. Thus, the readings in this book detail differences in income, employment, health, lifespan, education, targeting for violence, and the likelihood of arrest and imprisonment. In this essay, however, we will consider the more mundane difficulties created by stigmatization, particularly the sense of being "on stage."

The discredited often have the feeling of being watched or on display when they are in settings dominated by nonstigmatized people. For example, when women walk through male-dominated settings, they often feel they are on display in terms of their physical appearance. Asian, black, and Latino students in majority white universities often describe a sense of being on display in campus dining facilities. In such cases, the discredited are likely to feel that others are judging them in terms of their stigma.

As sociologist Rosabeth Moss Kanter (1980, 1993) has shown, this impression is probably true. When Kanter studied corporate settings in which one person was visibly different from the others, that person was likely to get a disproportionate share of attention. In fact, people in the setting were likely to closely monitor what the minority person did, which meant his or her mistakes were more likely to be noticed—and the mistakes of those in the rest of the group were more likely to be overlooked, since everyone was busy watching the minority person. Even in after-work socializing, the minority person was still subject to disproportionate attention.

Kanter also found that the minority person's behavior was likely to be interpreted in terms of the prevailing stereotypes about the members of that category. For example, when there were only a few men in a setting dominated by women, the men were subject to intense observation, and their behavior was filtered through the stereotypes about men. Perceptions were distorted to fit the preexisting beliefs.

Without the presence of a visibly different person, members of a setting are likely to see themselves as different from one another in various ways. Through contrast with the visibly different person, however, they notice their own similarities. In this way, majority group members may construct dichotomies—"us" and "them"—out of settings in which there are a few who are different. It is not surprising that those who are visibly different sometimes isolate themselves in response.

Still, none of this is inevitable. Kanter argues that once minority membership in a setting reaches 15 percent, these processes abate. Until that point, however, those who are in the minority (or visibly stigmatized) are the subject of a good deal of attention. As a consequence, they are often accused of flaunting their difference, of being "so" black, Latino, gay, and so on—of making a show of their status.

This is a charge that the nonstigmatized often level at those who are stigmatized. Although there are certainly occasions on which the discredited may deliberately make a show of their status, Kanter's work indicates that when their numbers are low in a setting, they are likely to be charged with being too visible no matter what they do. When they are subjected to a disproportionate amount of attention and viewed through the lenses of stereotypes, almost anything the discredited do is likely to be noticed and attributed to the category to which they belong.

Those who are visibly stigmatized react to this excess of attention in various ways. Some are careful to behave in ways contrary to expectations. At other times, however, people may deliberately make reference to their stigmatized status. For example, in adolescence, light-skinned black men are often derided by their black and white peers as not "really" black, and so they may go to great lengths to counter that charge.

Overt displays of one's stigmatized status may also have an entertaining side. For example, many bilingual Latino students talk about how much they enjoy a loud display of Spanish when Anglos are present; some Asian American students have described their pleasure in pursuing extended no-English-used card games in public spaces on campus. Black and gay adolescents sometimes entertain themselves by loudly affecting stereotypical behavior and then watching the disapproving looks from observers. Those who do not occupy stigmatized statuses may better appreciate these displays by remembering their experience of deliberately acting like "obnoxious teenagers" in public settings. Thus, for some, flaunting their difference may also be fun.

In all, those who are visibly stigmatized—who cannot or will not hide their identity—generate a variety of mechanisms to try to neutralize that stigma and the undue attention that follows. In addition to those already mentioned, *"covering,"* described by Kenji Yoshino in Reading 53, describes the effort to keep one's stigma from "looming large." Covering is not about denying the existence of the stigma, but about finding ways to reduce its impact on interaction.

Yoshino mentions President Franklin Delano Roosevelt's effort to downplay his use of a wheelchair as an example of covering but extends the analysis to question the legitimacy of employers' demands that employees "cover" their race, sex, or sexual orientation differences—for example, by maintaining silence about their sexual orientation. Yoshino describes these requests to cover as a kind of coerced assimilation that should be questioned not only on behalf of America's minority groups, but also in terms of the rights of all Americans.

European Ethnic Groups

Whites of European ancestry sometimes envy the ethnicity of African Americans, Hispanics, and Asian Americans. As one student said, "It makes me feel like I just don't have anything." While his ancestry was a mix of Russian Jew, Italian Catholic, and Scotch-Irish Protestant, none of these identities seemed as compelling as the black, Asian, and Hispanic identities he saw around him.

This student's reaction reflects the transformed ethnic identity of the grandchildren and great-grandchildren of people who arrived in the peak immigration period of 1880 to 1920. At that time, Hungarians, Bohemians, Slovaks, Czechs, Poles, Russians, and Italians differed culturally and linguistically from one another and from the Irish, German, Scandinavian, and English immigrants who preceded them. Over the generations—and through intermarriage—this ethnic distinctiveness has been replaced by a socioeconomic "convergence" (Alba, 1990). Among non-Hispanic whites, ethnic ancestry no longer shapes occupation, residence, or political interest, nor is it the basis of the creation of communities of interest.[5] While many enjoy ethnic food and celebrations or have strong feelings attached to stories of immigration, the attachment is likely to be symbolic rather than meaningful. Ethnic identifications are also more likely to be situational and self-selected—for example, highlighting the Russian but ignoring the Irish and German sides of the family.

> But what of the consequences of this symbolic ethnicity? Is it a harmless way for Saturday suburban ethnics to feel connected and special? Is it a useful way to unite Americans by reminding us that we are all descended from immigrants who had a hard time and sacrificed a bit? Is it a lovely way to show that all cultures can coexist and that the pluralist values of diversity and tolerance are alive and well in the United States?
>
> The answer is yes and maybe no. Because aside from all of the positive, amusing, and creative aspects to this celebration of roots and ethnicity, there is a subtle way in which this ethnicity has consequences for American race relations. After all, in much of this discussion the implicit and sometimes explicit comparison for this symbolic ethnicity has been the social

---

[5]An exception to the process of convergence among European-originated groups may be white, urban, Catholic ethnics. Throughout the 19th century, American Catholic churches were established as specifically ethnic churches (called "nationality churches"). These mostly urban churches were tailored to serve a particular ethnic group, which often included sending a priest from the home country who spoke the immigrants' native language. Thus, within a single urban area one might find separate Irish, Italian, and Polish Catholic churches, as well as effectively separate Catholic schools. The formation of ethnic churches meant that parishes also became ethnically segregated. On occasion, those parishes came to constitute stable, distinctive, working-class ethnic enclaves, for example, such as those found in Chicago. In these cases, ethnic identity continues as an active, viable reality.

reality of racial and ethnic identities of America's minority groups. For the ways in which ethnicity is flexible and symbolic and voluntary for white middle-class Americans are the very ways in which it is not so for non-whites and Hispanic Americans.

Thus the discussions of the influence of looks and surname on ethnic choice would look very different if one were describing a person who was one-quarter Italian and three-quarters African American or a woman whose married name changed from O'Connell to Martinez. The social and political consequences of being Asian or Hispanic or black are not symbolic for the most part, or voluntary. (Waters, 1990:155–156)

The Expectations of Those Who Share One's Stigma

The shame associated with stigma may keep people from affiliating with one another, as has sometimes been the case among disabled people; or stigma may be the grounds for coming together in collective pride, as has often been the case for American race and ethnic groups. For those stigmatized by color, sex, or social class, family members have often provided the lessons about what to expect from those in and outside the category. For those who are gay and lesbian, the lessons are usually provided later in life by members of the gay community.

Particularly for those with visible stigma, there are also frequent reminders that one will be seen as a representative of *all* members of the category. Thus, many in stigmatized categories must factor in virtually everyone's opinion: What will others in my category think? What will those who are not stigmatized think? Indeed, they may even be criticized for failing to deal with themselves as stigmatized—"After all, who do you think you are?" In a sense, members of stigmatized categories may monitor one another much as they are policed by those outside the category, with the difference that those within their category can at least claim to be defending them.

This point is illustrated in a story by the late tennis champion Arthur Ashe (1993). Ashe described watching his daughter play with a gift she had just received—a white doll—as they sat in the audience of a televised match in his honor. When the cameras panned his section of seats, he realized that he needed to get the doll away from his daughter or risk the anger of some black viewers who would argue that by letting his child play with a white doll, he appeared to be a bad role model for the black community.

A different example is provided by a Mexican American acquaintance who worked in an office with only a few other Hispanics, most of whom felt that the routes to upward mobility were closed to them. Together they drafted a letter to the firm's president detailing their concerns and seeking some corrective action. Although he had qualms about signing the letter, our acquaintance felt there was no alternative. Because he worked for management, he was then called in to explain his behavior, which his supervisor saw as disloyal. Thus, he was put in the position of having to explain that, as a Chicano, he could not have refused to sign the letter.

Codes of conduct for those in stigmatized categories often require loyalty to the group, a fact of life that in this case the supervisor was unaware of. Indeed, the operating rule for many in stigmatized categories is to avoid public disagreement with one another or public airing of the group's "dirty laundry." Such codes are not trivial, because when the codes are violated, members of stigmatized categories risk ostracism from a critical support network. The reality of discrimination makes it foolhardy to reject those who share one's stigma. What would it have meant to Arthur Ashe to lose the support of other African Americans? To whom would our acquaintance have turned in that organization had he refused to sign the letter? When they are unaware of these pressures, those in privileged categories may make impossible demands of those who are stigmatized; when aware of these pressures, however, such requests are clear tests of loyalty.

POINTS AND STAGES OF CONFLICT

This essay focused on how privilege and stigma yield different treatment and different world views. In this final section we examine varying conceptions of racism. Then we consider the stages of identity development within which privilege and stigma are experienced.

As we said earlier, overt displays of status sometimes leave those who are not members of the stigmatized category feeling excluded. For example, when Latino students talked about their pleasure in speaking Spanish, an Anglo friend immediately responded with a description of how excluded she felt on those occasions. While aware of this, the Latino students nonetheless made it clear that they were not willing to forgo these opportunities. Their non-Spanish-speaking friends would just have to understand that it wasn't anything personal. This may well mark the bottom line: Those who are not stigmatized will sometimes feel and be excluded by their friends.

But another question is implied here: If the Hispanics exclude the Anglos, can the Anglos similarly exclude the Hispanics? As a way to approach this, consider the following two statements about gays and straights. In what ways are the statements similar, and in what ways different?

> A heterosexual says, "I can't stand gays. I don't want to be anywhere around them."
> A gay says, "I can't stand straights. I don't want to be anywhere around them."

While the statements are almost identical, the speakers come from very different positions of power. A heterosexual could probably structure his or her life so as to rarely interact with anyone gay, or at least anyone self-identified as gay. Most important, however, the heterosexual's attitude is consistent with major social, political, legal, and religious practices. Thus, the heterosexual in this example speaks from a position of some power, if only that derived from alignment with dominant cultural practices.

This is not the case for the gay person in this example, who is unlikely to be able to avoid contact with straights—and who would probably pay a considerable economic cost for self-segregation if that were attempted. There are no powerful institutional supports for hatred of heterosexuals. Similarly, whatever pleasure there might be in exclusiveness it would exist against a backdrop of relative powerlessness, discrimination, and stigmatization. The same might be said of men's disparagement of women compared to women's disparagement of men. As one student wrote,

As a male I have at times been on the receiving end of comments like, "Oh, you're just like all men," or "Why can't men show more emotion?" but these comments or the sentiments behind them do not carry any power to affect my status. Even in the instance of a black who sees me as a representative of all whites, his vision of me does not change my privileged status.

Thus, the exclusiveness of those in nonstigmatized statuses exists in a context of relative powerfulness, a sense of entitlement, infrequent discrimination based on master status, and a general ability to avoid those who might be prejudiced against people like themselves. The forms of exclusion available to stigmatized people are unlikely to tangibly affect the lives of those in privileged statuses. Being able to exclude someone from a dance or a club is not as significant as being able to exclude that person from a job, residence, or an educational institution. This is what is meant when it is said that members of stigmatized categories may be prejudiced but not discriminatory; they do not have access to the institutional power by which to significantly affect the lives of those in nonstigmatized groups.

The term *racist* also carries different connotations for blacks and whites. Among whites, being color conscious is often considered to be a sign of being racist (Blauner, 1992). This understanding of what it means to be a racist has its basis in the civil rights movement. If, as the civil rights movement taught, color should not make a difference in the way people are treated, whites who make a point of *not* noticing race argue that they are being polite and not racist (Frankenberg, 1993).

But given America's historical focus on race, it seems unrealistic for any of us to claim that we are oblivious to it. While many consider it impolite to mention race, differential treatment does not disappear as a consequence. Further, a refusal to notice race conveys that being black, Asian, or Latino is a "defect" that is indelicate (for whites) to mention. Thus, it can be argued that colorblindness is not really a strategy of politeness; rather, it is a strategy of power evasion. Since race, sex, sexual orientation, or disability clearly make a difference in people's lives, pretending not to see those statuses is a way to avoid noticing their effect. The alternative would be a strategy of awareness, that is, of paying systematic attention to the impact of these statuses on oneself and others (Frankenberg, 1993).

Different conceptions of racism also emerge in the course of *racial and ethnic identity development,* which is the "understanding shared by members of ethnic groups, of what it means to be black, white, Chicano, Irish, Jewish, and so on" (White and Burke, 1987:311). In Reading 25, Beverly Daniel Tatum describes black adolescent identity development, but we offer here a brief composite sketch of what appear to be the stages of this development (Cross, 1971, 1978; Hazen, 1992, 1994; Helms, 1990; Morton and Atkinson, 1983; Thomas, 1970; Thomas and Thomas, 1971). These stages might also be applied to sex, class, and sexual orientation identities, although their application to disability is problematic. One important caution is necessary, however: Not everyone necessarily goes through each of these stages. For example, it is argued that African Americans are rarely found in the first of the stages we detail (Hazen, 1992).

For those in stigmatized statuses, the first stage of identity development involves an internalization of the culture's negative imagery. This stage may include the disparagement of others in one's group and a strong desire to be accepted by dominant group members. For women, this might mean being highly critical of other women. For those who are low income or gay, this stage might entail feelings of shame. For people of color, it might involve efforts to lighten one's skin, straighten one's hair, or have an eye tuck.

In the second stage, anger at the dominant culture emerges, usually as the result of specific encounters with discrimination. Philosopher Sandra Bartky (1990), focusing on women's discovery of the extent of sexism, describes this as a period in which sexism seems to be everywhere. Events and objects that previously had been neutral are discovered to be sexist; it becomes impossible to get through the day without becoming enraged—and the injustices one discovers are communicated to everyone within earshot. One's own behavior is also subject to increased scrutiny: "Am I being sexist to buy a doll for my niece?" Situations that used to be straightforward become moral tests.

The third stage is sometimes called an immersion stage, because it involves total involvement in one's own culture. In the previous stage, the individual is focused on evaluating and reacting to the dominant culture. In this stage, however, the focus shifts to one's own group. Dominant group members and the dominant group culture become less relevant to one's pursuits. This is often a period of participation in segregated activities and organizations as one seeks distance from dominant group members. While anger is somewhat lessened here, the process of reevaluating one's old identity continues.

The final stage is described as a period of integration as one's stigmatized status becomes integrated with the other aspects of one's life rather than taking precedence over them. Still, an opposition to prejudice and discrimination continues. At this point, one can distinguish between supportive and unsupportive dominant group members and thus one is more likely to establish satisfying relations with them.

For those who do not occupy stigmatized statuses, the first stage of race or ethnic identity development is identified as an unquestioning acceptance of dominant group values. This acceptance might take shape as being oblivious to discrimination or as espousing supremacist ideologies.

In the second stage, one becomes aware of stigmatization, often through an eye-opening encounter with discrimination. Such an experience may produce a commitment to social change or a sense of powerlessness. As is the case for those in stigmatized statuses, in this stage those in privileged statuses also find themselves overwhelmed by all the forms of discrimination they see, often accompanied by a sense of personal guilt. In an attempt to affiliate and offer assistance, they may seek alliances with those in stigmatized statuses. On college campuses this timing may not be promising, since many of those in stigmatized statuses are at a high level of anger at those in privileged groups.

In stage three, those in privileged statuses focus less on trying to win the approval of those in stigmatized groups and instead explore the history of privileged and stigmatized statuses. Learning how privilege has affected one's own life is often a central question in this period.

The final stage involves integrating one's privileged statuses with all the other aspects of one's life, recognizing those in stigmatized categorizations as distinctive individuals rather than romanticizing them as a category ("just because

oppressors are bad, doesn't mean that the oppressed are good" [Spivak, 1⁹
and understanding that many with privilege have worked effectively ₐ
discrimination.

The research on cognitive development in higher education bears inte'
on the stages of race and ethnic identity development and on the diversi,ᵤ
college population. For example,

> . . . Diversity experiences in the first year of college seem to be particularly important in devel-
> oping critical thinking. Indeed, diversity experiences at the beginning of college may positively
> affect a student's cognitive growth throughout his or her entire college career. . . . [R]acially
> oriented diversity experiences may be particularly important for the critical-thinking growth
> of white students. Indeed, experiences like making friends with students from a different race
> and attending a racial or cultural awareness workshop had positive impacts on growth in criti-
> cal thinking only for white men and women. (Pascarella, 2001:25)

> It appears that students see ethnic clusters but do not see the increasingly diverse peer
> groups that are emerging of which they are a part. It may also be that students on our
> campuses are reflecting some disappointment with the campuses' inability to capitalize
> fully on the potential created by increasing diversity on campus. These findings underscore
> the fact that individuals, groups, and institutions thrive under campus conditions that ac-
> knowledge multiple affiliations and identities and facilitate their engagement. (Smith and
> Schonfeld, 2000:19)

Overall, the more diversity in the racial and ethnic composition of the student
body, the higher was white students' satisfaction with college—even when students
did not feel that groups communicated well across their differences (Tanaka, 2005).
Unfortunately, however, "it is also clear that increasing the number of faculty of
color *negatively* impacted white students' overall satisfaction with college. . . ."
(Tanaka, 2005:74).

Passage through the stages of ethnic or racial identity is positively related to self-
esteem for all American race and ethnic groups, but the relationship is stronger for
those who are Asian American, African American, and Latino than for those who
are white (Hazen, 1994:55). Indeed, on various measures of self-esteem, African
Americans score significantly higher than those in other race or ethnic groups
(Hazen, 1992).

We once observed an African American student explain to his white classmates
that he and his sister both self-identified as black, even though their mother was
white. At that point a white student asked why he didn't call himself white since
he looked white and that status would yield him more privilege. In response, he
detailed all the qualities he prized in the black community and said he would
never give up that status to be white. Much of what he said was new to the white
students; many had never thought there was anything positive about being black
in America.

The student's question reflected the common assumption that those who are
stigmatized wish they belonged to the privileged group. Yet the woman who asked
the question was clear that she never wanted to be a male, which was equally surprising to the men in the class. Thus, many men presume there is nothing positive
about being female, many straights assume there is nothing positive about being

gay, many nondisabled people assume that disability ensures misery and loneliness (French, 1996), and many in the middle and upper classes assume there is nothing positive in life for those who are poor. But most people value and appreciate the statuses they occupy. We may wish those statuses weren't stigmatized or overprivileged, but that does not mean we would want to be other than who we are.

THE READINGS IN THIS SECTION

Our goal in this essay was to provide you with a framework by which to make sense of people's experience of privilege and stigma. Because there is a great deal of material that illustrates privilege and stigma, for this section we have tried to select readings with broad applicability.

KEY CONCEPTS

covering Trying to reduce the impact of a known or visible stigma. (pages 211–212)

discredited and discreditable The discredited are those whose stigma is known or apparent to others. The discreditable are those whose stigma is unknown or invisible to others; they are not yet discredited. (pages 206–212)

double consciousness A concept first offered by W. E. B. Du Bois to describe seeing oneself (or members of one's group) through the eyes of a critical, dominant group member. (page 210)

entitlement The belief that one has the right to respect, protection, reward, and other privileges. (page 201)

looping or rereading Interpreting (and usually dismissing) someone's words or actions because of the status that the person occupies. (page 203)

marked and unmarked statuses A marked status is one identified as "special" in some way, for example, a *blind* musician or a *woman* doctor. Unmarked statuses, such as musician or doctor, do not have such qualifiers. (page 201)

passing Not revealing a stigmatized identity. (pages 206–209)

privilege The advantages provided by some statuses. (pages 195–202)

REFERENCES

Alba, Richard D. 1990. *Ethnic Identity: The Transformation of White America.* New Haven, CT: Yale University Press.

Ashe, Arthur. 1993. *Days of Grace.* New York: Ballantine.

Associated Press. 2003. Are Legacy College Admissions Racist? March 5.

Bartky, Sandra. 1990. *Femininity and Domination: Studies in the Phenomenology of Oppression.* New York: Routledge.

Berke, Richard. 1998. Chasing the Polls on Gay Rights. *New York Times,* August 2, 4:3.

Blauner, Bob. 1992. Talking Past Each Other: Black and White Languages of Race. *The American Prospect,* Summer.

Carter, Tom. 2002. Profiling Is "Flawed" Tool to Beat Terror. *The Washington Times,* January 14, 12.

Cary, Lorene. 1991. *Black Ice.* New York: Knopf.

Cross, H., G. Kenney, J. Mell, and W. Zimmermann. 1990. *Employer Practices: Differential Treatment of Hispanic and Anglo Job Seekers.* Washington, DC: The Urban Institute.

Cross, W. E., Jr. 1971. The Negro-to-Black Conversion Experience: Toward a Psychology of Black Liberation. *Black World,* 20 (9):13–17.

———. 1978. The Thomas and Cross Models of Psychological Nigrescence: A Review. *The Journal of Black Psychology,* 5(1):13–31.

Davis, F. James. 1991. *Who Is Black? One Nation's Definition.* University Park, PA: Pennsylvania University Press.

Du Bois, W. E. B. 1982. *The Souls of Black Folk.* New York: Penguin. (Originally published in 1903.)

Ettinger, Maia. 1994. The Pocahontas Paradigm, or Will the Subaltern Please Shut Up? *Tilting the Tower,* edited by Linda Garber, 51–55. New York: Routledge.

Frankenberg, Ruth. 1993. *White Women, Race Matters: The Social Construction of Whiteness.* Minneapolis: University of Minnesota Press.

French, Sally. 1996. Simulation Exercises in Disability Awareness Training: A Critique. *Beyond Disability: Towards an Enabling Society,* edited by Gerald Hales, 114–23. London: Sage Publications.

Gallup Organization, Gallup Poll News Service. 2004. Homosexual Relations.

Goffman, Erving. 1961. *Asylums.* New York: Doubleday Anchor.

———. 1963. *Stigma: Notes on the Management of Spoiled Identity.* Englewood Cliffs, NJ: Prentice-Hall.

Hare, Nathan. 1982. W. E. Burghart Du Bois: An Appreciation, pp. xiii–xxvii in *The Souls of Black Folk.* New York: Penguin. (Originally published in 1969.)

Harris, David. 2002. Flying While Arab: Lessons from the Racial Profiling Controversy. *Civil Rights Journal,* 6(1):8–14.

———. 2003. The Reality of Racial Disparity in Criminal Justice: The Significance of Data Collection. *Law and Contemporary Problems,* 66(3):71–95.

Hazen, Sharlie Hogue. 1992. *The Relationship between Ethnic/Racial Identity Development and Ego Identity Development.* Ph.D. proposal, Department of Psychology, George Mason University.

———. 1994. *The Relationship between Ethnic/Racial Identity Development and Ego Identity Development.* Ph.D. dissertation, Department of Psychology, George Mason University.

Helms, J. E. 1990. An Overview of Black Racial Identity Theory. *Black and White Racial Identity: Theory, Research, and Practice,* edited by J. E. Helms, 9–33. New York: Greenwood Press.

Herek, Gregory M. 1992. The Social Context of Hate Crimes. *Hate Crimes: Confronting Violence against Lesbians and Gay Men,* edited by Gregory Herek and Kevin Berrill, 89–104. Newbury Park, CA: Sage.

———, and Eric K. Glunt. 1993. Heterosexuals Who Know Gays Personally Have More Favorable Attitudes. *The Journal of Sex Research,* 30:239–44.

Hocker, Cliff. 2004. Worst Labor Market for Black Professionals in 25 Years. *Black Enterprise,* May, 26.

hooks, bell. 1989. *Talking Back: Thinking Feminist, Thinking Black.* Boston: South End Press.

Institute of Medicine, Board on Health Sciences. 2003. *Unequal Treatment: Confronting Racial and Ethnic Disparities in Health Care.* Washington, DC: National Academy of Sciences.

Kanter, Rosabeth Moss. 1993. *Men and Women of the Corporation.* New York: Basic Books. (Originally published in 1976.)

———, with Barry A. Stein. 1980. *A Tale of 'O': On Being Different in an Organization.* New York: Harper and Row.

Kennedy, Florynce. 1976. *Color Me Flo: My Hard Life and Good Times.* Englewood Cliffs, NJ: Prentice-Hall.

Kimmel, Michael S., and Michael A. Messner, eds. 1989. *Men's Lives.* New York: Macmillan.

Kirp, David L. 2003. No-Brainer. *Nation,* November 10, 17–19.

Kocieniewski, David. 2002. New Jersey Troopers Avoid Jail in Case That Highlighted Profiling. *The New York Times,* January 15, A1.

Kroeger, Brooke. 2004. When a Dissertation Makes a Difference. *The New York Times,* March 20, B9.

Lester, Joan. 1994. *The Future of White Men and Other Diversity Dilemmas.* Berkeley, CA: Conari Press.

Massey, Douglas S. 2001. Residential Segregation and Neighborhood Conditions in U.S. Metropolitan Areas. *America Becoming: Racial Trends and Their Consequences,* edited by Neil J. Smelser, William Julius Wilson, and Faith Mitchell, 391–434. Washington, DC: National Academy Press.

McIntosh, Peggy. 1988. White Privilege and Male Privilege: A Personal Account of Coming to See Correspondences through Work in Women's Studies. Working Paper Number 189, Wellesley College, Center for Research on Women, Wellesley, MA.

Morton, G., and D. R. Atkinson. 1983. Minority Identity Development and Preference for Counselor Race. *Journal of Negro Education,* 52(2):156–61.

Pager, Devah. 2003. Discrimination in Hiring. *Northwestern University Newsfeed,* November 12.

Pascarella, Ernest T. 2001. Cognitive Growth in College. *Change,* November–December, 21–27.

Rosenhan, D. L. 1973. On Being Sane in Insane Places. *Science,* 179:250–58.

Ross, Stephen, and John Yinger. 2002. *The Color of Credit: Mortgage Discrimination, Research Methodology, and Fair-Lending Enforcement.* Cambridge, MA: MIT Press.

Schur, Edwin. 1984. *Labeling Women Deviant: Gender, Stigma, and Social Control.* New York: Random House.

Sedgwick, Eve Kosofsky. 1990. *The Epistemology of the Closet.* Berkeley: University of California Press.

Smith, Daryl G., and Natalie B. Schonfeld. 2000. The Benefits of Diversity: What the Research Tells Us. *About Campus,* November–December, 16–23.

Smith, Tom W. 2001. *Intergroup Relations in a Diverse America: Data from the 2000 General Social Survey.* The American Jewish Committee. www.ajc.org.

Spelman, Elizabeth. 1988. *Inessential Woman.* Boston: Beacon Press.

Spivak, Gayatre. 1994. George Mason University Cultural Studies presentation.

Tanaka, Greg. 2005. *The Intercultural Campus: Transcending Culture and Power in American Higher Education.* New York: Peter Lang.

Thomas, C. 1970. Different Strokes for Different Folks. *Psychology Today* 4(4):48–53, 78–80.

———, and S. Thomas. 1971. Something Borrowed, Something Black. In *Boys No More: A Black Psychologist's View of Community,* edited by C. Thomas. Beverly Hills, CA: Glencoe Press.

Tokarczyk, Michelle M. 2004. Promises to Keep: Working Class Students and Higher Education. *What's Class Got to Do with It? American Society in the Twenty-First Century,* edited by Michael Zweig, 161–167. Ithaca, NY: ILR Press.

Turner, Margery Austin, Michael Fix, and Raymond J. Struyk. 1991. *Opportunities Denied, Opportunities Diminished: Discrimination in Hiring.* Washington, DC: The Urban Institute.

U.S. Bureau of the Census. 1997. *Money Income in the United States.* Washington, DC: U.S. Government Printing Office.

———. 2003. *Money Income in the United States.* www.census.gov.

U.S. Department of Commerce. 1993. *Statistical Abstract of the United States, 1992.* Washington, DC: U.S. Government Printing Office.

Waters, Mary C. 1990. *Ethnic Options: Choosing Identities in America.* Berkeley: University of California Press.

White, C. L., and P. J. Burke. 1987. Ethnic Role Identity among Black and White College Students: An Interactionist Approach. *Sociological Perspectives,* 30(3):310–31.

Williams, Patricia J. 1991. Teleology on the Rocks. *The Alchemy of Race and Rights.* Cambridge, MA: Harvard University Press.

RACE AND ETHNICITY

READING 24

Latinos and the U.S. Race Structure

Clara E. Rodríguez

According to definitions common in the United States, I am a light-skinned Latina, with European features and hair texture. I was born and raised in New York City; my first language was Spanish, and I am today bilingual. I cannot remember when I first realized how the color of one's skin, the texture of one's hair, or the cast of one's features determined how one was treated in both my Spanish-language and English-language worlds. I do know that it was before I understood that accents, surnames, residence, class, and clothing also determined how one was treated.

Looking back on my childhood, I recall many instances when the lighter skin color and European features of some persons were admired and terms such as "pelo malo" (bad hair) were commonly used to refer to "tightly curled" hair. It was much later that I came to see that this Eurocentric bias, which favors European characteristics above all others, was part of our history and cultures. In both Americas and the Caribbean, we have inherited and continue to favor this Eurocentrism, which grew out of our history of indigenous conquest and slavery (Shohat and Stam 1994).

I also remember a richer, more complex sense of color than this simple color dichotomy of black and white would suggest, a genuine esthetic appreciation of people with some color and an equally genuine valuation of people as people, regardless of color. Also, people sometimes disagreed about an individual's color and "racial" classification, especially if the person in question was in the middle range, not just with regard to color, but also with regard to class or political position.[1]

As I grew older, I came to see that many of these cues or clues to status—skin color, physical features, accents, surnames, residence, and other class characteristics—changed according to place or situation. For example, a natural "tan" in my South Bronx neighborhood was attractive, whereas downtown, in the business area, it was "otherizing." I also recall that the same color was perceived differently in different areas. Even in Latino contexts, I saw some people as lighter or darker, depending on certain factors, such as their clothes, occupations, and families.[2] I suspect that others saw me similarly, so that in some contexts, I was very light, in others darker, and in still others about the same as everyone else. Even though my color stayed the same, the perception and sometimes its valuation changed.

I also realize now that some Latinos' experiences were different from mine and that our experiences affect the way we view the world. I know that not all Latinos have multiple or fluctuating identities. For a few, social context is irrelevant. Regardless of the context, they see themselves, and/or are seen, in only one way. They are what the Census Bureau refers to as *consistent;* that is, they consistently answer in the same way when asked about their "race." Often, but not always, they are at one or the other end of the color spectrum.

My everyday experiences as a Latina, supplemented by years of scholarly work, have taught me that certain dimensions of race are fundamental to Latino life in the United States and raise questions about the nature of "race" in this country. This does not mean that all Latinos have the same experiences, but that for most, these experiences are not surprising. For example, although some Latinos are consistently seen as having the same color or "race," many Latinos are assigned a multiplicity of "racial" classifications, sometimes in one day! I am reminded of the student who told me after class one day, "When people first meet me, they think I'm Italian, then when they find out my last name is Mendez, they think I'm Spanish, then when I tell them my mother is Puerto Rican, they think I'm nonwhite or Black." Although he had not

Clara E. Rodríguez is a professor of sociology at Fordham University's College at Lincoln Center.

changed his identity, the perception of it changed with each additional bit of information.

Latino students have also told me that non-Latinos sometimes assume they are African American. When they assert they are not "Black" but Latino, they are either reproved for denying their "race" or told they are out of touch with reality. Other Latinos, who see Whites as Other-than-me are told by non-Latinos, "But you're white." Although not all Latinos have such dramatic experiences, almost all know (and are often related to) others who have.

In addition to being reclassified by others (without their consent), some Latinos shift their own self-classifications during their lifetime. I have known Latinos, who became "black," then "white," then "human beings," and finally "Latino"—all in a relatively short time. I have also known Latinos for whom the sequence was quite different and the time period longer. Some Latinos who altered their identities came to be viewed by others as legitimate members of their new identity group. I also saw the simultaneously tricultural, sometimes trilingual, abilities of many Latinos who manifested or projected a different self as they acclimated themselves to a Latino, African American, or White context (Rodríguez 1989:77).

I have come to understand that this shifting, context-dependent experience is at the core of many Latinos' life in the United States. Even in the nuclear family, parents, children, and siblings often have a wide range of physical types. For many Latinos race is primarily cultural; multiple identities are a normal state of affairs; and "racial mixture" is subject to many different, sometimes fluctuating, definitions.

Some regard *racial mixture* as an unfortunate or embarrassing term, but others consider the affirmation of mixture to be empowering. Lugones (1994) subscribes to this latter view and affirms "mixture," *mestizaje,* as a way of resisting a world in which purity and separation are emphasized, and one's identities are controlled: "Mestizaje defies control through simultaneously asserting the impure, curdled multiple state and rejecting fragmentation into pure parts . . . the mestiza . . . has no pure parts to be 'had,' controlled." (p. 460) Also prevalent in the upper classes is the hegemonic view that rejects

or denies "mixture" and claims a "pure" European ancestry. This view also is common among middle- and upper-class Latinos, regardless of their skin color or place of origin. In some areas, people rarely claim a European ancestry, such as in indigenous sectors of Latin America, in parts of Brazil and in some coastal areas in Colombia, Venezuela, Honduras, and Panama (see, e.g., Arocha 1998; De la Fuente 1998). Recently, some Latinos have encouraged another view in which those historical components that were previously denied and denigrated, such as indigenous and African ancestry, were privileged (see, e.g., Moro; *La Revista de Nuestra Vida* [Bogota, Colombia, September 1998]; *La Voz del Pueblo Taino* [The Voice of the Taino People], official newsletter of the United Confederation of Taino People, U.S. regional chapter, New York, January 1998).

Many people, however—mostly non-Latinos—are not acquainted with these basic elements of Latino life. They do not think much about them; and when they do, they tend to see race as a "given," an ascribed characteristic that does not change for anyone, at any time. One is either white or not white. They also believe that "race" is based on genetic inheritance, a perspective that is just another construct of race.

Whereas many Latinos regard their "race" as primarily cultural, others, when asked about their race, offer standard U.S. race terms, saying that they are White, Black, or Indian. Still others see themselves as Latinos, Hispanics, or members of a particular national-origin group *and* as belonging to a particular race group.[3] For example, they may identify themselves as Afro-Latinos or white Hispanics. In some cases, these identities vary according to context, but in others they do not.

I have therefore come to see that the concept of "race" can be constructed in several ways and that the Latino experience in the United States provides many illustrations of this. My personal experiences have suggested to me that for many Latinos, "racial" classification is immediate, provisional, contextually dependent, and sometimes contested. But because these experiences apply to many non-Latinos as well, it is evident to me that the Latino construction of race and the racial reading of Latinos are not isolated phenomena. Rather, the government's recent deliberations on racial and ethnic classification standards reflect the experiences and complexities of many groups and individuals who are similarly involved in issues pertaining to how they see themselves and one another (U.S. Dept. of Commerce 1995; U.S. Office of Management and Budget 1995, 1997a, 1997b, 1999).

Throughout my life, I have considered racism to be evil and I oppose it with every fiber of my being. I study race to understand its influence on the lives of individuals and nations because I hope that honest, open, and well-meaning discussions of race and ethnicity and their social dynamics can help us appreciate diversity and value all people, not for their appearance, but for their character.

It was because of my personal experiences that I first began to write in this area and that I was particularly sensitive to Latinos' responses to the census' question about race. The U.S. Census Bureau's official position has been that race and ethnicity are two separate concepts. Thus, in 1980 and in 1990, the U.S. census asked people to indicate their "race"—white, black, Asian or Pacific Islander, American Indian or "other race"—and also whether or not they were Hispanic. Latinos responded to the 1990 census' question about race quite differently than did non-Latinos. Whereas less than 1% of the non-Hispanic population reported they were "other race," more than 40% of Hispanics chose this category. Latinos responded similarly in the previous decennial census (Denton and Massey 1989; Martin, DeMaio, and Campanelli 1990; Rodríguez 1989, 1990, 1991; Tienda and Ortiz 1986). Although the percentages of different Hispanic groups choosing this category varied, all chose it more than did non-Hispanics.

In addition, the many Hispanics who chose this category wrote—in the box explicitly asking for race—the name of their "home" Latino country or group, to "explain" their race—or "otherness."[4] The fact that these Latino referents were usually cultural or national-origin terms, such as Dominican, Honduran, or Boricua (i.e., Puerto Rican) underscores the fact that many Latinos viewed the question of race as a question of culture, national origin, and socialization rather than simply biological or genetic ancestry or color. Indeed, recent studies have found that many Latinos understand "race" to mean national origin, nationality, ethnicity, culture (Kissam, Herrera, and Nakamoto 1993), or a combination of these and skin color (Bates et al. 1994:109; Rodríguez 1991, 1992, 1994; Rodríguez and Cordero-Guzmán 1992). For many Latinos, the term *race* or *raza* is a reflection of these understandings and not of those often associated with "race" in the United States, e.g., defined by hypodescent.[5] Studies have found that Latinos also tend to see race along a continuum and not as a dichotomous variable in which individuals are either white or black (Bracken and de Bango 1992; Rodríguez and Hagan 1991; Romero 1992).

This does not mean that there is one Latino view of race. Rather, there are different views of race within different countries, classes, and even families. Latinos' views of race are dependent on a complex array of factors, one of which is the racial formation process in their country of origin. Other variables also influence their views of race, for example, generational differences, phenotype, class, age, and education. But even though there is not just one paradigm of Latin American race, there are some basic differences between the way that Latinos view race and the way that race is viewed overall in the United States.

In the United States, rules of hypodescent and categories based on presumed genealogical-biological criteria have generally dominated thinking about race. Racial categories have been few, discrete, and mutually exclusive, with skin color a prominent element. Categories for mixtures—for example, mulatto—have been transitory. In contrast, in Latin America, racial constructions have tended to be more fluid and based on many variables, like social class and phenotype. There also have been many, often overlapping, categories, and mixtures have been consistently acknowledged and have had their own terminology. These general differences are what Latinos bring with them to the United States, and they influence how they view their own and others' "identity."

Although Latinos may use or approach "race" differently, this does not mean that "race" as understood by Latinos does not have overtones of racism or implications of power and privilege—in either Latin America or the United States. The depreciation and denial of African and Amerindian characteristics are widespread.[6] Everywhere in Latin America can be found ". . . a pyramidal class structure, cut variously by ethnic lines, but with a local, regional and nation-state elite characterized as 'white.' And white rules over color within the same class; those who are lighter have differential access to some dimensions of the market" (Torres and Whitten 1998:23).

Suffice it to say at this point that in my many years of research in this area, I have noticed in my and others' work that "race" is a recurring, sometimes amusing and benign, and sometimes conflictual issue.[7] For Latinos' responses to questions of race are seldom as simple and straightforward as they tend to be for most non-Hispanic Whites (Rodríguez et al. 1991).

In the past, new immigrants immediately underwent a racialization process, which conveyed an implicit hierarchy of color and power. The two elements of this racialization process were (1) the acceptance of and participation in discrimination against people of color (Bell 1992; Du Bois 1962:700 ff; Morrison 1993) and (2) negotiations regarding the group's placement in the U.S. racial-ethnic queue (Jacobson 1998; Rodríguez 1974; Smith 1997; Takaki 1994). Immigrants undergoing this racialization process discriminated implicitly or explicitly against others because of their color and status. Indeed, some immigrants realized that one way to become "White," or more acceptable to Whites, was to discriminate against others seen as "nonwhite" (Ignatiev 1995; Kim 1999; Loewen 1971). Kim (1999) reviewed the historical experience of Asian Americans being triangulated with Blacks and Whites through a simultaneous process of valorization and ostracism. This racial triangulation continued to reinforce White racial

power and insulate it from minority encroachment or challenge.

Some immigrants discriminated against Blacks and/or other depreciated minorities, by not living with "them," not hiring "them" in enclave economies, or articulating prejudices against "them." Institutionalized discrimination and normative behavior aided racialization so that, for example, it became difficult to rent or sell to members of certain groups because of exclusionary practices. Nearly all immigrant groups experienced this seldom-mentioned, but indisputable dimension of the Americanization process. Critical to the racialization process was the belief that there is always some "other" group to which one is superior. Indeed, this process has been an effective means of protecting the status quo because it made it difficult to understand and pursue areas of common interest and resulted in divide-and-conquer outcomes.

Latinos—and many other groups—come to the United States with different views on race and with their own racial hierarchies. The relation of these people's racialization to their hierarchies in the United States has not been widely studied. But it is clear that when they arrive, they too become part of a racialization process in which they are differentiated according to the official perception of their race, which may or may not be the same as their own perception. This racial reclassification immerses immigrants in a social education process in which they first learn—and then may ignore, resist, or accept—the state-defined categories and the popular conventions about race (particularly one's own) (Rodríguez 1994).

The racialization process also includes contradictory views of the way that Hispanics are generally regarded. At one extreme, Hispanics are a Spanish-speaking white ethnic group, who are simply the most recent in the continuum of immigrant groups and are expected to follow the traditional path of assimilation. Another view holds that the term *Hispanic*—which has generally not been unknown to new immigrants from Latin America—is subtly "colored" by negative and racial associations. For example, the stereotyped image (for both Hispanics and non-Hispanics) of a Hispanic is "tan." Within this perspective, Hispanics are often referred to as "light skinned," not as white. Yet, many Hispanics would be seen as White, Black, or Asian if it were not known that they were Hispanic. But seeing Hispanics/Latinos as "light" clearly restricts their "Whiteness" and thus makes them nonwhite by default, but not a member of other race groups. Thus, many Hispanics entering this country become generically "nonwhite" to themselves, or to others, regardless of their actual phenotype or ancestry.

The United States' racialization process affects all groups' sense of who they are, and how they are seen, in regard to color and race. There are few studies of this concerning Latinos, but some autobiographies suggest that the racialization process has had a significant impact (see, e.g., Rivera 1983; Rodríguez 1992; Santiago 1995; Thomas 1967). Whether this has been a dissonant impact and has affected Latinos' mobility and the quality of life has not yet been determined.

Some Latinos, influenced by movements such as the Black Power movement, Afrocentrism, pan-Africanism and African diaspora philosophies, and the celebration of negritude, have come to see themselves, and sometimes their group, as Black. Terms like *Afro-Latino, black Cuban,* and *black Panamanian* are now common, and some Latinos celebrate their African roots. Others focus on their Amerindian or indigenous component, while still others see themselves only as white or mixed or identify themselves only ethnically.

A Dominican student of mine told me that each of her and her husband's children claimed a different identity. So they had one Black child, one White child, and one Dominican child. Each of the children had different friends and tastes. Many variables contribute to and interact with the racialization process to determine how individuals decide on their group affiliation. Generation, phenotype, previous and current class position, and the size and accessibility of one's cultural or national-origin group, as well as the relative size of other groups, all affect how individual Latinos identify themselves.

My own life experiences have demonstrated the social constructedness of race, and subsequent research has shown that "race" is not fixed, is imperfectly measured, is at variance with scientific principles, is often conflated with the concept of "ethnicity," and is under increasing scientific criticism and popular interrogation. Nonetheless, race is still real; it still exists.[8] We may question its necessity, the right of anyone to establish such markers, and its validity as a scientific concept. We may see it as unjust and want to change it. But we must acknowledge its significance in our lives. It can be deconstructed, but it cannot be dismissed.

DISCUSSION QUESTIONS

1. What do you think Rodríguez means when she says that for Latinos, race is "cultural"?
2. What do you think is the impact of American racial constructions on immigrant Latino Americans?

NOTES

1. In her study of Spanish speaking Caribbeans, Dominguez states that "An individual may be identified as *indio, trigueno, blanco, prieto,* or whatever in different contexts by different people or even by the same person" (1986:275).
2. Except when specifically referring to women, I use the word *Latino* to refer to both women and men. At the descriptive level, my analyses of how Latinas and Latinos classify themselves racially have not revealed significant differences. But under more controlled conditions, some labor market differences by race and gender have been noted (Gómez n.d.; Rodríguez 1991).
3. I use both *Hispanic* and *Latino*, in part because both terms are used in the literature and I've tried to use those of the authors I cite when discussing their work. Works based on census material, for example, tend to use the term *Hispanic*, mainly because this is the category under which the data were collected. Other works refer to surveys employing the term *Latino*. See the following for different arguments concerning the preferred term: Gimenez 1989; Hayes-Bautista and Chapa 1987; Oboler 1995; Treviño 1987.
4. According to Jorge del Pinal, 42.7% of the Hispanics who chose the "other race" category in the 1990 census gave a

PERSONAL ACCOUNT

What's in a Name?

What is in a name? For children, the letters of their name can be a doorway that leads to discovering elements for reading and writing. For some adults, names may represent personal traits or values. They may remind one of places or trades, and even hold personal messages. This has been my experience also, as my full name unveils many different aspects of my identity and heritage.

My first name is Ruth, I identify myself as Jewish. My second name, Carina, reflects my Latina background. I was born and raised in Buenos Aires, Argentina. My surname, Feldsberg, is the name of the city located on the border between Austria and the Czech Republic. But mainly, my last name carries the memories of my father, who was among the fortunate who saw the writing on the wall, and left Nazi-occupied Austria as a refugee. He lived in the Netherlands, Ecuador, and finally settled in Buenos Aires. There he married my mother, Edith Altschul, an Argentine Jew of Czech descent.

I grew up bilingual, speaking Spanish and German at school and at home. I practiced Argentine, European traditions and also observed the Jewish holidays. But the knowledge that we were the only family in the neighborhood to celebrate certain holidays made me feel isolated. Besides religion, I also felt different in terms of ethnicity and the language spoken at home. And although my mother was Argentine, her family's Czech origin also separated me from most of the children my age. Argentina's middle class is largely formed by Italian or Spanish immigrants, and the official religion is Catholicism. I knew that I could not share my background and felt alienated because others could not relate to my experience. Growing up, I learned to keep a low profile, to be cautious, and not to unveil my identity. I would listen and constantly evaluate whether or not it was safe for me to speak. As I entered adolescence, my own identity became a puzzle even to myself as I began to pose "existential" questions. Who am I really? Latina? Jewish? European? Where do I want to live? These questions ultimately motivated me to explore my roots, travel in Europe, and live in Latin America, the Middle East, and, finally, in the United States. Presently, I live in California, and I am not sure that I have been able to completely answer all those questions. I can relate to discrimination against Latinos, because being Jewish, I learned early on about discrimination. Yet not having been the target of racial or social class oppression, I can be a strong ally. If I heard a pejorative comment about Latinos, without feeling touched, I could quickly dismiss it and see it as lack of knowledge about the complexities, beauty, and diversity among Latinos. The place I still struggle and feel more vulnerable is in my Jewish heritage. I may have become what people call a citizen of the world, and I can live everywhere, but never feel truly at home anywhere.

— Ruth C. Feldsberg

Latino referent. However, 94.3% of "other race" persons who provided a write-in gave a Latino referent. (Personal communication, July 30, 1999.) In addition, two-thirds of all those who did not specify their race wrote in their Hispanic ethnicity (U.S. Office of Management and Budget 1995:44689).

5. *Hypodescent* is also referred to as the "one-drop rule," in which "one drop" of "nonwhite or Black blood" determines a person's "race."

6. The degree to which racism is perceived and experienced within the Latino framework may be related to phenotype. Consequently, those farthest from either the local mean or the ideal European model may be those most subject to, and therefore most aware of, racism and discrimination. In the dominant United States framework, those farthest from the stereotype "Latin look" may be those who are most acutely aware of, or in the best position to observe, discrimination.

7. See Davis et al. (1998a:III-22-23) for light and humorous discussions of skin color in cognitive interviews.

8. Marks (1994) maintains that folk concepts of race—flawed and scientifically deficient as they may be—are passed down from generation to generation, just as genetic material is inherited. This is part of what keeps the concept of "race" real.

REFERENCES

Arocha, Jaime. 1998. "Inclusion of Afro-Colombians: Unreachable National Goal?" *Latin American Perspectives* 25 (3) (May):70–89.

Bates, Nancy A., Manuel de la Puente, Theresa J. DeMaio, and Elizabeth A. Martin. 1994. "Research on Race and Ethnicity: Results from Questionnaire Design Tests." Paper presented at the U.S. Census Bureau's annual research conference, March 20–23, Rosslyn, VA.

Bell, Derrick. 1992. *Faces at the Bottom of the Well: The Permanence of Racism.* New York: Basic Books.

Bracken, Karen, and Guillermo de Bango. 1992. "Hispanics in a Racially and Ethnically Mixed Neighborhood in the Greater Metropolitan New Orleans Area." *Ethnographic Evaluation of the 1990 Decennial Census Report* 16. Prepared under Joint Statistical Agreement 89–45 with Hispanidad '87, Inc. Washington, DC: U.S. Bureau of the Census.

Davis, Diana K., Johnny Blair, Howard Fleischman, and Margaret S. Boone. 1998a. *Cognitive Interviews on the Race and Hispanic Origin Questions on the Census 2000 Dress Rehearsal Form.* Report prepared by Development Associates, Inc., Arlington, VA, under contract from the U.S. Census Bureau, Population Division, May 29.

De La Fuente, Alejandro. 1998. "Race, National Discourse, and Politics in Cuba: An Overview." *Latin American Perspectives* 25 (3) (May): 43–69. Issue 100 entitled "Race and National Identity in the Americas" and edited by Helen Safa.

Denton, N. A., and D. S. Massey. 1989. "Racial Identity among Caribbean Hispanics: The Effect of Double Minority Status on Residential Segregation." *American Sociological Review* 54:790–808.

Domínguez, Virginia R. 1986. *White by Definition: Social Classification in Creole Louisiana.* New Brunswick, NJ: Rutgers University Press.

Du Bois, W. E. B. 1962. *Black Reconstruction in America, 1860–1880.* Cleveland: World Publishing.

Gimenez, Martha. 1989. "Latino/'Hispanic'—Who Needs a Name? The Case against a Standardized Terminology." *International Journal of Health Services* 19 (3): 557–571.

Gómez, Christina. n.d. "The Continual Significance of Skin Color: An Exploratory Study of Latinos in the Northeast." *Hispanic Journal of Behavioral Sciences,* currently under review.

Hayes-Bautista, D. E., and J. Chapa. 1987. "Latino Terminology: Conceptual Basis for Standardized Terminology." *American Journal of Public Health* 77: 61–68.

Ignatiev, Noel. 1995. *How the Irish Became White.* New York: Routledge & Kegan Paul.

Jacobson, Mathew. 1998. *Becoming Caucasian: Whiteness and the Alchemy of the American Melting Pot.* Cambridge, MA: Harvard University Press.

Kim, Claire Jean. 1999. "The Racial Triangulation of Asian Americans." *Politics and Society* 27(1)(March): 105–138.

Kissam, Edward, Enrique Herrera, and Jorge M. Nakamoto. 1993. "Hispanic Response to Census Enumeration Forms and Procedures." Task order no. 46-YABC-2-0001, contract no. 50-YABC-2-66027, submitted by Aguirre International, 411 Borel Ave., Suite 402, San Mateo, CA 94402, to U.S. Bureau of the Census, Center for Survey Methods Research, March.

Lugones, María. 1994. "Purity, Impurity, and Separation." *Signs* 19 (2) (Winter): 459–479.

Marks, Jonathan. 1994. "Black, White, Other: Racial Categories Are Cultural Constructs Masquerading as Biology." *Natural History,* December, pp. 32–35.

Martin, E., T. J. DeMaio, and P. C. Campanelli. 1990. "Context Effects for Census Measures of Race and Hispanic Origin." *Public Opinion Quarterly* 54 (4): 551–566.

Morrison, Toni. 1993. "On the Backs of Blacks." *Time,* special issue (Fall), p. 57.

Oboler, Suzanne. 1995. *Ethnic Labels/Latino Lives: Identity and the Politics of (Re) Presentation in the United States.* Minneapolis: University of Minnesota Press.

Rivera, Edward. 1983. *Family Installments: Memories of Growing up Hispanic.* New York: Penguin Books.

Rodríguez, Clara. 1974. "Puerto Ricans: Between Black and White." *Journal of New York Affairs* 1 (4): 92–101.

———. 1989. *Puerto Ricans: Born in the USA.* Boston: Unwin Hyman.

———. 1990. "Racial Identification among Puerto Ricans in New York." *Hispanic Journal of Behavioral Sciences* 12 (4) (November): 366–79.

———. 1991. "The Effect of Race on Puerto Rican Wages." In *Hispanics in the Labor Force: Issues and Policies,* ed. Edwin Meléndez, Clara Rodríguez, and Janice Barry Figueroa. New York: Plenum Press.

———. 1992. "Race, Culture and Latino 'Otherness' in the 1980 Census." *Social Science Quarterly* 73 (4) (December): 930–937.

———. 1994. "Challenging Racial Hegemony. Puerto Ricans in the United States." In *Race,* ed. R. Sanjek and S. Gregory. New Brunswick, NJ: Rutgers University Press.

Rodríguez, Clara, Aida Castro, Oscar García, and Analisa Torres. 1991. "Latino Racial Identity: In the Eye of the Beholder?" *Latino Studies Journal* 2 (3) (December): 33–48.

Rodríguez, Clara, and Hector Cordero-Guzmán. 1992. "Placing Race in Context." *Ethnic and Racial Studies* 15 (4): 523–542.

Rodríguez, Nestor, and Jacqueline Hagan. 1991. *Investigating Census Coverage and Content among the Undocumented: An Ethnographic Study of Latino Immigrant Tenants in Houston. Ethnographic Evaluation of the 1990 Decennial Census Report* 3. Prepared under Joint Statistical Agreement 89-34 with the University of Houston, U.S. Bureau of the Census, Washington, DC.

Romero, Mary. 1992. *Ethnographic Evaluation of Behavioral Causes of Census Undercount of Undocumented Immigrants and Salvadorans in the Mission District of San Francisco, California. Ethnographic Evaluation of the 1990 Decennial Census Report* 18. Prepared under Joint Statistical Agreement 89-41 with the San Francisco State University Foundation, U.S. Bureau of the Census, Washington, DC.

Santiago, Roberto. 1995. "Black and Latino." In *Boricuas: Influential Puerto Rican Writings, an Anthology*, ed. Roberto Santiago. New York: Ballantine Books.

Shohat, Ella, and Robert Stam. 1994. *Unthinking Eurocentrism: Multiculturalism and the Media.* New York: Routledge & Kegan Paul.

Smith, Rogers M. 1997. *Civic Ideals: Conflicting Visions in U.S. History.* New Haven, CT: Yale University Press.

Takaki, Ronald. 1994. *From Different Shores: Perspectives on Race and Ethnicity in America.* 2d ed. New York: Oxford University Press.

Thomas, Piri. 1967. *Down These Mean Streets.* New York: Knopf.

Tienda, M., and V. Ortiz. 1986. "'Hispanicity' and the 1980 Census." *Social Science Quarterly* 67 (March): 3–20.

Torres, Arlene, and Norman E. Whitten Jr., eds. 1998. *Blackness in Latin America and the Caribbean.* Vol. 2. Bloomington: Indiana University Press.

Treviño, F. M. 1987. "Standardized Terminology for Standardized Populations." *American Journal of Public Health* 77: 69–72.

U.S. Department of Commerce. 1995. "1996 Race and Ethnic Targeted Test; Notice." *Federal Register,* 60:231:62010-62014. December 1. Washington, DC: U.S. Government Printing Office.

U.S. Office of Management and Budget (OMB). 1995. "Standards for the Classification of Federal Data on Race and Ethnicity; Notice." *Federal Register,* part 6, vol. 60, no. 166, pp. 44674–44693, August 28.

———. 1997a. "Recommendations from the Interagency Committee for the Review of the Racial and Ethnic Standards to the Office of Management and Budget Concerning Changes to the Standards for the Classification of Federal Data on Race and Ethnicity; Notice." *Federal Register,* 62:131:36874–36946, July 9.

———. 1997b. "Revisions to the Standards for the Classification of Federal Data on Race and Ethnicity; Notices." *Federal Register,* 62:210:58782-58790, October 30.

———. 1999. "Provisional Guidance on the Implementation of the 1997 Standards for the Collection of Federal Data on Race and Ethnicity." Prepared by Tabulation Working Group, Interagency Committee for the Review of Standards for Data on Race and Ethnicity, Washington, DC, February 17.

"Why Are All the Black Kids Sitting Together in the Cafeteria?"

Beverly Daniel Tatum

Walk into any racially mixed high school cafeteria at lunch time and you will instantly notice that in the sea of adolescent faces, there is an identifiable group of Black students sitting together. Conversely, it could be pointed out that there are many groups of White students sitting together as well, though people rarely comment about that. The question on the tip of everyone's tongue is "Why are the Black kids sitting together?" Principals want to know, teachers want to know, White students want to know, the Black students who aren't sitting at the table want to know.

How does it happen that so many Black teenagers end up at the same cafeteria table? They don't start out there. If you walk into racially mixed elementary schools, you will often see young children of diverse racial backgrounds playing with one another, sitting at the snack table together, crossing racial boundaries with an ease uncommon in adolescence. Moving from elementary school to middle school (often at sixth or seventh grade) means interacting with new children from different neighborhoods than before, and a certain degree of clustering by race might therefore be expected, presuming that children who are familiar with one another would form groups. But even in schools where the same children stay together from kindergarten through eighth grade, racial grouping begins by the sixth or seventh grade. What happens?

One thing that happens is puberty. As children enter adolescence, they begin to explore the question of identity, asking "Who am I? Who can I be?" in ways they have not done before. For Black youth,

Beverly Daniel Tatum is president of Spelman College. Prior to her appointment to the Spelman presidency in 2002, she spent 13 years at Mount Holyoke College as professor of psychology, department chair, dean of the college, and acting president.

asking "Who am I?" includes thinking about "Who am I ethnically and/or racially? What does it mean to be Black?"

As I write this, I can hear the voice of a White woman who asked me, "Well, all adolescents struggle with questions of identity. They all become more self-conscious about their appearance and more concerned about what their peers think. So what is so different for Black kids?" Of course, she is right that all adolescents look at themselves in new ways, but not all adolescents think about themselves in racial terms.

The search for personal identity that intensifies in adolescence can involve several dimensions of an adolescent's life: vocational plans, religious beliefs, values and preferences, political affiliations and beliefs, gender roles, and ethnic identities. The process of exploration may vary across these identity domains. James Marcia described four identity "statuses" to characterize the variation in the identity search process: (1) *diffuse,* a state in which there has been little exploration or active consideration of a particular domain, and no psychological commitment; (2) *foreclosed,* a state in which a commitment has been made to particular roles or belief systems, often those selected by parents, without actively considering alternatives; (3) *moratorium,* a state of active exploration of roles and beliefs in which no commitment has yet been made; and (4) *achieved,* a state of strong personal commitment to a particular dimension of identity following a period of high exploration.[1]

An individual is not likely to explore all identity domains at once, therefore it is not unusual for an adolescent to be actively exploring one dimension while another remains relatively unexamined. Given the impact of dominant and subordinate status, it is not surprising that researchers have found that adolescents of color are more likely to be actively engaged in an exploration of their racial or ethnic identity than are White adolescents.[2]

Why do Black youths, in particular, think about themselves in terms of race? Because that is how the rest of the world thinks of them. Our self-perceptions are shaped by the messages that we receive from those around us, and when young Black men and women enter adolescence, the racial content of those messages intensifies. A case in point: If you were to ask my ten-year-old son, David, to describe himself, he would tell you many things: that he is smart, that he likes to play computer games, that he has an older brother. Near the top of his list, he would likely mention that he is tall for his age. He would probably not mention that he is Black, though he certainly knows that he is. Why would he mention his height and not his racial group membership? When David meets new adults, one of the first questions they ask is "How old are you?" When David states his age, the inevitable reply is "Gee, you're tall for your age!" It happens so frequently that I once overheard David say to someone, "Don't say it, I know. I'm tall for my age." Height is salient for David because it is salient for others.

When David meets new adults, they don't say, "Gee, you're Black for your age!" If you are saying to yourself, of course they don't, think again. Imagine David at fifteen, six-foot-two, wearing the adolescent attire of the day, passing adults he doesn't know on the sidewalk. Do the women hold their purses a little tighter, maybe even cross the street to avoid him? Does he hear the sound of the automatic door locks on cars as he passes by? Is he being followed around by the security guards at the local mall? As he stops in town with his new bicycle, does a police officer hassle him, asking where he got it, implying that it might be stolen? Do strangers assume he plays basketball? Each of these experiences conveys a racial message. At ten, race is not yet salient for David, because it is not yet salient for society. But it will be.

UNDERSTANDING RACIAL IDENTITY DEVELOPMENT

Psychologist William Cross, author of *Shades of Black: Diversity in African American Identity,* has offered a theory of racial identity development that I have found to be a very useful framework for understanding what is happening not only with David, but with those Black students in the cafeteria.[3] According to Cross's model, referred to as the psychology of nigrescence, or the psychology of becoming Black, the five stages of racial identity development are *pre-encounter, encounter, immersion/emersion, internalization,* and *internalization-commitment.* For the moment, we will consider the first two stages as those are the most relevant for adolescents.

In the first stage, the Black child absorbs many of the beliefs and values of the dominant White culture, including the idea that it is better to be White. The stereotypes, omissions, and distortions that reinforce notions of White superiority are breathed in by Black children as well as White. Simply as a function of being socialized in a Eurocentric culture, some Black children may begin to value the role models, lifestyles, and images of beauty represented by the dominant group more highly than those of their own cultural group. On the other hand, if Black parents are what I call race-conscious—that is, actively seeking to encourage positive racial identity by providing their children with positive cultural images and messages about what it means to be Black—the impact of the dominant society's messages are reduced.[4] In either case, in the pre-encounter stage, the personal and social significance of one's racial group membership has not yet been realized, and racial identity is not yet under examination. At age ten, David and other children like him would seem to be in the pre-encounter stage. When the environmental cues change and the world begins to reflect his Blackness back to him more clearly, he will probably enter the encounter stage.

Transition to the encounter stage is typically precipitated by an event or series of events that force the young person to acknowledge the personal impact of racism. As the result of a new and heightened awareness of the significance of race, the individual begins to grapple with what it means to be a member of a group targeted by racism. Though Cross describes this process as one that unfolds in late adolescence and early adulthood, research suggests that an examination of one's racial or ethnic identity may begin as early as junior high school.

In a study of Black and White eighth graders from an integrated urban junior high school, Jean Phinney and Steve Tarver found clear evidence for the beginning of the search process in this dimension of identity. Among the forty-eight participants, more than a third had thought about the effects of ethnicity on their future, had discussed the issues with family and friends, and were attempting to learn more about their group. While White students in this integrated school were also beginning to think about ethnic identity, there was evidence to suggest a more active search among Black students, especially Black females.[5] Phinney and Tarver's research is consistent with my own study of Black youth in predominantly White communities, where the environmental cues that trigger an examination of racial identity often become evident in middle school or junior high school.[6]

Some of the environmental cues are institutionalized. Though many elementary schools have self-contained classrooms where children of varying performance levels learn together, many middle and secondary schools use "ability grouping," or tracking. Though school administrators often defend their tracking practices as fair and objective, there usually is a recognizable racial pattern to how children are assigned, which often represents the system of advantage operating in the schools.[7] In racially mixed schools, Black children are much more likely to be in the lower track than in the honors track. Such apparent sorting along racial lines sends a message about what it means to be Black. One young honors student I interviewed described the irony of this resegregation in what was an otherwise integrated environment, and hinted at the identity issues it raised for him.

> It was really a very paradoxical existence, here I am in a school that's 35 percent Black, you know, and I'm the only Black in my classes. . . . That always struck me as odd. I guess I felt that I was different from the other Blacks because of that.

In addition to the changes taking place within school, there are changes in the social dynamics outside school. For many parents, puberty raises anxiety about interracial dating. In racially mixed communities, you begin to see what I call the birthday party effect. Young children's birthday parties in multiracial communities are often a reflection of the community's diversity. The parties of elementary school children may be segregated by gender but not by race. At puberty, when the parties become sleepovers or boy-girl events, they become less and less racially diverse.

Black girls, especially in predominantly White communities, may gradually become aware that something has changed. When their White friends start to date, they do not. The issues of emerging sexuality and the societal messages about who is sexually desirable leave young Black women in a very devalued position. One young woman from a Philadelphia suburb described herself as "pursuing White guys throughout high school" to no avail. Since there were no Black boys in her class, she had little choice. She would feel "really pissed off" that those same White boys would date her White friends. For her, "that prom thing was like out of the question."[8]

Though Black girls living in the context of a larger Black community may have more social choices, they too have to contend with devaluing messages about who they are and who they will become, especially if they are poor or working-class. As social scientists Bonnie Ross Leadbeater and Niobe Way point out,

> The school drop-out, the teenage welfare mother, the drug addict, and the victim of domestic violence or of AIDS are among the most prevalent public images of poor and working-class urban adolescent girls. . . . Yet, despite the risks inherent in economic disadvantage, the majority of poor urban adolescent girls do not fit the stereotypes that are made about them.[9]

Resisting the stereotypes and affirming other definitions of themselves is part of the task facing young Black women in both White and Black communities.

As was illustrated in the example of David, Black boys also face a devalued status in the wider world. The all too familiar media image of a young Black man with his hands cuffed behind his back, arrested for a violent crime, has primed many to view young Black men with suspicion and fear. In the context of predominantly White schools, however, Black boys may enjoy a degree of social success, particularly if they are athletically talented. The culture has embraced the Black athlete, and the young man who can fulfill that role is often pursued by Black girls and White girls alike. But even these young men will encounter experiences that may trigger an examination of their racial identity.

Sometimes the experience is quite dramatic. *The Autobiography of Malcolm X* is a classic tale of racial identity development, and I assign it to my psychology of racism students for just that reason. As a junior high school student, Malcolm was a star. Despite the fact that he was separated from his family and living in a foster home, he was an A student and was elected president of his class. One day he had a conversation with his English teacher, whom he liked and respected, about his future career goals. Malcolm said he wanted to be a lawyer. His teacher responded, "That's no realistic goal for a nigger," and advised him to consider carpentry instead.[10] The message was clear: You are a Black male, your racial group membership matters, plan accordingly. Malcolm's emotional response was typical—anger, confusion, and alienation. He withdrew from his White classmates, stopped participating in class, and eventually left his predominately white Michigan home to live with his sister in Roxbury, a Black community in Boston.

No teacher would say such a thing now, you may be thinking, but don't be so sure. It is certainly less likely that a teacher would use the word *nigger,* but consider these contemporary examples shared by high school students. A young ninth-grade student was sitting in his homeroom. A substitute teacher was in charge of the class. Because the majority of students from this school go on to college, she used the free time to ask the students about their college plans. As a substitute she had very limited information about their academic performance, but she offered some suggestions. When she turned to this young man, one of few Black males in the class, she suggested that he consider a community college. She had recommended four-year colleges to the other students. Like Malcolm, this student got the message.

In another example, a young Black woman attending a desegregated school to which she was bussed was encouraged by a teacher to attend the upcoming school dance. Most of the Black students did not live in the neighborhood and seldom attended the extracurricular activities. The young woman indicated that she wasn't planning to come. The well-intentioned teacher was persistent. Finally the teacher said, "Oh come on, I know you people love to dance." This young woman got the message, too.

COPING WITH ENCOUNTERS: DEVELOPING AN OPPOSITIONAL IDENTITY

What do these encounters have to do with the cafeteria? Do experiences with racism inevitably result in so-called self-segregation? While certainly a desire to protect oneself from further offense is understandable, it is not the only factor at work. Imagine the young eighth-grade girl who experienced the teacher's use of "you people" and the dancing stereotype as a racial affront. Upset and struggling with adolescent embarrassment, she bumps into a White friend who can see that something is wrong. She explains. Her White friend responds, in an effort to make her feel better perhaps, and says, "Oh, Mr. Smith is such a nice guy, I'm sure he didn't mean it like that. Don't be so sensitive." Perhaps the White friend is right, and Mr. Smith didn't mean it, but imagine your own response when you are upset, perhaps with a spouse or partner. He or she asks what's wrong and you explain why you are offended. Your partner brushes off your complaint, attributing it to your being oversensitive. What happens to your emotional thermostat? It escalates. When feelings, rational or irrational, are invalidated, most people disengage. They not only choose to discontinue the conversation but are more likely to turn to someone who will understand their perspective.

In much the same way, the eighth-grade girl's White friend doesn't get it. She doesn't see the significance of this racial message, but the girls at the "Black table" do. When she tells her story there, one of them is likely to say, "You know what, Mr. Smith said the same thing to me yesterday!" Not only are Black adolescents encountering racism and reflecting on their identity, but their White peers, even when they are not the perpetrators (and sometimes they are), are unprepared to respond in supportive ways. The Black students turn to each other for the much needed support they are not likely to find anywhere else.

In adolescence, as race becomes personally salient for Black youth, finding the answer to questions such as, "What does it mean to be a young Black person? How should I act? What should I do?" is particularly important. And although Black fathers, mothers, aunts, and uncles may hold the answers by offering themselves as role models, they hold little appeal for most adolescents. The last thing many fourteen-year-olds want to do is to grow up to be like their parents. It is the peer group, the kids in the cafeteria, who hold the answers to these questions. They know how to be Black. They have absorbed the stereotypical images of Black youth in the popular culture and are reflecting those images in their self-presentation.

Based on their fieldwork in U.S. high schools, Signithia Fordham and John Ogbu identified a common psychological pattern found among African American high school students at this stage of identity development.[11] They observed that the anger and resentment that adolescents feel in response to their growing awareness of the systematic exclusion of Black people from full participation in U.S. society leads to the development of an oppositional social identity. This oppositional stance both protects one's identity from the psychological assault of racism and keeps the dominant group at a distance. Fordham and Ogbu write:

> Subordinate minorities regard certain forms of behavior and certain activities or events, symbols, and meanings as *not appropriate* for them because those behaviors, events, symbols, and meanings are

characteristic of white Americans. At the same time they emphasize other forms of behavior as more appropriate for them because these are *not* a part of white Americans' way of life. To behave in the manner defined as falling within a white cultural frame of reference is to "act white" and is negatively sanctioned.[12]

Certain styles of speech, dress, and music, for example, may be embraced as "authentically Black" and become highly valued, while attitudes and behaviors associated with Whites are viewed with disdain. The peer groups' evaluation of what is Black and what is not can have a powerful impact on adolescent behavior.

Reflecting on her high school years, one Black woman from a White neighborhood described both the pain of being rejected by her Black classmates and her attempts to conform to her peer's definition of Blackness:

> "Oh you sound White, you think you're White," they said. And the idea of sounding White was just so absurd to me. . . . So ninth grade was sort of traumatic in that I started listening to rap music, which I really just don't like. [I said] I'm gonna be Black, and it was just that stupid. But it's more than just how one acts, you know. [The other Black women there] were not into me for the longest time. My first year there was hell.

Sometimes the emergence of an oppositional identity can be quite dramatic, as the young person tries on a new persona almost overnight. At the end of one school year, race may not have appeared to be significant, but often some encounter takes place over the summer and the young person returns to school much more aware of his or her Blackness and ready to make sure that the rest of the world is aware of it, too. There is a certain "in your face" quality that these adolescents can take on, which their teachers often experience as threatening. When a group of Black teens are sitting together in the cafeteria, collectively embodying an oppositional stance, school administrators want to know not only why they are sitting together, but what can be done to prevent it.

We need to understand that in racially mixed settings, racial grouping is a developmental process in response to an environmental stressor, racism. Joining with one's peers for support in the face of stress is a positive coping strategy. What is problematic is that the young people are operating with a very limited definition of what it means to be Black, based largely on cultural stereotypes.

OPPOSITIONAL IDENTITY DEVELOPMENT AND ACADEMIC ACHIEVEMENT

Unfortunately for Black teenagers, those cultural stereotypes do not usually include academic achievement. Academic success is more often associated with being White. During the encounter phase of racial identity development, when the search for identity leads toward cultural stereotypes and away from anything that might be associated with Whiteness, academic performance often declines. Doing well in school becomes identified as trying to be White. Being smart becomes the opposite of being cool.

While this frame of reference is not universally found among adolescents of African descent, it is commonly observed in Black peer groups. Among the Black college students I have interviewed, many described some conflict or alienation from other African American teens because of their academic success in high school. For example, a twenty-year-old female from a Washington, D.C., suburb explained:

> It was weird, even in high school a lot of the Black students were, like, "Well, you're not really Black." Whether it was because I became president of the sixth-grade class or whatever it was, it started pretty much back then. Junior high, it got worse. I was then labeled certain things, whether it was "the oreo" or I wasn't really Black.

Others described avoiding situations that would set them apart from their Black peers. For example, one young woman declined to participate in a gifted program in her school because she knew it would separate her from the other Black students in the school.

In a study of thirty-three eleventh-graders in a Washington, D.C., school, Fordham and Ogbu found that although some of the students had once been academically successful, few of them remained so. These students also knew that to be identified as a "brainiac" would result in peer rejection. The few students who had maintained strong academic records found ways to play down their academic success enough to maintain some level of acceptance among their Black peers.[13]

Academically successful Black students also need a strategy to find acceptance among their White classmates. Fordham describes one such strategy as *racelessness*, wherein individuals assimilate into the dominant group by de-emphasizing characteristics that might identify them as members of the subordinate group.[14] Jon, a young man I interviewed, offered a classic example of this strategy as he described his approach to dealing with his discomfort at being the only Black person in his advanced classes. He said, "At no point did I ever think I was White or did I ever want to be White. . . . I guess it was one of those things where I tried to de-emphasize the fact that I was Black." This strategy led him to avoid activities that were associated with Blackness. He recalled, "I didn't want to do anything that was traditionally Black, like I never played basketball. I ran cross-country. . . . I went for distance running instead of sprints." He felt he had to show his White classmates that there were "exceptions to all these stereotypes." However, this strategy was of limited usefulness. When he traveled outside his home community with his White teammates, he sometimes encountered overt racism. "I quickly realized that I'm Black, and that's the thing that they're going to see first, no matter how much I try to de-emphasize my Blackness."

A Black student can play down Black identity in order to succeed in school and mainstream institutions without rejecting his Black identity and culture.[15] Instead of becoming raceless, an achieving Black student can become an *emissary*, someone who sees his or her own achievements as advancing the cause of the racial group. For example, social scientists Richard Zweigenhaft and

G. William Domhoff describe how a successful Black student, in response to the accusation of acting White, connected his achievement to that of other Black men by saying, "Martin Luther King must not have been Black, then, since he had a doctoral degree, and Malcolm X must not have been Black since he educated himself while in prison." In addition, he demonstrated his loyalty to the Black community by taking an openly political stance against the racial discrimination he observed in his school.[16]

It is clear that an oppositional identity can interfere with academic achievement, and it may be tempting for educators to blame the adolescents themselves for their academic decline. However, the questions that educators and other concerned adults must ask are, How did academic achievement become defined as exclusively White behavior? What is it about the curriculum and the wider culture that reinforces the notion that academic excellence is an exclusively White domain? What curricular interventions might we use to encourage the development of an empowered emissary identity?

An oppositional identity that disdains academic achievement has not always been a characteristic of Black adolescent peer groups. It seems to be a post-desegregation phenomenon. Historically, the oppositional identity found among African Americans in the segregated South included a positive attitude toward education. While Black people may have publicly deferred to Whites, they actively encouraged their children to pursue education as a ticket to greater freedom.[17] While Black parents still see education as the key to upward mobility, in today's desegregated schools the models of success—the teachers, administrators, and curricular heroes—are almost always White.

Black Southern schools, though stigmatized by legally sanctioned segregation, were often staffed by African American educators, themselves visible models of academic achievement. These Black educators may have presented a curriculum that included references to the intellectual legacy of other African Americans. As well, in the context of a segregated school, it was a given that the high achieving students would all be Black. Academic achievement did not have to mean separation from one's Black peers.

THE SEARCH FOR ALTERNATIVE IMAGES

This historical example reminds us that an oppositional identity discouraging academic achievement is not inevitable even in a racist society. If young people are exposed to images of African American academic achievement in their early years, they won't have to define school achievement as something for Whites only. They will know that there is a long history of Black intellectual achievement.

This point was made quite eloquently by Jon, the young man I quoted earlier. Though he made the choice to excel in school, he labored under the false assumption that he was "inventing the wheel." It wasn't until he reached college and had the opportunity to take African American studies courses that he learned about other African Americans besides Martin Luther King, Malcolm X, and Frederick Douglass—the same three men he had heard about year after year, from kindergarten to high school graduation. As he reflected on his identity struggle in high school, he said:

> It's like I went through three phases. . . . My first phase was being cool, doing whatever was particularly cool for Black people at the time, and that was like in junior high. Then in high school, you know, I thought being Black was basically all stereotypes, so I tried to avoid all of those things. Now in college, you know, I realize that being Black means a variety of things.

Learning his history in college was of great psychological importance to Jon, providing him with role models he had been missing in high school. He was particularly inspired by learning of the intellectual legacy of Black men at his own college:

> When you look at those guys who were here in the Twenties, they couldn't live on campus. They couldn't eat on campus. They couldn't get their hair cut in town. And yet they were all Phi Beta Kappa. . . . That's what being Black really is, you know, knowing who

you are, your history, your accomplishments. . . . When I was in junior high, I had White role models. And then when I got into high school, you know, I wasn't sure but I just didn't think having White role models was a good thing. So I got rid of those. And I basically just, you know, only had my parents for role models. I kind of grew up thinking that we were on the cutting edge. We were doing something radically different than everybody else. And not realizing that there are all kinds of Black people doing the very things that I thought we were the only ones doing. . . . You've got to do the very best you can so that you can continue the great traditions that have already been established.

This young man was not alone in his frustration over having learned little about his own cultural history in grade school. Time and again in the research interviews I conducted, Black students lamented the absence of courses in African American history or literature at the high school level and indicated how significant this new learning was to them in college, how excited and affirmed they felt by this newfound knowledge. Sadly, many Black students never get to college, alienated from the process of education long before high school graduation. They may never get access to the information that might have helped them expand their definition of what it means to be Black and, in the process, might have helped them stay in school. Young people are developmentally ready for this information in adolescence. We ought to provide it.

NOT AT THE TABLE

As we have seen, Jon felt he had to distance himself from his Black peers in order to be successful in high school. He was one of the kids *not* sitting at the Black table. Continued encounters with racism and access to new culturally relevant information empowered him to give up his racelessness and become an emissary. In college, not only did he sit at the Black table, but he emerged as a campus leader, confident in the support of his Black peers. His example illustrates that one's presence at the Black table is often an expression of one's identity development, which evolves over time.

Some Black students may not be developmentally ready for the Black table in junior or senior high school. They may not yet have had their own encounters with racism, and race may not be very salient for them. Just as we don't all reach puberty and begin developing sexual interest at the same time, racial identity development unfolds in idiosyncratic ways. Though my research suggests that adolescence is a common time, one's own life experiences are also important determinants of the timing. The young person whose racial identity development is out of synch with his or her peers often feels in an awkward position. Adolescents are notoriously egocentric and assume that their experience is the same as everyone else's. Just as girls who have become interested in boys become disdainful of their friends still interested in dolls, the Black teens who are at the table can be quite judgmental toward those who are not. "If I think it is a sign of authentic Blackness to sit at this table, then you should too."

The young Black men and women who still hang around with the White classmates they may have known since early childhood will often be snubbed by their Black peers. This dynamic is particularly apparent in regional schools where children from a variety of neighborhoods are brought together. When Black children from predominantly White neighborhoods go to school with Black children from predominantly Black neighborhoods, the former group is often viewed as trying to be White by the latter group. We all speak the language of the streets we live on. Black children living in White neighborhoods often sound White to their Black peers from across town, and may be teased because of it. This can be a very painful experience, particularly when the young person is not fully accepted as part of the White peer group either.

One young Black woman from a predominantly White community described exactly this situation in an interview. In a school with a lot of racial tension, Terri felt that "the worst thing that happened" was the rejection she experienced from the other Black children who were being bussed to her school. Though she wanted to be friends with them, they teased her, calling her an "oreo cookie" and sometimes beating her up. The only close Black friend Terri had was a biracial girl from her neighborhood.

Racial tensions also affected her relationships with White students. One White friend's parents commented, "I can't believe you're Black. You don't seem like all the Black children. You're nice." Though other parents made similar comments, Terri reported that her White friends didn't start making them until junior high school, when Terri's Blackness became something to be explained. One friend introduced Terri to another White girl by saying, "She's not really Black, she just went to Florida and got a really dark tan." A White sixth-grade "boyfriend" became embarrassed when his friends discovered he had a crush on a Black girl. He stopped telling Terri how pretty she was, and instead called her "nigger" and said, "Your lips are too big. I don't want to see you. I won't be your friend anymore."

Despite supportive parents who expressed concern about her situation, Terri said she was a "very depressed child." Her father would have conversations with her "about being Black and beautiful" and about "the union of people of color that had always existed that I needed to find. And the pride." However, her parents did not have a network of Black friends to help support her.

It was the intervention of a Black junior high school teacher that Terri feels helped her the most. Mrs. Campbell "really exposed me to the good Black community because I was so down on it" by getting Terri involved in singing gospel music and introducing her to other Black students who would accept her. "That's when I started having other Black friends. And I thank her a lot for that."

The significant role that Mrs. Campbell played in helping Terri open up illustrates the constructive potential that informed adults can have in the identity development process. She recognized Terri's need for a same-race peer group and helped her find one. Talking to groups of Black students about the variety of living situations Black people come from and the unique situation facing Black adolescents in White communities helps to expand the definition of what it means to be Black and increases intragroup acceptance at a time when that is quite important.

For children in Terri's situation, it is also helpful for Black parents to provide ongoing opportunities for their children to connect with other Black peers even if that means traveling outside the community they live in. Race-conscious parents often do this by attending a Black church or maintaining ties to Black social organizations such as Jack and Jill. Parents who make this effort often find that their children become bicultural, able to move comfortably between Black and White communities, and able to sit at the Black table when they are ready.

Implied in this discussion is the assumption that connecting with one's Black peers in the process of identity development is important and should be encouraged. For young Black people living in predominantly Black communities, such connections occur spontaneously with neighbors and classmates and usually do not require special encouragement. However, for young people in predominantly White communities they may only occur with active parental intervention. One might wonder if this social connection is really necessary. If a young person has found a niche among a circle of White friends, is it really necessary to establish a Black peer group as a reference point? Eventually it is.

As one's awareness of the daily challenges of living in a racist society increase, it is immensely helpful to be able to share one's experiences with others who have lived it. Even when White friends are willing and able to listen and bear witness to one's struggles, they cannot really share the experience. One young woman came to this realization in her senior year of high school:

> [The isolation] never really bothered me until about senior year when I was the only one in the class. . . . That little burden, that constant burden of you always having to strive to do your best and show that you can do just as much as everybody else. Your White friends can't understand that, and it's really hard to communicate to them. Only someone else of the same racial, same ethnic background would understand something like that.

When one is faced with what Chester Pierce calls the "mundane extreme environmental stress" of racism, in adolescence or in adulthood, the ability to see oneself as part of a larger group from which one can draw support is an important coping strategy.[18] Individuals who do not have such a strategy available to them because they do not experience a shared identity with at least some subset of their racial group are at risk for considerable social isolation.

DISCUSSION QUESTIONS

1. Could the stages of identity development that Tatum describes for African American adolescents apply to gay adolescents? Latino adolescents? Young women?

2. What are the positive and negative consequences of the adolescent choice to "sit at the table" with other African Americans?

3. When you were in high school, did the popular kids, the athletes, or other cliques eat lunch together? How does that compare to what Tatum describes?

NOTES

1. J. Marcia, "Development and validation of ego identity status," *Journal of Personality and Social Psychology* 3 (1966): 551–58.

2. For a review of the research on ethnic identity in adolescents, see J. Phinney, "Ethnic identity in adolescents and adults: Review of research," *Psychological Bulletin* 108, no. 3 (1990): 499–514. See also "Part I: Identity development" in B. J. R. Leadbeater and N. Way (Eds.), *Urban girls: Resisting stereotypes, creating identities* (New York: New York University Press, 1996).

3. W. E. Cross, Jr., *Shades of Black: Diversity in African-American identity* (Philadelphia: Temple University Press, 1991).

4. For an expanded discussion of "race-conscious" parenting, see B. D. Tatum, *Assimilation blues*, ch. 6.

5. J. S. Phinney and S. Tarver, "Ethnic identity search and commitment in Black and White eighth graders," *Journal of Early Adolescence* 8, no. 3 (1988): 265–77.

6. See B. D. Tatum, "African-American identity, academic achievement, and missing history," *Social Education* 56, no. 6 (1992): 331–34; B. D. Tatum, "Racial identity and relational theory: The case of Black women in White communities," in *Work in progress, no. 63* (Wellesley, MA: Stone Center Working Papers, 1992); B. D. Tatum, "Out there stranded? Black youth in White communities,"

pp. 214–33 in H. McAdoo (Ed.), *Black families,* 3d ed. (Thousand Oaks, CA: Sage, 1996).

7. For an in-depth discussion of the negative effects of tracking in schools, see J. Oakes, *Keeping track: How schools structure inequality* (New Haven: Yale University Press, 1985).

8. For further discussion of the social dynamics for Black youth in White communities, see Tatum, "Out there stranded?"

9. Leadbeater and Way, *Urban girls,* p. 5.

10. A. Haley and Malcolm X, *The autobiography of Malcolm X* (New York: Grove Press, 1965), p. 36.

11. S. Fordham and J. Ogbu, "Black students' school success: Coping with the burden of 'acting White,'" *Urban Review* 18 (1986): 176–206.

12. Ibid., p. 181.

13. For an expanded discussion of the "trying to be White" phenomenon, see Fordham and Ogbu, "Black students' school success," and S. Fordham, "Racelessness as a factor in Black students' school success: Pragmatic strategy or Pyrrhic victory?" *Harvard Educational Review* 58, no. 1 (1988): 54–84.

14. Fordham, "Racelessness as a factor in Black students' school success." See also S. Fordham, *Blacked out: Dilemmas of race, identity, and success at Capital High* (Chicago: University of Chicago Press, 1996).

15. For further discussion of this point, see R. Zweigenhaft and G. W. Domhoff, *Blacks in the White establishment? A study of race and class in America* (New Haven: Yale University Press, 1991), p. 155.

16. Ibid.

17. Ibid., p. 156.

18. C. Pierce, "Mundane extreme environment and its effects on learning," in S. G. Brainard (Ed.), *Learning disabilities: Issues and recommendations for research* (Washington, DC: National Institute of Education, 1975).

READING 26

Middle Eastern Lives in America

Amir Marvasti

Karyn D. McKinney

. . . Receiving and wanting attention from others is a natural part of human existence. We interact

Amir Marvasti is a professor of criminal justice and sociology at Penn State, Altoona. Karyn D. McKinney is a professor of sociology at Penn State, Altoona.

with other people and would like to be noticed by them. We especially want to be recognized for our achievements (e.g., when we excel in academics or sports). It is not, however, natural to be the focus of others' scorn or suspicion, especially when you have not done anything to evoke the negative attention. For example, it is not natural to be repeatedly subjected to so-called random searches at airports under the eyes of menacing men with hands on their guns simply because of one's appearance, as the first author, Amir, has. That kind of attention is neither desired nor deserved.

Sadly, this is an all too common experience for Middle Eastern Americans. Frequently, they find themselves in social encounters in which they are asked to essentially explain themselves, or to produce an account of their identity. We borrow the term "account" from Stanford Lyman and Marvin Scott to refer to encounters in which a person is called to "explain unanticipated or untoward behavior—whether that behavior is his or her own or that of others, and whether the approximate cause of the statement arises from the actor himself or someone else."[1] Thus accounts are given when an unusual situation or something or someone out of the ordinary is presented. . . .

In many ways, the case of Middle Eastern Americans is similar to that of Japanese Americans in the first half of the twentieth century. Turmoil in the Middle East and acts of terrorism committed in the United States by Middle Easterners have created an identity crisis for those who were either born or have ancestry from that part of the world. The issue of accountability has become an everyday reality for Middle Eastern people in light of official policies that systematically demand that they explain their every action. . . .

For the purpose of data analysis, our interviews and Amir's personal experiences were coded broadly into styles of accounting, or ways in which the respondents and Amir accounted for being Middle Eastern when either implicitly or explicitly required to do so. This approach is similar to Joe Feagin and Karyn McKinney's "resistance strategies" in their analysis of how blacks cope with racist incidents or racist situations.[2] Feagin and McKinney found that African Americans have learned a repertoire of coping mechanisms, both through personal experience and through collective memory.[3] Despite the fact that many white Americans believe that people of color react quickly or always with anger to discrimination, Feagin and McKinney's research showed that African Americans choose carefully from this complex set of responses each time they face a discriminatory incident. The repertoire includes two main types of responses: attitudinal coping mechanisms and action-oriented resistance strategies.[4] Attitudinal coping mechanisms reported by the African American respondents included being always prepared for discrimination, avoiding internalization of the discrimination or of feelings of anger and bitterness, knowing oneself, and using spirituality and mental withdrawal. The respondents also discussed more active resistance strategies. Some of these included verbal confrontation, educating whites, protesting through formal channels, using humor, and physical withdrawal.[5]

Several of these resistance strategies described by Feagin and McKinney are similar to the accounting practices of our Middle Eastern American respondents. In the following sections, excerpts from our interviews are presented in the form of encounter stories from the respondents' and Amir's everyday experiences. Several styles of accounting emerge from the analysis: humorous accounting, educational accounting, confrontational accounting, and passing.

HUMOROUS ACCOUNTING

When faced with questions about their ethnic identity, sometimes respondents use humor to present themselves. Consider, for example, the following cases that involve accounting for Middle Eastern–sounding names. A contractor named Ali[6] explains how he uses humor when questions about his name are raised:

Amir: Do you get any reactions about your name? Like people asking you what kind of name is that?

Ali: Sometimes they do; sometimes they don't. Sometimes, if they haven't met me or if they are sending me correspondence, they think it's a lady's name and a lot of correspondence comes in Ms. Ali. They think I'm either Alison or something like that. Nowadays, when my name comes up [in face-to-face contacts with clients], I use my sense of humor. For example, when they can't spell my name or ask questions about it, I say, "I'm the brother of Muhammad Ali, the boxer."

Another respondent, whose first name "Ladan" (the name of a flower in Persian) brings up unwelcome and troubling associations with the notorious terrorist Osama bin Laden, tells this story about how she used humor with an inquisitive customer:

Amir: With the name Ladan, do you run into any problems?

Ladan: Where I work [at a department store] we all wear nametags, with the name Ladan very clearly spelled out L A D A N. And this old couple, they approached me and I was very friendly with them—I usually chitchat with my customers. And he started asking me all these questions like, "You're so pretty, where're you from?" [I respond,] "I'm from Iran." [He says.] "What?" [I repeat,] "I'm from Iran." So he asks, "What's your name?" And I say, "Ladan." So he bent down to read my nametag and he just looked at me with a funny face and asked, "Are you related to Bin Laden?"

Amir: Was he joking?

Ladan: No, he was not. But I did joke back to him and I said, "Yes, he's my cousin and actually he's coming over for dinner tonight." [She chuckles.]

Amir: So, when this sort of thing happens, you use humor to deal with it?

Ladan: Yeah, I do, because otherwise, if I don't turn it into a joke or a laughing mood, I get upset. I get really, really offended.

Amir: So what was this guy's reaction? Did he laugh with you?

Ladan: When this guy realized my name is Ladan and I'm from Iran, he changed his attitude. He became reserved and he even went one step backward. When I noticed he was uncomfortable,

I completed the transaction with his wife and let them leave as soon as they wanted.

Note that in this case her use of humor does not necessarily result in the proverbial "happy ending," or any kind of clearly discernible resolution. The customer turned away and ended the interaction. Clearly, an account was called for and one was given in a way that allowed Ladan to highlight the ludicrousness of the account-taker's assumptions and his right to solicit an account.

The following is the story of how Amir accounted for his name using humor. This encounter took place at a voting precinct in a small town in Pennsylvania on Election Day, November 14, 2002. He was there to vote in the midterm elections. The encounter begins with the examination of his photo identification.

> *The Election Supervisor:* Okay . . . this is a hard one! [squinting at my driver's license] You're ready? [alerting her coworker] It says "AMAR." . . . It's "A" . . . *I wait, silent and motionless, as the three old women probe my ID. I fear that any sudden movement might send people running out of the building screaming for help. "Say something!" I scream in my head. The words finally roll out of my mouth:*
> *Amir:* You know, my dad gave me a long name, hoping that it would guarantee my success in life. [They laugh.]
> *Election Supervisor:* Well, you must be a doctor because you sure sign your name like one.
> *Amir:* [I can't resist] Actually, I am a doctor. . . . So maybe my dad had the right idea after all.

Here humor is a method of introduction. It was not clear to Amir what the election supervisors thought about him, but he did sense that there were unanswered questions, an account had to be given for who he was. Note that the immediate substance of Amir's identity was not in question—they had his photo identification in front of them and most likely could tell from his swarthy appearance that he was not a native Pennsylvanian. Humorous accounting allowed Amir to communicate something more important about himself than simply his name, namely, that he is from a "normal" family that aspires to the universal notion of "success in life"; and that he is aware that there are concerns about his identity and is capable of responding to them in a mutually sensible way. In humorous accounting the substance of the account is incidental, as it is deliberately trivialized. Middle Eastern Americans use this way of accounting as a way of acknowledging the need to explain themselves while at the same time subtly mocking the necessity of the encounter.

EDUCATIONAL ACCOUNTING

Sometimes accounting takes on a deliberate pedagogical form. In such cases Middle Eastern Americans assume the role of educators, informing and instructing their fellow citizens about relevant topics. For example, in response to suspicions and antagonism from his neighbors, a Pakistani Muslim, Hassan, did a sort of door-to-door educational accounting:

> After September 11, I walked the street the whole week and talked to every single one of my neighbors for at least 3 hours. And one of my neighbors—his brother was in Tower Two and he got out, and his mother was there and she was *furious* with Muslims and me. And we were there for three hours, my wife, my kids, her [the neighbor], her son and her other son that came out of the World Trade Center—he had come down by the time the buildings came down. And I was like, "Look, that's not Islam. That's not who Muslims are. Ask your son, what type of person am I? What type of person is my wife? Do I oppress my wife? Do I beat my wife? Have you ever heard me say anything extreme before?". . . They all know I don't drink, they all know that I pray five times a day, they all know I fast during the month of Ramadan. At the end of Ramadan, we have a big party and invite everyone over to help celebrate the end of fast. This year, they'll all probably fast one day with me so they can feel what it's like.

Hassan's approach is proactive, addressing potential questions before they are explicitly opened for accounting. . . . [He] tries to transform the relationship between him, as an account-giver, and the account-takers who suspect him of being an "evildoer."

Middle Eastern Americans have to be selective about which inquiries are worthy of an educational account. For example, an Iranian respondent, Mitra, speaks of how she filters the inquiries about her culture and identity before answering them:

> If they ask about the government or the senate over there [Iran]. I don't know anything about it. I know who the president is, but they ask me about the senate or the name of the senator over there, I don't know. Since I don't know I'm not going to get involved. I'll say I don't know or I'm not interested. If they say, "Oh, you are from *that* country!" or "You are from the Middle East and you are a terrorist," those kinds of comments I'm not going to get into. I'll just say, "*No,* I'm not." But if they ask me about the culture I'll tell them, "Alright," and inform them about it—as much as I know.

Mitra, while inclined to assume the role of an educator, is not willing or prepared to respond to every question. Part of her educational accounting strategy involves evaluating the degree of her expertise on the subject and the tone of the questions. As she says, if the account-taker begins with accusations, such as "you are a terrorist," the only reasonable reply might be to deny the accusation and end the interaction.

Educational accounting is a common strategy for Middle Eastern Muslim women who wear the hijab.[7] Many of them are approached by strangers who ask questions like: "Isn't it hot under there?" "Does that come in many colors?" or simply "Why do you wear that?" or "Are you going to make *them* [referring to the ten- and twelve-year-old girls who were standing in a grocery store line with their mother] wear it too?" Our respondents reported that whenever time and circumstances allowed, they provide detailed accounts based on their religious teachings. Some of these answers include: "I wear it because it is my culture," "I wear it so that you won't stare at my body when you are talking to me," or "It's cooler under my scarf than you think." It should be noted that some of these women did report being verbally harassed or physically attacked (one was pelted with spitballs when she was in high school, another reported that her friend's scarf was pulled off by a teenage boy at a grocery store, and another was repeatedly yelled at "Go home!" by people in passing cars as she walked to her office on campus). However, such overt acts of discrimination were fairly isolated. The pattern for these women was that of perfect strangers literally stopping them on the street and asking questions about the hijab, sometimes so directly as to be rude.

Similarly, as a Middle Eastern sociology professor, Amir is often asked by his students to explain a wide range of topics about the region and Islam, from customs and culture to the mind-set of terrorists. Like Mitra, he evaluates each question before providing an account. For example, a student in his undergraduate criminology seminar began every session with a trivial question about Iran, such as "Do they have trees over there?" At first, Amir provided a detailed educational account whenever asked to do so, even for seemingly inane items. Given the limited time he had to cover the assigned readings, later in the semester it became necessary for Amir to remind his students that he was not paid to educate them about the Middle East; the topic of the course was crime, specifically, the criminogenic aspects of American culture. For those interested in the topic, Amir recommended a trip to the library for references on the Middle East and Iran. In this case, the educational accounting became unfeasible simply because it was consuming too much time and diverting attention from the subject matter at hand.

Indeed, a recurring problem with being Middle Eastern in a professional context is that the process of accounting for oneself (be it educational, humorous, or otherwise) could hinder one's job performance. With rare exceptions, when professional duties and the accounting demands coincide . . . the work of answering for one's ethnic background and religion could become a considerable chore. Another problem with becoming a "cultural ambassador" is that it tests the limits of the account-giver's knowledge about the topic.[8] The Middle East is a vast and diverse cultural entity representing many people and religions. Unstructured attempts at educating others in everyday encounters inevitably translate into sketchy overgeneralizations. Therefore, while educational accounting may be the most intelligible and productive accounting strategy for one's identity, it is also the most time-consuming and potentially misleading approach.

CONFRONTATIONAL ACCOUNTING

When prompted to provide an account, some Middle Eastern Americans make their anger and frustrations with the encounter explicitly known. We refer to this as confrontational accounting. This strategy involves providing information while at the same time directly challenging the other's right and rationale to request it. For example, consider how a young Iranian woman speaks of her experiences with a coworker:

> She [the coworker] would tell me, "I don't know which country you come from but in America we do it like this or that." I let it go because I was older than her and we had to work together. . . . But one day I pulled her aside and I told her, "For your information where I come from has a much older culture. And what I know, you can't even imagine. So why don't you go get some more education. And if you mention this thing again—'my country is this your country is that'—I'm going to take it to management and they're going to fire you or they're going to fire me." And that was it.

Here the accounting is not intended to repair the interaction or to restore it to a state of equilibrium. On the contrary, the goal is to explicitly challenge the conventional format of the encounter. Instead of aiming for consensus, confrontational accounting foregrounds divergent and conflicting viewpoints as it signals the account-giver's objection to the entire affair.

Confrontational strategies are used especially in times when the accounting, while seemingly a rational concern for everyone involved, crosses the boundary of basic fairness in the eyes of the account-giver. Specifically, Middle Eastern Americans who are subjected to profiling may become confrontational in response to the practice. For example, when Amir learned that unlike himself, his white colleagues were not asked to show ID cards upon entering the campus gym, he felt justified in becoming confrontational. In one instance, while pulling out his ID card from his wallet, he asked the woman at the front counter why his white faculty friend, who had just walked in ahead of him, was not asked to present an ID. She explained that she had not noticed the other person entering or she would have asked that person to do the same.

This encounter highlights the risky nature of confrontational accounting for both parties involved in the interaction. At its core, this strategy counters an account request with another: They ask for his ID and Amir asks why he should be the only one subjected to this rule. In turn, the other side presents their account and so on. What follows is a chain of accounts and counteraccounts possibly escalating into a formal dispute. Though it is possible that in some cases, when confronted, the account-takers simply back down and cease their efforts, it is just as likely that they intensify their demands, especially when they are backed by policies or other public mandates.

Since September 11, when flying, Amir has been very conscious of this fact. While Amir is certain that he has been singled out for security checks, he fears that objecting and confronting these practices would lead to additional hardships (i.e., a direct confrontation with law enforcement agents in which they have the greater authority and likelihood to win). Even after boarding the plane, he is often questioned by those seated next to him. Their inquires typically begin with the ordinary (i.e., What is your name?) and proceed to the very personal and official matters (i.e., Are you a U.S. citizen? Do you have a green card?). In these encounters, Amir feels that to refuse to answer or to confront the other's right to ask about personal and private details of his life will lead to other more serious accounting demands.

So for Middle Eastern Americans confrontational accounting is a risky approach that could, on the one hand, rid them of a potentially humiliating process, or, on the other hand, generate additional requests and demands. Of course, confrontational accounting, when used by large numbers, can become a type of mass rebellion, as with African Americans and the passive resistance component of the Civil Rights Movement of the 1960s.

PASSING OR AVOIDING ACCOUNTS

Sometimes, the best accounting strategy is to put oneself in a position not to have to give an account at all.[9] One way of conceptualizing such strategies is to think of them as attempts at "passing."[10] We view passing as a strategy for eliminating the need for accounting for one's identity. For many Middle Eastern Americans, passing is accomplished by manipulating their appearance. The stereotypical image of a Middle Eastern person roughly translates into someone with dark hair, large facial features, swarthy skin, non-European foreign accent, and beards in the case of men and veils and scarves in the case of women. Faced with these stereotypes, some respondents consciously altered their looks to avoid anything that might associate them with being Middle Eastern. Ironically the ultimate dubious achievement in this game of passing is hearing something like the following: "I know you are from Iran, but you don't *really* look or sound Middle Eastern. . . . You could be Hispanic for all I know."

In fact, some Middle Eastern Americans try to pass by trading their own ethnic identity with a less controversial one. The simplest way to do this is to move to an ethnically diverse region. Some of the respondents from South Florida stated that one reason they don't experience negative episodes of ethnic accounting is because they are thought to be Hispanic. For example, an Iranian woman was asked what kind of Spanish she was speaking when she was at a shopping mall having a conversation in Farsi with her teenage daughter. Another Iranian

man tried to pass as Italian by placing an Italian flag vanity license plate on his car. As a general rule, displaying Western or patriotic symbols (e.g., an American flag) at work, in front of one's house, or on one's car are ways of avoiding ethnic accounting for Middle Eastern Americans. After September 11, Amir's neighbors gave him an American flag to place outside his apartment for his own safety. In a sense, the symbols of patriotism become accounting statements in their own right; they become declarations of loyalty to "the American culture."

Another strategy for passing is to give an ambiguous account in response to ethnic identity questions. For example, an Egyptian man in response to questions about his country of origin states that he is Coptic (the designation of people from pre-Islamic Egypt). He noted that in many cases the account-takers find it too embarrassing to ask follow-up questions and therefore pretend to know what "Coptic" means and drop the subject altogether. Iranians create this kind of ambiguity by stating that they are Persians (the designation of ancient Iranians).

Accounts are also circumvented by stating the name of the city of one's ancestral origin rather than one's country of birth. Amir once told a college classmate that he was from Tehran. To his astonishment, his classmate asked, "Is that near Paris?" Changing one's name is another way to pass. Some respondents change their Muslim names (e.g., Hossein) to typical American names (e.g., Michael). When asked why he changed his name, one person explained that he was tired of people slamming down the phone when he made inquiries about jobs. Some change from widely known ethnic-sounding names to lesser-known ones as in the change from Hossein to Sina. Finally, attention to clothes and grooming are equally important considerations for those who want to pass. For example, wearing jeans and having a clean shave draw less attention and lead to fewer occasions to have to account for oneself.

Passing strategies for Middle Eastern Americans are not without complications. To start with, for some, passing is tantamount to "selling out" (i.e., giving up one's native culture in favor of another).

More important, for Middle Eastern Americans, passing has been construed by the media as an extension of an evil terrorist plot. After September 11, numerous media reports referred to how the hijackers were specifically instructed to wear jeans and shave their faces. Therefore, rather than being viewed as a sign of cultural assimilation, Middle Eastern Americans' conspicuous attempts at passing are sometimes considered part of a diabolical plan to deceive and destroy Americans.

Finally, especially where passing for Hispanic is concerned, Middle Eastern Americans face direct opposition and disavowals from some members of the Hispanic community. On the one hand, according to some of our respondents in South Florida, Middle Eastern Americans have been "outed" by Hispanics who point them out in public and announce to everyone that they are really Middle Eastern and not to be confused with Hispanics. On the other hand, Hispanics are self-consciously changing their self-presentation as to not be mistaken for Middle Eastern. For example, a Mexican man was warned by his wife not to wear a certain hat for fear that it made him look "Middle Eastern."

NOT A KNEE-JERK REACTION

Our respondents did not go off half-cocked, as it were. In dealing with the situations they faced, they tried to select the most reasonable reaction. It is important to note that these respondents are not passive. Their strategies are about fighting back, about speaking in a way that preserves their dignity in the face of intimidation, scrutiny, and insults. . . .

This is not a mere exercise in social roles, but particularly in the context of the War on Terror, this relationship has very practical consequences for Middle Eastern Americans. Their lives have to be transparent. They have to be mindful of the fact that

their attempts to protect their privacy could be misread as a clandestine plan. Furthermore, legislation, such as the PATRIOT Act, can reinforce the lower status of this minority group in relation to the white majority. In essence, the roles are becoming more institutionalized, slowly expanding beyond informal encounters and entering the realm of official policy.

DISCUSSION QUESTIONS

1. Why do some Americans have to account for identity?
2. What are some of the potential problems of passing?
3. Is humorous accounting an effective response to questions of identity?

NOTES

1. Stanford Lyman and Marvin Scott, *A Sociology of the Absurd* (Dix Hills, N.Y.: General Hall, 1989), p. 112.
2. Joe Feagin and Karyn McKinney, *The Many Costs of Racism* (Lanham, Md.: Rowman & Littlefield, 2003): 147–79.
3. Feagin and McKinney, *The Many Costs of Racism*, p. 119.
4. Feagin and McKinney, *The Many Costs of Racism*, p. 123.
5. Feagin and McKinney, *The Many Costs of Racism*, pp. 124–67.
6. Most names have been fictionalized to protect the identity of respondents. In cases where it is necessary to use an actual first name, every effort is made to disguise other personal identifying information about a respondent.
7. Islamic word for modesty in dress that applies to both men and women. In the case of many Muslim women living in the United States, this means wearing a scarf that covers the hair and the neck, as well as wearing loose-fitting garments so that the outlines of the body are not exaggerated.
8. Bruce Jacobs, *Race Manners: Navigating the Minefield between Black and White Americans* (New York: Arcade Publishing, 1999), pp. 144–48.
9. See Lyman and Scott, *A Sociology of the Absurd*, pp. 126–27.
10. Erving Goffman, *Stigma: Notes on the Management of Spoiled Identity* (Englewood Cliffs, N.J.: Prentice Hall, 1963).

READING 27

Everybody's Ethnic Enigma

Jelita McLeod

The forty-something black man I was sharing an elevator with looked at me for a while before he asked the question I had been expecting. He wanted to know my ethnicity.

"I'm mixed," I told him. "Half-Caucasian, half-Asian."

"Oh," he said, disappointed. "I thought you were one of us."

I knew what the question would be because people have been asking me the same thing as long as I can remember. I've found that curiosity easily overrides courtesy. I am asked in stores, on the bus, on the street, in line at McDonald's, even in public bathrooms. Almost always the inquirers are total strangers, as if not knowing me allows them to abandon social graces they might otherwise feel the need to display. Sometimes they will ask me straight out, but very often they use coded language, as in "What's your background?" Then there's "Where are you from?" which is really a two-part question, to be followed by "Where are you *really* from?"

Why is it that people feel they can approach me for this personal information? Would they ask total strangers their age or marital status? What do they need the information for? Are they census takers? Once, in a truly surreal episode, a casino dealer stopped in the middle of a hand of poker to ask me, as if he couldn't stand to wait a second longer. After I offered my usual answer, he shook his finger in my face and said he wasn't convinced, that I didn't look white enough. He was Asian.

I wonder why, after having been subjected to this treatment for years, I still respond. I can't remember a time when doing so has resulted in a pleasant

encounter or a meaningful conversation. Yet I've never quite found the strength to meet such inquiries with "It's none of your business" or, better yet, silence. What's quite strange is that people often feel the need to comment, as if what I've told them is an opinion they can't quite agree with. Comedian Margaret Cho tells a story about a TV producer who asked her to act "a little more Chinese," to which she replied, "But I'm Korean." "Whatever," the producer said. I had a similar experience with a man in a bookstore, who crept out from behind a shelf of cookbooks to ask me where I was from. Before I had a chance to say anything, he guessed: "Japan?" I could have said Oregon, where my father is from, but I knew he wouldn't go for that, so I said, "Indonesia." "Ah," he said. "Close." It's not close. Not really. Not unless you consider London close to Djibouti. The distances are similar.

In the game of "Name that Ethnicity," I am the trick question. I have been mistaken for almost every Asian nationality, but also as Hispanic, Native American, Arab and, of course, African American. There's something in being a chameleon. It's human nature to look for unifying bonds. When people think that they have something in common with you, particularly something so personal as identity, they feel they know you and they imagine that you have an innate understanding of them, too. They will speak to you in a certain unguarded way. The idea that any person can be truly "colorblind" is a fallacy. As long as the human eye can detect differences in skin tone, eye shape, hair texture, these differences will play a role in how we interact with one another. Because of my ambiguous appearance, I have experienced from people the kind of familiarity they would normally reserve for one of their "own."

The unfortunate consequence of this ambiguity is the misunderstanding I frequently encounter from those who haven't gotten the full story. The Mexican immigration official who looks disgusted when I can't understand Spanish, as I surely should. The kindly Vietnamese waiter who helps me "remember" how to pronounce the names of dishes. This puts me in the slightly ridiculous position of being apologetic for not being what people expect me to be, however unreasonable.

Jelita McLeod is a writer-editor at Prince George's Community College in Largo, Maryland. Her work has appeared in *The Washington Post*, *The Sun*, and *International Educator*. She has also provided commentary for National Public Radio.

PERSONAL ACCOUNT

My Strategies

I speak differently around different people. When I am with white people I use my vocabulary, sharp wit, and smooth, concise statements. I try to keep my grammar in line and use acceptable slang and swearing. When I am in a formal setting, court, school, work, etc., I do the above, but I also change my inflection. I also use no slang or swearing. My white voice has gotten me loans, jobs, and makes my life easier. On the flip side when I am around black people, my speech is totally different. Black people, mostly, talk in a manner that is all inclusive. They don't want to talk down to anyone, or over anyone's head. Using a large vocabulary for no reason is considered rude and frowned upon. You are considered a snob. Black people worry about everyone understanding, seeing if you are on the level, and creating a relaxed environment. We are probably tired of talking in a fake manner all day, so the manner we choose has to be more relaxed.

White people size you up by the way you talk plus other things. If I were to use slang or talk in the manner I do around black people, I would be considered stupid and faking it. Yet when I talk with a high vocabulary and diction that is taken as the way I talk and assumed to be natural. Since it is the most comfortable for whites, and matches their own manner of speaking, they don't contest its authenticity. So when speaking I have to remember who I am talking to; context is, again, everything. I slip around my close friends often though, and they stare at me. "What it do Liz?" This will get no response beyond, ". . . what?" This isn't to say anything about all white people; these are general statements

from my life. I know plenty of white people who have learned or always knew how to talk in the manner that black people do, but they are the exceptions. The same goes for black people. It stands to reason that if we can talk in a different manner, that white people can also learn.

There are other things I have to remember when moving between groups. Eye contact is a big one, because most black people don't like it, yet white people think you are distracted if you don't use it. I also don't like eye contact, but have learned to use it as needed. Hand shakes are another issue, which factors in age, sex, race, etc. I won't go into the differences because it would be another paper. Needless to say, a lot of effort goes in to small tasks. I have to keep my ghetto pass and still not be thought silly and stupid.

Usually when someone figures out I am biracial, I'll have to pass some stupid test. It is usually a series of questions displaying their limited understanding. Here is a transcript:

Person A: I don't mean to be racist, but. . . . (This means that they are going to say something very racist, always.)
Eric: Sigh, I am biracial. (To try and stop them before they offend me.)
Person A: No you're not, really?
Eric: Father is a large black man.
Person A: NO WAY, laughter. You look so white.
Eric: Yep.

When I think back to the man in the elevator, I feel disappointed, too. The way he said "I thought you were one of us" made me feel as if we might have bonded but now couldn't, as if I'd been refused entry into a club because I didn't have the right password. My immediate reaction was that I was missing out on something. But I see the artificiality of this classification mentality. If the opportunity for bonding existed before he knew my ethnic makeup, wasn't it still there after he found out? After all, I was still the same person.

When my parents were married, my grandfather was against the union. His objection was that the children of mixed marriages had no foothold in any one community but instead were doomed to a lifetime of identity crises and disorientation.

If my grandfather were still alive, I'd tell him that the crisis comes not from within, but from without.

I know who I am. It's everyone else that's having trouble.

DISCUSSION QUESTIONS

1. Does an ambiguous appearance lead to stereotypic assumptions?
2. If you don't identify with the questioner, what are the likely consequences?

PERSONAL ACCOUNT *(Continued)*

Person A: Is he like all the way black, or like really light?

Eric: Nope, *as black as you think black is.*

Person A: (Now apologizes for their racist comment that started this.) Yeah, but aren't you like still white, you look white? Do you have siblings? Which parent did you live with?

Eric: Happy to meet such a race expert. Yes, my older brother, Gene, and I have the same parents and he looks black. I lived with my mother, but saw my father whenever I wished.

Person A: But you look white, phhhh, look at you, you're white.

Eric: Thank you I needed someone to tell me my race, thus saving all that time I would have spent already knowing.

Person A: Don't get mad or anything. I'm just saying, you look white, you act white.

Eric: *How is it that black people act?*

This could continue, but by now I usually end it by going to do something, or they start to get uncomfortable and change the subject. Things in italics are usually omitted if I have to work with the person at a job or in a class. No reason to be hostile if I am going to see them often. When I was very young I had to get used to people openly laughing at me. I still don't know why they laugh, but they always do. As if I said my father was a polar bear, thus making me half polar bear. That example is the only way I can try to make sense of it. I am so used to the tests that I can usually answer their questions before they ask.

Often the test is to prove you are black. My name is easy because Eric Michael Jackson is easy to pass as a black name. Most people will buy this right away. Then everything they knew about me gets converted to stigma mode, unless they are black, then it gets un-stigmatized. I also have to use stereotypes to prove who I am at times. I feel this is wrong, but it is better than punching someone in the face. Thus, all my actions for a limited time become black. I like chicken. This wasn't an issue when I was white, now it is. I can't say I know anyone, other than people who don't eat meat, who don't love chicken.

I enjoy seeing the looping and re-reading upon my newly discovered blackness. Before when I had an opinion on matters regarding race I was thought a tad extreme, but they could see my point. Now they either don't want to talk about it because any discussion of race outside ones own group is no longer pc, or because they feel I'll get all black on them. As if I'll stand up and shout, "Free Mumia and H. Rap Brown!" then curse them for years of oppression. In reality they just disregard what I say because I am "biased." They are not biased because being white apparently gives you this supreme understanding of how things work. I remind them I am also white, something they like to remind me of as well, and then I get a "not re-ally." So I am only white when it suits them, and then I am black the rest of the time. Where I am from, I was white enough to go in your home, but I won't be dating your daughter. I have often had people boast I was the first black man in their home. This usually makes me want to leave right away. Looking back on it, my entire life has been a sociological study and I just never knew it. I knew what ethnocentrism was when I was ten.

P. S. teachers hate it when you call them that, like twenty times a day.

Eric Jackson

READING 28

Adopted in China, Seeking Identity in America

Lynette Clemetson

Molly Feazel desperately wants to quit the Chinese dance group that her mother enrolled her in at

Lynette Clemetson is a reporter for *The New York Times.*

age 5, because it sets her apart from friends in her Virginia suburb. Her mother, though, insists that Molly, now 15, will one day appreciate the connection to her culture.

Qiu Meng Fogarty, 13, prefers her Chinese name (pronounced cho mung) to Cecilia, her English name. She volunteers in workshops for children in New York adopted from China "so that they know it can all work out fine," she said.

Since 1991, when China loosened its adoption laws to address a growing number of children abandoned because of a national one-child policy, American families have adopted more than 55,000 Chinese children, almost all girls. Most of the children are younger than 10, and an organized subculture has developed around them, complete with play groups, tours of China and online support groups.

Molly and Qiu Meng represent the leading edge of this coming-of-age population, adopted just after the laws changed and long before such placements became popular, even fashionable.

Molly was among 61 Chinese children adopted by Americans in 1991, and Qiu Meng was one of 206 adopted the next year, when the law was fully put into effect. Last year, more than 7,900 children were adopted from China.

As the oldest of the adopted children move through their teenage years, they are beginning—independently and with a mix of enthusiasm and trepidation—to explore their identities. Their experiences offer hints at journeys yet to come for thousands of Chinese children who are now becoming part of American families each year.

Those experiences are influenced by factors like the level of diversity in their neighborhoods and schools, and how their parents expose them to their heritage.

"We're unique," Qiu Meng said.

A view that Molly does not share. "I don't see myself as different at all," said Molly, whose friends, her mother said, all seem to be "tall, thin and blond."

The different outlooks are normal say experts on transracial adoption.

Most Americans who bring Chinese children to the United States are white and in the upper middle class.

Jane Brown, a social worker and adoptive parent who conducts workshops for adopted children and their families, says the families should directly confront issues of loss and rejection, which the children often face when they begin to understand the social and gender politics that caused their families in China to abandon them.

Ms. Brown also recommends that transracial adoptive families address American attitudes on race early, consistently and head on.

"Sometimes parents want to celebrate, even exoticize, their child's culture, without really dealing with race," said Ms. Brown, 52, who is white and who has adopted children from Korea and China.

"It is one thing to dress children up in cute Chinese dresses, but the children need real contact with Asian-Americans, not just waiters in restaurants on Chinese New Year. And they need real validation about the racial issues they experience."

The growing population is drawing the attention of researchers. The Evan B. Donaldson Adoption Institute, a research group based in New York, is surveying adopted children from Asia who are now adults to try to find ways to help the younger children form healthy identities.

Nancy Kim Parsons, a filmmaker who was adopted from Korea, is making a documentary comparing the experiences of adults who had been adopted a generation ago from Korea with the young children adopted from China.

South Korea was the first country from which Americans adopted in significant numbers, and it is still among the leaders in international adoptions, along with Russia, Guatemala, Ukraine, Kazakhstan, India and Ethiopia. The experiences of those adopted from Korea have provided useful lessons for families adopting from China.

Hollee McGinnis, 34, the policy director at the Donaldson institute, was adopted from South Korea by white parents and was raised in Westchester County. Ten years ago, she started an adult support group, called Also Known As, which now also mentors children adopted from China.

"College was when I really began trying to understand what other people saw in my face," she said. "Before then I didn't really understand what it meant to be Asian."

It is a process McKenzie Forbes, 17, who was adopted from China and raised in towns in Virginia and West Virginia where there are few other Asians, is just starting to absorb. For her, college holds the promise of something new.

"I am feeling ready to break out a little bit," McKenzie said. "When I am around other Asians, I feel a connection that I don't feel around other people. I can't explain it exactly. But I think it will be fun to meet other people and hear their stories."

McKenzie, who was accepted by Dickinson College in Pennsylvania, applied only to universities with Asian student groups. Confident and pensive, she likes classical music and punk rock. She is wild about Japanese anime, a hobby she hopes to turn into a career, and to travel to Japan. Exploring China, she said, "is what everyone would expect."

Adopted at 2, McKenzie is among the oldest of the current wave of children adopted from China. Like many Americans adopting from overseas at the time, McKenzie's family turned to China because of a movement started in 1972 by the National Association of Black Social Workers discouraging the placement of African-American children with white adoptive families.

"With an African-American child we had no guarantee that the mother or a social worker wouldn't come and take the child away," McKenzie's mother, Maree Forbes, said. "With the children from China, we felt safe that there wouldn't be anyone to come back to get them."

McKenzie has a younger sister, Meredyth, 15, also adopted from China, and brothers Robert and John, 11-year-old twins, adopted from Vietnam. The family left Culpeper, Va., when McKenzie was 5, after children at school ostracized her because she is Chinese.

More frequent than outright racism though, McKenzie and Meredyth said, are offenses of ignorance. They were called out of class at their current school, for example, because a counselor wanted them to take an English language test for immigrant students. "We probably spoke better English than the instructor," Meredyth said.

The experience has been different for Qiu Meng Fogarty. As she recovered from a fit of giggles about something having to do with a boy, Qiu Meng looked at her friends Celena Kopinski and Hope Goodrich, who were also adopted from China, and breathed a cheery sigh.

"It's like we're related," she said, sitting on her bed in her home on Manhattan's Upper West side. "It's nice because we're all on the same page. We don't have to be like, 'Oh, you're adopted?' or 'Oh, yeah, I'm Chinese,' It's just easy."

The three girls have been friends for as long as they can remember. Their parents helped form Families with Children from China, a support group started in 1993 that now has chapters worldwide.

Some teenagers lose interest in the group because many of its activities focus on younger children. But Qiu Meng, a perky wisp of a girl with an infectious laugh, is still enthusiastically involved. She sold "Year of the Dog" T-shirts at a Chinese New Year event in January, and is a mentor at group workshops.

She said she remembers how hard it was to talk about painful things when she was younger and children at school would stretch their eyes upward and tease her. "There aren't a lot of children who can talk openly and easily about things like that," she said. "So it feels good to be able to help them."

Last summer, Qiu Meng, Celena and Hope attended a camp for children adopted from around the world. When it ended, counselors gathered the campers in a circle and connected them with a string. The campers all went home with a section of the string tied to their wrists, as a reminder their shared experience.

When a volleyball coach later told Qiu Meng to cut off the string for a game, she carefully tucked it away, took it home and hung it on her bedroom wall among numerous Chinese prints and paintings.

The teenagers all acknowledge that they are just beginning a long process of self-definition, and even though Molly is still trying to persuade her parents to allow her to quit the Chinese dance class, she admits privately that she benefits from the struggle.

"If my parents didn't push, I know I would just drop it all completely," she said. "And then I wouldn't have anything to fall back on later."

Molly, Qiu Meng and McKenzie said they would not have wanted to grow up any other way, and they all said they would one day like to adopt from China. "It's a good thing to do," Qiu Meng said. "And since I'm Asian, they wouldn't look different."

DISCUSSION QUESTIONS

1. Why is it necessary to form an organization called Families with Children from China?
2. What factors do teenagers take into consideration when they self-identify race, ethnicity, or sexual orientation?

READING 29

Loot or Find: Fact or Frame?

Cheryl I. Harris

Devon W. Carbado

EVIDENCE OF THINGS SEEN

What do these images represent? What facts do they convey? We could say that image A depicts a man who, in the aftermath of Katrina, is wading through high waters with food supplies and a big black plastic bag. We might say that image B depicts a man and woman, both wearing backpacks. They, too, are wading through high waters in the aftermath of Katrina, and the woman appears to be carrying food supplies.

This is not how these images were presented in the press. The captions that appeared with the two photos, both of which ran on Yahoo! news, were quite different. The caption for image A read: "A young man walks through chest-deep flood water after looting a grocery store in New Orleans." The caption for image B read: "Two residents wade through chest-deep waters after finding bread and soda from a local grocery store after Hurricane Katrina came through the area." The caption for image A, then, tells us that a crime has been committed; the caption for image B tells that a fierce, poignant struggle for survival is under way—the subjects have just found food. Image A depicts a young black man; image B shows a white man and woman.

The images and their respective captions almost immediately stirred up significant controversy. People complained that the captions accompanying the images were racially suggestive: black people "loot" and white people "find." *Boston Globe* correspondent Christina Pazzanese wondered, "I am curious how one photographer knew the food was

Cheryl I. Harris is a professor of law at the University of California, Los Angeles. Devon W. Carbado is a professor of law at the University of California, Los Angeles.

AP Photo/Dave Martin

Chris Graythen/Getty Images

looted by one but not the other. Were interviews conducted as they swam by?"[1]

Not everyone agreed, however, that the images and captions reflected a racial problem. As one commentator put it:

It's difficult to draw any substantiated conclusions from these photos' captions. Although they were both carried by many news outlets, they were taken by two different photographers and came from two different services, the Associated Press (AP) and the Getty Images via Agence France-Presse (AFP). Services make different stylistic standards for how they caption photographs, or the dissimilar wordings may have been due to nothing more than the preferences of different photographers and editors, or the difference might be the coincidental result of a desire to avoid repetitive wording (similar photographs from the same news services variously describe the depicted actions as "looting," "raiding," "taking," "finding," and "making off"). The viewer also isn't privy to the contexts in which the photographs were taken—it's possible that in one case the photographer actually saw his subject exiting an unattended grocery store with an armful of goods, while in the other case the photographer came upon his subjects with supplies in hand and could only make assumptions about how they obtained them.[2]

For the most part, this controversy focused on a question of fact. Did the black person really loot the goods he was carrying? Did the white man and white woman really find the food they were carrying? Indeed, the director of media relations at the Associated Press suggested that, as to image A, "he [the photographer] saw the person go into the shop and take the goods. . . . that's why he wrote 'looting' in the article."[3] In other words, the fact of the matter was that the black man in image A was a looter.

The photographer of image B, Chris Graythen, maintained,

> I wrote the caption about the two people who "found" the items. I believed in my opinion, that they did simply find them, and not "looted" them in the definition of the word. The people were swimming in chest deep water, and there were other people in the water, both white and black. I looked for the best picture. There were a million items floating in the water—we were right near a grocery store that had 5+ feet of water in it. It had no doors. The water was moving, and the stuff was floating away. These people were not ducking into a store and busting down windows to get electronics. They picked up bread and Cokes that were floating in the water. They would have floated away anyhow.[4]

To some extent, the credibility of Graythen's explanation is beside the point here. That is, the loot-or-find problem of image A and image B cannot fully be addressed with reference to the individual intent of those who either took the picture or produced the accompanying interpretive text. Indeed, it is entirely plausible that had the photos appeared without any captions, they would have been read the same way.[5] This is because while neither "loot" nor "find" is written on either image, in the context of public disorder, the race of the subjects inscribes those meanings.

THE "COLOR-BLIND" FRAME

Drawing on facts about both Hurricane Katrina and the public's response to it, [we question] whether efforts to change the racial status quo and eliminate inequality should or can rely solely on facts or empiricism. There is a growing sense within the civil rights community that more empirical research is needed to persuade mainstream Americans that racism remains a problem in American society and that the elimination of racial disadvantage is not a do-it-yourself project. The idea seems to be that if only more Americans knew certain "facts" (for example, about the existence of implicit bias) they would be more inclined to support civil rights initiatives (for example, affirmative action). We agree that more empirical research is needed. Facts are important—indeed crucial—since so much of public opinion is grounded in misinformation. We simply do not think that there is a linear progression between raw empiricism and more enlightened public opinion about race and racism. Put another way, we do not believe that facts speak for themselves.

It is precisely the recognition that facts don't speak for themselves that helps to explain why scholars across academic fields and politicians across the political spectrum continue to pay significant attention to the social and cognitive processes that shape how we interpret facts. Of the variety of theories—in sociology, political science, law, anthropology, psychology, and economics—that attempt to explain these processes, most share the idea that we interpret events through frames—interpretational structures that, consciously and unconsciously, shape what we see and how we see it. In the words of one scholar, framing refers to "understanding a story you already know and saying, 'Oh yeah, that one.'"[6] As we process and make sense of an event, we take account of and simultaneously ignore facts that do not fit the frame, and sometimes we supply ones that are missing. Thus, it is sometimes said that "frames trump facts."[7]

The most relevant and dominant frame is color blindness, or the belief that race is *not* a factor in how we make sense of the world. Color blindness is a kind of metaframe that comprises three interwoven racial scripts: (1) because of *Brown v. Board of Education* and the civil rights reforms it inaugurated, racism is by and large a thing of the past; (2) when racism does rear its ugly head, it is the product of misguided and irrational behavior on the part of self-declared racial bigots, who are few and far between; and (3) racial consciousness—whether in the form of affirmative action or Jim Crow–like racism—should be treated with suspicion, if not rejected outright. The gradual ascendancy and eventual racial dominance of color blindness frames the facts of racial inequality (manifested, for example, in disparities in wealth and educational outcomes between blacks and whites) as a function of something other than racism. Because scientists have largely repudiated the notion of biological inferiority, color blindness frames the problem of racial disadvantage in terms of conduct. The problem is not genes but culture, not blood but behavior: were black people to engage in normatively appropriate cultural practices—work hard, attend school, avoid drugs, resist crime—they would transcend their current social status and become part of the truly advantaged. On this view, black disadvantage is both expected and deserved—a kind of natural disaster not produced by racism.

At least initially, Katrina challenged the supremacy of color blindness. The tidal wave of suffering that washed over New Orleans seemed incontrovertible evidence of the salience of race in contemporary U.S. society.[8] The simple fact that the faces of those left to fend for themselves or die were overwhelmingly black raised questions about the explanatory power of color blindness under which race is deemed irrelevant.[9] Racial suffering was everywhere. And black people

were dying—prime time live. One had to close one's eyes, or willfully blind oneself, not to see this racial disaster. Everyone, it seemed, except government officials, was riveted. And there was little disagreement that Katrina exposed shameful fissures in America's social fabric; that the precipitating event was an act of God, not the cultural pathology of the victims; and that the government's response, at least in the initial phases, was woefully inadequate. Seasoned mainstream journalists wept and railed, while ordinary Americans flooded relief organizations with money.

The tragedy of Katrina created a rupture in the racial-progress narrative that had all but erased the suffering of poor black people from the political landscape. In contrast to the pre-Katrina picture, black people were perceived to be innocent victims. Black people were perceived to have a legitimate claim on the nation-state. Black people were perceived to be deserving of government help. Katrina—or the *facts* the public observed about its effects—disrupted our tendency to *frame* black disadvantage in terms of cultural deficiency. But how did that happen? And doesn't this disruption undermine our central point about facts and frames?

Not at all. Frames are not static. Epic events like Katrina push up against and can temporarily displace them. All those people. All that suffering. This can't be America. How could we let this happen? That question—how could we let this happen?—reflected a genuine humanitarian concern for fellow human beings. Moreover, the compelling facts about Katrina raised a number of questions about racial inequality previously suppressed under color blindness. Indeed, as the humanitarian crisis peaked with the retreating floodwaters, a debate over the role of race in the disaster quickly emerged. The unrelenting spectacle of black suffering bodies demanded an explanation. Why were those New Orleans residents who remained trapped during Katrina largely black and poor? Was it, as hip-hop artist Kanye West argued, a case of presidential indifference to, or dislike of, poor black people?[10] Or was it, as Ward Connerly asserted, the predictable consequence of a natural disaster that befell a city that just happened to be predominantly black? Was it, as Linda Chavez claimed, the result of a culture of dependency combined with local bureaucratic incompetence? Was race a factor in de-termining who survived and who did not?[11] Or did class provide a better explanation?[12] Finally, could we ever fully understand Katrina without meaningfully engaging the legacy of slavery?[13] These and other, similar questions were pushed into the foreground by the force of Katrina's devastation.

But the frame of color blindness did not disappear. It manifested itself in the racial divide that emerged with respect to how people answered the foregoing questions. While there is some intraracial diversity of opinion among public figures about the role of race and racism in explaining what happened, there remains a striking racial difference in how the disaster is viewed. According to public opinion polls, whites largely reject the notion that race explains the governmental disregard, while blacks assert that the fact that the victims were black and poor was a significant part of the story.[14] This difference over the difference that race makes reflects competing racial frames. Thus, while the facts of what happened in Katrina's aftermath unsettled the familiar color-blind racial script that poor black people were the authors of their own plight, those facts did not ultimately displace core ideas embedded in the color-blind frame: race is irrelevant and racism largely does not exist. Most whites were able to see black people as victims, but they were unwilling to link their victim status to race or racism. A more acceptable story was that black people in New Orleans suffered only because of bureaucratic inefficiencies in the wake of a natural disaster. Race simply could not be a factor. Katrina then only partially desta-bilized the frame of color blindness. To the extent that our starting point for thinking about race is that it does not matter, other racial frames or scripts more easily fit within the overarching frame. These frames can both explicitly invoke race and, even more powerfully, implicitly play the race card. After the initial uncertainty, what emerged in the wake of Katrina was the frame of "law and order"—a racial script that permeated the debate over the iconic photographs with which we began our essay, and over the post-Katrina relief efforts. The media were both author and reader of events in ways that both challenged and underwrote this racial frame.

A PICTURE IS WORTH A THOUSAND WORDS

Recall Chris Graythen's response to the racial controversy concerning the images with which we began this [reading]. With regard to image B, Graythen asserted that he "looked for the best pic-ture." More specifically, Graythen searched for an image that would best narrate a particular factual story: that people were wading through water to find food. According to Graythen, both whites and blacks were finding food in the chest-high water. Unlike pre-Katrina New Orleans, this space was racially integrated. Graythen searched this racially integrated body of water for a picture that would most successfully convey the idea of people find-ing food (as distinct from people "ducking into a store and busting down windows to get electron-ics"). Graythen's "best picture"—his "Oh yeah, that one"—emerged when he saw the two white people photographed in image B. Their images best fit the caption that Graythen already had in mind, people wading through water to find food. Because people are more likely to associate blacks with looting ("ducking into a store and busting down win-dows to get electronics") than with finding food, Graythen's selection makes sense. Indeed, one can infer from Graythen's decision to photograph white people that it was easier to frame white people as despondent people finding food than it was to frame black people in that way. To put the point slightly differently, there would be some dissonance between the image of black people in those high waters and a caption describing people finding food. This dissonance is not about facts—whether in fact the black people were finding food; the dis-sonance is about frames—the racial association between black people and looting, particularly on the heels of a natural disaster or social upheaval.

Two caveats before moving on. First, nothing above is intended to suggest that Graythen's decision to photograph the two white people was racially conscious—that is, intentionally motivated by race. Frames operate both consciously and unconsciously; his selection of whites to photograph (and his "natu-ral selection" against blacks) converged with existing racial frames about criminality and perpetrators, on the one hand, and law-abidingness and victims, on the other. The two photos were perfect mirror images of each other. But only image B could convey a story of survival against adversity; image A was inconsistent with that script. The presence of a black man with a big plastic bag in the context of a natural disaster is already inscribed with meaning. In that sense, the black man in image A did not require a caption to be framed; nor did the white man and woman in image B. The stereotype of black criminality was activated by image A and the many images like it, which showed the central problem in New Orleans not to be the lack of humanitarian aid, but the lack of law and order.

The second caveat: our analysis should not be read as an argument against empiricism or a claim that facts are irrelevant. We simply mean to say that racial frames shape our perceptions of the facts. This does not mean that we are overdetermined by frames or that we are unable to escape their interpretative strictures. Rather, the point is that dependence on "just the facts" will seldom be enough to dislodge racial frames.[15] Partly this is because racial frames are installed not as the result of empiricism, but in spite of it. Consider color blindness. It is the dominant racial frame for understanding race not because of facts but because of a well-financed political project to entrench and naturalize a color-blind understanding of American race relations.[16] Accordingly, something more than facts is required to undo the racial work color blindness continues to perform; and something more than facts is required to dislodge the normativity of color blindness itself.

FROM RESCUE TO OCCUPATION: SEEING THE INVISIBLE

I'd rather have them here dead than alive. And at least they're not robbing you and you [don't] have to worry about feeding them.[17]

> A resident of St. Gabriel when asked for her reactions to the decision to designate the town as a collective morgue

To the extent that our discussion of the problem of racial frames has largely examined representational issues, one might reasonably ask: What are the material consequences of this problem? And how, if at all, did it injure black New Orleanians in the wake of Hurricane Katrina? The answer relates to two interconnected frames: the frame of law and order and the frame of black criminality. Working together, these frames rendered black New Orleanians dangerous, unprotectable, and unrescuable.

In the immediate aftermath of Katrina, the media pointedly criticized the slow pace at which the federal government was responding to the disaster. But the critical stance was short-lived and quickly gave way to a focus on the breakdown of law and order, a frame that activated a familiar stereotype about black criminality. While initially blacks were seen as victims of Hurricane Katrina and a failed governmental response, this victim status proved to be highly unstable. Implicit in the frame that "this can't be America" is the notion that the neglect in the wake of Katrina was a violation of the duty of care owed to all citizens of the nation. This social contract includes blacks as citizens; and indeed the claim by blacks, "We are American"—a statement vigorously asserted by those contained in the convention center[18]—responded to and relied upon that frame.[19]

As time progressed, the social currency of the image of blacks as citizens of the state to whom a duty of care is owed diminished. It rubbed uneasily against the more familiar racial framing of poor black people as lazy, undeserving, and inherently criminal. Concern over the looting of property gradually took precedence over the humanitarian question of when people might be rescued and taken off of the highways and rooftops. Thus, while armed white men were presumed to be defending their property, black men with guns constituted gangs of violent looters who had to be contained. Under this frame, the surrounding towns and parishes that constituted potential refuge for black New Orleans residents who had no means to evacuate before the storm became no-go areas because of concerns about black criminality.

A particularly stark example of this came during the CNN interview on September 8 between Christiane Amanpour and the resident of St. Gabriel quoted above. The sentiment that dead blacks were better than live ones was enforced not only by local authorities who, like the Gretna police, turned people away at gunpoint, but by the National Guard and other local authorities who purportedly denied the Red Cross permission to enter the city shortly after the storm because of concerns about the safety of the rescuers.[20]

These fears were grounded in what ultimately proved to be grossly exaggerated or completely unsubstantiated media accounts of violence and attacks particularly in the Superdome and the convention center.[21] The tone of these reports were hyperbolic, evoking all of the familiar racial subtexts: FOX News, for example, issued a news report the day before the Superdome was evacuated that "there were many reports of robberies, rapes, carjackings, rioters and murder and that violent gangs are roaming the streets at night, hidden by the cover of darkness." . . . These reports were taken as authoritative by police and other law enforcement officials. Indeed, even the mayor of the city, Ray Nagin, who is black, spoke of "hundreds of armed gang members" killing and raping people inside the Superdome, such that the crowd had descended to an "almost animalistic state."[22]

We are not arguing that there was no violence. There was. But the frames of black criminality and law and order overdetermined how we interpreted both the extent and nature of that violence. For example, consider how the "facts" about rape were interpreted and discussed. . . .

One of the more prominent examples of this official disregard was Charmaine Neville, a member of the family of renowned New Orleans musicians, who was raped by a roving group of men who invaded her community in the Lower Ninth Ward while she and her neighbors struggled unsuccessfully over a series of days to be evacuated and to obtain medical care.[23] Neville's searing account of what happened to her is a clear indictment of the government for its neglect: "What I want people

to understand is that if we hadn't been left down there like animals that they were treating us like, all of those things would not have happened." Neville reported that her efforts to tell law enforcement officers and the National Guard of her assault were ignored. Neville's prominence and her fortuitous encounter with a member of the Catholic archdiocese in New Orleans during an interview at a local news station meant that her assault received media attention. Others did not.

Obviously, we are not excusing the conduct of the rapists or blaming that conduct on the government. Our point is simply that the overall governmental response in the aftermath of Katrina, shaped as it was by the racial frame of law and order, created conditions of possibility for rape and increased the likelihood that those rapes would be unaddressed. The sexual assaults against women—the vast majority of them black—became markers of black disorder, chaos, and the "animalistic" nature of New Orleans residents; but black women themselves could not occupy the position of victims worthy of rescue. Their injuries were only abstractions that were marshaled to make the larger point about the descent of New Orleans into a literal and figurative black hole. Black women's rape was invoked but not addressed. . . .

The government focused its attention on violence directed against property and violence directed against the rescuers—reports of which have proven to be false or grossly embellished. While these acts of violence could fit comfortably within the frame of law and order, violence against black women's bodies could not. Images of black criminality could work concomitantly with and help to instantiate the law-and-order frame that relies on black disorder; images of black women as innocent victims could do neither. The frames of law and order and black criminality influenced both the exaggeration (overreporting) and the marginalization (underreporting) of violent crimes in ways that make clear that facts don't speak for themselves. . . .

Only one shooting was confirmed in the Superdome, when a soldier shot himself during a scuffle with an attacker. Though New Orleans police chief Eddie Compass reported that he and his officers had retrieved more than thirty weapons from criminals who had been shooting at the rescuers, he later modified his statement to say that this had happened to another unit, a SWAT team at the convention center. The director of the SWAT team, however, reported that his unit had heard gunshots only one time and that his team had recovered no weapons despite aggressive searches.

In retrospect, it is clear that the media both mischaracterized and exaggerated the security threat to the rescue mission. Certainly the chaos in the wake of Katrina and the breakdown of the communications network helped develop a climate in which rumors could and did flourish. Yet under similarly difficult conditions during other natural disasters and even war, reporters have adhered to basic journalistic standards. That they did not under these conditions could be explained as an isolated case of failure under extremely trying circumstances. That might very well be so. Yet, the important part of this story is not that the media failed to observe the basic rules of journalism; it is that the story they told was one people were all too ready to accept. It was a narrative that made sense within the commonly accepted racial frames of law and order and black criminality.

These frames made it difficult for us to make sense of reported instances of "guys who looked like thugs, with pants hanging down around their asses," engaged in frantic efforts to get people collapsing from heat and exhaustion out of the Superdome and into a nearby makeshift medical facility. These images did not make racial sense. There was no ready-made social frame within which the image of black male rescuers could be placed. Existing outside of standard racial frames, black male rescuers present a socially unintelligible image. That we have trouble *seeing* "guys who look like thugs" as rescuers is not a problem of facts. It is a problem of frames. Indeed, the very use of the term "thug" already frames the fact of what they might be doing in a particular way.

CONCLUSION

. . . Katrina offers profound insights into how race operates in American society, insights into how various facts about our social life are racially interpreted through frames. As a result of racial frames, black people are both visible (as criminals) and invisible (as victims). Racial frames both capture and displace us—discursively and materially. More than shaping whether we see black people as criminal or innocent, perpetrator or victim, these frames shape whether we see black people at all. Indeed, one might reasonably ask: Where have all the black people gone, long time passing? It is not hyperbolic to say that post-Katrina black New Orleanians have become a part of an emerging social category: the disappeared. A critical lesson of Katrina is that civil rights advocacy groups need to think harder about frames, particular when making interventions into natural disasters involving African Americans.

As Michele Landis Dauber reminds us, the template for the American social welfare system has been disaster relief, and the extent to which people are entitled to any form of government resources has always depended upon the claimants' ability to "narrat[e] their deprivation as a disaster—a sudden loss for which the claimant is not responsible."[24] In the case of Katrina, this disaster-relief conception of welfare would seem to promote an immediate national response to aid the hurricane victims. The problem for black people and for other nonwhites, however, as Dauber herself notes, is that racial minorities' claims to victim status have always been fraught "because they are highly likely to be cast as a 'disaster' for the dominant racial group."[25] Implicit in Dauber's analysis is the idea that the move to realign America's racial discourse and policy away from its current distortions must confront the complex problem of racial frames. The existence of racial frames makes it enormously difficult to incorporate "just the facts" into an argument about racism. . . .

What is required is likely to be more in the nature of a social movement than a social survey. Facts will always play a crucial role, but just as the successes of the civil rights movement were born of organized struggle,

PERSONAL ACCOUNT

He Hit Her

I was raised in Charleston, South Carolina, a city where racial and class lines are both evident and defined by street address. I had been taught all my life that black people were different than "us" and were to be feared, particularly in groups.

One summer afternoon when I was eighteen or nineteen, I was sitting in my car at a traffic light at the corner of Cannon and King streets, an area on the edge of the white part of the peninsular city, but progressively being inhabited by more and more blacks. It was hot, had been for weeks, and the sticky heat of South Carolina can be enraging by itself.

As I waited at the light, a young black couple turned the corner on the sidewalk and began to walk towards where I was sitting. The man was yelling and screaming and waving his arms about his head. The woman, a girl really, looked scared and was walking and trying to ignore his tirade. Perhaps it was her seeming indifference that finally did it, perhaps the heat, I don't know. As they drew right up next to my car though, he hit her. He hit her on the side of her head, open palmed, and her head bounced off the brick wall of the house on the corner and she sprawled to the ground, dazed and crying. The man stood over her, shaking his fist and yelling.

I looked around at the other people in cars around me, mostly whites, and at the other people on the sidewalks, mostly blacks, and I realized as everyone gaped that no one was going to do anything, no one was going to help, and neither was I. I don't think it was fear of the man involved that stopped me; rather, I think it was fear generated by what I had been told about the man that stopped me. Physically I was bigger than he was and I knew how to handle myself in a fight: I worked as a bouncer in a nightclub. What I was afraid of was what I had been told about blacks: that *en masse*, they hated

whites, and that given the opportunity they would harm me. I was afraid getting out of the car in that neighborhood would make me the focus of the fight and in a matter of time I would be pummeled by an angry black crowd. Also in my mind were thoughts of things I had heard voiced as a child: "They are different. Violence is a part of life for them. They beat, stab, and shoot each other all the time, and the women are just as bad as the men." So I sat and did nothing. The light changed and I pulled away.

The incident has haunted me over the last almost fifteen years. I have often thought about it and felt angry when I did. I believe that as I examined it over time the woman who had been hit, the victim, became less and less prominent, and the black man and myself more prominent. Then I had an epiphany about it.

What bothered me about the incident was not that a man had hit a woman and I had done nothing to intervene, not even to blow my horn, but that a man had hit a woman and I had done nothing to intervene and that this reflected on me as a man. "Men don't hit women, and other men don't let men hit women," was also part of my masculinity training as a boy. There was a whole list of things that "real" men did and things that "real" men didn't do, and somewhere on there was this idea that men didn't let other men hit women. I realized that the incident haunted me not because a man had hit a woman, but because my lack of response was an indictment of *my* masculinity. The horror had become that I was somehow less of a man because of my inaction. Part of the dichotomy that this set up was the notion that the black man had done something to *me*, not to the woman he hit, and it was here that my anger lay. I wonder how this influenced my perception of black men I encountered in the future.

Tim Norton

so too must our efforts to shift racial frames ground themselves in a broader and more organic orientation than raw empiricism. People came to see the facts of de jure segregation differently not because new facts emerged about its harms but because new interpretations of those facts were made possible by social organization on the ground that pushed the courts toward a new consensus. We believe the same is true today.

DISCUSSION QUESTIONS

1. Did the television pictures of Katrina victims challenge the color-blind perspective?
2. How did the images of the people of New Orleans contrast with the image of Americans?
3. Did the media report the facts?

NOTES

This chapter draws from and builds upon Cheryl I. Harris, "White Washing Race; Scapegoating Culture," *California Law Review* (2006) (forthcoming) (book review).

1. Cited in Aaron Kinney, " 'Looting' or 'Finding'?" *Salon,* September 1, 2005.
2. www.snopes.com/Katrina/photos/looters.asp.
3. Cited in Kinney, " 'Looting' or 'Finding'?"
4. Ibid.
5. One study of local television news stories on crime and public opinion illustrates the strong association between criminal behavior and racial identity. Participants were shown an identical news story under three different conditions: one group witnessed a version in which the perpetrator was white; another group saw a version in which the perpetrator was black; and a third group viewed a version in which there was no picture of the perpetrator. Following the screening, the participants in the first, white-perpetrator group were less likely to recall having seen a suspect than subjects in the second, black-perpetrator group. Among those in the third group, who saw no image of the perpetrator, over 60 percent erroneously recalled seeing a perpetrator, and in 70 percent of those cases viewers identified that nonexistent image as black. See Franklin Gilliam Jr. and Shanto Iyengar, "Prime Suspects: The Influence of Local Television News on the Viewing Public," *American Journal of Political Science* 44 (2000):560.
6. Roger Schank, "Tell Me a Story," *Narrative and Intelligence* 71 (1995).
7. A more nuanced formulation suggests, "Like well-accepted theories that guide our interpretation of data, schemas incline us to interpret data consistent with our biases." See Jerry Kang, "Trojan Horses of Races," *Harvard Law Review* 118 (2005):1489, 1515.
8. We do not intend to ignore the tremendous loss suffered in the Gulf region more broadly: we focus on New Orleans because of its unique position in the national imagination, as well as its pre-Katrina racial demographics. Indeed, New Orleans was not just a city that had come to be predominantly black; it was a city that was culturally marked as black. As one noted historian has stated, "The unique culture of south Louisiana derives from black Creole culture." Quoted in "Buffetted by Katrina, City's Complex Black Community Struggles to Regroup," Associated Press, October 4, 2005, www.msnbc.com.
9. Or fend for themselves and be punished for it. A particularly harrowing account of official indifference and hostility comes from the ordeal of two emergency room workers who had the misfortune of being in New Orleans for a conference when Hurricane Katrina struck. After their hotel in the French Quarter closed, they, along with several hundred others, collected money to hire buses for their evacuation, but the buses were prevented from entering the city. When the workers attempted to flee on foot, they were directed to wait on the interstate for rescue that never came. Neither the police nor the National Guard provided them with food or water. When the group managed to find food for themselves and set up a makeshift camp, they were repeatedly dispersed at gunpoint by the police. When they attempted to walk across the bridge into the neighboring city of Gretna, they were again turned back at gunpoint by Gretna police. See Larry Bradshaw and Lorrie Beth Slonsky, "Trapped in New Orleans," September 6, 2005, www.counterpunch.org/bradshaw09062005.html.
10. On a nationally broadcast telethon to raise money for the victims of Katrina, Kanye West departed from the scripted remarks to say, "I hate the way they portray us in the media. You see a black family: it says they are looting. You see a white family; it says they have been looking for food. And you know, it has been five days, because most of the people are black, and even for me to complain about it, I would be a hypocrite, because I have tried to turn away from the TV because it is too hard to watch. So now I am calling my business manager right now to see what is the biggest amount I can give. And just imagine if I was down there and those are my people down there." Commenting on the slow pace of the government's response, he said, "George Bush doesn't care about black people." NBC immediately cut to another star on the program and censored West's remarks from the West Coast feed of the program. It also issued the following disclaimer: "Kanye West departed from the scripted comments that were prepared for him, and his opinions in no way represent the views of the networks. It would be most unfortunate if the efforts of the artists who participated tonight and the generosity of millions of Americans who are helping those in need are overshadowed by one person's opinion." "Rapper Kanye West Accuses Bush of Racism; NBC Apologizes," *CBC Arts,* September 3, 2005, www.cbc.ca/story/arts/national/2005/09/03/Arts/kanye_west_Katrina20050903.html.
11. This was Howard Dean's view. In an address to the National Baptist Convention he stated, "As survivors are evacuated, order is restored, the water slowly begins to recede, and we sort through the rubble, we must also begin to come to terms with the ugly truth that skin color, age and economics played a deadly role in who survived and who did not." "Excerpts of DNC Chairman Howard Dean's Remarks to the National Baptist Convention of America, Inc.," U.S. Newswire, September 8, 2005, www.usnewswire.com.
12. While some have argued that class was a more salient factor than race in explaining who was affected, we do not think that given the country's history of de jure and de facto racial subordination, race can be so neatly disaggregated from class. Particularly in the context of

New Orleans—a city that was predominantly black and predominantly poor—the fact that those left on the overpasses and in the Superdome were black had everything to do with why they were poor. The point is not to reproduce another unhelpful version of the race-versus-class debate but to avoid sublimating the racial dimension of the issues raised by Katrina. Recent survey analysis suggests that race was in fact a crucial factor in explaining who was in harm's way. See "Katrina Hurts Blacks and Poor Victims Most," CNN/*USA Today*/Gallup Poll, October 25, 2005.

13. Both the Reverend Jesse Jackson and Representative Cynthia McKinney drew a link between the events in the Gulf and slavery. In response to a question by Anderson Cooper on CNN about whether race was a determinative factor in the federal government's response to Katrina, Jackson replied, "It is at least a factor. Today I saw 5,000 African Americans on the I–10 causeway desperate, perishing, dehydrated, babies dying. It looked like Africans in the hull of a slave ship. It was so ugly and so obvious. Have we missed this catastrophe because of indifference and ineptitude or is it a combination of both? And certainly I think the issue of race as a factor will not go away from this equation." Jesse Jackson, Remarks on *360 Degrees*, CNN, September 2, 2005. In an address on the floor of the House of Representatives on September 8, 2005, Representative McKinney said, "As I saw the African Americans, mostly African-American families ripped apart, I could only think about slavery, families ripped apart, herded into what looked like concentration camps." Cynthia McKinney, "Text of Remarks Delivered on the Floor of the House on Sept. 8, 2005," reprinted in "A Few Thoughts on the State of Our Nation," September 12, 2005, www.counterpunch.org/mckinney09122005.html.

14. "Huge Racial Divide over Katrina and Its Consequences," Report of the Pew Research Center for People and the Press, September 8, 2005, 2; available at http://people-press.org/reports/display.php3?Report ID=255.

15. As Gary Blasi contends, "If we store social categories in our heads by means of prototypes or exemplars rather than statistics, then our basic cognitive mechanisms not only predispose us toward stereotypes. . . , but also limit the potentially curative effect of information that contradicts the statistical assumptions about base rates that are embedded in our stereotypes." Gary Blasi, "Advocacy Against the Stereotype," *UCLA Law Review* 49 (2002):1241, 1256–57.

16. See Lee Cokorinos, *The Assault on Diversity* (Institute for Democracy Studies, 2002), tracing the network of conservative activists and organizations that have waged a well-funded campaign over two decades to change the corpus of civil rights laws, end affirmative action, and reframe the political discourse on race and racism.

17. This should not suggest that she was without any compassion. She went on to say, "[The bodies] have to go somewhere. These are people's families. They have to—they still have to have dignity." It's precisely our point that one can have compassion and still see black people through racial frames. *Paula Zahn Now,* CNN, September 8, 2005.

18. See Michael Ignatieff, "The Broken Contract," *New York Times,* September 25, 2005 (reporting that a woman held at the convention center asserted, "We are American" during a TV interview, demonstrating both anger and astonishment that she would have to remind Americans of that fact and that the social contract had failed).

19. Note that this frame is simultaneously inclusionary and exclusionary. To the extent that it asserts black citizenship, it seeks to include black people within the nation-state. However, it excludes noncitizens, black as well as others, from the circle of care based on lack of formal American belonging. This is deeply problematic but it reveals the limited space within which blacks could assert legitimate claims on national empathy.

20. See Anna Johnson, "Jackson Lashes Out at Bush over Hurricane Response, Criticizes Media for Katrina Coverage," AP Alert, September 3, 2005 (reporting that the Red Cross asserted that it could not enter New Orleans on orders from the National Guard and local authorities). A principal reason for the delay was that government officials believed that they had to prepare a complicated military operation rather than a relief effort. See "Misinformation Seen Key in Katrina Delays," UPI Top Stories, September 30, 2005.

21. See Brain Thevenot and Gordon Russell, "Reports of Anarchy at the Superdome Overstated," *Seattle Times,* September 26, 2005 (reporting that "the vast majority of reported atrocities committed by evacuees have turned out to be false, or at least unsupported by any evidence, according to key military, law enforcement, medical and civilian officers in a position to know." See also Andrew Gumbel, "After the Storm, US Media Held to Account for Exaggerated Tales of Katrina Chaos," *Los Angeles Times,* September 28, 2005.

22. Thevenot and Russell, "Reports of Anarchy."

23. See Charmaine Neville, "How We Survived the Flood," transcript of interview given to New Orleans media outlets, September 5, 2005, www.counterpunch.org/neville09072005.html.

24. Michele Landis Dauber, "Fate, Responsibility, and 'Natural' Disaster Relief: Narrating the American Welfare State," *Law and Society* 33 (1999):257, 264.

25. Ibid., 307.

SEX AND GENDER

READING 30

Chappals and Gym Shorts:
An Indian-Muslim Woman
in the Land of Oz

Almas Sayeed

It was finals week during the spring semester of my sophomore year at the University of Kansas, and I was buried under mounds of papers and exams. The stress was exacerbated by long nights, too much coffee and a chronic, building pain in my permanently splintered shins (left over from an old sports injury). Between attempting to understand the nuances of Kant's *Critique of Pure Reason* and applying the latest game-theory models to the 1979 Iranian revolution, I was regretting my decision to pursue majors in philosophy, women's studies *and* international studies.

My schedule was not exactly permitting much down time. With a full-time school schedule, a part-time job at Lawrence's domestic violence shelter and preparations to leave the country in three weeks, I was grasping to hold onto what little sanity I had left. Wasn't living in Kansas supposed to be more laid-back than this? After all, Kansas was the portal to the magical land of Oz, where wicked people melt when doused with mop water and bright red, sparkly shoes could substitute for the services of American Airlines, providing a quick getaway. Storybook tales aside, the physical reality of this period was that my deadlines were inescapable. Moreover, the most pressing of these deadlines was completely non-school related: my dad, on his way home to Wichita, was coming for a brief visit. This

Almas Sayeed is a Congressional Hunger Center Research Fellow with the Economic Mobility Program at the Center for American Progress. She graduated from the University of Kansas in 2002 and earned her MSc from the London School of Economics and Political Science in 2004.

would be his first stay by himself, without Mom to accompany him or act as a buffer.

Dad visited me the night before my most difficult exam. Having just returned from spending time with his family—a group of people with whom he historically had an antagonistic relationship—Dad seemed particularly relaxed in his stocky six-foot-four frame. Wearing one of the more subtle of his nineteen cowboy hats, he arrived at my door, hungry, greeting me in Urdu, our mother tongue, and laden with gifts from Estée Lauder for his only daughter. Never mind that I rarely wore makeup and would have preferred to see the money spent on my electric bill or a stack of feminist theory books from my favorite used bookstore. If Dad's visit was going to include a conversation about how little I use beauty products, I was not going to be particularly receptive.

"Almas," began my father from across the dinner table, speaking in his British-Indian accent infused with his love of Midwestern colloquialisms, "You know that you won't be a spring chicken forever. While I was in Philadelphia, I realized how important it is for you to begin thinking about our culture, religion and your future marriage plans. I think it is time we began a two-year marriage plan so you can find a husband and start a family. I think twenty-two will be a good age for you. You should be married by twenty-two."

I needed to begin thinking about the "importance of tradition" and be married by twenty-two? This, from the only Indian man I knew who had Alabama's first album on vinyl and loved to spend long weekends in his rickety, old camper near Cheney Lake, bass fishing and listening to traditional Islamic Quavali music? My father, in fact, was in his youth crowned "Mr. Madras," weightlifting champion of 1965, and had left India to practice medicine and be an American cowboy in his spare time. But he wanted *me* to aspire to be a "spring chicken," maintaining some unseen hearth and home to reflect my commitment to tradition and culture.

Dad continued, "I have met a boy that I like for you very much. Masoud's son, Mahmood. He is a good Muslim boy, tells great jokes in Urdu and is a promising engineer. We should be able to arrange something. I think you will be very happy with him!" Dad concluded with a satisfied grin.

Masoud, Dad's cousin? This would make me and Mahmood distant relatives of some sort. And Dad wants to "arrange something"? I had brief visions of being paraded around a room, serving tea to strangers in a sari or a shalwar kameez (a traditional South Asian outfit for women) wearing a long braid and chappals (flat Indian slippers), while Dad boasted of my domestic capabilities to increase my attractiveness to potential suitors, I quickly flipped through my mental Rolodex of rhetorical devices acquired during years of women's studies classes and found the card blank. No doubt, even feminist scholar Catherine MacKinnon would have been rendered speechless sitting across the table in a Chinese restaurant speaking to my overzealous father.

It is not that I hadn't already dealt with the issue. In fact, we had been here before, ever since the marriage proposals began (the first one came when I was fourteen). Of course, when they first began, it was a family joke, as my parents understood that I was to continue my education. The jokes, however, were always at my expense: "You received a proposal from a nice boy living in our mosque. He is studying medicine," my father would come and tell me with a huge, playful grin. "I told him that you weren't interested because you are too busy with school. And anyway you can't cook or clean." My father found these jokes particularly funny, given my dislike of household chores. In this way, the eventuality of figuring out how to deal with these difficult issues was postponed with humor.

Dad's marriage propositions also resembled conversations that we had already had about my relationship to Islamic practices specific to women, some negotiated in my favor and others simply shelved for the time being. Just a year ago, Dad had come to me while I was home for the winter holidays, asking me to begin wearing *hijab,* the traditional headscarf worn by Muslim women. I categorically refused, maintaining respect for those women who chose to do so. I understood that for numerous women, as well as for Dad, hijab symbolized something much more than

covering a woman's body or hair; it symbolized a way to adhere to religious and cultural traditions in order to prevent complete Western immersion. But even my sympathy for this concern didn't change my feeling that hijab constructed me as a woman first and a human being second. Veiling seemed to reinforce the fact that inequality between the sexes was a natural, inexplicable phenomenon that is impossible to overcome, and that women should cover themselves, accommodating an unequal hierarchy, for the purposes of modesty and self-protection. I couldn't reconcile these issues and refused my father's request to don the veil. Although there was tension—Dad claimed I had yet to have my religious awakening—he chose to respect my decision.

Negotiating certain issues had always been part of the dynamic between my parents and me. It wasn't that I disagreed with them about everything. In fact, I had internalized much of the Islamic perspective of the female body while simultaneously admitting to its problematic nature (To this day, I would rather wear a wool sweater than a bathing suit in public, no matter how sweltering the weather). Moreover, Islam became an important part of differentiating myself from other American kids who did not have to find a balance between two opposing cultures. Perhaps Mom and Dad recognized the need to concede certain aspects of traditional Islamic norms, because for all intents and purposes, I had been raised in the breadbasket of America.

By the time I hit adolescence, I had already established myself outside of the social norm of the women in my community. I was an athletic teenager, a competitive tennis player and a budding weightlifter. After a lot of reasoning with my parents, I was permitted to wear shorts to compete in tennis tournaments, but I was not allowed to show my legs or arms (no tank tops) outside of sports. It was a big deal for my parents to have agreed to allow me to wear shorts in the first place. The small community of South Asian Muslim girls my age, growing up in Wichita, became symbols of the future of our community in the United States. Our bodies became the sites to play out cultural and religious debates.

Much in the same way that Lady Liberty had come to symbolize idealized stability in the *terra patria* of America, young South Asian girls in my community were expected to embody the values of a preexisting social structure. We were scrutinized for what we said, what we wore, being seen with boys in public and for lacking grace and piety. Needless to say, because of disproportionate muscle mass, crooked teeth, huge Lucy glasses, and a disposition to walk pigeon-toed, I was not among the favored.

To add insult to injury, Mom nicknamed me "Amazon Woman," lamenting the fact that she—a beautiful, petite lady—had produced such a graceless, unfeminine creature. She was horrified by how freely I got into physical fights with my younger brother and arm wrestled boys at school. She was particularly frustrated by the fact that I could not wear her beautiful Indian jewelry, especially her bangles and bracelets, because my wrists were too big. Special occasions, when I had to slather my wrists with tons of lotion in order to squeeze my hands into her tiny bangles, often bending the soft gold out of shape, caused us both infinite amounts of grief. I was the snot-nosed, younger sibling of the Bollywood (India's Hollywood) princess that my mother had in mind as a more appropriate representation of an Indian daughter. Rather, I loved sports, sports figures and books. I hated painful makeup rituals and tight jewelry.

It wasn't that I had a feminist awakening at an early age. I was just an obnoxious kid who did not understand the politics raging around my body. I did not possess the tools to analyze or understand my reaction to this process of social conditioning and normalization until many years later, well after I had left my parents' house and the Muslim community in Wichita. By positioning me as a subject of both humiliation and negotiation, Mom and Dad had inadvertently laid the foundations for me to understand and scrutinize the process of conditioning women to fulfill particular social obligations.

What was different about my dinner conversation with Dad that night was a sense of immediacy and detail. Somehow discussion about a "two-year marriage plan" seemed to encroach on my personal space much more than had previous jokes about my inability to complete my household chores or pressure to begin wearing hijab. I was meant to understand that when it came to marriage, I was up against an invisible clock (read: social norms) that would dictate how much time I had left: how much time I had left to remain desirable, attractive and marriageable. Dad was convinced that it was his duty to ensure my long-term security in a manner that reaffirmed traditional Muslim culture in the face of an often hostile foreign community. I recognized that the threat was not as extreme as being shipped off to India in order to marry someone I had never met. The challenge was far more subtle than this. I was being asked to choose my community; capitulation through arranged marriage would show my commitment to being Indian, to being a good Muslim woman and to my parents by proving that they had raised me with a sense of duty and the willingness to sacrifice for my culture, religion and family.

There was no way to tell Dad about my complicated reality. Certain characteristics of my current life already indicated failure by such standards. I was involved in a long-term relationship with a white man, whose father was a prison guard on death row, an occupation that would have mortified my upper-middle-class, status-conscious parents. I was also struggling with an insurmountable crush on an *actress* in the Theater and Film Department. I was debating my sexuality in terms of cultural compatibility as well as gender. Moreover, there was no way to tell Dad that my social circle was supportive of these nontraditional romantic explorations. My friends in college had radically altered my perceptions of marriage and family. Many of my closest friends, including my roommates, were coming to terms with their own life-choices, having recently come out of the closet but unable to tell their families about their decisions. I felt inextricably linked to this group of women, who, like me, often had to lead double lives. The immediacy of fighting for issues such as queer rights, given the strength and beauty of my friends' romantic relationships, held far more appeal for me than the topics of marriage and security that my father broached over our Chinese dinner. There was no way to explain to my loving, charismatic, steadfastly religious father, who was inclined to the occasional violent outburst, that a traditional arranged marriage not only conflicted with the feminist ideology I had come to embrace, but it seemed almost petty in the face of larger, more pressing issues.

Although I had no tools to answer my father that night at dinner, feminist theory had provided me with the tools to understand *why* my father and I were engaged in the conversation in the first place. I understood that in his mind, Dad was fulfilling his social obligation as father and protector. He worried about my economic stability and, in a roundabout way, my happiness. Feminism and community activism had enabled me to understand these things as part of a proscribed role for women. At the same time, growing up in Kansas and coming to feminism here meant that I had to reconcile a number of different issues. I am a Muslim, first-generation Indian, feminist woman studying in a largely homogeneous white, Christian community in Midwestern America. What sacrifices are necessary for me to retain my familial relationships as well as a sense of personal autonomy informed by Western feminism?

There are few guidebooks for women like me who are trying to negotiate the paradigm of feminism in two different worlds. There is a delicate dance here that I must master—a dance of negotiating identity within interlinking cultural spheres. When faced with the movement's expectations of my commitment to local issues, it becomes important for me to emphasize that differences in culture and religion are also "local issues." This has forced me to change my frame of reference, developing from a rebellious tomboy who resisted parental imposition to a budding social critic, learning how to be a committed feminist and still keep my cultural, religious and community ties. As for family, we still negotiate despite the fact that Dad's two-year marriage plan has yet to come to fruition in this, my twenty-second year.

DISCUSSION QUESTIONS

1. Do you have your own example of "politics raging around my body"?
2. What are the symbols of a traditional lifestyle in your parents' cultural heritage?

READING 31

Proving Manhood

Timothy Beneke

Instead of coming to ourselves . . . we grow all manner of deformities and enormities.

Saul Bellow

. . . Why is it that successfully enduring distress is so central to proving manhood and proving superiority to women, not only in the United States, but in most of the cultures of the world? And why is it that manhood is something to be *proved?* And how do we confer manhood on men without also conferring upon them superiority to women? Or is the very business of conferring manhood inherently problematic? . . .

COMPULSIVE MASCULINITY

By compulsive masculinity I mean the compulsion or need to relate to, and at times create, stress or distress as a means of both proving manhood and conferring on boys and men superiority over women and other men. Failure to do so results in the social or private perception that one is less than a man. One must take distress "like a man" or run the risk of being perceived as feminine—a "sissy" or "mama's boy."

The content of the stress and distress can be usefully divided into three general categories:

1. That which would hurt anyone, e.g., physical pain, physical danger, large quantities of alcohol.
2. That which poses a psychological danger owing to the meaning it is given in relation to manhood, e.g., failing to win a sporting contest, losing physical strength and skill as one ages, and crying in public.
3. That which poses the greatest threat of all to manhood (a special case of category 2)—women. . . .

Timothy Beneke is a freelance writer and anti-rape activist.

I will further divide compulsive masculinity into what I witness (and manifest) as an American man and what can be gleaned from other cultures through anthropological and other data. It is useful to keep in mind the distinction between activities performed as masculinity-proving in themselves (like many rites of passage), and activities like work where proving masculinity is not the primary goal, but rather a secondary gratification that influences how work is done.

COMPULSIVE MASCULINITY IN THE UNITED STATES

American culture is replete with examples of compulsive masculinity. Witness Norman Mailer writing about Muhammad Ali, who had recently lost an agonizing championship fight to Joe Frazier, in *Life* magazine in March of 1971: "For Ali had shown America what we all had hoped was secretly true. He was a man. He could endure moral and physical torture and he could stand."[1]

It wasn't enough that Ali had shown himself to be a great fighter; winning had been too easy for him. Ali had taken Frazier's punishment "like a man" and remained competent and whole: "he could stand." He did not give up or burst into tears or go soft. According to Mailer "we *all*" could only be sure he was a man if he suffered and endured. Otherwise he was too much of a woman and not a real man, or he was a boy and, implicitly, too soft and attached to his mother—too feminine. Mailer assumes that admirers of Ali tacitly subscribed to this manhood ideology and that readers of *Life* magazine already understood it. No explanation was required.

That one of America's most famous writers could write this about America's (then) most famous athlete in one of America's most popular magazines suggests the pervasiveness of this ideology. It was, and largely still is, central to American culture.

Tom Wolfe wrote about the "right stuff" that was required of men to be test pilots and astronauts. What was this right stuff? It was the ability to repeatedly endure severe physical and psychological distress—high g's; intense, physically induced anxiety; and rapid heartbeats—while remaining cool, competent, and able to make snap, life-or-death decisions. And this right stuff—possessed only by the few—Wolfe says, is nothing other than masculinity itself.[2]

Sociologist Michael Kimmel offers many examples in his essay on the cult of masculinity in the United States.[3] The National Commission on the Causes and Prevention of Violence stated that "proving masculinity may require frequent rehearsals of toughness, the exploitation of women, and quick aggressive responses" (237). To "rehearse toughness" is to repeatedly prove one's ability to withstand stress as a preparation for greater stress. Kimmel quotes General Homer Lea, writing in 1898: "the greatest danger that a long period of profound peace offers to a nation is that of creating effeminate tendencies in young men" (241). Without war to "masculinize" men, they are in danger of becoming like women. And the Boy Scout Manual of 1914 states:

> The wilderness is gone, the Buckskin Man is gone, the painted Indian has hit the trail over the Great Divide, the hardships and privations of pioneer life which did so much to develop sterling manhood are now but a legend of history, and we must depend upon the Boy Scout movement to produce the MEN of the future. (243)

Again, without stress or distress through which men could test their manhood, they risk becoming women or remaining boys.

It seems that virtually anything men experience as stressful can serve as an occasion to prove manhood, so long as it is also something experienced as stressful by women. It would appear unlikely that American men could prove masculinity doing something women find easy to do. Although, with the advent of a "mythopoetic men's movement," where men take pride and may even compete in displaying their feelings, it is possible that the ability to cry in public, something women do more easily than men, may become a means of proving manhood.

American men take pride in handling alcohol like a man—getting sick or drunk, becoming incompetent, too easily can threaten one's manhood. Boys and even men feel superior to women and other men through their greater capacity to handle "grossness": unpleasant sounds and smells, insects and rodents, dirt, and so on.

The whole domain of male sports constitutes an occasion for proving manhood. The ability to withstand physical pain and intense psychological pressure, as Ali had done, and remain competent, is a central part of this. Moments of physical danger, like facing a fast-moving baseball when at bat or on the field, or evading tacklers while carrying a football, are similar occasions. The sheer psychological pressure exerted by the importance of winning or performing well enables one to prove manhood.

Hypermasculine G. Gordon Liddy, of radio talk and Watergate fame, as a child toughened himself by placing his hand on a burning flame without flinching and eating a cooked rat.[4] And part of what makes some popular aftershave lotions like Old Spice manly is the stinging pain they cause when rubbed on the face.

What defines a sissy on the playground is regression in the face of stress: bursting into tears when hurt, growing soft and "choking" at a crucial moment in a sporting event, giving in to fear and refusing to accept dares or take risks.

Work is another realm where the ethos of the playground is often transferred and where competence has often been equated with masculinity. It is an open question to what extent the training one receives to become a doctor, lawyer, or other professional is motivated by compulsive masculinity—and to what extent the entrance of large numbers of women into the higher levels of these professions will change them.[5] Nor is it clear the degree to which proving manhood constitutes a source of creativity in work.

Clearly, the army claims to make a man out of its entrants.[6] A popular television commercial for the army presents a solider about to parachute from a plane. We hear a voice-over of him writing to his father, telling him that he would have been proud of him today. The solider remembers what his father told him: "Being a man means putting your fear aside and doing your job."

The degree to which work is motivated by ulterior, manhood-proving needs is an issue that demands exploration. And, as technology increasingly renders men's superior physical strength of less value, mastering technology itself increasingly becomes an important realm for proving manhood, as the popularity of the television sitcom, *Home Improvement,* ironically attests.

Another means of proving manhood requires resisting the impulse to "go soft" and empathize with or nurture those who are suffering or weaker—a skill strongly needed to remain cold-blooded when confronting suffering or horror. It would appear that at least some of the evils of the world, e.g., sexism, fascism, homophobia, and racism, are, in varying degrees, then, ways that men prove their manhood. Men engaging in a gang bang, committing political torture, bashing a gay man; white men deriding blacks and boys torturing a bug, are all in danger of being regarded as less manly by other men if they empathize with or try to help the rape or torture victim, the gay or black man, even the bug. They resist the impulse to empathize with victims in order to prove manhood. Though men aren't likely to explicitly regard these experiences as suffering "taken like a man," it is what's expected of them.

And, similarly, men mock and feel superior to women or men whose need to nurture is easily aroused at the sight of babies or cuddly animals. The capacity to experience other beings as "cute" is the capacity to have one's desire to nurture aroused. Many men find this threatening to their manhood. Men rather often, and women seldom, refer sarcastically to the actions of others as "cute." Typically, it is a way of saying that, in trying to be clever, another man has been incompetent; "cute" is, in this sense, a denigration of manhood. If a baseball pitcher throws an odd pitch or a basketball player shoots a wild and spectacular shot, they may be accused of "trying to be cute," that is, of not being a real man. "Getting cute" is perceived as the equivalent of seeking nurturance, being feminine, and is thus unacceptable.

Learning to swear is an interesting domain for proving manhood; saying what (supposedly) no "good" woman would say is a way of advertising one's toughness and separation from women; one learns to endure the implicit fear of one's parents, and maybe, God. A good swear is the opposite of a good cry; it hardens one in a self-image of toughness and attempts to inspire fear in one's real or imagined cohorts and adversaries.

Symbols of masculinity often contain and express a history of suffering successfully endured. Think of tattoos, sculpted muscles, and scars. Such symbols convey a willingness and capacity to suffer for a masculine identity, an achieved and visible toughness.

Threats to manhood need not be explicit, conscious, or labeled; they can be deeply internalized and can manifest themselves as shadowy anxiety, guilt, or defensiveness, among other things. Proving manhood need not be dramatic or overt, rather, typically, it becomes internalized and characterological. What makes the need to prove manhood compulsive is that it can never be satisfied; one is momentarily a man and then the doubts reassert themselves—you're only as masculine as your last demonstration of masculinity. Men internalize a draconian model of masculinity that is inherently masochistic.

Relating to stress together is a common way that men bond—the greater the stress the stronger the bond. The extraordinary connection men feel at war has often been observed.[7] Compulsive masculinity is inherently social, no matter how isolated the man or boy engaging in it.[8]

Women constitute the third major category of stress that threatens manhood. . . .

First, the presence of women when a man is encountering masculinity-threatening stress compounds the stress. Part of proving manhood includes being perceived by women as a "real man."

Second, in the realm of sex, manhood is proved through one's capacity to find sexual partners and to remain potent with them. Sex is often dominative for men, and sexual problems are typically seen more as problems of failed manhood than as sexual problems.[9] In American culture we seldom explicitly regard sex as an occasion to take distress "like a man." But we do regard it as a proving ground for masculinity, either in terms of success at finding sexual partners or performance in sex.

Third, men's competition with women in the workplace is increasingly a threat to masculinity; competence at work has been a defining feature of male identity and men's superiority to women. . . .

COMPULSIVE MASCULINITY AND SEXISM

Compulsive masculinity is inexorably tied to sexism—in proving manhood a man is proving his superiority to women by enduring distress that women supposedly cannot endure. The domination and degradation of women are a basic defense used to bolster men's vulnerable masculinity. Where men are compulsively masculine, they are also sexist. What follows are some assumptions of sexist men, stated at their most extreme and stereotypical:[10]

> Men and women are inherently different.
> Real men are superior to women and superior to men who do not live up to models of masculinity.
> Activities normally associated with women are demeaning for men to engage in.
> Men should not feel or express vulnerable or sensitive emotions: the manly emotions are lust and anger.
> Toughness and the domination of others are central to men's identity.
> Sex is less about pleasure or relating and more about proving manhood and asserting power.
> Gay men are failed men.

Relatively few men may actively express such beliefs; far more men feel them than express them. But it is safe to say that all men in American society must—to some degree—negotiate their identities by way of such ideas. I am struck by the powerful psychic resonance such ideas have for me, even though I do not intellectually subscribe to them. They are far more alive in my emotions than I would like them to be. For instance, I react with anxiety to the thought of engaging in certain "women's activities"

PERSONAL ACCOUNT

Just Something You Did as a Man

In a class we had discussed the ways men stratify them-selves in terms of masculinity. I decided I would put that discussion to the test at work.

As I sat at a table, one of my coworkers approached me with a copy of a popular men's magazine, which portrays nude women. He said, "Frank, there is this bitch in here with the most beautiful big tits I have ever seen in my life." I told him that I wasn't interested in looking at the magazine because I had decided I did not agree with the objectification of women. His reply was, "What's the matter, are you getting soft on us?" I joked that it was not a matter of getting soft, it was simply a decision I had made due to a "new and improved consciousness."

At my job, talk about homosexuals, the women who walk by, and graphic (verbal) depictions of sexual ag-gression toward women abound, but on this occasion I either rejected the conversation or said nothing at all. By the end of the day I was being called, sometimes jok-ingly and sometimes not, every derogatory homosexual slur in the English language. I was no longer "one of the boys." I did not engage in the "manly" discourse of the day so therefore I was labeled (at best) a "sissy."

My coworkers assumed that I had had or was about to have a change of sexual orientation simply because I did not engage in their conversations about women and homosexuals. Since men decide how masculine another man is by how much he is willing to put down women and gays, I was no longer considered masculine.

This experience affected me as much as it did be-cause it opened my eyes to a system of stratification in which I have been immersed but still had no idea ex-isted. Demeaning women and homosexuals, to me, was just something you did as a man. But to tell you the truth, I don't think I could go back to talking like that. I am sure that my coworkers will get used to my new thinking, but even if they don't I believe that it is worth being rejected for a cause such as this. I had not thought about it, but I would not want men talking about my sisters and mother in such a demeaning way.

Francisco Hernandez

---

like sewing; I still have trouble acknowledging, much less expressing, vulnerable emotions; the element of performance as an end in itself is still more alive in my sex life than I want it to be. And it has been a struggle to acknowledge the liberatory potential that gay men offer straight men.

I find it impossible to imagine compulsive mas-culinity without sexism. The inability to empathize with women, to experience "vulnerable" emotions, to engage in egalitarian sex, or to empathize with gays is tied to the need to prove manhood by never regressing under stress.

DISCUSSION QUESTIONS

1. Is proving masculinity primarily about demon-strating superiority to women?
2. Do you think the need to prove manhood is as strong now as it was for your parents' generation?

NOTES

1. Norman Mailer, *Existential Errands* (New York: Signet, 1974), 43.
2. Tom Wolfe, *The Right Stuff* (New York: Bantam, 1980), 22.
3. Michael Kimmel, "The Cult of Masculinity: American Social Character and the Legacy of the Cowboy," in *Beyond Patriarchy*, ed. Michael Kaufman (Oxford: Oxford University Press, 1983). Also see Kimmel's lucid and rich *Manhood in America* (New York: The Free Press, 1995), which promises to establish manhood-proving as an independent force in American history.
4. Gordon Liddy, *Will* (New York: St. Martin's Press, 1980), 24.
5. The issue of how work, indeed the Weberian rationaliza-tion of modern society, is informed and motivated by manhood-proving motivations is one that awaits demysti-fication. For instance, will the massive entry of women into medical school alter the masochistic structure of medical training? The degree to which training for the professions is modeled on military training no doubt relates to the general militarization of society. The moral logic of the warrior still can be found throughout the world of work. Christine L. Williams has produced two thoughtful em-pirical studies about work and gender: *Still a Man's World:*

Men Who Do "Women's" Work (Berkeley: University of California Press, 1995), and *Gender Differences at Work: Women and Men in Nontraditional Occupations* (Berkeley: University of California Press, 1989).

6. The likelihood that one will have to go to war some day is no doubt a major, underdiscussed factor among the objective social forces constructing masculinity and sexism. If a sense that someday they will have to fight and kill is drilled into men, if they have to be willing to risk death, to die as part of their gendered identity, then childhood becomes war preparedness and women become objects of protection and thus inferior.

7. See Glenn Gray, *The Warriors* (New York: Harper and Row, 1967).

8. This is as good a place as any to suggest a possible relation between compulsive masculinity and creativity. To wit, I am intrigued by a parallel between creating and conquering stress as a means of proving manhood, and creating and conquering stress as a part of the creative process in art. Sometimes in the creative process, an internalized dare is produced as one writes the first line of a poem (or puts the first daub of paint on canvas), and prepares for the second. Does compulsive masculinity make such creative processes more psychically congenial to boys and men? There is considerable evidence that boys are more risk-taking in their cognitive styles than girls. And if creating and conquering distress separates men from mothers, does the same process in art gratify a need in men to emulate mothers by giving birth to something new? I owe this last observation to Jim Stockinger.

9. See Jeffrey Fracher and Michael Kimmel, "Hard Issues and Soft Spots: Counseling Men About Sexuality," in *Men's Lives,* eds. Michael Kimmel and Mike Messner (New York: Macmillan Publishing, 1989).

10. This summary is adopted from Harry Christian's useful *The Making of Anti-sexist Men* (London: Routledge and Kegan Paul, 1994), 10–11.

READING 32

Proud to Wear My Hijab

Syeda Rezwana Nodi

"Hey, I wanted to ask you something for a long time. Are you Rezwana from 10th-grade English

---

Syeda Rezwana Nodi is an author for *WireTap.*

class?" Priya asked me as I was going to the French office after first period.

It was the second semester of my junior year and I hadn't seen Priya since summer. She was one of my closest friends in 10th grade when she sat beside me in English class.

"Of course it's me, Priya. I don't know how you forgot about me so easily but I still remember you," I smiled.

"Honestly, I didn't recognize you at all," she said laughing. "I guess it's because of that hijab. I swear you look really different."

Priya's not my only friend who didn't recognize me after I started wearing my hijab last summer when I turned 16.

To me, my hijab is not just a piece of cloth that covers my hair. It's the most visible symbol of being a Muslim. One of the reasons Muslim women wear the hijab is to protect them from unwanted attention from men.

And it was my choice to wear one.

It bothers me that people think I'm different, now that I wear a hijab. Yes, it changes my appearance a little—it covers my hair and makes me look like I'm 12 instead of 17.

But caring more about my appearance than my culture would disrespect the honor of wearing it. So when my friends didn't recognize me, and made absurd labels like "one of the hijabis," I really felt hurt.

For example, last December, my friends and I gathered around the sign-up sheet for an upcoming annual talent show in our community center. We usually did the performances together, but this time it was different.

I was at the back of the line, and when my friends were nearly done signing up, a friend asked me, "Rez, you're not going to do any more performances right? 'Specially now that you're one of the hijabis."

A roar of laughter followed her comment. It was discouraging and disappointing, especially because I wanted to participate in the show.

Unfortunately, I care about what people say to me and I am a sensitive person. So I didn't perform because I didn't want to risk more comments like that.

People treated me differently after I started wearing my hijab, even though I was still friendly, fun loving and enthusiastic. And I didn't understand the label of "one of the hijabis." What did it mean exactly?

Surprisingly my friend circle was narrowing down to only Muslims. I didn't have enough courage to participate in sports or extracurricular activities. I was afraid people would make more bizarre comments about me and I would feel left out.

Finally, I told my mom about my feelings.

She said I should try to see the positive in the situation. I should confront my friends and tell them their assumptions aren't true. "What's wrong with looking different?" she asked me.

"Don't you think you should have more confidence in yourself? Being a hijabi is something you should be proud of. If that's what some people want to call you, then let them. Try to be more optimistic. Take things lightly instead of getting offended."

She was right. She made me realize I shouldn't underestimate myself and I became more confident of my appearance.

I didn't need to confront anyone, but if anyone asked me about my hijab, I would explain why I wear it. Otherwise, I decided it was no big deal. In fact, seeing me wear the hijab with pride, inspired some of my friends to wear it, too.

When school sports started, I joined the soccer and tennis teams. My hijab didn't get in the way. A lot of Muslim people play on our soccer team and the players greet me happily. The tennis group showed me some helpful tricks and encouraged me all the way. The heavy tennis rackets gave me more trouble than anything else.

The best thing is no one calls me a hijabi anymore. It's a meaningless label that made me doubt my decision to wear the symbol of my faith and modesty.

Though it was hard sticking to my beliefs, the experience has proven to me that wearing my hijab and tuning out people's negativity made me feel dignified, and so I shall continue to wear it with pride.

DISCUSSION QUESTIONS

1. Why did it bother Syeda Nodi when her friends described her as "one of the hijabis"?
2. Are women who wear the hijab stigmatized in contemporary America?

SEXUAL ORIENTATION

READING 33

Beyond the Closet: The Transformation of Gay and Lesbian Life

Steven Seidman

SEXUAL IDENTITY

Identities refer to the way we think of ourselves and the self image we publicly project.[1] No doubt our identities are related to how we feel about ourselves

---

Steven Seidman is a professor of sociology at SUNY Albany.

and to our character or personality; as such, the image we publicly fashion might feel like a spontaneous expression of who we really are. Yet we can project an identity only through acting purposefully. The decisions we make about the way we dress, walk, and talk, the language we use and how we use it, who we associate with, and where and with whom we live make a statement about who we are. These practices announce to the world something about our gender, sexuality, parental status, social class, ethnic identity, and countless other markers of identity. In other words, we fashion identities by drawing on a culture that already associates identities with certain behaviors, places, and things.

Identities are complex. We don't have just one and in the course of our lives we can alter—add or subtract—identities. We make choices about which identity or identities to make into a core part of our self-definition and which will be treated as "threads" or secondary.

If an identity such as being a wife is considered "core," it will shape an individual's decisions about friends, residence, social activities, and employment. A core identity will be a key part of one's public presentation; it will carry over to diverse situations and remain part of varied social roles. It will be a chief way you want friends, coworkers, acquaintances, and kin to see and respond to you. For example, if being Jewish is a core identity, an individual will fashion a public self that consistently signals this identity by means of clothes, language, social activities, and friends. Decisions about partners or lovers, work, residence, and donations of time and money will likely be shaped by a core identity. By contrast, approaching identity as a thread suggests that an identity is important or self-defining in only some situations. While we may have only one or two core identities, we have many identity threads. For example, when I'm at home my identity as a parent may be paramount but at work it's my identity as a professor that matters; while as an active member of the gay community it is being gay that is crucial.

Not all identities are chosen or easily managed. There may be social pressure to approach certain identities as core ones; other individuals may disregard your wish to make this or that identity into a core or a thread. For example, for many people, race and gender function as a core identity. If you're black, others will likely assume and react as if this racial identity is primary regardless of your wishes.

During what we might call the heyday of the closet era, between roughly 1950 and 1980, some closeted individuals downplayed their homosexuality as an identity. They managed what was publicly considered a deviant identity by defining homosexuality as a secondary part of themselves, something akin to a peculiar appetite or an unusual sexual impulse. Yet for some individuals the sheer magnitude of energy and focus spent managing this stigmatized identity, and the fact that avoiding suspicion and exposure sometimes shaped a whole way of life, meant that homosexuality functioned as a sort of hidden core identity.

For individuals who decided to come out during this period of heightened public homophobia, the intensity of the struggle for acceptance of the self, and the anticipation that disclosure would likely bring a major lifestyle change, pressured some individuals to make homosexuality a focus of their lives. The pervasiveness of public fear and loathing of homosexuals that sustained the closet made coming out a deliberate, intense life drama. It is hardly surprising that many of these individuals would come to define their homosexuality as a core identity. Also, during these years many individuals migrated to urban centers and built protective subcultures. Becoming a part of these enclaves often meant fashioning a life around a core gay identity, as one became integrated into the dense social networks of an exclusive outsider world.

To the extent that the closet has less of a role in shaping gay life, the dynamics of identity change somewhat. As the lives of at least some gays look more like those of straights, as gays no longer feel compelled to migrate to urban enclaves to feel secure and respected, gay identity is often approached in ways similar to heterosexual identity—as a thread. However, it is a thread of a minority rather than a dominant majority—more like being a Muslim-American than like being a Protestant American. Given gays' historically embattled status, individuals will often be deliberate in publicly asserting a gay identity in order to make a personal statement of pride or a political statement. Many people continue to claim a core gay identity, despite the lessening of public acts of homophobia and social repression. Today, individuals may choose to adopt a core gay identity as a lifestyle or for political reasons. For example, individuals may migrate to urban subcultures and fashion lives around being gay, but less to escape a claustrophobic, hostile social milieu than to find kindred spirits who share particular lifestyle choices.

It occurred to me, as my research progressed, that as some of us are living more openly and freely, heterosexuals are now routinely exposed to positive images of being gay and to actual gay individuals. I wondered whether straight Americans might alter the way they approach sexual identity. I decided to interview mostly younger folk, roughly age seventeen to early twenties. I figured that any change in the culture of heterosexual identity would be easier to detect in younger people.

I found contradictory patterns. On the one hand, as straight individuals viewed gays as normal, some reported being less attached to or less assertive of a heterosexual identity. These individuals told me that they do not act to avoid gays or any suspicion of being gay by deliberately flagging a heterosexual identity. They have deemphasized heterosexuality as an identity and some have said they no longer consider sexuality an important marker of identity. They prefer to identify themselves and others in nonsexual ways; for example, in terms of gender, social values, occupation, or as just "people." On the other hand, some individuals respond to the new gay visibility by becoming more purposeful about being seen as heterosexual. I was particularly interested in those individuals who said they view gays as ordinary people. Many of these individuals told me that they want to be recognized as straight. Some said that it's because that's who they are. Perhaps that's true, but it's also the case that claiming a heterosexual identity confers real social and cultural privileges.

The heightened sense of identity among heterosexuals and their deliberateness about asserting a heterosexual identity is, I think, something new. In the era of the closet, everyone was simply assumed to be straight; to be sure, individuals also projected a straight identity by being homophobic or gender conventional. Today, as it becomes less acceptable to be publicly homophobic, and as many gays and straights look and act alike, some individuals are deliberate in presenting a public heterosexual identity.

HETEROSEXUAL DOMINANCE

I work in one of the most liberal institutions in America, a research university, in one of the most liberal states in the nation, New York. Among colleagues and administrators, I feel respected as an individual and as a scholar who studies and writes about gay life. I have never experienced anything remotely close to discrimination or disrespect—at least not for reasons of sexual orientation. Still, my institution does not offer domestic partnership benefits for same-sex partners; gays are not included in the university policy of promoting respect for social diversity; there has never been any effort to hire openly gay professors; and except for myself and a handful of faculty who teach women's studies and English, I know of no faculty that includes lesbian and gay scholarship as part of his or her regular course offerings. In short, the personal aspects of my work life are "virtually normal," but my public status is that of a second-class citizen.

If gay life is freer and more open for many of us today, it is not because heterosexual dominance has ended. Discriminatory social policies and laws continue to organize American institutional life. Still, there has been something of a shift, at least in emphasis, in the way that heterosexual privilege is enforced. In many social settings, homophobic and blatantly repressive institutional practices are losing legitimacy as gays are seen as ordinary, "normal" human beings deserving rights and respect. We have cautiously been invited to join the community of Americans, but so far the invitation has not extended beyond tolerance of a minority; heterosexual dominance has not been seriously challenged. How is it that gays can be viewed as normal but are still unequal?[2]

To understand changes in patterns of heterosexual dominance, I decided to look at commercial films. Since the early 1960s, homosexuals have regularly appeared on the screen. However, the dramatic rise in their visibility since the 1990s makes film useful for charting shifts in how homosexuality is understood and regulated.

After analyzing almost fifty films that appeared between 1960 and 2000, I've concluded that for most of these years heterosexual dominance worked by polluting homosexuality. The homosexual was viewed as such a despicable and disgusting figure that no one would want to openly declare herself a homosexual. Conversely, the heterosexual was defined as a pure and ideal status. Moreover, to the extent that homosexuals were imagined as predators, child molesters, disease spreaders, or cultural subversives, the state and other social institutions were given a broad social mandate to protect respectable citizens by purging America of any visible signs of homosexuality. This culture of homosexual pollution contributed significantly to creating the conditions that we have come to call "the closet."

Until the mid-1990s, the image of the polluted homosexual dominated the screen. Then there was a striking change: the rise of the "normal gay." In films such as *Philadelphia, In and Out, The Object of My Affection, As Good as It Gets,* and *My Best Friend's Wedding,* gays step forward as "normal" human beings. Normality carries ambiguous political meaning. The status of normality means that gays are just like any other citizens. We have the same needs, feelings, commitments, loyalties, and aspirations as straight Americans. Accordingly, we deserve the same rights and respect. But normal also carries another normative sense: the normal gay is expected to exhibit specific kinds of traits and behaviors. He is supposed to be gender conventional, well adjusted, and integrated into mainstream society; she is committed to home, family, career, and nation.

This claim to normality justifies social integration but only for normal-looking and acting gays and lesbians. Moreover, to the extent that the normal gay aspires only to be a full-fledged citizen or to be accepted into America as is, her integration does not challenge heterosexual dominance. The politics of the normal gay involves minority rights, not the end of heterosexual privilege.

THE POLITICS OF SEXUAL CITIZENSHIP

The closet was not only a response to a culture that polluted and scandalized homosexuality. Stigma and the shame it induced would surely create ambivalence around being seen as homosexual, but they would not necessarily keep homosexuals silent

and secretive. If many gay individuals chose to organize public heterosexual lives, it was in no small part because of a government that waged a war against homosexuals. From the 1950s onward, the state enacted laws and policies that persecuted and prosecuted homosexuals. If exposure risked public disgrace and the loss of job and family, is it any wonder that many individuals opted for a closeted life?

Throughout most of American history homosexuals were not the targets of state control. From the beginning of the republic through much of the nineteenth century, homosexuality was not viewed as the basis for a distinct self-identity, and homosexual behavior was not the focus of specific laws. Homosexual behavior was outlawed as an act of "sodomy," which referred to a wide range of nonmarital, nonprocreative acts. This changed in the late nineteenth and early twentieth centuries as a variety of powerful social groups enlisted the state to battle what they saw as the spread of vice, divorce, and sexual and gender deviance. The state became heavily involved in regulating the intimate affairs of its citizens. Still, it wasn't until the 1950s and 1960s that the government mobilized its considerable resources and authority to crack down on homosexuals. At this point, the closet became the defining reality of gay life in America.

Homosexual repression and pollution was met with political resistance. From the beginning, the modern gay movement has been divided between a rights-oriented assimilationist and a liberationist agenda. Both wings of the movement made dismantling the closet a chief political aim. Except for a short period in the early 1970s and a brief flourish in the late 1980s and early 1990s (ACT UP and Queer Nation), a rights agenda has dominated the chief organizations of the gay movement. Its aim, roughly speaking, is to bring gays into the circle of citizenship and social respectability.

The rights-oriented movement has had many successes. Repressive laws have been repealed or now go unenforced; and positive rights have been established in many municipalities, workplaces, and institutions of all sorts. These social gains have made it possible for many of us to organize fairly routine personal and public lives. And, as many of us have come to feel a strong sense of self-integrity and social entitlement, mainstream gay politics has responded by shifting its agenda from gaining tolerance (decriminalization) to achieving civil and political equality. In this regard, it is not accidental that battles around gay marriage and gays in the military have gained prominence. There cannot be real equality without equal marital and military rights.

As the rights wing of the gay movement moved forward confidently, as there developed multimillion-dollar national organizations battling for our rights, the voices of some critics have also grown sharper and louder. Liberationism didn't, after all, expire in the mid-1970s or the mid-1990s. It survived on the margins, in the culture of academics, artists, writers, and some activists. And, as the rights movement has helped gays gain a footing in the social mainstream, liberationists have expressed concerns. While some critics wrongly interpret the struggle for rights as a desire to mimic straight life, liberationists have also understood, in a way that rights advocates have not, that heterosexual dominance is deeply rooted in the institutions and culture of American society. Gaining equal rights, including the right to marry and serve in the military, will not bring about full social equality. Without challenging a culture of advertising, television, film, music, literature, and news that makes heterosexuality the norm and the ideal, there cannot be social equality. Until our public schools hire openly gay teachers and administrators, and incorporate the teaching of gay lives, families, culture, and politics into the curriculum, there may be tolerance but not social equality. Until our workplaces celebrate events such as Coming Out Day and the anniversary of Stonewall, until companies advertise to attract gay consumers, promote openly gay employees to managerial and supervisory positions, encourage gay employees to bring their partners and dates to work-related social events, and offer the full range of health and other social benefits to gay employees, civic equality will remain an unrealized promise. We need a movement that broadens rights activism to include an agenda of across-the-board institutional equality and cultural justice.[3]

The struggle for gay equality should not be isolated from other social and sexual conflicts. From lesbian feminists and gay liberationists to queer activists, a liberationist tradition has sought to broaden our thinking about the politics of sexuality. They invite us to view the politics of sexual identity as part of a larger network of sexual and social conflicts.

From a liberationist perspective, bringing gays into the circle of good sexual citizens would still leave in place a sexual order that unnecessarily restricts the range of desires, behaviors, and relationships that are considered acceptable and worthy of value and social support. In other words, the idea of a good sexual citizen is associated with specific sexual-gender norms—what we might call a notion of "normal sexuality." Only sexual desires and acts that are viewed as normal are acceptable. Behaviors between consenting adults that fall outside the boundaries of normal sexuality may be labeled "abnormal," "diseased," or "unhealthy"; individuals who engage in these behaviors may be perceived as sick, immoral, and socially dangerous.

My sense is that, despite some dissent and conflict, there is a dominant culture that associates normal sexuality with sex that is exclusively between adults, that conforms to dichotomous gender norms that is private, tender, caring, genitally centered, and linked to love, marriage, and monogamy. There is then a wide range of consensual adult practices that are potentially vulnerable to stigma and social punishment; for example, rough or S/M (sadomasochistic) sex, "casual" sex, multiple-partner sex, group and fetishistic sex, and commercial and public sex. Individuals who engage in some of these acts will be scandalized as "bad citizens"; demands will be heard to use repressive or therapeutic interventions to protect good citizens from contamination—that is, being seduced, molested, or infected by disease-carrying sexual deviants.

The gay movement should not ignore this broader sexual political context. Like it or not, a movement seeking gay equality inevitably supports or challenges a wide network of sexual control. Obviously, it challenges the outsider status of gays.

But, to the extent that this movement appeals to a narrow set of sexual norms associated with the good citizen to justify its claim for rights and respect, it reinforces the outsider status of many sexual agents who engage in consensual, victimless practices. In fact, as the "normal gay" is integrated as a good citizen, other sexual outsiders may stand in for the homosexual as representing the "bad" or dangerous sexual citizen. Polluting specific sexual citizens as "bad" and dangerous (for example, sex workers, libertines, sexually aggressive women, sexually active youth, pregnant young women) establishes certain sexual acts or lifestyles (commercial sex, multiple-partner sex, youthful sexuality) as unacceptable; those who engage in these acts risk public disgrace or worse. Bringing gays into the fold of the good citizen may not then bring about expanded choice for all citizens. It may evoke fears of disorder, and this may bring about the tightening of sexual control for all citizens.

Liberationists remind gays that there are many types of outsiders. There are outsiders among insiders (for example, straights whose desires run to the nonconventional) and insiders among outsiders (gays who are thoroughly straight-looking-and-acting). So, yes, gays need and deserve equal rights and full, across-the-board social equality. But there are battles around sexual regulation that need to be waged beyond gay rights and equality. Liberationist voices need to be heard.

A MULTICULTURAL AMERICA

Gays' changing social status is connected to the making of America as a multicultural nation. The United States is becoming a society that is more socially diverse than it has been at any other time in its history. And, for many of its citizens, respecting and valuing group differences is a key part of this nation's identity.

Today, many Americans see themselves as national citizens but also as members of particular cultural communities. We are proud to be American but also to be women, African American, Chinese, Irish, Catholic, Muslim, Latino/a, gay, or part of a disabled community. And we don't confine our differences to private life; we assert our group identities in social and political life. We bring our differences into the cultural and institutional arena and expect them to be respected.

Outsider groups, including gays, have benefited from this multicultural remaking of America. For example, Americans are today expected to initially withhold judgment when encountering individuals who are culturally different. We are encouraged to consider varied points of view on sexuality, family, politics, education, and faith. For individuals and groups who are marginal or who have been outside of what is considered "the mainstream," a multicultural national ideal makes it possible for them to at least get a public hearing. In a multicultural society, public space, however cramped and marginal, is created for outsider groups to make their case to be respected as part of the spectrum of legitimate social difference.

At a deeper level, as a national culture takes shape that values group differences, there is occurring something of a shift from "absolutist" to "pragmatic" types of moral reasoning. The former makes judgments on the basis of transcendent worldviews. For example, divorce might be criticized because it violates a fixed, absolute norm of permanent marriage established by religion, tradition, or natural-law thinking. By contrast, a pragmatic approach offers loose guidelines in making judgments; it acknowledges that there can be varied legitimate moral points of view and that these should be reckoned with. This approach encourages a more situation-specific style of moral decision making; individual needs, purposes, and possible social consequences should be considered. Judgments about the ethics of divorce should weigh issues of individual well-being and public welfare and perhaps involve some sort of calculus of advantage and disadvantage. Absolute thinking is not so much declining as making room for pragmatic moral styles.

A pragmatic moral culture encourages gay integration. If an identity or way of life can be deemed worthy of social respect because it promotes personal and social well-being, and cannot be shown to have clear social harm, gays need only make the case that homosexuality is both victimless and, like heterosexuality, essential to personal happiness. To the extent that a pragmatic moral style gains a social footing, those who aim to deny gays' rights and respect by relying on absolutist arguments (for example, that homosexuality is a sin or disease) may be put on the defensive, as they are accused of intolerance, authoritarianism, or cultural backwardness.

Changes in America's moral culture pressure institutions to accommodate group differences. In the past few decades, we've seen institutions make real efforts to incorporate people of color, women, ethnic minorities, the disabled, and gays. In each case, though, social accommodation has meant tolerance, not full social equality.

Group differences are recognized but understood as products of prejudice and discrimination. Inequalities are to be remedied by education and the establishment of equal rights and opportunity. In effect, complex cultural communities such as those of blacks, the deaf, or gays, are viewed as temporary social adaptations to intolerance. Individual members of these groups are assumed to share core national values, beliefs, and social goals. As outsiders are tolerated and integrated into the social mainstream, their participation in these particular cultural communities is expected to weaken. These ethnic-like identities will become merely personal or symbolic, if they do not entirely disappear. At least that's the expectation and hope. In this view of a multicultural America, group differences are recognized, but integration through legal rights and identity normalization leaves the dominant social norms and hierarchies in place.

For example, confronted with the women's movement the state and other social institutions responded by narrowing its agenda to one of granting women's formal equality. As men and women become equal national citizens or bearers of equal rights as workers, family members, and political citizens, gender differences other than those that relate to rights, equal opportunity, and respect are understood as personal. However, many in the women's movement claim that there are important differences in social values and outlook between men and women; these differences have mostly been ignored by our institutions.

The way multiculturalism currently works in the United States leaves in place the dominant social groups and social norms. A social order that is disproportionately shaped by the interests of, say, men, whites, the abled, or straights is not seriously threatened by enfranchising gays, women or blacks. Still, integrating outsider groups such as these improves the quality of their lives and may have important unintended consequences. For example, the state, pressured by various groups, has passed a great deal of legislation that expands individual control over bodily, sexual, and intimate expression. Thus, the legalization of abortion in *Roe v. Wade* and a wave of legislation aimed at protecting women from sexual harassment and violence has expanded women's capacity to make sexual-intimate choices. Appealing to an ideal of sexual autonomy that is implicit in this legislation, women may claim a right to remain single, to be single parents, or to choose other women as their partners.

Although this liberal state practice promotes tolerance, it has considerable limits and can be stalled or reversed. In general, as the agenda of social movements has shifted from abstract civil rights to actual institutional equality, the state has retreated from an agenda of promoting diversity. Thus, as gay marriage became a national issue after the Hawaii Court of Appeals case, the U.S. Congress passed, with the overwhelming support of the Democrats and the president, the Defense of Marriage Act, which restricted marriage to heterosexuals. Nevertheless, to the extent that the state endorses the right of individuals to control their own bodies and sexual expression, gays can appeal to this principle to make demands for tolerance and equality. . . .

DISCUSSION QUESTIONS

1. Under what circumstances would sexual identity be a thread identity, and when would it be a core identity?
2. How does the film and popular culture image of the "normal gay" both help and hinder the gay rights movement?
3. Do you find yourself more inclined to the civil rights or the liberationist approach to sexual citizenship? Why?

NOTES

1. My ideas about identity have benefited from the sociological views of Erving Goffman, in particular *The Presentation of the Self in Everyday Life* (Garden City, N.Y.: Doubleday, 1959) and *Stigma: Notes on the Management of Sexual Identity* (Englewood Cliffs, N.J.: Prentice-Hall, 1963). I have also drawn considerably from poststructural approaches that emphasize the relational and performative character of identity. In this regard, see Judith Butler, *Gender Trouble: Gender and the Subversion of Identity* (New York: Routledge, 1990), and Diana Fuss, *Essentially Speaking: Feminism, Nature, and Difference* (New York: Routledge, 1990), and "Inside/Out," in *Inside/Out. Lesbian Theories, Gay Theories,* ed. Diana Fuss (New York: Routledge, 1991). The work of historians and social scientists has been crucial in recent discussion of sexual identity. For a sampling of this work, see Jeffrey Weeks, *Coming Out: Homosexual Politics in Britain from the Nineteenth Century to the Present* (London: Quarter, 1977), and *Sexuality and Its Discontents* (London: Routledge, 1985); John D'Emilio, *Sexual Politics, Sexual Communities: The Making of a Homosexual Minority in the United States, 1940–1970* (Chicago: University of Chicago Press, 1983); Lillian Faderman, *Odd Girls and Twilight Lovers: A History of Lesbian Life in Twentieth-Century America* (New York: Columbia University Press, 1991); George Chauncey, *Gay New York: Gender, Urban Culture, and the Making of the Gay Male World, 1890–1940* (New York: Basic Books, 1994); Kenneth Plummer, *Sexual Stigma: An Interactionist Account* (London: Routledge, 1975); Kristin Esterberg, *Lesbian and Bisexual Identities: Constructing Communities, Constructing Selves* (Philadelphia: Temple University Press, 1997); Arlene Stein, *Sex and Sensibility: Stories of a Lesbian Generation* (Berkeley: University of California Press, 1997); Joshua Gamson, *Freaks Talk Back: Tabloid Talk Shows and Sexual Nonconformity* (Chicago: University of Chicago Press, 1998); and Viviane Namaste, *Invisible Lives: The Erasure of Transsexual and Transgendered People* (Chicago: University of Chicago Press, 2000).

2. In thinking about heterosexual dominance. I've drawn considerably from gay liberationism and lesbian feminism. Key texts include Dennis Altman, *Homosexual Oppression and Liberation* (New York: Avon Books, 1971); Nancy Myron and Charlotte Bunch, eds. *Lesbianism and the Women's Movement* (Baltimore: Diana Press, 1975); Karla Jay and Allen Young, eds., *Out of the Closets: Voices of Gay Liberationism* (New York: New York University Press, 1992 [1972]); and Mark Blasius and Shane Phelan, eds., *We Are Everywhere: A Historical Sourcebook of Gay and Lesbian Politics* (New York: Routledge, 1997). Among the key works inspired by these traditions are Adrienne Rich, "Compulsory Heterosexuality and Lesbian Existence," *Signs* 5 (Summer 1980): 631–60; Michael Warner, "Fear of a Queer Planet," *Social Text* 9 (1991): 3–17; Eve Sedgwick, *Epistemology of the Closet* (Berkeley: University of California Press, 1990); and, in the British context, Stevie Jackson, *Heterosexuality in Question* (London: Sage, 1999). In the past few years there has emerged an empirical literature that speaks to the ways compulsory heterosexuality operates in different institutions and societies. See Mary Louise Adams, *The Trouble with Normal: Postwar Youth and the Making of Heterosexuality* (Toronto: University of Toronto Press, 1997); Karen Dubinsky, *Improper Advances: Rape and Heterosexual Conflict in Ontario, 1880–1929* (Chicago: University of Chicago Press, 1993); Debbie Epstein and Richard Johnson, *Schooling Sexualities* (Buckingham: Open University Press, 1998); Chrys Ingraham, *White Weddings: Romancing Heterosexuality in Popular Culture* (New York: Routledge, 1999); Mairtin Mac An Ghaill, *The Making of Men: Masculinities, Sexualities, and Schooling* (Buckingham: Open University Press, 1994); Anna Marie Smith, "The Good Homosexual and the Dangerous Queer: Resisting the 'New Homophobia,'" in *New Sexual Agendas,* ed. Lynn Segal (New York: New York University Press, 1997); D. Steinberg, D. Epstein, and R. Johnson, eds., *Border Patrols: Policing the Boundaries of Heterosexuality* (London: Cassell, 1997); and Lisa Duggan, "The Social Enforcement of Heterosexuality and Lesbian Resistance," in *Class, Race, and Sex: The Dynamics of Control,* eds. Amy Swerdlow and Hannah Lessinger (Boston: G. K. Hall, 1983), 75–92.

3. In thinking about lesbian and gay politics beyond questions of rights and equality, my ideas have been sharpened by the work of Michel Foucault, *The History of Sexuality, Vol. 1: An Introduction* (New York: Vintage, 1980); Gayle Rubin, "Thinking Sex: Notes for a Radical Theory of the Politics of Sexuality," in *Pleasure and Danger: Exploring Female Sexuality,* ed. Carole Vance (Boston: Routledge, 1984); Pat Califia, *Public Sex: The Culture of Radical Sex* (Pittsburgh: Cleis, 1994); Sedgwick, *Epistemology of the Closet;* Vaid, *Virtual Equality;* Combahee River Collective, "A Black Feminist

Statement," in *All the Women Are White, All the Blacks Are Men, But Some of Us Are Brave: Black Women's Studies,* eds. Gloria Hull, Patricia Bell Scott, and Barbara Smith (Old Westbury, N.Y.: Feminist Press, 1982); Shane Phelan, *Getting Specific: Postmodern Lesbian Politics* (Minneapolis: University of Minnesota Press, 1994); Diane Richardson, "Constructing Sexual Citizenship: Theorizing Sexual Rights," *Critical Social Policy 20* (2000): 100–35; Jeffrey Weeks, "The Sexual Citizen," in *Love and Eroticism,* ed. Mike Featherstone (London: Sage, 1999), pp. 35–52.

READING 34

Sexual Orientation and Sex in Women's Lives: Conceptual and Methodological Issues

Esther D. Rothblum

In the novel *Never Say Never* (Hill, 1996), two co-workers, Leslie, who is a lesbian, and Sara, who is heterosexual, become close friends. Though it is obvious to the reader and to both women that they are sexually attracted to each other, the suspense builds as to whether or not Leslie and Sara will "consummate" their relationship—that is, become genitally sexual. Whether or not the women do "it" will affect the reader's perception as to whether the book had a happy ending (they became lovers) or an unhappy one (they remained "just friends"). It will also determine whether Sara "becomes" a lesbian.

What is sexual orientation? What does it mean to be a heterosexual, bisexual, or lesbian woman? Are these terms on a continuum or separate categories? Can all women categorize themselves in one of these three ways? This article will discuss conceptual issues of sexual orientation in women. Closely related to sexual orientation is the concept of sexual behavior. Sexual orientation is usually defined in terms of the gender of one's sexual partner.

Esther D. Rothblum is a professor of women's studies at San Diego State University.

This article will ask the question, what is "sex" for women? Finally, there has been so little research addressing these concepts that some methodological issues for future research will be presented.

CONCEPTUAL ISSUES IN SEXUAL ORIENTATION

Dichotomous Definitions

Fehr (1988) views categorical definitions as "classical" in the sense that they are defined by specific inclusion and exclusion criteria. She states:

> Category membership is therefore an all-or-none phenomenon; any instance that meets the criterion is a member; all others are non-members. Boundaries between concepts are thus clearly defined. Because each member must possess the particular set of attributes that is the criterion for category inclusion, all members have a full and equal degree of membership and therefore are equally representative of the category. (p. 558)

Similarly, Rosch (1978) has argued that categories in language can be structured into a model of best fits, followed by examples that resemble these best fits to some extent.

In a categorical definition of sexual orientation, all aspects of sexual orientation—desire, behavior, and identity—are presumed to be congruent. The terms "heterosexual" and "lesbian" are often used in ways that presume these are unidimensional. When a woman says that she is a "lesbian," we may take for granted that this identity includes homogeneity of sexual behavior, sexual fantasies, and participation in a lesbian community, for example. Consider the following quotation:

> I have been heterosexual as some homosexuals say they have been homosexual: forever. Already, at the age of 5, I was attracted (in some diffuse sense of "attract") to male movie stars in ways that were different from my fascination with female stars. Demands by lesbian separatists earlier in the Second Wave that heterosexual feminists vacate their relationships with men seemed to me then and seem to me still both cruel and impossible. . . . The impossibility, for

women like me, is akin to the impossibility I would feel if, in obedience to political fiat, I were asked to change my fingerprints. (Bartky, 1992, p. 426)

This quotation is noteworthy for highlighting several issues usually assumed about sexual orientation: that it forms at an early age, that it involves sexual attraction, and that it can't be changed. The quote is unusual in that heterosexual women are rarely asked to describe their own sexuality, since heterosexuality is the "default" sexual orientation in Western societies.

Let us assume that sexual orientation is categorical. This would imply that there is a distinct boundary between being a lesbian on the one hand and a heterosexual woman on the other. At one extreme, we could picture a woman who has felt sexual/affectional desire only toward females since she was a girl. Similarly, this woman has had sexual relations only with other females. She considers herself a lesbian and has integrated into the lesbian community.

In reality, few women fit this image. Young girls who are attracted to other girls and women quickly learn to hide these feelings from others and even from themselves. They may date boys and even get married in order to fit the dominant heterosexual lifestyles. Women who do have the courage to express sexual desire and relations with other women may avoid using the term "lesbian" to describe themselves because of its negative connotations.

At the other extreme, a woman may always have been attracted to males and had sexual relations only with men. Yet we know little about heterosexuality among women. Media images of women depict them as very sexual, but in passive, objectified roles (see Umiker-Sebeok, 1981, for a review of this literature). At the same time, there may be pressure by parents and schools for young women to remain celibate, and there are few approved roles for women to be heterosexually active outside of marriage (see Hyde and Jaffee, 2000). Consequently, even heterosexual women may know little about their own sexual desire and attraction.

Some of the earliest writings about sexual orientation focused on "stages" that gay men and lesbians go through in the process of coming out. Generally these stages described an initial sense of difference and identity confusion that eventually was replaced by identity acceptance and synthesis (see Cass, 1979; Coleman, 1981). In this way, lesbians were presumed to move from lack of congruence to congruence between identity and behavior.

How would a categorical definition of sexual orientation include bisexuality? Bisexuality may be viewed as a separate category for women who are attracted to and have sexual relationships with women and men. In the past, categorical definitions of sexual orientation would have excluded bisexuality, viewing bisexuals as women in transition to be lesbians, or as lesbians who wanted a less stigmatizing self-description (Rust, 2000b). Development of a strong bisexual movement and bisexual communities has demonstrated that bisexuality is not transient and in fact may be an even more stigmatized term than lesbianism.

In sum, a dichotomous definition of sexual orientation is bipolar, with heterosexual women and lesbians as opposite constructs. Bisexuality is seen as either nonexistent or as a transitional phase between being heterosexual and lesbian (this point is discussed in detail by Rust, 2000a). There is congruence between sexual identity, behavior, and desire. Thus, if a woman experiences any same-gender behavior or attraction, she is presumed to be a lesbian with a same-gender identity as well.

Continuous Definitions

On the other hand, sexual orientation can be conceptualized as multifaceted. Consider this quotation:

How does my heterosexuality contribute to my feminist politics? That is an impossible question for me to answer because, although I have lived monogamously with a man I love for over 26 years, I am not and never have been a "heterosexual." But neither have I ever been either a "lesbian" or a "bisexual." What I am—and have been for as long as I can remember—is someone whose gender and sexuality have just never seemed to mesh very well with the available cultural categories, and *that*—rather than my presumed heterosexuality—is what has most profoundly informed my feminist politics (Bem, 1992. p. 436)

This statement describes the experience of many women who have unsuccessfully tried to "fit" into categorical definitions. Even as new terminology has entered counterculture vocabularies (e.g., "queer" to describe people who do not have a mainstream sexual orientation), these individuals continue to feel marginalized and disenfranchised. . . .

In sum, from a continuous perspective, sexual orientation is a multidimensional concept that varies in degree and intensity. Sexual orientation is viewed as diverse, with each individual having a unique template of erotic and affectional identity, behavior, fantasies, relationships (including relationship status), and emotional attachments, all of which can change over time (Garnets & Kimmel, 1993). These components can be (and often are) incongruous, so there is no simple relationship among behavior, identity, and desire. For example, many more people engage in same-gender sexual behavior than those who identify as lesbian, gay, or bisexual.

RESEARCH ON SEXUAL ORIENTATION

Most research in this area has used categorical definitions of sexual orientation, such as asking participants to check off whether they are lesbian, bisexual, or heterosexual. Furthermore, a survey entitled "Lesbian Mental Health Survey" (Oetjen & Rothblum, 2000) is unlikely to obtain many respondents who identify as bisexual or heterosexual. Nor will it interest women who are sexually involved with women but who do not identify as lesbian. Such categorical methods introduce a level of artificiality that may not in fact correspond with the identity or experiences of women respondents. . . .

In a recent study, Jessica Morris and I (1999) examined the interrelationships among various dimensions of sexual orientation. The study examined the way in which over 2,000 women who answered a "Lesbian Wellness Survey" were distributed on five aspects of lesbian sexuality and the coming out process. The five aspects were sexual orientation on the "Kinsey Scale" (Kinsey, Pomeroy, & Martin, 1948; Kinsey, Pomeroy, Martin, & Gebhard, 1953); years out (length of

time of self-identity as lesbian/gay/bisexual); outness/disclosure (amount of disclosure of sexual orientation to others); sexual experience (proportion of sexual relationships with women compared to men); and lesbian activities (extent of participation in lesbian community events). The intercorrelations among these dimensions were quite low, indicating that being lesbian is not a homogeneous experience.

Closer examination by the demographic characteristics of race/ethnicity and age revealed a diversity of experience. African American, Native American, and Latina respondents had moderate correlations among the aspects of the lesbian experience, whereas the intercorrelations of White and Asian American respondents tended to be mild or nonsignificant. The results indicate that researchers who are studying one aspect of the lesbian experience (e.g., outness to others) need to ensure that they are not assuming such behavior based on other dimensions (such as frequent participation in lesbian community activities or years of being out), especially among White and Asian American lesbians. Most studies of sexual orientation have focused on members of the visible gay and lesbian communities (there is still relatively little research on people who are bisexual). By recruiting participants at lesbian community events or using mailing lists of lesbian newsletters, for example, researchers are stratifying by lesbian *self-identity*. . . .

The limited research on dimensions of women's sexual orientation, whether conducted directly in lesbian/bisexual women's communities or via national surveys, indicates that identity as lesbian or bisexual, sexual activity with women, and sexual desire are separate and (somewhat) overlapping dimensions. This raises the question whether sexual orientation for women should be defined on the basis of sexual activity/attraction and, if so, what *does* sex mean for women?

CONCEPTUAL ISSUES IN FEMALE SEXUAL ACTIVITY

In the United States, the concept of "sex" is so closely linked with genital intercourse that most heterosexual women will not "count" experiences that didn't include this aspect of sexual activity. When asked when they first had "sex," women who have sex with men will often "count" the first time they had sexual intercourse with a man, even if this experience was not particularly sexual for them and even if they had prior sexual experiences that were quite arousing and even led to orgasm (see Rothblum, 1994, for a review). Loulan (1993) has described how female adolescents who have engaged in a variety of sexual activities but have not had intercourse will say that they have not "gone all the way." Thus, women's definition of what constitutes sexual activity with a male partner is often separate from their own sexual arousal and desire.

"Sex" when both partners are female is even more complex. On the one hand, lesbians and bisexual women will say that sex between women allows for a greater variety of sexual expression, exactly because it is not focused on intercourse (see Rothblum, 1999, for a review). On the other hand, sexual activity between women is socially constructed in the lesbian/bisexual communities to mean certain activities and not others. Two women who are "just" kissing and cuddling, for example, have not "gone all the way" (Rothblum, 1999). Interestingly, the current Vermont Youth Behavior Risk Survey (Vermont Department of Health, 1999) asks respondents whether they have had "intercourse" with males only, females only, both males and females, or neither. It is difficult to say how female adolescents will conceptualize "intercourse" between two females, but the wording of this item reflects the salience of the word "intercourse" to mean sexual activity in research.

Research on female sexuality has found lesbians to engage in sexual activity with relatively low frequency. A major survey of sexual activity among 12,000 people (Blumstein & Schwartz, 1983) indicated that lesbians are less likely to have genital sex than are married heterosexual, cohabiting heterosexual, or gay male couples. Loulan (1988) surveyed over 1,500 lesbians and found the majority (78%) to have been celibate for some period of time. Most had been celibate for less than 1 year, 35% had been celibate from 1 to 5 years, and 8% for 6 years or more. The national survey by Laumann et al. (1994)

similarly found women to be lower than men on rates of sexual behavior.

The results of these surveys were interpreted as reflecting women's lack of socialization to initiate sexual encounters. Survey authors also indicated that lesbians, being women, placed more focus on love, affection, and romance than on genital sexual activity (e.g., Klinkenberg & Rose, 1994). Thus, heterosexual and bisexual women may have sex more often because men are more likely to want and initiate sexual activity.

It is difficult to obtain accurate data on sexual behavior. Sexual activity is private, and women in particular are not socialized to discuss details of sexual activity. This issue is confounded for lesbians and bisexual women, who may live in areas where same-gender sexual activity is against the law and who may lose their jobs or custody of their children if such knowledge became public. Most sex surveys have been criticized for being of questionable accuracy, as people may not respond honestly for a variety of reasons (see Laumann et al., 1994, for a discussion).

Certainly the low rates of sexual "activity" found in these surveys may in part be due to how sexual behavior is traditionally defined. What are the implications of lesbians engaging in genital sex less than heterosexual women or than men, yet at the same time using a genital-based definition to define "sex"? Is there a way that women of all sexual orientations should discuss the relative devaluation of alternatives to genital sex? Can we reclaim erotic, nongenital experiences as "real" sex?

CONCEPTUAL ISSUES IN FEMALE SEXUAL DESIRE

The lack of congruence between female sexual behavior and desire implies that sexual behavior per se may not be what is most important to women and may not define their sexual identity. On the one hand, women in Western societies live in a culture of sex (Rothblum, 1994) in which images of women being sexual are everywhere in the media and are used to promote a wide range of products in the economy. On the other hand, the overemphasis on sex ignores the reality that women have related passionately and emotionally to other women all their lives.

Some years ago, Kathy Brehony and I (Rothblum & Brehony, 1993) interviewed self-identified lesbians who considered themselves to be in a couple but who were not currently sexual with their partners (and may never have had sex with these partners). Here are some examples of the ways of relating that we found (all names are pseudonyms):

Laura became attracted to her heterosexual roommate, Violet. Violet seemed to encourage the relationship in multiple ways, such as having heart-shaped tattoos made with each other's names and telling Laura it was okay that people mistook them for lovers. When Laura suggested they become lovers, Violet said she couldn't do it. Laura was devastated.

Elizabeth and Marianne were briefly genitally sexual, then Marianne broke that off, saying that the age difference of 20 years was too great for her. Marianne, the younger of the two, became involved sexually with another woman, Eve, and Elizabeth decided to move out of state to get away. Elizabeth and Marianne continued their relationship over the telephone, and both agree that they are the most important people in each other's lives. Elizabeth says about Eve, Marianne's sexual partner, "she will never have access to the total person that I have."

Sarah and Hannah have a primary relationship, but without sex. They have an agreement that they can have other lovers, but only men. Sarah is confused because she is a lesbian, and now her friends only see her with male lovers. It has shaken her whole identity as a lesbian. Hannah is primarily heterosexual. They are both afraid that sex would make them even more intense, given their closeness already.

These examples bring up a number of themes related to sexual desire. When two members of a couple disagree on what constitutes sex and thus whether or not they are having sex, they may also differ on whether or not they are in a real relationship. Even when both members of the couple agree that their genitally asexual relationship makes them a real couple, society in general may not agree with this definition. The couple may hide their asexuality from their community in much the same way that women in past centuries hid their sexuality from the community at large. Societal validation is especially important for women who are not heterosexual, in light of the fact that many of these women felt invisible to society at large when growing up or while coming out. Furthermore, the examples above came from self-identified lesbians; others may exist among women who are passionate about women yet who are married to men, in celibate religious orders, or extremely closeted even to themselves.

METHODOLOGICAL ISSUES FOR FUTURE RESEARCH

. . . In conclusion, what can we say about female sexuality at the end of the millennium? Sexual behavior is still defined in genital ways that may not accurately reflect the totality of women's sexual experiences. Sexual behavior is only one dimension of women's sexuality, and not highly interrelated with sexual desire, attraction, sexual orientation, and so on. There is increasing knowledge that even the concept of gender itself is flexible, complex, and multidimensional, so that knowing who is a "woman" is not as clear-cut as once believed. Far fewer women may be heterosexual in the traditional sense, indicating that more research on women's sexuality is necessary to learn about women's ways of being in sexual relationships. Even for women who *are* heterosexual, little is known about this "mainstream" group, such as how they came to be heterosexual, the ways that they might question their heterosexuality, and how their sexual desire and attraction differs from those of women who are bisexual or lesbian. Women's sexuality is an area in which we don't even know what most of the questions are, let alone the answers.

DISCUSSION QUESTIONS

1. What are the social consequences of operating from categorical definitions of sexuality?
2. What assumptions about women's sexuality does this article encourage us to question?
3. Should "sex" be defined as only genital intercourse?

REFERENCES

Bartky, S. L. (1992). Hypatia unbound: A confession. *Feminism & Psychology, 2,* 426–428.

Bem, S. L. (1992). On the inadequacy of our sexual categories: A personal perspective. *Feminism & Psychology, 3,* 436–437.

Blumstein, P., & Schwartz, P. (1983). *American couples.* New York: William Morrow.

Cass, V. C. (1979). Homosexual identity formation: A theoretical model. *Journal of Homosexuality, 4,* 219–235.

Coleman, E. (1981). Developmental stages of the coming out process. *Journal of Homosexuality, 4,* 31–43.

Fehr, B. (1988). Prototype analysis of the concepts of love and commitment. *Journal of Personality and Social Psychology, 55*(4), 557–579.

Garnets, L. D., & Kimmel, D. C. (1993). Introduction: Lesbian and gay male dimensions in the psychological study of human diversity. In L. D. Garnets & D. C. Kimmel (Eds.), *Psychological perspectives on lesbian and gay male experiences* (pp. 1–51). New York: Columbia University Press.

Hill, L. (1996). *Never say never.* Tallahassee, FL: Naiad Press.

Hyde, J. S., & Jaffee, S. R. (2000). Becoming a heterosexual adult: The experiences of young women. *Journal of Social Issues, 56*(2), 283–296.

Kinsey, A. C., Pomeroy, W., & Martin, C. (1948). *Sexual behavior in the human male.* Philadelphia: W. B. Saunders.

Kinsey, A. C., Pomeroy, W. B., Martin, C. F., & Gebhard, P. H. (1953). *Sexual behavior in the human female.* Philadelphia: Saunders.

Klinkenberg, D., & Rose, S. (1994). Dating scripts of lesbians and gay men. *Journal of Homosexuality, 26,* 23–35.

Laumann, E. O., Gagnon, J. H., Michael, R. T., & Michaels S. (1994). *The social organization of sexuality: Sexual practices in the Untied States.* Chicago: University of Chicago Press.

Loulan. J. (1988). Research on the sex practices of 1566 lesbians and the clinical applications. *Women and Therapy, 7,* 221–234.

Loulan, J. (1993). Celibacy. In E. D. Rothblum & K. A. Brehony (Eds.), *Boston marriages: Romantic but asexual relationships among contemporary lesbians.* Amherst, MA: University of Massachusetts Press.

Morris, J. F., & Rothblum, E. D. (1999). Who fills out a "lesbian" questionnaire? The interrelationship of sexual orientation, years out, disclosure of sexual orientation, sexual experience with women, and participation in the lesbian community. *Psychology of Women Quarterly, 23*(3), 537–557.

Oetjen, H., & Rothblum, E. D. (2000). When lesbians aren't gay: Factors affecting depression among lesbians. *Journal of Homosexuality, 39*(1), 49–73.

Rosch, E. (1978). Principles of categorization. In E. Rosch & B. B. Lloyd (Eds.), *Cognition and categorization* (pp. 27–48). Hillsdale, NJ: Erlbaum.

Rothblum, E. D. (1994). I only read about myself on bathroom walls: The need for research on the mental health of lesbians and gay men. *Journal of Consulting and Clinical Psychology, 62,* 213–220.

Rothblum, E. D. (1999). Poly-friendships. *Journal of Lesbian Studies, 3,* 71–83.

Rothblum, E. D., & Brehony, K. A. (Eds.). (1993). *Boston marriages: Romantic but asexual relationships among contemporary lesbians.* Amherst, MA: University of Massachusetts.

Rust, P. C. (2000a). Bisexuality: A contemporary paradox for woman. *Journal of Social Issues, 56*(2), 205–221.

Rust, P. C. (2000b). *Bisexuality in the United States: A reader and guide to the literature.* New York: Columbia University Press.

Umiker-Sebeok, J. (1981). The seven ages of woman: A view from American magazine advertisements. In C. Mayo & N. M. Henley (Eds.), *Gender and nonverbal behavior* (pp. 209–252). New York: Springer-Verlag.

Vermont Department of Health. (1999). Vermont Youth Behavior Risk Survey. Unpublished survey currently in progress.

READING 35

Anti-Gay Slurs Common at School: A Lesson in Cruelty

Laura Sessions Stepp

Emmett English, a cheerful, easygoing boy, started third grade last year at a new school, Chevy Chase Elementary in Bethesda, Maryland. On his first day he proudly wore a new red Gap sweatshirt and almost immediately wished he had chosen something else.

"A girl called me 'gay,'" he remembered. "I didn't know what that meant but I knew it was something bad." His mother, Christina Files, confirmed this. "He came home quite upset," she said.

"That's soooo gay." "Faggot." Or "lesbo." For all the outcry over harassment of gays following the murder of college student Matthew Shepard two years ago, anti-gay insults are still the slang of

---

Laura Sessions Stepp is a staff writer for the *Washington Post*.

choice among children and teenagers, according to teachers, counselors and youths themselves. Some say the insults are increasing in school classrooms and hallways—among children as young as 8 or 9—partly because gay youths and their supporters have become more visible and more active.

"Schools are seen as a safe place to say things and get away with it," said Jerry Newberry, director of health information for the National Education Association, a teachers' union. A recent survey of students in seven states backs up his impression. Human Rights Watch, an international research and advocacy group, reported last month that 2 million U.S. teenagers were having serious problems in school because they were taunted with anti-gay slurs.

Young people use these slurs in two different ways, one generally derogatory and one referring insultingly to sexual orientation. Schools have a hard time policing either use.

Taunts and slurs, particularly the words "fag" and "faggot," were cited in more than half of the publicized schoolyard shootings of the last three years, according to Newberry. Columbine shooters Eric Harris and Dylan Klebold were called fags. So was Andy Williams, who sprayed a San Diego high school with gunfire [in 2001], killing two people.

Anti-gay language first appears on elementary school playgrounds. "Kids at our school say, 'That kid is sooo gay,'" said Julia Pernick, a classmate of Emmett's in fourth grade at Chevy Chase Elementary. "They think it means stupid or unusual or strange."

The insults multiply in the emotionally precarious years of early adolescence. "If you're too short, too tall, too fat, too skinny, you get targeted in middle school," said David Mumaugh, now a junior at Walter Johnson High School in Bethesda. "Kids sign their yearbooks, 'See you next year, fag.'"

Sarah Rothe, an eighth-grader at Lake Braddock Middle School in Burke, [Virginia,] said such words "are as common as the word 'like'" at her school. Classmate Christina Jagodnick said "there's a big difference" between anti-gay slurs and other derogatory terms. "If we were to say other words

which we all know are wrong," she said, "someone would stop us."

At Lake Braddock this year, according to students, a boy was targeted by classmates who glued his locker shut, writing the word "gay" on the outside. No one knew the boy's sexual orientation, but the bullies called him names until, recently, he transferred to another school. The school would not comment on the situation.

Gay teens are reluctant to discuss personal harassment on the record for fear of attracting more. But when they're offered anonymity, they won't stop talking.

A junior at Magruder High School in Rockville, [Maryland,] said: "I have a lot of friends who say, 'Oh, that's so gay.' They don't associate it with homosexuality. You could plant that word in the dictionary for 'stupid.' Do I face a whole life of this?"

At Herndon High School in Herndon, [Virginia,] a junior said, "I was walking with a friend down the hall and this kid yells, 'Faggot.' How am I supposed to defend who I am?"

When straight students are bullied, they usually can count on an adult coming to their aid, counselors say. Gays don't have that assurance. According to several surveys, four out of five gay and lesbian students say they don't know one supportive adult at school.

"Teachers are aware they may offend someone if they speak about homosexuality in anything other than negative terms," said Deborah Roffman, who teaches sex education in the Baltimore and Washington areas. "They don't know how to cross that street safely, so they don't even step off the curb."

A LONELY CAMPAIGN

Jerry Newberry and other educators suggest that anti-gay insults are increasing partly because gay youths and their supporters have become more assertive in trying to stop them. Justen Deal, 16, has fought such a campaign alone.

A cherubic-looking blond kid from south of Charleston, W.Va., Justen heard anti-gay words from the time he could talk, even used them himself on occasion. But by the age of 12, when he first suspected he was gay, "they made my skin crawl," he said.

Unlike children in other minority groups, he had no natural support group to comfort him. His parents had relinquished custody of him to his paternal grandmother, Patty Deal, when he was born, and her only knowledge of homosexuals was what she had seen on the TV comedy "Ellen."

She did her best once she found out in his eighth-grade year that he was gay. He had written a letter to his school counselor that Patty Deal read. She immediately sought psychiatric help for him, took him to a hospital on the night he overdosed on antidepressants, [and] enrolled him in a new middle school in Boone County.

Neither she nor Justen knows how, but rumors started flying at Sherman Junior High. "I was asked eight times a day if I was gay," Justen remembered. "I'd say no, or not say anything. That year is when I learned for sure that the things you hear about words not hurting is a fairy tale."

Justen thought he'd be safe from gay-bashing once he reached Sherman Senior High. He knew principal Theresa Lonker, a tough-looking administrator who sends students to detention for cursing. When she told Justen, "We'll look out for you," she seemed to mean it.

But she couldn't be everywhere. Name-calling started slowly in his freshman year and picked up this year, according to Justen's friend Lindsey Light. Fed up this past spring, Justen tried to do something about language in a very visible way.

He drafted a new harassment policy for Sherman High to include sexual orientation and left it on Lonker's desk. He lobbied the county school superintendent, Steve Pauley, to rewrite the county's harassment policy.

He visited West Virginia Gov. Robert Wise's office asking the governor to convene a task force to investigate harassment. He testified before the legislature on an amendment to the state's hate crime bill that would have included protection based on sexual orientation. His comments made both Charleston newspapers, including the front page of the *Daily Mail*.

Some of his classmates were not exactly thrilled with the attention. They threw coins and paper wads at him on a school bus during a field trip and also one afternoon in a science class. "Everyone [in the class] heard me tell them to stop, but the teacher was in his own little world," Justen said.

The science teacher, Robert Britton, said he didn't realize at the time there was any harassment going on. "I heard [Justen] say something about stuff being thrown at him but I thought he was just talking about words," Britton said.

Justen's one-person language crusade was rebuffed at every turn. Principal Lonker said she never saw the recommendation for changing the school's harassment policy. Superintendent Pauley said he was reluctant to single out gay students for special mention. Gov. Wise's office declined to appoint a task force on the needs of gay students. The legislature voted against adding sexual orientation to its anti-harassment statute. By mid-April, Justen, feeling defeated, decided to change what he could: his school.

He transferred to Huntington High, about 90 miles north. The school has a sizable population of openly gay students, and friends found a gay couple with whom he could live.

On his last day at Sherman High, his grandmother waited for him in her blue Chevy Impala. She appeared both nervous and sad.

"I've always taught Justen to tell the truth," she said. "I reckon he just listened too good. I knew he'd leave one day—I just didn't know it would be so soon."

Justen didn't want to leave his grandma. But despite Lonker's efforts to keep him safe at school, he said, he didn't *feel* safe and thus had a hard time keeping his mind on equations and Civil War battles. His pals had told him to shrug off the verbal digs, but he could not.

"My friends don't understand that every time I hear the word 'fag' it really hurts," he said. "It reminds me that I'm so far away from what kids see as normal."

Walking out of Sherman on that soggy Tuesday, buoyed by the hugs of several students and his principal, he said, "It was a good day. I only heard the word 'faggot' four times."

PERSONAL ACCOUNT

An Opportunity to Get Even

When I was a freshman in high school, my parents sent me to a private school. I got harassed a lot by a few of the sophomore guys there because I wore pants with the uniform (instead of the pleated mini-skirts), I didn't wear makeup, and probably most important, I would not date any of them (and couldn't give a reason for that). Most of this harassment was anti-gay slurs with specific references to me on the bathroom walls. One of the guys often yelled comments such as "Hey Dyke, I got what you need right here" while grabbing his crotch. My name was written on many of the bathroom stalls (both male and female), with my sexual orientation, and a rhyme about a gang bang.

After about six weeks of this, I confided in my soccer coach. I told her about the harassment and came out to her. I don't know what I expected, but I did not expect any positive reaction. She told me she was glad I came out to her, and she promised to keep my confidentiality. She also offered me an opportunity to get back at the three guys who were harassing me the most. She told me that this was my battle and that I was going to have to learn how to fight.

She knew that the three guys were part of the boys' soccer team, and made arrangements so that, as part of the homecoming festivities, our soccer team would play theirs. By doing this she gave me the opportunity to "show them up" and make them look bad in front of the school. I did my best to accomplish that. For example, every time any of them came near me, I would run into them or trip them. My goal was to embarrass them in front of the school. It did not look good for the guys because a "dyke" challenged and defeated the "jocks."

What my soccer coach did for me meant a lot. First, she was literally the only person I was out to at that time, so she was a source of support. Further, she went out of her way to help me get even with the harassers. Because of what she did for me, the harassment stopped.

Gillian Carroll

DISCUSSION QUESTIONS

1. Were antigay insults common among students in the secondary schools you attended? Were racist insults also present? If so, what was the response of parents, teachers, and administrators to the behavior?

2. What would you recommend school administrators do to eliminate antigay insults in the schools?

SOCIAL CLASS

READING 36

Nickel and Dimed: On (Not) Getting by in America

Barbara Ehrenreich

You might think that unskilled jobs would be a snap for someone who holds a Ph.D. and whose normal line of work requires learning entirely new things every couple of weeks. Not so. The first thing I discovered is that no job, no matter how lowly, is truly "unskilled." Every one of the six jobs I entered into in the course of this project required concentration, and most demanded that I master new terms, new tools, and new skills—from placing orders on restaurant computers to wielding the backpack vacuum cleaner. None of these things came as easily to me as I would have liked; no one ever said, "Wow, you're fast!" or "Can you believe she just started?" Whatever my accomplishments in the rest of my life, in the low-wage work world I was a person of average ability—capable of learning the job and also capable of screwing up.

I did have my moments of glory. There were days at The Maids when I got my own tasks finished fast enough that I was able to lighten the load on others, and I feel good about that. There was my breakthrough at Wal-Mart, where I truly believe that, if I'd been able to keep my mouth shut, I would have progressed in a year or two to a wage of $7.50 or more an hour. And I'll bask for the rest of my life in the memory of that day at the

Woodcrest when I fed the locked Alzheimer's ward all by myself, cleaned up afterward, and even managed to extract a few smiles from the vacant faces of my charges in the process. . . .

But the real question is not how well I did at work but how well I did at life in general, which includes eating and having a place to stay. The fact that these are two separate questions needs to be underscored right away. In the rhetorical buildup to welfare reform, it was uniformly assumed that a job was the ticket out of poverty and that the only thing holding back welfare recipients was their reluctance to get out and get one. I got one and sometimes more than one, but my track record in the survival department is far less admirable than my performance as a jobholder. On small things I was thrifty enough; no expenditures on "carousing," flashy clothes, or any of the other indulgences that are often smugly believed to undermine the budgets of the poor. True, the $30 slacks in Key West and the $20 belt in Minneapolis were extravagances; I now know I could have done better at the Salvation Army or even at Wal-Mart. Food, though, I pretty much got down to a science: lots of chopped meat, beans, cheese, and noodles when I had a kitchen to cook in; otherwise, fast food, which I was able to keep down to about $9 a day. But let's look at the record.

In Key West, I earned $1,039 in one month and spent $517 on food, gas, toiletries, laundry, phone, and utilities. Rent was the deal breaker. If I had remained in my $500 efficiency, I would have been able to pay the rent and have $22 left over (which is still $78 less than the cash I had in my pocket at the start of the month). This in itself would have been a dicey situation if I had attempted to continue for a few more months, because sooner or later I would have had to spend something on medical and dental care or drugs other than ibuprofen. But my move to the trailer park—for the purpose, you will recall, of taking a second job—made me responsible for $625 a month in rent alone, utilities not included. Here I might have economized by giving

Barbara Ehrenreich is the author of twelve books, including *The Worst Years of Our Lives, Blood Rites,* and *Fear of Falling,* which was nominated for a National Book Critics Award.

Editors' note: To learn about the lives of the working poor, professional journalist Barbara Ehrenreich traveled the United States working as a waitress, hotel maid, house cleaner, nursing aid, and Wal-Mart salesperson.

up the car and buying a used bike (for about $50) or walking to work. Still, two jobs, or at least a job and a half, would be a necessity, and I had learned that I could not do two physically demanding jobs in the same day, at least not at any acceptable standard of performance.

In Portland, Maine, I came closest to achieving a decent fit between income and expenses, but only because I worked seven days a week. Between my two jobs, I was earning approximately $300 a week after taxes and paying $480 a month in rent, or a manageable 40 percent of my earnings. It helped, too, that gas and electricity were included in my rent and that I got two or three free meals each weekend at the nursing home. But I was there at the beginning of the off-season. If I had stayed until June 2000 I would have faced the Blue Haven's summer rent of $390 a week, which would of course have been out of the question. So to survive year-round, I would have had to save enough, in the months between August 1999 and May 2000, to accumulate the first month's rent and deposit on an actual apartment. I think I could have done this—saved $800 to $1,000—at least if no car trouble or illness interfered with my budget. I am not sure, however, that I could have maintained the seven-day-a-week regimen month after month or eluded the kinds of injuries that afflicted my fellow workers in the housecleaning business.

In Minneapolis—well, here we are left with a lot of speculation. If I had been able to find an apartment for $400 a month or less, my pay at Wal-Mart—$1,120 a month before taxes—might have been sufficient, although the cost of living in a motel while I searched for such an apartment might have made it impossible for me to save enough for the first month's rent and deposit. A weekend job, such as the one I almost landed at a supermarket for about $7.75 an hour, would have helped, but I had no guarantee that I could arrange my schedule at Wal-Mart to reliably exclude weekends. If I had taken the job at Menards and the pay was in fact $10 an hour for eleven hours a day, I would have made about $440 a week after taxes—enough to pay for a motel room and still have something left over to

save up for the initial costs of an apartment. But were they really offering $10 an hour? And could I have stayed on my feet eleven hours a day, five days a week? So yes, with some different choices, I probably could have survived in Minneapolis. But I'm not going back for a rematch.

All right, I made mistakes, especially in Minneapolis, and these mistakes were at the time an occasion for feelings of failure and shame. I should have pulled myself together and taken the better-paying job; I should have moved into the dormitory I finally found (although at $19 a night, even a dorm bed would have been a luxury on Wal-Mart wages). But it must be said in my defense that plenty of other people were making the same mistakes: working at Wal-Mart rather than at one of the better-paying jobs available (often, I assume, because of transportation problems); living in residential motels at $200 to $300 a week. So the problem goes beyond my personal failings and miscalculations. Something is wrong, very wrong, when a single person in good health, a person who in addition possesses a working car, can barely support herself by the sweat of her brow. You don't need a degree in economics to see that wages are too low and rents too high.

The problem of rents is easy for a noneconomist, even a sparsely educated low-wage worker, to grasp: it's the market, stupid. When the rich and the poor compete for housing on the open market, the poor don't stand a chance. The rich can always outbid them, buy up their tenements or trailer parks, and replace them with condos, McMansions, golf courses, or whatever they like. Since the rich have become more numerous, thanks largely to rising stock prices and executive salaries, the poor have necessarily been forced into housing that is more expensive, more dilapidated, or more distant from their places of work. . . . In Key West, the trailer park [that was convenient to my hotel job] was charging $625 a month for a half-size trailer, forcing low-wage workers to search for housing farther and farther away in less fashionable keys. But rents were also skyrocketing in the touristically challenged city of Minneapolis, where the last bits of near-affordable housing lie deep in the city, while job growth has occurred on the city's periphery, next to distinctly unaffordable suburbs. Insofar as the poor have to work near the dwellings of the rich—as in the case of so many service and retail jobs—they are stuck with lengthy commutes or dauntingly expensive housing.

If there seems to be general complacency about the low-income housing crisis, this is partly because it is in no way reflected in the official poverty rate, which has remained for the past several years at a soothingly low 13 percent or so. The reason for the disconnect between the actual housing nightmare of the poor and "poverty," as officially defined, is simple: the official poverty level is still calculated by the archaic method of taking the bare-bones cost of food for a family of a given size and multiplying this number by three. Yet food is relatively inflation-proof, at least compared with rent. In the early 1960s, when this method of calculating poverty was devised, food accounted for 24 percent of the average family budget (not 33 percent even then, it should be noted) and housing 29 percent. In 1999, food took up only 16 percent of the family budget, while housing had soared to 37 percent.[1] So the choice of food as the basis for calculating family budgets seems fairly arbitrary today; we might as well abolish poverty altogether, at least on paper, by defining a subsistence budget as some multiple of average expenditures on comic books or dental floss.

When the market fails to distribute some vital commodity, such as housing, to all who require it, the usual liberal-to-moderate expectation is that the government will step in and help. We accept this principle—at least in a halfhearted and faltering way—in the case of health care, where government offers Medicare to the elderly, Medicaid to the desperately poor, and various state programs to the children of the merely very poor. But in the case of housing, the extreme upward skewing of the market has been accompanied by a cowardly public sector retreat from responsibility. Expenditures on public housing have fallen since the 1980s, and the expansion of public rental subsidies came to a halt in the mid-1990s. At the same time, housing subsidies for home owners—who tend to be far more affluent than renters—have remained at their usual munificent levels. It did not escape my attention, as a temporarily low-income person, that the housing subsidy I normally receive in my real life—over $20,000 a year in the form of a mortgage-interest deduction—would have allowed a truly low-income family to live in relative splendor. Had this amount been available to me in monthly installments in Minneapolis, I could have moved into one of those "executive" condos with sauna, health club, and pool.

But if rents are exquisitely sensitive to market forces, wages clearly are not. Every city where I worked in the course of this project was experiencing what local businesspeople defined as a "labor shortage"—commented on in the local press and revealed by the ubiquitous signs saying "Now Hiring" or, more imperiously, "We Are Now Accepting Applications." Yet wages for people near the bottom of the labor market remain fairly flat, even "stagnant." "Certainly," the *New York Times* reported in March 2000, "inflationary wage gains are not evident in national wage statistics."[2] Federal Reserve chief Alan Greenspan, who spends much of his time anxiously scanning the horizon for the slightest hint of such "inflationary" gains, was pleased to inform Congress in July 2000 that the forecast seemed largely trouble-free. He went so far as to suggest that the economic laws linking low unemployment to wage increases may no longer be operative, which is a little like saying that the law of supply and demand has been repealed.[3] Some economists argue that the apparent paradox rests on an illusion: there is no real "labor shortage," only a shortage of people willing to work at the wages currently being offered.[4] You might as well talk about a "Lexus shortage"—which there is, in a sense, for anyone unwilling to pay $40,000 for a car.

In fact, wages *have* risen, or did rise, anyway, between 1996 and 1999. When I called around to various economists in the summer of 2000 and complained about the inadequacy of the wages available to entry-level workers, this was their first response: "But wages are going up!" According to the Economic Policy Institute, the poorest 10 percent of American workers saw their wages rise from $5.49 an hour (in 1999 dollars) in 1996 to $6.05 in 1999. Moving up the socioeconomic ladder, the next 10 percent–sized slice of Americans—which is roughly where I found myself as a low-wage worker—went from $6.80 an hour in 1996 to $7.35 in 1999.[5]

Obviously we have one of those debates over whether the glass is half empty or half full; the increases that seem to have mollified many economists do not seem so impressive to me. To put the wage gains of the past four years in somewhat dismal perspective: they have not been sufficient to bring low-wage workers up to the amounts they were earning twenty-seven years ago, in 1973. In the first quarter of 2000, the poorest 10 percent of workers were earning only 91 percent of what they earned in the distant era of Watergate and disco music. Furthermore, of all workers, the poorest have made the least progress back to their 1973 wage levels. Relatively well-off workers in the eighth decile, or 10 percent–sized slice, where earnings are about $20 an hour, are now making 106.6 percent of what they earned in 1973. When I persisted in my carping to the economists, they generally backed down a bit, conceding that while wages at the bottom are going up, they're not going up very briskly. Lawrence Michel at the Economic Policy Institute, who had at the beginning of our conversation taken the half-full perspective, heightened the mystery when he observed that productivity—to which wages are theoretically tied—has been rising at such a healthy clip that "workers should be getting much more."[6]

The most obvious reason why they're not is that employers resist wage increases with every trick they can think of and every ounce of strength they can summon. I had an opportunity to query one of my own employers on this subject in Maine . . . when Ted, my boss at The Maids, drove me about forty minutes to a house where I was needed to reinforce a shorthanded team. In the course of complaining about his hard lot in life, he avowed that he could double his business overnight if only he could find enough reliable workers. As politely as possible, I asked him why he didn't just raise the

pay. The question seemed to slide right off him. We offer "mothers' hours," he told me, meaning that the workday was supposedly over at three—as if to say, "With a benefit like that, how could anybody complain about wages?"

In fact, I suspect that the free breakfast he provided us represented the only concession to the labor shortage that he was prepared to make. Similarly, the Wal-Mart where I worked was offering free doughnuts once a week to any employees who could arrange to take their breaks while the supply lasted. As Louis Uchitelle has reported in the *New York Times,* many employers will offer almost anything—free meals, subsidized transportation, store discounts—rather than raise wages. The reason for this, in the words of one employer, is that such extras "can be shed more easily" than wage increases when changes in the market seem to make them unnecessary.[7] In the same spirit, automobile manufacturers would rather offer their customers cash rebates than reduced prices; the advantage of the rebate is that it seems like a gift and can be withdrawn without explanation.

But the resistance of employers only raises a second and ultimately more intractable question: Why isn't this resistance met by more effective counterpressure from the workers themselves? In evading and warding off wage increases, employers are of course behaving in an economically rational fashion; their business isn't to make their employees more comfortable and secure but to maximize the bottom line. So why don't employees behave in an equally rational fashion, demanding higher wages of their employers or seeking out better-paying jobs? The assumption behind the law of supply and demand, as it applies to labor, is that workers will sort themselves out as effectively as marbles on an inclined plane—gravitating to the better-paying jobs and either leaving the recalcitrant employers behind or forcing them to up the pay. "Economic man," that great abstraction of economic science, is supposed to do whatever it takes, within certain limits, to maximize his economic advantage.

I was baffled, initially, by what seemed like a certain lack of get-up-and-go on the part of my fellow workers. Why didn't they just leave for a better-paying job, as I did when I moved from the Hearth-side to Jerry's? Part of the answer is that actual humans experience a little more "friction" than marbles do, and the poorer they are, the more constrained their mobility usually is. Low-wage people who don't have cars are often dependent on a relative who is willing to drop them off and pick them up again each day, sometimes on a route that includes the babysitter's house or the child care center. Change your place of work and you may be confronted with an impossible topographical problem to solve, or at least a reluctant driver to persuade. Some of my coworkers, in Minneapolis as well as Key West, rode bikes to work, and this clearly limited their geographical range. For those who do possess cars, there is still the problem of gas prices, not to mention the general hassle, which is of course far more onerous for the carless, of getting around to fill out applications, to be interviewed, to take drug tests. I have mentioned, too, the general reluctance to exchange the devil you know for one that you don't know, even when the latter is tempting you with a better wage-benefit package. At each new job, you have to start all over, clueless and friendless.

There is another way that low-income workers differ from "economic man." For the laws of economics to work, the "players" need to be well informed about their options. The ideal case—and I've read that the technology for this is just around the corner—would be the consumer whose Palm Pilot displays the menu and prices for every restaurant or store he or she passes. Even without such technological assistance, affluent job hunters expect to study the salary-benefit packages offered by their potential employers, watch the financial news to find out if these packages are in line with those being offered in other regions or fields, and probably do a little bargaining before taking a job.

But there are no Palm Pilots, cable channels, or Web sites to advise the low-wage job seeker. She has only the help-wanted signs and the want ads to go on, and most of these coyly refrain from mentioning numbers. So information about who earns what and where has to travel by word of mouth,

and for inexplicable cultural reasons, this is a very slow and unreliable route. Twin Cities job market analyst Kristine Jacobs pinpoints what she calls the "money taboo" as a major factor preventing workers from optimizing their earnings. "There's a code of silence surrounding issues related to individuals' earnings," she told me. "We confess everything else in our society—sex, crime, illness. But no one wants to reveal what they earn or how they got it. The money taboo is the one thing that employers can always count on."[8] I suspect that this "taboo" operates most effectively among the lowest-paid people, because, in a society that endlessly celebrates its dot-com billionaires and centimillionaire athletes, $7 or even $10 an hour can feel like a mark of innate inferiority. So you may or may not find out that, say, the Target down the road is paying better than Wal-Mart, even if you have a sister-in-law working there.

Employers, of course, do little to encourage the economic literacy of their workers. They may exhort potential customers to "Compare Our Prices!" but they're not eager to have workers do the same with wages. . . . The hiring process seems designed, in some cases, to prevent any discussion or even disclosure of wages—whisking the applicant from interview to orientation before the crass subject of money can be raised. Some employers go further; instead of relying on the informal "money taboo" to keep workers from discussing and comparing wages, they specifically enjoin workers from doing so. The *New York Times* recently reported on several lawsuits brought by employees who had allegedly been fired for breaking this rule—a woman, for example, who asked for higher pay after learning from her male coworkers that she was being paid considerably less than they were for the very same work. The National Labor Relations Act of 1935 makes it illegal to punish people for revealing their wages to one another, but the practice is likely to persist until rooted out by lawsuits, company by company.[9]

But if it's hard for workers to obey the laws of economics by examining their options and moving on to better jobs, why don't more of them take a stand where they are—demanding better wages and work conditions, either individually or as a group? This is a huge question, probably the subject of many a dissertation in the field of industrial psychology, and here I can only comment on the things I observed. One of these was the co-optative power of management, illustrated by such euphemisms as *associate* and *team member*. At The Maids, the boss—who, as the only male in our midst, exerted a creepy, paternalistic kind of power—had managed to convince some of my coworkers that he was struggling against difficult odds and deserving of their unstinting forbearance. Wal-Mart has a number of more impersonal and probably more effective ways of getting its workers to feel like "associates." There was the profit-sharing plan, with Wal-Mart's stock price posted daily in a prominent spot near the break room. There was the company's much-heralded patriotism, evidenced in the banners over the shopping floor urging workers and customers to contribute to the construction of a World War II veterans' memorial (Sam Walton having been one of them). There were "associate" meetings that served as pep rallies, complete with the Wal-Mart cheer: "Gimme a 'W,'" etc.

The chance to identify with a powerful and wealthy entity—the company or the boss—is only the carrot. There is also a stick. What surprised and offended me most about the low-wage workplace (and yes, here all my middle-class privilege is on full display) was the extent to which one is required to surrender one's basic civil rights and—what boils down to the same thing—self-respect. I learned this at the very beginning of my stint as a waitress, when I was warned that my purse could be searched by management at any time. I wasn't carrying stolen salt shakers or anything else of a compromising nature, but still, there's something about the prospect of a purse search that makes a woman feel a few buttons short of fully dressed. After work, I called around and found that this practice is entirely legal: if the purse is on the boss's property—which of course it was—the boss has the right to examine its contents.

Drug testing is another routine indignity. Civil libertarians see it as a violation of our Fourth Amendment freedom from "unreasonable search"; most jobholders and applicants find it simply embarrassing. In some testing protocols, the employee has to strip to her underwear and pee into a cup in the presence of an aide or technician. Mercifully, I got to keep my clothes on and shut the toilet stall door behind me, but even so, urination is a private act and it is degrading to have to perform it at the command of some powerful other. I would add preemployment personality tests to the list of demeaning intrusions, or at least much of their usual content. Maybe the hypothetical types of questions can be justified— whether you would steal if an opportunity arose or turn in a thieving coworker and so on—but not questions about your "moods of self-pity," whether you are a loner or believe you are usually misunderstood. It is unsettling, at the very least, to give a stranger access to things, like your self-doubts and your urine, that are otherwise shared only in medical or therapeutic situations.

There are other, more direct ways of keeping low-wage employees in their place. Rules against "gossip," or even "talking," make it hard to air your grievances to peers or—should you be so daring— to enlist other workers in a group effort to bring about change, through a union organizing drive, for example. Those who do step out of line often face little unexplained punishments, such as having their schedules or their work assignments unilaterally changed. Or you may be fired; those low-wage workers who work without union contracts, which is the great majority of them, work "at will," meaning at the will of the employer, and are subject to dismissal without explanation. The AFL-CIO estimates that ten thousand workers a year are fired for participating in union organizing drives, and since it is illegal to fire people for union activity, I suspect that these firings are usually justified in terms of unrelated minor infractions. Wal-Mart employees who have bucked the company—by getting involved in a unionization drive or by suing the company for failing to pay overtime—have been fired for breaking the company rule against using profanity.[10]

So if low-wage workers do not always behave in an economically rational way, that is, as free agents within a capitalist democracy, it is because they dwell in a place that is neither free nor in any way democratic. When you enter the low-wage workplace—and many of the medium-wage workplaces as well—you check your civil liberties at the door, leave America and all it supposedly stands for behind, and learn to zip your lips for the duration of the shift. The consequences of this routine surrender go beyond the issues of wages and poverty. We can hardly pride ourselves on being the world's preeminent democracy, after all, if large numbers of citizens spend half their waking hours in what amounts, in plain terms, to a dictatorship.

Any dictatorship takes a psychological toll on its subjects. If you are treated as an untrustworthy person—a potential slacker, drug addict, or thief—you may begin to feel less trustworthy yourself. If you are constantly reminded of your lowly position in the social hierarchy, whether by individual managers or by a plethora of impersonal rules, you begin to accept that unfortunate status. To draw for a moment from an entirely different corner of my life, that part of me still attached to the biological sciences, there is ample evidence that animals—rats and monkeys, for example—that are forced into a subordinate status within their social systems adapt their brain chemistry accordingly, becoming "depressed" in humanlike ways. Their behavior is anxious and withdrawn; the level of serotonin (the neurotransmitter boosted by some antidepressants) declines in their brains. And—what is especially relevant here—they avoid fighting even in self-defense.[11]

Humans are, of course, vastly more complicated; even in situations of extreme subordination, we can pump up our self-esteem with thoughts of our families, our religion, our hopes for the future. But as much as any other social animal, and more so than many, we depend for our self-image on the humans immediately around us—to the point of altering our perceptions of the world so as to fit in with theirs.[12] My guess is that the indignities imposed on so many low-wage workers—the drug tests, the constant surveillance, being "reamed out" by managers—are

part of what keeps wages low. If you're made to feel unworthy enough, you may come to think that what you're paid is what you are actually worth.

It is hard to imagine any other function for workplace authoritarianism. Managers may truly believe that, without their unremitting efforts, all work would quickly grind to a halt. That is not my impression. While I encountered some cynics and plenty of people who had learned to budget their energy, I never met an actual slacker or, for that matter, a drug addict or thief. On the contrary, I was amazed and sometimes saddened by the pride people took in jobs that rewarded them so meagerly, either in wages or in recognition. Often, in fact, these people experienced management as an obstacle to getting the job done as it should be done. Waitresses chafed at managers' stinginess toward the customers; housecleaners resented the time constraints that sometimes made them cut corners; retail workers wanted the floor to be beautiful, not cluttered with excess stock as management required. Left to themselves, they devised systems of cooperation and work sharing; when there was a crisis, they rose to it. In fact, it was often hard to see what the function of management was, other than to exact obeisance.

There seems to be a vicious cycle at work here, making ours not just an economy but a culture of extreme inequality. Corporate decision makers, and even some two-bit entrepreneurs like my boss at The Maids, occupy an economic position miles above that of the underpaid people whose labor they depend on. For reasons that have more to do with class—and often racial—prejudice than with actual experience, they tend to fear and distrust the category of people from which they recruit their workers. Hence the perceived need for repressive management and intrusive measures like drug and personality testing. But these things cost money—$20,000 or more a year for a manager, $100 a pop for a drug test, and so on—and the high cost of repression results in ever more pressure to hold wages down. The larger society seems to be caught up in a similar cycle: cutting public services for the poor, which are sometimes referred to collectively as the "social wage," while investing ever more heavily in prisons and cops. And in the larger society, too, the cost of repression becomes another factor weighing against the expansion or restoration of needed services. It is a tragic cycle, condemning us to ever deeper inequality, and in the long run, almost no one benefits but the agents of repression themselves.

But whatever keeps wages low—and I'm sure my comments have barely scratched the surface—the result is that many people earn far less than they need to live on. How much is that? The Economic Policy Institute recently reviewed dozens of studies of what constitutes a "living wage" and came up with an average figure of $30,000 a year for a family of one adult and two children, which amounts to a wage of $14 an hour. This is not the very minimum such a family could live on; the budget includes health insurance, a telephone, and child care at a licensed center, for example, which are well beyond the reach of millions. But it does not include restaurant meals, video rentals, Internet access, wine and liquor, cigarettes and lottery tickets, or even very much meat. The shocking thing is that the majority of American workers, about 60 percent, earn less than $14 an hour. Many of them get by by teaming up with another wage earner, a spouse or grown child. Some draw on government help in the form of food stamps, housing vouchers, the earned income tax credit, or—for those coming off welfare in relatively generous states—subsidized child care. But others—single mothers for example—have nothing but their own wages to live on, no matter how many mouths there are to feed.

Employers will look at that $30,000 figure, which is over twice what they currently pay entry-level workers, and see nothing but bankruptcy ahead. Indeed, it is probably impossible for the private sector to provide everyone with an adequate standard of living through wages, or even wages plus benefits, alone: too much of what we need, such as reliable child care, is just too expensive, even for middle-class families. Most civilized nations compensate for the inadequacy of wages by providing relatively generous public services such as health insurance, free or subsidized child care, subsidized housing, and effective public transportation. But the United States, for all its wealth, leaves its citizens to fend for themselves—facing market-based rents, for example, on their wages alone. For millions of Americans, that $10—or even $8 or $6—hourly wage is all there is.

It is common, among the nonpoor, to think of poverty as a sustainable condition—austere, perhaps, but they get by somehow, don't they? They are "always with us." What is harder for the nonpoor to see is poverty as acute distress: The lunch that consists of Doritos or hot dog rolls, leading to faintness before the end of the shift. The "home" that is also a car or a van. The illness or injury that must be "worked through," with gritted teeth, because there's no sick pay or health insurance and the loss of one day's pay will mean no groceries for the next. These experiences are not part of a sustainable lifestyle, even a lifestyle of chronic deprivation and relentless low-level punishment. They are, by almost any standard of subsistence, emergency situations. And that is how we should see the poverty of so many millions of low-wage Americans—as a state of emergency.

In the summer of 2000 I returned—permanently, I have every reason to hope—to my customary place in the socioeconomic spectrum. I go to restaurants, often far finer ones than the places where I worked, and sit down at a table. I sleep in hotel rooms that someone else has cleaned and shop in stores that others will tidy when I leave. To go from the bottom 20 percent to the top 20 percent is to enter a magical world where needs are met, problems are solved, almost without any intermediate effort. If you want to get somewhere fast, you hail a cab. If your aged parents have grown tiresome or incontinent, you put them away where others will deal with their dirty diapers and dementia. If you are part of the upper-middle-class majority that employs a maid or maid service, you return from work to find the house miraculously restored to order—the toilet bowls shit-free and gleaming, the socks that you left on the floor levitated back to their normal dwelling place. Here, sweat is a metaphor for hard work, but seldom its consequence. Hundreds of little things get done, reliably and routinely every day, without anyone's seeming to do them.

The top 20 percent routinely exercises other, far more consequential forms of power in the world. This stratum, which contains what I have termed in an earlier book the "professional-managerial class," is the home of our decision makers, opinion shapers, culture creators—our professors, lawyers, executives, entertainers, politicians, judges, writers, producers, and editors.[13] When they speak, they are listened to. When they complain, someone usually scurries to correct the problem and apologize for it. If they complain often enough, someone far below them in wealth and influence may be chastised or even fired. Political power, too, is concentrated within the top 20 percent, since its members are far more likely than the poor—or even the middle class—to discern the all-too-tiny distinctions between candidates that can make it seem worthwhile to contribute, participate, and vote. In all these ways, the affluent exert inordinate power over the lives of the less affluent, and especially over the lives of the poor, determining what public services will be available, if any, what minimum wage, what laws governing the treatment of labor.

So it is alarming, upon returning to the upper middle class from a sojourn, however artificial and temporary, among the poor, to find the rabbit hole close so suddenly and completely behind me. You were *where,* doing *what?* Some odd optical property of our highly polarized and unequal society makes the poor almost invisible to their economic superiors. The poor can see the affluent easily enough—on television, for example, or on the covers of magazines. But the affluent rarely see the poor or, if they do catch sight of them in some public space, rarely know what they're seeing, since—thanks to consignment stores and, yes, Wal-Mart—the poor are usually able to disguise themselves as members of the more comfortable classes. Forty years ago the hot journalistic topic was the "discovery of the poor" in their inner-city and Appalachian "pockets of poverty." Today you are more likely to find commentary on their "disappearance," either as a supposed demographic reality or as a shortcoming of the middle-class imagination.

In a 2000 article on the "disappearing poor," journalist James Fallows reports that, from the vantage point of the Internet's nouveaux riches, it is "hard to understand people for whom a million dollars would be a fortune . . . not to mention those for whom $246 is a full week's earnings."[14] Among the reasons he and others have cited for the blindness of the affluent is the fact that they are less and less likely to share spaces and services with the poor. As public schools and other public services deteriorate, those who can afford to do so send their children to private schools and spend their off-hours in private spaces—health clubs, for example, instead of the local park. They don't ride on public buses and subways. They withdraw from mixed neighborhoods into distant suburbs, gated communities, or guarded apartment towers; they shop in stores that, in line with the prevailing "market segmentation," are designed to appeal to the affluent alone. Even the affluent young are increasingly unlikely to spend their summers learning how the "other half" lives, as lifeguards, waitresses, or housekeepers at resort hotels. The *New York Times* reports that they now prefer career-relevant activities like summer school or interning in an appropriate professional setting to the "sweaty, low-paid and mind-numbing slots that have long been their lot."[15]

Then, too, the particular political moment favors what almost looks like a "conspiracy of silence" on the subject of poverty and the poor. The Democrats are not eager to find flaws in the period of "unprecedented prosperity" they take credit for; the Republicans have lost interest in the poor now that "welfare-as-we-know-it" has ended. Welfare reform itself is a factor weighing against any close investigation of the conditions of the poor. Both parties heartily endorsed it, and to acknowledge that low-wage work doesn't lift people out of poverty would be to admit that it may have been, in human terms, a catastrophic mistake. In fact, very little is known about the fate of former welfare recipients because the 1996 welfare reform legislation blithely failed to include any provision for monitoring their postwelfare economic condition. Media accounts persistently bright-side the situation, highlighting the occasional success stories and downplaying the acknowledged increase in hunger.[16] And sometimes there seems to be almost deliberate deception. In June 2000, the press rushed to hail a study supposedly showing that Minnesota's welfare-to-work program had sharply reduced poverty and was, as *Time* magazine put it, a "winner."[17] Overlooked in these reports was the fact that the program in question was a pilot project that offered far more generous child care and other subsidies than Minnesota's actual welfare reform program. Perhaps the error can be forgiven—the pilot project, which ended in 1997, had the same name, Minnesota Family Investment Program, as Minnesota's much larger, ongoing welfare reform program.[18]

You would have to read a great many newspapers very carefully, cover to cover, to see the signs of distress. You would find, for example, that in 1999 Massachusetts food pantries reported a 72 percent increase in the demand for their services over the previous year, that Texas food banks were "scrounging" for food, despite donations at or above 1998 levels, as were those in Atlanta.[19] You might learn that in San Diego the Catholic Church could no longer, as of January 2000, accept homeless families at its shelter, which happens to be the city's largest, because it was already operating at twice its normal capacity.[20] You would come across news of a study showing that the percentage of Wisconsin food-stamp families in "extreme poverty"—defined as less than 50 percent of the federal poverty line—has tripled in the last decade to more than 30 percent.[21] You might discover that, nationwide, America's food banks are experiencing "a torrent of need which [they] cannot meet" and that, according to a survey conducted by the U.S. Conference of Mayors, 67 percent of the adults requesting emergency food aid are people with jobs.[22]

One reason nobody bothers to pull all these stories together and announce a widespread state of emergency may be that Americans of the newspaper-reading professional middle class are used to thinking of poverty as a consequence of unemployment. During the heyday of downsizing in the Reagan years, it very often was, and it still is for many inner-city residents who have no way of getting to the proliferating entry-level jobs on urban peripheries. When unemployment causes poverty, we know how to state the problem—typically, "the economy isn't growing fast enough"—and we know what the traditional liberal solution is—"full employment." But when we have full or nearly full employment, when jobs are available to any job seeker who can get to them, then the problem goes deeper and begins to cut into that web of expectations that make up the "social contract." According to a recent poll conducted by Jobs for the Future, a Boston-based employment research firm, 94 percent of Americans agree that "people who work full-time should be able to earn enough to keep their families out of poverty."[23] I grew up hearing over and over, to the point of tedium, that "hard work" was the secret of success: "Work hard and you'll get ahead" or "It's hard work that got us where we are." No one ever said that you could work hard—harder even than you ever thought possible—and still find yourself sinking ever deeper into poverty and debt.

When poor single mothers had the option of remaining out of the labor force on welfare, the middle and upper middle class tended to view them with a certain impatience, if not disgust. The welfare poor were excoriated for their laziness, their persistence in reproducing in unfavorable circumstances, their presumed addictions, and above all for their "dependency." Here they were, content to live off "government handouts" instead of seeking "self-sufficiency," like everyone else, through a job. They needed to get their act together, learn how to wind an alarm clock, get out there and get to work. But now that government has largely withdrawn its "handouts," now that the overwhelming majority of the poor are out there toiling in Wal-Mart or Wendy's—well, what are we to think of them? Disapproval and condescension no longer apply, so what outlook makes sense?

Guilt, you may be thinking warily. Isn't that what we're supposed to feel? But guilt doesn't go anywhere near far enough; the appropriate emotion is shame—shame at our *own* dependency, in this case, on the underpaid labor of others. When someone works for less pay than she can live on—when, for example, she goes hungry so that you can eat more cheaply and conveniently—then she has made a great

PERSONAL ACCOUNT

How I Learned to Appreciate Printers

One thing I will never take for granted are printers. I grew up living in an apartment complex located in Fairfax County. My dad has worked two jobs as a maintenance engineer since we immigrated to the United States from Bolivia, while my mom worked and took care of my sister and me. Although we lived comfortably, we did not have enough money to purchase a new computer. Instead, my dad would occasionally bring home a variety of parts from old computers that the white collar employees at his job discarded.

When I was in sixth grade, we had finally accumulated enough pieces to put together an entire computer with mouse, monitor, and keyboard. Although it was not new, it worked and I was delighted. However, the problem with my computer was that the printer did not work. One night I had to print out an eight-page story for my sixth grade English class, which meant that my mom and dad had to take me to Kinko's. I hated Kinko's! The amount of money we needed to pay for some ink and paper astounded me. My heart would sink each time we had to go. My dad would get so mad every time we would walk up to the front desk to pay for my pages. I did not know much about computers, so there were also lots of things that went wrong on our visits to Kinko's. My dad would get impatient, and I would get frustrated as my mom tried her best to figure out the problem. Every minute there felt like an hour! It has been years since my family first purchased our very own home printer, yet the sense of relief and appreciation has yet to fade every time my printer prints.

Sandra Pamela Maida

---

sacrifice for you, she has made you a gift of some part of her abilities, her health, and her life. The "working poor," as they are approvingly termed, are in fact the major philanthropists of our society. They neglect their own children so that the children of others will be cared for; they live in substandard housing so that other homes will be shiny and perfect; they endure privation so that inflation will be low and stock prices high. To be a member of the working poor is to be an anonymous donor, a nameless benefactor, to everyone else. As Gail, one of my restaurant coworkers put it, "you give and you give."

Someday, of course—and I will make no predictions as to exactly when—they are bound to tire of getting so little in return and to demand to be paid what they're worth. There'll be a lot of anger when that day comes, and strikes and disruption. But the sky will not fall, and we will all be better off for it in the end.

DISCUSSION QUESTIONS

1. Why might the poverty of low-wage workers be invisible to America's middle and upper classes?

2. Ehrenreich describes an American culture of "repressive management," at least in the world of low-wage work. If you have worked in low-wage jobs, has that been your experience?

3. Did it surprise you when Ehrenreich referred to the tax deduction she receives for the interest on her mortgage as a "housing subsidy"? Why or why not?

NOTES

1. Jared Bernstein, Chauna Brocht, and Maggie Spade-Aguilar, "How Much Is Enough? Basic Family Budgets for Working Families," Economic Policy Institute, Washington, D.C., 2000, p. 14.
2. "Companies Try Dipping Deeper into Labor Pool," *New York Times*, March 26, 2000.
3. "An Epitaph for a Rule That Just Won't Die," *New York Times*, July 30, 2000.
4. "Fact or Fallacy: Labor Shortage May Really Be Wage Stagnation," *Chicago Tribune*, July 2, 2000; "It's a Wage Shortage, Not a Labor Shortage," *Minneapolis Star Tribune*, March 25, 2000.
5. I thank John Schmidt at the Economic Policy Institute in Washington, D.C., for preparing the wage data for me.

6. Interview, July 18, 2000.

7. "Companies Try Dipping Deeper into Labor Pool," *New York Times,* March 26, 2000.

8. Personal communication, July 24, 2000.

9. "The Biggest Company Secret: Workers Challenge Employer Practices on Pay Confidentiality," *New York Times,* July 28, 2000.

10. Bob Ortega, *In Sam We Trust,* p. 356; "Former Wal-Mart Workers File Overtime Suit in Harrison County," *Charleston Gazette,* January 24, 1999.

11. See, for example, C. A. Shively, K. Laber-Laird, and R. F. Anton, "Behavior and Physiology of Social Stress and Depression in Female Cynomolgous Monkeys," *Biological Psychiatry* 41:8 (1997), pp. 871–82, and D. C. Blanchard et al., "Visible Burrow System as a Model of Chronic Social Stress: Behavioral and Neuroendocrine Correlates," *Psychoneuroendocrinology* 20:2 (1995), pp. 117–34.

12. See, for example, chapter 7, "Conformity," in David G. Myers, *Social Psychology* (McGraw-Hill, 1987).

13. *Fear of Falling: The Inner Life of the Middle Class* (Pantheon, 1989).

14. "The Invisible Poor," *New York Times Magazine,* March 19, 2000.

15. "Summer Work Is Out of Favor with the Young," *New York Times,* June 18, 2000.

16. The *National Journal* reports that the "good news" is that almost six million people have left the welfare rolls since 1996, while the "rest of the story" includes the problem that "these people sometimes don't have enough to eat" ("Welfare Reform, Act 2," June 24, 2000, pp. 1, 978–93).

17. "Minnesota's Welfare Reform Proves a Winner," *Time,* June 12, 2000.

18. Center for Law and Social Policy, "Update," Washington, D.C., June 2000.

19. "Study: More Go Hungry since Welfare Reform," *Boston Herald,* January 21, 2000; "Charity Can't Feed All while Welfare Reforms Implemented," *Houston Chronicle,* January 10, 2000; "Hunger Grows as Food Banks Try to Keep Pace," *Atlanta Journal and Constitution,* November 26, 1999.

20. "Rise in Homeless Families Strains San Diego Aid," *Los Angeles Times,* January 24, 2000.

21. "Hunger Problems Said to Be Getting Worse," *Milwaukee Journal Sentinel,* December 15, 1999.

22. Deborah Leff, the president and CEO of the hunger-relief organization America's Second Harvest, quoted in the *National Journal,* op. cit.; "Hunger Persists in U.S. despite the Good Times," *Detroit News,* June 15, 2000.

23. "A National Survey of American Attitudes toward Low-Wage Workers and Welfare Reform," Jobs for the Future, Boston, May 24, 2000.

READING 37

Cause of Death: Inequality

Alejandro Reuss

INEQUALITY KILLS

You won't see inequality on a medical chart or a coroner's report under "cause of death." You won't see it listed among the top killers in the United States each year. All too often, however, it is social inequality that lurks behind a more immediate cause of death, be it heart disease or diabetes, accidental injury or homicide. Few of the top causes of death are "equal opportunity killers." Instead, they tend to strike poor people more than rich people, the less educated more than the highly educated, people lower on the occupational ladder more than those higher up, or people of color more than white people.

Statistics on mortality and life expectancy do not provide a perfect map of social inequality. For example, the life expectancy for women in the United States is about six years longer than the life expectancy for men, despite the many ways in which women are subordinated to men. Take most indicators of socioeconomic status, however, and most causes of death, and it's a strong bet that you'll find illness and injury (or "morbidity") and mortality increasing as status decreases.

Men with less than 12 years of education are more than twice as likely to die of chronic diseases (e.g., heart disease), more than three times as likely to die as a result of injury, and nearly twice as likely to die of communicable diseases, compared to those with 13 or more years of education. Women with family incomes below $10,000 are more than three times as likely to die of heart disease and nearly three times as likely to die of diabetes, compared to those with family incomes above $25,000.

Alejandro Reuss is a doctoral candidate in economics at the University of Massachusetts, Amherst.

...re more likely than whites to ...stroke; lung, colon, prostate, ...well as all cancers combined; ...AIDS; accidental injury; and ...all, the lower you are in a social hier-...chy, the worse your health and the shorter your life are likely to be.

THE WORSE OFF IN THE UNITED STATES ARE NOT WELL OFF BY WORLD STANDARDS

You often hear it said that even poor people in rich countries like the United States are rich compared to ordinary people in poor countries. While that may be true when it comes to consumer goods like televisions or telephones, which are widely available even to poor people in the United States, it's completely wrong when it comes to health.

In a 1996 study published in the New England Journal of Medicine, University of Michigan researchers found that African-American females living to age 15 in Harlem had a 65% chance of surviving to age 65, about the same as women in India. Meanwhile, Harlem's African-American males had only a 37% chance of surviving to age 65, about the same as men in Angola or the Democratic Republic of Congo. Among both African-American men and women, infectious diseases and diseases of the circulatory system were the prime causes of high mortality.

It takes more income to achieve a given life expectancy in a rich country like the United States than it does to achieve the same life expectancy in a less affluent country. So the higher money income of a low-income person in the United States, compared to a middle-income person in a poor country, does not necessarily translate into a longer life span. The average income per person in African-American families, for example, is more than five times the per capita income of El Salvador. The life expectancy for African-American men in the United States, however, is only about 67 years, the same as the average life expectancy for men in El Salvador.

HEALTH INEQUALITIES IN THE UNITED STATES ARE NOT JUST ABOUT ACCESS TO HEALTH CARE

Nearly one-sixth of the U.S. population lacks health insurance, including about 44% of poor people. A poor adult with a health problem is only half as likely to see a doctor as a high-income adult. Adults living in low-income areas are more than twice as likely to be hospitalized for a health problem that could have been effectively treated with timely outpatient care, compared with adults living in high-income areas. Obviously, lack of access to health care is a major health problem.

But so are environmental and occupational hazards; communicable diseases; homicide and firearm-related injuries; and smoking, alcohol consumption, lack of exercise, and other risk factors. These dangers all tend to affect lower-income people more than higher-income, less educated people more than more-educated, and people of color more than whites. African-American children are more than twice as likely as white children to be hospitalized for asthma, which is linked to air pollution. Poor men are nearly six times as likely as high-income men to have elevated blood-lead levels, which reflect both residential and workplace environmental hazards. African-American men are more than seven times as likely to fall victim to homicide as white men; African-American women, more than four times as likely as white women. The less education someone has, the more likely they are to smoke or to drink heavily. The lower someone's income, the less likely they are to get regular exercise.

Michael Marmot, a pioneer in the study of social inequality and health, notes that so-called diseases of affluence—disorders, like heart disease, associated with high calorie and high-fat diets, lack of physical activity, etc.—are most prevalent among the least affluent people in rich societies. While recognizing the role of such "behavioral" risk factors as smoking in producing poor health, he argues, "It is not sufficient . . . to ask what contribution smoking makes to generating the social gradient in ill health, but we must ask, why is there a social gradient in smoking?" What appear to be individual "lifestyle" decisions often reflect a broader social epidemiology.

GREATER INCOME INEQUALITY GOES HAND IN HAND WITH POORER HEALTH

Numerous studies suggest that the more unequal the income distribution in a country, state, or city, the lower the life expectancies for people at all income levels. One study published in the *American Journal of Public Health*, for example, shows that U.S. metropolitan areas with low per capita incomes and low levels of income inequality have lower mortality rates than areas with high median incomes and high levels of income inequality. Meanwhile, for a given per capita income range, mortality rates always decline as inequality declines.

R. G. Wilkinson, perhaps the researcher most responsible for relating health outcomes to overall levels of inequality (rather than individual income levels), argues that greater income inequality causes worse health outcomes independent of its effects on poverty. Wilkinson and his associates suggest several explanations for this relationship. First, the bigger the income gap between rich and poor, the less inclined the well off are to pay taxes for public services they either do not use or use in low proportion to the taxes they pay. Lower spending on public hospitals, schools, and other basic services does not affect wealthy people's life expectancies very much, but it affects poor people's life expectancies a great deal. Second, the bigger the income gap, the lower the overall level of social cohesion. High levels of social cohesion are associated with good health outcomes for several reasons. For example, people in highly cohesive societies are more likely to be active in their communities, reducing social isolation, a known health risk factor. (See Thad Williamson, "Social Movements Are Good for Your Health")

Numerous researchers have criticized Wilkinson's conclusions, arguing that the real reason income inequality tends to be associated with worse health outcomes is that it is associated with higher rates of poverty. But even if they are right and inequality causes worse health simply by bringing about greater poverty, that hardly makes for a defense of inequality. Poverty and inequality are like partners in crime. "[W]hether public policy focuses primarily on the elimination of poverty or on reduction in income disparity," argue Wilkinson critics Kevin Fiscella and Peter Franks, "neither goal is likely to be achieved in the absence of the other."

DIFFERENCES IN STATUS MAY BE JUST AS IMPORTANT AS INCOME LEVELS

Even after accounting for differences in income, education, and other factors, the life expectancy for African Americans is less than that for whites. U.S. researchers are beginning to explore the relationship between high blood pressure among African Americans and the racism of the surrounding society. African Americans tend to suffer from high blood pressure, a risk factor for circulatory disease, more often than whites. Moreover, studies have found that, when confronted with racism, African Americans suffer larger and longer-lasting increases in blood pressure than when faced with other stressful situations. Broader surveys relating blood pressure in African Americans to perceived instances of racial discrimination have yielded complex results, depending on social class, gender, and other factors.

Stresses cascade down social hierarchies and accumulate among the least empowered. Even researchers focusing on social inequality and health, however, have been surprised by the large effects on mortality. Over 30 years ago, Michael Marmot and his associates undertook a landmark study, known as Whitehall I, of health among British civil servants. Since the civil servants shared many characteristics regardless of job classification—an office work environment, a high degree of job security, etc.—the researchers expected to find only modest health differences among them. To their surprise, the study revealed a sharp increase in mortality with each step down the job hierarchy—even from the highest grade to the second highest. Over ten years, employees in the lowest grade likely to die as those in the high- was that people in lower grades lence of many "lifestyle" risk ... oor diet, and lack of exercise. ... researchers controlled for such factors, ... owever, more than half the mortality gap remained.

Marmot noted that people in the lower job grades were less likely to describe themselves as having "control over their working lives" or being "satisfied with their work situation," compared to those higher up. While people in higher job grades were more likely to report "having to work at a fast pace," lower-level civil servants were more likely to report feelings of hostility, the main stress-related risk factor for heart disease. Marmot concluded that "psycho-social" factors—the psychological costs of being lower in the hierarchy—played an important role in the unexplained mortality gap. Many of us have probably said to ourselves, after a trying day on the job, "They're killing me." Turns out it's not just a figure of speech. Inequality kills—and it starts at the bottom.

DISCUSSION QUESTIONS

1. What explanation can you offer for why the rich are less likely to support public services in communities with a wide income gap between the rich and poor?
2. Why do you think there might be social class differences in smoking, drinking, or exercise?
3. What are all the factors that produce higher illness and mortality rates for poor Americans?

REFERENCES

Lisa Berkman, "Social Inequalities and Health: Five Key Points for Policy-Makers to Know," February 5, 2001, Kennedy School of Government, Harvard University.

Kevin Fiscella and Peter Franks, "Poverty or income inequality as predictors of mortality: longitudinal cohort study," British Medical Journal 314: 1724–8, 1997.

Arline T. Geronimus, et al., "Excess Mortality among Blacks and Whites in the United States," The New England Journal of Medicine 335 (21), November 21, 1996.

Health, United States, 1998, with Socioeconomic Status and Health Chartbook, National Center for Health Statistics, www.cdc.gov/nchs.

Human Development Report 2000, UN Development Programme.

Ichiro Kawachi, Bruce P. Kennedy, and Richard G. Wilkinson, eds., The Society and Population Health Reader, Volume I: Income Inequality and Health, 1999.

Nancy Krieger, Ph.D., and Stephen Sidney, M.D., "Racial Discrimination and Blood Pressure: The CARDIA Study of Young Black and White Adults," American Journal of Public Health 86 (10), October 1996.

Michael Marmot, "Social Differences in Mortality: The Whitehall Studies," Adult Mortality in Developed Countries: From Description to Explanation, Alan D. Lopez, Graziella Caselli, and Tapani Valkonen, eds., 1995.

Michael Marmot, "The Social Pattern of Health and Disease," Health and Social Organization: Towards a Health Policy for the Twenty First Century, David Blane, Eric Brunner, and Richard Wilkinson, eds., 1996.

Thad Williamson, "Social Movements Are Good for Your Health," Dollars and Sense, May/June, 2001.

World Development Indicators 2000, World Bank.

READING 38

Why Are Droves of Unqualified, Unprepared Kids Getting into Our Top Colleges? Because Their Dads Are Alumni

John Larew

Growing up, she heard a hundred Harvard stories. In high school, she put the college squarely in her sights. But when judgment day came in the winter of 1988, the Harvard admissions guys were frankly unimpressed. Her academic record was solid—not special. Extracurriculars, interview, recommendations? Above average, but not by much. "Nothing really stands out" one admissions officer scribbled on her application folder. Wrote another, "Harvard not really the right place."

John Larew wrote this article when he was editor of Harvard's student newspaper, The Harvard Crimson.

At the hyperselective Harvard, where high school valedictorians, National Merit Scholar finalists, musical prodigies—11,000 ambitious kids in all—are rejected annually, this young woman didn't seem to have much of a chance. Thanks to Harvard's largest affirmative action program, she got in anyway. No, she wasn't poor, black, disabled, Hispanic, native American, or even Aleutian. She got in because her mom went to Harvard.

Folk wisdom at Harvard holds that "Mother Harvard does not coddle her young." She sure treats her grandkids right, though. For more than 40 years, an astounding one-fifth of Harvard's students have received admissions preference because parents attended the school. Today, these overwhelming affluent, white children of alumni—"legacies"—are three times more likely to be accepted to Harvard than high school kids who lack that handsome lineage.

Yalies, don't feel smug: Offspring of the Old Blue are two-and-a-half times more likely to be accepted than their unconnected peers. Dartmouth this year admitted 57 percent of its legacy applicants, compared to 27 percent of nonlegacies. At the University of Pennsylvania, 66 percent of legacies were admitted last year—thanks in part to an autonomous "office of alumni admissions" that actively lobbies for alumni children before the admissions committee. "One can argue that it's an accident, but it sure doesn't look like an accident," admits Yale Dean of Admissions Worth David.

If the legacies' big edge seems unfair to the tens of thousands who get turned away every year, Ivy League administrators have long defended the innocence of the legacy stat. Children of alumni are just smarter; they come from privileged backgrounds and tend to grow up in homes where parents encourage learning. That's what Harvard Dean of Admissions William Fitzsimmons told the campus newspaper, the *Harvard Crimson*, when it first reported on the legacy preference last year. Departing Harvard President Derek Bok patiently explained that the legacy preference worked only as a "tie-breaking factor" between otherwise equally qualified candidates.

Since Ivy League admissions data is a notoriously classified commodity, when Harvard officials said in previous years that alumni kids were just better, you had to take them at their word. But then federal investigators came along and pried open those top-secret files. The Harvard guys were lying.

This past fall, after two years of study, the U.S. Department of Education's Office for Civil Rights (OCR) found that, far from being more qualified or even equally qualified, the average admitted legacy at Harvard between 1981 and 1988 was significantly *less* qualified than the average admitted nonlegacy. Examining admissions office ratings on academics, extracurriculars, personal qualities, recommendations, and other categories, the OCR concluded that "with the exception of the athletic rating, [admitted] nonlegacies scored better than legacies in *all* areas of comparison."

Exceptionally high admit rates, lowered academic standards, preferential treatment . . . hmmm. These sound like the cries heard in the growing fury over affirmative action for racial minorities in America's elite universities. Only no one is outraged about legacies.

- In his recent book, *Preferential Policies,* Thomas Sowell argues that doling out special treatment encourages lackluster performance by the favored and resentment from the spurned. His far-ranging study flits from Malaysia to South Africa to American college campuses. Legacies don't merit a word.
- Dinesh D'Souza, in his celebrated jeremiad *Illiberal Education,* blames affirmative action in college admissions for declining academic standards and increasing racial tensions. Lowered standards for minority applicants, he hints, may soon destroy the university as we know it. Lowered standards for legacies? The subject doesn't come up.
- For all his polysyllabic complaints against preferential admissions, William F. Buckley Jr. (Yale '50) has never bothered to note that son Chris (Yale '75) got the benefit of a policy that more than doubled his chance of admission.

With so much silence on the subject, you'd be excused for thinking that in these enlightened times hereditary preferences are few and far between. But you'd be wrong. At most elite universities during the eighties, the legacy was by far the biggest piece of the preferential pie. At Harvard, a legacy is about twice as likely to be admitted as a black or Hispanic student. As sociologists Jerome Karabel and David Karen point out, if alumni children were admitted to Harvard at the same rate as other applicants, their numbers in the class of 1992 would have been reduced by about 200. Instead, those 200 marginally qualified legacies outnumbered all black, Mexican-American, native American, and Puerto Rican enrollees put together. If a few marginally qualified minorities are undermining Harvard's academic standards as much as conservatives charge, think about the damage all those legacies must be doing.

Mind you, colleges have the right to give the occasional preference—to bend the rules for the brilliant oboist or the world-class curler or the guy whose remarkable decency can't be measured by the SAT. (I happened to benefit from a geographical edge: It's easier to get into Harvard from West Virginia than from New England.) And until standardized tests and grade point average perfectly reflect the character, judgment, and drive of a student, tips like these aren't just nice, they're fair. Unfortunately, the extent of the legacy privilege in elite American colleges suggests something more than the occasional tie-breaking tip. Forget meritocracy. When 20 percent of Harvard's student body gets a legacy preference, aristocracy is the word that comes to mind.

A CASTE OF THOUSANDS

If complaining about minority preferences is fashionable in the world of competitive colleges, bitching about legacies is just plain gauche, suggesting an unhealthy resentment of the privileged. But the effects of the legacy trickle down. For every legacy that wins, someone—usually someone less privileged—loses. And higher education is a high-stakes game.

High school graduates earn 59 percent of the income of four-year college graduates. Between high school graduates and alumni of prestigious colleges, the disparity is far greater. A *Fortune* study of

American CEOs shows the usual suspects—graduates of Yale, Princeton, and Harvard—leading the list. A recent survey of the Harvard Class of 1940 found that 43 percent were worth more than $1 million. With some understatement, the report concludes, "A picture of highly advantageous circumstances emerges here, does it not, compared with American society as a whole?"

An Ivy League diploma doesn't necessarily mean a fine education. Nor does it guarantee future success. What it *does* represent is a big head start in the rat race—a fact Harvard will be the first to tell you. When I was a freshman, a counselor at the Office of Career Services instructed a group of us to make the Harvard name stand out on our résumés: "Underline it, boldface it, put it in capital letters."

Of course, the existence of the legacy preference in this fierce career competition isn't exactly news. According to historians, it was a direct result of the influx of Jews into the Ivy League during the twenties. Until then, Harvard, Princeton, and Yale had admitted anyone who could pass their entrance exams, but suddenly Jewish kids were outscoring the WASPs. So the schools began to use nonacademic criteria—"character," "solidity," and, eventually, lineage—to justify accepting low-scoring blue bloods over their peers. Yale implemented its legacy preference first, in 1925—spelling it out in a memo four years later: The school would admit "Yale sons of good character and reasonably good record . . . regardless of the number of applicants and the superiority of outside competitors." Harvard and Princeton followed shortly thereafter.

Despite its ignoble origins, the legacy preference has only sporadically come under fire, most notably in 1978's affirmative action decision, *University of California Board of Regents v. Bakke*. In his concurrence, Justice Harris Blackmun observed, "It is somewhat ironic to have us so deeply disturbed over a program where race is an element of consciousness, and yet to be aware of the fact, as we are, that institutions of higher learning . . . have given conceded preferences to the children of alumni."

If people are, in fact, aware of the legacy preference, why has it been spared the scrutiny given other preferential policies? One reason is public ignorance of the scope and scale of those preferences—an ignorance carefully cultivated by America's elite institutions. It's easy to maintain the fiction that your legacies get in strictly on merit as long as your admissions bureaucracy controls all access to student data. Information on Harvard's legacies became publicly available not because of any fit of disclosure by the university, but because a few civil rights types noted that the school had a suspiciously low rate of admission for Asian-Americans, who are statistically stronger than other racial groups in academics.

While the ensuing OCR inquiry found no evidence of illegal racial discrimination by Harvard, it did turn up some embarrassing information about how much weight the "legacy" label gives an otherwise flimsy file. Take these comments scrawled by admissions officers on applicant folders:

- "Double lineage who chose the right parents."
- "Dad's [deleted] connections signify lineage of more than usual weight. That counted into the equation makes this a case which (assuming positive TRs [teacher recommendations] and Alum IV [alumnus interview]) is well worth doing."
- "Lineage is main thing."
- "Not quite strong enough to get the clean tip."
- "Classical case that would be hard to explain to dad."
- "Double lineage but lots of problems."
- "Not a great profile, but just strong enough #'s and grades to get the tip from lineage."
- "Without lineage, there would be little case. With it, we'll keep looking."

In every one of these cases, the applicant was admitted.

Of course, Harvard's not doing anything other schools aren't. The practice of playing favorites with alumni children is nearly universal among private colleges and isn't unheard of at public institutions, either. The rate of admission for Stanford's alumni children is "almost twice the general population," according to a spokesman for the admissions office. Notre Dame reserves 25 percent of each freshman class for legacies. At the University of Virginia, where native Virginians make up two-thirds of each class, alumni children are automatically treated as Virginians even if they live out of state—giving them a whopping competitive edge. The same is true of the University of California at Berkeley. At many schools, Harvard included, all legacy applications are guaranteed a read by the dean of admissions himself—a privilege nonlegacies don't get.

LITTLE WHITE ELIS

Like the Harvard deans, officials at other universities dismiss the statistical disparities by pointing to the superior environmental influences found in the homes of their alums. "I bet that, statistically, [legacy qualifications are] a little above average, but not by much," says Paul Killebrew, associate director of admissions at Dartmouth. "The admitted group [of legacies] would look exactly like the profile of the class."

James Wickenden, a former dean of admissions at Princeton who now runs a college consulting firm, suspects otherwise. Wickenden wrote of "one Ivy League university" where the average combined SAT score of the freshman class was 1,350 out of a possible 1,600, compared to 1,280 for legacies. "At most selective schools, [legacy status] doubles, even trebles the chances of admission," he says. Many colleges even place admitted legacies in a special "Not in Profile" file (along with recruited athletes and some minority students), so that when the school's SAT scores are published, alumni kids won't pull down the average.

How do those kids fare once they're enrolled? No one's telling. Harvard, for one, refuses to keep any records of how alumni children stack up academically against their nonlegacy classmates—perhaps because the last such study, in 1956, showed Harvard sons hogging the bottom of the grade curve.

If the test scores of admitted legacies are a mystery, the reason colleges accept so many is not. They're afraid the alumni parents of rejected children will stop giving to the colleges' unending fundraising campaigns. "Our survival as an institution depends on having support form alumni," says Richard Steele, director of undergraduate admissions at Duke University, "so according advantages to alumni kids is just a given."

In fact, the OCR exonerated Harvard's legacy preference precisely because legacies bring in money. (OCR cited a federal district court ruling that a state university could favor the children of out-of-state alumni because "defendants showed that the alumni provide monetary support for the university.") And there's no question that alumni provide significant support to Harvard: Last year, they raised $20 million for the scholarship fund alone.

In a letter to OCR defending his legacies, Harvard's Fitzsimmons painted a grim picture of a school where the preference did not exist—a place peeved alumni turned their backs on when their kids failed to make the cut. "Without the fundraising activities of alumni," Fitzsimmons warned darkly, "Harvard could not maintain many of its programs, including needs-blind admissions."

Ignoring, for the moment, the question of how "needs-blind" a system is that admits one-fifth of each class on the assumption that, hey, their parents might give us money, Fitzsimmons's defense doesn't quite ring true. The "Save the Scholarship Fund" line is a variation on the principle of "Firemen First," whereby bureaucrats threatened with a budget cut insist that essential programs rather than executive perks and junkets will be the first to be slashed. Truth be told, there is just about nothing that Harvard, the richest university in the world, could do to jeopardize needs-blind admissions, provided that it placed a high enough priority on them.

But even more unclear is how closely alumni giving is related to the acceptance of alumni kids. "People whose children are denied admission are initially upset," says Wickenden, "and maybe for a year or two their interest in the university wanes. But typically they come back around when they see that what happened was best for the kids." Wickenden has put his money where his mouth is: He rejected two sons of a Princeton trustee involved in a $420 million fundraising project, not to mention the child of a board member who managed the school's $2 billion endowment, all with no apparent ill effect.

Most university administrators would be loath to take such a chance, despite a surprising lack of evidence of the legacy/largess connection. Fitzsimmons admits Harvard knows of no empirical research to support the claim that diminishing legacies would decrease alumni contributions, relying instead on "hundreds, perhaps thousands of conversations with alumni whose sons and daughters applied."

No doubt some of Fitzsimmons's anxiety is founded: It's only natural for alumni to want their kids to have the same privileges they did. But the historical record suggests that alumni are far more tolerant than administrators realize. Admit women and blacks? *Well, we would,* said administrators earlier this century—*but the alumni just won't have it.* Fortunately for American universities, the bulk of those alumni turned out to be less craven than administrators thought they'd be. As more blacks and women enrolled over the past two decades, the funds kept pouring in, reaching an all-time high in the eighties.

Another significant historical lesson can be drawn from the late fifties, when Harvard's selectiveness increased dramatically. As the number of applications soared, the rate of admission for legacies began declining from about 90 percent to its current 43 percent. Administration anxiety rose inversely, but Harvard's fundraising machine has somehow survived. That doesn't mean there's *no* correlation between alumni giving and the legacy preference, obviously; rather, it means that the people who would withhold their money at the loss of the legacy privilege were far outnumbered by other givers. "It takes time to get the message out," explains Fitzsimmons, "but eventually people start responding. We've had to make the case [for democratization] to alumni, and I think that they generally feel good about that."

HEIR CUT

When justice dictates that ordinary kids should have as fair a shot as the children of America's elite, couldn't Harvard and its sister institutions trouble themselves to "get the message out" again? Of course they could. But virtually no one—liberal or conservative—is pushing them to do so.

"There must be no goals or quotas for any special group or category of applicants," reads an advertisement in the right-wing *Dartmouth Review*. "Equal opportunity must be the guiding policy. Males, females, blacks, whites, Native Americans, Hispanics . . . can all be given equal chance to matriculate, survive, and prosper based solely on individual performance."

Noble sentiments from the Ernest Martin Hopkins Institute, an organization of conservative Dartmouth alumni. Reading on, though, we find these "concerned alumni" aren't sacrificing *their* young to the cause. "Alumni sons and daughters," notes the ad further down, "should receive some special consideration."

Similarly, Harvard's conservative *Salient* has twice in recent years decried the treatment of Asian-Americans in admissions, but it attributes their misfortune to favoritism for blacks and Hispanics. What about legacy university favoritism—a much bigger factor? *Salient* writers have twice endorsed it.

What's most surprising is the indifference of minority activists. With the notable exception of a few vocal Asian-Americans, most have made peace with the preference for well-off whites.

Mecca Nelson, the president of Harvard's Black Students Association, leads rallies for the hiring of more minority faculty. She participated in an illegal sit-in at an administration building in support of Afro-American studies. But when it comes to the policy that Asian-American activist Arthur Hu calls "a 20-percent-white quota," Nelson says, "I don't have any really strong opinions about it. I'm not very clear on the whole legacy issue at all."

Joshua Li, former co-chair of Harvard's Asian-American Association, explains his complacency differently: "We understand that in the future Asian-American students will receive these tips as well."

At America's elite universities, you'd expect a somewhat higher standard of fairness than that—

especially when money is the driving force behind the concept. And many Ivy League types *do* advocate for more just and lofty ideals. One of them, as it happens, is Derek Bok. In one of Harvard's annual reports, he warned that the modern university is slowly turning from a truth-seeking enterprise into a money-grubbing corporation—at the expense of the loyalty of its alums. "Such an institution may still evoke pride and respect because of its intellectual achievements," he said rightly. "But the feelings it engenders will not be quite the same as those produced by an institution that is prepared to forgo income, if need be, to preserve values of a nobler kind."

Forgo income to preserve values of a nobler kind—it's an excellent idea. Embrace the preferences for the poor and disadvantaged. Wean alumni from the idea of the legacy edge. And above all, stop the hypocrisy that begrudges the great unwashed a place at Harvard while happily making room for the less qualified sons and daughters of alums.

After 70 years, it won't be easy to wrest the legacy preference away from the alums. But the long-term payoff is as much a matter of message as money. When the sons and daughters of today's college kids fill out *their* applications, the legacy preference should seem not a birthright, but a long-gone relic from the Ivy League's inequitable past.

DISCUSSION QUESTIONS

1. Do you think legacy preferences are unfair? Why or why not? How do you think they compare to minority preferences?
2. John Larew, then editor of the *Harvard Crimson*, was the first to bring the subject of legacy preference to national attention. Since then, these preferences have received a good deal of media attention. Do you think that legacy admissions are now stigmatized admissions like affirmative action admissions?

READING 39

The Opportunity for a College Education: Real Promise or Hollow Rhetoric?

Brian K. Fitzgerald

. . . Americans hold strong views about the relationship between hard work and the opportunity to attend college. Peter Sacks's recent essay for the *Chronicle of Higher Education* suggests that the egalitarian belief, so reminiscent of the nineteenth-century's Horatio Alger novels, that one's place in American higher education is "limited only by one's talent and determination," is alive and well. Three statements best capture this egalitarian view of educational opportunity:

> Most students who are motivated and willing to work hard in high school can go to college.
>
> Academic qualifications are most responsible for keeping high school graduates out of college.
>
> Very few students who are qualified can't go to college and attain a bachelor's degree if they have the ambition.

If you find yourself agreeing with these statements, you are in good company. The perception is widely held that a college education and bachelor's degree are attainable for all students who are willing to do the hard work necessary to get into college and to graduate. This linkage of hard work and success—that is, meeting high standards—has affected education at all levels. It has propelled elementary and secondary school reform onto every governor's agenda, and most recently onto the federal agenda through the No Child Left Behind Act of 2001. School reform is inextricably linked to college

opportunity because these initiatives seek to ensure that all students graduate from high school meeting high standards, thus reducing the dropout rate and increasing the proportion of graduates who are qualified to attend college. . . .

Yet the reality of college opportunity today, even for those students who have met the standards that reform initiatives seek to achieve for all students, is starkly different from the perceptions of most Americans. Decades after establishing the national goal of providing access to college for all qualified students by offering financial aid to those who cannot afford college, significant barriers to college remain. [In 2002] alone, record-high financial barriers erected by recent trends in tuition and financial aid policies prevented hundreds of thousands of college-qualified high school graduates from enrolling in degree-granting four-year colleges, or in any college at all. Over the current decade, these losses will balloon into the millions as the number of high school graduates skyrockets. How could this happen in a nation like ours? This article describes the real limits on opportunity that exist for students from low- and moderate-income families, the policy drift that has produced the record-high financial barriers faced by these students, the implications and challenges that these trends present, and what can be done to address them.

THE REALITY OF COLLEGE OPPORTUNITY

Two conditions are necessary for college enrollment: a student must be qualified to attend the institution to which she or he aspires, and she or he must be able to afford to enroll. Clearly, not all students are qualified to attend four-year colleges; the high number of high school dropouts constitutes the largest such group. For students who have graduated from high school academically qualified to attend four-year colleges, however, financial need is the most significant barrier to enrollment.

The most important gauge of college opportunity today is whether students who graduate from high

Brian K. Fitzgerald is executive director of the Business-Higher Education Forum.

school qualified to attend a four-year college can do so or are prevented in large numbers from enrolling because of financial barriers. Fortunately, an analysis of the latest data available—a 1997 U.S. Department of Education study entitled *Access to Postsecondary Education for the 1992 High School Graduates*—provides a window on the level of opportunity for students from low-income (less than $25,000 per year) and moderate-income ($25,000–$50,000 per year) families who meet the department's definition of college-qualified high school graduates. The analysis takes into account high school curriculum, grades, class rank, and test scores, among other factors. All of the students in this analysis were at least minimally qualified to attend a four-year college, most planned to attend immediately after graduation, and most were well-informed about college costs and financial aid. These characteristics suggest that they were highly likely to attend four-year colleges and—if Americans' perceptions of college opportunity are correct—that they would enroll in college despite their family's inability to pay, at virtually the same rate as all college qualified students. Indeed, if financial aid were adequate to level the playing field, comparably qualified low-income students would enjoy the same opportunity to attend college as students from high-income ($75,000 and above in income) families, who face very low financial barriers on average.

However, the challenges these students face in paying for college deter them at each step of the process leading to college enrollment. For example, low-income students are six times less likely to take entrance exams and apply to four-year colleges than their high-income peers. These barriers have their clearest effect on college enrollment decisions: 48 percent of college-qualified low-income students do not attend a four-year college within two years of graduation, and 22 percent attend no college at all, compared with 17 percent and 4 percent, respectively, of their high-income peers.

Even among the most highly qualified students, these enrollment differences do not narrow. The highest-achieving poor students attend college at the same rate (78 percent) as the lowest-achieving wealthy students (77 percent), and 22 percent of

the highest-achieving poor students do not attend college, which is seven times higher than the rate at which the highest achieving wealthy students do not attend (3 percent).

Financial barriers also have a substantial and comparable impact on the expectations, plans, and enrollment behavior of college-qualified moderate-income high school graduates: 43 percent do not enroll in a four-year college within two years of graduation and 16 percent do not attend any college at all.

The substantial proportion of college-qualified high school graduates who were unable to enroll in a four-year college—or in any college at all—by the mid-1990s suggests that large numbers of students were denied access to college in 2001–02 because the financial barriers they face today are comparable to or higher than those of the mid-1990s. . . .[O]f the nearly 900,000 college-qualified high school students from low- and moderate-income families who graduated in that year, 406,000 were prevented from enrolling in a four-year college, and 168,000 of them did not enroll in any college at all.

This large group of college-qualified high school graduates who today are denied access also portends substantial losses over the course of the current decade as the number of high school graduates rises to historic levels. [Statistics indicate that] 4.4 million of these students will not attend a four-year college, and 2 million students will not attend college at all. This staggering toll suggests that one of the core values we hold as a nation—equal educational opportunity—starkly contrasts with the reality of opportunity in America today.

THE SHIFTING FOCUS OF INVESTMENTS IN HIGHER EDUCATION

Grant aid has been recognized for nearly forty years as especially important to ensuring access for low- and moderate-income students in general, who are highly sensitive to the cost of college.

Despite this long-standing recognition, a shift in policy priorities at the federal and state levels has increased financial barriers for low- and moderate-income families. This shift from a political and policy focus on low-income access to a more politically popular focus on middle- and upper-income afford-ability has fueled a shortfall in need-based grant aid. Throughout the past quarter century, college expenses remaining for low-income students who receive the maximum Pell Grant award have doubled in constant dollars at public four-year colleges. The erosion in the purchasing power of the Pell Grant maximum over two decades, from a high of 84 per-cent of public college tuition in the mid-1970s to a low of 34 percent in the mid-1990s, has resulted in work-study and loans constituting an ever-larger percentage of federal student aid. Student loans now total $42 billion, or three quarters of the Department of Education's 2003 budget request, and loans now total 60 percent of all aid offered.

The single most important manifestation of this policy shift at the federal level, however, has involved using the federal tax code, in the form of tax credits and deductions, to support higher education. The Department of Education's 2003 budget indicates that recently added provisions in the tax code, including the Hope Scholarship Tax Credit, will provide nearly $10 billion in credits and deductions for direct educational expenses and student loan interest. A recent General Accounting Office report, however, indicates that low-income families receive few of these tax benefits because they have no tax liability against which to take the credits and deductions, or student aid reduces their eligibility for tax relief. Consequently, the newest federal initiative to assist families with the cost of college, nearly equaling Pell Grant funding, sup-ports middle- and upper-income families, not the neediest families.

A report from the National Center on Public Policy and Higher Education cites several state trends that have made college less accessible for low- and moderate-income families. First, state policies per-mitting tuition increases have outstripped growth in family income, except for high-income families. Second, exacerbating the decline in the purchasing power of Pell Grants, the purchasing power of state

grants fell for five straight years in the 1990s. Third, and most troubling, the steepest increases in tuition were imposed when families faced the greatest finan-cial hardship—for example, during the recession of 1991 and the current recession.

The College Board's *Trends in College Pricing* indi-cates that falling state support for public institutions as a result of recent state deficits has caused the largest public four-year tuition increases in a decade—nearly 10 percent in 2002. Dale Russakoff and Amy Arget-singer reported in the *Washington Post* that many states planned to impose tuition increases as high as 40 percent for fall 2003. These deficits have also caused many states to impose across-the-board reduc-tions for student aid for all students and, in the case of Illinois, additional targeted cuts to eliminate grants of up to $5,000 for fifth-year students. After years of falling or frozen tuition in Massachusetts, state college tuition rose 24 percent [in 2003] while state funding for student aid dropped 24 percent, substantially wid-ening the gap between college cost and student aid.

Neither the dramatic cuts in higher education funding during the recession of the early 1990s nor the [recent] fiscal crises in many states have resulted in policies designed to insulate low- and moderate-income students from tuition increases through addi-tional need-based grant aid. Rather, during the 1990s, states implemented politically popular merit-based aid programs, resulting in staggering growth in fund-ing. Since the inception of the first large-scale merit program, the Georgia Hope Scholarship program, in 1993, state merit aid nationwide has experienced a 336 percent increase in real dollars, compared to an 88 percent increase in state need-based aid. Merit aid constituted nearly a quarter of all state aid by the end of the decade, up from less than 10 percent in 1982.

Some of these programs, despite good intentions, have had deleterious effects on the neediest students. Analysis of several state programs in the Civil Rights Project of Harvard University's report on merit aid found that most state programs subsidize students who can afford to pay for college and affect enroll-ment decisions in fairly minor ways while not lower-ing financial barriers for low-income students and improving their chances of attending college. . . .

RISING FINANCIAL BARRIERS TO COLLEGE ACCESS

Two decades of underfunding of grant aid, the substitution of loans, and the more recent focus on tax credits and merit-based aid have erected substantial financial barriers to college for low- and moderate-income students. As a result, unmet need (the portion of college expenses not covered by what the family can reasonably pay for college, the so-called expected family contribution, and student aid) has reached unprecedented levels. On average, annual unmet need for low-income families in the late 1990s reached $3,200 at community colleges, $3,800 at four-year public colleges, and $6,200 at four-year private colleges. In contrast, high-income families face only $400 in unmet need at four-year public colleges.

This gap between college expenses and financial aid, however, belies the true magnitude of the financing challenges facing these families, and the extraordinary efforts they must make to finance a college education. Most low-income families are extremely sensitive to the price of college because they are able to contribute only a small portion of college expenses and are highly dependent on grant aid. Yet for these students, although all aid (grants, work-study, and loans) covers two-thirds of the average cost of a moderately priced four-year public college, grants constitute only one-third of this cost. To ensure enrollment, families of low-income students must commit $8,200, one-third of family income each year, in the form of work and loans by the parents and the student. This gap between grant aid and college cost represents the true net price of college for these students and the barrier that must be overcome before access to college can become a reality.

In the face of these financial barriers, work is an essential component of many low-income students' financing strategies, but one that often lowers the probability of degree completion considerably. Sixty-five percent of all low-income college students work while enrolled, and these students work an average of twenty-four hours a week. Many students work more, however, nearly a third work more than thirty-five hours a week, and 80 percent of students enrolled at two-year public colleges work an average of twenty-seven hours a week. For low-income students, such decisions are a necessary response to high levels of unmet need. Excessive work reduces persistence and degree completion from 79 percent for low-income students who work relatively few hours to 47 percent for students who work more than thirty-five hours a week—and nearly a third of low-income students work at least that much. Only 22 percent of college-qualified low-income high school graduates will earn a bachelor's degree, compared with 62 percent of similar high-income students, as a result of these barriers.

In contrast to the time-honored tradition of working one's way through college, working to close the unmet need gap has become a cruel hoax. Because the federal work-study program, which provides wages that are considered student aid, limits work to twenty hours a week, students who must work more hours or seek higher-paying jobs to meet their college expenses must work off-campus. The wages from these off-campus jobs are taxable income, however, and not considered student aid, as work-study wages are. Consequently, as students earn wages to pay the large portion of college expenses for one year, they actually reduce their eligibility for aid, especially grant aid, for the subsequent year because they must report these off-campus earnings on their student aid applications. Thus, working one year to narrow the student aid gap widens this gap in subsequent years, ironically, requiring even more work to close an even larger gap. . . .

Inadequate grant aid also increased annual borrowing among low-income students. . . . Low-income minority students in particular borrow at much higher rates than high-income students and often borrow much more than all other students. A recent report on student debt, *The Burden of Borrowing*, published by the State Public Interest Research Group's Higher Education Project, indicates that 71 percent of low-income students graduate with debt, compared to 44 percent of high-income students. African American students borrow $2,000 more than other students and more than half of both African American and Hispanic students graduate with debt levels considered unmanageable by student loan industry standards.

Moderate-income students confront similar financial barriers of unmet need and work-loan burden. They face $2,700 in unmet need at community colleges, $3,000 at four-year public colleges, and $4,900 at four-year private colleges. They also face $5,641 a year in work and loan burden at public colleges. The financial barriers confronting moderate-income students, though slightly lower than those facing low-income students, pose serious challenges for enrollment in college and completion of a degree.

IMPLICATIONS

The social and economic consequences of this loss of college access for millions of qualified students are considerable and will affect the nation over the course of a generation. The degree of access to college enjoyed by low- and moderate-income students will determine whether social stratification will grow, as the sons and daughters of those who cannot pay for college are consigned to low-paying jobs with declining real wages, and whether economic growth will be dampened by a shortage of college-educated workers.

The issue of college access and its implications for social stratification is crucial for the next generation of Americans because powerful demographic forces already at work will not only increase the number of college-age Americans but also change the face of American higher education. This demographic wave will expand the traditional college-age population of eighteen- to twenty-four-year-olds by five million in 2015; 80 percent of those students will be minority and 50 percent will be Hispanic. This growth will cause the number of high school graduates to swell to unprecedented levels over the course of the current decade as the children of the baby-boom generation and new immigrants flood high schools and colleges. Department of Education data indicate that this demographic trend will peak in 2008, when the largest number of students in the history of our nation graduate from high school. The ability of our largest generation to gain access to college, and particularly to a bachelor's degree, will determine the extent to which its members will have a realistic chance of joining the middle class. Failure to provide this chance will inflict a heavy social toll: increasing stratification as the sons and daughters of janitors and food service workers are consigned to low-paying jobs. . . .

This demographic wave of students will also increase the demand for student aid dollars, because a higher percentage of these students will be from low-income, minority families. These students will be disproportionately dependent on grant aid. Students from low-income families will represent an ever-increasing proportion of high school attendees, and each successive graduating class will increase the demand for grant funds in order to make access to college and pursuit of a baccalaureate degree a reality. In [2001 and 2002] the federal Pell Grant program faced a shortfall in excess of a billion dollars as eligibility for grants has exceeded appropriated funds. At the state level, such growth in demand for grants will confront both the commitment to merit aid in many states and reductions in need-based grant aid resulting from deficits. Consequently, the financial barriers confronting these students will likely rise significantly as demand for grants outstrips availability and as tuition rises as a result of the same deficits. If financial barriers increase and the unmet need gap grows, large numbers of additional low- and moderate-income students—beyond the millions identified earlier—will be denied access to a college education.

David Breneman, an economist and dean of the Curry School of Education at the University of Virginia, has explored the implications of diminished opportunity in an essay written for members of Congress. Breneman argues that because the difference in economic returns between graduating from high school and dropping out is *de minimus,* the real economic benefit of graduating from high school results from the opportunity to attend college, where the returns are significantly higher. Thus the single largest incentive for students to

PERSONAL ACCOUNT

That Moment of Visibility

I never realized how much my working-class background and beliefs played a role in my education. My family, friends, and neighbors never placed much importance on college. Instead, we were strongly encouraged to find work immediately after high school so we could support ourselves financially. My sisters and I were encouraged to do secretarial work until we married. There was no particular positive status attached to obtaining a degree except maybe the chance of making a lot of money. In fact, friends who went to college were looked at somewhat suspiciously. Among my reference group, college was often seen as a way to get out of having to work.

No one in my family had ever gone to college. It was not financially feasible and a college environment was equal to the unknown. It really was scary terrain. When I decided to go to a local community college after having worked for five years in a secretarial position, family and friends could not understand my decision. Why would I choose college when I already had a job? I could pay bills, buy what I needed, and I had a savings account. So I started by taking a course a semester—and I barely got through the first course. Although I received a good grade, I felt incredibly isolated, like I was an impostor who did not belong in a classroom. I had no idea how someone in college was supposed to act. I stayed silent, scared, and consciously invisible most of the time. I was not even close to making a commitment to a college education when I signed up for a second course—but because my job payed for it (one of the benefits), I felt I had nothing to lose. I signed up for Introduction to Juvenile Delinquency and midway through, our class received an assignment to do a fifteen-page self-analysis applying some of the theories we were learning. The thought of consciously revealing myself when I was trying so hard not to look, act, or be different was not something I was willing (or, I think, able at the time) to do. When I discussed the assignment with the people close to me, they agreed that the assignment was too personal and revealing. I decided not to do it and I also decided that college was probably not for me.

I went to see my professor (who was the only woman in her department) to let her know that I was refusing to do the assignment and would not complete the course. We had spoken two or three times outside of class and she knew a little about me. I knew that she was also from a working-class background and had returned to school after working some years. I felt the least I could do was tell her I was quitting the class. When I said that I was unwilling to do the assignment, she stared at me for some time, and then asked me what I would prefer to write about. I was stunned that I was noticed and was being asked what I would like to do. When I had no reply, she asked if I would write a paper on the importance of dissent. All I could think to say was yes. I completed the course successfully and found an ally in my department. I can't overstate the importance of that moment of acknowledgment. It was the first time I felt listened to. It was the moment when you feel safe enough to reveal who you are, the deep breath you can finally take when you figure out that the person you're talking to understands, appreciates, and may even share your identity.

I think of this experience as a turning point for me—when I realized that despite all my conscious efforts to be invisible and to "pass," it was that moment of visibility and acknowledgment that kept me in school.

Rose B. Pascarell

---

meet higher educational standards is not to achieve a high school diploma per se, but to gain access to the benefits that a high school diploma affords: entry to college and the opportunity to attain a bachelor's degree. Breneman cautions, however, that reduced opportunity could undermine school reform efforts by eliminating one of the greatest motivations for achieving high standards and graduating from high school.

In addition to these social and educational issues, large losses of college-qualified students pose serious workforce issues. These students will graduate from high school when they will be desperately needed as replacement workers in our nation's economy, as aging, college-educated baby boomers retire in increasing numbers from various sectors during the coming decade. Projections by the Employment Policy Foundation indicate that demand will create a shortage of six million college-educated workers early in the next decade. To maintain economic growth, the nation will have to increase the enrollment and degree completion rates of low- and moderate-income students or bring in highly skilled foreign workers to meet the demand—a dubious proposition in this post–September 11 world. Failure to educate these workers will create a serious drag on our economic growth. . . . Ironically, simply ensuring access for students who are qualified to attend four-year colleges would go a long way toward addressing the anticipated shortage of workers and its potential effect on economic growth. . . .

DISCUSSION QUESTIONS

1. What are the social consequences of the fact that the highest-achieving poor students attend college at the same rate as the lowest-achieving wealthy students?

2. What are the ways that having a job affects students' college experience?

3. Why do you think attention has focused on the affordability of a college education rather than access to it?

NOTES

Advisory Committee on Student Financial Assistance. *Access Denied: Restoring the Nation's Commitment to Equal Educational Opportunity.* Washington, D.C.: Advisory Committee on Student Financial Assistance, 2001.

Advisory Committee on Student Financial Assistance. *Empty Promises: The Myth of College Access in America.* Washington, D.C.: Advisory Committee on Student Financial Assistance, 2002.

Advisory Committee on Student Financial Assistance. Letter to the Honorable Judd Gregg, Chairman, Committee on Health, Education, Labor and Pensions, United States Senate, May 23, 2003.

Breneman, D. W. "Declining Access: A Potential—If Slow Moving—Train Wreck." *National Crosstalk,* 2002, 11(2), 2002.

College Board. *Trends in College Pricing 2002.* Washington, D.C.: College Board, 2002.

Employment Policy Foundation. *Challenges Facing the American Workplace.* Washington, D.C.: Employment Policy Foundation, 2002.

Heller, D. E., and Marin, P. (eds.) *Who Should We Help: The Negative Social Consequences of Merit Scholarships.* Cambridge, Mass.: Civil Rights Project. Harvard University, 2002.

King, T., and Bannon, E. *The Burden of Borrowing: A Report on the Rising Rates of Student Loan Debt.* Washington, D.C.: State PIRG's Higher Education Project, 2002.

National Center for Public Policy and Higher Education. *Losing Ground: A National Status Report on the Affordability of American Higher Education.* San Jose, Calif.: National Center for Public Policy and Higher Education, 2002.

No Child Left Behind Act of 2001. U.S. Public Law 107–110. 107th Cong., Jan, 8, 2002.

Russakoff, D., and Argetsinger, A. "States Plan Big Tuition Increases." *Washington Post,* July 22, 2003, p. 1.

Sacks, P. "Class Rules: The Fiction of Egalitarian Higher Education." *Chronicle of Higher Education,* July 25, 2003, 49(46), p. B7.

St. John, E. P., Droogsma Musoba, G., Simmons, A. B., and Chung, C. *Meeting the Access Challenge: Indiana's Twenty-First Century Scholars Program.* Bloomington: Indiana Education Policy Center, 2002.

U.S. Department of Education. *2003 Budget Summary.* Washington, D.C.: U.S. Government Printing Office, 2002.

U.S. Department of Education, National Center for Educational Statistics. *Access to Postsecondary Education for the 1992 High School Graduates.* NCES 98–105. Washington, D.C.: National Center for Educational Statistics, 1997.

U.S. Department of Education, National Center for Education Statistics. *Projections of Education Statistics to 2011.* NCES 2001–083. Washington, D.C.: National Center for Educational Statistics, 2001.

U.S. Department of Education, National Center for Education Statistics. *Changes in the Net Price of College Attendance: 1992–1993 to 1999–2000.* Washington, DC: National Center for Education Statistics, 2002.

U.S. General Accounting Office. *Student Aid and Tax Credits: Better Research and Guidance Will Facilitate Comparison and Effectiveness of Student Use.* GAO–02–751. Washington, D.C.: U.S. General Accounting Office, 2002.

DISABILITY

Public Transit

John Hockenberry

New York was not like Iran.

It was a shock to return to the United States in 1990, where it routinely took an act of God to hail a taxi. There was nothing religious about New York City, even on Christmas Eve. I had taken a cab from midtown to Riverside Church on the west side of Manhattan only to find that my information about a Christmas Eve service there was mistaken. The church was padlocked, which I only discovered after getting out of the cab into the forty-mile-an-hour wind and the twenty-degree weather. I tried all of the doors of the church and found myself alone at close to midnight, without a taxi, on December 24 at 122d Street and Riverside Drive.

I was wearing a wool sports jacket and a heavy scarf, but no outer jacket. There were no cars on the street. Being wrong about the service and having come all the way uptown was more than a little frustrating. I suspected that I was not in the best psychological condition to watch the usual half-dozen or so New York cabs pass me by and pretend not to see me hailing them. I knew the most important thing was to try and not look like a panhandler. This was always hard. Many times in New York I had hailed a cab only to have the driver hand me a dollar. Once I was so shocked that I looked at the cabbie and said, as though I were correcting his spelling, "No, I give you the money."

"You want a ride?" he said. "Really?"

The worst were the taxis that stopped but had some idea that the wheelchair was going to put itself into the trunk. After you hopped into the backseat, these drivers would look at you as though you were trying to pull a fast one, tricking them into having to get out of their cabs and load something in the trunk that you had been cleverly hiding. Some cabbies would say that I should have brought someone with me to put the chair in, or that it was too heavy for them to lift. My favorite excuse was also the most frequent, "Look, buddy, I can't lift that chair. I have a bad back."

"I never heard of anyone who became paralyzed from lifting wheelchairs," I'd say. My favorite reply never helped. If the drivers would actually load the chair, you could hear them grumbling, throwing it around to get it to fit, and smashing the trunk lid down on it. When we would arrive at our destination, the driver would throw the chair at me like it was a chunk of nuclear waste and hop back behind the wheel. The only thing to do in these situations was to smile, try not to get into a fight, and hope the anger would subside quickly so you could make it wherever you were going without having a meltdown.

There were some drivers who wouldn't load the chair at all. For these people, at one time, I carried a Swiss army knife. The rule was, if I had to get back out of a cab because a driver wouldn't load my chair, then I would give the driver a reason to get out of his cab shortly after I was gone. I would use the small blade of the knife to puncture a rear tire before the cab drove away, then hail another one. A few blocks ahead, when the first driver had discovered his difficulties, he was generally looking in his trunk for the tire jack when I passed by, waving.

The trouble with this idea was that other people often did not have the same righteous attitude that I did about tire puncturing in Manhattan traffic, and using knives to get freelance revenge in New York City under any circumstances. Most of my friends put me in the same league with subway vigilante Bernard Goetz, and concluded that I needed serious help. So I had stopped using the Swiss army knife and was without it that Christmas Eve on 122d and Riverside Drive.

John Hockenberry is a correspondent for *Dateline NBC*. He has been a broadcast journalist for National Public Radio and *ABC News*, and is the author of *Moving Violations: War Zones, Wheelchairs, and Declarations of Independence*.

The first cab drove toward me and slowed down; the driver stared, then quickly drove by. A second cab approached. I motioned emphatically. I smiled and tried to look as credible as I could. Out in this December wind, I was just another invisible particle of New York misery. The driver of the second cab shook his head as he passed with the lame, catch-all apologetic look New York cabbies use to say, "No way, Mac. Sorry, no way I can take you."

I had one advantage. At least I was white. Black males in New York City have to watch at least as many cabs go by as someone in a wheelchair does before getting a ride. Black male friends of mine say they consciously have to rely on their ritzy trench coats or conservative "Real Job" suits to counter skin color in catching a cab. If I could look more white than crippled, I might not freeze to death on Christmas Eve. I was a psychotic, twentieth-century hit man named Tiny Tim, imagining all sorts of gory ways to knock off a cabbie named Scrooge. The wind was blowing furiously off the Hudson, right up over Riverside Drive.

A third cab drove by. I wondered if I could force a cab to stop by blocking the road. I wished I had a baseball bat. For a period of a few minutes, there was no traffic. I turned and began to roll down Riverside. After a block, I turned around, and there was one more empty cab in the right lane coming toward me. I raised my hand. I was sitting directly under a streetlight. The cabbie clearly saw me, abruptly veered left into the turn lane, and sat there, signaling at the red light.

I rolled over to his cab and knocked on the window. "Can you take a fare?" The driver was pretending I had just landed there from space, but I was freezing and needed a ride, so I tried not to look disgusted. He nodded with all of the enthusiasm of someone with an abscessed tooth, I opened the door and hopped onto the backseat. I folded the chair and asked him to open the trunk of his cab.

"Why you want me to do that?" he said.

"Put the chair in the trunk, please." I was half-sitting in the cab, my legs still outside. The door was open and the wheelchair was folded next to the cab. "No way, man," he said. "I'm not going to do that.

It's too damn cold." I was supposed to understand that I would now simply thank him for his trouble, get back in my wheelchair, and wait for another cab. "Just put the chair in the trunk right now. It's Christmas Eve, pal. Why don't you just pretend to be Santa for five fucking minutes?" His smile vanished. I had crossed a line by being angry. But he also looked relieved, as though now he could refuse me in good conscience. It was all written clearly on his face. "You're crazy, man. I don't have to do nothing for you." I looked at him once more and said, "If you make me get back into this chair, you are going to be very sorry." It was a moment of visceral anger. There was no turning back now. "Go away, man. It's too cold."

I got back into the chair. I placed my backpack with my wallet in it on the back of my chair for safekeeping. I grabbed his door and, with all of my strength, pushed it back on its hinges until I heard a loud snap. It was now jammed open. I rolled over to his passenger window, and two insane jabs of my right fist shattered it. I rolled around to the front of the cab, and with my fist in my white handball glove took out first one, then the other headlight. The light I was bathed in from the front of the cab vanished. The face of the driver could now be seen clearly, illuminated by the dashboard's glow.

I could hear myself screaming at him in a voice that sounded far away. I knew the voice, but the person it belonged to was an intruder in this place. He had nothing to do with this particular cabbie and his stupid, callous insensitivity; rather, he was the overlord to all such incidents that had come before. Whenever the gauntlet was dropped, it was this interior soul, with that screaming voice and those hands, who felt no pain and who surfed down a wave of hatred to settle the score. This soul had done the arithmetic and chosen the weapons. I would have to live with the consequences.

I rolled over to the driver's seat and grabbed the window next to his face. I could see that he was absolutely terrified. It made me want to torture him. I hungered for his fear; I wanted to feel his presumptions of power and physical superiority in my hands as he sank up to his neck in my rage, my fists closed around his throat. I attacked his half-open window. It cracked, and as I hauled my arm back to finish it, I saw large drops of blood on the driver's face. I looked at him closely. He was paralyzed with fear and spattered with blood. There was blood on his window, as well. A voice inside me screamed, "I didn't touch you, motherfucker. You're not bleeding. Don't say that I made you bleed. You fucking bastard. Don't you dare bleed!"

I rolled back from the cab. It was my own blood shooting from my thumb. It gushed over the white leather of my glove: I had busted an artery at the base of my thumb, but I couldn't see it because it was inside the glove. Whatever had sliced my thumb had gone neatly through the leather first, and as I rolled down the street I could hear the cabbie saying behind me, "You're crazy, man, you're fucking crazy." I rolled underneath a street lamp to get a closer look. It was my left hand, and it had several lacerations in addition to the one at the base of my thumb. It must have been the headlight glass. The blood continued to gush. Wind blew it off my fingers in festive red droplets, which landed stiffly on the frozen pavement under the street lamp. Merry Christmas.

Up the street, a police squad car had stopped next to the cab, which still had its right rear door jammed open. I coasted farther down the street to see if I could roll the rest of the way home. With each push of my hand on the wheel rim of my chair, blood squirted out of my glove. I could feel it filled with blood inside. The cops pulled up behind me. "Would you like us to arrest that cabbie? Did he attack you?" All I could think of was the indignity of being attacked by him. I thought about scream- ing, "That piece of human garbage attacked me? No way. Maybe it was me who attacked him as a public service. Did you donut eaters ever think of that? I could have killed the bastard. I *was* trying to kill him, in fact. I insist that you arrest me for attempted murder right now, or I will sue the NYPD under the Americans with Disabilities Act." I thought better of this speech. Intense pain had returned my mind to practical matters. Spending the night in jail for assaulting a cabbie after bragging about it while bleeding to death seemed like a poor way to cap off an already less than stellar Christmas Eve.

"Everything's fine, officer. I'll just get another taxi" I continued to roll one-handed and dripping down Riverside Drive. The cops went back to talk to the cabbie, who was screaming now. I began to worry that he was going to have me arrested, but the cops drove back again. Once more, the officer asked if I wanted to file a complaint against the cab- bie. As more blood dripped off my formerly white glove, the officers suggested that I go to the hospi- tal. They had figured out what had happened. As I started to explain, they told me to get in the squad car. "Let's just say it was an unfortunate accident," one officer said. "I don't think he'll ever stop for someone in a wheelchair again. If we can get you to the emergency room in time, maybe you won't lose your thumb."

I got in the backseat while the cops put the chair in the trunk. Seven blocks away was the emergency room of St. Luke's Hospital. Christmas Eve services at St. Luke's included treatment of a young woman's mild overdose. An elderly man and his worried- looking wife were in a corner of the treatment room. His scared face looked out from beneath a green plastic oxygen mask. A number of men stood around watching CNN on the waiting-room television. A woman had been brought in with fairly suspicious- looking bruises on her face and arms. One arm was broken and being set in a cast. She sat quietly while two men talked about football in loud voices. The forlorn Christmas decorations added to the hope- lessness of this little band of unfortunates in the emergency room.

When I arrived, everything stopped. Police of- ficers are always an object of curiosity, signaling the arrival of a shooting victim or something more spectacular. For a Christmas Eve, the gushing artery at the base of my thumb was spectacular enough. The men sitting around the emergency room shook their heads. The overdose patient with the sunken cocaine eyes staggered over to inspect the evening's best carnage. "Where did you get that wheelchair?" She looked around as though she was familiar with all of the wheelchairs in this emergency room from previous visits. "It's my own," I replied. "That's a good idea," she said. "Why didn't I think of that?"

I got nine stitches from a doctor who suggested politely that whatever my complaint with the taxi driver, I was one person on the planet who could ill afford to lose a thumb. The deep laceration was just a few millimeters from the nerve and was just as close to the tendon. Severing either one would have added my thumb to an already ample chorus of numbness and paralysis. The thought of losing the use of my thumb was one thing, but what was really disturbing was the thought of its isolation on my hand, numb in the wrong zone. Trapped on a functional hand, a numb and paralyzed thumb would have no way of communicating with my numb and paralyzed feet. It would be not only paralyzed, it would be in exile: an invader behind enemy lines, stuck across the checkpoint on my chest.

Today, there is a one-inch scar that traces a half circle just to the left of my knuckle. The gloves were a total loss, but they no doubt saved my thumb. Nothing could save my pride, but pride is not always salvageable in New York City. I have taken thousands of cabs, and in each case the business of loading and unloading delivers some small verdict on human nature. Often it is a verdict I am in no mood to hear, as was the case on that Christmas Eve. At other times, the experience is eerie and sublime. At the very least, there is the possibility that I will make a connection with a person, not just stare at the back of an anonymous head.

In my life, cabbies distinguish themselves by being either very rude and unhelpful or sympathetic and righteous. Mahmoud Abu Holima was one of the latter. It was his freckles I remembered, along with his schoolboy nose and reddish-blond hair, which made his Islamic tirades more memorable. He was not swarthy like other Middle Eastern cabbies. He had a squeaky, raspy voice. He drove like a power tool carving Styrofoam. He used his horn a lot. He made constant references to the idiots he said were all around him.

He was like a lot of other New York cabbies. But out of a sea of midtown yellow, Mahmoud Abu Holima was the one who stopped one afternoon in 1990, and by stopping for me he wanted to make it clear to everyone that he was not stopping for anyone else, especially the people in expensive-looking suits waiting on the same street corner I was. His decision to pick me up was part of some protest Mahmoud delivered to America every day he drove the streets of Manhattan.

His cab seemed to have little to do with transporting people from place to place. It was more like an Islamic institute on wheels. A voice in Arabic blared from his cassette player. His front seat was piled with books in Arabic and more cassettes. Some of the books were dog-eared Korans. There were many uniformly bound blue and green books open, marked, and stacked in cross-referenced chaos, the arcane and passionate academic studies of a Muslim cabbie studying hard to get ahead and lose his day job, interrupting his studies in midsentence to pick up a man in a wheelchair.

I took two rides with him. The first time I was going somewhere uptown on Third Avenue. Four cabs had passed me by. He stopped. He put the chair in the trunk and, to make more space there, brought stacks of Arabic books from the trunk into the front seat. He wore a large, knit, dirty-white skullcap and was in constant motion. He seemed lost in the ideas he had been reading about before I got in. At traffic lights, he would read. As he drove, he continually turned away from the windshield to make eye contact with me. His voice careened from conversation to lecture, like his driving. He ignored what was going on around him on the street. He told me he thought my wheelchair was unusually light. He said he knew many boys with no legs who could use such a chair. There were no good wheelchairs in Afghanistan.

"Afghanistan, you know about the war in Afghanistan?" he asked.

I said I knew about it. He said he wasn't talking about the Soviet invasion of Afghanistan and the American efforts to see that the Soviets were defeated. He said that the war was really a religious war. "It is the war for Islam." On a lark, in my broken, rudimentary Arabic, I asked him where he was from. He turned around abruptly and asked,

"Where did you learn Arabic?" I told him that I had learned it from living in the Middle East. I apologized for speaking so poorly. He laughed and said that my accent was good, but that non-Muslims in America don't speak Arabic unless they are spies. "Only the Zionists really know how to speak," he said, his voice spitting with hatred.

I thanked him for picking me up. He removed my chair from his trunk, and as I hopped back into it I explained to him that it was difficult sometimes to get a cab in New York. He said that being in America was like being in a war where there are only weapons, no people. "In Islam," he said, "the people are the weapons."

"Why are you here?" I asked him.

"I have kids, family." He smiled once, and the freckles wrinkled on his nose and face, making him look like Tom Sawyer in a Muslim prayer cap. The scowl returned as he drove away. He turned up the cassette. The Arabic voice was still audible a block away.

The second time I saw him, I remembered him and he remembered me. He had no cassettes this time. There were no books in the car, and there was plenty of room in the trunk for my chair this time. Where were all of the books? He said he had finished studying. I asked him about peace in Afghanistan and the fact that Iran and Iraq were no longer at war. He said something about Saddam Hussein I didn't catch, and then he laughed. He seemed less nervous but still had the good-natured intensity I remembered from before. "Are you from Iran?" I asked him, and this time he answered. He told me he was from Egypt. He asked me if I knew about the war in Egypt, and I told him I didn't.

Before he dropped me off, he said that he wanted me to know when we would lose the war against Islam. He said that we won't know when we have lost. "Americans never say anything that's important." He looked out the window. His face did not express hatred as much as disappointment. He shook his head. "It is quiet now."

He ran a red light and parked squarely in the middle of an intersection, stopping traffic to let me out. Cars honked and people yelled as I got into the wheelchair. He scowled at them and laughed. I laughed too. I think I said to him, "*Salaam,*" the Arabic word for peace and good-bye. He said something that sounded like "*Mish Salaam fi Amerika,*" no peace in America. Then he said, "*Sa'at.*" In Arabic, it means difficult. He got into his cab, smiled, and drove away. On February 26, 1993, cabbie, student of Islam, and family man Mahmoud Abu Holima, along with several others, planted a bomb that blew up in the World Trade Center. Today, he is serving a life sentence in a New York prison. . . .

When I returned to New York City from the Middle East in 1990, I lived in Brooklyn, just two blocks from the Carroll Street subway stop on the F train. It was not accessible, and as there appeared to be no plans to make it so, I didn't think much about the station. When I wanted to go into Manhattan, I would take a taxi, or I would roll up Court Street to the walkway entrance to the Brooklyn Bridge and fly into the city on a ribbon of oak planks suspended from the bridge's webs of cable that appeared from my wheelchair to be woven into the sky itself. Looking down, I could see the East River through my wheelchair's spokes. Looking up, I saw the clouds through the spokes of the bridge. It was always an uncommon moment of physical integrity with the city, which ended when I came to rest at the traffic light on Chambers Street, next to city hall.

It was while rolling across the bridge one day that I remembered my promise to Donna, my physical therapist, about how I would one day ride the rapid transit trains in Chicago. Pumping my arms up the incline of the bridge toward Manhattan and then coasting down the other side in 1990, I imagined that I would be able physically to accomplish everything I had theorized about the subway in Chicago in those first days of being a paraplegic back in 1976. In the Middle East, I had climbed many stairways and hauled myself and the chair across many filthy floors on my way to interviews, apartments, and news conferences. I had also lost my fear of humiliation from living and working there. I was even intrigued with the idea of taking the train during the peak of rush hour when the greatest number of people of all kinds would be underground with me.

I would do it just the way I had told Donna back in the rehab hospital. But this time, I would wire myself with a microphone and a miniature cassette machine to record everything that happened along the way. Testing my own theory might make a good commentary for an upcoming National Public Radio program about inaccessibility. Between the Carroll Street station and city hall, there were stairs leading in and out of the stations as well as to transfer from one line to another inside the larger stations. To get to Brooklyn Bridge/City Hall, I had to make two transfers, from the F to the A, then from the A to the 5, a total of nearly 150 stairs.

I rolled up to the Brooklyn Carroll Street stop on the F train carrying a rope and a backpack and wired for sound. Like most of the other people on the train that morning I was on my way to work. Taking the subway was how most people crossed the East River, but it would have been hard to come up with a less practical way, short of swimming, for a paraplegic to cover the same distance. Fortunately, I had the entire morning to kill. I was confident that I had the strength for it, and unless I ended up on the tracks, I felt sure that I could get out of any predicament I found myself in, but I was prepared for things to be more complicated. As usual, trouble would make the story more interesting.

The Carroll Street subway station has two staircases. One leads to the token booth, where the fare is paid by the turnstiles at the track entrance, the other one goes directly down to the tracks. Near the entrance is a newsstand. As I rolled to the top of the stairs, the man behind the counter watched me closely and the people standing around the newsstand stopped talking. I quickly climbed out of my chair and down onto the top step.

I folded my chair and tied the length of rope around it, attaching the end to my wrist. I moved down to the second step and began to lower the folded chair down the steps to the bottom. It took just a moment. Then, one at a time, I descended the first flight of stairs with my backpack and seat cushion in my lap until I reached a foul-smelling landing below street level. I was on my way. I looked up. The people at the newsstand who had been peering sheepishly down at me looked away. All around me, crowds of commuters with briefcases and headphones walked by, stepping around me without breaking stride. If I had worried about anything associated with this venture, it was that I would just be in the way. I was invisible.

I slid across the floor to the next flight of stairs, and the commuters arriving at the station now came upon me suddenly from around a corner. Still, they expressed no surprise and neatly moved over to form an orderly lane on the side of the landing opposite me as I lowered my chair once again to the bottom of the stairs where the token booth was.

With an elastic cord around my legs to keep them together and more easily moved (an innovation I hadn't thought of back in rehab), I continued down the stairs, two steps at a time, and finally reached the chair at the bottom of the steps. I stood it up, unfolded it, and did a two-armed, from-the-floor lift back onto the seat. My head rose out of the sea of commuter legs, and I took my place in the subway token line.

"You know, you get half price," the tinny voice through the bulletproof glass told me, as though this were compensation for the slight inconvenience of having no ramp or elevator. There, next to his piles of tokens, the operator had a stack of official half-price certificates for disabled users. He seemed thrilled to have a chance to use them. "No, thanks, the tokens are fine." I bought two and rolled through the rickety gate next to the turnstiles and to the head of the next set of stairs. I could hear the trains rumbling below.

I got down on the floor again, and began lowering the chair. I realized that getting the chair back up again was not going to be as simple as this lowering maneuver. Most of my old theory about riding the trains in Chicago had pertained to getting up to the tracks, because the Chicago trains are elevated. Down was going well, as I expected, but up might be more difficult.

Around me walked the stream of oblivious commuters. Underneath their feet, the paper cups and straws and various other bits of refuse they dropped were too soiled by black subway filth to be recognizable as having any connection at all to their world above. Down on the subway floor, they seemed evil, straws that could only have hung from diseased lips, plastic spoons that could never have carried anything edible. Horrid puddles of liquid were swirled with chemical colors, sinister black mirrors in which the bottoms of briefcases sailed safely overhead like rectangular airships. I was freshly showered, with clean white gloves and black jeans, but in the reflection of one of these puddles, I too looked as foul and discarded as the soda straws and crack vials. I looked up at the people walking by, stepping around me, or watching me with their peripheral vision. By virtue of the fact that my body and clothes were in contact with places they feared to touch, they saw and feared me much as they might fear sudden assault by a mugger. I was just like the refuse, irretrievable, present only as a creature dwelling on the rusty edge of a dark drain. By stepping around me as I slid, two steps at a time, down toward the tracks, they created a quarantine space, just for me, where even the air seemed depraved.

I rolled to the platform to wait for the train with the other commuters. I could make eye contact again. Some of the faces betrayed that they had seen me on the stairs by showing relief that I had not been stuck there, or worse, living there. The details they were too afraid to glean back there by pausing to investigate, they were happy to take as a happy ending which got them off the hook. They were curious as long as they didn't have to act on what they had learned. As long as they didn't have to act, they could stare.

I had a speech all prepared for the moment anyone asked if I needed help. I felt a twinge of satisfaction over having made it to the tracks without having to give it. My old theory, concocted while on painkillers in an intensive care unit in Pennsylvania, had predicted that I would make it. I was happy to do it all by myself. Yet I hadn't counted on being completely ignored. New York is such a far cry from the streets of Jerusalem, where Israelis would come right up to ask how much you wanted for your wheelchair, and Arabs would insist on carrying you up a flight of stairs whether you wanted to go or not. . . .

I rolled to the stairs and descended into a corridor crowded with people coming and going. "Are you all right?" A black woman stopped next to my chair. She was pushing a stroller with two seats, one occupied by a little girl, the other empty, presumably for the little boy with her, who was standing next to a larger boy. They all beamed at me, waiting for further orders from Mom.

"I'm going down to the A train," I said. "I think I'll be all right, if I don't get lost."

"You sure you want to go down there?" She sounded as if she was warning me about something. "I know all the elevators from having these kids," she said. "They ain't no elevator on the A train, young man." Her kids looked down at me as if to say, *What can you say to that?* I told her that I knew there was no elevator and that I was just seeing how many stairs there were between Carroll Street and city hall. "I can tell you, they's lots of stairs." As she said good-bye, her oldest boy looked down at me as if he understood exactly what I was doing, and why. "Elevators smell nasty," he said.

Once on the A train, I discovered at the next stop that I had chosen the wrong side of the platform and was going away from Manhattan. If my physical therapist, Donna, could look in on me at this point in my trip, she might be more doubtful about my theory than I was. By taking the wrong train, I had probably doubled the number of stairs I would have to climb.

I wondered if I could find a station not too far out where the platform was between the tracks, so that all I had to do was roll to the other side and catch the inbound train. The subway maps gave no indication of this, and the commuters

I attempted to query on the subject simply ignored me or seemed not to understand what I was asking. Another black woman with a large shopping bag and a brown polka-dotted dress was sitting in a seat across the car and volunteered that Franklin Avenue was the station I wanted. "No stairs there," she said.

At this point, every white person I had encountered had ignored me or pretended that I didn't exist, while every black person who had come upon me had offered to help without being asked. I looked at the tape recorder in my jacket to see if it was running. It was awfully noisy in the subway, but if any voices at all were recorded, this radio program was going to be more about race than it was going to be about wheelchair accessibility. It was the first moment that I suspected the two were deeply related in ways I have had many occasions to think about since.

At Franklin Avenue I crossed the tracks and changed direction, feeling for the first time that I was a part of the vast wave of migration in and out of the Manhattan that produced the subway, all the famous bridges, and a major broadcast industry in traffic reporting complete with network rivals and local personalities, who have added words like *rubbernecking* to the language. I rolled across the platform like any other citizen and onto the train with ease. As we pulled away from the station, I thought how much it would truly change my life if there were a way around the stairs, if I could actually board the subway anywhere without having to be Sir Edmund Hillary.

DISCUSSION QUESTIONS

1. As Hockenberry notes, black men and disabled people share the inability to get cabs to pick them up. Why does that experience make them so angry?
2. Is this story limited to New York City?
3. Why do people shun interaction with the disabled?

READING 41

"Can You See the Rainbow?" The Roots of Denial

Sally French

CHILDHOOD

Some of my earliest memories are of anxious relatives trying to get me to see things. I did not understand why it was so important that I should do so, but was acutely aware of their intense anxiety if I could not. It was aesthetic things like rainbows that bothered them most. They would position me with great precision, tilting my head to precisely the right angle, and then point to the sky saying "Look, there it is; look, there, there . . . THERE!" As far as I was concerned there was nothing there, but if I said as much their anxiety grew even more intense; they would rearrange my position and the whole scenario would be repeated.

In the end, despite a near total lack of color vision and a complete indifference to the rainbow's whereabouts, I would say I could see it. In that way I was able to release the mounting tension and escape to pursue more interesting tasks. It did not take long to learn that in order to avert episodes such as these and to protect the feelings of the people around me, I had to deny my disability.

The adults would also get very perturbed if ever I looked "abnormal." Being told to open my eyes and straighten my face, when all I was doing was trying to see, made me feel ugly and separate. Having adults pretend that I could see more than I could, and having to acquiesce in the pretence, was a theme throughout my childhood.

Adults who were not emotionally involved with the issue of whether or not I could see also led me along the path of denial. This was achieved by their tendency to disbelieve me and interpret my

---

Sally French is a senior lecturer in Health and Human Services at the University of Hertfordshire.

behavior as "playing up" when I told them I could not see. Basically they were confused and unable to cope with the ambiguities of partial sight and were not prepared to take instruction on the matter from a mere child. One example of this occurred in the tiny country primary school that I attended. On warm, sunny days we had our lessons outdoors where, because of the strong sunlight, I could not see to read, write or draw. It was only when the two teachers realized I was having similar difficulties eating my dinner that they began to doubt their interpretation that I was a malingerer. On several occasions I was told off by opticians when I failed to discriminate between the different lenses they placed before my eyes. I am not sure whether they really disbelieved me or whether their professional pride was hurt when nothing they could offer seemed to help; whatever it was I rapidly learned to say "better" or "worse," even though all the lenses looked the same.

It was also very difficult to tell the adults, when they had scraped together the money and found the time to take me to the pantomime or wherever, that it was a frustrating and boring experience. I had a strong sense of spoiling other people's fun, just as a sober person among a group of drunken friends may have. As a child, explaining my situation without appearing disagreeable, sullen and rude was so problematic that I usually denied my disability and suffered in silence. All of this taught me from a very early age that, while the adults were working themselves up about whether or not I could see rainbows, my own anxieties must never be shared.

These anxieties were numerous and centered on getting lost, being slow, not managing and, above all, looking stupid and displaying fear. I tried very hard to be "normal," to be anonymous and to merge with the crowd. Beaches were a nightmare; finding my way back from the sea to specific people in the absence of landmarks was almost impossible, yet giving in to panic was too shameful to contemplate. Anticipation of difficulties could cause even greater anguish than the difficulties themselves and was sufficient to ruin whole days. The prospect of outings with lots of sighted children to unfamiliar

places was enough to make me physically ill, and with a bewildering mix of remorse and relief, I would stay at home.

Brownie meetings were worrying if any degree of independent movement was allowed; in the summer when we left the confines and safety of our hut to play on the nearby common, the other children would immediately disperse, leaving me alone among the trees, feeling stupid and frightened and wondering what to do next. The adults were always adamant that I should join in, that I should not miss out on the fun, but how much they or the other children noticed my difficulties I do not know; I was never teased or blamed for them, they were simply never discussed, at least not with me. This lack of communication gave me a powerful unspoken message that my disability must be denied.

By denying the reality of my disability I protected myself from the anxiety, disapproval, frustration and disappointment of the adults in my life. Like most children I wanted their acceptance, approval and warmth, and quickly learned that this could best be gained by colluding with their perceptions of my situation. I denied my disability in response to their denial, which was often motivated by a benign attempt to integrate me in a world which they perceived as fixed. My denial of disability was thus not a psychopathological reaction, but a sensible and rational response to the peculiar situation I was in.

Special School

Attending special school at the age of nine was, in many ways, a great relief. Despite the crocodile walks,[1] the bells, the long separations from home, the regimentation and the physical punishment, it was an enormous joy to be with other partially sighted children and to be in an environment where limited sight was simply not an issue. I discovered that many other children shared my world and, despite the harshness of institutional life, I felt relaxed, made lots of friends, became more confident and thrived socially. For the first time in my life I was a standard product and it felt very good. The sighted adults who looked after us were few in number with purely custodial roles, and although they seemed to be in a permanent state of anger, provided we stayed out of trouble we were basically ignored. We lived peer-orientated, confined and unchallenging lives where lack of sight rarely as much as entered our heads.

Although the reality of our disabilities was not openly denied in this situation, the only thing guaranteed to really enthuse the staff was the slightest glimmer of hope that our sight could be improved. Contact lenses were an innovation at this time, and children who had previously been virtually ignored were nurtured, encouraged and congratulated, as they learned to cope with them, and were told how good they looked without their glasses on. After I had been at the school for about a year, I was selected as one of the guinea pigs for the experimental "telescopic lenses" which were designed, at least in part, to preserve our postures (with which there was obsessive concern) by enabling us to read and write from a greater distance. For most of us they did not work.

I remember being photographed wearing the lenses by an American man whom I perceived to be very important. First of all he made me knit while wearing them, with the knitting held right down on my lap. This was easy as I could in any case knit without looking. He was unduly excited and enthusiastic and told me how much the lenses were helping. I knew he was wrong. Then he asked me to read, but this changed his mood completely; he became tense, and before taking the photograph he pushed the book, which was a couple of inches from my face, quite roughly to my knees. Although I knew he had cheated and that what he had done was wrong, I still felt culpable for his displeasure and aware that I had failed an important test.

We were forced to use equipment like the telescopic lenses even though it did not help, and sometimes actually made things worse; the behavior of the adults clearly conveyed the message, "You are not acceptable as you are." If we dared to reject the equipment we were reminded of the cost, and asked to reflect on the clever and dedicated people who were tirelessly working for the benefit of ungrateful

creatures like ourselves. No heed was ever taken of our own suggestions; my requests to try tinted lenses were always ignored and it was not until I left school that I discovered how helpful they would be.

The only other times that lack of sight became an issue for us at the school were during the rare and clumsy attempts to integrate us with able-bodied children. The worst possible activity, netball,[2] was usually chosen for this. These occasions were invariably embarrassing and humiliating for all concerned and could lead to desperate maneuvers on the part of the adults to deny the reality of our situation—namely that we had insufficient sight to compete. I am reminded of one netball match, with the score around 20/nil, during which we overheard the games mistress[3] of the opposing team anxiously insisting that they let us get some goals. It was a mortifying experience to see the ball fall through the net while they stood idly by. Very occasionally local Brownies would join us for activities in our extensive grounds. We would be paired off with them for a treasure hunt through the woods, searching for milk-bottle tops—the speed at which they found them was really quite amazing. They seemed to know about us, though, and would be very kind and point the "treasure" out, and even let us pick it up ourselves sometimes, but relying on their bounty spoiled the fun and we wished we could just talk to them or play a different game.

Whether the choice of these highly visual activities was a deliberate denial of our disabilities or simply a lack of imagination on the part of the adults, I do not know. Certainly we played such games successfully among ourselves, and as we were never seen in any other context, perhaps it was the latter. It was only on rare occasions such as these that our lack of sight (which had all but been forgotten) and the artificiality of our world became apparent.

As well as denying the reality of their disabilities, disabled children are frequently forced to deny painful feelings associated with their experiences because their parents and other adults simply cannot cope with them. I am reminded of a friend who, at the age of six or seven, was repeatedly promised expensive toys and new dresses provided she did not cry when taken back to school; we knew exactly how we must behave. Protecting the feelings of the adults we cared about became an arduous responsibility which we exercised with care.

Bravery and stoicism were demanded by the institution too; any outward expression of sadness was not merely ridiculed and scorned, it was simply not allowed. Any hint of dejection led to stern reminders that, unlike most children, we were highly privileged to be living in such a splendid house with such fantastic grounds—an honor which was clearly not our due. There was no one to turn to for comfort or support, and any tears which were shed were, of necessity, silent and private. In contrast to this, the institution, normally so indifferent to life outside its gates, was peculiarly concerned about our parents' states of mind. Our letters were meticulously censored to remove any trace of despondency and the initial letter of each term had a compulsory first sentence: "I have settled down at school and am well and happy." Not only were we compelled to deny our disabilities, but also the painful feelings associated with the lifestyles forced upon us because we were disabled.

Such was our isolation at this school that issues of how to behave in the "normal" world were rarely addressed, but at the next special school I attended, which offered a grammar school education and had an entirely different ethos, much attention was paid to this. The headmaster, a strong, resolute pioneer in the education of partially sighted children, appeared to have a genuine belief not only that we were as good as everyone else, but that we were almost certainly better, and he spent his life tirelessly battling with people who did not share his view.

He liked us to regard ourselves as sighted and steered us away from any connection with blindness; for example, although we were free to go out by ourselves to the nearby town and beyond, the use of white canes was never suggested although many of us use them now. He delighted in people who broke new, visually challenging ground, like acceptance at art school or reading degrees in mathematics, and "blind" occupations, like physiotherapy, were rarely encouraged. In many ways

his attitudes and behavior were refreshing, yet he placed the onus to achieve and succeed entirely on ourselves; there was never any suggestion that the world could adapt, or that our needs could or should be accommodated. The underlying message was always the same: "Be superhuman and deny your disability."

ADULTHOOD

In adulthood, most of these pressures to deny disability persist, though they become more subtle and harder to perceive. If disabled adults manage to gain control of their lives, which for many is very difficult, these pressures may be easier to resist. This is because situations which pose difficulties, create anxieties or cause boredom can be avoided, or alternatively adequate assistance can be sought; many of the situations I was placed in as a child I now avoid. As adults we are less vulnerable and less dependent on other people, we can more easily comprehend our situation, and our adult status makes the open expression of other people's disapproval, frustration and disbelief less likely. In addition, disabled adults arouse less emotion and misplaced optimism than disabled children, which serves to dilute the insatiable drive of many professionals to cure or "improve" us. Having said this, many of the problems experienced by disabled adults are similar to those experienced by disabled children.

Disabled adults frequently provoke anxiety and embarrassment in others simply by their presence. Although they become very skillful at dealing with this, it is often achieved at great cost to themselves by denying their disabilities and needs. It is not unusual for disabled people to endure boredom or distress to safeguard the feelings of others. They may, for example, sit through lectures without hearing or seeing rather than embarrass the lecturer, or endure being carried rather than demanding an accessible venue. In situations such as these reassuring phrases such as "I'm all right" or "Don't worry about me" become almost automatic.

One of the reasons we react in this way, rather than being assertive about our disabilities, is to avoid the disapproval, rejection and adverse labeling of others, just as we did when we were children. Our reactions are viewed as resulting from our impairments rather than from the ways we have been treated. Thus being "up front" about disability and the needs which emanate from it can easily lead us to be labeled "awkward," "selfish" or "warped." Such labeling is very difficult to endure without becoming guilty, anxious and depressed; it eats away at our confidence, undermining our courage and leading us to deny our disabilities.

Disbelief remains a common response of able-bodied people when we attempt to convey the reality of our disabilities. If, for example, I try to explain my difficulty in coping with new environments, the usual response is, "Don't worry we all get lost" or "It looks as if you're doing fine to me." Or when I try to convey the feelings of isolation associated with not recognizing people or not knowing what is going on around me, the usual response is "You will in time" or "It took me ages too." This type of response renders disabled people "just like everyone else." For those of us disabled from birth or early childhood, where there is no experience of "normality" with which to compare our situation, knowing how different we really are is problematic and it is easy to become confused and to have our confidence undermined when others insist we are just the same.

An example of denial through disbelief occurred when I was studying a statistics component as part of a course in psychology. I could see absolutely nothing of what was going on in the lectures and yet my frequent and articulate requests for help were met with the response that all students panic about statistics and that everything would work out fine in the end. As it happens it did, but only after spending many hours with a private tutor. As people are generally not too concerned about how we "got there," our successes serve to reinforce the erroneous assumption that we really are "just like everyone else." When I finally passed the examination, the lecturer concerned informed me, in a jocular and patronizing way, that my worries had clearly been unfounded! When people deny our disabilities they deny who we really are.

This tendency to disbelieve is exacerbated by the ambiguous nature of impairments such as partial sight. It is very hard for people to grasp that although I appear to manage "normally" in many situations, I need considerable help in others. The knowledge of other people's perceptions of me is sufficiently powerful to alter my behavior in ways which are detrimental to myself; for example, the knowledge that fellow passengers have seen me use a white cane to cross the road, can be enough to deter me from reading a book on the train. A more common strategy among people with limited sight is to manage roads unaided, thereby risking life and limb to avoid being labeled as frauds.

A further reaction, often associated with the belief that we are really no different, is that because our problems are no greater than anyone else's we do not deserve any special treatment or consideration. People who react in this way view us as whining and ungrateful complainers whenever we assert ourselves, explain our disabilities, ask that our needs be met or demand our rights. My most recent and overt experience of this reaction occurred during a visit to Whitehall to discuss the lack of transport for disabled people. Every time I mentioned a problem which disabled people encounter, such as not being able to use the underground system or the buses, I was told in no uncertain terms that many other people have transport problems too; what about old people, poor people, people who live in remote areas? What was so special about disabled people, and was not a lot being done for them anyway? I was the only disabled person present in this meeting and my confidence was undermined sufficiently to affect the quality of my argument. Reactions such as this can easily give rise to feelings of insecurity and doubt; it is, of course, the case that many people do have problems, but disabled people are among them and cannot afford to remain passive or to be passed by.

College

At the age of 19, after working for two years, I started my physiotherapy training at a special segregated college for blind and partially sighted students. For the first time in my life my disability was, at least in part, defined as blindness. Although about half the students were partially sighted, one of the criteria for entry to the college was the ability to read and write braille (which I had never used before) and to type proficiently, as, regardless of the clarity of their handwriting, the partially sighted students were not permitted to write their essays or examinations by hand, and the blind students were not permitted to write theirs in braille. No visual teaching methods were used in the college and, for those of us with sight, it was no easy matter learning subjects like anatomy, physiology and biomechanics without the use of diagrams.

The institution seemed unable to accept or respond to the fact that our impairments varied in severity and gave rise to different types of disability. We were taught to use special equipment which we did not need and were encouraged to "feel" rather than "peer" because feeling, it was thought, was aesthetically more pleasing, especially when dealing with the poor, unsuspecting public. There was great concern about the way we looked in our professional roles; white canes were not allowed inside the hospitals where we practiced clinically, even by totally blind students, and guide dogs were completely banned. It appeared that the blind students were expected to be superhuman whereas the partially sighted students were expected to be blind. Any attempt to defy or challenge these rules was very firmly quashed so, in the interests of "getting through," we outwardly denied the reality of our disabilities and complied.

Employment

Deciding whether or not to deny disability probably comes most clearly to the fore in adult life when we attempt to gain employment. Until very recently it was not uncommon to be told very bluntly that, in order to be accepted, the job must be done in exactly the same way as everyone else. In many ways this was easier to deal with than the situation now, where "equal opportunity" policies have simultaneously raised expectations and pushed negative attitudes underground, and where, in reality, little

has changed. Although I have no way of proving it, I am convinced that the denial of my disability has been absolutely fundamental to my success in gaining the type of employment I have had. I have never completely denied it (it is not hidden enough for that) but rather, in response to the interviewers' skeptical and probing questions, I have minimized the difficulties I face and portrayed myself in a way which would swell my headmaster's pride.

Curiously, once in the job, people have sometimes decided that certain tasks, which I can perform quite adequately, are beyond me, while at the same time refusing to relieve me of those I cannot do. At one college where I worked it was considered impossible for me to cope with taking the minutes of meetings, but my request to be relieved of invigilating large numbers of students, on the grounds that I could not see them, was not acceded to; once again the nature of my disability was being defined by other people. On the rare occasions I have been given "special" equipment or consideration at work it has been regarded as a charitable act or donation for which I should be grateful and beholden. This behavior signals two distinct messages: first that I have failed to be "normal" (and have therefore failed), and second that I must ask for nothing more.

In these more enlightened days of "equal opportunities," we are frequently asked and expected to educate others at work about our disabilities. "We know nothing about it, you must teach us" is the frequent cry. In some ways this is a positive development but, on the other hand, it puts great pressure on us because few formal structures have been developed in which this educative process can take place. In the absence of proactive equal opportunity policies, we are rarely taken seriously and what we say is usually forgotten or ignored. Educating others in this way can also mean that we talk of little else but disability, which, as well as becoming boring to ourselves, can lead us to be labeled adversely or viewed solely in terms of problems. Challenging disabling attitudes and structures, especially as a lone disabled person, can become frustrating and exhausting, and in reality it is often easier and (dare I say) more functional, in the short term at least, to cope with inadequate conditions rather than fight to improve them. We must beware of tokenistic gestures which do little but put pressure on us.

CONCLUSION

The reasons I have denied the reality of my disability can be summarized as follows:

1. To avoid other people's anxiety and distress.
2. To avoid other people's disappointment and frustration.
3. To avoid other people's disbelief.
4. To avoid other people's disapproval.
5. To live up to other people's ideas of "normality."
6. To avoid spoiling other people's fun.
7. To collude with other people's pretences.

I believe that from earliest childhood denial of disability is totally rational given the situations we find ourselves in, and that to regard it as a psycho-pathological reaction is a serious mistake. We deny our disabilities for social, economic and emotional survival and we do so at considerable cost to our sense of self and our identities; it is not something we do because of flaws in our individual psyches. For those of us disabled from birth or early childhood, denial of disability has deeply penetrating and entangled roots; we need support and encouragement to make our needs known, but this will only be achieved within the context of genuine structural and attitudinal change.

In this paper I have drawn upon my life experiences and personal reactions to elucidate the pressures placed upon disabled people to deny the reality of their experience of disability. This approach is limited inasmuch as personal experiences and responses can never be divorced from the personality and biography of the person they concern. In addition these pressures will vary according to the individual's impairment. But with these limitations in mind, I am confident that most disabled people will identify with what I have described and that only the examples are, strictly speaking, mine.

DISCUSSION QUESTIONS

1. What are all the ways that French and those around her conspire to deny that she is disabled?
2. Would those in other stigmatized statuses have experiences similar to French's?

NOTES

1. Walking two-by-two in a long file.
2. Girls' basketball.
3. Physical education teacher.

READING 42

Not Blind Enough: Living in the Borderland Called Legal Blindness

Beth Omansky

. . . Human beings are uncomfortable with uncertainty. For instance, when waiting for medical test results or news about a missing loved one, how often we hear people say, "It's the not knowing that's so hard." The human mind, including sight and vision, seeks to make order out of chaos—to organise and categorise, and to find comfort in closure, which relieves the anxieties of uncertainty. Moreover, in an ocularcentric world, the predominant method of making sense of the surrounding environment is sight (Elkins 1996). After all, social culture informs us that "seeing is believing." Because legal blindness is abundantly ambiguous, the sighted might fail to apprehend how borderland blind people make sense of the physical world; what is more, they feel tentative about how to treat borderland blind people or

Beth Omansky is a researcher and writer involved in the international disability studies community and is engaged in disability advocacy in Portland, Oregon. She researched the social construction of blindness as part of her Ph.D. in social work from the University of Queensland, Australia.

even to trust that those who claim the identity of legal blindness are, in fact, blind.

Unlike totally blind people, borderland blind people are often accused of fraud because they act too sighted. John Hull (1990, pp. 67–69) describes this social phenomenon in a journal entry titled, "You Bastard! You're Not Blind." Hull tells of a passerby repeatedly yelling at him, insisting that he was not *really* blind; Hull's orientation and mobility skills failed to replicate societal stereotypes of how blindness presents itself in everyday life.

Borderland blind people are subjected to pressures that totally blind people do not endure; they are pushed and pulled back and forth across the border between sightedness and blindness, resulting in disallowance of citizenship in both lands, which leaves them in a state of what Black American pacifist civil rights leader, Bayard Rustin, aptly called "social dislocation" (D'Emilio 2004).

Totally blind people fall into a discrete stereotyped classification of blindness as darkness (Monbeck 1973), which in many ways is comforting to sighted people because they do not have to guess what the blind person can or cannot see. In an effort to relieve their own dubiety, sighted people might try to force borderland blind people to choose one side or the other—usually pushing them into the socially preferred land of the sighted—a land in which they experience egregious inequality. Borderland blind people are vulnerable to attempted regulation by disquieted but well-meaning acquaintances, friends and family, who yearn for their loved one to be "normal"; in reaction, borderland blind people might internally regulate their own behaviour or else succumb to external pressures as they try to "pass" even during times when they clearly reside on the blind side of the pale. The dynamics of such interactions press everyone concerned into denial (French 1993). Participants in this study reported experiences which echo these phenomena.

PATROLLING THE BORDER

. . . This subtheme is consistent with Sally French's personal account, "Can You See the Rainbow?" [Reading 41], which receives the most reprint permission requests of her entire body of work (personal communication, September 2003). . . .

Two of [one of my informant's] anecdotes are consistent with French's reminiscences. Uncomfortable with the contradictions of "border" behaviour, a companion requested that Larry refrain from reading the newspaper in restaurants while his guide dog lay at his side because it would "confuse" sighted restaurant-goers and give them false impressions of what blindness is. Perhaps she was afraid observers would disbelieve Larry's claim of blindness, and by association, might just reflect on her own character. She also urged him to call colours by the names most commonly used by sighted people despite the fact that he saw them as another colour. For example, if he sees a building as brown even though he knows it's red, he calls it brown, but she thinks he should call it red because that's what it is to sighted people and also, to how he used to see it. She is more comfortable with him pretending to see as sighted people do, and as he used to even though she did not know him before he went blind. Colours are important to Larry's profession as an artist and photographer; so now he encounters a conundrum common to legal blindness. Which is more valid? An accurate description of what the borderland blind person sees, or is the sighted population's naming and interpretation of things *more* valid because it is the majority opinion? And if the latter is accepted as "truth," does this place borderland blind people in the position of having to lie about their own experience to satisfy sighted people's perception of "reality"—of truth? . . .

I, too, have often experienced people placing me on the sighted ("normal") side of the border despite my own choice to stake my claim on the blindness side. On two separate occasions, sighted people grabbed my white cane away from me when my picture was about to be taken. As I posed in front of a statue of George Mason on the campus where we had just attended my master's degree graduation ceremony, one of my relatives walked up and took my cane from my hand. I understood and appreciated his good intentions, but I didn't like it. I didn't say anything because I didn't want to cause tension between us or hurt his feelings. Another time I was getting my picture taken at the Molly Malone statue in Dublin, Ireland. The man in charge of the statue looked through his camera to set the pose, and then reached up in an attempt to remove my cane from my hand. I was not as surprised as I was at graduation, so this time I refused to hand it over and got my picture taken as I am. I guess they both thought the cane was unsightly, which, come to think of it, is a pretty telling word.

Stephen Kuusisto's (1998, p. 13) family left him with a mixed message that placed him on the fence of the border, ill-equipped to fit in on either side; first, that he was blind, and next, that he "was taught to disavow it." He explains the emotional consequences thus, "I grew bent over like the dry tinder grass. I couldn't stand up proudly, nor could I retreat" (Kuusisto 1998, p. 13).

Sighted people do not always attempt to place blind people on the sighted side: a critical factor is acceptance of their loved one's blindness. For example, Larry's daughter accepted his blindness from the outset, and she understands the limitations of an ocularcentric built environment. Every year, she sends him a new bright yellow parka because she wants him to be easily seen by motorists. Soon after Larry told his family that he had become blind, one of his sons offered to act as driver on a trip across the country—a role Larry traditionally assumed. His son told him that he would drive, and Larry still could take photographs of the Southwest desertscape, just as he had always done on previous trips.

RESISTANCE AND CHALLENGE IN EVERYDAY LIFE

Larry, Catherine, J. R. and I have been subjected to social treatment based on common myths about blind people, and we each found various ways to challenge these stereotypes. We all used humour as a strategy to resist and challenge societal misperceptions about blindness. J. R. believes that those who use humour are the ones who "survive" blindness.

For instance, when Larry shook hands with someone to whom he was introduced, he made a "lucky guess" that the person was a piano player. The person making the introduction cried out in amazement, "Oh, my God! How did you get that?" Larry then spun a yarn about how his blindness gave him special hypersensitivity to touch. Larry laughed as he told me, "So you know I am definitely just perpetrating a hoax."

One of J. R.'s anecdotes speaks directly to the stereotype that blindness means darkness (Monbeck, 1973), and it also highlights what it is like to be both observer and observed. When J. R. goes to the optician's office he observes that people notice that he wears tinted (not dark) glasses, yet he carries a white cane. He jokes, "They think, 'Oh you have glasses you're not blind.'" But then, there is the presence of the white cane. J. R. suspects the observers wonder about the optician's abilities, thinking, "This is the best they can do?" His anecdote illustrates the cognitive dissonance sighted people experience when they witness the alterity of legal blindness. But J. R.'s social commentary was not as funny to me once I connected the dots back to when I was fired from my much-needed receptionist job at the optician's office because, "It looked bad" for the optical company.

J. R. told about when he was using his white cane during an outing, and a child asked her mother, "Why is that man using that white stick?" The mother explained that he used the cane because he is blind. As J. R. passed them, he said to the mother, "Don't tell her about the 25 bonus points," which refers to the old joke about drivers earning "bonus points" for running over a blind person. He made his point that he is well aware of "blind" jokes.

None of the participants reported engaging in self-demeaning humour; instead, they turned the joke onto society in the form of social observation, and they all used humour to resist internalised oppression—a strategy used by many authors (e.g., Hull 1990; Knipfel 1999; Kudlick 2005; Kuusisto 1998; Michalko 1998, 1999).

Blind People as Public Property

Frequently, acting blind (i.e., using low vision aids and other blindness skills) elicits invasive, infantilising questions from strangers such as, "Oh my, what happened to you?" or, "How do you cross the street by yourself?" or, "Aren't you afraid?" Sometimes this line of questioning is followed with something along the lines of, "Oh, you're just so brave," or, "You're such an inspiration." Strangers seem to have no compunction about prying into private medical and even financial matters as if they have a right to know; and if the blind person refuses to answer, the strangers either redouble their efforts or turn away as if they were the ones insulted. Larry manages blindness questions in different ways depending upon whether they come from strangers, acquaintances or family. He said:

> It's like they wonder what it is that you see . . . if it's like my niece . . . I'll take more care in analogies and stuff like that whereas if it's my brother or my sister-in-law or one of the guys I'm with, um, I would just give them a couple of different things.

Larry reports, however, that as for the general public, he doesn't "give a shit what they think." Be that as it may, he remains aware of how people might perceive him.

Borderland blind people report that they make decisions about whether they should disclose their visual impairment from moment to moment and situation to situation. Act sighted or flaunt blindness? Or should they just do what they need to do to get around without feeling the need to explain themselves to anyone? Self-disclosure decisions are aroused by the needs of embodied consequences of blindness; by awareness of societal attitudes and predictable consequences of presenting oneself as blind; and by issues around identity. All these factors influence how blind (and other disabled) people negotiate a world "from the vantage point of the atypical" (Linton 1998, p. 6).

As illustration, fast-food restaurants almost always hang their menus high up on walls several feet behind the service counter. Blind people cannot read the sign for two reasons; first, their impairment limits their sensory ability to read print from a distance; and second, the location, position and font size of the menu is rendered inaccessible because the restaurant designers falsely assumed

their customers are all sighted. Faced with the barrier of an inaccessible menu, borderland blind customers must decide whether to "ask for help" (request access), knowing through past experience their request might evoke pity, disdain, or that they will be outright shunned. One alternative I adopted in the past is to memorize what I wish to order and just order the same thing every time I go to that restaurant. Blind people often choose this option to avoid making themselves vulnerable to stigmatization, rudeness, public embarrassment or pity, but the downside is that they surrender gastronomic variety (Gordon 1996; Linton 1998).

Restaurants can be particularly troublesome for borderland blind people because the ocular-centric environment and the embodied experience bump up against the pressure of social graces. The fancier the restaurant, the dimmer the lighting most likely is. People sit across from each other, so the table width breaches any possibility of eye contact; add flickering candles, an undercurrent of simultaneously humming conversations punctuated with loud laughter, and now the setting becomes a recipe for social *faux pas* and other mishaps. Catherine said:

> [t]hey just think you're absolutely stupid. And it's just like you can't get away from that. That's your embarrassment . . . And then it's all over. It's all over. [Laughs] And then you go to the bathroom and cry . . . breathe . . . panic attack. It's like, Christ! Why can't anything go right? Why couldn't the mashed potatoes be over here? Why couldn't the butter be . . . ?

Finding the bathroom in a dark restaurant is like running an obstacle course—wending one's way through tables, booths, wait staff carrying head-level trays, feet and handbags in aisles, coats on chair backs, swinging kitchen doors with wait staff moving quickly in all directions, and the dark hallway that inevitably houses the rest rooms, which are more than likely not clearly marked because the signs are hung high above eye level, written in fancy script, or marked with artistically gender-specific designs with no print as clues:

I cannot count on both hands how many times I've walked into the men's room in restaurants because no one was around to whom I could ask direction. When I see a urinal on the wall, I turn around and head off into the restroom next door, hoping no one saw me enter or leave.

ASKING FOR HELP

When borderland blind people ask for impairment-related assistance, they must identify themselves as blind. It is very difficult to pass as sighted and ask for help reading a street sign six feet above where you are standing. Identity is a two-way social process; people identify themselves and people are identified by others (Rosenblum & Travis 1996). Since borderland blind people may not use typical blindness artifacts (e.g., white cane, dark glasses) the sighted public may respond to requests for assistance in demeaning, curt or other unhelpful ways. Sighted people might be more ready to offer help to someone who is obviously blind; yet they may feel intruded upon by an unidentifiable borderland blind person. Catherine said:

> Yeh, you have to ask everyone, and it's like people, they can be really; brush you off mean. You have to be really cordial and demure as a blind person.

Larry's reluctance to ask for help is bound up in his desire for self-sufficiency. He said:

> . . . to find out that yeah you know damn it I need help reading this label because I don't know if it's apple juice or apple vinegar . . . So um, there was a time when I wouldn't have bought it. That's, that's the thing that can eat at you. You know?

POLICING ONE'S SELF

The traditional medical establishment, indeed, all of society, teaches disabled people to act like everyone else if they hope to lead successful lives—they have to act "normal," which requires them to "overcome" their impairments. But as Linton (1998), Michalko (2002), and others note, people do not "overcome" as that is impossible;

people live with their impairments. As Linton (1998) observes:

> "overcoming" disability [sic] assumes that there is something inferior about their group membership, and the responsibility is left on the individual to work harder to be successful and to triumph over what otherwise would be a tragic life (p. 17).

Another message in the concept of "overcoming" is that the person has gone beyond societal expectations of what people with impairments can achieve; the person has overcome the "social stigma of having a disability" (Linton 1998, p. 17).

I Can See Clearly Now: Passing as Sighted

"Passing" is an interactional social tool employed by all people, in one way or another, as they produce personal identities within (and influenced by) the cultural contexts in which they live. Some blind people employ premeditated strategies as they attempt to pass as sighted and/or to engage in social interaction in ways that are understood and unquestioned by sighted people. Michalko (1999) and Hull (1990) describe intricate ways they negotiate meeting and greeting oncoming people beyond their field of vision. Michalko (1998) uses eye contact with sighted people. He stays aware not only of his seeing, but of how and where he directs his eyes so that sighted people assume he is making direct eye contact. If he gazes where he needs to in order to see them, he appears as though he is not looking at the other person at all. I have central vision loss, so when I look at a person's face, they often think I am looking behind them or looking at their hair instead of into their eyes:

> Depending on where I am and who I'm with, I might try to appear as if I'm making eye contact. Sometimes I will tell people that even though it appears I'm not looking at them, I really am, but I have to feel emotionally ready for an onslaught of nosy questions before I do that.

Catherine said she has problems with relationships just because of her vision. She can't pick up signals such as body language or a "certain look" to know, for example, if someone is "getting pissed off." In concert with Michalko (1999) and Hull (1990), Catherine can't identify people approaching her. She has to learn the sound of their walk. She said, "I have to know them because you can feel people's energy in a way." But, when borderland blind people use familiar clues to identify people or things, sighted people disbelieve their blindness, and then they have to re-assert that, yes, they really are blind, which is another social pitfall distinctive to the borderland. The struggle to be believed can be emotionally draining because such disbelief assaults their integrity and essential as well as social identity. Catherine said:

> . . . it's like you're always having to confirm "I'm blind but I'm not too blind." It's like back and forth, and you're just like constantly pulling at them and you don't realize that; and they don't realize that you feel like you're manipulating the crap out of them and that they're invalidating you. And they're invalidating your blindness. You're just like, either way I go they hate me. [Laughs] It's like you just feel like you're hated even though you know yes, no it's not about you.

Borderland blind people might attempt to pass or, at the very least, to remain unnoticed, which keeps things simpler in social situations. Explaining one's blindness several times a day to several different strangers gets tiresome, distracting and boring. Catherine believes sighted people act like "little anthropologists" trying to figure out blindness culture, and ". . . in the process they're destroying the living hell out of it and objectifying your blindness, and objectifying you, and, oh. This is *huge*."

Sometimes borderland blind people deny themselves use of access equipment such as white canes or low vision glasses; or they might take unnecessary risks such as not asking a passerby what colour the traffic light is at an idle intersection—all to avoid the attention that a "spoiled identity" attracts (Goffman 1986). *Passing* is *acting,* that is, to practice in a creative, methodical way, how to perform as something they are not—sighted. Larry said that his need for perfectionism drives how he presents himself in public:

Yeah, the challenge is greater; therefore the perfection has to be greater . . . See, if people come up to you and say, "Gee I didn't know you were blind." I say I hit a home run.

Catherine hesitates to use her blindness as an excuse even when it is a quite legitimate reason for a particular behaviour, explaining, "You don't want to blame it on you being blind though, that's the problem." She describes her reticence to be judged by sighted people:

> . . . when a lot of things are caused by not seeing you don't want to keep saying it over and over again because people get kind of like, okay, you're going to blame everything on that, you know . . . You have to be really self sufficient sounding, even if you're kind of leaving outs bits of the reason. . . .

I understand Catherine's reasoning. I think long and hard before invoking blindness as a reason for something I did or did not do because I am concerned that people will think I'm using my blindness—as Sally French (1993) writes, "playing up"; they might think I'm a complainer or not "adjusted." Multiple identities further confound the dilemma. For example:

> I think people might misconstrue my holding money close up to my face to read the denominations on bills, or feel the edges of coins to tell quarters with their ridged edges apart from smooth-edged pennies and nickels. I'm concerned that people will think I'm doing all this because I am Jewish; that is, inviting them to invoke stereotypes about Jews having an extreme attachment to money. I guess I'd rather be thought of as a pitiful blind person than a money-hungry Jew. So, I try to be inconspicuous.

Personal Costs of Passing or Coming Out

A lot of thought, creativity, time and energy gets spent carrying out strategies for passing as sighted, and the personal costs can be high. Catherine said that when she self-discloses her blindness, she feels vulnerable, and she does her best to resist falling prey to the negative societal stereotypes that blind people are "fools" (Monbeck 1973). She said:

[Y]ou don't see it. And so you're constantly dealing with these things that come at you and you don't know what it is . . . Um, ah, and you know it's like having to explain to people. It's like yeah I might not see but . . . you *cannot* pull one over on me.

Sometimes people choose not to disclose their blindness, which results in exclusion from activities not because of sighted people leaving them out, but because they have left themselves out. On the other hand, they might disclose their impairments and ask for what they need despite feeling awkward and running the risk of being treated as different. Either way, there is a trade-off. . . .

Just because someone asks for what he or she needs does not guarantee they will get it. J. R. talked about people who think they know what blind people are going through, and say something like, "Oh gee, my brother knew a friend who was, had a friend who was blind, or something like that," and then proceed to give unwanted or the wrong kind of assistance. Blind people tell stories about sighted people grabbing them by the arm at street corners, and then tugging them across the street even though they had not asked for assistance or even wanted to go across the street in the first place. One evening, a woman grabbed me as I made my way through a theatre aisle and literally pulled me to where she thought I wanted to go without ever asking if I needed assistance (Omansky Gordon 2003, p. 224). Apparently, my white cane drafted her into do-gooder duty. Rod Michalko (1998) relates a story about someone pressing a dollar in his hand as he and his dog guide stood at a traffic light together. He told the man he did not need it, and asked him to take it back. The man insisted Rod take it. So, he did, and then gave it to a panhandler. . . .

DISCUSSION QUESTIONS

1. How do the stereotypes of sighted people affect those who are "borderland blind"?

2. Why would people who are legally blind be reluctant to ask for help?

3. What are the costs and benefits of passing as sighted?

REFERENCES

D'Emilio, John, 2004. *Lost Prophet: The Life and Times of Bayard Rustin.* Chicago: University of Chicago Press.

Elkins, James, 1996. *The Object Stares Back.* New York: Simon & Schuster.

French, Sally, 1993. Can You See the Rainbow? The Roots of Denial. In John Swain, Vic Finkelstein, Sally French & Michael Oliver (eds.), *Disabling Barriers, Enabling Environments.* London: Open University Press.

Goffman, Erving, 1986. *Stigma: Notes on the Management of a Spoiled Identity.* Englewood Cliffs, NJ: Prentice-Hall.

Gordon, Beth. 1996. I am Legally Blind. In Rosenblum, Karen E. & Toni-Michele C. Travis (eds.) *The Meaning of Difference: American Constructions of Race, Sex and Gender, Social Class, and Sexual Orientation.* New York: McGraw-Hill.

Hull, John, 1990. *Touching the Rock: An Experience of Blindness.* New York: Pantheon Books.

Knipfel, Jim, 1999. *Slack Jaw.* New York: Penguin Putnam.

Kudlick, Catherine J., 2005. The Blind Man's Harley: White Canes and Gender Identity in America. In *Signs: Journal of Women and Culture in Society,* vol. 30, no. 2, pp. 1589–1606.

Kuusisto, Stephen, 1998. *Planet of the Blind: A Memoir.* New York: G. K. Hall.

Linton, Simi, 1998. *Claiming Disability: Knowledge and Identity.* New York: New York University Press.

Michalko, Rod, 1998. *Mystery of the Eye and the Shadow of Blindness.* Toronto: University of Toronto Press.

———, 1999. *The Two in One: Walking with Smokie, Walking with Blindness.* Philadelphia: Temple University Press.

———, 2002. *The Difference That Disability Makes.* Philadelphia: Temple University Press.

Monbeck, Michael, 1973. *The Meaning of Blindness: Attitudes Toward Blindness and Blind People.* Bloomington: Indiana University Press.

Omansky Gordon, Beth, 2003. I am Legally Blind. In Rosenblum, Karen E. & Toni-Michelle C. Travis (eds.), *The Meaning of Difference: American Constructions of Race, Sex and Gender, Social Class, and Sexual Orientation.* New York: McGraw-Hill.

Rosenblum, Karen E. & Toni-Michelle C. Travis, 1996, (eds.). *The Meaning of Difference: American Constructions of Race, Sex and Gender, Social Class, and Sexual Orientation.* New York: McGraw-Hill.

THE MEANING OF DIFFERENCE

FRAMEWORK ESSAY

The first framework essay in this book considered how contemporary American master statuses are named, dichotomized, and stigmatized. The second essay focused on the experience of privilege and stigma that accompanies those master statuses. In this section, we will look at the *meaning* that is attributed to difference. What significance are differences of race, sex, class, disability, and sexual orientation presumed to have? What difference does difference make? The concept of ideology is critical to understanding the specific meanings that are attributed to differences, and so we will focus on ideology in this essay.

Ideology

The concept of *ideology* was first elaborated by Marx and Engels, particularly in *The German Ideology* (1846). It is now a concept used throughout the social sciences and humanities. In general, an ideology can be defined as a widely shared belief or idea that has been constructed and disseminated by the powerful, primarily reflects their experiences, and functions for their benefit.

Ideologies are anchored in the experiences of their creators; thus, they offer only a partial view of the world. "Ideologies are not simply false, they can be 'partly true,' and yet also incomplete [or] distorted. . . . [They are not] consciously crafted by the ruling class and then injected into the minds of the majority; [they are] instead *produced* by specifiable, complex, social conditions" (Brantlinger, 1990:80). Because those who control the means of disseminating ideas have a better chance of having their ideas prevail, Marx and Engels concluded that "the ideas of the ruling class are in every epoch the ruling ideas." Ideologies have the power to supplant, distort, or silence the experiences of those outside their production.

The idea that people are rewarded on the basis of their merit is an example of an ideology. It is an idea promoted by those with power—for example, teachers and supervisors—and many opportunities are created for the expression of the belief. Report cards, award banquets, and merit raises are all occasions for the expression of the belief that people are rewarded on the basis of their merit.

But certainly, most know this idea is not really true: People are not rewarded only, or even primarily, on the basis of their merit. The idea that merit is rewarded is only partly true and reflects only *some* people's experiences. The frequent repetition of the idea, however, has the potential to overwhelm contrary experience. Even those whose experience has not generally been that people are rewarded based on merit are likely to subscribe to this philosophy, because they hear it so often. In any event, there are few safe opportunities to describe beliefs to the contrary or have those beliefs widely disseminated.

Thus, the idea that people are rewarded on the basis of merit is an ideology. It is a belief that reflects primarily the experiences of those with power, but it is presented as universally valid. The idea overwhelms and silences the voices of those who are outside its production. In effect, ideologies ask us to discount our own experience.

This conflict between one's own experience and the ideas conveyed by an ideology is implied in W. E. B. Du Bois's description of the "double consciousness" experienced by African Americans discussed in Framework Essay II (page 194). It is also what many feminists refer to as the double or fractured consciousness experienced by women. In both cases, the dominant ideas fail to reflect the real-life experiences of people in these categories. For example, the *actual* experience of poverty, discrimination, teen motherhood, disability, sexual assault, life in a black neighborhood, or in a gay relationship rarely coincides with the public discussion on these topics. Because those in stigmatized categories do not control the production or distribution of the prevailing ideas, *their* experience is not likely to be reflected in them. The ideology not only silences their experience; it may invalidate it even in their own minds: "I must be the one who's crazy!" In this way, the dominant discourse can invade and overwhelm our own experience (Kasper, 1986; D. Smith, 1978, 1990).

An ideology that so dominates a culture as to become the prevailing and unquestioned belief was described in the 1920s by Italian political theorist Antonio Gramsci as the *hegemonic*, or ruling, ideology. Gramsci argued that social control was primarily accomplished by the control of ideas, and that whatever was considered to be "common sense" was especially effective as a mechanism of social control (Omi and Winant, 1994:67). Commonsense beliefs are likely to embody widely shared ideas primarily reflecting the interests and experience of those who are powerful. We are all encouraged to adhere to common sense even when that requires discounting our own experience. The discussion of natural-law language that follows highlights that process.

Conveying Ideologies: Natural-Law Language and Stereotypes

Hegemonic, or ruling, ideologies often take the form of commonsense beliefs that are especially embodied in stereotypes and what is called *natural-law language.*

Natural-Law Language   When people use the word *natural,* they usually mean that something is inevitable, predetermined, or outside human control (Pierce, 1971). *Human nature* and *instinct* are often used in the same way. For example, "It's only natural to care about what others think," "It's human nature to want to get ahead," or "It's just instinctive to be afraid of someone different" all convey the sense that something is inevitable, automatic, and independent of one's will.

Thus, it is not surprising when, in discussions about discrimination, someone says, "It's only natural for people to be prejudiced" or "It's human nature to want to be with your own kind." Each of these commonsense ideas conveys a belief in the inevitability of discrimination and prejudice, as if such processes emerged independently of anyone's will.

Even for issues of which we disapprove, the word *natural* can convey this sense of inevitability. For example, "I am against racism, but it's only natural" puts nature on the side of prejudice. Arguing that something is natural because it happens frequently has the same consequence. "All societies have discriminated against women," implies that something that happens frequently is therefore inevitable. But in truth, something that happens frequently could just as likely mean there is an extensive set of social controls ensuring the outcome.

At least three consequences follow from using natural-law language. First, it brings discussion to a close, as if having described something as natural makes any further exploration of the topic unnecessary. This makes sense given that the word *natural* is equated with inevitability: If something is inevitable, there is little sense in questioning it.

Second, because natural-law language treats behavior as predetermined, it overlooks the actual cultural and historical variation of human societies. If something is natural, it should always happen. Yet virtually no human behavior emerges everywhere and always; all social life is susceptible to change. Thus, natural-law language ignores the variability of social life.

Third, natural-law language treats individuals as passive, lacking an interest in or control over social life. If it is "natural" to dislike those who are different, then there is really nothing we can do about that feeling. It is no one's responsibility; it is just natural. If there is nothing I can do about my own behavior, there is little I could expect to do about the behavior of others. Human nature thus is depicted as a limitation beyond which people cannot expect to move (Gould, 1981). Describing certain behavior as "only natural" implies that personal and social change are impossible.

In all these ways—by closing off discussion, masking variation and change, and treating humans as passive—natural-law language tells us not to question the world that surrounds us. Natural-law language has this effect no matter what context it emerges in: "It's only natural to discriminate," "It's only natural to want to have children," "It's only natural to marry and settle down," "Inequality is only natural; the poor will always be with us," "Aggression and war are just human nature," "Greed is instinctive." In each case, natural-law language not only discourages questions, it carries a covert recommendation about what you *ought* to do. If something is "just natural," you cannot prevent others from doing it, and you are well advised to do it yourself. Thus, natural-law language serves as a forceful mechanism of social control (Pierce, 1971).

Natural-law language is used to reinforce hegemonic ideologies. It reduces the complexity and historic variability of the social world to a claim for universal processes, offering a partial and distorted truth that silences those with contrary experience. Natural-law language can make discrimination appear to be natural, normal, and inevitable. It tells us simply to accept the world around us and not seek to improve it. Thus, natural-law language itself creates and maintains ideas about difference.

Stereotypes A *stereotype* is a prediction that "members of a group will behave in certain ways" (Andre, 1988:259)—that black men will have athletic ability or that Asian American students will excel in the sciences. As Frank Wu wrote in Reading 52, "Before I can talk about Asian American experiences at all, I have to kill off the model minority myth because the stereotype obscures many realities."

Stereotypes assume that all the individuals in a category possess the same characteristics. Stereotypes persist despite evidence to the contrary because they are not formulated in a way that is testable or falsifiable (Andre, 1988). In this way stereotypes differ from descriptions. Descriptions offer no prediction; they can be tested for accuracy and rejected when they are wrong; they encourage explanation and a consideration of historical variability.

For example, "Most great American athletes are African American" is a description. First, there is no prediction that a particular African American can be expected to be a good athlete, or that someone who is white will be a poor one. Second, the claim is falsifiable; that is, it can be tested for accuracy and proven wrong (e.g., by asking what proportion of the last two decades' American Olympic medal winners were African American). Third, the statement turns our attention to explanation and historical variation: Why might this be the case? Has this always been the case?

In contrast, "African Americans are good athletes" is a stereotype. It attempts to characterize a whole population, thus denying the inevitable differences among the people in the category. It predicts that members of a group will behave in a particular way. It cannot be falsified since there is no direct way to test the claim. Further, the stereotype denies the reality of historical and cultural variation by suggesting that this has always been the case. Thus, stereotypes essentialize: they assume that if you know something about the physical package someone comes in, you can predict that person's behavior.

Both stereotypes and natural-law language offer broad-based predictions about behavior. Stereotypes predict that members of a particular category will possess particular attributes; natural-law language predicts that certain behavior is inevitable. Neither stereotypes nor natural-law language is anchored in any social or historical context, and, for that reason, both are frequently wrong. Basketball great Bill Russell's reaction when asked if he thought African Americans were "natural" athletes makes clear the similarity of natural-law language and stereotyping. As Russell said, this was a stereotypic image of African American athletes that deprecated the skill and effort he brought to his craft—as if he were great because he was black rather than because of the talent he cultivated in hours of practice.

Stereotyping and Asian Americans As we have said, stereotypes explain life outcomes by attributing some essential, shared quality to all those in a particular category. The current depiction of Asian Americans as a "model minority" is a good example of this. This stereotype masks the considerable economic, educational, and occupational heterogeneity among Asian Americans. For example, the proportion of those holding college degrees varies considerably among Asian American groups, at rates of 64 percent for Asian Indians, 46 percent for Chinese, 42 percent for Filipinos, 40 percent for Japanese, 44 percent for Koreans, and 14 percent for Vietnamese (Le, 2007). The model-minority stereotype is itself a fairly recent invention. Among those now called "model minority" are categories of people who have been previously categorized as undesirable immigrants, denied citizenship through naturalization, and placed in internment camps as potential traitors.

In American culture, stereotypes are often driven by the necessity to explain why some categories of people succeed more than others (Steinberg, 1989). Thus, the model-minority stereotype is often used to claim that if racism has not been an impediment to Asian Americans' success, it could not have hurt African Americans'.

The myth of the Asian-American "model minority" has been challenged, yet it continues to be widely believed. One reason for this is its instructional value. For whom are Asian Americans supposed to be a "model"? Shortly after the Civil War, southern planters recruited Chinese immigrants in order to pit them against the newly freed blacks as "examples" of laborers willing to work hard for low wages. Today, Asian Americans are again being used to discipline blacks. . . . Our society needs an Asian-American "model minority" in an era anxious about a growing black underclass. (Takaki, 1993:416)

A brief review of American immigration policy explains the misguided nature of the comparison between African and Asian Americans. Until 1965, U.S. immigration was restricted by quotas that set limits on the number of immigrants from each nation based on the percentage of people from that country residing in the United States at the time of the 1920 census. This had the obvious and intended effect of severely restricting immigration from Asia, as well as that from Southern and Eastern Europe and Africa. The civil rights movement of the 1960s raised such national embarrassment about this quota system that in 1965 Congress replaced national-origin quotas with an annual 20,000-person limit for every nation regardless of its size. Within that quota, preference went first to those who were relatives of U.S. citizens and then to those with occupational skills needed in America.

The result was a total increase in immigration and a change in its composition. Because few individuals from non-European countries could immigrate on the grounds of having family in America—previous restrictions would have made that almost impossible—the quotas were filled with people meeting designated *occupational* needs. Thus, those immigrating to the United States since 1965 have had high educational and occupational profiles. The middle- and upper-class professionals and entrepreneurs who have immigrated to the United States did not suddenly become successful here; rather, they continued their home-country success here. These high occupational and educational profiles have characterized immigrants from African as well as Asian countries.

The high Asian American educational and occupational profile has yielded the country's highest median *household* income, but not its highest *individual* income. The chart below compares family and individual income by race and shows the degree to which family size affects household income.

FAMILY, HOUSEHOLD, AND PER CAPITA INCOME BY RACE AND ETHNICITY

Race/ethnicity	Median family income	Median household size	Median per capita Income
White (non-Hispanic)	$45,904	2.45	$25,278
Black	$30,439	2.67	$15,159
Latino	$33,447	3.49	$12,306
Asian American	$55,521	3.10	$22,352

Source: U.S. Census Bureau, 2001.
Note: Between 2000 and 2001, "median household money income did not change for households with a non-Hispanic White householder, or for those with a householder who reported a single race of Asian. However, income fell for Blacks by 2.5 to 3.0 percent, for Asians who reported more than one race by 4.0 to 4.5 percent, and for Hispanics by 2.9 percent" (Weinberg, 2003).

Despite a higher educational profile, Asian Americans' per capita income lags behind that of non-Hispanic whites. The following 1999 data compare college graduation with unemployment and poverty rates.

EDUCATION, UNEMPLOYMENT, AND POVERTY RATES BY RACE AND ETHNICITY

Race/ethnicity	Percent with college degree	Unemployment rate	Percent of families in poverty
Whites	25.9	3.7	8.0
Blacks	15.4	8.0	23.4
Latinos	10.9	6.4	22.7
Asian Americans	42.4	4.2	11.0

Source: U.S. Census Bureau, 2000; in Le, 2001.

A more telling statistic is how much more money a person earns with each additional year of schooling completed, or what sociologists call "returns on education." Using this measure, research consistently shows that for each additional year of education attained, Whites earn another $522 [a year.] That is, beyond a high school degree, a White [worker] with four more years of education (equivalent to a college degree) can expect to earn $2,088 [more] per year in salary.

In contrast, return on each additional year of education for a Japanese American is only $438 [a year]. For a Chinese American, it's $320. For Blacks, it's even worse at only $284. What this means is that, basically, a typical Asian American has to get more years of education just to make the same amount of money that a typical White [worker] makes with less education. (Le, 2001)

While selective immigration goes a long way toward explaining the success of some recent immigrants from Asian countries, it's important to distinguish between immigrants and those who are refugees. The circumstances of arrival and resettlement for those who have fled their home countries make the refugee population exceedingly heterogeneous and quite different from those who have immigrated to the United States (Haines, 1989). Thus, Vietnamese, Laotian, Cambodian, and Hmong refugees are unlikely to have the high occupational or educational profiles of other Asian immigrants.

Interestingly, the contemporary comparison—if Asian Americans can make it, why can't African Americans?—echoes an earlier question: If European immigrants can make it, why can't African Americans? The answer to that question is summarized as follows:

Conditions within the cities to which they had migrated [beginning in the 1920s], not slavery, strained blacks' ability to retain two-parent families. Within those cities, blacks faced circumstances that differed fundamentally from those found earlier by European immigrants. They entered cities in large numbers as unskilled and semiskilled manufacturing jobs were leaving, not growing. The discrimination they encountered kept them out of the manufacturing jobs into which earlier immigrants had been recruited. One important goal of public schools had been the assimilation and "Americanization" of immigrant children; by contrast, they excluded and segregated blacks. Racism enforced housing segregation, and residential concentration among blacks increased at the same time it lessened among immigrants and their children.

Political machines had embraced earlier immigrants and incorporated them into the system of "city trenches" by which American cities were governed; they excluded blacks from effective political power until cities had been so abandoned by industry and deserted by whites that resistance to black political participation no longer mattered. All the processes that had opened opportunities for immigrants and their children broke down for blacks. (Katz, 1989:51)

Stereotyping and African Americans Currently Asian Americans suffer the effects of what may be called a positive stereotype, while African Americans experience just the opposite. The trajectory, nature, and impact of racial stereotypes have been examined extensively in terms of whites' attitudes toward blacks. The picture is a complicated one.

Certainly, in terms of belief in the principles of racial equality and integration, the research has shown a significant and sustained improvement in whites' attitudes across the board—but the *degree* of that improvement has varied by the topic. About public transportation and jobs, virtually all whites endorsed the ideas of equal access and integration by the mid-1970s. But it wasn't until the mid-1990s that a 95 percent level of white support was reached on the question of school integration, and white support of unconstrained access to housing is only about 60 percent (Bobo, 2001). The acceptance of interracial marriage has reached 70 percent among whites (and 80 percent among blacks), with 66 percent saying they would approve their child or grandchild marrying outside their race (Ludwig, 2004).

Alongside this increased commitment to equality and integration, research also shows a persistence of negative stereotypes about blacks among whites.

> Bobo and Kluegel (1997:100–101) show that 31 percent of Whites gave Blacks a low absolute rating in terms of intelligence, 47 percent did so in terms of laziness, 54 percent did so concerning proclivity to violence, and 59 percent did so concerning preference to live off welfare. . . . These negative stereotypes often also apply in terms of Whites' views of Hispanics (T. Smith, 1990). Although Whites' views of Asians and Pacific Islanders are seldom as negative as those regarding Blacks and Hispanics, Asians and Pacific Islanders typically receive unfavorable relative ratings. The 1990 General Social Survey reported that considerably more than 50 percent of Whites rated Blacks and Hispanics as less intelligent. A similar percentage rated Blacks and Hispanics as prone to violence. Considerably more than two-thirds of Whites rated Blacks and Hispanics as actually preferring to live off welfare. (Bobo, 2001: 277–278)

Not surprisingly, these stereotypes affect everthing from support of social policies to interpersonal interactions.

> Research indicating Whites' fearfulness of a Black stranger is indicative [of interpersonal interactions]. Based on a survey that involved the use of sophisticated experimental vignettes, St. John and Heald-Moore (1995) found that Whites were more fearful of a Black stranger than of a White stranger. This was true irrespective of other situational factors such as time of day or neighborhood characteristics. The degree of fear was strongly conditioned by only two factors: age and gender of the Black person (young Black males were feared more than others) and age of the White person (feelings of fear and vulnerability were greatest among older Whites). . . .
> This work implies that the interaction between Blacks and Whites in many public settings is rife with the potential for missteps, misunderstanding, and insult. Precisely this sort of dynamic is suggested by events and experiences recounted in qualitative interviews with middle-class Blacks (Feagin, 1991; Cose, 1993; Feagin and Sikes, 1994). (Bobo, 2001:278–279)

The work of social psychologists Samuel Gaertner and John Dovidio offers insight into the nature of these difficult interactions. Gaertner and Dovidio have spent thirty years researching prejudice, focusing especially on *aversive racism*. Unlike those who are overtly prejudiced, aversive racists are unaware of their negative attitudes, instead considering themselves unprejudiced and even supportive of racial equality. Despite endorsing the principles of fair treatment, they feel personally so uneasy with blacks that they to avoid interracial interaction.

> When interracial interaction is unavoidable, aversive racists experience anxiety and discomfort, and consequently they try to disengage from the interaction as quickly as possible. In addition, because part of the discomfort that aversive racists experience is due to a concern about acting inappropriately and appearing prejudiced, aversive racists are motivated primarily by avoiding wrongdoing in interracial interactions. (Gaertner and Dovidio, 2005:619)

Out of their discomfort and desire to minimize interaction—especially in the absence of situational norms compelling engagement—aversive racists are likely to discriminate against blacks but in ways they are unaware of—for example, by failing to help blacks in emergencies to the same extent that they would help whites. As Gaertner and Dovidio summarize the research literature, "Taken together, the results from a substantial number of studies drawing on a range of different paradigms demonstrate the systematic operation of aversive racism producing in Whites a failure to help, to hire or admit, and to treat Blacks fairly under the law" (Gaertner and Dovidio, 2005:623).

When considering the ultimate effect of stereotypes—that is, discriminatory behavior—whites and blacks disagree about the extent of discrimination. Response to the annual Gallop poll about how different groups are treated in American society is typical: In a 2003 survey, 73 percent of whites, but only 39 percent of blacks felt that blacks and whites were treated the same in their local community. When the question is about the treatment of blacks and whites in the country as a whole, 39 percent of whites but only 11 percent of blacks feel that treatment is the same (Ludwig, 2003). These gaps in the perception of discrimination also appear between whites and Asians and Latinos, although they are somewhat smaller.

Finally, African Americans and other people of color are likely to understand discrimination as institutionally based, and whites are more likely to attribute it to isolated events or individuals.

> In short, to Whites, the [New York City police] officers who tortured Abner Louima constitute a few bad apples. To Blacks, these officers represent only the tip of the iceberg. [Hatian immigrant Abner Louima was beaten and sexually assaulted by police after he was arrested outside a Brooklyn nightclub in 1997.]
>
> To Whites, the Texaco tapes are shocking. To Blacks, the tapes merely reflect that in this one instance the guilty were caught. [In 1996, a Texaco executive turned over audiotapes of Texaco executives making racist remarks and plotting to purge the documents in a discrimination case. Ultimately, Texaco paid more than $115 million for having failed to hire, promote, and treat its black staff with general decency.]
>
> But differences in perception cut deeper than this. . . . Although many Whites recognize that discrimination plays some part in higher rates of unemployment, poverty, and a range of hardships in life that minorities often face, the central cause is usually understood to be the

level of effort and cultural patterns of the minority group members themselves (Schuman, 1971; Apostle et al., 1983; Kluegel and Smith, 1986; Schuman, et al., 1997). For minorities, especially Blacks, it is understood that the persistence of race problems has something to do with how our institutions operate. For many Whites, larger patterns of inequality are understood as mainly something about minorities themselves. . . . [T]he most popular view holds that blacks should "try harder," should get ahead "without special favors," and fall behind because they "lack motivation." (Bobo, 2001:281–282)

Social Institutions and the Support of Ideologies

The specific messages carried by natural-law language and stereotypes are often echoed by social institutions. The term *social institution* refers to the established mechanisms by which societies meet their predictable needs. For example, the need to socialize new members of the society is met by the institutions of the family and education. In addition to these, social institutions include science, law, religion, politics, the economy, military, medicine, mass media, and popular culture. Ideologies—in our case ideologies about the meaning of difference—naturally play a significant role in the operation of social institutions. In the discussion that follows, we will consider how late-19th- and early-20th-century science and popular culture constructed the meaning of race, class, sex, disability, and sexual orientation differences. Throughout, there is a striking congruence among scientific pronouncements, popular culture messages, and the prejudices of the day.

Science   The need to explain the meaning of human difference forcefully emerged when 15th-century Europeans encountered previously unknown regions and peoples. "Three centuries of exploration brought home as never before the tremendous diversity of human behavior and life patterns within environments and under circumstances dramatically different from those of Europe. . . . Out of that large laboratory of human experience was born the [idea of the] conflict between nature and nurture" (Degler, 1991:4–5).

The "nature-nurture" conflict offered two ways to explain human variation. Explanations from the nature side stressed that the diversity of human societies—and the ability of some to conquer and dominate others—reflected significant biological differences among populations. Explanations from the nurture side argued that human diversity resulted from historical, environmental, and cultural difference. From the nature side, humans were understood to act out behaviors that are biologically driven. From the nurture side, humans were something of a *tabula rasa,* a blank slate, on which particular cultural expectations were inscribed.

Whether nature or nurture was understood to dominate, however, the discussion of the meaning of human difference always assumed that people could be ranked as to their worth (Gould, 1981). Thus, the real question was whether the rankings reflected in social hierarchies were the result of nature, and thus inevitable and fixed, or whether they could be affected by human action and were thus subject to change.

The question was not merely theoretical. The 1800s in America witnessed appropriation of Native American territories and the forced relocation of vast numbers of people under the Indian Removal Act of 1830; the 1848 signing of the Treaty of

Guadalupe Hidalgo ending the Mexican-American War and ceding what is now Texas, New Mexico, California, Utah, Nevada, Colorado, and Arizona to the United States with the 75,000 Mexican nationals residing in those territories becoming U.S. citizens; passage of the 1892 Chinese Exclusion Act; a prolonged national debate about slavery and women's suffrage; and the arrival of an unprecedented number of poor and working-class immigrants from Southern and Eastern Europe. The century closed with the internationally publicized trial of Irish playwright Oscar Wilde, who was sentenced to two years' hard labor for "gross indecency," which in this case meant homosexuality.

Thus, a profound question was whether social hierarchy reflected natural, permanent, and inherent differences in capability (the nature side) or was the product of specific social and historical circumstances and therefore susceptible to change. Because Africans were held by whites in slavery, did that mean Africans were by their nature inferior to whites? Were Native Americans literally "savages" occupying some middle ground between animals and civilized humans, and did they therefore benefit from domination by those who supposedly were more advanced? Did the dissimilarity of Chinese immigrants from American whites mean they were not "human" in the way whites were? If homosexuality was congenital, did that mean homosexuals were profoundly different from heterosexuals? Were women closer to plants and animals than to civilized men? Were the deaf also "dumb"? Were the poor and working classes composed of those who not only lacked the talents by which to rise in society but also passed their defects on to their children? In all, were individuals and categories of people located in the statuses for which they were best suited? This was the question driving public debate (Degler, 1991). If one believed that the social order simply reflected immutable biological differences, the answer to the question would probably be yes. That would not have been the case, however, for those who believed these differences were the outcome of specific social and historical processes overlaying a shared humanity. In all, the question behind the nature-nurture debate was about the *meaning* of what appeared to be *natural* difference. The answer to that question was shaped by the hegemonic ideologies of the time—especially those informed by science.

Charles Darwin's publication of *The Origin of the Species* (1859) and *The Descent of Man* (1871) shifted the weight of popular and scholarly opinion toward the nature side of the equation (Degler, 1991). In its broadest terms, Darwin's conclusions challenged the two central beliefs of the time. (Darwin himself was quite distressed to have arrived at these conclusions [Shipman, 1994].) First, the idea of evolutionary change challenged "traditional, Christian belief in a single episode of creation of a static, perfect, and unchanging world." The significance of evolutionary change was clear: "If the world were not created perfect, then there was no implicit justification for the way things were . . ." (Shipman, 1994:18).

Second, Darwin's work implied that all humans share a common ancestry. If differences among birds were the result of their adaptation to distinctive environments, then *their differences existed within an overall framework of similarity and common ancestry.* By analogy, the differences within human populations might also be understood as "variability within overall similarity" (Shipman, 1994:22)—a shocking possibility at the time. "It was the age of imperialism and most non-Europeans were regarded, even by Darwin, as 'barbarians'; he was astonished and taken aback by their wildness and animality. The differences among humans seemed so extreme that the humanity . . . of some living groups was scarcely credible" (Shipman, 1994:19).

Darwin's idea that change in the physical environment resulted in the perpetuation of some species and demise of others (the idea of natural selection) bolstered a pre-existent concept of "survival of the fittest." This phrase had been coined by English sociologist Herbert Spencer, who had been considering the evolutionary principles of human societies several years before Darwin published *The Origin of the Species.*

Spencer's position, eventually called *social Darwinism,* was extremely popular in America. Spencer strongly believed that modern societies are inevitably improvements over earlier forms of social organization and that progress would necessarily follow from unimpeded competition for social resources. In all, social Darwinism argued that those who are more advanced naturally rise to the top of any stratification ladder.

Through social Darwinism, the prevailing hierarchies—slave owner over people held in slavery, white over Mexican and Native American, native born over immigrant, upper class over poor, male over female—could be attributed to natural processes and justified as a reflection of inherent differences among categories of people. As one sociologist at the turn of the century framed it, "under the tutelage of Darwinism the world returns again to the idea that *might* as evidence of fitness has something to do with *right*" (Degler, 1991:13). Social Darwinism lacked a socially or historically grounded explanation for social stratification. Instead, it treated those hierarchies as a reflection of the biological merit of categories of people. Thus, the ideology of social Darwinism was used to justify slavery, colonialism, immigration restrictions, the criminalization of homosexuality, the forced relocation of Native Americans, and the legal subordination of women. Because social Darwinism affirmed that difference meant defect, it was also compatible with the historical oppression of disabled people.

The social Darwinist position was also used by those opposed to providing equal education for women. Just when American institutions of higher education were opening to women—Vassar College was founded in 1865, Smith and Wellesley colleges ten years later, and by 1870 many state universities had become coeducational—biologist Edward Clarke published a book (1873) that argued that the physical energy education required would endanger women's reproductive abilities (an idea first put forward by Spencer). Clarke's case was based on meager and questionable empirical evidence: seven clinical cases, only one of which actually supported his position (Sayers, 1982:14). His work was a response to *social* rather than scientific developments, since it was prompted by no new discoveries in biology. Nonetheless, the book was an immediate and enduring success. For the next thirty years it was used in the argument against equal education despite the accumulation of evidence refuting its claims. While Clarke's research should have been suspect, it instead became influential in policymaking. In part, "the reason why Clarke's argument seemed so serviceable to those opposed to women's higher education was that it was couched in biological terms and thus appeared to offer a legitimate scientific basis for conservative opposition to equal education" (Sayers, 1982:11).

In a similar fashion, science shaped ideas about the meaning of same-sex relationships. By the turn of the century in Europe, a gay rights movement had arisen in Germany and gay themes had emerged in French literature (Adam, 1987). At the same time, however, an international move to criminalize sexual relations between men gathered momentum: a revision of the German criminal code increased the penalties for male homosexuality, the British imprisoned Oscar Wilde, and Europe and the United States experienced a social reform movement directed against prostitution and male homosexuality. The possibility of sexual relations between women was not considered until later.

The move to criminalize homosexuality was countered by physicians arguing, from a social Darwinist position, that homosexuality is the product of "hereditary weakness" and is thus beyond individual control. Though their hope was for increased tolerance, those who took this position offered the idea of "homosexuality as a medical entity and the homosexual as a distinctive kind of person" (Conrad and Schneider, 1980:184). Thus, they contributed to the idea that heterosexual and homosexual people were biologically different from each other.

Science also supported the argument that people of different skin colors were different in significant, immutable ways. Certainly Spencer's idea of the survival of the fittest was understood to support the ideology that whites are superior to all people of color: "The most prevalent form of social Darwinism at the turn of the century was actually racism, that is, the idea that one people might be superior to another because of differences in their biological nature" (Degler, 1991:15).

The scientific defense of American slavery first emerged with the work of two eminent scientists, Swiss naturalist Louis Agassiz and Philadelphia physician Samuel Morton. Agassiz immigrated to America in 1840 and became a professor at Harvard. There he garnered immense popularity by countering the biblically based theory of the unity of all people (which attributed racial differences to "degeneration" from a shared origin) with a "scientific" theory that different races had descended from different moments of creation—"different Adams" as it was called (Gould, 1981:39). Morton tested Agassiz's theories by measuring the skull capacity of people of different races. His idea was that the size of the skull would correlate with the intelligence of the race, and his results "matched every good Yankee's prejudices—whites on top, Indians in the middle, and blacks on the bottom; and among whites, Teutons and Anglo-Saxons on top, Jews in the middle, and Hindus on the bottom" (Gould, 1981:53).

As we now know, Morton's findings were simply wrong. Others who replicated his measurements did not arrive at the same conclusions about skull capacity: There were "*no* significant differences among races for Morton's own data" (Gould, 1981:67). There is no evidence that Morton intended to deceive. Rather, his assumptions of white superiority were so firm that he was oblivious to his own errors and illogic, errors that yielded the conclusion of white superiority only because of his miscalculations.

The use of questionable research to support prevailing beliefs was also evident in the development of intelligence testing. In 1904, Alfred Binet, director of the psychology lab at the Sorbonne, was commissioned by the French minister of public education to develop a test to identify children whose poor performance in school might indicate a need for special education. Binet developed a test with a series of tasks that children of "normal" intelligence were expected to have mastered. Binet's own claims for the test were fairly limited. He did not equate intelligence with the score produced by his test, arguing that intelligence was too complex a factor to be reduced to a simple number. Nor did he construe his test as measuring inborn, permanent, or inherited limitations (Gould, 1981).

Binet's hesitations regarding the significance of the test, however, were ignored by the emerging field of American psychology, which used intelligence as a way to explain social hierarchies. "The people who are doing the drudgery are, as a rule, in their proper places," wrote H. H. Goddard, who introduced the Binet test to America. Stanford psychologist Lewis M. Termin (author of the Stanford-Binet IQ test) argued that "the children of successful and cultured parents test higher than children from wretched and ignorant homes for the simple reason that their heredity is better" (Degler, 1991:50). Indeed, "Terman believed that class boundaries had been set by innate intelligence" (Gould, 1981:183).

Such conclusions were used to shape decisions about the distribution of social resources. For example, intelligence was described as a capacity like the capacity of a jug to hold a certain amount of milk. A pint jug could not be expected to hold a quart of milk; similarly, it was pointless to waste "too much" education on someone whose capacity was supposedly limited. IQ tests were used to assess mental deficiency, including the newly developed categories of idiots, imbeciles, and morons. Morons were judged the highest of the "mental defectives," with the potential to be trained to function in society. Nonetheless, Goddard recommended that they be "institutionalized, carefully regulated, made happy by catering to their limits, . . . prevented from breeding" (Gould, 1981:160), and not allowed into the country as immigrants. Toward that end, intelligence tests were used to identify the "mental defectives" as they landed at Ellis Island:

> [C]onsider a group of frightened men and women who speak no English and who have just endured an oceanic voyage in steerage. Most are poor and have never gone to school; many have never held a pencil or pen in their hand. They march off the boat; one of Goddard's intuitive women [inspectors] takes them aside shortly thereafter, sits them down, hands them a pencil, and asks them to reproduce on paper a figure shown to them a moment ago, but now withdrawn from their sight. Could their failure be a result of testing conditions, of weakness, fear, or confusion, rather than of innate stupidity? Goddard considered the possibility, but rejected it. (Gould, 1981:166)

In the early decades of the 20th century, the eugenics movement, a form of social Darwinism, spearheaded the use of forced sterilization to limit the growth of "defective" populations. Eugenicists lobbied for state laws endorsing the sterilization of the "feebleminded, insane, criminalistic, epileptic, inebriate, diseased, blind, deaf; deformed, and dependent" (Lombardo, n.d.). The practice was approved by the Supreme Court in *Buck v. Bell* in 1927, with Justice Oliver Wendell Holmes, Jr., writing the majority opinion:

> It is better for all the world, if instead of waiting to execute degenerate offspring for crime or to let them starve for the imbecility, society can prevent those who are manifestly unfit from continuing their kind. . . . Three generations of imbeciles are enough.

Only in 1942, in *Skinner v. Oklahoma*, did the Supreme Court back away from its position, but by that point thirteen states had laws allowing the sterilization of criminals. Thus,

> sterilization of people in institutions for the mentally ill and mentally retarded continued through the mid-1970's. At one time or another, 33 states had statutes under which more than 60,000 Americans endured involuntary sterilization. The *Buck v. Bell* precedent allowing sterilization of the so-called "feebleminded" has never been overturned." (Lombardo, n.d.)

The findings of intelligence testers were also used to advocate particular social policies such as restrictions on immigration. While it is not clear that the work of intelligence testers directly affected the Immigration Restriction Act of 1924 (Degler, 1991), the ultimate shape of the legislation limited immigration from Southern and Eastern Europe, which was consistent with intelligence testers' claims about the relative intelligence of the "races" in Europe. These quotas barred the admission of European Jews fleeing the impending holocaust (Gould, 1981).

Still, by about 1930 a considerable body of research showed that social environment more than biology accounted for differing IQ scores and that the tests themselves measured not innate intelligence but familiarity with the culture of those who wrote the tests. In the end, the psychologists who had promoted intelligence testing were forced to repudiate the idea that intelligence is inherited or that it can be separated from cultural knowledge.[1]

Whether measuring cranial capacity, developing paper-and-pencil intelligence tests, worrying about the effect of education on women, or arguing for hereditary weakness as an explanation of homosexuality, the work of these scientists supported the prevailing ideologies about the merit and appropriate social position of people of different sexes, races, ethnic groups, sexual orientations, and social classes. Most of these scientists were not overtly motivated by ideology; indeed they were sometimes troubled by their own findings. Still, their research was riddled with technical errors and questionable findings. Their research proved "the surprising malleability of 'objective,' quantitative data in the interest of a preconceived idea" (Gould, 1981:147). Precisely because their research confirmed prevailing beliefs, it was more likely to be celebrated than scrutinized.

Why were these findings eventually repudiated? Since they offered a defense of the status quo and confirmed the prevailing ideology, who would have criticized them?

First, the scientific defense of immutable hierarchy was eroded by the steady accumulation of evidence about the "intellectual equality and therefore the equal

---

[1]". . . There is also a lot of evidence for the whole American population, for American ethnic groups, and for populations wherever tests are given that IQ is changing in ways that can't possibly be genetic because they happen too fast. It is widely recognized that average IQs are increasing fairly rapidly. These changes in IQ clearly must have more to say about relationships between testing and real performance, or about social patterns of learning, than about biologically rooted 'intelligence.' The genes of a large population don't change that fast unless there is a very dramatic episode of natural selection such as an epidemic" (Cohen, 1998:210).

cultural capacity of all peoples" (Degler, 1991:61). A good deal of the research that made that point was produced by the many "prominent or soon to be prominent" scholars of African American, Chinese, and European immigrant ancestry who, after finally being admitted to institutions of higher education, were pursuing scientific research. Black scholars such as W. E. B. Du Bois and E. Franklin Frazier, and scholars of recent European immigrant ancestry such as anthropologists Franz Boas, Alfred Kroeber, and Edward Sapir, trenchantly criticized the social science of the day and by their very presence challenged the prevailing expectations about the "inherent inferiority" of people like themselves (Degler, 1991).

The presumptions about the meaning of race were also challenged by increased interracial contact. The 1920s began the Great Migration, in which hundreds of thousands of African Americans from the rural South moved to northern cities. This movement continued through two world wars as black, Latino, Asian, and Native American men joined the armed forces and women followed wartime employment opportunities. The 1920s also brought the Harlem Renaissance, an outpouring of creativity from black writers, scholars, and artists in celebration of African and African American culture. Overall, white social scientists "gained an unprecedented opportunity to observe blacks in a fresh and often transforming way" (Degler, 1991:197). Their attitudes and expectations changed as a result of this increased contact.

In sum, the scientific argument for the inherent inferiority of some groups of people was advanced by upper-class, native-born, white male faculty members of prestigious universities. Few others would have had the means with which to disseminate their ideas or the prestige to make those ideas influential. These theories of essential difference were not written by Native Americans, Mexicans, women, gays, African Americans, or immigrants from Asia or Southern and Eastern Europe. Most of these people lacked access to the public forums to present their experiences until the rise of the antislavery, suffrage, labor, and gay rights movements. Insofar as the people in these categories could be silenced, it was easier to depict them as essentially and profoundly different.

Popular Culture   Like the sciences, popular culture (the forms of entertainment available for mass consumption such as popular music, theater, film, literature, and television) may convey ideologies about difference and social stratification. At virtually the same time that social Darwinism gained popularity in America—indeed within two years of Louis Agassiz's arrival in the United States in 1840—America's first minstrel show was organized. Like social Darwinism, minstrel shows offered a defense of slavery.

Minstrel shows, which became an enormously popular form of entertainment, were musical variety shows in which white males in "blackface" ridiculed blacks, abolitionism, and women's suffrage. Their impact can be seen in the movies and cartoons of the 1930s and 1940s and in current American stereotypes. As the shows traveled the country, their images were impressed on whites who often had no direct contact with blacks and thus no information to contradict the minstrel images.

The three primary characters of the minstrel show were the happy slave, Zip Coon, and the mammy (Riggs, 1987). The image of the happy slave—singing and dancing, naive and childlike, taken care of through old age by the white master, as a virtual member of the family—asserted that blacks held in slavery were both content and cared for. Zip Coon was a northern, free black man characterized by an improper use of language and laughable attempts to emulate whites; the caricature was used to show that blacks lacked the intelligence to handle freedom. The mammy was depicted as a large and presumably unattractive black woman fully devoted to the white family she served. Like the happy slave, the mammy was unthreatening and content—no sexual competition to the white mistress of the house, no children of her own needing attention, committed to and fulfilled by her work with her white family. Thus, the characters of the minstrel show hid the reality of slavery. The happy slave and mammy denied the brutality of the slave system. Zip Coon denied the reality of blacks' organization of the underground railroad, their production of slave narratives in books and lectures, and their undertaking of slave rebellions and escapes.

In all, minstrel shows offered an ideology about slavery constructed by and in the interests of those with power. They ridiculed antislavery activists and legitimatized the status quo. Minstrel shows asserted that blacks did not mind being held as slaves and that they did not suffer loss and pain in the same way whites did. The minstrel show was not the only source of this ideology, but as a form of popular entertainment it was a very effective means of disseminating such beliefs. The shows traveled to all parts of the country, with a hostile racial message masked as mere entertainment.

But within popular culture, an effective counter to the ideology of the minstrel show emerged through the speakers of the antislavery lecture circuit and the publication of numerous slave narratives. Appearing as early as 1760, these narratives achieved an enormous and enduring popularity among northern white readers. Frederick Douglass, former slave and the renowned antislavery activist, was the most famous public lecturer on the circuit and wrote a best-selling slave narrative. Whether as book or lecture, slave narratives provided an image of blacks as human beings. Access to these life histories provided the first opportunity for most whites to see a shared humanity between themselves and those held in slavery (Bodziock, 1990). Thus, slave narratives directly countered the images of the minstrel show. While popular culture may offer a variety of messages, all parties do not meet equally on its terrain. Those with power have better access and more legitimacy, but popular culture cannot be so tightly controlled as to entirely exclude the voice of the less powerful.

Conclusion

As Karl Marx noted, ideology was "the mechanism whereby there can occur a difference between how things really are in the economy and the wider society and how people think they are" (Marshall, 1994:234). Continuing this framework essay's focus on ideologies and social institutions, the first readings in this section address intersectionality, exploring people's experience of multiple master statuses and how that is shaped by ideologies and social institutions.

Following intersectionality, the readings turn to law, public policy, the economy, and language as social institutions that construct the meanings attributed to difference. Indeed, each of the Supreme Court decisions described in Reading 49 is ultimately about the *meaning* of difference—for example, in the determination of citizenship or access to higher education, what meaning are we going to attribute to race differences, or to sex differences? At the level of social institutions, the meaning that is made of difference has the potential for far-reaching impact.

KEY CONCEPTS

aversive racism Unrecognized prejudices that affect behavior. (page 341)

hegemonic Dominating or ruling. A **hegemonic ideology** is a belief that is pervasive in a culture. (page 335)

ideology A widely shared belief that primarily reflects the experiences of those with power, but is presented as universally valid. (pages 334–335)

natural-law language Language that treats human behavior as bound by natural law. (pages 335–336)

social Darwinism The belief that those who dominate a society are necessarily the fittest. (page 344)

social institution Established system for meeting societal needs; for example, the family. (page 342)

stereotype A characterization of a category of people as all alike, as possessing the same set of characteristics and likely to behave in the same ways. (pages 336–342)

REFERENCES

Adam, Barry D. 1987. *The Rise of a Gay and Lesbian Movement.* Boston: G. K. Hall & Co.

Andre, Judith. 1988. Stereotypes: Conceptual and Normative Considerations. *Racism and Sexism: An Integrated Study,* edited by Paula S. Rothenberg, 257–62. New York: St. Martin's Press.

Apostle, Richard, Charles Glock, Thom Piazza, and Marijean Suelzle. 1983. *The Anatomy of Racial Attitudes.* Berkeley, CA: University of California Press.

Bobo, Lawrence D. 2001. Racial Attitudes and Relations at the Close of the Twentieth Century. *America Becoming: Racial Trends and Their Consequences,* edited by Neil J. Smelser, William Julius Wilson, and Faith Mitchell, 264–301. Washington, DC: National Academy Press.

———, and James Kluegel. 1997. Status, Ideology, and Dimensions of Whites' Racial Beliefs and Attitudes: Progress and Stagnation. *Racial Attitudes in the 1990s: Continuity and Change,* edited by S. Tuch and J. Martin, 93–120. Westport, CT: Praeger.

Bodziock, Joseph. 1990. The Weight of Sambo's Woes. *Perspectives on Black Popular Culture,* edited by Harry B. Shaw, 166–79. Bowling Green, OH: Bowling Green State University Popular Press.

Brantlinger, Patrick. 1990. *Crusoe's Footprints: Cultural Studies in Britain and America.* New York: Routledge.

Cohen, Mark Nathan. 1998. *Culture of Intolerance: Chauvinism, Class, and Race in the United States.* New Haven, CT: Yale University Press.

Conrad, Peter, and Joseph W. Schneider. 1980. *Deviance and Medicalization.* Philadelphia: Temple University Press.

Cose, Eliott. 1993. *The Rage of a Privileged Class.* New York: HarperCollins.

Degler, Carl N. 1991. *In Search of Human Nature: The Decline and Revival of Darwinism in American Social Thought.* New York: Oxford University Press.

Feagin, Joe. 1991. The Continuing Significance of Race: Anti-black Discrimination in Public Places. *American Sociological Review,* 56:101–116.

———, and Melvin Sikes. 1994. *Living with Racism: The Black Middle Class Experience.* Boston: Beacon.

Gaertner, Samuel L., and John F. Dovidio. 2005. Understanding and Addressing Contemporary Racism: From Aversive Racism to the Common Ingroup Identity Model. *Journal of Social Issues* 61:615–639.

Gould, Stephen Jay. 1981. *The Mismeasure of Man.* New York: W. W. Norton.

Haines, David W. 1989. *Refugees as Immigrants.* Totowa, NJ: Rowman and Littlefield.

Kasper, Anne. 1986. Consciousness Re-evaluated: Interpretive Theory and Feminist Scholarship. *Sociological Inquiry* 56(1).

Katz, Michael B. 1989. *The Undeserving Poor.* New York: Pantheon Books.

Kluegel, James, and Eliot Smith. 1986. *Beliefs about Inequality: Americans' Views of What Is and What Ought to Be.* New York: Aldine de Gruyter.

Le, C. N. 2001. The Model Minority Image. *Asian-Nation.* www.asian-nation.org/issues2.html.

———. 2007. Socioeconomic Statistics & Demographics," *Asian-Nation: The Landscape of Asian America.* http://www.asian-nation.org/model-minority.shtml (accessed May 2007).

Lombardo, P. n.d. "Eugenic Sterilization Laws," *The Eugenics Archive,* Dolan DNA Learning Center, Cold Spring Harbor Laboratory. http://www.eugenicsarchive.org/eugenics/list3.pl (accessed June 2005).

Ludwig, Jack. 2003. Blacks and Whites Still Perceive Local Treatment of Blacks Differently. Gallup Organization, Gallup Poll News Service. May 27.

——— 2004. Acceptance of Interracial Marriage at Record High. Gallup Organization, Gallup Poll News Service. June 1.

Marshall, Gordon. 1994. *The Concise Oxford Dictionary of Sociology.* Oxford, UK: Oxford University Press.

Omi, Michael, and Howard Winant. 1994. *Racial Formation in the United States.* New York: Routledge.

Pierce, Christine. 1971. Natural Law Language and Women. *Woman in Sexist Society,* edited by Vivian Gornick and Barbara K. Moran, 242–58. New York: New American Library.

Riggs, Marlon. 1987. *Ethnic Notions.* California Newsreel (video).

St. John, C., and T. Heald-Moore. 1995. Fear of Black Strangers. *Social Science Research* 24:262–280.

Sayers, Janet. 1982. *Biological Politics: Feminist and Anti-feminist Perspectives.* London: Tavistock Publications.

Schuman, Howard. 1971. Free Will and Determinism in Beliefs about Race. *Majority and Minority: The Dynamics of Racial and Ethnic Relations,* edited by N. Yetman and C. Steeh, 375–380. Boston: Allyn & Bacon.

———, Charlotte Steeh, Lawrence Bobo, and Maria Krysan. 1997. *Racial Attitudes in America: Trends and Interpretations.* Rev. ed. Cambridge: Harvard University Press.

Shipman, Pat. 1994. *The Evolution of Racism: Human Differences and the Use and Abuse of Science.* New York: Simon and Schuster.

Smith, Dorothy. 1978. A Peculiar Eclipsing: Women's Exclusion from Men's Culture. *Women's Studies International Quarterly* 1:281–95.

———. 1990. *The Conceptual Practices of Power: A Feminist Sociology of Knowledge.* Boston: Northeastern University Press.

Smith, Tom. 1990. Ethnic Images. General Social Survey Technical Report, No. 19, National Opinion Research Center. University of Chicago.

Steinberg, Steven. 1989. *The Ethnic Myth: Race, Ethnicity, and Class in America.* Boston: Beacon Press.

Takaki, Ronald. 1993. *A Different Mirror: A History of Multicultural America.* Boston: Little, Brown.

U.S. Census Bureau. 2000. *Statistical Abstract of the United States: 2000* (120th ed.). Washington DC: United States Department of Commerce.

U.S. Census Bureau. 2001. *Money Income in the United States: 2000.* Current Population Reports. P60-213. September.

Weinberg, Daniel H. 2003. Press Briefing on 2002 Income and Poverty Estimates. U.S. Census Bureau. September 26.

INTERSECTIONALITY

READING 43

It's All in the Family: Intersections of Gender, Race, and Nation

Patricia Hill Collins

When former vice president Dan Quayle used the term *family values* near the end of a speech at a political fundraiser in 1992, he apparently touched a national nerve. Following Quayle's speech, close to three hundred articles using the term *family values* in their titles appeared in the popular press. Despite the range of political perspectives expressed on "family values," one thing remained clear—"family values," however defined, seemed central to national well-being. The term *family values* constituted a touchstone, a phrase that apparently tapped much deeper feelings about the significance of ideas of family, if not actual families themselves, in the United States.

Situated in the center of "family values" debates is an imagined traditional family ideal. Formed through a combination of marital and blood ties, ideal families consist of heterosexual couples that produce their own biological children. Such families have a specific authority structure; namely, a father-head earning an adequate family wage, a stay-at-home wife, and children. Those who idealize the traditional family as a private haven from a public world see family as held together by primary emotional bonds of love and caring. Assuming a relatively fixed sexual division of labor, wherein women's roles are defined as primarily in the home and men's in the public world of work, the traditional family ideal also assumes the separation of work and family. Defined as a natural or biological arrangement based on heterosexual attraction, this monolithic family type articulates with governmental structures. It is organized not around a biological core, but a state-sanctioned, heterosexual

marriage that confers legitimacy not only on the family structure itself but on children born into it (Andersen 1991).[1]

The power of this traditional family ideal lies in its dual function as an ideological construction and as a fundamental principle of social organization. As ideology, rhetoric associated with the traditional family ideal provides an interpretive framework that accommodates a range of meanings. Just as reworking the rhetoric of family for their own political agendas is a common strategy for conservative movements of all types, the alleged unity and solidarity attributed to family is often invoked to symbolize the aspirations of oppressed groups. For example, the conservative right and Black nationalists alike both rely on family language to advance their political agendas.

Moreover, because family constitutes a fundamental principle of social organization, the significance of the traditional family ideal transcends ideology. In the United States, understandings of social institutions and social policies are often constructed through family rhetoric. Families constitute primary sites of belonging to various groups: to the family as an assumed biological entity; to geographically identifiable, racially segregated neighborhoods conceptualized as imagined families; to so-called racial families codified in science and law; and to the U.S. nation-state conceptualized as a national family.

The importance of family also overlaps with the emerging paradigm of intersectionality. Building on a tradition from Black Women's Studies, intersectionality has attracted substantial scholarly attention in the 1990s.[2] As opposed to examining gender, race, class, and nation, as separate systems of oppression, intersectionality explores how these systems mutually construct one another, or, in the words of Black British sociologist Stuart Hall, how they "articulate" with one another (Slack 1996). Current scholarship deploying intersectional analyses suggests that certain ideas and practices surface repeatedly across multiple systems of oppression and serve as focal points or privileged social locations for these intersecting systems.[3]

Patricia Hill Collins is a professor of sociology at the University of Maryland.

The use of the traditional family ideal in the United States may function as one such privileged exemplar of intersectionality.[4] In this [essay], I explore how six dimensions of the traditional family ideal construct intersections of gender, race, and nation. Each dimension demonstrates specific connections between family as a gendered system of social organization, race as ideology and practice in the United States, and constructions of U.S. national identity. Collectively, these six dimensions illuminate specific ways that ideological constructions of family, as well as the significance of family in shaping social practices, constitute an especially rich site for intersectional analysis. . . .

MANUFACTURING NATURALIZED HIERARCHY

One dimension of family as a privileged exemplar of intersectionality lies in how it reconciles the contradictory relationship between equality and hierarchy. The traditional family ideal projects a model of equality. A well-functioning family protects and balances the interests of all its members—the strong care for the weak, and everyone contributes to and benefits from family membership in proportion to his or her capacities. In contrast to this idealized version, actual families remain organized around varying patterns of hierarchy. As Ann McClintock observes, "the family image came to figure *hierarchy within unity* [emphasis in original] as an organic element of historical progress, and thus became indispensable for legitimating exclusion and hierarchy within nonfamilial social forms such as nationalism, liberal individualism and imperialism" (McClintock 1995, 45). Families are expected to socialize their members into an appropriate set of "family values" that simultaneously reinforce the hierarchy within the assumed unity of interests symbolized by the family and lay the foundation for many social hierarchies. In particular, hierarchies of gender, wealth, age, and sexuality within actual family units correlate with comparable hierarchies in U.S. society. Individuals typically learn their assigned place in hierarchies of

race, gender, ethnicity, sexuality, nation, and social class in their families of origin. At the same time, they learn to view such hierarchies as natural social arrangements, as compared to socially constructed ones. Hierarchy in this sense becomes "naturalized" because it is associated with seemingly "natural" processes of the family.

The "family values" that underlie the traditional family ideal work to naturalize U.S. hierarchies of gender, age, and sexuality. For example, the traditional family ideal assumes a male headship that privileges and naturalizes masculinity as a source of authority. Similarly, parental control over dependent children reproduces age and seniority as fundamental principles of social organization. Moreover, gender and age mutually construct one another; mothers comply with fathers, sisters defer to brothers, all with the understanding that boys submit to maternal authority until they become men. Working in tandem with these mutually constructing age and gender hierarchies are comparable ideas concerning sexuality. Predicated on assumptions of heterosexism, the invisibility of gay, lesbian, and bisexual sexualities in the traditional family ideal obscures these sexualities and keeps them hidden. Regardless of how individual families grapple with these hierarchical notions, they remain the received wisdom to be confronted.

In the United States, naturalized hierarchies of gender and age are interwoven with corresponding racial hierarchies, regardless of whether racial hierarchies are justified with reference to biological, genetic differences or to immutable cultural differences (Goldberg 1993). The logic of the traditional family ideal can be used to explain race relations. One way that this occurs is when racial inequality becomes explained using family roles. For example, racial ideologies that portray people of color as intellectually underdeveloped, uncivilized children require parallel ideas that construct Whites as intellectually mature, civilized adults. When applied to race, family rhetoric that deems adults more developed than children, and thus entitled to greater power, uses naturalized ideas about age and authority to legitimate racial hierarchy. Combining age and gender hierarchies adds additional complexity. Whereas White men and White women enjoy shared racial privileges provided by Whiteness, within the racial boundary of Whiteness, women are expected to defer to men. People of color have not been immune from this same logic. Within the frame of race as family, women of subordinated racial groups defer to men of their groups, often to support men's struggles in dealing with racism. . . .

This notion of naturalized hierarchy learned in family units frames issues of U.S. national identity in particular ways. If the nation-state is conceptualized as a national family with the traditional family ideal providing ideas about family, then the standards used to assess the contributions of family members in heterosexual, married-couple households with children become foundational for assessing group contributions to overall national well-being. Naturalized hierarchies of the traditional family ideal influence understandings of constructions of first- and second-class citizenship. For example, using a logic of birth order elevates the importance of time of arrival in the country for citizenship entitlements. Claims that early-migrating, White Anglo-Saxon Protestants are entitled to more benefits than more recent arrivals resemble beliefs that "last hired, first fired" rules fairly discriminate among workers. Similarly, notions of naturalized gender hierarchies promulgated by the traditional family ideal—the differential treatment of girls and boys regarding economic autonomy and free access to public space—parallel practices such as the sex-typing of occupations in the paid labor market and male domination in government, professional sports, the streets, and other public spaces.

As is the case with all situations of hierarchy, actual or implicit use of force, sanctions and violence may be needed to maintain unequal power relations. However, the very pervasiveness of violence can lead to its invisibility. For example, feminist efforts to have violence against women in the home taken seriously as a bona fide form of violence and not just a private family matter have long met with resistance. In a similar fashion, the extent of the violence against Native American, Puerto Rican, Mexican-American, African-American, and other groups who were incorporated into the United States not through voluntary migration but via conquest and slavery remains routinely overlooked. Even current violence against such groups remains underreported unless captured in a dramatic fashion, such as the videotaped beating of motorist Rodney King by Los Angeles police officers. Despite their severity and recent increase, hate crimes against gays, lesbians, and bisexuals also remain largely invisible. Through these silences, these forms of violence not only are neglected, they become legitimated. . . .

Subordinated groups often face difficult contradictions in responding to such violence (Crenshaw 1991). One response consists of analyzing one or more hierarchies as being socially constructed while continuing to see others as naturalized. In African-American civil society, for example, the question of maintaining racial solidarity comes face-to-face with the question of how naturalized hierarchies construct one another. Maintaining racial solidarity at all costs often requires replicating hierarchies of gender, social class, sexuality, and nation in Black civil society.

LOOKING FOR A HOME: PLACE, SPACE, AND TERRITORY

The multiple meanings attached to the concept of "home"—home as family household, home as neighborhood, home as native country—speak to its significance within family as a privileged exemplar of intersectionality. In the United States, the traditional family ideal's ideas about place, space, and territory suggest that families, racial groups, and nation-states require their own unique places or "homes." Because "homes" provide spaces of privacy and security for families, races, and nation-states, they serve as sanctuaries for group members. Surrounded by individuals who seemingly share similar objectives, these homes represent idealized, privatized spaces where members can feel at ease.

This view of home requires certain gendered ideas about private and public space. Because women are so often associated with family, home space becomes seen as a private, feminized space that is distinct from the public, masculinized space that lies outside its borders. Family space is for members only—outsiders can be invited in only by family members or else they are intruders. Within these gendered spheres of private and public space, women and men again assume distinctive roles. Women are expected to remain in their home "place." Avoiding the dangerous space of public streets allows women to care for children, the sick, and the elderly, and other dependent family members. Men are expected to support and defend the private, feminized space that houses their families. Actual U.S. families rarely meet this ideal. . . .

ON "BLOOD TIES": FAMILY, RACE, AND NATION

Presumptions of "blood ties" that permeate the traditional family ideal reflect another dimension of how family operates as a privileged exemplar of intersectionality. In the United States, concepts of family and kinship draw strength from the flow of blood as a substance that regulates the spread of rights (Williams 1995). While the legal system continues to privilege heterosexual married couples as the preferred family organization, the importance given to bonds between mothers and children, brothers and sisters, grandmothers and grandchildren, illustrates the significance of biology in definitions of family. Representing the genetic links among related individuals, the belief in blood ties naturalizes the bonds among members of kinship networks. Blood, family, and kin are so closely connected that the absence of such ties can be cause for concern. As the search of adoptees for their "real" families or blood relatives suggests, blood ties remain highly significant for definitions of family.

Given the significance attached to biology, women of different racial groups have varying responsibilities in maintaining blood ties. For example, White women play a special role in keeping family bloodlines pure. Historically, creating White families required controlling White women's sexuality, largely through social norms that advocated pre-marital virginity. By marrying White men

and engaging in sexual relations only with their husbands, White women ensured the racial purity of White families. Thus, through social taboos that eschewed pre-marital sexuality and interracial marriage for White women, White families could thereby avoid racial degeneration (Young 1995). When reinserted into naturalized hierarchies of gender, race, class, and nation, and institutionally enforced via mechanisms such as segregated space and state-sanctioned violence, efforts to regulate sexuality and marriage reinforced beliefs in the sanctity of "blood ties."

. . . Definitions of race as family in the United States traditionally rested on biological classifications legitimated by science and legally sanctioned by law. By grouping people through notions of physical similarity, such as skin color, facial features, or hair texture, and supported by law and custom, scientific racism defined Whites and Blacks as distinctive social groups (Gould 1981). Just as members of "real" families linked by blood were expected to resemble one another, so were members of racial groups descended from a common bloodline seen as sharing similar physical, intellectual, and moral attributes. Within this logic, those lacking biological similarities became defined as family outsiders, while racially different groups became strangers to one another.

. . . U.S. national identity may be grounded more in ethnic nationalism than is typically realized. Notions of U.S. national identity that take both family and race into account result in a view of the United States as a large national family with racial families hierarchically arranged within it. Representing the epitome of racial purity that is also associated with U.S. national interests. Whites constitute the most valuable citizens. In this racialized nation-state, Native Americans, African-Americans, Mexican Americans, and Puerto Ricans become second-class citizens, whereas people of color from the Caribbean, Asia, Latin America, and Africa encounter more difficulty becoming naturalized citizens than immigrants from European nations. Because all of these groups are not White and thereby lack appropriate blood ties, they are deemed to be less-worthy actual and potential U.S. citizens. . . .

MEMBERSHIP HAS ITS PRIVILEGES: RIGHTS, OBLIGATIONS AND RULES

By suggesting an ideal relationship between the rights and responsibilities of family membership, the traditional family ideal operates as a privileged exemplar of intersectionality in yet another way. In a situation in which notions of belonging to a family remain important to issues of responsibility and accountability, individuals feel that they "owe" something to, and are responsible for, members of their families. For example, people within family units routinely help their family members by babysitting, lending money, helping relatives find employment and housing, or caring for the elderly. Family members linked by blood are entitled to these benefits merely by belonging. Even when family members lack merit, they are entitled to benefits simply because they belong. Beyond this issue of access to entitlements, individuals incur differential responsibilities that depend on their placement in family hierarchies. For example, women are expected to perform much of the domestic labor that keeps the family going, whereas men's duties lie in providing financial support.

In a similar fashion, U.S. citizens by birth or naturalization acquire certain rights and responsibilities that accrue from membership. Citizens are promised entitlements such as equal protection under the law, access to unemployment insurance, old age pensions, free public education, and other social welfare benefits. Citizens are also expected to fulfill certain obligations to one another. U.S. citizens are expected to pay taxes, observe the law, and engage in military service when required. In contrast to the rights and responsibilities provided insiders, outsiders lack both the entitlements provided group members and the obligations attached to belonging. Similar to non-family members, non-U.S. citizens are neither entitled to citizenship benefits nor responsible for national duties. . . .

In a situation of naturalized hierarchy, conceptualizing U.S. national identity as composed of racial groups that collectively comprise a U.S. national family fosters differential patterns of enforcement of the rights and obligations of citizenship. Members of some racial families receive full benefits of membership while others encounter inferior treatment. Gender hierarchies add additional complexity. African-American women's experiences with entitlement criteria for 1930s Social Security programs, for example, illustrate how institutionalized racism and gender-specific ideology public policies shaped national public policy. Race was a factor in deciding which occupations would be covered by Social Security. Two occupational categories were expressly excluded from coverage: agricultural and domestic workers, the two categories that included most African-American women. Also, by providing differential benefits to men and women through worker's compensation (for which Black women did not qualify) and mother's aid, from its inception, Social Security encompassed ideas about gender. Eligibility rules rewarded women who remained in marriages and were supported by their husbands but penalized women who became separated or divorced or who remained single and earned their own way. Black women who were not in stable marriages lacked access to spousal and widows benefits that routinely subsidized White women. In this case, the combination of race-targeted polices concerning occupational category and gender-targeted policies concerning applicants' marital status worked to exclude Black women from benefits (Gordon 1994). On paper, Black women may have been first-class U.S. citizens, but their experiences reveal their second-class treatment.

FAMILY GENEALOGY: INHERITANCE AND THE FAMILY WAGE

. . . Focusing on wealth not only references contemporary economic inequality but also incorporates the historical origins and reproduction of class differences over time. Despite ideas that social mobility is widespread, U.S. children routinely enjoy or suffer the economic status of their parents. Families constitute important sites for inheritance, not solely of cultural values, but of property. Families use wealth to create opportunities, secure a desired standard of living, and pass their social class status to their children. In this process, the family home becomes more than a private respite from the demands of the public sphere. When "family values" and "property values" become intertwined, homes in racially segregated neighborhoods become important investments. The traditional family ideal shows the family not only occupying a home, but owning it. Ensconced in tax policies that provide lucrative benefits for homeowners, for many Americans, the single-family home as a tangible symbol of wealth remains central to the American dream (Coontz 1992). Wealth matters because, if one adheres to rules of marriage and childbearing, it is directly transferable from generation to generation.

. . . Despite the historical concentration of wealth among a small percentage of families, the intergenerational transmission of wealth through family also operates among working-class families. Traditional analyses view working-class families in purely wage-earning terms. Such families are thought to have no property to pass on to their children, and are seen as mere employees of other more wealthy families. However, the notion of working-class men being entitled to a "family wage" emerges at the intersection of expectations of family inheritance and a naturalized gender hierarchy. In this situation, working-class men inherit opportunities to earn a wage and are expected to use that wage to support their families. According to this logic, women's and children's social class status derives from that of men.

When these relationships regulating intergenerational property transmission are racialized, as they are in the United States, another level of complexity emerges. In her analysis of how racism undermined the War on Poverty program, Jill Quadagno describes the resistance that craft unions put forth when pressured to change entrenched patterns of racial discrimination. As Quadagno points out, the right of unions to select their own members was seen as a "property right of the working class. This

was a most compelling argument for nepotism—the tradition of passing on the craft from fathers to sons" (Quadagno 1994, 65). Among Philadelphia plumbers, 40 percent of the apprentices were sons of members. Fathers wanted their sons to be trained as plumbers and to continue in the business. Practices such as these virtually ensured that African-Americans and other groups were excluded from lucrative positions. Quadagno quotes one construction worker who explains the concept of property rights and property transmission in White working-class families:

> Some men leave their sons money, some large investments, some business connections and some a profession. I have none of these to bequeath to my sons. I have only one worthwhile thing to give: my trade. . . . For this simple father's wish it is said that I discriminate against Negroes. Don't all of us discriminate? Which of us when it comes to choice will not choose a son over all others? (quoted in Quadagno 1994, 65)

In effect, racial discrimination in education, employment, and housing historically reflected White working-class understandings of these social locations as "private property" to be disposed of as inherited wealth. . . .

FAMILY PLANNING

The significance of the family as an exemplar of intersectionality can also be seen in one final dimension of family rhetoric. Family planning comprises a constellation of options, ranging from coercion to choice, from permanence to reversibility regarding reproduction of actual populations. In the case of individual families, decision-making lies with family members; they decide whether to have children, how many children to have, and how those children will be spaced. Feminist scholars in particular have identified how male control over women's sexual and reproductive capacities has been central to women's oppression (see, for example, Raymond 1993). . . .

Social policies designed to foster the health of the United States conceptualized as a national family follow a family planning logic, as demonstrated via eugenic thinking. Early twentieth century "racial hygiene" or eugenic movements compellingly illustrate the thinking that underlies population policies designed to control the motherhood of different groups of women for reasons of nationality and race (Haller 1984; Proctor 1988). Eugenic philosophies and the population policies they supported emerged in political economies with distinctive needs, and in societies with particular social class relations. Common to eugenic movements throughout the world was the view that biology was central to solving social problems. Societies that embraced eugenic philosophies typically aimed to transform social problems into technical problems amenable to biological solutions effected via social engineering. Eugenic approaches thus combined a "philosophy of biological determinism with a belief that science might provide a technical fix for social problems" (Proctor 1988, 286).

Three elements of eugenic thinking seem remarkably similar to themes in American public policy. Those embracing eugenic thinking saw "race and heredity—the birth rates of the fit and the unfit—as the forces that shape[d] . . . political and social developments" (Haller 1984, 78). First, eugenic thinking racializes segments of a given population by classifying people into mutually exclusive racial groups. Because the United States has operated as a racialized state since its inception, race remains a fundamental principle of U.S. social organization. While racial meanings change in response to political and economic conditions, the fundamental belief in race as a guiding principle of U.S. society remains remarkably hardy. Associating diverse racial groups with perceived national interests, a second element of eugenic thinking, also has a long history in the United States. The third feature of eugenic thinking, the direct control of different racial groups through various measures also is present in U.S. politics. So-called positive eugenic—efforts to increase reproduction among the better groups who allegedly carried the outstanding qualities of their group in their genes—and negative eugenic—efforts to prevent the propagation by less desirable groups—also have affected U.S. public policy. . . .

With the civil rights, women's, anti-war, and other social movements of the 1950s and 1960s, as well as the growing nonwhite immigrant population of the 1970s and 1980s, the United States experienced profound change. Omi and Winant (1994) interpret the expanding conservative social projects that emerged during this period as a direct response to the perceived gains of Blacks and women. One core feature characterizing the rhetoric of social projects of the Right was a return to the family values of the traditional U.S. family. By associating the ideal family with U.S. national interests, these movements linked those interests to their own political agendas concerning race and gender. Returning to "family values" not only invoked racial and gendered meanings, it set the stage for reviving a logic of eugenic that could be applied to adolescent pregnancy, women's poverty, street crime, and other social issues.

In this context, contemporary American social policies from the 1960s through the "family values" debate of the 1990s become more comprehensible. When attached to state policy in a racialized nation-state, questions of controlling the sexuality and fertility of women from diverse race, social class, and citizenship groups become highly politicized. For example, White women, especially those of the middle class, are encouraged to reproduce. In contrast, women of color, especially those lacking economic resources or not in state sanctioned marriages, are routinely discouraged from having children (Raymond 1993). Population policies such as providing lavish services to combat infertility for White, middle class women, while offering a limited range of Norplant, Depo Provera, and sterilization to poor African-American women constitute contemporary reflections of the logic of eugenic thinking (Davis 1981; Nsiah-Jefferson 1989). . . .

RECLAIMING FAMILY

Family occupies such a prominent place in the language of public discourse in the United States that rejecting it outright might be counterproductive for groups aiming to challenge hierarchies. Because the family functions as a privileged exemplar of intersectionality in structuring hierarchy, it potentially can serve a similar function in challenging that hierarchy. . . .

Given the power of family as ideological construction and principle of social organization, Black nationalist, feminist, and other political movements in the United States dedicated to challenging social inequality might consider recasting intersectional understandings of family in ways that do not reproduce inequality. Instead of engaging in endless criticism, reclaiming the language of family for democratic ends and transforming the very conception of family itself might provide a more useful approach.

DISCUSSION QUESTIONS

1. What is an example of a subordinated group other than African Americans that has contradictions?
2. How realistic is the traditional family ideal today?
3. What is the role of family and race in U.S. national identity?

NOTES

1. By dislodging beliefs in the naturalness or normality of any one family form, feminist scholarship analyzes the significance of specific notions of family to gender oppression (Thorne 1992). As Stephanie Coontz (1992) reports, this traditional family ideal never existed, even during the 1950s, a decade that is often assumed to be the era of its realization. Feminist anthropologists also challenge the traditional family ideal by demonstrating that the heterosexual, married couple form in the United States is neither "natural," universal, nor cross-culturally normative (Collier et al. 1992). Recent family scholarship suggests that large numbers of U.S. families never experienced the traditional family ideal, and those who may have once achieved this form are now abandoning it (Coontz 1992; Stacey 1992).
2. In the early 1980s, several African-American women scholar-activists called for a new approach to analyzing Black women's lives. They claimed that African-American women's experiences were shaped not just by race but also by gender, social class, and sexuality. In this tradition, works such as *Women, Race, and Class* by Angela Davis (1981), "A Black Feminist Statement" drafted by the Combahee River Collective (1982), and Audre Lorde's (1984) classic volume *Sister Outsider* stand as groundbreaking works that explore interconnections among systems of oppression. Subsequent work aimed to name this interconnected relationship with terms such as *matrix of domination* (Collins 1990), and

intersectionality (Crenshaw 1991). Because Black lesbians were at the forefront in raising the issue of intersectionality, sexuality was one of the emphases in early work by African-American women. However, pervasive homophobia in African-American communities, as evidenced by the reaction to the works of Alice Walker, Ntosake Shange, Michele Wallace and other early modern Black feminists, diverted attention from intersectional analyses that emphasized sexuality. The absence of a developed tradition of queer theory in the academy also worked against more comprehensive intersectional analyses. For early intersectional analyses that included sexuality, see the essays in Barbara Smith's (1983) edited volume *Home Girls: A Black Feminist Anthology.*

3. A wide range of topics, such as the significance of primatology in framing gendered, raced views of nature in modern science (Haraway 1989); the social construction of Whiteness among White women in the United States (Frankenberg 1993); race, gender, and sexuality in the colonial conquest (McClintock 1995); and the interplay of race, class, and gender in welfare state policies in the United States (Brewer 1994: Quadagno 1994) have all received an intersectional treatment. Moreover, the initial emphasis on race, social class, and gender has expanded to include intersections involving sexuality, ethnicity, and nationalism (Anthias and Yuval-Davis 1992; Parker et al. 1992; Daniels 1997).

4. Theoretical and empirical work on women of color's location in work and family not only challenges the traditional family ideal, but paves the way for the more general question of family as a privileged site of intersectionality. For work in this tradition, see Dill 1988, Zinn 1989, and Glenn 1992.

REFERENCES

Andersen, Margater L. 1991. Feminism and the American family ideal. *Journal of Comparative Family Studies* 22(2) (Summer): 235–46.

Anthias, Floya, and Nira Yuval-Davis. 1992. *Racialized boundaries: Race, nation, gender, colour and class in the anti-racist struggle.* New York: Routledge.

Brewer, Rose, 1994. Race, gender and US state welfare policy: The nexus of inequality for African American families. In *Color, class and country: Experiences of gender,* ed. Gay Young and Bette Dickerson. London: Zed Books.

Collier, Jane, Michelle Z. Rosaldo, and Sylvia Yanagisako. 1992. Is there a family?: New anthropological views. In *Rethinking the family.* See Thorne and Yalom 1992.

Collins, Patricia Hill. 1990. *Black feminist thought: Knowledge, consciousness, and the politics of empowerment.* New York: Routledge, Chapman and Hall.

Combahee River Collective. 1982. A Black feminist statement. In *But some of us are brave,* ed. Gloria T. Hull, Patricia

Bell Scott, and Barbara Smith. Old Westbury, NY: Feminist Press.

Coontz, Stephanie. 1992. *The way we never were: American families and the nostalgia trap.* New York: Basic Books.

Crenshaw, Kimberle. 1991. Mapping the margins: Intersectionality, identity politics, and violence against women of color. *Stanford Law Review* 43(6): 1241–99.

Daniels, Jessie. 1997. *White lies.* New York: Routledge.

Davis, Angela Y. 1981. *Women, race, and class.* New York: Random House.

Dill, Bonnie Thornton. 1988. Our mothers' grief: Racial ethnic women and the maintenance of families. *Journal of Family History* 13(4): 415–31.

Frankenberg, Ruth. 1993. *The social construction of whiteness: White women, race matters.* Minneapolis: University of Minnesota Press.

Glenn, Evelyn Nakano. 1992. From servitude to service work: Historical continuities in the racial division of paid reproductive labor. *Signs* 18(1): 1–43.

Goldberg, David Theo. 1993. *Racist culture: Philosophy and the politics of meaning.* Cambridge, MA: Blackwell.

Gordon, Linda. 1994. *Pitied but not entitled: Single mothers and the history of welfare.* Cambridge: Harvard University Press.

Gould, Stephen Jay. 1981. *The mismeasure of man.* New York: W. W. Norton.

Haller, Mark H. 1984 [1963]. *Eugenics: Hereditarian attitudes in American thought.* New Brunswick: Rutgers University Press.

Haraway, Donna. 1989. *Primate visions: Gender, race, and nature in the world of modern science.* New York: Routledge, Chapman and Hall.

Lorde, Audre. 1984. *Sister outsider.* Trumansberg, NY: Crossing Press.

McClintock, Anne. 1995. *Imperial leather.* New York: Routledge.

Nsiah-Jefferson, Lautie. 1989. Reproductive laws, women of color, and low-income women. In *Reproductive laws for the 1990s,* ed. Sherrill Cohen and Nadine Taub. Clifton, NJ: Humana Press.

Omi, Michael, and Howard Winant. 1994. *Racial formation in the United States: From the 1960s to the 1990s.* New York: Routledge.

Parker, Andrew, Mary Russo, Doris Sommer, and Patricia Yaeger, eds. 1992. *Nationalisms and sexualities.* New York: Routledge.

Proctor, Robert N. 1988. *Racial hygiene: Medicine under the Nazis.* Cambridge: Harvard University Press.

Quadagno, Jill. 1994. *The color of welfare: How racism undermined the war on poverty.* New York: Oxford University Press.

Raymond, Janice. 1993. *Women as wombs: Reproductive technologies and the battle over women's freedom.* San Francisco: Harper San Francisco.

Slack, Jennifer Daryl. 1996. The theory and method of articulation in cultural studies. In *Stuart Hall: Critical dialogues in cultural studies,* ed. David Morley and Kuan-Hsing Chen. New York: Routledge.

Smith, Barbara, ed. 1983. *Home girls: A Black feminist anthology.* New York: Kitchen Table Press.

Stacey, Judith. 1992. Backward toward the postmodern family: Reflections on gender, kinship, and class in the Silicon Valley. In *Rethinking the family.* See Thorne and Yalom 1992.

Thorne, Barrie. 1992. Feminism and the family: Two decades of thought. In *Rethinking the family: Some feminist questions.* See Thorne and Yalom 1992.

Thorne, Barrie, and Marilyn Yalom, eds. 1992. *Rethinking the family: Some feminist questions,* Boston: Northeastern University Press.

Williams, Brackette F. 1995. Classification systems revisited: Kinship, caste, race, and nationality as the flow of blood and the spread of rights. In *Naturalizing power: Essays in feminist cultural analysis,* ed. Sylvia Yanagisako and Carol Delaney. New York: Routledge.

Young, Robert J. C. 1995. *Colonial desire: Hybridity in theory, culture and race.* New York: Routledge.

Zinn, Maxine Baca. 1989. Family, race, and poverty in the eighties. *Signs* 14(4): 875–84.

READING 44

Toward a Theory of Disability and Gender

Thomas J. Gerschick

. . . Comprehensive theories about the relationship between disability and gender remain elusive. This essay contributes to the development of such theory by addressing the following questions: How does disability affect the gendering process? How does it affect the experience of gender? How does having a disability affect women's and men's abilities to enact gender? In what ways are the experiences of women and men with disabilities similar and different?[1]

Thomas Gerschick is a professor of sociology at Illinois State University.

Developing a theory of disability and gender provides insight into the lives of a large number of people. The U.S. Census Bureau estimates that in 1994 more than 20.6 percent of the U.S. population, or about fifty-four million people, had some level of physical or mental disability; for 9.9 percent of the population, or twenty-six million people, this disability was severe (McNeil 1997, 1).[2] After women, then, people with disabilities represent the largest minority population in the United States. Given that the likelihood of developing a disability increases with age, and given that the baby-boom generation is aging, the proportion of the U.S. population with disabilities will likely continue to increase. Moreover, accounting for the experiences of women and men with disabilities makes feminist theories of gender more inclusive, complex, and nuanced. Finally, a theory of the relation between gender and disability provides another tool that people with disabilities can use to understand and challenge their oppression.

In order to contextualize the experiences of women and men with physical disabilities, we need to attend to three sets of social dynamics: the stigma assigned to disability, gender as an interactional process, and the importance of the body to enacting gender.

To have a disability is not only a physical or mental condition; it is also a social and stigmatized one (Goffman 1963). As anthropologist Robert Murphy observes, "Stigmatization is less a by-product of disability than its substance. The greatest impediment to a person's taking full part in this society are not his physical flaws, but rather the tissue of myths, fears, and misunderstandings that society attaches to them" (1990, 113). Thus, stigmatization is embedded in the daily interactions between people with disabilities and the temporarily able-bodied.[3] In order to enact gender, people with disabilities must be recognized by others as "appropriately" masculine or feminine (West and Zimmerman 1987). Much is at stake in this process, as one's sense of self rests precariously on others' validation or rejection of one's gender performance. Successful enactment bestows status and acceptance; failure invites embarrassment and humiliation (West and Zimmerman 1987). Thus, people with disabilities

are engaged in an asymmetrical power relationship with their temporarily able-bodied counterparts.

Bodies are central to achieving recognition as appropriately gendered beings. Bodies operate socially as canvases on which gender is displayed and kinesthetically as the mechanisms by which it is physically enacted. Thus, the bodies of people with disabilities make them vulnerable to being denied recognition as women and men. The type of disability, its visibility, its severity, and whether it is physical or mental in origin mediate the degree to which the body of a person with a disability is socially compromised. For instance, a severe case of the Epstein-Barr virus can lead to disability; however, typically the condition is not readily apparent and, as a consequence, does not trigger stigmatization and devaluation. Conversely, having quadriplegia and using a wheelchair for mobility is highly visual, is perceived to be severe, and frequently elicits invalidation.[4] Moreover, the degree to which a person with a disability is legitimized or delegitimized is context-specific and has both material and nonmaterial consequences.

Disability affects the gendering process in many ways. My current research suggests that the age of onset combines with the type, severity, and visibility of a person's disability to influence the degree to which she or he is taught and subjected to gendered expectations. As C. West and D. H. Zimmerman (1987) note, no one escapes being gendered, including people with disabilities. However, all people do not experience the same degree and type of gender socialization and expectations. For instance, if an infant has a congenital disability and if that disability is severe, as in the case of spina bifida, parents and others in the infant's social world will assign her or him to sex and gender categories but will likely hold fewer gender expectations than for an infant who has a milder disability, such as a visual impairment. Conversely, when the onset of a disability occurs later in a child's life, she or he already will have experienced a significant amount of gender socialization and internalized many gendered expectations. Thus, her or his struggles for social validation as a woman or man will begin with a different level of awareness and commitment to gender. For people with disabilities, then, gendering is conditional.

Furthermore, theories of gender presume that everyone has the same ability to learn, understand, respond to, and be held accountable for gendered expectations. However, for people with a mental disability, these abilities are compromised to different degrees. For example, a person with profound mental retardation may not be able to comprehend many aspects of gender and consequently would largely be beyond the reach of sanctions, while the same does not hold true for a person with a learning disability. Additionally, mental illness can vary individuals' gender enactment. Kay Redfield Jamison (1995), for instance, eloquently describes how her gender performance varied depending on whether she was manic or depressed.

Although women and men with disabilities share similar experiences of devaluation, isolation, marginalization, and discrimination, their fortunes diverge in important ways. Two stigmatized statuses converge in the lives of women with disabilities, further diminishing their already devalued gender status. As M. Fine and A. Asch note, they experience "sexism without the pedestal" (1988, 1). Conversely, for men with physical disabilities, masculine gender privilege collides with the stigmatized status of having a disability, thereby causing status inconsistency, as having a disability erodes much, but not all, masculine privilege.

Although there is much that we do not know regarding the extent of violence that people with disabilities experience, research suggests that children with disabilities are 70 percent more likely to be physically or sexually abused than their able-bodied counterparts (Crosse, Kaye, and Ratnofsky 1993). This abuse is likely to be chronic rather than episodic and to be perpetuated by someone the victim knows, such as a family member or personal attendant (Sobsey and Doc 1991). Furthermore, this abuse is gendered; females with disabilities are more likely to be sexually assaulted, whereas males with disabilities are more likely to experience other forms of physical abuse (Sobsey, Randall, and Parrila 1997). Thus, having a disability exacerbates one of the worst, most direct elements of oppression.

In the contemporary United States, to be perceived as physically attractive is to be socially and sexually desirable. As a result of their invalidated condition, women and men with disabilities are constrained in their opportunities to nurture and to be nurtured, to be loved and to love, and to become parents if they so desire (Fine and Asch 1988, 13). Writer Susan Hannaford explains, "I discovered on becoming officially defined as 'disabled' that I lost my previous identity as a sexually attractive being" (1985, 17). This dynamic, in addition to being mediated by degree, type, and severity of disability, may also be gendered. For example, Hannaford maintains that women are four times as likely as men to divorce after developing a disability (18) and only one-third to one-fourth as likely to marry (76). Fine and Asch (1988, 12–23) provide a range of supporting evidence. Ironically, this may also mean that women with disabilities are less likely than their able-bodied counterparts to be limited by many of the gendered expectations and roles that feminists have challenged.

Women and men with physical disabilities are also economically more vulnerable than nondisabled people. Among people of working age, women with disabilities are less likely to participate in the labor force than both nondisabled women and men with disabilities. This gap varies by gender and the severity of the disability. For instance, according to the U.S. Census Bureau, nondisabled women's labor force participation rate in 1994 was 74.5 percent. For women with a mild disability, the percentage dropped to 68.4 percent, and it plunged to 24.7 percent for women with severe disabilities. For men, the respective numbers were 89.9 percent, 85.1 percent, and 27.8 percent (McNeil 1997). Women with disabilities are also more susceptible to being tracked into low-wage service-sector jobs.

Similarly, gender and the severity of one's disability affect median monthly earnings. Among women 21–64 years of age in 1994, median monthly earnings were $1,470 among those with no disability, $1,200 among those with a nonsevere disability, and $1,000 among those with a severe disability. Comparable figures for men were $2,190, $1,857, and $1,262 (McNeil 1997). As a consequence, women and men with disabilities are poorer than their able-bodied counterparts, and women with disabilities fare worst of all (LaPlante et al. 1999).

In brief summary, disability has a profound effect on the material and nonmaterial experience of gender. Yet, there is still much we do not know about this dynamic: How and under what conditions do social characteristics such as race, class, age, and sexual orientation further mediate the relationship between gender and disability? How does gender affect the experience of disability? How do the dynamics identified in this essay vary by culture in a global context? How might the stigmatization and marginalization that women and men with disabilities face contribute to the creation of alternative gender identities? As we enter a new millennium, I [hope we can] take up these questions . . . so that we can soon develop more comprehensive theories about the relationship between disability and gender.

DISCUSSIONS QUESTIONS

1. How are people affected by occupying two stigmatized statuses?
2. Why is it difficult to develop a theory of disability?
3. Why will disability coupled with gender only become a bigger issue in U.S. society?

NOTES

This essay is dedicated to the memory of Adam S. Miller (1971–99), friend and frequent coauthor. I would like to thank Bob Broad and Georganne Rundblad for their comments on previous drafts of this essay and Ryan Hieronymous for research assistance.

1. Space limitations necessitate that I focus on disabilities primarily in the United States in this essay. See Lynn and Wilkinson 1993 for a number of international perspectives on women and disability.
2. McNeil 1997 provides Census Bureau definitions and measures of disability.
3. I intentionally use the term *temporarily able-bodied* to highlight the facts that aging is often disabling and that many of us will develop a disability during our lifetime. In 1994, e.g., the disability rate among the U.S. population ages 65–79 years was 47.3 percent; for those ages 80 years and older, it rose to 71.5 percent (McNeil 1997).
4. Of course, the degree to which one's body is compromised is also affected by other social characteristics, including

race and ethnicity, social class, age, and sexual orientation. Unfortunately, exploring these other characteristics is beyond the scope of this essay.

REFERENCES

Crosse, S. B., E. Kaye, and A. C. Ratnofsky. 1993. *Report on the Maltreatment of Children with Disabilities.* Washington, D.C.: National Center on Child Abuse and Neglect.

Fine, M., and A. Asch. 1988. "Introduction: Beyond Pedestals." In *Women with Disabilities: Essays in Psychology, Culture, and Politics,* ed. M. Fine and A. Asch, 1–37. Philadelphia: Temple University Press.

Goffman, E. 1963. *Stigma: Notes on the Management of Spoiled Identity.* New York: Touchstone.

Hannaford, S. 1985. *Living Outside Inside: A Disabled Woman's Experience.* Berkeley, Calif.: Canterbury.

Jamison, K. R. 1995. *An Unquiet Mind.* New York: Knopf.

LaPlante, M. P., J. Kennedy, H. S. Kaye, and B. L. Wenger. 1999. *Disability and Employment.* Available on-line at http://dsc.ucsf.edu/default.html.

Lynn, M., and S. Wilkinson, eds. 1993. "Women and Disability," special issue of *Canadian Woman Studies,* vol. 13, no. 4.

McNeil, J. M. 1997. *Americans with Disabilities, 1994–95.* Current Population Report No. P70-61. Washington, D.C.: Bureau of the Census.

Murphy, R. F. 1990. *The Body Silent.* New York: Norton.

Sobsey, D., and T. Doc. 1991. "Patterns of Sexual Abuse and Assault." *Sexuality and Disability* 9(3): 243–59.

Sobsey, D., W. Randall, and R. K. Parrila. 1997. "Gender Differences in Abused Children with and without Disabilities." *Child Abuse and Neglect* 21(8): 707–20.

West, C., and D. H. Zimmerman. 1987. "Doing Gender." *Gender & Society* 1(2): 125–51.

READING 45

Oppression

Marilyn Frye

It is a fundamental claim of feminism that women are oppressed. The word "oppression" is a strong word. It repels and attracts. It is dangerous and dangerously fashionable and endangered. It is much misused, and sometimes not innocently.

Marilyn Frye is a professor of philosophy at Michigan State University.

The statement that women are oppressed is frequently met with the claim that men are oppressed too. We hear that oppressing is oppressive to those who oppress as well as to those they oppress. Some men cite as evidence of their oppression their much-advertised inability to cry. It is tough, we are told, to be masculine. When the stresses and frustrations of being a man are cited as evidence that oppressors are oppressed by their oppressing, the word "oppression" is being stretched to meaninglessness; it is treated as though its scope includes any and all human experience of limitation or suffering, no matter the cause, degree or consequence. Once such usage has been put over on us, then if ever we deny that any person or group is oppressed, we seem to imply that we think they never suffer and have no feelings. We are accused of insensitivity; even of bigotry. For women, such accusation is particularly intimidating, since sensitivity is one of the few virtues that has been assigned to us. If we are found insensitive, we may fear we have no redeeming traits at all and perhaps are not real women. Thus are we silenced before we begin: the name of our situation drained of meaning and our guilt mechanisms tripped.

But this is nonsense. Human beings can be miserable without being oppressed, and it is perfectly consistent to deny that a person or group is oppressed without denying that they have feelings or that they suffer.

We need to think clearly about oppression, and there is much that mitigates against this. I do not want to undertake to prove that women are oppressed (or that men are not), but I want to make clear what is being said when we say it. We need this word, this concept, and we need it to be sharp and sure.

The root of the word "oppression" is the element "press." *The press of the crowd; pressed into military service; to press a pair of pants; printing press; press the button.* Presses are used to mold things or flatten them or reduce them in bulk, sometimes to reduce them by squeezing out the gasses or liquids in them. Something pressed is something caught between or among forces and barriers which are so related to each other that jointly they restrain, restrict or prevent the thing's motion or mobility. Mold. Immobilize. Reduce.

The mundane experience of the oppressed provides another clue. One of the most characteristic and ubiquitous features of the world as experienced by oppressed people is the double bind situations in which options are reduced to a very few and all of them expose one to penalty, censure or deprivation. For example, it is often a requirement upon oppressed people that we smile and be cheerful. If we comply, we signal our docility and our acquiescence in our situation. We need not, then, be taken note of. We acquiesce in being made invisible, in our occupying no space. We participate in our own erasure. On the other hand, anything but the sunniest countenance exposes us to being perceived as mean, bitter, angry or dangerous. This means, at the least, that we may be found "difficult" or unpleasant to work with, which is enough to cost one one's livelihood; at worst, being seen as mean, bitter, angry or dangerous has been known to result in rape, arrest, beating and murder. One can only choose to risk one's preferred form and rate of annihilation.

Another example: It is common in the United States that women, especially younger women, are in a bind where neither sexual activity nor sexual inactivity is all right. If she is heterosexually active, a woman is open to censure and punishment for being loose, unprincipled or a whore. The "punishment" comes in the form of criticism, snide and embarrassing remarks, being treated as an easy lay by men, scorn from her more restrained female friends. She may have to lie and hide her behavior from her parents. She must juggle the risks of unwanted pregnancy and dangerous contraceptives. On the other hand, if she refrains from heterosexual activity, she is fairly constantly harassed by men who try to persuade her into it and pressure her to "relax" and "let her hair down"; she is threatened with labels like "frigid," "uptight," "manhater," "bitch" and "cocktease." The same parents who would be disapproving of her sexual activity may be worried by her inactivity because it suggests she is not or will not be popular, or is not sexually normal. She may be charged with lesbianism. If a woman is raped, then if she has been heterosexually active she is subject to the presumption that she liked it (since her activity is presumed to show that she likes sex), and if she has not been heterosexually active, she is subject to the presumption that she liked it (since she is supposedly "repressed and frustrated"). Both heterosexual activity and heterosexual nonactivity are likely to be taken as proof that you wanted to be raped, and hence, of course, weren't *really* raped at all. You can't win. You are caught in a bind, caught between systematically related pressures.

Women are caught like this, too, by networks of forces and barriers that expose one to penalty, loss or contempt whether one works outside the home or not, is on welfare or not, bears children or not, raises children or not, marries or not, stays married or not, is heterosexual, lesbian, both or neither. Economic necessity; confinement to racial and/or sexual job ghettos; sexual harassment; sex discrimination; pressures of competing expectations and judgments about *women, wives* and *mothers* (in the society at large, in racial and ethnic subcultures and in one's own mind); dependence (full or partial) on husbands, parents or the state; commitment to political ideas; loyalties to racial or ethnic or other "minority" groups; the demands of self-respect and responsibilities to others. Each of these factors exists in complex tension with every other, penalizing or prohibiting all of the apparently available options. And nipping at one's heels, always, is the endless pack of little things. If one dresses one way, one is subject to the assumption that one is advertising one's sexual availability; if one dresses another way, one appears to "not care about oneself" or to be "unfeminine." If one uses "strong language," one invites categorization as a whore or slut; if one does not, one invites categorization as a "lady," one too delicately constituted to cope with robust speech or the realities to which it presumably refers.

The experience of oppressed people is that the living of one's life is confined and shaped by forces and barriers which are not accidental or occasional and hence avoidable, but are systematically related to each other in such a way as to catch one between and among them and restrict or penalize motion in any direction. It is the experience of being caged in: all avenues, in every direction, are blocked or booby trapped.

Cages. Consider a birdcage. If you look very closely at just one wire in the cage, you cannot see the other wires. If your conception of what is before you is determined by this myopic focus, you could look at that one wire, up and down the length of it, and be unable to see why a bird would not just fly around the wire any time it wanted to go somewhere. Furthermore, even if, one day at a time, you myopically inspected each wire, you still could not see why a bird would have trouble going past the wires to get anywhere. There is no physical property of any one wire, *nothing* that the closest scrutiny could discover, that will reveal how a bird could be inhibited or harmed by it except in the most accidental way. It is only when you step back, stop looking at the wires one by one, microscopically, and take a macroscopic view of the whole cage, that you can see why the bird does not go anywhere; and then you will see it in a moment. It will require no great subtlety of mental powers. It is perfectly *obvious* that the bird is surrounded by a network of systematically related barriers, no one of which would be the least hindrance to its flight, but which, by their relations to each other, are as confining as the solid walls of a dungeon.

It is now possible to grasp one of the reasons why oppression can be hard to see and recognize: one can study the elements of an oppressive structure with great care and some good will without seeing the structure as a whole, and hence without seeing or being able to understand that one is looking at a cage and that there are people there who are caged, whose motion and mobility are restricted, whose lives are shaped and reduced.

The arresting of vision at a microscopic level yields such common confusion as that about the male door opening ritual. This ritual, which is remarkably widespread across classes and races, puzzles many people, some of whom do and some of whom do not find it offensive. Look at the scene of the two people approaching a door. The male steps slightly ahead and opens the door. The male holds the door open while the female glides through. Then the male goes through. The door closes after them. "Now how," one innocently asks, "can those crazy womenslibbers say that is oppressive? The guy *removed* a barrier to the lady's smooth and unruffled progress." But each repetition of this ritual has a place in a pattern, in fact in several patterns. One has to shift the level of one's perception in order to see the whole picture.

The door-opening pretends to be a helpful service, but the helpfulness is false. This can be seen by noting that it will be done whether or not it makes any practical sense. Infirm men and men burdened with packages will open doors for able bodied women who are free of physical burdens. Men will impose themselves awkwardly and jostle everyone in order to get to the door first. The act is not determined by convenience or grace. Furthermore, these very numerous acts of unneeded or even noisome "help" occur in counterpoint to a pattern of men not being helpful in many practical ways in which women might welcome help. What *women* experience is a world in which gallant princes charming commonly make a fuss about being helpful and providing small services when help and services are of little or no use, but in which there are rarely ingenious and adroit princes at hand when substantial assistance is really wanted either in mundane affairs or in situations of threat, assault or terror. There is no help with the (his) laundry; no help typing a report at 4:00 a.m.; no help in mediating disputes among relatives or children. There is nothing but advice that women should stay indoors after dark, be chaperoned by a man, or when it comes down to it, "lie back and enjoy it."

The gallant gestures have no practical meaning. Their meaning is symbolic. The door-opening and similar services provided are services which really are needed by people who are for one reason or another incapacitated—unwell, burdened with parcels, etc. So the message is that women are incapable. The detachment of the acts from the concrete realities of what women need and do not need is a vehicle for the message that women's actual needs and interests are unimportant or

irrelevant. Finally, these gestures imitate the behavior of servants toward masters and thus mock women, who are in most respects the servants and caretakers of men. The message of the false helpfulness of male gallantry is female dependence, the invisibility or insignificance of women, and contempt for women.

One cannot see the meanings of these rituals if one's focus is riveted upon the individual event in all its particularity, including the particularity of the individual man's present conscious intentions and motives and the individual woman's conscious perception of the event in the moment. It seems sometimes that people take a deliberately myopic view and fill their eyes with things seen microscopically in order not to see macroscopically. At any rate, whether it is deliberate or not, people can and do fail to see the oppression of women because they fail to see macroscopically and hence fail to see the various elements of the situation as systematically related in larger schemes.

As the cageness of the birdcage is a macroscopic phenomenon, the oppressiveness of the situations in which women live our various and different lives is a macroscopic phenomenon. Neither can be *seen* from a microscopic perspective. But when you look macroscopically you can see a network of forces and barriers which are systematically related and which conspire to the immobilization, reduction and molding of women and the lives we live. . . .

It seems to be the human condition that in one degree or another we all suffer frustration and limitation, all encounter unwelcome barriers, and all are damaged and hurt in various ways. Since we are a social species, almost all of our behavior and activities are structured by more than individual inclination and the conditions of the planet and its atmosphere. No human is free of social structures, nor (perhaps) would happiness consist in such freedom. Structure consists of boundaries, limits and barriers; in a structured whole, some motions and changes are possible, and others are not. If one is looking for an excuse to dilute the word "oppression," one can use the fact of social structure as an excuse and say that everyone is oppressed. But if one would rather get clear about what oppression is and is not, one needs to sort out the sufferings, harms and limitations and figure out which are elements of oppression and which are not.

From what I have already said here, it is clear that if one wants to determine whether a particular suffering, harm or limitation is part of someone's being oppressed, one has to look at it *in context* in order to tell whether it is an element in an oppressive structure: one has to see if it is part of an enclosing structure of forces and barriers which tends to the immobilization and reduction of a group or category of people. One has to look at how the barrier or force fits with others and to whose benefit or detriment it works. As soon as one looks at examples, it becomes obvious that not everything which frustrates or limits a person is oppressive, and not every harm or damage is due to or contributes to oppression.

If a rich white playboy who lives off income from his investments in South African diamond mines should break a leg in a skiing accident at Aspen and wait in pain in a blizzard for hours before he is rescued, we may assume that in that period he suffers. But the suffering comes to an end; his leg is repaired by the best surgeon money can buy and he is soon recuperating in a lavish suite, sipping Chivas Regal. Nothing in this picture suggests a structure of barriers and forces. He is a member of several oppressor groups and does not suddenly become oppressed because he is injured and in pain. Even if the accident was caused by someone's malicious negligence, and hence someone can be blamed for it and morally faulted, that person still has not been an agent of oppression.

Consider also the restriction of having to drive one's vehicle on a certain side of the road. There is no doubt that this restriction is almost unbearably frustrating at times, when one's lane is not moving and the other lane is clear. There are surely times, even, when abiding by this regulation would have harmful consequences. But the restriction is obviously wholesome for most of us most of the time. The restraint is imposed for our benefit, and does

benefit us; its operation tends to encourage our *continued* motion, not to immobilize us. The limits imposed by traffic regulations are limits most of us would cheerfully impose on ourselves given that we knew others would follow them too. They are part of a structure which shapes our behavior, not to our reduction and immobilization, but rather to the protection of our continued ability to move and act as we will.

Another example: The boundaries of a racial ghetto in an American city serve to some extent to keep white people from going in, as well as to keep ghetto dwellers from going out. A particular white citizen may be frustrated or feel deprived because s/he cannot stroll around there and enjoy the "exotic" aura of a "foreign" culture, or shop for bargains in the ghetto swap shops. In fact, the existence of the ghetto, of racial segregation, does deprive the white person of knowledge and harm her/his character by nurturing unwarranted feelings of superiority. But this does not make the white person in this situation a member of an oppressed race or a person oppressed because of her/his race. One must look at the barrier. It limits the activities and the access of those on both sides of it (though to different degrees). But it is a product of the intention, planning and action of whites for the benefit of whites, to secure and maintain privileges that are available to whites generally, as members of the dominant and privileged group. Though the existence of the barrier has some bad consequences for whites, the barrier does not exist in systematic relationship with other barriers and forces forming a structure oppressive to whites; quite the contrary. It is part of a structure which oppresses the ghetto dwellers and thereby (and by white intention) protects and furthers white interests as dominant white culture understands them. This barrier is not oppressive to whites, even though it is a barrier to whites.

Barriers have different meanings to those on opposite sides of them, even though they are barriers to both. The physical walls of a prison no more dissolve to let an outsider in than to let an insider out, but for the insider they are confining and limiting while to the outsider they may mean protection from what s/he takes to be threats posed by insiders—freedom from harm or anxiety. A set of social and economic barriers and forces separating two groups may be felt, even painfully, by members of both groups and yet may mean confinement to one and liberty and enlargement of opportunity to the other.

The service sector of the wives/mommas/assistants/girls is almost exclusively a woman-only sector; its boundaries not only enclose women but to a very great extent keep men out. Some men sometimes encounter this barrier and experience it as a restriction on their movements, their activities, their control or their choices of "lifestyle." Thinking they might like the simple nurturant life (which they may imagine to be quite free of stress, alienation and hard work), and feeling deprived since it seems closed to them, they thereupon announce the discovery that they are oppressed, too, by "sex roles." But that barrier is erected and maintained by men, for the benefit of men. It consists of cultural and economic forces and pressures in a culture and economy controlled by men in which, at every economic level and in all racial and ethnic subcultures, economy, tradition—and even ideologies of liberation—work to keep at least local culture and economy in male control.*

DISCUSSION QUESTIONS

1. What are the central elements of Marilyn Frye's definition of oppression and an oppressed group?
2. Frye argues that the concept of "oppression" needs to be clearly defined. Why? Do you agree with her?
3. Do you find Frye's birdcage metaphor to be convincing?

---

*Of course this is complicated by race and class. Machismo and "Black manhood" politics seem to help keep Latin or Black men in control of more cash than Latin or Black women control; but these politics seem to me also to ultimately help keep the larger economy in *white* male control.

READING 46

White Privilege: Unpacking the Invisible Knapsack

Peggy McIntosh

Through work to bring materials from Women's Studies into the rest of the curriculum, I have often noticed men's unwillingness to grant that they are over-privileged, even though they may grant that women are disadvantaged. They may say they will work to improve women's status, in the society, the university, or the curriculum, but they can't or won't support the idea of lessening men's. Denials which amount to taboos surround the subject of advantages which men gain from women's disadvantages. These denials protect male privilege from being fully acknowledged, lessened or ended.

Thinking through unacknowledged male privilege as a phenomenon, I realized that since hierarchies in our society are interlocking, there was most likely a phenomenon of white privilege which was similarly denied and protected. As a white person, I realized I had been taught about racism as something which puts others at a disadvantage, but had been taught not to see one of its corollary aspects, white privilege, which puts me at an advantage.

I think whites are carefully taught not to recognize white privilege, as males are taught not to recognize male privilege. So I have begun in an untutored way to ask what it is like to have white privilege. I have come to see white privilege as an invisible package of unearned assets which I can count on cashing in each day, but about which I was "meant" to remain oblivious. White privilege is like an invisible weightless knapsack of special provisions, maps, passports, codebooks, visas, clothes, tools and blank checks.

Describing white privilege makes one newly accountable. As we in Women's Studies work to

---

Peggy McIntosh is associate director of the Wellesley College Center for Research on Women.

reveal male privilege and ask men to give up some of their power, so one who writes about having white privilege must ask, "Having described it, what will I do to lessen or end it?"

After I realized the extent to which men work from a base of unacknowledged privilege, I understood that much of their oppressiveness was unconscious. Then I remembered the frequent charges from women of color that white women whom they encounter are oppressive. I began to understand why we are justly seen as oppressive, even when we don't see ourselves that way. I began to count the ways in which I enjoy unearned skin privilege and have been conditioned into oblivion about its existence.

My schooling gave me no training in seeing myself as an oppressor, as an unfairly advantaged person, or as a participant in a damaged culture. I was taught to see myself as an individual whose moral state depended on her individual moral will. My schooling followed the pattern my colleague Elizabeth Minnich has pointed out: whites are taught to think of their lives as morally neutral, normative, and average, and also ideal, so that when we work to benefit others, this is seen as work which will allow "them" to be more like "us."

I decided to try to work on myself at least by identifying some of the daily effects of white privilege in my life. I have chosen those conditions which I think in my case *attach somewhat more to skin-color privilege* than to class, religion, ethnic status, or geographical location, though of course all these other factors are intricately intertwined. As far as I can see, my African American co-workers, friends and acquaintances with whom I come into daily or frequent contact in this particular time, place, and line of work cannot count on most of these conditions.

1. I can if I wish arrange to be in the company of people of my race most of the time.
2. If I should need to move, I can be pretty sure of renting or purchasing housing in an area which I can afford and in which I would want to live.
3. I can be pretty sure that my neighbors in such a location will be neutral or pleasant to me.
4. I can go shopping alone most of the time, pretty well assured that I will not be followed or harassed.
5. I can turn on the television or open to the front page of the paper and see people of my race widely represented.
6. When I am told about our national heritage or about "civilization," I am shown that people of my color made it what it is.
7. I can be sure that my children will be given curricular materials that testify to the existence of their race.
8. If I want to, I can be pretty sure of finding a publisher for this piece on white privilege.
9. I can go into a music shop and count on finding the music of my race represented, into a supermarket and find the staple foods which fit with my cultural traditions, into a hairdresser's shop and find someone who can cut my hair.
10. Whether I use checks, credit cards, or cash, I can count on my skin color not to work against the appearance of financial reliability.
11. I can arrange to protect my children most of the time from people who might not like them.
12. I can swear, or dress in second hand clothes, or not answer letters, without having people attribute these choices to the bad morals, the poverty, or the illiteracy of my race.
13. I can speak in public to a powerful male group without putting my race on trial.
14. I can do well in a challenging situation without being called a credit to my race.
15. I am never asked to speak for all the people of my racial group.
16. I can remain oblivious of the language and customs of persons of color who constitute the world's majority without feeling in my culture any penalty for such oblivion.
17. I can criticize our government and talk about how much I fear its policies and behavior without being seen as a cultural outsider.
18. I can be pretty sure that if I ask to talk to "the person in charge," I will be facing a person of my race.

19. If a traffic cop pulls me over or if the IRS audits my tax return, I can be sure I haven't been singled out because of my race.

20. I can easily buy posters, postcards, picture books, greeting cards, dolls, toys, and children's magazines featuring people of my race.

21. I can go home from most meetings of organizations I belong to feeling somewhat tied in, rather than isolated, out-of-place, outnumbered, unheard, held at a distance, or feared.

22. I can take a job with an affirmative action employer without having coworkers on the job suspect that I got it because of race.

23. I can choose public accommodation without fearing that people of my race cannot get in or will be mistreated in the places I have chosen.

24. I can be sure that if I need legal or medical help, my race will not work against me.

25. If my day, week, or year is going badly, I need not ask of each negative episode or situation whether it has racial overtones.

26. I can choose blemish cover or bandages in "flesh" color and have them more or less match my skin.

I repeatedly forgot each of the realizations on this list until I wrote it down. For me white privilege has turned out to be an elusive and fugitive subject. The pressure to avoid it is great, for in facing it I must give up the myth of meritocracy. If these things are true, this is not such a free country; one's life is not what one makes it; many doors open for certain people through no virtues of their own.

In unpacking this invisible knapsack of white privilege, I have listed conditions of daily experience which I once took for granted. Nor did I think of any of these perquisites as bad for the holder. I now think that we need a more finely differentiated taxonomy of privilege, for some of these varieties are only what one would want for everyone in a just society, and others give licence to be ignorant, oblivious, arrogant and destructive.

I see a pattern running through the matrix of white privilege, a pattern of assumptions which were passed on to me as a white person. There

was one main piece of cultural turf; it was my own turf, and I was among those who could control the turf. *My skin color was an asset for any move I was educated to want to make.* I could think of myself as belonging in major ways, and of making social systems work for me. I could freely disparage, fear, neglect, or be oblivious to anything outside of the dominant cultural forms. Being of the main culture, I could also criticize it fairly freely.

In proportion as my racial group was being made confident, comfortable, and oblivious, other groups were likely being made inconfident, uncomfortable, and alienated. Whiteness protected me from many kinds of hostility, distress, and violence, which I was being subtly trained to visit in turn upon people of color.

For this reason, the word "privilege" now seems to me misleading. We usually think of privilege as being a favored state, whether earned or conferred by birth or luck. Yet some of the conditions I have described here work to systematically overempower certain groups. Such privilege simply *confers dominance* because of one's race or sex.

I want, then, to distinguish between earned strength and unearned power conferred systemically. Power from unearned privilege can look like strength when it is in fact permission to escape or to dominate. But not all of the privileges on my list are inevitably damaging. Some, like the expectation that neighbors will be decent to you, or that your race will not count against you in court, should be the norm in a just society. Others, like the privilege to ignore less powerful people, distort the humanity of the holders as well as the ignored groups.

We might at least start by distinguishing between positive advantages which we can work to spread, and negative types of advantages which unless rejected will always reinforce our present hierarchies. For example, the feeling that one belongs within the human circle, as Native Americans say, should not be seen as privilege for a few. Ideally it is an *unearned entitlement.* At present, since only a few have it, it is an *unearned advantage* for them. This paper results from a process of coming to see that some of the power which I originally saw as attendant

PERSONAL ACCOUNT

My Secret

It is 1992; I'm in the first grade. I am an impressionable little white girl with a racist white teacher. There were two or three black children in the class. I remember a little black girl with braids and multiple barrettes holding them in place. The same barrettes I used on my hair except she had a whole bunch of almost every color. "Just like me," I remember thinking.

Our teacher had an interesting system of rewards and punishments. If we did something good, we got a "yellow mark" in the little pouch by our name that hung on the wall. If we did something bad, we got a "black mark." I remember thinking how horrible it would be to get a black mark. I also remember who got those most of the time. I remember being scared I might get one. Eight black marks were the worst, with a bad phone call home, and eight yellow the opposite, a good phone call home.

One day, a little white girl had her watch stolen. The teacher made a huge deal about it and even had a police officer at the school come to investigate and talk to us. She told everyone, "If you admit to taking the watch now, I'll only give you two black marks." No one confessed. We must have stood there for a while, waiting for the "criminal" among us. I kept double-checking with myself internally: had I stolen the watch? Finally, the teacher said she was going to give eight black marks and a bad phone call home either way. She said if the person did not give up the watch, the police officer was going to arrest them.

I was scared for whoever stole it. I remember scanning the room and noticing that, following the teacher's lead, many of us had begun glancing over at the little black girl in class (who had a record for getting black marks). After awhile, the teacher dug into the little girl's pockets and ripped the watch out. I can still see the little girl standing there afterward, with her hands in her pockets, looking at the floor. How smart the teacher must be, I thought, to suspect her first. I couldn't get over how horrible it would be to be that little girl and have eight black marks and a bad phone call home. Why hadn't she just admitted it earlier? She must be different from me. She must not think stealing or getting in trouble is bad. I was so shocked at my little compadre. I was afraid of her now.

It is difficult for me to share this story. I have to carry the guilt of my teacher's racist construction of reality. I am afraid of how it affected my impressionable mind. I hate to think that any of the racism she planted is still there. I know that it is. As open-minded as I am, it is very difficult for me to ever feel completely equal with a black friend. It makes me angry. I wanted to protect her from punishment. I wanted her to be innocent. I wanted Ms. Sovie to be wrong. I can't erase this memory. I have to constantly overcome it. Now you know my secret.

Sarah Herschler

---

on being a human being in the U.S. consisted in *unearned advantage* and *conferred dominance*.

I have met very few men who are truly distressed about systemic, unearned male advantage and conferred dominance. And so one question for me and others like me is whether we will be like them, or whether we will get truly distressed, even outraged, about unearned race advantage and conferred dominance and if so, what we will do to lessen them. In any case, we need to do more work in identifying how they actually affect our daily lives. Many, perhaps most, of our white students in the U.S. think that racism doesn't affect them because they are not people of color; they do not see "whiteness" as a racial identity. In addition, since race and sex are not the only

advantaging systems at work, we need similarly to examine the daily experience of having age advantage, or ethnic advantage, or physical ability, or advantage related to nationality, religion, or sexual orientation.

Difficulties and dangers surrounding the task of finding parallels are many. Since racism, sexism, and heterosexism are not the same, the advantaging associated with them should not be seen as the same. In addition, it is hard to disentangle aspects of unearned advantage which rest more on social class, economic class, race, religion, sex and ethnic identity than on other factors. Still, all of the oppressions are interlocking, as the Combahee River Collective Statement of 1977 continues to remind us eloquently.

One factor seems clear about all of the interlocking oppressions. They take both active forms which we can see and embedded forms which as a member of the dominant group one is taught not to see. In my class and place, I did not see myself as a racist because I was taught to recognize racism only in individual acts of meanness by members of my group, never in invisible systems conferring unsought racial dominance on my group from birth.

Disapproving of the systems won't be enough to change them. I was taught to think that racism could end if white individuals changed their attitudes. [But] a "white" skin in the United States opens many doors for whites whether or not we approve of the way dominance has been conferred on us. Individual acts can palliate, but cannot end, these problems.

To redesign social systems we need first to acknowledge their colossal unseen dimensions. The silences and denials surrounding privilege are the key political tool here. They keep the thinking about equality or equity incomplete, protecting unearned advantage and conferred dominance by making these taboo subjects. Most talk by whites about equal opportunity seems to me now to be about equal opportunity to try to get into a position of dominance while denying that *systems* of dominance exist.

It seems to me that obliviousness about white advantage, like obliviousness about male advantage, is kept strongly inculturated in the United States so as to maintain the myth of meritocracy, the myth that democratic choice is equally available to all. Keeping most people unaware that freedom of confident action is there for just a small number of people props up those in power, and serves to keep power in the hands of the same groups that have most of it already.

Though systemic change takes many decades, there are pressing questions for me and I imagine for some others like me if we raise our daily consciousness on the perquisites of being light-skinned. What will we do with such knowledge? As we know from watching men, it is an open question whether we will choose to use unearned advantage to weaken hidden systems of advantage, and whether we will use any of our arbitrarily awarded power to try to reconstruct power systems on a broader base.

NOTE

This essay is excerpted from her working paper, "White Privilege and Male Privilege: A Personal Account of Coming to See Correspondences Through Work in Women's Studies," copyright © 1988 by Peggy McIntosh. Available for $4.00 from address below. The paper includes a longer list of privileges. Permission to excerpt or reprint must be obtained from Peggy McIntosh, Wellesley College Center for Research on Women, Wellesley, MA 02181; (781) 283–2522; FAX: (781) 283–2504

DISCUSSION QUESTIONS

1. Is meritocracy a myth?
2. What are some examples of unearned advantages and conferred dominance?
3. Why are so many people oblivious to white advantage?

READING 47

Ethnic Identity and Racial Formations: Race and Racism American-Style and *a lo Latino*

Marta Cruz-Janzen

I am a Latinegra. Racism has been with me all my life. Born and raised a U.S. citizen in the U.S. Commonwealth of Puerto Rico, I completed most of my schooling on the island. In high school I moved back and forth between the island and the mainland. On the island, I became aware of Latina/o racism at an early age. On the mainland, U.S. racism was added to my consciousness and understanding. Today my life is affected not only by U.S. racism

Marta Cruz-Janzen is a professor of multicultural education at Florida Atlantic University.

but also by Latina/o racism and the intersection of the two. Latina/o and U.S. racial ideologies seem to represent fundamentally divergent systems of social order. U.S. racism enforces the black-versus-white dichotomy; Latina/o racism appeases it. U.S. racism is sharp and clear; Latina/o racism is stratified and nebulous. The intersection of these doctrines unleashes a dilemma for Latinas/os in the United States: What to do with a racial heritage shrouded in secrecy? What to do with a long history of blurred racial lines and deeply hidden family secrets in a world controlled by a rigid color line? I am rejected by both U.S. and Latina/o forms of racism. Latinas/os in Latin America accept me marginally; Latinas/os in the United States openly spurn me. The repudiation by Latinas/os has intensified over the years, and I know why. Through me Latinas/os see the blackness in themselves; I am a living reminder of the ancestors they thought they had left behind. Oppressors rely on their victims' shame and silence. Breaking the shackles of oppression requires telling what is really happening and addressing all the sources of racism. With this chapter I break my own psychological shackles of oppression. I explore the forces impacting racism in Latinas/os today, among them: (1) racism in Latin America, especially Mexico, Puerto Rico, and Cuba, (2) Spanish racism before colonization, (3) U.S. racism, and (4) the intersection of U.S. and Latina/o racial doctrines.

Mucho que poco, todos tenemos la mancha de platano (Much or little, we all have the plantain stain). Latina/o cultures are rich in oral traditions. Popular expressions bear witness to a long and complex history. Oral histories tell more and are often closer to the truth than what is written in books or discussed in polite society. This popular adage states what is known but not acknowledged in most Latina/o cultures—that everyone has some non-European blood. A green vegetable resembling a banana, the plantain is white inside but, when touched, quickly produces a stain that darkens to black and sets permanently. *La mancha de platano*—black and Indian heritage—may or may not be apparent but is present in all Latinas/os and cannot be washed away. When I was growing up, my father's [black] family called me

trigueña (wheat-colored), whereas the favorite term of my mother's [white] family was *morena* (black), considered a step down. Sometimes, they both called me *negra,* or some variation of the term. When my black grandma called me *negrita* (little black) it was usually with pride and accompanied by a loving hug. When my white grandma called me *negra,* it signaled anger and impending punishment. Outside of the family the labels varied, but when *negra* was used it was as a derisive reminder of my race and lower status. In the latter instances, *negra* tended to be followed by *sucia* (immoral, but literally "dirty") or *parejera* (arrogant). *Parejero/a* is not used for whites, only for blacks and Indians. It denotes people who do not accept *su lugar* (their place) beneath whites and do not remain quiet like children or humbly obey (Zenon Cruz, 1975). An equivalent term, used in Mexico and many other parts of Latin America, is *igualada/o.* Both terms signify a false sense of equality and belonging among superiors.

It has always intrigued me that my father's birth certificate defines him as mestizo. The explanation for this was that because his parents, both black, were educated and middle-class they were *mejorando la raza* (improving the race). They had moved out of Barrio San Antón, the black quarters of the coastal town of Ponce, and lived in a predominantly white neighborhood. They maintained an impeccable home with a beautiful front garden and, aware of their neighbors' scrutiny, never ventured out unless well groomed. When I visited, though, I recall always playing alone, never having friends in the neighborhood. A white girl next door and I sometimes played together through the iron fence but never at each other's home. As I played in the front yard I saw children from across the street watching but knew that we could not get together. My black grandparents had five children. While concerned for all of them, they worried most about their two daughters; one attended the university, became a teacher, and taught in a remote rural school, while the other was considered fortunate for marrying a white man. San Antón was known as an *arrabal,* an impoverished slum beyond the city limits. Grandma was admired and respected there and often took me with her while distributing food and clothes. The differences in living conditions between my grandparents' neighborhood and San Antón were staggering: streets were narrow and unpaved, buildings were in disrepair and lacked indoor plumbing, most houses were makeshifts built of discarded wood and cardboard with zinc roofs. Distinctively, most residents were dark-skinned *puros prietos* (pure blacks).

My two sets of grandparents lived in what appeared to be two separate worlds. I do not recall a single time when they or their families visited each other. My siblings and I were shuttled between them on weekends and holidays. On one side we were *mejorando la raza,* on the other *una pena* (disgrace, sorrow, shame). On one side we were *trigueños finos* (wheat-colored and refined), on the other *morenos y prietos* (black and dark). My paternal black grandma reminded me to pinch my nose between my fingers each day to sharpen its roundness; my maternal white grandma wanted my *greñas* and *ceretas* (curly, wild hair) restrained at all times. Uninhibitedly, my mother's family voiced concerns for me and my siblings as black persons, and especially for me and my sisters as Latinegras in a white, male-dominated Latina/o society. Whereas my father "elevated" his family and himself by marrying a white, my mother was openly chastised for marrying *ese negro feo* (that ugly black), lowering herself and her entire family. Repeatedly, she was told, *Cada oveja con su pareja* (Each sheep with its pair), a reminder that interracial marriages were frowned upon even by the Catholic Church, which preached that we were all *ovejas de Dios* (God's sheep). . . .

RACISM IN MEXICO, PUERTO RICO, AND CUBA

Aqui, el que no tiene dinga tiene mandinga. El que no tiene congo tiene carabali. Y pa' los que no saben na', ¿y tu abuela a'onde esta? (Here, those who don't have Dinga have Mandinga. Those who don't have Congo have Carabali. And for those who don't know anything, where's your grandma?) Carabalis, Congos,

and Mandingas were African nations; Dingas and Ingas were Indians. This aphorism makes clear the preponderance of interracial bloodlines within the Latino world. At the same time, *Hoy dia los negros quieren ser blancos y los mulatos caballeros* (Nowadays blacks want to be whites and mulattoes knights) reveals the rancor of white Latinas/os over the social advances of Latinas/os of color.

Mexicans have a long history of interracial unions between Africans, Indians, and Spaniards. The contributions of Africans have influenced every aspect of Mexican culture, history, and life. Esteban el Negro explored northern Mexico; the hit song "La Bamba" comes from the Bamba or Mbamba people of Veracruz, and the national *corrido* song style is partially African in origin; the muralist and painter Diego Rivera was of African descent. The African presence is apparent, but it is denied in Mexico and by Mexicans in the United States. In spite of their impressive contributions, Afro-Mexicans remain a marginalized group, not yet even recognized as full citizens (Muhammad, 1995). Mexican historians and academicians endorse the claim that the "discovery" of Mexico represented an encounter of two worlds, the Indian and the Spanish, with little if any mention of the Africans brought there (Muhammad, 1995). By the middle of the eighteenth century, Mexico's second-largest population group was largely of African extraction. In 1810 blacks represented 10.2 percent of the Mexican population (Muhammad, 1995). It is estimated that about two hundred thousand Spaniards and two hundred and fifty thousand Africans had migrated to Mexico up to 1810 (Forbes, 1992), and the African population was largely assimilated by the rapidly emerging interracial population. Although Mexico identifies itself as a nation of mestizos, the term "mestizo" is normally not used for identifiable Afro-Mexicans, who are instead referred to as *morenos*. The 1921 census was the last in which racial categories were used in Mexico. Today it is estimated that mestizos make up approximately 85–90 percent of the Mexican population and indigenous persons only 8–10 percent (Fernandez, 1992). There are no current data, demographic or otherwise, for Afro-Mexicans, but Miriam Jiménez Romón of New York's

Schomburg Center for Research in Black Culture estimates that 75 percent of the population of Mexico has some African admixture (Muhammad, 1995). Mexicans will boast about their Spanish relatives and may even admit to Indian ones but will rarely admit to a black forebear. Whereas indigenous groups have gained national and international visibility and support, Afro-Mexicans remain suppressed and unheard. Contemporary social research in Mexico tends to exclude Afro-Mexican communities, and no major study on Mexican race relations has ever been done (Muhammad, 1995). Within the past decade anthropologists and others have visited Afro-Mexican communities and reported their deplorable living conditions and rampant illiteracy, their inadequate schools and medical facilities, and their lack of electricity, potable water, plumbing, sewerage, drainage, and paved streets. Visiting Mexico in 1988, I searched for and found Afro-Mexicans living in a clearly segregated shanty town outside of Guadalajara. The squalor of their homes and community was appalling. They openly talked about blatant racism and their financial and legal inability to migrate to the United States. These Afro-Mexicans have been ignored and neglected by government agencies; they receive little or no assistance (Muhammad, 1995).

Puerto Rico, after four centuries of Spanish colonial rule, had developed into a multiracial society. French people and multiracial Creoles went to Puerto Rico after the U.S. Louisiana Purchase from France and migrated from Haiti when the slaves revolted (U.S. Commission on Civil Rights, 1976). Labor shortages throughout the island in the 1840s brought Chinese, Italians, Corsicans, Lebanese, Germans, Scots, Irish, and many others. As the twentieth century approached, the racial composition of Puerto Rico covered the spectrum from whites to blacks with a large in-between interracial group known as *trigueños* (U.S. Commission on Civil Rights, 1976). Racially speaking, most Puerto Ricans are of interracial black, Taino, and white origin. It is believed that racial mixing has touched at least 70 percent of Puerto Rico's population. With U.S. invasion of the island and installation of military rule in 1898, citizenship in 1917, and

the establishment of the Commonwealth in 1952, U.S. whites became first-class citizens. Elite Puerto Rican whites were quick to ingratiate themselves with the new upper class by impressing them with their whiteness (Toplin, 1976). The advent of U.S. racism brought the exclusion of social whites who declared themselves white in official U.S. demographic surveys. Whereas the 1846 census reported 51.24 percent of the Puerto Rican population as African or Negro, in 1959 the count dropped to only 23 percent (Toplin, 1976). Members of Congress were not discreet in expressing their low opinion of Puerto Ricans and wondering how there could be so many whites in a "black man's country." Several were openly angered by the degree of racial mixture, stating that the "horror" of racial mixing had gone too far and prevented them from establishing clear racial categorization. They concluded that it was the "duty" of the United States to impose a strict color code on Puerto Rican society in order to ensure propagation of the white race, that is, the newly established elite (Toplin, 1976).

Racial prejudice increased with U.S. occupation of the island (Toplin, 1976; Zenon Cruz, 1975) and became prevalent in public places during the 1950s and 1960s. It persists in social clubs, public and private universities, businesses, banks, tourist facilities, public and private schools, and housing today. Although the local government stopped using racial classifications in 1950, the legal and penal systems, which remain predominantly white, continue to use them against black and dark-skinned poor urban youth (Santiago-Valles, 1995). Little if anything is done to correct the open racism, and many areas remain "hermetically closed" to the darker-skinned Puerto Rican (Toplin, 1976). The Puerto Rican elite, comprised mostly of the descendants of Spaniards with increasing numbers of U.S. whites and European immigrants, treat darker Puerto Ricans with visible contempt. Few Puerto Ricans of African descent explicitly identify as such because of a long history of discrimination and a present fear of police brutality and persecution (Santiago-Valles, 1995). Elite Puerto Ricans still claim that the Spanish white race prevailed in the island, making it the "whitest of all the Antilles," and seek closer ties with Spain (Santiago-Valles, 1995). The 1992 Columbus Quincentennial was celebrated with much emphasis on the Spanish roots of the island. Subsequent annual "Nuestra Hispanidad" (Our Hispanicism) celebrations have focused on Spain and white Puerto Ricans. There is a dearth of information about black and dark-skinned Puerto Ricans but a strong association between black and poor. Black and dark-skinned Puerto Ricans live disproportionately in slums under extremely deprived conditions. U.S. citizenship granted all Puerto Ricans, including those of black heritage, an open door to the continental United States. The enormous loss of jobs between 1940 and 1970 created a massive exodus of Puerto Ricans to the U.S. mainland (U.S. Commission on Civil Rights, 1976). This immense socioeconomic dislocation brought increased visibility to the predominantly black and interracial Puerto Ricans on the mainland.

The Cuban population has historically been African and Spanish (Fernandez, 1992). Almost all Cuban-born Latinas/os came to the United States as refugees from the Revolution of 1959 and the Mariel boatlift in 1980. Although the vast majority of Cubans today are black, most Cuban-Americans are white (McGarrity and Cardenas, 1995). Revolution refugees were mostly educated middle- and upper-class white Cubans with backgrounds in the professions, businesses, and government who soon became integrated into the U.S. middle class. The "less congenial" Marielos were mainly uneducated and poor lower-class black Cubans (Rivera, 1991). The long-standing racism of white Cubans against black Cubans is well known. In Cuba, blacks were excluded from certain schools, especially private Catholic schools, public beaches, hotels, restaurants, and parks. They could not rent homes in some areas (McGarrity and Cardenas, 1995). Before the Marielos, Cubans were welcomed in the United States and given preferential treatment with much transitional support. These elite Cubans were "proudly and adamantly white," uncontaminated, as they emphasized (McGarrity and Cardenas, 1995). Social and elite white Cuban Americans did not welcome the visibility brought on

by the Marielos, the black compatriots they thought they had left behind in Cuba (Rivera, 1991). White Cubans are the most successful of the three major U.S. Latina/o groups; Mexicans follow, and Puerto Ricans, with more apparent African bloodlines, are the least (Forbes, 1992). . . .

THE INTERSECTION OF LATINA/O AND U.S. RACISM

Individuals in the United States may believe that times have changed—that conditions for Latinegros have improved. After all, many U.S. educational institutions advocate multicultural education, the affirmation of diversity, and the teaching of tolerance. The sad reality is that racism continues to be part of everyday life among Latinas/os in the United States and is today confounded by U.S. racism. Latina/o racial antagonism has been transported to U.S. soil. Elite white Latinas/os, seeking acceptance by U.S. whites, quickly disown compatriots of known African lineage even when they appear white and are socially accepted as white in their home countries. In the United States these social white Latinas/os become *negros mal agradecidos* (ungrateful), *changos* (insolent), and *alzaos* (uppity) for wanting the privileges that elite white Latinas/os take for granted. Essentially, social white Latinas/os seek a closeness to elite white Latinas/os that remains simply unacceptable within the U.S. racial and social structure. In this struggle for acceptance, many social white Latinas/os fear focusing attention on themselves and their African legacy. When I moved to the mainland United States, I was told by some Latinas/os that since I would be perceived and treated as black I should identify with African Americans. Others advised me to accentuate my Latina attributes and deemphasize the black ones. Gone were most of the polite, if superficial, niceties—it no longer surprises me when I encounter Latinas/os whom I know in public places and they pretend not to see me. When U.S. Latinas/os emphasize their Hispanicism, they also tend to make sure that I understand my lack of it and the social abyss that separates us. Just three years ago, a

"Hispanic" educator in Colorado told me that I was not one of them: "Hispanics are from Spain. You are not Hispanic. Everyone knows you are black." At a Latina/o educators' meeting where I raised concerns about the educational needs of African American students I was addressed scornfully: "You ought to know; you are black like 'them.'" A Latino friend explained, "Some Hispanics here don't want you to be one of them because you represent everything they don't want to be. 'How dare this black woman speak Spanish and claim to be one of us?' They see you as black, and they don't want to be black." In 1993 a "Hispanic" reader from New Mexico wrote to *Hispanic* magazine, in response to its earlier coverage of Latino major-league baseball players, including black Latinos: "I would appreciate knowing how the writer arrived at the classification of apparent Blacks as Hispanics. Does the fact that men come from Spanish-speaking countries such as Puerto Rico or Cuba automatically give them the Hispanic title designation? History shows that Africans were transported to the Americas as slaves and took the names of their slave masters."...

One of the most insidious and pervasive forms of racism, one that appears to be escalating through globalized technology, is the promotion of images that exalt whiteness (Forbes, 1992). Historically, people of African background in Latin America have been stereotyped and vilified in popular culture in a number of ways. Media programs from Latin America and particularly Mexico are very popular among Latinas/os worldwide, especially in the United States, and are rapidly gaining other international audiences. *Telenovelas* (soap operas) and television programming are Mexico's largest export, sold throughout Latin America, the United States, and 125 other countries (Quinones, 1997). In these programs dark-skinned persons, particularly Latinegros, are presented as beggars, criminals, and servants. Latinegras are cooks, maids, nannies, and prostitutes. A term broadly used for dark-skinned Latinos in these programs is "Ladino," which also means a "liar" and a "thief." The upper class usually reflects the Nordic ideal, with light-colored eyes and hair and black and/or Indian servants.

Latinegros are also promoted as either athletes or singers but are mostly depicted in a distorted way and made the object of ridicule.

CONCLUSION

Clearly, Latinas/os present a dilemma for the United States—what to do with a rapidly increasing population of mixed racial ancestry that defies categorization, resists homogenization, and cannot be readily assimilated. Today some Latinas/os mock the term as "His Panic," to signify the perceived fear of the white male-dominated U.S. government of non-white Latina/o population growth. Through its racial policies and the "Hispanic" category the United States has chosen to advance Spanishness or put bluntly, whiteness, among Latinas/os (Forbes, 1992). It has established a system whereby Latinas/os are deluded into believing that they are all members of this new Hispanic group. While being reminded of my lack of "Hispanicness," I am reminded that politically my self-identification as a "Hispanic" is needed. What is concealed is that Latinas/os with uninterrupted descent from white Spaniards are glorified and established as the group's leaders. Most Latinas/os in the United States migrated in search of opportunities denied and/or made unavailable to them by the white elites of their homelands. They do not realize that the United States is re-creating this power structure among them. Perhaps "His Panic" is Latinas/os' own panic—their own, even greater dilemma. The U.S. color line makes no allowance for middle groups; it is designed to disperse the middle cloud in opposite directions. Individuals are either white or "something else" (Cruz-Janzen, 1997). That "something else" may be African American, Asian American, Native American, or Hispanic, but only white Europeans—more specifically, white Europeans with the exception of Spaniards—can be white. As Hispanics, Latinas/os are spuriously classified as Europeans and white Latinas/os are deluded into believing that they are accepted as White Europeans. Latinos fail to recognize that ultimately, U.S. rejection is directed at all of them. Although their predecessors were present in this hemisphere before the arrival of the Pilgrims, U.S. Latinas/os are relegated to foreign status, forever designated as immigrants from Spain, whereas other Europeans are integrated as "Americans." Latinas/os of color are rendered invisible as only white Latinas/os are recognized.

Issues of race and racism are not talked about openly in Latina/o cultures in the United States because many Latinas/os argue that they are discriminated against as an ethnic group and discussions of internal racism divide the group and prevent coalescence against White/European-American oppression. But Latinegras/os in the United States as elsewhere resent their oppression. They are aware of the *tapujos*—the secrets, contradictions, and hypocrisy—among Latinas/os that provide fertile ground for U.S. racial policies. They express their anger and frustration over a situation that has been with them all their lives and is getting worse. Many realize that the stringent black-versus-white dichotomy is widening the racial divide that has existed among Latinas/os.

DISCUSSION QUESTIONS

1. Does education whiten one's color?
2. Does having a higher income whiten?
3. Does racism operate on the same principles across cultures?

REFERENCES

Cruz-Janzen, Marta I. 1997. *Curriculum and the Self-Concept of Biethnic and Biracial Persons*. Ann Arbor, MI: UMI Dissertation Services.

Fernandez, Carlos A. 1992. "*La raza* and the Melting Pot: A Comparative Look at Multiethnicity/Multiraciality," pp. 126–43 in Maria P. Root (ed.), *Racially Mixed People in America*. Newbury Park, CA: Sage.

Forbes, Jack D. 1992. "The Hispanic Spin: Party Politics and Governmental Manipulation of Ethnic Identity." *Latin American Perspectives* 19 (Fall): 59–78.

McGarrity, Gayle and Osvaldo Cardenas. 1995. "Cuba," pp. 77–108 in Minority Rights Group (ed.), *No Longer Invisible: Afro-Latin Americans Today*. London: Minority Rights Publications.

Muhammad, Jameelah S. 1995. "Mexico and Central America," pp. 163–80 in Minority Rights Group (ed.),

No Longer Invisible: Afro-Latin Americans Today. London: Minority Rights Publications.

Quinones, Sam. 1997. "Hooked on *Telenovelas*." *Hemispheres* (November): 125–29.

Rivera, Mario A. 1991. *Decision and Structure: U.S. Refugee Policy in the Mariel Crisis*. Lanham, MD: University Press of America.

Santiago-Valles, Kelvin A. 1995. "Puerto Rico," pp. 139–62 in Minority Rights Group (ed.), *No Longer Invisible: Afro-Latin Americans Today*. London: Minority Rights Publications.

Toplin, Robert B. 1976. *Slavery and Slave Relations in Latin America*. Westport, CT: Greenwood Press.

U.S. Commission on Civil Rights. 1976. *Puerto Ricans in the Continental United States: An Uncertain Future*.

Zenon Cruz, Isabelo. 1975. *Narciso descrube su trasero: El negro en la cultura puertorriqueña*. Vol. 2. Humacao, PR: Editorial Furidi.

READING 48

I/Me/Mine—Intersectional Identities as Negotiated Minefields

Shuddhabrata Sengupta

Identities can occasionally be weapons of mass destruction (lite). They can be invading armies and besieged cities. They can be maps waiting to be redrawn. Or a people, anticipating measures of "freedom" and "occupation" to come their way from an armored vehicle, or a cluster bomb, or depleted uranium.

To speak of identities in times of war and in the aftermath of war is to be compelled to recognize how certain methods of identification—the ascription of citizenship to a subject of a nation-state, for instance—also automatically confers on the being so described partisanship vis-à-vis one or the other forces engaged in the battle. The same could be said

Shuddhabrata Sengupta is a media practitioner, filmmaker, and writer with the Raqs Media Collective and one of the initiators of Sarai. His work involves textual explorations of aesthetics, surveillance, and cyberculture.

of religious or ethnic identity, or color, and in some cases of gender, and the battlefields that lie on the terrain within and between these categories. Let me sketch a few scenarios for you, to make all my dilemmas when talking about identities explicit.

Are you the internationally recognized and feted artist or academic woman of color who considers herself to be more oppressed than the working-class Caucasian woman in prison—let's say a blonde Bosnian Muslim immigrant sex worker who happens to have charges of manslaughter against her for killing her abusive Jamaican pimp? Here, the index of oppression is melanin, not life.

Are you a Caucasian, which translates as "black" in Russia?

Or are you the African American man in prison who considers himself to be less oppressed, because he is a man, than the African American woman on the street, whom he is happy to call a "ho"?

Are you the African American Gl in Iraq, sucked into a war by the poverty draft at home and face to face with the anger of a subject population that considers you to be the brutal enforcer of an occupying army that possesses the greatest number of weapons of mass destruction on earth? In combat fatigues, and under camouflage striping, white shades into dark, and dark can pale to white.

Are you the white working-class woman, perhaps a single mother, who is herself a victim of insidious sexism within the military and within working-class subcultures, who nevertheless becomes a willing enforcer of the apparatus of humiliation in the Abu Ghraib prison?

Are you the South Asian illegal alien in New York who washes dishes in a restaurant, is hoping to be a taxi driver, and really wishes he could be a Chinese grocer on the make?

Are you the recently arrived, already battered, non-English-speaking Indian or Pakistani "passport bride" caught between her aggressive husband, notions of community honor, shame, and the (amended) marriage fraud provisions of the 1952 Immigration and Naturalization Act of the United States?

Are you the Palestinian teenager throwing rocks at an Israeli military bulldozer who wishes he were a black rap artist from the Bronx with a Jewish record producer?

Are you the Iraqi woman, relieved that Saddam Hussein is no more, angry about U.S. bombs landing in her neighborhood, worried about the calls for the veil that emanate from Shiite clerics asserting their long oppressed identities by demanding a Shiite Islamic state in Iraq, and equally worried about having been "liberated" from a dictator only to be delivered as a subject to a convicted fraudster,[1] all in the name of her freedom, her honor, and her dignity as an Iraqi?

Are you the rich Indian racist who thinks that white women were made white in order for him to harass them on the streets of New Delhi? Are you the British exchange student of Nigerian origin in an Indian city who can't find a room to rent because of her color and who listens patiently to stories about how Indians suffer racism in the city where she grew up?

Are you one of the 15 million Bangladeshi illegal immigrants whom the Indian government now plans to identify and deport? Have you given thought to how you might change your accent, or your name, or adjust a few facts in your biography, and tell your children a few stories so that they don't let slip that you walked across the border when the police, accompanied by ethnographers, come knocking on your shack in New Delhi for an interview? Can you exchange one biography of oppression for another that might be more suitable for survival under the present circumstances?

Are you the anti-Semitic black Muslim descendent of slaves? Are you the racist Jewish granddaughter of concentration camp survivors? Are you the white supremacist descendent of refugees from the potato famine in Ireland? Are you the Hindu fundamentalist who has fantasies of raping Muslim women and who will defend the honor of his sister with an automatic weapon? Are you the Kashmiri Muslim woman suicide bomber with a sharp memory of being raped by an Indian army major when you were a teenager?

Is what you call your identity a weapon, a shield, a fortress, a battering ram, an unexploded land mine?

The trouble with the deployment of identities as means of offense or defense is that, given a change in the equations of violence in any instance, which may have to do with anything from local politics to broader geopolitical crosscurrents, the victim very quickly becomes the oppressor. And so the idealist builder of Zion becomes a tyrant. Yesterday's Kurdish peshmarga (guerrilla fighter), forgotten by the world, becomes today's policeman for an occupying power because of the way the cartographic dice happen to be loaded at present. The players in the game may change; the Kurd may well go back up the mountain, fleeing like he had to the last time Saddam Hussein gassed him with helicopters that were bought with the help of today's "liberators."

The history of the twentieth century bears witness to the fact that the project of national liberation has inevitably turned the dream of freedom into the nightmare of refugee and prison camps and exile. The victims have changed; the rules haven't. And the assertion of the identity of an oppressed people becomes the excuse for silencing any question about the networks of power and privilege within the community.

As someone carrying an Indian passport, I am only too keenly aware that the rhetoric of nationalism and anticolonialism, a constituent of the chimera of what an Indian identity is seen to be, is the currency that enables the Indian state to act exactly as brutally as any colonial or imperial power within the borders of the republic. I do not doubt that colonialism was brutal, but I see colonialism as the instance by which a network of oppression stretched across the world. The white convict in Australia, the East Indian indentured worker in Trinidad, the pauperized peasant in Bihar, and the dispossessed African pastoralist were as much at the receiving end of violence as local landed elites—native princes, rubber plantation owners, administrators, and policemen of all colors—were perpetuators of that violence. I long to be able to recover what I call the history and buried memory of the detritus of empire that enables me to see the flow and network of power in structures and institutions that, though they may on occasion take on the patina of race and color, were just as able to discard it when

it suited their purpose. Sometimes they could do both at once, as in the upper-class railway carriages in India during British rule, which were always desegregated so that the Indian prince, no matter how dark, could drink gin and tonic with the English colonist, and the second- and third-class carriages, which were often segregated so that the Irish subaltern could always be kept at arm's length from the Indian sepoy, cootie, or pilgrim.

Once you position or foreground a particular circumstance of victimhood, it enables a scotoma, an inability to see oneself as anything other than a victim, and this, if anything, propels and unleashes the greatest violence. And so it is that the United States can disperse depleted uranium in faraway lands because Americans have been persuaded that 9/11, a tragedy for the whole world like any tragedy (be it the violence in Kashmir, or Afghanistan, or Palestine, or Rwanda, or Vietnam), comes to be seen as the special, particular tragedy of the American people and thereby the launching pad for the exclusive claim to the righteous use of force on their behalf by the U.S. government.

It is only when we examine identities as fields of intersection and therefore always of contestation that we can imagine possibilities other than the binaries of "Are you with the besieged dictator or are you with the invading army?" It is possible to be neither. Or in the case of another example, "Are you critical of patriarchy within the African American community and of racism in the United States?" or "Can you be critical of patriarchy in the minority Muslim community in India and be critical at the same time of the anti-Muslim prejudices of Hindu fundamentalists?" It is possible to be both. And can you break your silences about being neither, in the first instance, and about being both in the latter two instances? Or will you choose to voice one opposition and be silent about another because of fears of betrayal, of letting who you are in one sense be held against who you are in another? Being neither in the first instance and being both in the second are concomitant to our admitting to our identities as force fields of different kinds of motivations, of different and sometimes conflicting intersections, of varied yet interlinked trajectories and histories of power and powerlessness.

Kimberle Williams Crenshaw puts this quite succinctly in her essay "Mapping the Margins: Intersectionality, Identity Politics, and Violence against Women of Color" (1991) when she says, and I quote:

> Among the most troubling political consequences of the failure of antiracist and feminist discourses to address the intersections of racism and patriarchy is the fact that, to the extent they forward the interest of people of color and "women," respectively, one analysis often implicitly denies the validity of the other. The failure of feminism to interrogate race means that the resistance strategies of feminism will often replicate and reinforce the subordination of people of color, and the failure of antiracism to interrogate patriarchy means that antiracism will frequently reproduce the subordination of women. These mutual elisions present a particularly difficult political dilemma for women of color. Adopting either analysis constitutes a denial of a fundamental dimension of our subordination and works to preclude the development of a political discourse that more fully empowers women of color.

A call center worker in a suburb of Delhi, the city where I live, performs a Californian accent as she pursues a loan defaulter in a poor Los Angeles neighborhood on the telephone. She threatens and cajoles him. She scares him, gets underneath his skin, because she is scared that he won't agree to pay and that this will translate as a cut in her salary. Latitudes away from him, she has a window open on her computer telling her about the weather in his backyard, his credit history, his employment record, his prison record. Her skin is darker than his, but her voice is trained to be whiter on the phone. Her night is his day. She is a remote agent with a talent for impersonation in the information-technology-enabled industry in India. She never gets paid extra for the long hours she puts in. He was laid off a few months ago and hasn't been able to sort himself out, which is why she is calling him on behalf of the company she works for. He lives in a third-world neighborhood in a first-world city; she works in a free trade zone in a third-world country. The army of the government that rules him is busy with shock and awe; the army of the government that rules her is always prepared to go to war on her behalf. She wants a green card; he wants credit. They both want out. Neither knows the other as anything other than as case and agent. The conversation between them is a denial of their realities and an assertion of many identities, each with their truths, all at once.

Identities are minefields, and the mines have been lain by armies that have forgotten the map. The arsenal is familiar; it's just that we don't know which mine (as in "weapon" and as in "first-person possessive singular personal pronoun") will claim which part of me. I negotiate them at my peril, never very sure about what I am stepping on and which aspect of my beings will blow up in my face. . . .

An understanding of the networked nature of the contemporary world and of the history of this world will help us understand that there are crosscutting histories of oppression and violence, that no one is innocent, and that all of us are implicated somewhere in our histories or in the histories of our ancestors as victims and as aggressors. If you take, for instance, the Middle East, it is easy to blame the current mess on the shortsighted policies of European colonialism. While the latter dynamic is to a large extent totally true, European colonialism in the Middle East has a comparatively recent history. We forget, for instance, that it was immediately preceded by the no less lethal achievement of the Islamic Ottoman Empire, which, right up to the closing of the first decade of the twentieth century, underlay by its many vexations the further complexities that the enterprise of competing European colonialisms was due to unleash. A vulgar Eurocentric view of history would not even recognize the Ottoman project or the Islamicate achievement as worthy of consideration and would mistakenly consider itself (Europe) to be the harbinger of "civilization and urbanity" in the Arab and Islamic world. But a counter-Eurocentric or even a specifically Turkic Islamist project, one that seeks to invert Eurocentrism, would no doubt either neglect to mention that a non-European power had a pretty lethal record of colonialism, even in fairly recent times, or romanticize the Ottoman achievement in terms of its tolerance, its catholicity, and so on—all of which, of course, have some basis in truth.

The understanding of the dynamics of power versus powerlessness, however, lies in taking account of both the interweaving of the histories of the Ottoman and European enterprises and their many internal contradictions. Consequently, looking for this interwovenness as well as acknowledging the gaps—those spaces of incommensurability that make it difficult to speak in binaries of Ottoman versus European, or black versus white—is a project of vastly different epistemological challenges to the projects that dominate the current scene and tend to oversimplify these histories. Just as parallel lines meet and intersect when one moves from Euclidean two-dimensional geometry to non-Euclidean three-dimensional geometry, so too an entirely different vision of the same realities becomes contingent on how one chooses to see. . . .

Acknowledgments

This text is revised from a talk given at a conference on "Identities and Intersectional Feminism" organized by the Center for Ideas and Society at the University of California, Riverside, April 26, 2003. I would like to acknowledge the debt I owe to the ongoing conversation with Monica Narula and Jeebesh Bagchi, my colleagues in the Raqs Media Collective and at the Sarai Programme, Centre for the Study of Developing Societies, Delhi, for many of the ideas in this text.

DISCUSSION QUESTIONS

1. Explain how identity can be used as a shield.
2. How are identities fields of intersection?
3. What impact did British colonialism have on Indian identity?

NOTE

1. Convicted fraudster here refers to Ahmed Husain Chalabi. Chalabi, an Iraqi politician, belongs to the Shia community and is associated with the Iraqi National Congress (INC). One of the key figures to emerge in the political scenario of post-Saddam Hussein Iraq, Chalabi was a favorite of his Pentagon backers and occupied a prominent position in the new Iraqi regime. He fell from grace in August 2004 when corruption charges against him resurfaced but was reinducted into the interim Iraqi authority as a deputy prime minister in April 2005. In 1992 he was sentenced in absentia by a Jordanian court to twenty-two years in prison with hard labor for bank fraud after the 1990 collapse of Petra Bank, which he had founded in 1977. Although he has always maintained that the case was a plot to frame him by Baghdad, the issue was revisited later when the State Department raised questions about the INC's accounting practices.

REFERENCES

Crenshaw, Kimberle Williams. 1991. "Mapping the Margins: Intersectionality, Identity Politics, and Violence against Women of Color." http://www.hsph.harvard.edu/Organizations/healthnet/WoC/feminisms/crenshaw.html.

LAW, PUBLIC POLICY, AND ECONOMY

READING 49

Thirteen Key Supreme Court Cases and the Civil War Amendments

Individuals' lives are affected not only by social practices but also by law as interpreted in the courts. Under U.S. federalism Congress makes laws, the president swears to uphold the law, and the Supreme Court interprets the law. When state laws appear to be in conflict with the United States Constitution or when the terminology of the Constitution is vague, the Supreme Court interprets such laws. We will focus here on Supreme Court rulings that have defined the roles individuals are allowed to assume in American society.

As the supreme law above laws enacted by Congress, the U.S. Constitution determines individual and group status. A brief document, the Constitution describes the division of power between the federal and state governments, as well as the rights of individuals. Only 16 amendments to the Constitution have been added since the ratification of the Bill of Rights (the first 10 amendments). Although the Constitution appears to be sweeping in scope—relying on the principle that all men are created equal—in reality the Constitution is an exclusionary document. It omitted women, Native Americans, and African Americans except for the purpose of determining a population count. In instances where the Constitution was vague on the rights of each of these groups, clarification was later sought through court cases.

Federalism provides four primary methods by which citizens may influence the political process. First, the Constitution grants citizens the right to petition the government, that is, the right to lobby. Second, as a civic duty, citizens are expected to vote and seek office. Once in office citizens can change conditions by writing new legislation, known as *statutory law*. Third, changes can be achieved through the lengthy procedure of passing constitutional amendments, which affect all citizens.

Controversial amendments have often become law after social movement activists advocated passage for several years or after a major national upheaval, such as the Civil War.

Last, the Constitution provides that citizens can sue to settle disputes. Through this method, sweeping social changes can take place when Supreme Court decisions affect all the individuals in a class. Thus, the assertion of individual rights has become a key tool of those who were not privileged by the Constitution to clarify their status in American society.

An examination of landmark cases reveals the continuous difficulties some groups have had in securing their rights through legal remedy. The Court has often taken a narrow perspective on what classes of people were to receive equal protection of the law, or were covered under the privileges and immunities clause.[1] Each group had to bring suit in every area where barriers existed. For example, white women who were citizens had to sue to establish that they had the right to inherit property, to serve on juries, to enter various professions, and in general to be treated as a class apart from their husband and family. Blacks sued to attend southern state universities and law schools, to participate in the all-white Democratic Party primary election,[2] to attend public schools which had been ordered to desegregate by the Supreme Court, and to vote without having to pay a poll tax. When these landmark cases were decided, they were perceived to herald sweeping changes in policy. Yet they proved to be only a guide to determining the rights of individuals.

I. *DRED SCOTT V. SANFORD* (1857)

Prior to the Civil War the Constitution was not precise on whether one was simultaneously a citizen of a given state and of the entire United States. Slavery further complicated the matter because the status of slaves and free persons of color was not specified in the Constitution, nor were members of either group considered citizens. Each state had the option of determining the status and rights of these nonwhites.

A federal form of government permitted flexibility by allowing states to differ on matters such as rights for its citizens. Yet as a newly invented form of government, a number of issues that were clear under British law were not settled until the Thirteenth, Fourteenth, and Fifteenth Amendments were added to the United States Constitution. Federalism raised questions about rights and privileges because a citizen was simultaneously living under the laws of a state and of the United States. Who had rights and privileges guaranteed by the Constitution? Did all citizens have all rights and privileges?

For example, what was the status of women? The Constitution provided for citizenship, but did not specify which rights and privileges were granted to female citizens. State laws considered white men and white women citizens, yet white women were often not allowed to own property, sue in court, or vote. Under federalism, each state enacted laws determining the rights and status of free blacks, slaves, white men, and white women so long as the laws did not conflict with the United States Constitution.

The *Dred Scott* case of 1846 considered the issues of slavery, property, citizenship, and the supremacy of the United States over individual states when a slave was taken to a free territory. The Court's holding primarily affected blacks, now called African Americans,[3] who sought the benefits of citizenship. Broadly, the case addressed American citizenship, a matter not clearly defined until passage of the Fourteenth Amendment in 1868.

Dred Scott was an enslaved man owned by Dr. John Emerson, a U.S. Army surgeon stationed in Missouri. When Emerson was transferred to Rock Island, Illinois, where slavery was forbidden, he took Dred Scott with him. Emerson was subsequently transferred to Fort Snelling, a territory (now Minnesota) where slavery was forbidden by the Missouri Compromise of 1820. In 1838, he returned to Missouri with Dred Scott.

In 1846 Scott brought suit in a Missouri circuit court to obtain his freedom on the grounds he had resided in free territory for periods of time. Scott won the case and his freedom. However, the judgment was reversed by the Missouri Supreme Court.

Later, when John Sanford, a citizen of New York and the brother of Mrs. Emerson, arranged for the sale of Scott, the grounds were established for Scott to take his case to the federal circuit court in Missouri. The federal court ruled that Scott and his family were slaves and therefore the "lawful property" of Sanford. With the financial assistance of abolitionists, Scott appealed his case to the Supreme Court.

The Court's decision addressed these key questions:

1. Are blacks citizens?
2. Are blacks entitled to sue in court?
3. Can one have all the privileges and immunities of citizenship in a state, but not the United States?
4. Can one be a citizen of the United States and not be qualified to vote or hold office?

Excerpts from the Supreme Court Decision in *Dred Scott v. Sanford*[4]

Mr. Chief Justice Taney delivered the opinion of the Court:

. . . The question is simply this: Can a Negro, whose ancestors were imported into this country and sold as slaves, become a member of the political community formed and brought into existence by the Constitution of the United States, and as such become entitled to all the rights, and privileges and immunities, guaranteed by that instrument to the citizen? One of which rights is the privilege of suing in a court of the United States. . . .

The question before us is whether the class of persons described are constituent members of this sovereignty? We think they are not, and that they are not included, and were not intended to be included, under the word "citizens" in the Constitution, and can therefore claim none of the rights and privileges which that instrument provides for and secures to citizens of the United States.

In discussing this question, we must not confound the rights of citizenship which a State may confer within its own limits and the rights of citizenship as a member of the Union. It does not by any means follow, because he has all the rights and privileges of a citizen of a State, that he must be a citizen of the United States. He may have all of the rights and privileges of a citizen of a State, and yet not be entitled to the rights and privileges of a citizen in any other State. . . .

Undoubtedly a person may be a citizen . . . although he exercises no share of the political power, and is incapacitated from holding particular office. Those who have not the necessary qualifications cannot vote or hold the office, yet they are citizens.

The court is of the opinion, that . . . Dred Scott was not a citizen of Missouri within the meaning of the Constitution of the United States, and not entitled as such to sue in its courts: and, consequently, that the Circuit Court had no jurisdiction. . . .

II. THE CIVIL WAR AMENDMENTS

The Civil War (1861–1865) was fought over slavery, as well as the issue of supremacy of the national government over the individual states.

After the Civil War, members of Congress known as the Radical Republicans sought to protect the freedom of the former slaves by passing the Thirteenth, Fourteenth, and Fifteenth Amendments. These amendments, especially the Fourteenth, have provided the foundation for African Americans, as well as women, gays, Native Americans, immigrants, and those who are disabled to bring suit for equal treatment under the law.

Amendment XIII, 1865

(Slavery)

This amendment prohibited slavery and involuntary servitude in the United States. The entire amendment follows:

Section 1. Neither slavery nor involuntary servitude, except as a punishment whereof the party shall have been duly convicted, shall exist within the United States, or any place subject to their jurisdiction.

Section 2. Congress shall have power to enforce this article by appropriate legislation.

Amendment XIV, 1868

(Citizenship, Due Process, and Equal Protection of the Laws)

This amendment defined citizenship; prohibited the states from making or enforcing laws that abridged

the privileges or immunities of citizenship; forbade states to deprive persons of life, liberty, or property without due process of law; and forbade states to deny equal protection of the law to any person. Over time the Fourteenth Amendment became the most important of the Reconstruction amendments. Key phrases such as "privileges and immunities," "deprive any person of life, liberty, or the pursuit of justice," and "deny to any person within its jurisdiction equal protection of the law" have caused this amendment to be the subject of more Supreme Court cases than any other provision of the Constitution. The entire amendment follows:

Section 1. All persons born or naturalized in the United States, and subject to the jurisdiction thereof, are citizens of the United States and of the State wherein they reside. No State shall make or enforce any law which shall abridge the privileges or immunities of citizens of the United States; nor shall any State deprive any person of life, liberty, or property, without due process of law; nor deny to any person within its jurisdiction the equal protection of the laws.

Section 2. Representatives shall be apportioned among the several States according to their respective numbers, counting the whole number of persons in each State, excluding Indians not taxed. But when the right to vote at any election for the choice of electors for President and Vice President of the United States, Representatives in Congress, the Executive and Judicial officers of a State, or the members of the Legislature thereof, is denied to any of the male inhabitants of such State, being twenty-one years of age, and citizens of the United States, or in any way abridged, except for participation in rebellion, or other crime, the basis of representation therein shall be reduced in proportion which the number of such male citizens shall bear to the whole number of male citizens twenty-one years of age in such State.

Section 3. No person shall be a Senator or Representative in Congress, or elector or President and Vice President, or hold any office, civil or military, under the United States, or under any State, who, having previously taken an oath, as a member of Congress, or as an officer of the United States, or as a member of any State legislature, or as an executive or judicial officer of any State, to support the Constitution of the United States, shall have engaged in insurrection or rebellion against the same, or given aid or comfort to the enemies thereof. But Congress may by a vote of two-thirds of each House, remove such disability.

Section 4. The validity of the public debt of the United States, authorized by law, including debts incurred for payments of pensions and bounties for services in suppressing insurrection or rebellion, shall not be questioned. But neither the United States nor any State shall assume or pay any debt or obligation incurred in aid of insurrection or rebellion against the United States, or any claim for the loss or emancipation of any slave, but all such debts, obligations and claims shall be held illegal and void.

Section 5. The Congress shall have power to enforce, by appropriate legislation, the provisions of this article.

Amendment XV, 1870
(The Right to Vote)

The entire amendment follows:

Section 1. The right of citizens of the United States to vote shall not be denied or abridged by the United States or by any State on account of race, color, or previous condition of servitude.

Section 2. The Congress shall have power to enforce this article by appropriate legislation.

As we have seen, the Thirteenth, Fourteenth, and Fifteenth Amendments were added to the Constitution expressly with former slaves in mind. In Section 1 of the Fourteenth Amendment, the definition of *citizenship* was clarified and granted to blacks. In the Fifteenth Amendment black males, former slaves, were granted the right to vote. For women, however, the situation was different.

During the 19th century there was no doubt that white females were U.S. citizens, but their rights as citizens were unclear. For example, although they were citizens, women were not automatically enfranchised. Depending on state laws, they were barred from owning property, holding office, or voting. The 1872 case of *Bradwell v. The State of Illinois* specifically tested whether women as United States citizens had the right to become members of the bar. More generally, it addressed whether the rights of female citizens included the right to pursue any employment.

III. *MINOR V. HAPPERSETT* (1875)

The Fifteenth Amendment was not viewed as a triumph for women because it specifically denied them the vote. Section 2 of the Fourteenth Amendment for the first time made reference to males as citizens. Since black men were included but women of all races were omitted, women were left to continue to seek changes through the courts. This was a difficult route because in subsequent cases, judges often held a narrow view that the legislators wrote the amendment only with black males in mind. Thus, a pattern was soon established in which white women followed black men and women in asserting their rights as citizens as seen in the 1875 case of *Minor v. Happersett*. In *Dred Scott* the question was whether Scott was a citizen; in *Minor* the question was whether *Minor* as a citizen had the right to vote. In both cases the Supreme Court said no.

Virginia Minor, a native-born, free, white citizen of the United States and the state of Missouri, and over the age of 21 wished to vote for president, vice president, and members of Congress in the election of November 1872. She applied to the registrar of voters but was not allowed to vote because she was not a "male citizen of the United States." As a citizen of the United States, Minor sued under the privileges and immunities clause of the Fourteenth Amendment.

The Court's decision addressed these key questions:

1. Who is covered under the term *citizen*?
2. Is suffrage one of the privileges and immunities of citizenship?
3. Did the Constitution, as originally written, make all citizens voters?
4. Did the Fifteenth Amendment make all citizens voters?
5. Can a state confine voting to only male citizens without violating the Constitution?

While women were citizens of the United States and the state where they resided, they did not automatically possess all the privileges granted to male citizens, such as suffrage. This landmark case was not overturned until the passage of the Nineteenth Amendment, which enfranchised women, in 1920.[5]

Excerpts from the Supreme Court Decision in *Minor v. Happersett*[6]

Mr. Chief Justice Waite delivered the opinion of the Court:

. . . It is contended [by Minor's counsel] that the provisions of the Constitution and laws of the State of Missouri which confine the right of suffrage and registration therefore to men, are in violation of the Constitution of the United States, and therefore void. The argument is, that as a woman, born or naturalized in the United States is a citizen of the United States and of the State in which she resides, she has the right of suffrage as one of the privileges and immunities of her citizenship, which the State cannot by its laws or Constitution abridge.

There is no doubt that women may be citizens. . . .

. . . From this it is apparent that from the commencement of the legislation upon this subject alien women and alien minors could be made citizens by naturalization, and we think it will not be contended that native women and native minors were already citizens by birth.

. . . More cannot be necessary to establish the fact that sex has never been made one of the elements of citizenship in the United States. In this respect men have never had an advantage over women. The same laws precisely apply to both. The Fourteenth amendment did not affect the citizenship of women any more than it did of men . . . therefore, the rights of Mrs. Minor do not depend upon the amendment. She has always been a citizen from her birth, and entitled to all the privileges and immunities of citizenship. The amendment prohibited the State, of which she is a citizen, from abridging any of her privileges and immunities as a citizen of the United States.

. . . The direct question is, therefore, presented whether all citizens are necessarily voters.

The Constitution does not define the privileges and immunities of citizens. For that definition we must look elsewhere.

. . . The [Fourteenth] amendment did not add to the privileges and immunities of a citizen. It simply furnished an additional guarantee for the protection of such as he already had. No new voters were necessarily made by it.

. . . No new State has ever been admitted to the Union which has conferred the right of suffrage upon women, and this has never been considered a valid objection to her admission.

. . . Certainly, if the courts can consider any question settled, this is one. For nearly ninety years the people have acted upon the idea that the Constitution, when it conferred citizenship, did not necessarily confer the right of suffrage. . . . Our province is to decide what the law is, not to declare what it should be.

The *Dred Scott, Bradwell,* and *Minor* cases point to the similarity in the status of black men and women of all races in 19th-century America. As one judicial scholar noted, race and sex were comparable classes, distinct from all others. Historically, these "natural classes" were considered permanent and unchangeable.[7] Thus, both slavery and the subjugation of women have been described as a caste system where one's status is fixed from birth and not alterable based on wealth or talent.[8]

Indeed, the connection between the enslavement of black people and the legal and social standing of women was often traced to the Old Testament. Historically slavery was justified on the grounds that one should look to Abraham; the Bible refers to Abraham's wives, children, men servants, maid servants, camels, and cattle as his property. A man's wife and children were considered his slaves. By the logic of the 19th century, if women were slaves, why shouldn't blacks be also?

Thus, the concepts of race and sex have been historically linked. Since "the doctrines were developed by the same people for the same purpose it is not surprising to find anti-feminism to be an echo of racism, and vice versa."[9]

Additional constitutional amendments were necessary for women and African Americans to exercise the privileges of citizenship that were automatically granted to white males. Nonetheless, even after amendments were enacted, African Americans still had to fight for enforcement of the law.

IV. *PLESSY V. FERGUSON* (1896)

After the Civil War the northern victors imposed military rule on the South.[10] White landowners and former slaveholders often found themselves with unproductive farmland and no free laborers. Aside from the economic loss of power, white males were in a totally new political environment: Black men had been elevated to citizens; former slaves were now eligible to vote, run for office, and hold seats in the state or national legislature. To ensure the rights of former slaves, the U.S. Congress passed the Civil War Amendments and provided federal troops to oversee federal elections.

However, when federal troops were withdrawn from the southern states in 1877, enfranchised black men became vulnerable to former masters who immediately seized political control of the state legislatures. In order to solidify political power, whites rewrote state constitutions to disenfranchise black men. To ensure that all blacks were restricted to a subordinate status, southern states systematically enacted "Jim Crow" laws, rigidly segregating society into black and white communities. These laws barred blacks from using the same public facilities as whites, including schools, hospitals, restaurants, hotels, and recreation areas. With the cooperation of southern elected officials, the Ku Klux Klan, a white supremacist, terrorist organization, grew in membership. The return of political power to whites without any federal presence to protect the black community set the stage for "separate but equal" legislation to become a constitutionally valid racial doctrine.

Under slavery, interracial sexual contact was forbidden but white masters nonetheless had the power to sexually exploit the black women who worked for them. The children of these relationships, especially if they looked white, posed potential inheritance problems because whites feared that such children might seek to exercise the privileges accorded to their white fathers. In order to keep all children of such relationships subordinate in the two-tiered racial system, descent was based on the race of the mother. Consequently, regardless of color, all the children of black women were defined as black.

This resulted in a rigid biracial structure where all persons with "one drop" of black blood were labeled black. Consequently, the "black" community consisted of a wide range of skin color based on this one-drop rule. Therefore, at times individuals with known black ancestry might look phenotypically white. This situation created a group of African Americans who had one-eighth or less African ancestry.

Louisiana was one of the few states to modify the one-drop rule of racial categorization because it considered mulattoes a valid racial category. A term derived from Spanish, *mulatto* refers to the offspring of a "pure African Negro" and a "pure white." Over time, *mulatto* came to encompass children of whites and "mixed Negroes."

These were the social conditions in 1896, when Homer Adolph Plessy, a mulatto, sought to test Louisiana laws that imposed racial segregation. Plessy and other mulattoes decided to test the applicability of the law requiring racial separation on railroad cars traveling in interstate transportation.

In 1890, Louisiana had followed other southern states in enacting Jim Crow laws that were written in compliance with the Equal Protection Clause of Section 1 of the Fourteenth Amendment. These laws required separate accommodations for white and black railroad passengers. In this case, Plessy, a U.S. citizen and a resident of Louisiana who was one-eighth black, paid for a first-class ticket on the East Louisiana Railway traveling from New Orleans to Covington, Louisiana. When he entered the passenger train, Plessy took a vacant seat in a coach designated for white passengers. He claimed that he was entitled to every "recognition, right, privilege, and immunity" granted to white citizens of the United States by the Constitution. Under Louisiana law, the conductor, who knew Plessy, was required to ask him to sit in a coach specifically assigned to nonwhite persons. By law, passengers who sat in the inappropriate coach were fined or imprisoned. When Plessy refused to comply with the order, he was removed from the train and imprisoned.

Plessy v. Ferguson is the one case that solidified the power of whites over blacks in southern states. Through state laws, and with the additional federal weight in the *Plessy* decision, whites began to enforce rigid separation of the races in every aspect of life.

In *Plessy*, Justice John Marshall Harlan wrote the only dissenting opinion. Usually in Supreme Court cases, attention is focused on the majority, rather than the dissenting opinion. However, in this case Justice Harlan's dissent is noteworthy because his views on race and citizenship pointed out a line of reasoning that eventually broke down segregation and second-class citizenship for blacks.

Justice Harlan's background as a Kentucky slaveholder who later joined the Union side during the Civil War is cited as an explanation of his views. Some scholars speculate that his shift from slaveholder to a defender of the rights of blacks was caused by his observation of beatings, lynchings, and the use of intimidation tactics against blacks in Kentucky after the Civil War. In a quirk of history, when *Plessy v. Ferguson* was overturned in 1954 by a unanimous opinion in *Brown v. Board of Education,* Justice Harlan's grandson was a member of the Supreme Court.

The Court's decision addressed these key questions:

1. How is a black person defined?
2. Who determines when an individual is black or white?
3. Does providing separate but equal facilities violate the Thirteenth Amendment?
4. Does providing separate but equal facilities violate the Fourteenth Amendment?
5. Does a separate but equal doctrine imply inferiority of either race?
6. Can state laws require the separation of the two races in schools, theaters, and railway cars?
7. Does the separation of the races when applied to commerce within the state of Louisiana abridge the privileges and immunities of the "colored man,"[11] deprive him of equal protection of the law, or deprive him of his property without due process of law under the Fourteenth Amendment?

Excerpts from the Supreme Court Decision in *Plessy v. Ferguson*[12]

Mr. Justice Brown delivered the opinion of the Court:

> . . . An [1890] act of the General Assembly of the State of Louisiana, provid[ed] for separate railway carriages for the white and colored races.

. . . No person or persons, shall be admitted to occupy seats in coaches, other than the ones assigned to them on account of the race they belong to.

. . . The constitutionality of this act is attacked upon the ground that it conflicts both with the Thirteenth Amendment of the Constitution, abolishing slavery, and the Fourteenth Amendment, which prohibits certain restrictive legislation.

. . . A statute which implied merely a legal distinction between the white and colored races . . . has no tendency to destroy the legal equality of the two races, or reestablish a state of servitude.

. . . The object of the amendment [the Fourteenth Amendment] was undoubtedly to enforce the absolute equality of the two races before the law, but in the nature of things it could not have been intended to abolish distinctions based upon color, or a commingling of the two races upon terms unsatisfactory to either.

Laws permitting and even requiring their separation in places where they are liable to be brought into contact do not necessarily imply the inferiority of either race to the other, and have been generally, if not universally recognized as within the competency of the state legislatures in the exercise of their police power. The most common instance of this is connected with the establishment of separate schools for white and colored children, which has been held to be a valid exercise of the legislative power even by courts of States where the political rights of the colored race have been longest and most earnestly enforced. One of the earliest of these cases is that of *Roberts v. City of Boston*, 5 Cush. 198, in which the Supreme Judicial Court of Massachusetts held that the general school committee of Boston had power to make provision for the instruction of colored children in separate schools established exclusively for them, and to prohibit their attendance upon the other schools.

. . . We are not prepared to say that the conductor, in assigning passengers to the coaches according to their race, does not act at his peril. . . . The power to assign to a particular coach obviously implies the power to determine to which race the passenger belongs, as well as the power to determine who, under the laws of the particular State, is to be deemed a white, and who is a colored person.

. . . We consider the underlying fallacy of the plaintiff's argument to consist in the assumption that the enforced separation of the two races stamps the colored race with a badge of inferiority. If this be so, it is not by reason of anything found in the act, but solely because the colored race chooses to put that construction upon it. . . . The argument also assumes that social prejudices may be overcome by legislation, and that equal rights cannot be secured to the negro except by an enforced commingling of the two races. We cannot accept this proposition. If the two races are to meet upon terms of social equality, it must be the result of natural affinities, a mutual appreciation of each other's merits and a voluntary consent of individuals.

. . . If the civil and political rights of both races be equal one cannot be inferior to the other civilly or politically. If one race be inferior to the other socially, the Constitution of the United States cannot put them upon the same plane.

It is true that the question for the proportion of colored blood necessary to constitute a colored person, as distinguished from a white person, is one upon which there is a difference of opinion in the different States, some holding that any visible admixture of black blood stamps the persons as belonging to the colored races, others that it depends upon the preponderance of blood . . . still others that the predominance of white blood must only be in the proportion of three fourths. . . . But these are questions to be determined under the laws of each State. . . .

Mr. Justice Harlan in the dissenting opinion:

. . . It was said in argument that the statute of Louisiana does not discriminate against either race, but prescribes a rule applicable alike to white and colored citizens. . . . [But] everyone knows that the statute in question had its origin in the purpose, not so much to exclude white persons from railroad cars occupied by blacks, as to exclude colored people from coaches occupied by or assigned to white persons.

. . . It is one thing for railroad carriers to furnish, or to be required by law to furnish, equal accommodations for all whom they are under a legal duty to carry. It is quite another thing for government to forbid citizens of the white and black races from traveling in the same public conveyance, and to punish officers of railroad companies for permitting persons of the two races to occupy the same passenger coach. If a State can prescribe, as a rule of civil conduct, that whites and blacks shall not travel as passengers in the same railroad coach, why may it not so regulate the use of the streets of its cities and towns as to compel white citizens to keep on one side of a street and black citizens to keep on the other? Why may it not, upon like grounds, punish whites and blacks who ride together in street cars or in open vehicles on a public road or street? Why may it not require sheriffs to assign whites to one side of a court-room and blacks to the other? And why may it not also prohibit the commingling of the two races in the galleries of legislative halls or in public assemblages convened for the consideration of the political questions of the day? Further, if this statute of Louisiana is consistent with the personal liberty of citizens, why may not the State require the separation in railroad coaches of native and naturalized citizens of the United States, or of Protestants and Roman Catholics?

. . . In my opinion, the judgment this day rendered will, in time, prove to be quite pernicious as the decision made by this tribunal in the Dred Scott case.

. . . The thin disguise of "equal" accommodations for passengers in railroad coaches will not mislead anyone, nor atone for the wrong this day done.

Thus, the *Plessy v. Ferguson* decision firmly established the separate but equal doctrine in the South until the National Association for the Advancement of Colored Persons (NAACP) began to systematically attack Jim Crow laws. It is ironic that in *Plessy* the systematic social, political, and economic suppression of blacks in the South through Jim Crow laws was justified in terms of a case decided in the northern city of Boston, where the segregation of schools occurred in practice (*de facto*), but not by force of law (*de jure*). In that 1849 case (*Roberts v. City of Boston*, 5 Cush. 198), a parent had unsuccessfully sued on behalf of his daughter to attend a public school. Thus, educational access became both the first and last chapter—in the 1954 case of *Brown v. Board of Education*—of the doctrine of separate but equal.

V. BROWN V. BOARD OF EDUCATION (1954)

Unlike many of the earlier cases brought by individual women, blacks, or Native Americans, *Brown v. Board of Education* was the result of a concerted campaign against racial segregation led by Howard University School of Law graduates and the NAACP. In the 1930s, the NAACP Legal Defense Fund began to systematically fight for fair employment, fair housing, and desegregation of public education. Key lawyers in the campaign against segregation were Charles Houston, Thurgood Marshall, James Nabrit, and William Hastie. Marshall later became a Supreme Court justice, Nabrit became president of Howard University, and Hastie became a federal judge.

By using the Fourteenth Amendment, *Brown* became the key case in an attempt to topple the 1896 separate but equal doctrine. Legal strategists knew that educational opportunity and better housing conditions were essential if black Americans were to achieve upward mobility. While one group of lawyers focused on restrictive covenant cases,[13] which prevented blacks from buying housing in white neighborhoods, another spearheaded the drive for blacks to enter state-run professional schools.

In 1954, suits were brought in Kansas, South Carolina, Virginia, and Delaware on behalf of black Americans seeking to attend nonsegregated public schools. However, the case is commonly referred to as *Brown v. Board of Education*. The plaintiffs in the suit contended that segregation in the public schools denied them equal protection of the laws under the Fourteenth Amendment. The contention was that since segregated public schools were not and could not be made equal, black American children were deprived of equal protection of the laws.

The Court's unanimous decision addressed these key questions:

1. Are public schools segregated by race detrimental to black children?
2. Does segregation result in an inferior education for black children?
3. Does the maintenance of segregated public schools violate the Equal Protection Clause of the Fourteenth Amendment?
4. Is the maintenance of segregated public school facilities *inherently* unequal?
5. What was the intent of the framers of the Fourteenth Amendment regarding distinctions between whites and blacks?
6. Is the holding in *Plessy v. Ferguson* applicable to public education?
7. Does segregation of children in public schools *solely on the basis of race,* even though the physical facilities and other "tangible" factors may be equal, deprive the children of the minority group of equal educational opportunities?

Excerpts from the Supreme Court Decision in *Brown v. Board of Education*[14]

Mr. Chief Justice Warren delivered the opinion of the Court:

. . . In each of these cases [NAACP suits in Kansas, South Carolina, Virginia, and Delaware] minors of the Negro race, through their legal representatives, seek the aid of the courts in obtaining admission to the public schools of their community on a non-segregated basis. . . . This segregation was alleged to deprive the plaintiffs of the equal protection of the laws under the Fourteenth Amendment. In each of the cases other than the Delaware case, a three-judge federal district court denied relief to the plaintiffs on the so-called "separate but equal" doctrine announced by this Court in *Plessy v. Ferguson,* 163 U.S. 537. Under that doctrine, equality of treatment is accorded when the races are provided substantially equal facilities, even though these facilities be separated. . . .

The plaintiffs contend that segregated schools are not "equal" and cannot be made "equal," and that hence they are deprived of the equal protection of the laws.

. . . The most avid proponents of the post–[Civil] War amendments undoubtedly intended them to remove all legal distinctions among "all persons born or naturalized in the United States."

In the first cases in this Court construing the Fourteenth Amendment, decided shortly after its adoption, the Court interpreted it as prescribing all state imposed discriminations against the Negro race. The doctrine of "separate but equal" did not make its appearance in this Court until 1896 in the *Plessy v. Ferguson, supra,* involving not education but transportation.

In these days, it is doubtful that any child may reasonably be expected to succeed in life if he is denied the opportunity of an education. Such an opportunity where the state has undertaken to provide it, is a right which must be made available to all on equal terms.

We come then to the question presented: Does segregation of children in public schools solely on the basis of race, even though the physical facilities and other "tangible" factors may be equal, deprive the children of the minority group of equal educational opportunities? We believe that it does.

To separate them [the children] from others of similar age and qualifications solely because of their race generates a feeling of inferiority as to their status in the community that may affect their hearts and minds in a way unlikely ever to be undone.

We conclude that in the field of public education the doctrine of "separate but equal" has no place. Separate educational facilities are inherently unequal. Therefore, we hold that the plaintiffs and others similarly situated for whom the actions have been brought are, by reason of the segregation complained of, deprived of the equal protection of the laws guaranteed by the Fourteenth Amendment.

. . . We have now announced that such segregation is a denial of the equal protection of the laws.

VI. *YICK WO V. HOPKINS* (1886)

In the 1880s, the questions of citizenship and the rights of citizens were raised again by Native Americans and Asian immigrants. While the status of citizenship for African Americans was settled by the Thirteenth and Fourteenth Amendments, the extent of the privileges and immunities clause still needed clarification. Yick Wo, a Chinese immigrant living in San Francisco, brought suit under the Fourteenth Amendment to see if it covered all persons in the territorial United States regardless of race, color, or nationality.

The Chinese were different from European immigrants because they came to the United States under contract to work as laborers building the transcontinental railroad. When Chinese workers remained, primarily in California, after the completion of the railroad in 1869, Congress became anxious about this "foreign element" that was non-Christian and non-European. Chinese immigrants were seen as an economic threat because they would work for less than white males. To address the issue of economic competition, the Chinese Exclusion Act was passed in 1882 to prohibit further immigration to the United States. This gave the Chinese the unique status among immigrants of being the only group barred from entry into the United States and barred from becoming naturalized U.S. citizens.

Yick Wo, a subject of the Emperor of China, went to San Francisco in 1861, where he operated a laundry at the same premise for 22 years with consent from the Board of Fire Wardens. When the consent decree expired on October 1, 1885, Yick Wo routinely reapplied to continue to operate a laundry. He was, however, denied a license. Of the over 300 laundries in the city and county of San Francisco, about 240 were owned by Chinese immigrants. Most of these laundries were wooden, the most common construction material used at that time, although it posed a fire hazard. Yick Wo and more than 150 of his countrymen were arrested and charged with carrying on business without having special consent, while those who were not subjects of China and were operating some 80 laundries under similar conditions, were allowed to conduct business.

Yick Wo stated that he and 200 of his countrymen with similar situations petitioned the Board of Supervisors for permission to continue to conduct business in the same buildings they had occupied for more than 20 years. The petitions of all the Chinese were denied, while all petitions of those who were not Chinese were granted (with one exception).

Did this prohibition of the occupation and destruction of the business and property of the Chinese laundrymen in San Francisco constitute the proper regulation of business, or was it discrimination and a violation of important rights secured by the Fourteenth Amendment?

The Court's decision addressed these key questions:

1. Does this municipal ordinance regulating public laundries within the municipality of San Francisco violate the United States Constitution?
2. Does carrying out this municipal ordinance violate the Fourteenth Amendment?
3. Does the guarantee of protection of the Fourteenth Amendment extend to all persons

within the territorial jurisdiction of the United States regardless of race, color, or nationality?

4. Are the subjects of the Emperor of China who, temporarily or permanently, reside in the United States entitled to enjoy the protection guaranteed by the Fourteenth Amendment?

Excerpts from the Supreme Court Decision in *Yick Wo v. Hopkins*[15]

Mr. Justice Matthews delivered the opinion of the Court:

. . . In both of these cases [*Yick Wo v. Hopkins* and *Wo Lee v. Hopkins*] the ordinance involved was simply a prohibition to carry on the washing and ironing of clothes in public laundries and washhouses, within the city and county of San Francisco, from ten o'clock p.m. until six o'clock a.m. of the following day. This provision was held to be purely a police regulation, within the competency of any municipality.

. . . The rights of the petitioners are not less because they are aliens and subjects of the Emperor of China.

The Fourteenth amendment to the Constitution is not confined to the protection of citizens. It says: "Nor shall any State deprive any person of life, liberty, or property without due process of law; nor deny to any person within its jurisdiction the equal protection of the laws." These provisions are universal in their application, to all persons within the territorial jurisdiction, without regard to any differences of race, or color, or of nationality; and the equal protection from the laws is a pledge of the protection of equal laws. . . .

Though the law itself be fair on its face and impartial in appearance, yet, it is applied and administered by public authority with an evil eye and unequal hand, so as practically to make unjust and illegal discriminations between persons in similar circumstances. . . .

. . . No reason whatever, except the will of the supervisors, is assigned why they should not be permitted to carry on, in the accustomed manner, their harmless and useful occupation, on which they depend for a livelihood. And while this consent of the supervisors is withheld from them and from two hundred others who have also petitioned, all of whom happened to be Chinese subjects, eighty others, not Chinese subjects, are permitted to carry on similar business under similar conditions. The fact of this discrimination is admitted. No reason for it is shown, . . . no reason for it exists except hostility to the race and nationality to which the petitioners belong, and which in the eye of the law is not justified. The discrimination is, therefore, illegal, and the public administration which enforces it is a denial of the equal protection of the laws and a violation of the Fourteenth amendment of the Constitution. The imprisonment of the petitioners is, therefore illegal, and they must be discharged.

The decision in *Yick Wo* demonstrated the Court's perspective that the Fourteenth Amendment applied to all persons, citizens and noncitizens.

VII. *ELK V. WILKINS* (1884)

In the late 19th century, Native Americans constituted a problematic class when the Supreme Court considered citizenship. Although Native Americans were the original inhabitants of the territory that became the United States, they were considered outside the concept of citizenship. They were viewed as a separate nation, and described as uncivilized, alien people who were not worthy of citizenship in the political community. As Native Americans were driven from their homeland and pushed farther west, the United States government developed a policy of containment by establishing reservations. Native Americans who lived with their tribes on such reservations were presumed to be members of "not strictly speaking, foreign states, but alien nations." The Constitution made no provisions for naturalizing Native Americans or defining the status of those who chose to live in the territorial United States rather than be assigned to reservations. It was presumed that Native Americans would remain on the reservations. The framers of the Constitution had not given any thought as to when or how a Native American might become a U.S. citizen. When the Naturalization Law of 1790 was written, only Europeans were anticipated as future citizens. The citizenship of Native Americans was not settled until 1924, when a statutory law, not a constitutional amendment, granted citizenship.

Elk v. Wilkins raised the question of citizenship and voting behavior as a privilege of citizenship. In 1857, the Court had easily dismissed Dred Scott's suit on the grounds that he was not a citizen. Since he did not hold citizenship, he could not sue. *Minor v. Happersett* in 1872 considered the citizenship and voting issue with a female plaintiff. In that case, citizenship was not in doubt but the court stated that citizenship did not automatically confer the right to suffrage. In *Elk*, a Native American claimed citizenship and the right to vote. Before considering the right to vote, the Court first examined whether Elk was a citizen and the process by which one becomes a citizen.

As midwestern cities emerged from westward expansion in the 1880s, a few Native Americans left their reservations to live and work in those cities. John Elk left his tribe and moved to Omaha, Nebraska, under the jurisdiction of the United States. In April 1880, he attempted to vote for members of the city council. Elk met the residency requirements in Nebraska and Douglas County for voting. Claiming that he complied with all of the statutory provisions, Elk asserted that under the Fourteenth and Fifteenth Amendments, he was a citizen of the United States who was entitled to exercise the franchise, regardless of race or color. He further claimed that Wilkins, the voter registrar, "designedly, corruptly, willfully, and maliciously" refused to register him for the sole reason that he was a Native American.

The Court's decision addressed these key questions:

1. Is a Native American still a member of an Indian tribe when he voluntarily separates himself from his tribe and seeks residence among the white citizens of the state?
2. What was the intent of the Fourteenth Amendment regarding who could become a citizen?
3. Can Native Americans become naturalized citizens?
4. Can Native Americans become citizens of the United States without the consent of the U.S. government?
5. Must Native Americans adopt the habits of a "civilized" life before they become U.S. citizens?
6. Is a Native American who is taxed a citizen?

Excerpts from the Supreme Court Decision in *Elk v. Wilkins*[16]

Mr. Justice Gray delivered the opinion of the Court.

. . . The plaintiff . . . relies on the first clause of the first section of the Fourteenth amendment of the Constitution of the United States, by which "all persons born or naturalized in the United States, and subject to the jurisdiction thereof, are citizens of the United States and of the State wherein they reside"; and on the Fifteenth amendment, which provides that "the right of citizens of the United States to vote shall be denied or abridged by the United States or by any State on account of race, color, or previous condition of servitude."

. . . The question then is, whether an Indian, born a member of the Indian tribes within the United States, is, merely by reason of his birth within the United States, and of his afterwards voluntarily separating himself from his tribe and taking up his residence among white citizens, a citizen of the United States, within the meaning of the first section of the Fourteenth amendment of the Constitution.

. . . The Indian tribes, being within the territorial limits of the United States, were not, strictly speaking, foreign States; but they were alien nations, distinct political communities, with whom the United States might and habitually did deal, as they thought fit, either through treaties made by the President and Senate, or through acts of Congress in the ordinary forms of legislation. The members of those tribes owed immediate allegiance to their several tribes, and were not a part of the United States. They were in a dependent condition, a state of pupilage, resembling that of a ward to his guardian.

. . . They were never deemed citizens of the United States, except under explicit provisions of treaty or statute to that effect, either declaring a certain tribe, or such members of it as chose to remain behind on the removal of the tribe westward, to be citizens, or authorizing individuals of particular tribes to become citizens. . . .

This [opening] section of the Fourteenth amendment contemplates two sources of citizenship, and two sources only: birth and naturalization.

. . . Slavery having been abolished, and the persons formerly held as slaves made citizens. . . . But Indians not taxed are still excluded from the count

[U.S. Census count for apportioning seats in the U.S. House of Representatives],[17] for the reason that they are not citizens. Their absolute exclusion from the basis of representation, in which all other persons are now included, is wholly inconsistent with their being considered citizens.

. . . Such Indians, then, not being citizens by birth, can only become so in the second way mentioned in the Fourteenth amendment, by being "naturalized in the United States," by or under some treaty or statute.

. . . The treaty of 1867 with the Kansas Indians strikingly illustrates the principle that no one can become a citizen of a nation without its consent, and directly contradicts the supposition that a member of an Indian tribe can at will be alternately a citizen of the United States and a member of the tribe.

. . . But the question whether any Indian tribes, or any members thereof, have become so far advanced in civilization, that they should be let out of the state of pupilage, and admitted to the privileges and responsibilities of citizenship, is a question to be decided by the nation whose wards they are and whose citizens they seek to become, and not by each Indian for himself.

. . . And in a later case [Judge Deady in the District Court of the United States for the District of Oregon] said: "But an Indian cannot make himself a citizen of the United States without the consent and co-operation of the government. The fact that he has abandoned his nomadic life or tribal relations, and adopted the habits and manners of civilized people, may be a good reason why he should be made a citizen of the United States, but does not of itself make him one. To be a citizen of the United States is a political privilege which no one, not born to, can assume without its consent in some form."

Mr. Justice Harlan in the dissenting opinion:

. . . We submit that the petition does sufficiently show that the plaintiff is taxed, that is, belongs to the class which, by the laws of Nebraska, are subject to taxation.

. . . The plaintiff is a citizen and *bona fide* resident of Nebraska. . . . He is subject to taxation, and is taxed, in that State. Further: The plaintiff has become so far incorporated with the mass of the people of Nebraska that . . . he constitutes a part of her militia.

By the act of April 9, 1866, entitled "An Act to protect all persons in the United States in their civil rights, and furnish means for their vindication" (14 Stat. 27), it is provided that "all persons born in the United States and not subject to any foreign power, excluding Indians not taxed, are hereby declared to be citizens of the United States." . . . Beyond question, by that act, national citizenship was conferred directly upon all persons in this country, of whatever race (excluding only "Indians not taxed"), who were born within the territorial limits of the United States, and were not subject to any foreign power. Surely every one must admit that an Indian, residing in one of the States, and subject to taxation there, became by force alone of the act of 1866, a citizen of the United States, although he may have been, when born, a member of a tribe.

. . . If he did not acquire national citizenship on abandoning his tribe [moving from the reservation] and . . . by residence in one of the States, subject to the complete jurisdiction of the United States, then the Fourteenth amendment has wholly failed to accomplish, in respect of the Indian race, what, we think, was intended by it, and there is still in this country a despised and rejected class of persons, with no nationality; who born in our territory, owing no allegiance to foreign power, and subject, as residents of the States, to all the burdens of government, are yet not members of any political community nor entitled to any of the rights, privileges, or immunities of citizens of the United States.

In all, the Court never addressed Elk's right to vote because the primary question involved Elk's citizenship. By excluding him from citizenship because he had not been naturalized and because there was no provision for naturalization, John Elk was left outside of the political community as was Dred Scott.

VIII. *LAU V. NICHOLS* (1974)

In the 19th century, Native Americans and Asian immigrants sought to exercise rights under the Fourteenth Amendment although it had been designed explicitly to protect blacks. In the 20th century, issues first raised by African Americans, such as equality in public education, again presented other minority groups with an opportunity to test their rights under the Constitution.

Brown v. Board of Education forced the Court to consider the narrow question of the distribution of resources between black and white school systems. The *Brown* decision addressed only education. It did not extend to the other areas of segregation in American society, such as the segregation of public transportation (e.g., buses) or public accommodations (e.g., restaurants and hotels). Indeed, *Brown* had not even specified how the integration of the school system was to take place. All of these questions were taken up by the Civil Rights movement that followed the *Brown* decision.

Once the separate but equal doctrine was nullified in education, immigrants raised other issues of equality. In the 1970s, suits were brought on behalf of the children of illegal immigrants, non-English-speaking children of Chinese ancestry, and children of low-income parents.

In *Lau v. Nichols,* a non-English-speaking minority group questioned equality in public education. The case was similar to *Brown* because it concerned public education, the Equal Protection Clause of the Fourteenth Amendment, and the suit was brought on behalf of minors; but the two cases also differed in many respects. The 1954 decision in *Brown* was part of a series of court cases attacking segregated facilities primarily in southern states. It addressed only the issues of black-white interaction.

In *Lau v. Nichols,* a suit was brought on behalf of children of Chinese ancestry who attended public schools in San Francisco. Although the children did not speak English, their classes in school were taught entirely in that language. (Some of the children received special instruction in the English language; others did not.) The suit did not specifically ask for bilingual education, nor did the Court require it, but *Lau* led to the development of such programs. In bilingual education, the curriculum is taught in children's native language, but they are also given separate instruction in the English language, and over time they are moved into English throughout their courses.

The *Lau* decision hinged in part on Department of Health, Education, and Welfare guidelines that prohibited discrimination in federally assisted programs. The decision was narrow because it instructed only the lower court to provide appropriate relief. The Court's ruling did not guarantee minority language rights, nor did it require bilingual education.

The Court's decision addressed these key questions:

1. Does a public school system that provides for instruction only in English violate the equal protection clause of the Fourteenth Amendment?
2. Does a public school system that provides for instruction only in English violate section 601 of the Civil Rights Act of 1964?
3. Do Chinese-speaking students who are in the minority receive fewer benefits from the school system than the English-speaking majority?
4. Must a school system that has a minority of students who do not speak English provide bilingual instruction?

Excerpts from the Supreme Court Decision in *Lau v. Nichols*[18]

Mr. Justice Douglas delivered the opinion of the Court:

> The San Francisco, California, school system was integrated in 1971 as a result of a federal court decree. The District Court found that there are 2,856 students of Chinese ancestry in the school system who do not speak English. Of those who have that language deficiency, about 1,000 are given supplemental courses in the English language. About 1,800 however, do not receive that instruction.
>
> This class suit brought by non-English-speaking Chinese students against officials responsible for the operation of the San Francisco Unified School District seeks relief against the unequal educational opportunities, which are alleged to violate, *inter alia,* the Fourteenth Amendment. No specific remedy is urged upon us. . . .
>
> The Court of Appeals [holding that there was no violation of the Equal Protection Clause of the Fourteenth Amendment or of section 601 of the Civil Rights Act of 1964] reasoned that "[e]very student brings to the starting line of his educational career different advantages and disadvantages caused in part by social, economic and cultural background, created

and continued completely apart from any contribution by the school system." . . . Section 71 of the California Education Code states that "English shall be the basic language of instruction in all schools." That section permits a school district to determine "when and under what circumstances instruction may be given bilingually." . . .

Under these state-imposed standards there is no equality of treatment merely by providing students with the same facilities, textbooks, teachers, and curriculum; for students who do not understand English are effectively foreclosed from any meaningful education.

. . . We know that those who do not understand English are certain to find their classroom experiences wholly incomprehensible and in no way meaningful.

We do not reach the Equal Protection Clause argument which has been advanced but rely solely on section 601 of the Civil Rights Act of 1964, 42 U.S.C. section 2000d. to reverse the Court of Appeals.

That section bans discrimination based "on the ground of race, color, or national origin, in any program or activity receiving Federal financial assistance." The school district involved in this litigation receives large amounts of federal financial assistance. The Department of Health, Education, and Welfare (HEW), which has authority to promulgate regulations prohibiting discrimination in federally assisted school systems, in 1968 issued one guideline that "[s]chool systems are responsible for assuring that students of a particular race, color, or national origin are not denied the opportunity to obtain the education generally obtained by other students in the system." In 1970 HEW made the guidelines more specific, requiring school districts that were federally funded "to rectify the language deficiency in order to open" the instruction to students who had "linguistic deficiencies." . . .

It seems obvious that the Chinese-speaking minority receive fewer benefits than the English-speaking majority from respondents' school system which denies them a meaningful opportunity to participate in the educational program—all earmarks of the discrimination banned by the regulations. . . .

Lau differed from *Brown* because it was decided not on the basis of the Fourteenth Amendment but on the Civil Rights Act of 1964. In reference to *Brown*, the justices noted that equality of treatment was not achieved by providing students with the same facilities, textbooks, teachers, or curriculum. *Lau* underscores the idea that equality may not be achieved by treating different categories of people in the same way.

IX. *SAN ANTONIO SCHOOL DISTRICT V. RODRIGUEZ* (1973)

The 1973 case of *San Antonio School District v. Rodriguez* raised the question of equality in public education from another perspective. As was the case in *Brown* and *Lau*, the Fourteenth Amendment required interpretation. However, unlike the earlier cases, the issue was the financing of local public schools.

Education is not a right specified in the Constitution. Under a federal system, education is a local matter in each state. This allows for the possibility of vast differences among states and even within states on the quality of instruction, methods of financing, and treatment of nonwhite students. Whereas the *Brown* decision examined inequality between races, *San Antonio* considered inequality based on financial resources through local property taxes. *San Antonio* raised the question of the consequence of the unequal distribution of wealth among Texas school districts. As with *Brown* and *Lau*, minors were involved; however, the issue was not race or language instruction but social class. Did the Texas school system discriminate against the poor?

Traditionally, the states have financed schools based on property tax assessments. Since wealth is not evenly distributed, some communities are able to spend more on education and provide greater resources to children. This is the basis of the *San Antonio* case, where the charge was that children in less affluent communities necessarily received an inferior education because those communities had fewer resources to draw on. The Rodriguez family contended that the Texas school system of financing public schools through local property taxes denied them equal protection of the laws in violation of the Fourteenth Amendment.

Financing public schools in Texas entailed state and local contributions. About half of the revenues were derived from a state-funded program that provided a minimal educational base; each district then supplemented state aid with a property tax. The Rodriguez family brought a class action suit on behalf of school children who claimed to be members of poor families who resided in school districts with a low property tax base. The contention was that the Texas system's reliance on local property taxation favored the more affluent and violated equal protection requirements because of disparities between districts in per-pupil expenditures.

The Court's decision addressed these key questions:

1. Does Texas's system of financing public school education by use of a property tax violate the Equal Protection Clause (Section 1) of the Fourteenth Amendment?
2. Does the Equal Protection Clause apply to wealth?
3. Is education a fundamental right?
4. Does this state law impinge on a fundamental right?
5. Is a state system for financing public education by a property tax that results in interdistrict disparities in per-pupil expenditures unconstitutionally arbitrary under the Equal Protection Clause?

Excerpts from the Supreme Court Decision in *San Antonio School District v. Rodriguez*[19]

Mr. Justice Powell delivered the opinion of the Court:

. . . The District Court held that the Texas system [of financing public education] discriminates on the basis of wealth in the manner in which education is provided for its people. Finding that wealth is a "suspect" classification and that education is a "fundamental" interest, the District Court held that the Texas system could be sustained only if the State could show that it was premised upon some compelling state interest.

. . . We must decide, first, whether the Texas system of financing public education operates to the disadvantage of some suspect class or impinges upon a fundamental right explicitly or implicitly protected by the Constitution, thereby requiring strict judicial

scrutiny. If so, the Texas scheme must still be examined to determine whether it rationally furthers some legitimate, articulated state purpose and therefore does not constitute an invidious discrimination in violation of the Equal Protection Clause of the Fourteenth Amendment.

. . . In concluding that strict judicial scrutiny was required, the [District] court relied on decisions dealing with the rights of indigents to equal treatment in the criminal trial and appellate processes, and on cases disapproving wealth restrictions on the right to vote. Those cases, the District Court concluded, established wealth as a suspect classification. Finding that a local property tax system discriminated on the basis of wealth, it regarded those precedents as controlling. It then reasoned, based on decisions of this Court affirming the undeniable importance of education, that there is a fundamental right to education and that, absent some compelling state justification, the Texas system could not stand.

We are unable to agree that this case, which in significant aspects is *sui generis,* may be so neatly fitted under the Equal Protection Clause. Indeed, we find neither the suspect-classification nor the fundamental-interest analysis persuasive.

The wealth discrimination discovered by the District Court in this case, and by several other courts that have recently struck down school financing in other States, is quite unlike any of the forms of wealth discrimination heretofore reviewed by this Court.

. . . First, in support of their charge that the system discriminates against the "poor," appellees have made no effort to demonstrate that it operates to the peculiar disadvantage of any class fairly definable as indigent, or as composed of persons whose incomes are beneath any designated poverty level. Indeed, there is reason to believe that the poorest families are not necessarily clustered in the poorest property districts. . . .

Second, neither appellees nor the District Court addressed the fact that . . . lack of personal resources has not occasioned an absolute deprivation of the desired benefit. The argument here is not that the children in districts having relatively low assessable property values are receiving no public education; rather, it is that they are receiving a poorer quality education than that available to children in districts having more assessable wealth. Apart from the unsettled and disputed question whether the quality of education may be determined by the amount of money expended for it, a sufficient answer to appellee's argument is that, at least where wealth is involved, the Equal Protection Clause does not require absolute equality or precisely equal advantages....

For these two reasons ... the disadvantaged class is not susceptible of identification in traditional terms....

... [I]t is clear that appellee's suit asks this Court to extend its most exacting scrutiny to review a system that allegedly discriminates against a large, diverse, and amorphous class, unified only by the common factor of residence in districts that happen to have less taxable wealth than other districts. The system of alleged discrimination and the class it defines have none of the traditional indicia of suspectness: the class is not saddled with such disabilities, or subjected to such a history of purposeful unequal treatment, or relegated to such a position of political powerlessness as to command extraordinary protection from the majoritarian political process.

We thus conclude that the Texas system does not operate to the peculiar disadvantage of any suspect class....

Education, of course, is not among the rights afforded explicit protection under our Federal Constitution. Nor do we find any basis for saying it is implicitly so protected....

In sum, to the extent that the Texas system of school financing results in unequal expenditures between children who happen to reside in different districts, we cannot say that such disparities are the product of a system that is so irrational as to be invidiously discriminatory....

Mr. Justice White, with whom Mr. Justice Douglas and Mr. Justice Brennan join, dissenting:

> ... In my view, the parents and children in Edgewood, and in like districts, suffer from an invidious discrimination violative of the Equal Protection Clause....
>
> There is no difficulty in identifying the class that is subject to the alleged discrimination and that is entitled to the benefits of the Equal Protection Clause. I need go no further than the parents and children in the Edgewood district, who are plaintiffs here and who assert that they are entitled to the same choice as Alamo Heights to augment local expenditures for schools but are denied that choice by state law. This group constitutes a class sufficiently definite to invoke the protection of the Constitution....

In *San Antonio v. Rodriguez,* the Court did not find that the differences between school districts constituted invidious discrimination. A majority of the justices felt that Texas satisfied constitutional standards under the Equal Protection Clause. On the other hand, four justices in dissenting opinions saw a class (the poor) that was subject to discrimination and that lacked the protection of the Constitution.

X. *BOWERS V. HARDWICK* (1986)

In most of the cases we have considered, plaintiffs have sued on the basis that their rights under the Fourteenth Amendment were violated. However, cases can reach the Supreme Court by several routes, one of which is a *writ of certiorari,* which is directed at an inferior court to bring the record of a case into a superior court for re-examination and review. This was the case in *Bowers v. Hardwick,* in which the constitutionality of a Georgia sodomy statute was challenged. This became a key case in the battle for constitutional rights for gay women and men.

The case of *Bowers v. Hardwick* began on the issue of privacy because the behavior in question took place in Michael Hardwick's home. In deciding the case, however, the justices shifted from the issue of privacy to question whether gays have a fundamental right to engage in consensual sex.

Michael Hardwick's suit was based on the following facts. On August 3, 1982, a police officer went to Hardwick's home to serve Hardwick a warrant for failure to pay a fine. Hardwick's roommate answered the door, but was not sure if Hardwick was at home. The roommate allowed the officer to enter and approach Hardwick's bedroom. The officer found the bedroom door partly open and observed Hardwick engaged in oral sex with another man. The officer arrested both men, charged them with sodomy, and held them in the local jail for 10 hours.

The Georgia sodomy statute under which the men were charged made "any sexual act involving the sex organs of one person and the mouth or anus of another" a felony punishable by imprisonment for up to 20 years. When the district attorney decided not to submit the case to a grand jury, Hardwick brought suit attacking the constitutionality of the Georgia statute. Later, a divided court of appeals held that the Georgia statute violated Hardwick's fundamental rights. The attorney general of Georgia appealed that judgment to the Supreme Court.

The Court's decision on the case was split. Five justices ruled that the constitutional right of privacy did not apply to Hardwick's case; four argued that it did. While the Georgia statute did not specify that only homosexual sodomy was prohibited, the Court's majority opinion was framed in those terms. (Most legal prohibitions are directed at nonprocreative acts irrespective of the sex of the participants.) The majority opinion also equated consensual sex within the home to criminal conduct within the home, an equation criticized by both gay rights activists and the dissenting justices.

> [The majority opinion] emphasized that the home does not confer immunity for criminal conduct, comparing gay sex first to drugs, firearms, and stolen goods and then to adultery, incest, and bigamy. In so doing, the Court evoked images of dissolution, fear, seizure, and instability. . . . [and] the stereotypical fear of gay men as predators and child molesters. . . . The majority [opinion] advances, mostly by implication, its view of gay sexuality as unrelated to recognized forms of sexual activity or intimate relationships, and as exploitative, predatory, threatening to personal and social stability. [Writing for the dissent] Justice Blackmun excoriates the majority's choice of analogies and its failure to explain why it did not use nonthreatening analogies such as private, consensual heterosexual activity or even sodomy within marriage for comparison.[20]

While the majority argued that the past criminalization of sodomy argued for its continued criminalization, critics responded that "Whereas the task of the Court was to decide whether the criminalization of sodomy is consistent with the Constitution, the majority treated the fact of past criminalization as determinative. . . . It had no answer to Justice Blackmun's contention 'that by such lights, the Court should have no authority to invalidate miscegenation laws.'"[21]

The Court's decision addressed these key questions:

1. Does Georgia's sodomy law violate the fundamental rights of gays?
2. Does the Constitution confer the fundamental right to engage in homosexual sodomy?
3. Is Georgia's sodomy law selectively being enforced against gays?

Excerpts from the Supreme Court Decision in *Bowers v. Hardwick*[22]

Mr. Justice White delivered the opinion of the Court:

> This case does not require a judgment on whether laws against sodomy between consenting adults in general, or between homosexuals in particular, are wise or desirable. . . . The issue presented is whether the Federal Constitution confers a fundamental right upon homosexuals to engage in sodomy and hence invalidates the laws of the many States that still makes such contact illegal and have done so for a very long time.
>
> We first register our disagreement with the Court of Appeals and with respondent that the Court's prior cases have construed the Constitution to confer a right of privacy that extends to homosexual sodomy. . . .
>
> Precedent aside, however, respondent would have us announce, as the Court of Appeals did, a fundamental right to engage in homosexual sodomy. This we are quite unwilling to do. . . .
>
> It is obvious to us that neither of these formulations [*Palko v. Connecticut,* 302 U.S. 319 (1937) and *Moore v. East Cleveland,* 431 U.S. 494 (1977)] would extend a fundamental right to homosexuals to engage in acts of consensual sodomy. Proscriptions against that conduct have ancient roots. . . . Sodomy was a criminal offense at common law and was forbidden by the laws of the original thirteen States when they ratified the Bill of Rights. In 1868, when the Fourteenth Amendment was ratified, all but 5 of the 37 States in the Union had criminal sodomy laws. In fact, until 1961, all 50 States outlawed sodomy, and today 24 States and the District of Columbia continue to provide criminal penalties for sodomy performed in private and between consenting adults. . . . Against this background, to claim that a right to engage in such conduct is "deeply rooted in

this Nation's history and tradition" or "implicit in the concept of ordered liberty" is, at best, facetious. . . .

Respondent . . . asserts that the result should be different where the homosexual conduct occurs in the privacy of the home. He relies on *Stanley v. Georgia,* 394 U.S. 557, (1969) . . . where the Court held that the First Amendment prevents conviction for possessing and reading obscene material in the privacy of one's home: "If the First Amendment means anything, it means that a State has no business telling a man, sitting alone in his house, what books he may read or what films he may watch." . . .

Stanley did protect conduct that would not have been protected outside the home, and it partially prevented the enforcement of state obscenity laws; but the decision was firmly grounded in the First Amendment. The right pressed upon us here has no similar support in the text of the Constitution, and it does not qualify for recognition under the prevailing principles for construing the Fourteenth Amendment. Its limits are also difficult to discern. Plainly enough, otherwise illegal conduct is not always immunized whenever it occurs in the home. Victimless crimes, such as the possession and use of illegal drugs, do not escape the law where they are committed at home. *Stanley* itself recognized that its holding offered no protection for the possession in the home of drugs, firearms, or stolen goods. . . . And if respondent's submission is limited to the voluntary sexual conduct between consenting adults, it would be difficult, except by fiat, to limit the claimed right to homosexual conduct while leaving exposed to prosecution adultery, incest, and other sexual crimes even though they are committed in the home. We are unwilling to start down that road. . . .

Justice Blackmun, with whom Justice Brennan, Justice Marshall, and Justice Stevens join, dissenting:

This case is no more about "a fundamental right to engage in homosexual sodomy," as the Court purports to declare, . . . than *Stanley v. Georgia,* 394 U.S. 557 (1969), . . . was about a fundamental right to watch obscene movies. . . . Rather, this case is about "the most comprehensive of rights and the right most valued by civilized men," namely, "the right to be let alone." *Olmstead v. United States,* 277 U.S. 438, (1928) (Brandeis, J., dissenting).

The statute at issue, Ga. Code Ann. section 16-6-2 (1984), denies individuals the right to decide for themselves whether to engage in particular forms of private,

consensual sexual activity. The Court conclu[des] section 16-6-2 is valid essentially because "the [laws] of . . . many States . . . still make such conduct illeg[al] and have done so for a very long time . . ." (Holmes, J., dissenting). Like Justice Holmes [dissenting in *Lochner v. New York,* 198 U.S. 45 (1905)], I believe that "[i]t is revolting to have no better reason for a rule of law than that it was laid down in the time of Henry IV. It is still more revolting if the grounds upon which it was laid down have vanished long since, and the rule simply persists from blind imitation of the past." Holmes, The Path of Law, 10 *Harvard Law Review* 457, 469 (1897). I believe we must analyze Hardwick's claim in the light of the values that underlie the constitutional right to privacy. If that right means anything, it means that, before Georgia can prosecute its citizens for making choices about the most intimate aspects of their lives, it must do more than assert that the choice they have made is an "'abominable crime not fit to be named among Christians.'"

Like the statute that is challenged in this case, the rationale of the Court's opinion applies equally to the prohibited conduct regardless of whether the parties who engage in it are married or unmarried, or are of the same or different sexes. Sodomy was condemned as an odious and sinful type of behavior during the formative period of the common law. That condemnation was equally damning for heterosexual and homosexual sodomy. Moreover, it provided no special exemption for married couples. The license to cohabit and to produce legitimate offspring simply did not include any permission to engage in sexual conduct that was considered a "crime against nature."

The Court's decision did not uphold Michael Hardwick's contention that his sexual conduct in the privacy of his own home was constitutionally protected. While the decision was seen as a blow to the assertion of gay rights, the majority's narrow one-vote margin also indicated the Court's shifting opinion on this issue.

XI. *REGENTS OF THE UNIVERSITY OF CALIFORNIA V. BAKKE* (1978)

The Supreme Court has reviewed several cases concerning equitable treatment in public education. Key cases include racially separate public schools *ducation,* 1954); the practice uction for Chinese students *u v. Nichols,* 1974); and the public schools based solely property taxes (*San Antonio iguez,* 1973).

African Americans not only had to fight for equity in public schools but also had to sue to gain admission to law and medical schools in state universities. See *Sipuel v. Oklahoma,* 1948; *Missouri ex rel Gaines,* 1938; and *Sweatt v. Painter,* 1950.

In 1978, race-based admissions became an issue again when a *white* person sued for admission to the medical school at the University of California at Davis. The case of *The Regents of the University of California v. Bakke,* however, must be seen in light of the policy of affirmative action, which sought to redress historic injustices against racial minorities and other specified groups by providing educational and employment opportunities to members of these groups.

In 1968, the University of California at Davis opened a medical school with a track admission policy for a 100-seat class. In 1974, applicants who identified themselves as economically and/or educationally disadvantaged or a member of a minority group (blacks, Chicanos, Asians, American Indians) were reviewed by a special committee. They could also compete for the remaining 84 seats. However, no disadvantaged white was ever admitted to the school through the special admissions program, although some applied. Bakke, a white male, applied to the medical school in 1973 and 1974 under the general admissions program. He was rejected both times because he did not meet the requisite cutoff score. In both years, special applicants with significantly lower scores than Bakke were admitted. After his second rejection Bakke sued for admission to the medical school, alleging that the special admissions program excluded him on the basis of his race in violation of the Equal Protection Clause of the Fourteenth Amendment, a provision of the California Constitution, and section 601 of Title VI of the Civil Rights Act of 1964, which provides that no person shall, on the ground of race or color, be excluded from participating in any program

receiving federal financial assistance. The California Supreme Court applied a strict-scrutiny standard. It concluded that the special admissions program was not the least intrusive means of achieving the goals of the admittedly compelling state interests of integrating the medical profession and increasing the number of doctors willing to serve minority patients. The California court held that Davis's special admissions program violated the Equal Protection Clause of the U.S. Constitution. The Davis Medical School was ordered to admit Bakke.

The Court's divided opinion addressed these key questions:

1. Does the University of California, Davis Medical School's admission policy violate the Fourteenth Amendment?
2. Does giving preference to a group of nonwhite applicants constitute discrimination?
3. Does the University of California, Davis Medical School use a racial classification that is suspect?
4. Was Bakke denied admission to the University of California, Davis Medical School on the basis of race?
5. Can race be used as a criterion for admission to a university?

Excerpts from the Supreme Court Decision in *The Regents of the University of California v. Bakke*[23]

Mr. Justice Powell delivered the opinion of the Court:

> The guarantees of the Fourteenth Amendment extend to all persons. Its language is explicit: "No State shall . . . deny to any person within its jurisdiction the equal protection of the laws." . . . The guarantee of equal protection cannot mean one thing when applied to one individual and something else when applied to a person of another color. . . .
>
> . . . the [Fourteenth] Amendment itself was framed in universal terms, without reference to color, ethnic origin, or condition of prior servitude.
>
> Petitioner [University of California, Davis] urges us to adopt for the first time a more restrictive view of the Equal Protection Clause and hold that discrimination

against members of the white "majority" cannot be suspect if its purpose can be characterized as "benign."

. . . Moreover, there are serious problems of justice connected with the idea of preference itself. First, it may not always be clear that a so-called preference is in fact benign. . . . Second, preferential programs may only reinforce common stereotypes holding that certain groups are unable to achieve success without special protection based on a factor having no relationship to individual worth. Third, there is a measure of inequity in forcing innocent persons in respondent's position to bear the burdens of redressing grievances not of their making.

. . . When a classification denies an individual opportunities or benefits enjoyed by others solely because of his race or ethnic background, it must be regarded as suspect.

If petitioner's purpose is to assure within its student body some specified percentage of a particular group merely because of its race or ethnic origin, such a preferential purpose must be rejected. . . . Preferring members of any one group for no reason other than race or ethnic origin is discrimination for its own sake. This the Constitution forbids.

. . . [A] goal asserted by petitioner is the attainment of a diverse student body. This clearly is a constitutionally permissible goal for an institution of higher education. Academic freedom, though not a specifically enumerated constitutional right, long has been viewed as a special concern of the First Amendment. . . .

Ethnic diversity, however, is only one element in a range of factors a university properly may consider in attaining the goal of a heterogeneous student body.

It may be assumed that the reservation of a specified number of seats in each class for individuals from the preferred ethnic groups would contribute to the attainment of considerable ethnic diversity in the student body. But petitioner's argument that this is the only effective means of serving the interest of diversity is seriously flawed. . . . Petitioner's special admissions program, focused solely on ethnic diversity, would hinder rather than further attainment of genuine diversity.

. . . In summary, it is evident that the Davis special admissions program involves the use of an explicit racial classification never before countenanced by this Court. It tells applicants who are not Negro, Asian, or Chicano that they are totally excluded from a specific percentage of the seats in the class.

The fatal flaw in petitioner's preferential program is its disregard of individual rights as guaranteed by the Fourteenth Amendment. Such rights are not absolute.

Mr. Justice Brennan, Mr. Justice White, Mr. Justice Marshall, and Mr. Justice Blackmun, concurring in part and dissenting in part:

We conclude . . . that racial classifications are not *per se* invalid under the Fourteenth Amendment.

Unquestionably we have held that a government practice or statute which restricts "fundamental rights" or which contains "suspect classifications" is to be subjected to "strict scrutiny" and can be justified only if it furthers a compelling government purpose. . . . But no fundamental right is involved here. Nor do whites as a class have any of the "traditional indicia of suspectness; the class is not saddled with such disabilities, or subjected to such a history of purposeful unequal treatment, or relegated to such a history of purposeful unequal treatment, or relegated to such position of political powerlessness as to command extraordinary protection from the majoritarian political process." . . .

Certainly . . . Davis had a sound basis for believing that the problem of under-representation of minorities was substantial and chronic. . . . Until at least 1973, the practice of medicine in this country was, in fact, if not in law, largely the prerogative of whites. In 1950, for example, while Negroes constituted 10% of the total population, Negro physicians constituted only 2.2% of the total number of physicians. The overwhelming majority of these . . . were educated in two predominantly Negro medical schools, Howard and Meharry. By 1970, the gap between the proportion of Negroes in medicine and their proportion in the population had widened: The number of Negroes employed in medicine remained frozen at 2.2% while the Negro population had increased to 11.1%. The number of Negro admittees to predominantly white medical schools, moreover, had declined in absolute numbers during the years 1955 to 1964.

Moreover, Davis had very good reason to believe that the national pattern of under-representation of minorities in medicine would be perpetuated if it retained a single admissions standard. . . .

Davis clearly could conclude that the serious and persistent under-representation of minorities in medicine depicted by these statistics is the result of handicaps under which minority applicants labor as a consequence of . . . deliberate, purposeful discrimination against minorities in education and in society generally, as well as in the medical profession. . . .

It is not even claimed that Davis' program in any way operates to stigmatize or single out any discrete . . . or even any identifiable, nonminority group. Nor will harm comparable to that imposed upon racial minorities by exclusion or separation on grounds of race be the likely result of the program. . . .

Nor was Bakke in any sense stamped as inferior by the Medical School's rejection of him. Indeed, it is conceded by all that he satisfied those criteria regarded by the school as generally relevant to academic performance better than most of the minority members who were admitted. Moreover, there is absolutely no basis for concluding that Bakke's rejection that was a result of Davis' use of racial preference will affect him throughout his life in the same way as the segregation of the Negro schoolchildren in *Brown I* would have affected them. Unlike discrimination against racial minorities, the use of racial preferences for remedial purposes does not inflict a pervasive injury upon individual whites in the sense that wherever they go or whatever they do there is a significant likelihood that they will be treated as second-class citizens because of their color. . . .

In addition, there is simply no evidence that the Davis program discriminated intentionally or unintentionally against any minority group which it purports to benefit. The program does not establish a quota in the invidious sense of a ceiling on the number of minority applicants to be admitted. . . .

Finally, Davis' special admissions program cannot be said to violate the Constitution. . . .

. . . we would reverse the judgment of the Supreme Court of California holding the Medical School's special admissions program unconstitutional and directing respondent's admission.

Justices Stevens and Stewart, along with Chief Justice Rehnquist, concurred and dissented in part. They found that the university's special admissions program violated Title VI of the Civil Rights Act of 1964, which prohibits discrimination under any program or activity receiving federal funding assistance. This dissent found that Bakke was not admitted to the Davis Medical School because of his race.

Race-based admissions were again considered in *Hopwood v. Texas,* a 1994 case in the Western District of Texas. The suit, brought by four white Texas residents, claimed that the affirmative action admissions program of the University of Texas School of Law violated the Equal Protection Clause of the Fourteenth Amendment and Title VI of the Civil Rights Act of 1964. The district court agreed that the plaintiffs' equal protection rights had been violated, but refused to direct the school to cease making admission decisions based on race. The case was subsequently appealed in the Court of Appeals for the Fifth Circuit, which held that the University of Texas School of Law could not use race as an admissions factor in order to achieve a diverse student body. The holding of the circuit court stands because the Supreme Court refused to hear the case.

This decision in effect overruled Justice Powell's opinion in *Bakke,* which held that universities can take account of an applicant's race in some circumstances. He asserted that the goal of achieving a diverse student body was permissible under the Constitution.

XII. *TENNESSEE V. LANE* (2004)

Historically, disabled people have been thought of as possessed or wicked. Often they were scorned and shut off from society in mental institutions. Today, however, the medical model is the dominant perspective that "those with disabilities have some kind of physical, mental, or emotional defect that not surprisingly limits their performance." Essentially, we don't expect those who are "flawed" to function as well as other people.[24]

Disabled people constantly face discrimination resulting in exclusion from housing, public buildings, and public transportation. This has prevented them from attending school, visiting museums, shopping, or living without assistance.

The 1990 Americans with Disabilities Act forbids discrimination against persons with disabilities in three key areas of public life. Title I covers employment; Title II encompasses public services, programs, and activities; and Title III covers public accommodations. In 2001 Casey Martin sued the PGA Tour,[25] under the public accommodations provisions of Title III to allow him to play golf on the tour while riding a golf cart because he suffers from Klippel-Trenaunay-Weber syndrome, a degenerative circulatory disorder that causes severe pain in his lower leg. Martin won his case when the Court held that the PGA walking rule was not compromised by allowing him to use a cart.

The provisions of Title II, which include access to the services, programs, or activities of a public entity such as a courthouse are questioned in *Tennessee v. Lane.* In this case, residents of the state who are paraplegics sued Tennessee because they were denied access to a courthouse under Title II of the Americans with Disabilities Act (ADA). Because this case involves a suit by an individual against a state, the Supreme Court has to consider the provisions of the Eleventh Amendment,[26] which provides state immunity against suits by citizens seeking equity and the enforcement clause, Section 5 of the Fourteenth Amendment.[27] After Tennessee was unsuccessful in getting the case dismissed because the plaintiffs sought damages, the case went to the Supreme Court. This issue then became an interpretation of Congress's power to enforce by appropriate legislation (Section 5) the guarantee that "no State shall make or enforce any law which shall abridge the privileges or immunities of citizens of the United States; nor shall any State deprive any person of life, liberty, or property, without due process of law; nor deny to any person within its jurisdiction the equal protection of the laws."

In 1998 George Lane and Beverly Jones, both paraplegics who use wheelchairs, filed suit against the state of Tennessee and a number of counties under Title II of the ADA, which states that no qualified individual with a disability shall, because of the disability be excluded from participation or denied the benefits of the services, programs, or activities of a public entity. Both parties claimed that they were denied access to the state court system because of their disability. Lane alleged that he was forced to appear to answer criminal charges on the second floor of a county courthouse. The courthouse had no elevator. In his first court appearance Lane crawled up two flights to reach the courtroom. When Lane had to return for a second time, he refused to crawl or to be carried to the courtroom. He was arrested and sent to jail for failure to appear for his hearing. Jones, a certified court reporter, claimed that she had not been able to obtain work because she could not gain access to several county courthouses.

The court's decision addressed these key questions:

1. Is Title II a valid exercise of Congress's Section 5 enforcement powers under the Fourteenth Amendment?
2. Does Title II enforce a variety of basic constitutional guarantees such as the right of access to the courts?
3. Does Title II validly enforce these constitutional rights?
4. Is Title II an appropriate response to this history of discrimination and pattern of unequal treatment?

Excerpts from the Supreme Court Decision in *Tennessee v. George Lane et al.*[28]

Mr. Justice Stevens delivered the opinion of the Court:

> The ADA was passed by large majorities in both Houses of Congress after decades of deliberation and investigation into the need for comprehensive legislation to address discrimination against persons with disabilities.
>
> . . . Title II, sections 12131–12134, prohibits any public entity from discrimination against "qualified" persons with disabilities in the provision or operation of public services, programs, or activities. The Act defines the term "public entity" to include state and local governments. . . .
>
> Title II, like Title I, seeks to enforce this prohibition on irrational disability discrimination. But it also seeks to enforce a variety of other basic constitutional guarantees, infringements of which are subject to more searching judicial review. . . . These rights include some, like the right of access to the courts at issue in this case, that are protected by the Due

Process Clause of the Fourteenth Amendment. The Due Process Clause [as] applied to the states via the Fourteenth Amendment both guarantee to a criminal defendant such as respondent Lane the "right to be present at all stages of the trial where his absence might frustrate the fairness of the proceedings." . . . The Due Process Clause also requires the States to afford certain civil litigants a "meaningful opportunity to be heard" by removing obstacles to their full participation in judicial proceedings. . . . And, finally, we have recognized that members of the public have a right of access to criminal proceedings secured by the First Amendment.

. . . It is not difficult to perceive the harm that Title II is designed to address. Congress enacted Title II against a backdrop of pervasive unequal treatment in the administration of state services and programs, including systematic deprivations of fundamental rights.

. . . With respect to the particular services at issue in this case, Congress learned that many individuals, in many States across the country, were being excluded from courthouses and court proceedings by reason of their disabilities. A report before Congress showed that some 76% of public services and programs housed in state-owned buildings were inaccessible to and unusable by persons with disabilities. . . .

The conclusion that Congress drew from this body of evidence is set forth in the text of the ADA itself: "Discrimination against individuals with disabilities persists in such critical areas as . . . education, transportation, communication, recreation, institutionalization, health services, voting, and access to public services. . . . This finding, together with the extensive record of disability discrimination that underlies it, makes clear beyond peradventure that inadequate provision of public services and access to public facilities was an appropriate subject for prophylactic legislation.

. . . Whatever might be said about Title II's other applications, the question presented in this case is not whether Congress can validly subject the States to private suits for money damages for failing to provide reasonable access to hockey rinks, or even to voting booths, but whether Congress had the power under Section 5 to enforce the constitutional right of access to the courts. Because we find that Title II unquestionably is valid Section 5 legislation as it applies to the class of cases implicating the accessibility of judicial services, we need go no further.

. . . Title II's affirmative obligation to accommodate persons with disabilities in the administration of justice cannot be said to be "so out of proportion to a supposed remedial or preventive object that it cannot be understood as responsive to, or designed to prevent, unconstitutional behavior. . . . It is, rather, a reasonable prophylactic measure, reasonably targeted to a legitimate end.

For these reasons, we conclude that Title III, as it applies to the class of cases implicating the fundamental right of access to the courts, constitutes a valid exercise of Congress's Section 5 authority to enforce the guarantees of the Fourteenth Amendment.

XIII. THE MICHIGAN CASES

Gratz v. Bollinger et al. (2003) and *Grutter v. Bollinger et al.* (2003) considered admission standards for the University of Michigan's undergraduate program and its Law School. This marked the first time in the 25 years since the *Bakke* decision that the Supreme Court had considered the legal status of race-conscious admissions. In *Bakke*, Justice Powell held that race could be taken into consideration if it served a compelling government interest. He then held that the goal of achieving a diverse student body was a circumstance where race could be considered. However, the *Bakke* decision generated six separate opinions, but no majority opinion.[29]

The University of Michigan cases question whether Justice Powell's opinion set a precedent for considering diversity a constitutional justification for race-conscious admissions.

Gratz v. Bollinger et al. (2003)

Jennifer Gratz and Patrick Hamacher were both white residents of Michigan who applied for admission to the University of Michigan's College of Literature, Science, and the Arts (LSA). Both were considered qualified for admission. However, both were denied early admission, and upon further review neither was admitted to the university. The university's Undergraduate Admissions Office uses a written guideline system which includes such factors as high school grades, standardized test scores, the quality of the high school, curriculum strength, geography, alumni relationships, leadership, and race. Although the guidelines have changed since 1995, the university consistently considered African Americans, Hispanics, and Native Americans as "underrepresented minorities." The guidelines provided that all applicants from an underrepresented racial or ethnic minority group were automatically given 20 points out of the 100 needed for admission. The university never disputed the claim that practically every qualified applicant from these groups was admitted.

In 1997 Gratz and Hamacher filed a class-action suit alleging violation of their rights under the Fourteenth Amendment and the Civil Rights Act of 1964. The Equal Protection Clause of the Fourteenth Amendment provides that a state cannot act unfairly or arbitrarily toward or discriminate against a person within its jurisdiction because the individual has "the equal protection of the laws." Title VI of the Civil Rights Act prohibits discrimination on the grounds of race, color, or national origin against anyone participating in a program or activity which receives federal financial assistance.

The Court's decision addressed these key questions:

1. Under strict scrutiny does the university's use of race in its current admission policy constitute narrowly tailored measures that further compelling government interests?
2. Does the undergraduate admission policy violate the Equal Protection Clause of the Fourteenth Amendment?
3. Does the undergraduate admission policy violate Title VI of the Civil Rights Act of 1964?

Excerpts from the Supreme Court Decision in *Gratz v. Bollinger et al.* (2003)[30]

Chief Justice Rehnquist delivered the opinion of the Court:

... Because the University's use of race in its current freshman admission policy is not narrowly tailored to

achieve respondents' asserted interest in diversity, the policy violates the Equal Protection Clause. For the reasons set forth in *Grutter v. Bollinger*... the Court has today rejected petitioners' argument that diversity cannot constitute a compelling state interest. However, the Court finds that the University's current policy, which automatically distributes 20 points, or one-fifth of the points needed to guarantee admission, to every single "underrepresented minority" applicant solely because of race, is not narrowly tailored to achieve educational diversity. In *Bakke*, Justice Powell explained his view that it would be permissible for a university to employ an admissions program in which "race or ethnic background may be deemed a 'plus' in a particular applicant's file" . . . he emphasized, however, the importance of considering each particular applicant as an individual, assessing all of the qualities that individual possesses, and in turn, evaluating that individual's ability to contribute to the unique setting of higher education. The admissions program Justice Powell described did not contemplate that any single characteristic automatically ensured a specific and identifiable contribution to a university's diversity. . . . The current LSA policy does not provide the individualized consideration Justice Powell contemplated. The only consideration that accompanies the 20-point automatic distribution to all applicants from underrepresented minorities is a factual review to determine whether an individual is a member of one of these minority groups. Moreover, unlike Justice Powell's example, where the race of a "particular black applicant" could be "considered without being decisive" . . . the LSA's 20-point distribution has the effect of making "the factor of race . . . decisive" for virtually every minimally qualified underrepresented minority applicant. The fact that the LSA has created the possibility of an applicant's file being flagged for individualized consideration only emphasizes the flaws of the University's system as a whole when compared to that described by Justice Powell. The record does not reveal precisely how many applications are flagged, but it is undisputed that consideration is the exception and not the rule in the LSA's program. Also, this individualized review is only provided *after* admissions counselors automatically distribute the University's version of a "plus" that makes race a decisive factor for virtually every minimally qualified underrepresented minority applicant. . . . Nothing in Justice Powell's *Bakke* opinion signaled that a university may employ whatever means it desires to achieve diversity without regard to the limits imposed by strict scrutiny. Because the University's use of race in its current freshman admission policy violates the Equal Protection Clause, it also violates Title VI.

Grutter v. Bollinger et al. (2003)

Barbara Grutter, a white Michigan resident, applied to the University of Michigan Law School in 1996. She was originally placed on a waiting list but was ultimately not admitted. She alleged that her application was rejected because the Law School used race as a "predominant" factor, which gave applicants from certain minority groups "a significantly greater chance of admission than students with similar credentials from disfavored racial groups." The Law School asserted that it had a compelling interest in obtaining the educational benefits derived from a diverse student body. Law School officials contended that the admissions staff was not directed to admit a specific percentage or number of minority students, but rather to consider race among several factors. The goal was to obtain a "critical mass" of underrepresented minority students in order to realize the educational benefits of a diverse student body. The critical mass concept was never stated in terms of a fixed number, or percentage, or even a range of numbers or percentages. Admission officers acknowledged that minority group membership was a strong factor in the acceptance decisions and that applicants from minority groups were given large allowance for admission compared to applicants from nonfavored groups. However, it was asserted that race was not considered the predominant factor in the Law School's admission formula.

The Court's decision addressed these key questions:

1. Was race a predominant or a plus factor when reviewing the files of Law School applicants?
2. Did the Law School have a compelling interest in creating a diverse study body?
3. Does seeking a critical mass of minority students equal a quota?
4. Does the Law School admissions policy violate the Fourteenth Amendment and Title VI of the Civil Rights Act of 1964?

Excerpts from the Supreme Court Decision in *Grutter v. Bollinger et al.*[31]

Justice O'Connor delivered the opinion of the Court:

We last addressed the use of race in public higher education over 25 years ago. In the landmark *Bakke* case, we reviewed a racial set-aside program that reserved 16 out of 100 seats in a medical school class for members of certain minority groups. . . . The decision produced six separate opinions, none of which commanded a majority of the Court. . . . The only holding for the court in *Bakke* was that a "State has a substantial interest that legitimately may be served by a properly devised admissions program involving the competitive consideration of race and ethnic origin."

. . . Public and private universities across the nation have modeled their own admissions programs on Justice Powell's views on permissible race-conscious policies.

. . . Justice Powell approved the university's use of race to further only one interest: "the attainment of a diverse student body" . . . Justice Powell grounded his analysis in the academic freedom emphasized that nothing less than the "'nation's future depends upon leaders trained through wide exposure' to the ideas and mores of students as diverse as the nation of many peoples." . . . Both "tradition and experience lend support to the view that the contribution of diversity is substantial."

Justice Powell was, however, careful to emphasize that in his view race "is only one element in a range of factors a university properly may consider in attaining the goal of a heterogeneous student body." . . . For Justice Powell "[i]t is not an interest in simple ethnic diversity, in which a specified percentage of the student body is in effect guaranteed to be members of selected ethnic groups," that can justify the use of race. . . . Rather, "[t]he diversity that furthers a compelling state interest encompasses a far broader array of qualifications and characteristics of which racial or ethnic origin is but a single though important element."

. . . We have held that all racial classifications imposed by government "must be analyzed by a reviewing court under strict scrutiny." . . . This means that such classifications are constitutional only if they are narrowly tailored to further compelling governmental interests.

. . . The Law School asks us to recognize, in the context of higher education, a compelling state interest in student body diversity.

. . . Today, we hold that the Law School has a compelling interest in attaining a diverse student body.

. . . Our conclusion that the Law School has a compelling interest in a diverse student body is informed by our view that attaining a diverse student body is at the heart of the Law School's proper institutional mission, and that "good faith" on the part of a university is "presumed" absent "a showing to the contrary."

. . . The Law School's concept of critical mass is defined by reference to the educational benefits that diversity is designed to produce.

These benefits are substantial. As the District Court emphasized, the Law School's admissions policy promotes "cross-racial understanding," helps to break down racial stereotypes, and "enables [students] to better understand persons of different races."

. . . The Law School has determined, based on its experience and expertise, that a "critical mass" of underrepresented minorities is necessary to further its compelling interest in securing the educational benefits of a diverse student body.

. . . To be narrowly tailored, a race-conscious admissions program cannot use a quota system—it cannot "insulat[e] each category of applicants with certain desired qualifications from competition with all other applicants" (opinion of Justice Powell). Instead, a university may consider race or ethnicity only as a "'plus' in a particular applicant's file," without "insulat[ing] the individual from comparison with all other candidates for the available seats."

. . . We find that the Law School's admissions program bears the hallmarks of a narrowly tailored plan. As Justice Powell made clear in *Bakke*, truly individualized consideration demands that race be used in a flexible, nonmechanical way.

. . . We are satisfied that the Law School's admissions program . . . does not operate as a quota. Properly understood, a "quota" is a program in which a certain fixed number or proportion of opportunities are "reserved exclusively for certain minority groups."

. . . The Law School's goal of attaining a critical mass of underrepresented minority students does not transform its program into a quota. . . . "[S]ome attention to numbers," without more, does not transform a flexible admissions system into a rigid quota.

. . . The Law School affords this individualized consideration to applicants of all races. There is no policy, either *de jure* or *de facto*, of automatic acceptance or rejection based on any single "soft" variable. Unlike the program at issue in *Gratz v. Bollinger* the Law School awards no mechanical, predetermined diversity "bonuses" based on race or ethnicity.

. . . What is more, the Law School actually gives substantial weight to diversity factors besides race. The Law School frequently accepts nonminority applicants with grades and test scores lower than underrepresented minority applicants (and other nonminority applicants) who are rejected.

. . . We agree that, in the context of its individualized inquiry into the possible diversity contributions of all applicants, the Law School's race-conscious admissions program does not unduly harm nonminority applicants.

. . . the Equal Protection Clause does not prohibit the Law School's narrowly tailored use of race in admissions decisions to further a compelling interest in obtaining the educational benefits that flow from a diverse student body.

NOTES

1. *Privileges and immunities* refer to the ability of one state to discriminate against the citizens of another state. A resident of one state cannot be denied legal protection, access to the courts, or property rights in another state.
2. In *Smith v. Allwright,* 321 U.S. 649 (1944), the Supreme Court held that a 1927 Texas law that authorized political parties to establish criteria for membership in the state Democratic party violated the Fifteenth Amendment. In effect, the criteria excluded nonwhites from the Democratic party. Since only party members could vote in the primary election, the result was a whites-only primary. The Democratic party so dominated politics in the southern states after the Civil War that winning the primary was equivalent to winning the general election.
3. Americans of African descent have been called *blacks, Negroes, colored,* or *African Americans,* depending on the historical period.
4. 19 Howard 393 (1857).
5. The Nineteenth Amendment that was ratified on August 18, 1920, stated, "The right of citizens of the United States to vote shall not be denied or abridged by the United States or by any state on account of sex. Congress shall have the power to enforce this article by appropriate legislation."
6. 21 Wallace 162 (1875).

7. Crozier, "Constitutionality of Discrimination Based on Sex," 15 *B.U.L. Review*, 723, 727–28 (1935) as quoted in William Hodes, "Women and the Constitution: Some Legal History and a New Approach to the Nineteenth Amendment" *Rutgers Law Review*, Vol. 25, 1970, p. 27.

8. Hodes, p. 45.

9. Gunnar Myrdal, *An American Dilemma: The Negro Problem and Modern Democracy*. New York: Harper and Row (2d ed. 1962 [1944]), pp. 1073–74, as quoted in Hodes, p. 29. This same biblical ground has yielded the idea that a woman is an extension of her husband and his status.

10. The states under military rule were Virginia, North Carolina, South Carolina, Georgia, Florida, Tennessee, Alabama, Mississippi, Texas, Louisiana, and Arkansas.

11. The term *colored* was used in Louisiana to describe persons of mixed race who had some African ancestry.

12. 163 U.S. 537 (1896).

13. Restrictive covenants were written in deeds restricting the use of the land. Covenants could prohibit the sale of land to nonwhites or non-Christians.

14. 347 U.S. 483 (1954).

15. 118 U.S. 356 (1886).

16. 112 U.S. 94 (1884).

17. Native Americans and slaves posed a problem when taking the census count, which was the basis for apportioning seats in the U.S. House of Representatives. Some states stood to lose representation if some of their slave or Native American population was not counted. Blacks were counted as three-fifths of a white man, and only those Native Americans who were taxed were counted.

18. 414 U.S. 563 (1974).

19. 411 U.S. 1 (1973).

20. Rhonda Copelon, "A Crime Not Fit to Be Named: Sex, Lies, and the Constitution," p. 182. In David Kairys (ed.), *The Politics of Law*, pp. 177–94, New York: Pantheon.

21. Copelon, p. 184.

22. 478 U.S. 186 (1986).

23. 438 U.S. 265 (1978).

24. Paul C. Higgins, *Making Disability*. Springfield, IL: Charles C. Thomas (1992), pp. 26–27.

25. *PGA Tour, Inc. v. Casey Martin*, 532 U.S. 661.

26. The Eleventh Amendment pertains to suits against the states. The interpretation is that a state cannot be sued by U.S. citizens of that state or another state nor by a foreign country.

27. Section 5 of the Fourteenth Amendment grants Congress the power to enforce the provisions of this amendment by appropriate legislation.

28. 124 S. Ct. 1978 (2004).

29. Four justices supported the University of California's admissions program against all objections on the ground that the government could use race "to remedy disadvantages cast on minorities by past racial prejudice."

Four other justices did not interpret *Bakke* on constitutional grounds, but instead struck down the program on statutory grounds. Justice Powell's position was against the set-aside admissions policy, but was also for "reversing the state court's injunction against any use of race whatsoever." The holding in *Bakke* was that a "State has a substantial interest that legitimately may be served by a properly devised admissions program involving the competitive consideration of race and ethnic origin."

30. 539 U.S. 244 (2003).

31. 539 U.S. 982 (2003).

READING 50

The Minority Rights Revolution

John D. Skrentny

On January 6, 1969, Senator Barry Goldwater, Republican of Arizona, sent a letter to the new presidential administration of Richard M. Nixon. Goldwater personified the right wing of the Republican Party, argued passionately for limited government, and had previously written a book entitled *The Conscience of a Conservative*.[1] He had also famously stuck to his principles and voted against the Civil Rights Act of 1964, the landmark law that ended racial segregation. On this day, however, Goldwater offered a lesson in political savvy for dealing with a disadvantaged group. The senator reminded the new administration that Nixon had promised a White House conference on Mexican American issues during his campaign, and that Nixon wanted to have "Mexicans" serve in his administration. Goldwater explained that this group preferred to be called "Mexican-Americans" and that the administration should avoid referring to them as Latin American—save that term for South America, coached Goldwater. The White House conference should occur "at the earliest possible

John D. Skrentny is a professor of sociology at the University of California, San Diego.

time because these people are watching us to see if we will treat them the way the Democrats have." He reminded them that New York was the largest Spanish-speaking city in the United States and that nationwide there were 6 million in this category. "You will hear a lot on this subject from me," the strident, states' rights conservative warned, "so the faster you move, the less bother I will be."[2]

A few years later, Robert H. Bork, who would become a famously right-leaning federal judge and author of the 1996 book *Slouching towards Gomorrah: Modern Liberalism and American Decline,* also promoted the cause of federal recognition of disadvantaged groups. In 1974, Bork was Nixon's solicitor general, and in that year co-authored a brief to the Supreme Court arguing that the failure to provide special language education for immigrant children was racial discrimination, according to both the Constitution and the Civil Rights Act of 1964. The Supreme Court agreed with the statutory argument, though it did not wish to go as far as Bork and create constitutional language rights in schools.[3]

Goldwater and Bork were not alone in promoting rights for minorities. The 1965–75 period was a minority rights revolution. After the mass mobilization and watershed events of the black civil rights movement, this later revolution was led by the Establishment. It was a bipartisan project, including from both parties liberals and conservatives—though it was hard to tell the difference. Presidents, the Congress, bureaucracies, and the courts all played important roles. In the signature minority rights policy, affirmative action, the federal government went beyond African Americans and declared that certain groups were indeed "minorities"—an undefined term embraced by policymakers, advocates, and activists alike—and needed new rights and programs for equal opportunity and full citizenship. In the parlance of the period, minorities were groups seen as "disadvantaged" but not defined by income or education. African Americans were the paradigmatic minority, but there were three other ethnoracial minorities: Latinos, Asian Americans, and American Indians. Immigrants, women, and the disabled of all ethnic groups were also included and won new rights during this revolutionary period.

Bipartisanship was not the only notable aspect of the minority rights revolution. Consider also the *speed* of the development of its laws and regulations. While they appeared to have global momentum on their side, it still took two decades from the first proposition in 1941 that blacks be ensured nondiscrimination in employment to the law (Title VII of the Civil Rights Act of 1964) guaranteeing that right. Similarly, it took about twenty years between the first efforts to allow expanded immigration from outside northern and western Europe and the Immigration Act of 1965, ending all national origin discrimination in immigration. Following these landmarks, however, the government passed other laws and regulations almost immediately after first proposal. In most cases, it took only a few years to have a new law passed and there was little lobbying pressure. Bilingual education for Latinos, equal rights for women in education, and equal rights for the disabled all became law within two years of first proposal. Affirmative action expanded beyond blacks almost immediately. Such rapid success in American politics is rare. It is especially rare when achieved by groups that were defined precisely by their powerlessness and disadvantage in American society.

The rapidity and ease of the minority rights revolution brings up another puzzle. If minority rights were so easy to establish, why were not more groups included? For example, government officials perceived eastern and southern European Americans (Italians, Poles, Jews, Greeks, etc.) to be discriminated against, economically disadvantaged, or both. These "white ethnics" also had strong advocates. Yet they were never made the subjects of special policies for aid, protection, or preference. Despite widespread perceptions of their oppression, gays and lesbians similarly failed to gain a federal foothold in the minority rights revolution. Some members of Congress first submitted a bill to protect Americans from discrimination on the basis of sexual orientation in 1974. There still is no law ensuring this protection.

TABLE 1

WORLD AND AMERICAN RIGHTS DEVELOPMENTS

World developments	U.S. developments
1941 "Four Freedoms" 1945 UN Charter	1941 Executive Order 8802
	1947 President's Committee on Civil Rights
1948 UN Universal Declaration of Human Rights 1950s–60s Emerging nations in Africa and Asia	1954 *Brown v. Board of Education* 1964 Civil Rights Act
1965 International Convention on the Elimination of All Forms of Racial Discrimination 1966 International Covenant on Economic, Social and Cultural Rights; International Covenant on Civil and Political Rights	1965 Voting Rights Act; Immigration Reform Act
	1968 Bilingual Education Act, developing Affirmative Action policies

Another curious aspect of this minority rights revolution is that the 1960s recognition of the right to be free from discrimination was not just an American phenomenon. Nondiscrimation was quite suddenly a *world* right, a *human* right. That is, the United States was anything but alone in its recognition of minority rights.[4] Consider the dates of major American minority-rights developments and United Nations conventions and covenants guaranteeing human-rights protections (see Table 1). Though usually (and notoriously) unperturbed by world trends, Americans were guaranteeing nondiscrimination and other rights at the same time that much of the world was coming to a formal consensus on these same issues. Was it just a coincidence that America and many other nations traveled on parallel paths? Moreover, was it happenstance that Africans and Asians simultaneously threw off the yoke of colonialism and their new nations joined the UN while American citizens of third-world ancestry also gained more control of their destinies? The minority rights revolution is not only an intellectual puzzle. It was an event of enormous significance. It shaped our current understanding of American citizenship, which is more inclusive than ever before, while also drawing lines of difference between Americans. It was a major part of the development of the American regulatory state, later decried by those same conservatives who joined with liberals in building it up. And it offers a unique look at American democracy. When the stars and planets line up in just the right way, politicians, bureaucrats, and judges can offer a range of efforts to help disadvantaged Americans—even if those Americans did not ask for them.

WHAT DO WE KNOW ABOUT THE MINORITY RIGHTS REVOLUTION?

The minority rights revolution was a sudden growth of federal legislation, presidential executive orders, bureaucratic rulings, and court decisions that established nondiscrimination rights. It targeted groups of Americans understood as disadvantaged but not defined by socioeconomic class. Many of these laws and regulations, especially affirmative action, were novel in that they created the new category of "minority" Americans and sought to guarantee nondiscrimination by giving positive recognition of group differences.

There is much research debating the fairness or efficacy of human rights laws. But how did we get them in the first place? . . .

The image that comes to most Americans' minds when they think of the period is angry protest—radical blacks, feminists, and Latinos shouting slogans, a white ethnic "backlash," newly assertive disabled and gay people, all joining Vietnam War protesters in creating a climate of upheaval. These images exist because there was, of course, a very large amount of social-movement activity. One account of the minority rights revolution might therefore emphasize the role of grassroots mobilizing. . . .

[But this discussion] fundamentally challenges the social-movement approach to understanding the late 1960s and early 1970s. One theme [here] is that while white men dominated government, by no means were social movements and minority advocates excluded. Scholars almost always assume social movements are discrete entities that exist *outside of* government.[5] There are "challenges from outside the polity" confronting "elites within it." In the late 1960s and early 1970s, however, formal members of social-movement organizations held positions of power in Congress and the bureaucracy, and strong advocates also worked out of the White House. They played crucial roles in formulating and pushing new rights. The images conjured up [here] are therefore mostly not of angry minority protests, raised fists, picket lines, and placards. The images of the minority rights revolution are mostly of mainstream Euro-American males and minority advocates, wearing suits, sitting at desks, firing off memos, and meeting in government buildings to discuss new policy directions. While these are not romantic images, they are the images of power. . . .

DYNAMICS OF CHANGE: UNDERSTANDING THE MINORITY RIGHTS REVOLUTION

To explain the minority rights revolution, this [discussion] emphasizes the importance of two factors: the perceived needs of national security and the various legacies of the black civil rights movement. . . . Significant themes throughout are the ways that prior policy developments and cultural meanings matter. Initial policymaking can make later policy development possible, easy, and quick. But understanding rapid policy development requires seeing the political importance of meanings—perceptions of what a thing, person, policy, or action *is*.

The Sequence of History and the Legacies of National Policy

An important concept used to study historical sequences in politics is the policy legacy (sometimes called "policy feedback").[6] The basic idea is simple: new policies remake politics. Government leaders, interest groups, and the public adjust their interests to take into account the existence of the new policy. This sometimes requires greatly changing their preferences. Policies may even call into being entirely new political organizations. This all means that the sequence of historical events matters greatly. For the present case, World War II and the Cold War helped make the minority rights (especially black) revolution possible, and the black civil rights movement helped make the rest of the revolution possible—and rapid.

National Security and Equal Rights The minority rights revolution could not have occurred without the prior world battle against the Nazis and Japanese and the Cold War struggle with the Soviet Union.[7] World War II and especially the Cold War's broadly defined "national security" policy had important legacies in domestic politics. In some ways this was direct and obvious: the perceived need for national security led to great investment in the means of warfare, driving a large part of the economy and building up firms that created weapons and other equipment. But there were other, more far-reaching effects.

During this dynamic period, war threats were staggering and horrifying, and national security prompted policies that included everything from education to highways to racial and ethnic equality. The latter became part of national security because American strategy in World War II set in motion the creation of global human-rights norms that gave a cause for the Allies and a structure to the later Cold War struggle with the Soviet Union. World War II marked the beginning of an unprecedented global cultural integration and the establishment of a global public sphere, held together by the UN and a few basic premises. The sanctity of human rights was one. At the top of the rights list was nondiscrimination. Race or ethnic discrimination, especially when practiced by those of European ancestry, was wrong. In short, geopolitical developments set into motion a dynamic where policies defined as furthering the goal of national security by fighting Nazism or global communism—including equal rights policies—found bipartisan support and rapid change in political fortunes.

Legacies of Black Civil Rights   The legacies of black civil rights policy were complex and varied. One important legacy was the creation of new "institutional homes" (to borrow Chris Bonastia's term) for rights advocates to have positions of real policy-making power.[8] Most important here were the Equal Employment Opportunity Commission (EEOC), the Department of Health, Education and Welfare's Office for Civil Rights, and the Department of Labor's Office of Federal Contract Compliance. All were created to enforce rights laws for blacks, and all attracted employees who supported equal-opportunity rights. Though they usually kept black rights as their priority, this was not uniformly true. The EEOC played a crucial role by implicitly designating four ethnoracial groups, plus women, as America's official minorities to be given special attention and included in affirmative action. These new sites of rights advocacy allowed the designated groups to concentrate their lobbying efforts to a sometimes very receptive audience, usually out of the public view.

Other policy legacies of the black civil rights movement were more cultural in character, though equally important. The Civil Rights Act of 1964, as well as other efforts to help blacks, created a tool kit or repertoire of policy models that could be extended again and again and adapted to deal with the problems of groups other than black Americans.[9] Through their own initiative, or when pressured by nonblack minority advocates, civil-rights bureaucrats responded with affirmative action—regardless of the specific demands of the minority advocates. Policymakers sometimes simply anticipated what minority constituents wanted. They created an "anticipatory politics" based on these policy tools and the new legitimacy of minority targeting.[10] Activist members of Congress used the Civil Rights Act's Title VI, barring federal funds for any program that discriminated on the basis of race, national origin, or religion, as part of a policy repertoire when seeking votes or social movement goals. Congress thus created Title IX of the Education Amendments of 1972, barring sex discrimination on the part of educational institutions receiving federal funds, and Section 504 of the Rehabilitation Act of 1973, which addressed discrimination on the basis of disability also by using the Civil Rights Act model.

. . . There are limits to the use of a policy as a model. The constellation of strategic interests that political actors have in particular contexts are based on the *meanings* they perceive in certain things. Meanings are constitutive—they tell us the identity of a person or thing. . . . Meanings may make a policy acceptable for one goal or group, but not for others. . . . Cultural meanings help us understand the speed of the revolution as well as its limits. . . .

Meaning and the Minority Rights Revolution

. . . To attract support for the Allied side during World War II, President Franklin Delano Roosevelt strongly promoted the United States as a symbol of human rights and race equality. These efforts then invited first the Axis and then the Soviet Union's propaganda strategies highlighting American racism and ethnic inequality. Especially with the parts of government aware of this propaganda and engaged with foreign audiences, specifically presidents and State Department officials, there was a rapid recategorization of domestic nondiscrimination as part of foreign policy and national security. This is apparent in both Democratic and Republican administrations. Comprehensive policy change, however, required convincing Congress and the American public, and both government leaders and rights groups actively promoted the meaning of nondiscrimination as national security. Change was incremental and needed mass mobilization for black civil rights and lobbying campaigns for immigration reform before breakthrough victories finally came in the mid-1960s.

Other rights could not be categorized as easily as national security. Women, for example, made few gains because gender was not a dividing principle in geopolitics as was race. Gender equality was not a part of Nazi, Japanese, or Communist propaganda and therefore served no national security interest. Social rights and welfare state development similarly did not become part of national security policy, even during the Cold War when America confronted an ideology based on economic egalitarianism. This was in part because many business and professional interest groups and Republican party leaders could quite plausibly argue that excessive interference with the market economy and market-based wealth distributions would push America *toward* socialism, rather than save it from this threat.

Recognition of the role of meanings is necessary to understand aspects of the minority rights revolution besides national security linkages and categorizations. If meanings are the foundations of the logics of appropriate action, then politicians will consciously or unreflectively use similar or different policies to appeal to different groups depending on their deservingness or some other meaning.[11] A key theme . . . is that different categories of Americans varied in their analogical similarity to African Americans, creating boundaries of appropriate or legitimate policies relating to them.

This was not only a matter of simple voting power, lobbying, or protest strength. Success and the speed at which it was achieved in the minority rights revolution depended greatly on the meaning of the group in question. After advocates for black Americans helped break the taboo on targeting policy at disadvantaged groups, government officials quickly categorized some groups as "minorities"—a never-defined term that basically

meant "analogous to blacks." These classifications were *not* based on study, but on simple, unexamined prototypes of groups.[12] Most obviously, government officials saw the complex category of Latinos (then usually called "Spanish-surnamed" or "Spanish-speaking") in terms of a simple racial prototype, obscuring the fact that many Latinos consider themselves white. Racialized in this way, Latinos needed little lobbying to win minority rights. Women, who faced ridicule like no other group, needed significant meaning entrepreneurship. Their advocates pushed hard to make the black analogy. Though Asian Americans presumably possessed a clearer group racial definition than did Latinos, the analogy between Asians and blacks was weaker than that between Latinos and blacks. Policymakers sometimes dropped Asian Americans from their lists. This was apparently just a cognitive forgetting—it required only small reminders for them to be included in minority policy, at least formally. While rights for the disabled were included easily and without debate, gay rights were a political nonstarter. Government officials saw white ethnics in a multifaceted way that shifted policy away from the minority-rights paradigm, despite the efforts of ethnic advocates. Moreover, though seen as disadvantaged, policymakers saw white ethnics as insufficiently disadvantaged to be categorized as minorities. In fact, federal government officials never spelled out what were the necessary and sufficient conditions or qualities for minorityhood. They classified groups just the same, and had little trouble doing so.

Meanings of groups also greatly affected the types of justice each group received.[13] Being analogous to blacks served as an initial classification, but groups retained distinctiveness. Equal opportunity meant different things depending on the group in question. In the late 1960s, equal opportunity in education for blacks meant a rejection of the "separate-but-equal" policy of the Jim Crow south. It meant zealous integration of schools, the bussing of students around cities so that blacks and whites could learn together. For Latinos, it meant *rejection* of the zealous integration practiced in some southwestern schools which included forced English-language usage. Instead, Latino children were to receive special bilingual education. For women, it meant a combination of different approaches, including integration in classrooms while segregated dormitories, sororities, and sports teams flourished. Readers may protest that these differences in policies were based on "real" differences between groups, yet this claim neglects the fact that lawmakers see some differences as real and relevant and others as not.[14] For example, the one-drop rule (which until recently was broadly taken for granted) defines anyone with any black ancestry as black and the European ancestry in an estimated 75–90 percent of African Americans as unreal.[15] The whiteness of Latinos is similarly denied reality. Despite the footnotes that may appear at the bottom of census tables, federal policy and national debates do not acknowledge that many Latinos are physically indistinguishable from Euro-Americans and consider themselves white. Orlando Patterson was thus able to point out the absurdity of ubiquitous news media predictions of a decline in the percentage of US citizens who are white due to the 2000 census's reports of the growing Latino presence.[16] ...

Meanings for Whom?

...While I stress the importance of policy legacies and meanings, creative, willful people are at the center of [the] story, though their identities and power may be constituted by institutions and meanings. Policy elites make decisions and those decisions matter. ... After the meanings of certain groups shifted, and the groups became "minorities" and legitimate targets of policy, presidents, bureaucrats and members of Congress [followed] a "logic of consequences," they pursued support from and justice for these groups with public recognition and targeted policies. But these policymakers were always basing their appeals in the universe of social meanings, especially the black analogy, and using policy and discourses originating in black civil rights. This is clear because, once started, the expansion of minority rights policies could have gone further than it did. Instead, creativity and risk raking reached limits.

DISCUSSION QUESTIONS

1. Was Skrentny's review of the bipartisan global agenda behind affirmative action a surprise to you? Why might you have been unaware of this background?

2. How did the minority rights revolution for blacks help later groups?

3. How do blacks differ from other minority groups?

NOTES

1. Barry M. Goldwater, *The Conscience of a Conservative* (New York: McFadden Books, 1964 [1960]).

2. Letter from Barry Goldwater to Ray Price, January 6, 1969, in Hugh Davis Graham, ed., *Civil Rights during the Nixon Administration, 1969–74* (Bethesda: University Publications of America, 1989), Part I, Reel 1, frame 21. Also see the letter from John Rhodes to Peter M. Flanigan, June 17, 1969, in Graham, *Civil Rights during Nixon*, Part I, Reel 2, frame 2.

3. The brief was for *Lau v. Nichols*, 94 U.S. 786 (1974). ... In his 1996 book, Bork writes, "Part of our national lore, and glory, is the fact that youngsters speaking not a word of English were placed in public schools where only English was used and very shortly were proficient in the language. That was crucial to the formation of American identity." Bork goes on to criticize bilingual education without mentioning his own role in the establishment of federal language rights. See Robert H. Bork, *Slouching towards Gomorrah: Modern Liberalism and American Decline* (New York: Regan Books, 1996), pp. 300–3.

4. Work by the sociologist John Meyer and his colleagues has examined the world development of rights protections as a part of the modern state, but has not clearly traced the processes through which this has occurred in the United States. The most recent statement is John Boli and George M. Thomas, eds., *Constructing World Culture* (Stanford: Stanford University Press, 1999). Philip Epp's work has examined processes of change in a comparative perspective, but concentrates solely on developments in courts. Philip Epp, *The Rights Revolution* (Chicago: University of Chicago Press, 1997).

5. For a rare dissenting view, see Mayor N. Zald and Michael A. Berger, "Social Movements in Organizations: Coup d'Etat, Insurgency, and Mass Movements," *American Journal of Sociology* 83 (1978): 823–61; and Meyer N. Zald, "Social Movements as Ideologically Structured Action: An Enlarged Agenda," *Mobilization* 5 (2000): 1–16.

6. Skocpol, *Protecting Soldiers and Mothers: The Political Origins of Social Policy in the U.S.* (Cambridge, Harvard

University Press, 1992). Paul Pierson, *Dismantling the Welfare State?* (New York: Cambridge University Press, 1994); Margaret Weir, *Politics and Jobs: The Boundaries of Employment Policy in the United States* (Princeton: Princeton University Press, 1992).

7. Scholars have long linked war with state building and policymaking. In social science, the importance of national security, or war, in state building was recognized since Max Weber's writing, but has been most developed in the work of Charles Tilly. Charles Tilly, ed., *The Formation of National States in Western Europe* (Princeton: Princeton University Press, 1975); Tilly, "War Making and State Making as Organized Crime," in Peter B. Evans, Dietrich Rueschemeyer, and Theda Skocpol, eds., *Bringing the State Back In* (New York: Cambridge University Press, 1985), pp. 169–91. A more recent statement is Miguel Centeno, *Blood and Debt: War and the Nation-State in Latin America* (University Park: Pennsylvania State University Press, 2002). Michael Sherry's work surveys the relationship of national security to domestic politics. Michael Sherry, *In the Shadow of War* (New Haven: Yale University Press, 1994).

8. Chris Bonastia, "Why Did Affirmative Action in Housing Fail during the Nixon Era? Exploring the 'Institutional Homes' of Social Policies," *Social Problems* 47 (2000): 523–42.

9. The classic statement is Ann Swidler, "Culture in Action: Symbols and Strategies," *American Sociological Review* 51 (1986): 273–86. Elisabeth S. Clemens, *The People's Lobby* (Chicago: University of Chicago Press, 1997), Chapter 2, discusses repertoires as tool kits of organizational models. It is a simple adaptation to use the concept for models of policy. See Rogers Brubaker, *Citizenship and Nationhood in France and Germany* (Cambridge, Mass.: Harvard University Press, 1992), pp.

16–17, on the related concept of cultural "idioms." On "policy paradigms," a more cognitively oriented concept, see Frank Dobbin, *Forging Industrial Policy* (New York: Cambridge University Press, 1994).

10. I thank Steve Teles for this concept. He traces it to Daniel Patrick Moynihan, "The Professionalization of Reform," *Public Interest* 1 (1965): 6–16.

11. As the economist Glenn Loury has written about racial groups, these meanings "bear on the identity, the status, and even the humanity of those who carry them" and "once established, these meanings may come to be taken for granted, enduring essentially unchallenged for millennia." Glenn Loury, *The Anatomy of Racial Inequality: Stereotypes, Stigma, and the Elusive Quest for Racial Justice* (Cambridge, Mass.: Harvard University Press, 2001).

12. See Lakoff and Johnson, *Metaphors We Live By*, p. 165, for a discussion of prototypes and how this process works on a cognitive level. On race and cognition, *see* Rogers Brubaker, Mara Loveman, and Peter Stamatov, "Reviving Constructivism: The Case for a Cognitive Approach to Race, Ethnicity and Nationalism," unpublished manuscript.

13. Other scholars have identified plural justices but have not linked them to specific meanings, instead identifying them with "spheres." Michael Walzer, *Spheres of Justice* (New York: Basic Books, 1983) ("spheres"); Jennifer Hoschschild, *What's Fair? American Beliefs about Distributive Justice* (Cambridge, Mass.: Harvard University Press, 1981) ("domains").

14. Lakoff and Johnson, *Metaphors We Live By*, pp. 141–46.

15. F. James Davis, *Who Is Black?* (University Park: Pennsylvania State University Press, 1991), p. 21.

16. Orlando Patterson, "Race by the Numbers," *New York Times*, May 8, 2001.

The Bankruptcy of Virtuous Markets: Racial Inequality, Poverty, and "Individual Failure"

Michael K. Brown

Martin Carnoy

Elliott Currie

Troy Duster

David B. Oppenheimer

Marjorie M. Shultz

David Wellman

Almost forty years after the civil rights revolution ended, two questions bedevil most discussions of racial economic inequality: (1) Why has deep poverty endured in the black community alongside a burgeoning black middle class? (2) Why do large gaps remain in family income, wages, and employment between blacks and whites? For many people this is the paradox and the bane of the civil rights revolution. How is it, they ask, that civil rights laws ended racial discrimination and left behind an unruly black underclass and substantial racial inequality? . . .

Michael K. Brown is a professor and chair of the Department of Politics at the University of California, Santa Cruz. Martin Carnoy is a professor of education and economics at Stanford University. Elliott Currie is a lecturer in legal studies at the University of California, Berkeley, and a visiting professor in the School of Criminology and Criminal Justice, Florida State University. Troy Duster is a professor of sociology and a senior fellow at the Institute for the History of the Production of Knowledge at New York University. David B. Oppenheimer is a professor of law and associate dean for academic affairs at Golden Gate University. Marjorie M. Shultz is a professor of law at Boalt Hall School of Law, University of California, Berkeley. David Wellman is a professor of community studies at the University of California, Santa Cruz, and a research sociologist at the Institute for the Study of Social Change at the University of California, Berkeley.

THE CHANGING STRUCTURE OF RACIAL INEQUALITY

In one respect, both black and white workers had similar experiences in the periods of economic growth and stagnation of the past sixty years: each group gained in real wages from 1940 to 1970, and each suffered from income stagnation and higher levels of unemployment after 1973. But in a racially stratified society, neither the gains nor the pains of economic change are distributed randomly. Because whites have historically controlled labor markets, black workers have been denied the economic benefits that white workers have received from increased education and they have been disproportionately unemployed. Between 1940 and 1970, at the same time that wages of black workers rose relative to those of whites, black employment *decreased* relative to white employment. By 1953, the unemployment rate for black men in their prime working years, twenty-five to forty-four years of age, was three times the white unemployment rate. And since then the rate has been two to two and one-half times as high. All black men, not just the unskilled or poorly educated, routinely experience more unemployment than their white male counterparts. Black unemployment is substantially higher than white unemployment regardless of education, age, occupation, or industry.[1] Even if one were to assume that black workers have the same education as white workers, black unemployment rates would still be 20 percent higher than the rates for whites.[2]

No doubt labor market discrimination has diminished in the past sixty years, and whites are clearly less prejudiced today than they were in 1940. But these developments tell us very little about contemporary patterns of racial discrimination and racial inequality. Why is it that twice as many blacks as whites are unemployed, regardless of the unemployment rate and long-run increases in black educational attainment? Reynolds Farley and Walter Allen pointed out some time ago that "if blacks had been incorporated into the economic mainstream and if racial discrimination declined, we would expect that their incomes would approach those of whites."[3] Why, then, did racial disparities in income and earnings widen over the 1980s, even though both black and white workers faced the same labor market environment: declining demand for unskilled labor, widening income and earnings inequality, and higher levels of unemployment? . . .

The Blue-Collar Breakthrough

. . . Contrary to the assumption that income always rises with increases in education, educated black workers [have been] more vulnerable to unemployment and wage discrimination than less educated blacks. Charles Killingsworth found that black-white unemployment ratios rose with education. In 1964 the unemployment rate for blacks with four years of college was more than three times the unemployment rate of college-educated white workers; but black workers with only four years or less of education had lower unemployment rates than comparable white workers. Baron and Hymer observe that wage gaps in the 1950s were not affected by education, noting that the "gap is greater at higher levels of education." In their study of the Chicago labor market, they discovered a stunning discrepancy. Black managers and sales workers earned just 57 percent and 54 percent of what whites in their respective occupations earned. But the wages of black operatives and laborers were 80 percent and 91 percent of whites in their occupations.[4] . . .

The White-Collar Breakthrough

Postwar occupational ceilings were undermined in the late 1960s and early 1970s by government policies and growing public sector employment. In this period, black workers made sharp income gains relative to white workers and significant occupational gains as they moved into professional, managerial, and technical positions. This white-collar breakthrough was due to the massive number of blacks moving into higher-ranking positions in the public sector and to the implementation of affirmative action policies that eliminated job

ceilings and other exclusionary devices aimed at educated black workers. Federal policies also enabled blue-collar black workers to pull down the barriers erected by skilled white craftsmen. Segregated jobs in the South were abolished, and industries that had historically excluded black workers were opened up when antidiscrimination laws were enforced.[5]

This white-collar breakthrough indicates that one of the core conservative arguments against antidiscrimination legislation is misleading. Gains in education did not produce the growth of the African American middle class in the 1960s; rather, it was government policies—the very factor that conservatives consider irrelevant—that led to the white-collar breakthrough. Although historically blacks have been more likely to work in the public sector than whites, prior to the 1960s they were concentrated predominantly in low-level jobs in agencies like the U.S. Post Office. The growth of federal spending in the 1960s generated an enormous number of professional, managerial, and technical jobs in state and local government. As a result, until the 1970s most of the gains blacks made in high-ranking jobs were in publicly funded social welfare and education agencies.[6]

College-educated blacks were the main beneficiaries of the growth in public sector jobs. By 1970, half of all black male college graduates and three-fifths of black female college graduates worked for the government. Public employment was crucial to the wage and salary gains made by African Americans relative to white workers in the 1960s because the wage gap between black and white workers is far narrower in the public sector. There is also evidence that, unlike white workers, black public employees were paid a higher salary than their counterparts in the private sector.[7]

By the 1970s, blacks were also making job gains in the private sector. Among black male workers, the proportion working as professionals or managers rose from 6.8 percent in 1960 to 17.4 percent by 1980. These private sector gains were chiefly due to affirmative action. . . . Enforcement of these policies opened up employment in industries and occupations previously closed to blacks, raised the

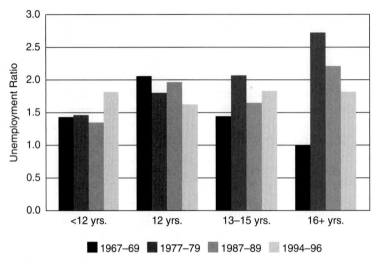

FIGURE 1
Black-White Male Unemployment Ratios by Years of Education, 1967–96.
Source: Chinhui Juhn, "Black-White Employment Differential in a Tight Labor Market," In Robert Cherry and William Rodgers III, *Prosperity for All? The Economic Boom and African Americans* (New York: Russell Sage Foundation, 2000), Table 3.2, p. 93.

incomes of college-educated blacks, and reduced wage discrimination for both black men and black women.[8]

Blacks were not the only group to benefit from government policies in this period. The white middle class also gained, expanding after 1945 because of a variety of public programs forged in the crucibles of the depression and war. . . .

THE 1980S RACIAL BACKLASH

Blacks lost ground in the Reagan years, and some of these reversals are quite startling. They also clearly fly in the face of conservative assertions that education brings economic advancement. For example, in this period young (twenty-five to thirty-four years of age) college-educated black men's earnings dropped to 72 percent of the white median income from a high of more than 80 percent, a serious setback by any measure. Compared to white men and women in the 1980s, black men made fewer occupational gains, and they were more likely to be downwardly mobile.

Unemployment rose for all black men relative to white workers, but especially for highly educated black workers. By the end of the 1960s the ratio of unemployed college-educated black workers to similarly unemployed white workers was even, a stunning reversal of the pattern Charles Killingsworth found in the 1950s and early 1960s. By 1980, as figure 1 shows, college-educated black workers were once again at an employment disadvantage relative to college-educated whites. They were almost three times as likely to be unemployed as college-educated white workers were. While black high school dropouts also experienced high unemployment rates during the 1980s, they were just one and one-half times as likely to be unemployed as white high school dropouts.

These reversals are not explained by a failure of black workers to learn or acquire job skills. By the 1970s, the difference between the proportions of black and white youth attending secondary schools had all but disappeared. Despite this, some conservative writers insist that racial gaps in earnings and occupation result from deep differences in educational and job skills between educated blacks and whites. In other words, they assume that the attainments of college-educated blacks and whites are not comparable. Yet as Martin Carnoy points out, black Scholastic Aptitude Test (SAT) and Graduate Record Examination (GRE) scores *increased* relative to whites in the 1980s. Thus, the notion that college-educated blacks lost ground to whites because of an increase in the gap between so-called unmeasured educational skills is simply wrong.[9]

Nor can the widening pay gap between black and white workers be explained by the increase in wage inequality among all workers. Although both white and black workers lost jobs and income, it is usually assumed that black workers lost more ground in the shift to a service economy because they were concentrated in the high-wage manufacturing jobs that were eliminated in the 1970s and 1980s. The notion that blacks just happened to be in the wrong place at the wrong time oversimplifies matters and ignores persistent discrimination. As the President's Council of Economic Advisers (CEA) recently concluded, there is "indirect evidence that discrimination also contributed to widening pay gaps across racial groups" in the 1980s.[10]

The evidence that labor market discrimination persisted in the 1980s is even stronger than the CEA's measured statement suggests. In some cases labor market discrimination endures despite repeated efforts to regulate an industry. Certain sectors of the economy are impervious to antidiscrimination policies. For example, black workers have been consistently excluded from construction jobs that do not require high levels of education. As Roger Waldinger and Thomas Bailey conclude, "The low levels of black penetration into construction's skilled trades are prima facie evidence of continuing discrimination." They show that flagrant discrimination continues in the construction industry because white-controlled unions resist efforts to break down the color barrier.[11] Another more recent study confirms the persistence of labor market discrimination. Deirdre Royster systematically followed the experiences of an evenly divided group of fifty young black and white men searching for entry-level jobs. All of these men had graduated from a vocational high school and had similar grades, attendance records, motivation and character, and commitment to hard work. Royster found that white male students gained the inside track to jobs routinely thought to be available only because of standard interviews and institutionally certified qualifications. Skill deficits in human capital could not explain why young black men were denied blue-collar jobs.[12]

The major reason why black economic progress was reversed is that competition for jobs intensified between black and white workers in the 1980s. Like the immediate postwar years, the Reagan era was good for white upward mobility. In this period, deindustrialization and rising wage inequality reduced the middle-class jobs and incomes that were the backbone of economic progress after World War II. Although both black and white low-income workers saw their wages decline, the earnings gap between low-income, young (sixteen to twenty-four years of age) black and white male family heads widened in the 1980s. The earnings ratio of white high school dropouts to white college-educated males remained mostly stable from 1970 to 1988. In contrast, however, the earnings ratio of poorly educated young black male family heads to black college graduates sharply declined. The problem, as William Darity Jr. and Samuel Myers Jr. point out, is that if "the widening [income] gap between black and white families . . . is to be attributed to the higher representation of blacks among the less skilled and the uneducated, then why is there a widening gap between black and white family heads with the *same* low degree of educational preparation?"[13] The answer will not be found by examining who had the necessary job and educational skills. Rather one must look at how black and white workers fared in the scramble for jobs after deindustrialization. The evidence indicates that blacks lost out.

In the period after 1970 as blacks lost blue-collar jobs (mostly work as operatives because few made it into the ranks of skilled craftworkers), they found employment in white-collar sales jobs. But they also took a 13 percent pay cut. White workers who had also been pushed out of good manufacturing jobs, on the other hand, moved into well-paying sales jobs, which gave them a 36 percent pay increase. Thus, black-white income ratios in 1989 were lower for white-collar jobs (67 percent) than for blue-collar jobs (75 percent).[14] The important change during the 1980s was that black workers moved from good (high-paying) jobs to bad (low-paying) jobs. The employment rates of young black and white workers also differed depending on whether they worked in manufacturing or service industries. Employment rates for white and black youth in the manufacturing sector have been relatively equal over the past four decades. In the service industry, however, which is where nearly all the new jobs are found, whites enjoy an accumulated advantage of nearly three times the employment rate of blacks.

The problem black workers faced was that there were fewer good jobs to go around, and they lost out in the racially competitive and discriminatory labor markets of the 1980s. Convincing evidence indicates that retail establishments, one of the fastest growing sectors of the economy, are far more likely to discriminate against black youth than manufacturing firms. One group of researchers sent matched pairs of white and black high school graduates from the Newark, New Jersey, class of 1983 out in the world to seek employment. These job applicants were not faking an interest in employment. They had been screened to make sure they were actually seeking work and were matched for academic achievement. In the manufacturing sector, blacks and whites had about equal success in obtaining employment. In the service sector, however, whites were four times as likely as blacks to be fully employed.[15] In fact, in audit studies, whites or males are 5 to 20 percent more likely on the average to receive job offers than blacks or women.[16]

Although both black and white workers lost good jobs, persuasive evidence demonstrates that blacks lost a greater share of the good jobs and gained more of the bad jobs than whites. Darity and Myers report a 30 percent decline in the ratio of good jobs held by blacks compared to whites

and a 1 percent increase in the ratio of bad jobs.[17] Carnoy discovered a similar pattern. He showed that the proportion of white males in low-paying jobs was mostly constant throughout the 1980s, about 31 percent, while the proportion of black and Latino males in these jobs increased sharply. The proportions of black, Latino, and white workers in midlevel jobs declined in the 1980s. Unlike white men and women, however, who made large gains in high-paying jobs, black and Latino workers were downwardly mobile.[18]

Competition between black and white workers for good jobs escalated during this period, a "classic case of protecting one's occupational turf from darker rivals," much like white workers did during the Great Depression. Declining wages and sluggish economic growth exacerbated competition over layoffs, reemployment, and job credentials. Downwardly mobile white workers in the 1980s acted just like unemployed white workers in the 1930s: they played the race card to keep or acquire good jobs.[19]

White workers were not the only culprits responsible for the exclusion of young blacks from high-paying jobs. Employers, as the matched-pairs studies of black and white youth seeking work demonstrate, are less likely to hire young blacks, particularly in service sector jobs. Indeed, some of the most powerful evidence for the persistence of labor market discrimination comes from recent studies of employers' attitudes and decisions. These studies show that many employers strongly prefer to hire white men and avoid hiring black men. Employers prefer white workers because they assume that black workers are less qualified and that there is a "lack of fit" between their own expectations and the cultural values of black employees. Faced with stiff competition, employers demand workers with more soft skills—motivation and the ability to interact with customers and other employees—to the detriment of black workers. Employers believe that black workers lack the soft skills necessary to stay competitive and frequently use negative stereotypes to characterize blacks' abilities.[20] Irate customers who complain about black workers reinforce employers' reluctance to hire them. One employer told researchers, "You do get customers coming in and they'll tell you, 'You need to hire more whites.'" Another study of employers' hiring decisions found that employers with mostly white customers were less likely to hire blacks.[21]

In their study of racial inequality in four cities, Philip Moss and Chris Tilly found that suburban employers were more likely to hire white women, Latinos, and black women than black men. The ratio of the percentage of black males hired in suburban firms to the percentage of black applicants was just .51. The ratio for whites was 1.22 and for Latinos, .87. Among central city employers the pattern was the same, though it was marginally better.[22] Other research shows that employers recruit applicants primarily in white neighborhoods to avoid potential black applicants, or advertise only in suburban or white ethnic newspapers.[23]

Many employers have cleverly taken advantage of these negative stereotypes of black workers. One study in New York City showed that as whites vacated desirable jobs, employers reclassified these well-paying jobs as low-skilled work. They did so partly for economic reasons—reclassification lowers labor costs. But they also assumed that black and Latino workers were incapable of anything but the most rudimentary of tasks. As a result, as "nonwhite New Yorkers get more jobs and have greater access to previously white occupations, [they] still find themselves locked into the [low-wage, dead-end jobs of the] secondary labor market."[24]

Blacks lost out in the 1980s for another reason. Republican policies hostile to affirmative action and labor intensified racial labor market competition. The enforcement of antidiscrimination laws was relaxed, and this was crucial in unleashing racial competition over jobs. Evaluations of affirmative action show that one of the traditional advantages whites have used to cope with economically tough times was restored when antidiscrimination laws were not strictly enforced in the 1980s. . . .

This is the context that set the stage for the recent political conflict over affirmative action. . . . White voters clearly understand the stakes in this controversy. A 1995 poll of likely voters on California's anti-affirmative action ballot proposition (Proposition 209) discovered that white voters were more concerned about losing jobs or promotions because of affirmative action policies (45 percent) than about the potential effects of racial discrimination for blacks and Latinos (25 percent). On the other hand, 80 percent of African Americans and 54 percent of Latinos were concerned that minorities would lose out because of discrimination.[25] Whatever the reality—and there is very little evidence that whites have lost jobs to affirmative action—white workers see themselves as an embattled group whose economic well-being is seriously threatened by affirmative action.

DISCUSSION QUESTIONS

1. Why do you think this article is titled "The Bankruptcy of Virtuous Markets"?
2. What most surprised you in this article?

NOTES

1. Reynolds Farley and Walter R. Allen, *The Color Line and the Quality of America* (New York: Oxford University Press, 1989), p. 225; Cordelia W. Reimers, "The Effect of Tighter Labor Markets on Unemployment of Hispanics and African Americans: The 1990s Experiences," in Robert Cherry and Williams Rodgers III, eds., *Prosperity for All? The Economic Boom and African Americans* (New York: Russell Sage Foundation, 2000), pp. 3–49.
2. William E. Spriggs and Rhonda M. Williams, "What Do We Need to Explain about African American Unemployment?" in Cherry and Rodgers, eds., *Prosperity for All?* pp. 195, 200.
3. Farley and Allen, *The Color Line and the Quality of Life in America*, p. 295.
4. Charles C. Killingsworth, "Negroes in a Changing Labor Market," in Arthur M. Ross and Herbert Hill, eds., *Employment, Race, and Poverty* (New York: Harcourt, Brace and World, 1967), p. 60; Harold Baron and Bennett Hymer, "The Negro Worker in the Chicago Labor Market," p. 255 in Julius Jacobson, ed., *The Negro and the Labor Movement*. New York: Anchor Books, 1968; Gerald David Jaynes and Robin M. Williams, eds., *A Common Destiny: Blacks and American Society* (Washington, D.C.: National Academy Press, 1989), p. 301.
5. Herbert R. Northrup, *Negro Employment in Basic Industry: A Study of Racial Policies in Six Industries* (Philadelphia:

University of Pennsylvania Press, 1970), p. 30; James J. Heckman, "The Central Role of the South in Accounting for the Economic Progress of Black Americans," *American Economic Review* 80 (May 1990): 245

6. Michael K. Brown and Steven P. Erie, "Blacks and the Legacy of the Great Society: The Economic and Political Impact of Federal Social Policy," *Public Policy* 29 (1981): 299–330.

7. Carnoy, *Faded Dreams*, pp. 162–65.

8. Ibid., p. 185; Jaynes and Williams, *A Common Destiny*, pp. 316–18.

9. Carnoy, *Faded Dreams*, pp. 82–83.

10. Council of Economic Advisers, *Economic Report of the President*, 1998 (Washington, D.C.: U.S. Government Printing Office, 1998), p. 150.

11. Roger Waldinger and Thomas Bailey, "The Continuing Significance of Race: Racial Conflict and Racial Discrimination in Construction," *Politics and Society* 19 (1991): 293. This is a classic example of opportunity hoarding; see introduction, "Group Hoarding and the Economic Theory of Discrimination."

12. Deirdre Royster, *Race and the "Invisible Hand"* (Berkeley and Los Angeles: University of California Press, 2003).

13. William Darity Jr. and Samuel L. Myers Jr., *Persistent Disparity: Race and Economic Inequality in the United States since 1945* (Northhampton, Mass.: Edward Elgar Publishing, 1998), pp. 9, 65–67, 69.

14. Darity and Myers, *Persistent Disparity*, pp. 47–48. The salaries of black workers moving from jobs as operatives to sales workers declined from $16,220 to $14,114; the salaries of white workers increased from $18,526 to $25,292.

15. Jerome Culp and Bruce H. Dunson, "Brothers of a Different Color: A Preliminary Look at Employer Treatment of White and Black Youth," in Richard B. Freeman and Harry J. Holzer, eds., *The Black Youth Unemployment Crisis* (Chicago: University of Chicago Press, 1986), p. 241.

16. Harry J. Holzer and David Neumark, "Assessing Affirmative Action," *Journal of Economic Literature* 38 (2000): 496. For a summary of recent research on discrimination, see Darity and Mason, "Evidence on Discrimination in Employment," pp. 79–81. Audit studies have been criticized on both conceptual and empirical grounds, but Deirdre Royster's study of employment discrimination takes the matched-pairs analysis common to audit studies to a new level of sophistication and overcomes the limits of previous studies. See Royster, *Race and the "Invisible Hand."*

17. Darity and Myers, *Persistent Disparity*, pp. 29–30.

18. Carnoy, *Faded Dreams*, pp. 95–99.

19. Darity and Myers, *Persistent Disparity*, p. 51. For a description of the experience of black workers during the depression, see Arthur M. Ross, "The Negro Worker in the Depression," *Social Forces* 18 (1940): 550–59.

20. Philip Moss and Chris Tilly, "'Soft' Skills and Race: An Investigation of Black Men's Employment Problems," *Work and Occupations* 23 (1996): 252–76; Philip Moss and Chris Tilly, "Why Opportunity Isn't Knocking: Racial Inequality and the Demand for Labor," in Alice O'Connor, Chris Tilly, and Lawrence D. Bobo, eds., *Urban Inequality: Evidence from Four Cities* (New York: Russell Sage Foundation, 2001), pp. 444–95.

21. Philip Moss and Chris Tilly, *Stories Employers Tell: Race, Skill, and Hiring in America* (New York: Russell Sage Foundation, 2001), p. 106; Harry J. Holzer, "Employer Hiring Decisions and Antidiscrimination Policy," in Richard B. Freeman, ed., *Generating Jobs: How to Increase Demand for Less-Skilled Workers* (New York: Russell Sage Foundation, 1998), p. 241.

22. Moss and Tilly, "Why Isn't Opportunity Knocking?" pp. 482–83.

23. Kathryn M. Neckerman and Joleen Kirschenman, "Hiring Strategies, Racial Bias, and Inner-City Workers," *Social Problems* 38 (1991): 433–47.

24. Gordon Lafer, "Minority Employment, Labor Market Segmentation, and the Failure of Job-Training Policy in New York City," *Urban Affairs Quarterly* 28 (1992): 224.

25. "Discrimination and Affirmative Action," *California Opinion Index*, (San Francisco: The Field Institute, May 1995), p. 2.

REFERENCES

Baron, Harold and Bennett Hymer. "The Negro Worker in the Chicago Labor Market," in Julius Jacobson, ed., *The Negro and the Labor Movement*. New York: Anchor Books, 1968.

Brown, Michael K., and Steven P. Erie. "Blacks and the Legacy of the Great Society: The Economic and Political Impact of Federal Social Policy." *Public Policy* 29 (1981): 299–330.

Carnoy, Martin. *Faded Dreams: The Politics and Economics of Race in America*. New York: Cambridge University Press, 1994.

Cherry, Robert, and William M. Rodgers III, eds. *Prosperity for All? The Economic Boom and African Americans*. New York: Russell Sage Foundation, 2001.

Council of Economic Advisers. *Economic Report of the President*, 1998. Washington, D.C.: U.S. Government Printing Office, 1998.

Culp, Jerome, and Bruce H. Dunson. "Brothers of a Different Color: A Preliminary Look at Employer Treatment of White and Black Youth." In Richard B. Freeman and Harry J. Holzer, eds., *The Black Youth Unemployment Crisis*. Chicago: University of Chicago Press, 1986.

Darity, William A. Jr., and Patrick L. Mason. "Evidence on Discrimination in Employment: Codes of Color, Codes of Gender." *Journal of Economic Perspectives* 12 (1998): 63–90.

PERSONAL ACCOUNT

Just Like My Mama Said

I remember when I was just a little boy, my mother used to tell me, "Anthony you have to work twice as hard in life as everyone else, because being black means that you already have one strike against you." When I was growing up in a predominately black area, I did not know what she meant by this. Then we moved to an area that was filled with white people. I found myself constantly lagging behind, and I couldn't figure out why.

When I was 19 years old, I hit rock bottom and had nothing. I then remembered what my mama had said, and I began to work twice as hard as everyone else. I managed to afford my own apartment and eventually get married.

My wife is white, but her parents dislike me because of my color. They told her all the stereotypes about "the black male" and swore to her that I would follow suit. Soon after we moved in together, I was laid off from my job. I began to worry that she would think her parents were correct, so I tried to teach her about the black experience. I began to worry that her parents would negatively influence her and I would lose her. I was ready to give in and let her parents win, when I remembered something that my mama had said: "Sometimes you can't teach people; they have to learn on their own." Little did I know an appropriate lesson would soon follow.

As I was going through the want ads, I saw an advertisement for a job delivering pianos. The job paid nine dollars an hour, more money than I had ever earned. I set up an interview for that evening. When my then-fiancée arrived home, I put on a shirt and a tie, grabbed my résumé, and headed for the interview. When I asked her if she thought I would get the job, she said, "I don't see why not. You work hard, you have good references, and you are enrolled in school." Needless to say I felt pretty good about my chances. I interviewed with a middle-aged white lady. The interview went very well. She nearly assured me that I had the job, but said that she just needed to run it by the storeowner. She left and returned with the owner minutes later. He was a middle-aged man of apparently white and Asian descent. He looked at me for a few seconds, and our eyes met. Then he shook his head and said, "No this is not who I want for the job" and walked out. The lady and I dejectedly looked at each other. She attempted to make an excuse for him, but I told her, "Don't worry, it's not your fault." I walked out and told my fiancée what had happened. We rode home in silence. She had just gotten her first taste of what it is like to be black in America.

Anthony McNeill

Darity, William Jr., and Samuel L. Myers Jr. *Persistent Disparity: Race and Economic Inequality in the United States since 1945.* Northhampton, Mass.: Edward Elgar Publishing, 1998.

Farley, Reynolds, and Walter Allen. *The Color Line and the Quality of Life in America.* New York: Oxford University Press, 1989.

Heckman, James J. "The Central Role of the South in Accounting for the Economic Progress of Black Americans." *American Economic Review* 80 (May 1990): 242–46.

Holzer, Harry J. "Employer Hiring Decisions and Antidiscrimination Policy." In Richard B. Freeman, ed., *Generating Jobs: How to Increase Demand for Less-Skilled Workers.* New York: Russell Sage Foundation, 1998.

Holzer, Harry J., and David Neumark. "Assessing Affirmative Action." *Journal of Economic Literature* 38 (2000): 483–568.

Jaynes, Gerald David and Robin M. Williams, eds., *A Common Destiny: Blacks and American Society.* Washington, D.C.: National Academy Press, 1989.

Killingsworth, Charles C. "Negroes in a Changing Labor Market," in Arthur M. Ross and Herbert Hill, eds., *Employment, Race, and Poverty.* New York: Harcourt, Brace and World, 1967.

Lafer, Gordon. "Minority Employment, Labor Market Segmentation, and the Failure of Job-Training Policy in New York City." *Urban Affairs Quarterly* 28 (1991): 206–35.

Moss, Philip, and Chris Tilly. "'Soft' Skills and Race: An Investigation of Black Men's Employment Problems." *Work and Occupations* 23 (1996): 252–76.

———. "Why Opportunity Isn't Knocking: Racial Inequality and the Demand for Labor." In Alice O'Connor, Chris Tilly, and Lawrence D. Bobo, eds., *Urban Inequality: Evidence from Four Cities.* New York: Russell Sage Foundation, 2001.

———. *Stories Employers Tell: Race, Skill, and Hiring in America.* New York: Russell Sage Foundation, 2001.

Neckerman, Kathryn M., and Joleen Kirschenman. "Hiring Strategies, Racial Bias, and Inner-City Workers." *Social Problems* 38 (1991): 433–47.

t. *Negro Employment in Basic Industry: Policies in Six Industries.* Philadelphia: nsylvania Press, 1970.

hris Tilly, and Lawrence D. Bobo, eds., *Evidence from Four Cities,* New York: Russell Sage ndation, 2001.

Oddone, Eugene, et al. "Race, Presenting Signs and Symptoms, Use of Carotid Artery Imaging, and Appropriateness of Carotid Endarterectomy." *Stroke* 30 (1999).

Reimers, Cordelia W. "The Effect of Tighter Labor Markets on Unemployment of Hispanics and African Americans: The 1990s Experiences." In Robert Cherry and Williams Rodgers III, eds., *Prosperity for All? The Economic Boom and African Americans.* New York: Russell Sage Foundation, 2000.

Ross, Arthur M. "The Negro Worker in the Depression." *Social Forces* 18 (1940): 550–59.

Royster, Deirdre. *Race and the "Invisible Hand."* Berkeley: University of California Press, 2003.

Spriggs, William E., and Rhonda M. Williams. "What Do We Need to Explain about African American Unemployment?" In Robert Cherry and Williams Rodgers III, eds., *Prosperity for All? The Economic Boom and African Americans.* New York: Russell Sage Foundation, 2000.

Waldinger, Roger, and Thomas Bailey. "The Continuing Significance of Race: Racial Conflict and Racial Discrimination in Construction." *Politics and Society* 19 (1991).

READING 52

The Model Minority: Asian American "Success" as a Race Relations Failure

Frank Wu

Student: "Asians are threatening our economic future. . . . We can see it right here in our own school. Who are getting into the best colleges, in disproportionate numbers? Asian kids! It's not fair."

Frank Wu is the dean of Wayne State University's Law school. He was the first Asian American to serve as a law professor at the Howard University School of Law, in Washington, D.C. He has written for a range of publications including *The Washington Post, The Los Angeles Times, The Chicago Tribune,* and *The Nation,* and he writes a regular column for *Asian Week.*

Teacher: "Uh . . . That certainly was an unusual essay. . . . Unfortunately, it's racist."

Student: "Um . . . are you sure? My parents helped me."

Garry Trudeau
Recycled Doonesbury: Second
Thoughts on a Gilded Age

REVENGE OF THE NERDS

I am not the model minority. Before I can talk about Asian American experiences at all, I have to kill off the model minority myth because the stereotype obscures many realities. I am an Asian American, but I am not good with computers. I cannot balance my checkbook, much less perform calculus in my head. I would like to fail in school, for no reason other than to cast off my freakish alter ego of geek and nerd. I am tempted to be very rude, just to demonstrate once and for all that I will not be excessively polite, bowing, smiling, and deferring. I am lazy and a loner, who would rather reform the law than obey it and who has no business skills. I yearn to be an artist, an athlete, a rebel, and, above all, an ordinary person.

I am fascinated by the imperviousness of the model minority myth against all efforts at debunking it. I am often told by nice people who are bewildered by the fuss, "You Asians are all doing well. What could you have to complain about anyway? Why would you object to a positive image?" To my frustration, many people who say with the utmost conviction that they would like to be color blind revert to being color conscious as soon as they look at Asian Americans, but then shrug off the contradiction. They are nonchalant about the racial generalization, "You Asians are all doing well," dismissive in asking "What could you have to complain about anyway?" and indifferent to the negative consequences of "a positive image."

Even people who are sympathetic to civil rights in general, including other people of color, sometimes resist mentioning civil rights and Asian

Americans together in the same sentence. It is as if Asian American civil rights concerns can be ruled out categorically without the need for serious consideration of the facts, because everyone knows that Asian Americans are prospering.

Consider the term "overachiever." I am reluctant to accept the title for myself, and not out of Asian modesty. To be called an "overachiever" begs the question: What, exactly, is it that individuals have achieved over—what others expected of them or what they deserve?

In either case, overachievers have surprised observers by surpassing the benchmark, and their exploits are not quite right. They will get their come-uppance sooner or later. Applied to an entire racial group, as "overachiever" is to Asian Americans, the implications are troubling. Asian Americans, often thought of as intellectuals, will be consigned to the same fate as intellectuals. As Columbia University historian Richard Hofstadter stated in the opening pages of his *Anti-intellectualism in American Life*, "The resentment from which the intellectual has suffered in our time is a manifestation not of a decline in his position but of his increasing prominence."[1]

And so it is with Asian Americans. "You Asians are all doing well anyway" summarizes the model minority myth. This is the dominant image of Asians in the United States. Ever since immigration reforms in 1965 led to a great influx of Asian peoples, we have enjoyed an excellent reputation. As a group, we are said to be intelligent, gifted in math and science, polite, hard working, family oriented, law abiding, and successfully entrepreneurial. We revere our elders and show fidelity to tradition. The nation has become familiar with the turn-of-the-century Horatio Alger tales of "pulling yourself up by your own bootstraps" updated for the new millennium with an "Oriental" face and imbued with Asian values.

This miracle is the standard depiction of Asian Americans in fact and fiction, from the news media to scholarly books to Hollywood movies. From the 1960s to the 1990s, profiles of whiz kid Asian Americans became so common as to be cliches. In 1971, *Newsweek* magazine observed that we were "outwhiting the whites."[2] *People* magazine one year made celebrities of the five Asian American teenagers who swept the highest prizes in the annual Westinghouse science talent search in an article headlined "Brain Drain Boon for the U.S.," and it followed up the next year by profiling an entire family of Asian American winners.[3] Brown University history professor Stephen Graubard wrote an op-ed for *The New York Times* asking "Why Do Asian Pupils Win Those Prizes?"[4] The Asian refugee who was a finalist in a spelling bee, but who lost on the word "enchilada," has become legendary.[5] *Time, Newsweek, Sixty Minutes,* and other media outlets have awarded Asian Americans the title "model minority."[6] *Fortune* magazine dubbed us the "superminority."[7] The *New Republic* heralded, "the triumph of Asian Americans" as "America's greatest success story" and *Commentary* magazine referred to Asian Americans as "a trophy population."[8] The *New York Times* announced that we are "going to the head of the class."[9] The *Washington Post* said in a headline, "Asian Americans Outperform Others at School and Work."[10] Smith College sociologist Peter Rose has described Asian Americans as making a transition "from pariahs to paragons."[11] Memoirist Richard Rodriguez and Washington Post columnist William Raspberry have wondered whether Hispanics and blacks, respectively, might be able to emulate Asian immigrants.[12] A minority group could become the equivalent of a white real estate developer: *Advertising Age* quoted a consultant who opined that Asian Americans were "the Donald Trumps of the 1990s."[13]

Conservative politicians especially like to celebrate Asian Americans. President Ronald Reagan called Asian Americans "our exemplars of hope."[14] President George [H.] Bush, California Governor Pete Wilson, House Speaker Newt Gingrich—all have been unduly awed by the model minority myth. In a brief for the *Heritage Foundation Policy Review*, California politician Ron Unz said that Asian Americans come from an "anti-liberal Confucian tradition" that "leaves them a natural constituency for conservatives."[15] In the *National Review*, author William McGurn made the model minority myth a partisan parable: "Precisely because Asian Americans are making it in their adoptive land, they hold the potential not only to add to Republican rolls but to define a bona-fide American language of civil rights."[16]

According to the model minority myth, Asian immigrants have followed the beacon of economic opportunity from their homes in China, Japan, Korea, the Philippines, India, Vietnam, and all the other countries on the Asian continent and within the Pacific Rim. They might be fleeing despotism or Communism, backwardness or the deprivations of war and famine, but whatever the conditions of their past they know that the legend of Golden Mountain, to use the Cantonese phrase, guides their future.

They arrive in America virtually penniless. They bring barely more than the clothes on their backs. Their meager physical possessions are less important than their mental capacity and work ethic. Thanks to their selfless dedication to a small business or an advanced degree in electrical engineering—or both—they are soon achieving the American Dream.

They run a corner grocery in Manhattan, offering the freshest fruits and vegetables and serving up a take-out luncheon buffet priced by the pound. They buy a dry cleaning establishment in Los Angeles, featuring one-hour turnaround times and giving discounts to police officers. They start a motel franchise, which spreads throughout the Midwest, boasting such low rates with amenities like free cable television that other proprietors have no choice but to post signs identifying their accommodations inaccurately as "Native American Owned." They begin a computer chip manufacturing plant in the Silicon Valley, inventing the hottest miniaturized gadgets before selling their shareholdings and retiring at thirty-five. Or they open a boutique in Washington, D.C., with a display case of real-hair wigs on the wall above a bevy of manicurists chatting among themselves in another language while painting their customers' nails....

They come to dominate their trades after less than a decade, reducing their competition to the verge of bankruptcy and then buying up their warehouse stocks. Their associations become monopolies, lending money cooperatively among their own members to preserve their collective advantage. In some cities, they hold more than half the commercial licenses and operate a majority of the downtown "mom and pop" retail outlets. Hospitals and universities have departments wholly staffed by Asian immigrants. Private industries ranging from automobile manufacturers to software developers to government agencies, such as the Defense Department, depend on them for research and development.

In turn, their American-born progeny continue the tradition with their staggering academic prowess. They start off speaking pidgin, some of them even being held back a grade to adjust. They are willing to do as they are told, changing their given names to Anglicized Christian names chosen with the help of their teachers and their friends and told matter of factly to their parents. Above all, they study, study, study.

They are brought up under the strict tutelage of parents who have sacrificed everything in the hopes that their children will garner more than what they themselves have lost. The parents defer everything for themselves and invest it in their young, giving them the mission of redeeming the family. They maintain that anything less than a straight-A report card will shame the ancestors, and they beat their children for receiving a single B-plus. The elders have faith in the school system. They instill respect for educators. They take their children to weekend language lessons instead of allowing them to watch Saturday morning cartoons on television.

The no-nonsense regimen works wonders. A parade of prodigies named Chang, Nguyen, and Patel takes the prizes at piano recitals and proceeds to graduate from high school with honors as valedictorian, salutatorian, and the rest of the top ten of the class, receiving full scholarships to the Ivy League colleges en route to graduate school and advanced professional training....

In the view of other Americans, Asian Americans vindicate the American Dream. A publicity campaign designed to secure the acceptance of Asian Americans could hardly improve perceptions. They have done better here than they ever could have dreamed of doing in their homelands. They are living proof of the power of the free market and the absence of racial discrimination. Their good fortune flows from individual self-reliance and community self-sufficiency, not civil rights activism or government welfare benefits. They believe that merit and effort pay off handsomely and justly, and so they do. Asian Americans do not whine about racial discrimination; they only try harder. If they are told that they have a weakness that prevents their social acceptance, they quickly agree and earnestly attempt to cure it. If they are subjected to mistreatment by their employer, they quit and found their own company rather than protesting or suing.

This caricature is the portrait of the model minority. It is a parody of itself. . . .

Regrettably, the model minority myth embraced by the pundits and the public alike is neither true nor truly flattering. Instead, it is a stock character that plays multiple roles in our racial drama. Like any other myth forming our collective narrative of race, it is ultimately more revealing than reassuring. Complimentary on its face, the model minority myth is disingenuous at its heart.

As well-meaning as it may be, the model minority myth ought to be rejected for three reasons. First, the myth is a gross simplification that is not accurate enough to be seriously used for understanding 10 million people. Second, it conceals within it an invidious statement about African Americans along the lines of the inflammatory taunt: "They made it; why can't you?" Third, the myth is abused both to deny that Asian Americans experience racial discrimination and to turn Asian Americans into a racial threat.

GERMS OF TRUTH WITHIN THE MYTH

Like many racial stereotypes, the model minority myth has a germ of truth. The problem, however, is that the germ becomes exaggerated and distorted. On its own terms, the myth is not even persuasive as a description of the status of Asian Americans.

In earning power, for example, the evidence points toward a disparity between what individual white Americans and what individual Asian Americans are paid—and not for lack of trying on the part of Asian Americans.

To figure out the facts, University of Hawaii sociology professor Herbert Barringer led a team that conducted the most comprehensive review of the research literature ever done. Barringer concludes that with respect to income, "in almost every category . . . whites showed advantages over most Asian Americans."[17]

Barringer proceeds cautiously because he is contesting the model minority myth. Even controlling for nativity—that is, native-born versus foreign-born—Barringer finds that Asian Americans who are native-born earn less money than white Americans who are native-born and possibly even than white Americans who are foreign-born. That means that Asians without cultural and language difficulties may earn less than white Americans who may have such difficulties. Barringer observes that "there seems to be no compelling reason to argue for parity" between Asian Americans and white Americans, but he does agree that Asian Americans "have certainly done much better with incomes than have blacks and Hispanics." He states that Asian Americans, including such ethnic groups as Vietnamese immigrants, might show "decided improvements" over time. He prefers "the most favorable interpretation," that "most Asian Americans are overeducated compared to whites for the incomes they earn."[18]

That interpretation, however, is most favorable to white Americans and not Asian Americans. Translated into practical terms, it means that white Americans are paid more than Asian Americans who are equally qualified. Either Asian Americans are not hired for the higher-paying jobs, or they are hired but are still paid less. . . .

The fact that Asian Americans are better educated than white Americans on average undermines rather than supports the model minority myth. The gap between Asian Americans and white Americans that appears with income reverses itself with education. It was consistent throughout the 1980s and 1990s. In 1980, approximately 36 percent of foreign-born Asian Americans had finished college compared with 16 percent of native-born citizens. In 1990, about 42 percent of Asian Americans had finished college compared with 25 percent of the general population. Every Asian American ethnic group, except Filipinos, attends college at higher rates than do white Americans. Chinese Americans, Indian Americans, and Korean Americans attend college at about twice the rate of white Americans. The entering classes of Ivy League schools are now as high as 20 percent Asian American, California schools such as University of California–Berkeley and UCLA as much as twice that percentage as Asian Americans become a plurality on campuses with no majority. Considering all educational institutions, Asian American overrepresentation is much lower but still significant: As of 1993, Asian Americans made up 5.3 percent of the college student body but approximately 2.9 percent of the general population. Their desire for education is increasing even as that of other groups is decreasing. Between 1979 and 1989, Asian Americans increased their numbers of Ph.D. recipients by 46 percent while whites and blacks decreased their numbers by 6 and 23 percent, respectively. By 1997, Asian Americans were receiving 12 percent of the doctorates conferred by U.S. universities, and they received more than one-quarter of the doctorates in engineering disciplines.

Although the average educational levels of Asian Americans might be taken as substantiating the model minority myth, the more plausible reading is that Asian Americans have had to overcompensate. Asian Americans receive a lower return on investment in education. They gain less money than white Americans on average for each additional degree. . . .

Moreover, Asian immigrants start off relatively privileged. This admission must be made gingerly, so that it will not be taken as corroboration of the model minority myth. In actuality, it undercuts the myth. Most Asian Americans are not rich. But some Asian immigrants are relatively fortunate compared to the many Asians who reside in Asia, and some of them are relatively fortunate compared

to native-born Americans (including, incidentally, native-born Asian Americans), even though they have not had an easy time of it in coming to the United States and even though they experience prejudice. A major study of diversity in the power elite found that almost none of the Chinese Americans who served on the boards of directors for Fortune 1000 companies were "authentic bootstrappers."[19] Almost all of them had come from well-to-do families in China, Taiwan, and Hong Kong.

University of California at Santa Cruz sociologist Deborah Woo examined more closely the media coverage of "a Korean-born immigrant who once worked the night shift at 7-Eleven to put himself through school" and who sold his company for $1 billion, as well as another Korean-born immigrant, a Silicon Valley entrepreneur who lived on ramen noodles and had to pawn his belongings to pay his phone bill, but gave $15 million to the San Francisco Asian Art Museum, "mak[ing] Horatio Alger look like a slacker."[20] Woo delved into the backgrounds of these examples of the model minority myth. In the former instance, the individual was able to start his company because he had received a government contract through a minority set-aside program. In the latter, the man was descended from the royal family that ruled Korea until the Japanese takeover of 1905, and he had been a university professor and an executive in the family business in Korea before emigrating. They are still impressive people, but they have not come from the ghetto. The sheen comes off the model minority myth once the real stories are revealed.

Asian immigrants personify "brain drain": the selective nature of immigration. More than half of the professional immigrants to the United States are Asian; Asian men are well over a majority of the professional immigrants in technical occupations. Indian doctors are the single largest ethnic group in the medical profession in this country, at about 4 percent of the total number of physicians; 11 percent of Indian men in the United States and 7 percent of Indian women hold medical degrees. Filipina women are over half the total number of registered nurses who were trained abroad; thousands more come every year. In 1990, 20 percent of all Filipino Americans listed their area of employment as health care. For many Asian ethnicities in the United States, such as Indians, the earliest cohort of immigrants following immigration policy reforms are the most qualified, and the continuing stream is less elite. Among some Asian ethnicities, such as Filipinos, the foreign-born generally make more money than the native-born. Under restrictive immigration policies, individuals who have skills that are in high demand in the United States have greater opportunities to acquire a green card. . . .

The model minority myth also masks great disparities among Asian ethnic groups. Japanese Americans and Chinese Americans are closest to equality with whites, but Vietnamese Americans and other Southeast Asian refugees languish at the bottom of the economic pyramid, along with blacks. . . .

Finally, the figures for Asian Americans are rendered unreliable by the careless inclusion of Asians who reside in the United States but who are not Asian Americans at all.[21] Hundreds of business executives with Japanese-based multinational companies spend stints of up to a few years here. Their upper-management salaries add to the average Asian American income, but they are no more representative of either Asians overseas or Asian immigrants than a white American vice president of a Fortune 500 company who was an expatriate manager in Europe would be either average of Americans or of Europeans themselves. They are part of a transnational overclass. . . .

Upon anything more than cursory reflection, the model minority myth becomes mystifying. The model minority myth is misleading not only because it takes for granted that racial groups rather than individual persons are the best basis for thinking about human lives, but also because it equates status and conduct. These most pernicious qualities of the myth are hidden in the open. Whatever else might be said about the myth, it cannot be disputed that it is a racial generalization. As such, it contains the premise that people can be arranged by racial group, and, furthermore, that

the differences between racial groups are more significant than either the similarities between racial groups or the differences within them. It makes race the main feature of an individual as well as the leading division among people. . . .

The model minority myth persists, despite violating our societal norms against racial stereotyping and even though it is not accurate. Dozens of amply documented and heavily annotated government studies and scholarly papers, along with a handful of better magazine and newspaper articles supplemented by television segments and public speeches, all intended to destroy the myth, have had negligible effect on popular culture. . . .

The myth has not succumbed to individualism or facts because it serves a purpose in reinforcing racial hierarchies. Asian Americans are as much a "middleman minority" as we are a model minority. We are placed in the awkward position of buffer or intermediary, elevated as the preferred racial minority at the expense of denigrating African Americans. Asian American writers and scholars have not hesitated to call the phenomenon what it is. Novelist Frank Chin has described it as "racist love," contrasting it with "racist hate" of other people of color. DePaul University law professor Sumi Cho has explained that Asian Americans are turned into "racial mascots," giving right-wing causes a novel messenger, camouflaging arguments that would look unconscionably self-interested if made by whites about themselves. University of California at Irvine political scientist Claire Kim has argued that Asian Americans are positioned through "racial triangulation," much as a Machiavellian would engage in political triangulation for maximum advantage. Law professor Mari Matsuda famously declared, "we will not be used" in repudiating the model minority myth.[22]

Whatever the effects are called, Asian Americans become pawns. We are not recognized in our own right but advanced for ulterior motives. Michael S. Greve, a leading advocate against racial remedies, said that the controversy over anti-Asian discrimination could be used to attack affirmative action: It presented "an opportunity to call, on behalf of a racial minority (i.e., the Asian applicants), for an end to discrimination. It was an appeal that, when made on behalf of whites, is politically hopeless and, perhaps, no longer entirely respectable."[23] . . .

BACKLASH FROM THE MYTH

The model minority myth hurts Asian Americans themselves. It is two-faced. Every attractive trait matches up neatly to its repulsive complement, and the aspects are conducive to reversal. If we acquiesced to the myth in its favorable guise, we would be precluded from rejecting its unfavorable interpretations. We would already have accepted the characteristics at issue as inherent.

The turnaround is inevitable during a military crisis or economic downturn. To be intelligent is to be calculating and too clever; to be gifted in math and science is to be mechanical and not creative, lacking interpersonal skills and leadership potential. To be polite is to be inscrutable and submissive. To be hard working is to be an unfair competitor for regular human beings and not a well-rounded, likable individual. To be family oriented is to be clannish and too ethnic. To be law abiding is to be self-righteous and rigidly rule-bound. To be successfully entrepreneurial is to be deviously aggressive and economically intimidating. To revere elders is to be an ancestor-worshipping pagan, and fidelity to tradition is reactionary ignorance.

Asian Americans cannot win by winning. . . .

The model minority myth does more than cover up racial discrimination; it instigates racial discrimination as retribution. The hyperbole about Asian American affluence can lead to jealousy on the part of non-Asian Americans, who may suspect that Asian Americans are too comfortable or who are convinced [that] Asian American gains are their losses. Through the justification of the myth, the humiliation of Asian Americans or even physical attacks directed against Asian Americans become compensation or retaliation. . . .

It would be bad enough if the model minority myth were true. Everyone else would resent Asian Americans for what Asian Americans possess.

It is worse that the model minority myth is false. Everyone else resents Asian Americans for what they believe Asian Americans possess. Other Americans say that their resentment is about riches and not race, but they assume that Asian Americans are rich on the basis of race; there is no escaping that the resentment is racial. Above all, the model minority myth is a case study in the risks of racial stereotypes of any kind. It is the stereotyping itself, not the positive or negative valence it assumes temporarily, that is dangerous. A stereotype confines its subjects. The myth was neither created by nor is it controlled by Asian Americans. It is applied to but not by Asian Americans.

DISCUSSION QUESTIONS

1. Is being a model minority a burden?
2. What are some of the consequences of the model minority myth for Asian Americans?
3. How would you feel about "positive stereotypes" being applied to a group that you were a member of?

NOTES

1. Richard Hofstadter, *Anti-intellectualism in American Life* (New York: Knopf, 1963), 6.
2. "Success Story: Outwhiting the Whites," *Newsweek*, June 21, 1971, 24.
3. David Grogan, "Brain Drain Boon for the U.S.: Students of Asian-American Families with Rare Genetic Gifts and a Reverence for Learning Sweep a Science Contest for the Nation's High-Schoolers," *People*, April 21, 1986, 30; Mary Shaughnessy, "When the Westinghouse Talent Scout Dealt Out Their Awards, They Gave the Kuos a Full House," *People*, June 8, 1987, 149.
4. Stephen G. Graubard, "Why Do Asian Pupils Win Those Prizes?" *New York Times*, January 29, 1988, A35.
5. "Minestrone, Ratatouille and Strudel," *Washington Post*, June 14, 1983, A18.
6. David Brand, "The New Whiz Kids: Why Asian Americans Are Doing So Well, and What It Costs Them," *Time*, August 31, 1987, 42; Martin Kasindorf, "Asian Americans: A Model Minority," *Newsweek*, December 6, 1982, 39.
7. Anthony Ramirez, "America's Super Minority," *Fortune*, November 24, 1986, 148.

PERSONAL ACCOUNT

Let Me Work for It!

I remember once in a sociology of education class that I was asked to describe my educational experience. At first, I was quick to say that it was very positive. Although racial remarks and jokes were passed around school, teachers and administrators paid little or no attention to them. I always felt uneasy with such remarks, but because the teachers and administrators would play ignorant to what was being said, I felt that maybe I was being too sensitive. Therefore, I learned to suck it up and was taught to view such comments as harmless.

Still, at a very young age I was very aware of racism and sexism. Both of my Vietnamese parents came to the United States when they were 20 years old. They arrived right before the Vietnam War ended, which explains the stigmatization they experienced. "VC" was a common epithet addressed to my dad along with "Gook" and "Charlie." My mom, on the other hand, struggled with gender/racial stereotypes such as being labeled mindless, dependent, and subservient. I can recall many times watching people mentally battering my parents. Numerous looks of disgust and intolerance of my parents' accent or confusion with the English language were some unpleasant cases that I experienced. Yet the snide remarks and mistreatment thrown at my parents remain the most hurtful. Many times my parents were told that their lack of proficiency in English would doom them from success and from any self-worth. They were also ostracized for holding on to their Vietnamese culture and were persuaded to assimilate to the American culture. The accumulation of these events reinforced the idea that being different, in this case Vietnamese, was negative. As far as I was concerned, my family was my only community. It was only within my family that I felt the sense of security, love, support, and, most importantly, connection. After all, I was just a "Gook" like my parents.

Yet I experienced support and love at school. I can trace this feeling all the way back to third grade. I remember how I was constantly praised for being so bright, even before turning in my first assignment. This did not send alarms to my brain. As a student, I felt great. I felt validated. But looking back on it now, there are alarms going off for me. Why? Because now I wonder if I was being labeled as a model student, a positive stereotype. Many Americans have held positive stereotypes about Asians and their work/study ethic, and making these stereotypes prior to a person's performance can create the possibility of drowning in the pressure of high expectations. Teachers have always had unreasonably high expectations for me. Although I did not experience this as pressure, I do feel that I have been robbed of the equal chance to prove myself, to see my mistakes and grow. I feel that I have so much to give, but my audience is content with what they "know" of me (which is usually built upon assumptions). I was never given the chance to work for the standing ovation; nor was I given the privilege of criticism.

At the personal level, the model minority stereotype has denied me human dignity, individuality, and the acknowledgment of my own strengths and weaknesses. I feel that I have been prejudged in this fictitious view of Asian Americans. These positive portrayals depict Asians as so flawless that they are robbed of any humanity. Some may feel indifferent to my story or ask if I really reject the positive stereotype. My only reply is this: positive and negative stereotyping are different sides of the same coin. Both invalidate individuals as human beings and lead to negative consequences.

Isabelle Nguyen

8. Daniel A. Bell, "The Triumph of Asian Americans: America's Greatest Success Story," *New Republic*, July 15, 1985, 24; Louis Winnick, "America's 'Model Minority,'" *Commentary* (August 1990): 23.

9. Fox Butterfield, "Why Asians Are Going to the Head of the Class: Some Fear Colleges Use Quotas to Limit Admissions," *New York Times*, August 3, 1986, Educational Supplement, 18.

10. Spencer Rich, "Asian Americans Outperform Others in School and at Work: Census Data Outlines 'Model Minority,'" *Washington Post*, October 10, 1985, A1.

11. Peter I. Rose, *Tempest-Tost: Race, Immigration, and the Dilemmas of Diversity* (New York: Oxford University Press, 1997).

12. Richard Rodriguez, "Asians: A Class by Themselves; A Formal Model for Minority Education," *Los Angeles Times*,

October 11, 1987, E1. Among William Raspberry's several articles on Asian Americans are "Asian Americans—Too Successful?" *Washington Post,* February 10, 1990, A23; "The Curse of Low Expectations," *Washington Post,* March 4, 1988, A25; and "When White Guilt Won't Matter," *Washington Post,* November 4, 1987, A23.

13. Alice Z. Cuneo, "Asian Americans: Companies Disoriented about Asians: Fast-Growing but Diverse Market Holds Key to Buying Power," *Advertising Age,* July 9, 1990, S2.

14. Rose, *Tempest-Tost,* 4.

15. Ron K. Unz, "Immigration or the Welfare State: Which Is Our Real Enemy?" *Heritage Foundation Policy Review* (Fall 1994): 33.

16. William McGurn, "The Silent Majority: Asian Americans' Affinity with Republican Party Principles," *National Review,* June 24, 1991, 19. Stuart Rothenberg and William McGurn, "The Invisible Success Story: Asian Americans and Politics," *National Review,* Sept. 15, 1989, 17. After the 2000 Presidential elections, in which Asian Americans supported Gore over Bush, the editor of *National Review* changed his mind about the prospects of Asian Americans belonging to the conservative "investor class" rather than representing the liberal "impact of immigration." John O'Sullivan, "Following the Returns: Investor Class or Immigrant Tide?" *National Review,* Dec. 18, 2000, 30.

17. Herbert R. Barringer, *Asians and Pacific Islanders in the United States* (New York: Russell Sage Foundation, 1993), 265.

18. Ibid., 266–67. *See* U.S. Department of Labor, Federal Glass Ceiling Commission, *A Solid Investment: Making Full Use of the Nation's Human Capital* (Washington, D.C.: Government Printing Office, 1995) and Federal Glass Ceiling Commission, *Good for Business: Making Full Use of the Nation's Human Capital* (Washington, D.C.: Government Printing Office, 1995).

19. Richard L. Zweigenhaft and G. William Domhoff, *Diversity in the Power Elite: Have Women and Minorities Reached the Top?* (New Haven, Conn.: Yale University Press, 1998), 140–57.

20. Deborah Woo, *Glass Ceilings and Asian Americans: The New Fear of Workplace Barriers* (Walnut Creek, Calif.: Alta Mira Press, 2000), 26–30.

21. U.S. Civil Rights Commission, *The Economic Status of Asian Americans* (Washington, D.C.: Government Printing Office, 1988), 86.

22. Frank Chin and Jeffrey Paul Chan, "Racist Love," in Richard Kostelanetz, ed., *Seeing Through the Shuck* (New York: Ballantine, 1972), 65; Sumi Cho, "Redeeming Whiteness in the Shadow of Internment: Earl Warren, Brown, and a Theory of Racial Redemption," *Boston College Law Review* 40 (1988): 120; Clair Jean Kim, "The Racial Triangulation of Asian Americans," in Gordon H. Chang, ed., *Asian Americans and Politics: Perspectives, Experiences, Prospects* (Washington, D.C.: Woodrow Wilson Center/

Stanford University Press 2001), 39–78; Mari Matsuda, "We Will Not Be Used: Are Asian Americans the Racial Bourgeoisie?" in *Where Is Your Body* (Boston: Beacon Press, 1996), 149–159. Matsuda delivered the talk at the 1990 dinner of the Asian Law Caucus in San Francisco, California, where she first used the phrase.

23. Michael S. Greve, "The Newest Move in Law Schools' Quota Game," *Wall Street Journal,* October 5, 1992, A12. Recognizing the divisive role Asian Americans were being inserted into, the Japanese American Citizens League withdrew its support for proposed legislation attacking affirmative action in 1989. One of the sponsors of the bill had said of the effort: "So, in a way, we want to help Asian Americans, but at the same time we're using it as a vehicle to correct what we consider to be a societal mistake on the part of the United States." Robert W. Stewart, "'Merit Only' College Entry Proposal Failing: Opposition by Japanese Americans to Admissions Policy Change Frustrates GOP Sponsor," *Los Angeles Times,* December 9, 1989, B12.

READING 53

The Pressure to Cover

Kenji Yoshino

When I began teaching at Yale Law School in 1998, a friend spoke to me frankly. "You'll have a better chance at tenure," he said, "if you're a homosexual professional than if you're a professional homosexual." Out of the closet for six years at the time, I knew what he meant. To be a "homosexual professional" was to be a professor of constitutional law who "happened" to be gay. To be a "professional homosexual" was to be a gay professor who made gay rights his work. Others echoed the sentiment in less elegant formulations. Be gay, my world seemed to say. Be openly gay, if you want. But don't flaunt.

I didn't experience the advice as antigay. The law school is a vigorously tolerant place, embedded in a university famous for its gay student population. (As the undergraduate jingle goes: "One in four, maybe more/One in three, maybe me/One in two, maybe you.") I took my colleague's words as generic

---

Kenji Yoshino is a professor of law at Yale Law School.

counsel to leave my personal life at home. I could see that research related to one's identity—referred to in the academy as "mesearch"—could raise legitimate questions about scholarly objectivity.

I also saw others playing down their outsider identities to blend into the mainstream. Female colleagues confided that they would avoid references to their children at work, lest they be seen as mothers first and scholars second. Conservative students asked for advice about how open they could be about their politics without suffering repercussions at some imagined future confirmation hearing. A religious student said he feared coming out as a believer, as he thought his intellect would be placed on a 25 percent discount. Many of us, it seemed, had to work our identities as well as our jobs.

It wasn't long before I found myself resisting the demand to conform. What bothered me was not that I had to engage in straight-acting behavior, much of which felt natural to me. What bothered me was the felt need to mute my passion for gay subjects, people, culture. At a time when the law was transforming gay rights, it seemed ludicrous not to suit up and get in the game.

"Mesearch" being what it is, I soon turned my scholarly attention to the pressure to conform. What puzzled me was that I felt that pressure so long after my emergence from the closet. When I stopped passing, I exulted that I could stop thinking about my sexuality. This proved naïve. Long after I came out, I still experienced the need to assimilate to straight norms. But I didn't have a word for this demand to tone down my known gayness.

Then I found my word, in the sociologist Erving Goffman's book *Stigma*. Written in 1963, the book describes how various groups—including the disabled, the elderly and the obese—manage their "spoiled" identities. After discussing passing, Goffman observes that "persons who are ready to admit possession of a stigma . . . may nonetheless make a great effort to keep the stigma from looming large." He calls this behavior covering. He distinguishes passing from covering by noting that passing pertains to the visibility of a characteristic, while covering pertains to its obtrusiveness. He relates how F.D.R. stationed

himself behind a desk before his advisers came in for meetings. Roosevelt was not passing, since everyone knew he used a wheelchair. He was covering, playing down his disability so people would focus on his more conventionally presidential qualities.

As is often the case when you learn a new idea, I began to perceive covering everywhere. Leafing through a magazine, I read that Helen Keller replaced her natural eyes (one of which protruded) with brilliant blue glass ones. On the radio, I heard that Margaret Thatcher went to a voice coach to lower the pitch of her voice. Friends began to send me e-mail. Did I know that Martin Sheen was Ramon Estevez on his birth certificate, that Ben Kingsley was Krishna Bhanji, that Kirk Douglas was Issur Danielovitch Demsky and that Jon Stewart was Jonathan Leibowitz?

In those days, spotting instances of covering felt like a parlor game. It's hard to get worked up about how celebrities and politicians have to manage their public images. Jon Stewart joked that he changed his name because Leibowitz was "too Hollywood," and that seemed to get it exactly right. My own experience with covering was also not particularly difficult—once I had the courage to write from my passions, I was immediately embraced.

It was only when I looked for instances of covering in the law that I saw how lucky I had been. Civil rights case law is peopled with plaintiffs who were severely punished for daring to be openly different. Workers were fired for lapsing into Spanish in English-only workplaces, women were fired for behaving in stereotypically "feminine" ways and gay parents lost custody of their children for engaging in displays of same-sex affection. These cases revealed that far from being a parlor game, covering was the civil rights issue of our time.

THE NEW DISCRIMINATION

In recent decades, discrimination in America has undergone a generational shift. Discrimination was once aimed at entire groups, resulting in the exclusion of all racial minorities, women, gays, religious minorities and people with disabilities. A battery of civil rights laws—like the Civil Rights Act of 1964 and the Americans with Disabilities Act of 1990—sought to combat these forms of discrimination. The triumph of American civil rights is that such categorical exclusions by the state or employers are now relatively rare.

Now a subtler form of discrimination has risen to take its place. This discrimination does not aim at groups as a whole. Rather, it aims at the subset of the group that refuses to cover, that is, to assimilate to dominant norms. And for the most part, existing civil rights laws do not protect individuals against such covering demands. The question of our time is whether we should understand this new discrimination to be a harm and, if so, whether the remedy is legal or social in nature.

Consider the following cases:

- Renee Rogers, an African-American employee at American Airlines, wore cornrows to work. American had a grooming policy that prevented employees from wearing an all-braided hairstyle. When American sought to enforce this policy against Rogers, she filed suit, alleging race discrimination. In 1981, a federal district court rejected her argument. It first observed that cornrows were not distinctively associated with African-Americans, noting that Rogers had only adopted the hairstyle after it "had been popularized by a white actress in the film '10.'" As if recognizing the unpersuasiveness of what we might call the Bo Derek defense, the court further alleged that because hairstyle, unlike skin color, was a mutable characteristic, discrimination on the basis of grooming was not discrimination on the basis of race. Renee Rogers lost her case.

- Lydia Mikus and Ismael Gonzalez were called for jury service in a case involving a defendant who was Latino. When the prosecutor asked them whether they could speak Spanish, they answered in the affirmative. The prosecutor struck them, and the defense attorney then brought suit on their behalf, claiming national-origin discrimination. The prosecutor responded that he had not removed the potential jurors for their ethnicity but for their ability to speak Spanish. His stated concern was that they would not defer to the court translator in listening to Spanish-language testimony. In 1991, the Supreme Court credited this argument. Lydia Mikus and Ismael Gonzalez lost their case.

- Diana Piantanida had a child and took a maternity leave from her job at the Wyman Center, a charitable organization in Missouri. During her leave, she was demoted, supposedly for previously having handed in work late. The man who was then the Wyman Center's executive director, however, justified her demotion by saying the new position would be easier "for a new mom to handle." As it turned out, the new position had less responsibility and half the pay of the original one. But when Piantanida turned this position down, her successor was paid Piantanida's old salary. Piantanida brought suit, claiming she had been discharged as a "new mom." In 1997, a federal appellate court refused to analyze her claim as a sex-discrimination case, which would have led to comparing the treatment she received to the treatment of "new dads." Instead, it found that Piantanida's (admittedly vague) pleadings raised claims only under the Pregnancy Discrimination Act, which it correctly interpreted to protect women only while they are pregnant. Diana Piantanida lost her case.

- Robin Shahar was a lesbian attorney who received a job offer from the Georgia Department of Law, where she had worked as a law student. The summer before she started her new job, Shahar had a religious same-sex commitment ceremony with her partner. She asked a supervisor for a late starting date because she was getting married and wanted to go on a celebratory trip to Greece. Believing Shahar was marrying a man, the supervisor offered his congratulations. Senior officials in the office soon learned, however, that Shahar's partner was a woman. This news caused a stir, reports of which reached Michael Bowers, the attorney general of Georgia who had successfully defended his state's prohibition of sodomy before the United States Supreme Court. After deliberating with his lawyers, Bowers rescinded her job offer. The staff member who informed her read from a script, concluding, "Thanks again for coming in, and have a nice day." Shahar brought suit, claiming discrimination on the basis of sexual orientation. In court, Bowers testified that he knew Shahar was gay when he hired her, and would never have terminated her for that reason. In 1997, a federal appellate court accepted that defense, maintaining that Bowers had terminated Shahar on the basis of her conduct, not her status. Robin Shahar lost her case.

- Simcha Goldman, an Air Force officer who was also an ordained rabbi, wore a yarmulke at all times. Wearing a yarmulke is part of the Orthodox tradition of covering one's head out of deference to an omnipresent god. Goldman's religious observance ran afoul of an Air Force regulation that prohibited wearing headgear while indoors. When he refused his commanding officer's order to remove his yarmulke, Goldman was threatened with a court martial. He brought a First Amendment claim, alleging discrimination on the basis of religion. In 1986, the Supreme Court rejected his claim. It stated that the Air Force had drawn a reasonable line between "religious apparel that is visible and that which is not." Simcha Goldman lost his case.

These five cases represent only a fraction of those in which courts have refused to protect plaintiffs from covering demands. In such cases, the courts routinely distinguish between immutable and mutable traits, between being a member of a legally protected group and behavior associated with that group. Under this rule, African-Americans cannot be fired for their skin color, but they could be fired for wearing cornrows. Potential jurors cannot be struck for their ethnicity but can be struck for speaking (or even for admitting proficiency in) a foreign language. Women cannot be discharged for having two X chromosomes but can be penalized (in some jurisdictions) for becoming mothers. Although the weaker protections for sexual orientation mean gays can sometimes be fired for their status alone, they will be much more vulnerable if they are perceived to "flaunt" their sexuality. Jews cannot be separated from the military for being Jewish but can be discharged for wearing yarmulkes.

This distinction between being and doing reflects a bias toward assimilation. Courts will protect traits like skin color or chromosomes because such traits cannot be changed. In contrast, the courts will not protect mutable traits, because individuals can alter them to fade into the mainstream, thereby escaping discrimination. If individuals choose not to engage in that form of self-help, they must suffer the consequences.

The judicial bias toward assimilation will seem correct and just to many Americans. Assimilation, after all, is a precondition of civilization—wearing clothes, having manners and obeying the law are all acts of assimilation. Moreover, the tie between assimilation and American civilization may be particularly strong. At least since Hector St. John de Crèvecoeur's 1782 "Letters from an American Farmer," this country has promoted assimilation as the way Americans of different backgrounds would be "melted into a new race of men." By the time Israel Zangwill's play "The Melting Pot" made its debut in 1908, the term had acquired the burnish of an American ideal. Theodore Roosevelt, who believed hyphenations like "Polish-American" were a "moral treason," is reputed to have yelled, "That's a great play!" from his box when it was performed in Washington. (He was wrong—it's no accident the title has had a longer run than the play.) And notwithstanding challenges beginning in the 1960's to move "beyond the melting pot" and to "celebrate diversity," assimilation has never lost its grip on the American imagination.

If anything, recent years have seen a revival of the melting-pot ideal. We are currently experiencing a pluralism explosion in the United States. Patterns of immigration since the late 1960's have made the United States the most religiously various country in the history of the world. Even when the demographics of a group—like the number of individuals with disabilities—are presumably constant, the number of individuals claiming membership in that group may grow exponentially. In 1970, there were 9 disability-related associations listed in the Encyclopedia of Associations; in 1980, there were 16; in 1990, there were 211; and in 2000, there were 799. The boom in identity politics has led many thoughtful commentators to worry that we are losing our common culture as Americans. Fearful that we are breaking apart into balkanized fiefs, even liberal lions like Arthur Schlesinger have called for a recommitment to the ethic of assimilation.

Beyond keeping pace with the culture, the judiciary has institutional reasons for encouraging assimilation. In the yarmulke case, the government argued that ruling in favor of the rabbi's yarmulke would immediately invite suits concerning the Sikh's turban, the yogi's saffron robes and the Rastafarian's dreadlocks. Because the courts must articulate principled grounds for their decisions, they are particularly ill equipped to protect some groups but not others in an increasingly diverse society. Seeking to avoid judgments about the relative worth of groups, the judiciary has decided instead to rely on the relatively uncontroversial principle of protecting immutable traits.

Viewed in this light, the judiciary's failure to protect individuals against covering demands seems eminently reasonable. Unfortunately, it also represents an abdication of its responsibility to protect civil rights.

THE CASE AGAINST ASSIMILATION

The flaw in the judiciary's analysis is that it casts assimilation as an unadulterated good. Assimilation is implicitly characterized as the way in which groups can evade discrimination by fading into the mainstream—after all, the logic goes, if a bigot cannot discriminate between two individuals, he cannot discriminate against one of them. But sometimes assimilation is not an escape from discrimination, but precisely its effect. When a Jew is forced to convert to Protestantism, for instance, we do not celebrate that as an evasion of anti-Semitism. We should not blind ourselves to the dark underbelly of the American melting pot.

Take the cornrows case. Initially, this case appears to be an easy one for the employer, as hairstyle seems like such a trivial thing. But if hair is so trivial, we might ask why American Airlines made it a condition of Renee Rogers's employment. What's

frustrating about the employment discrimination jurisprudence is that courts often don't force employers to answer the critical question of why they are requiring employees to cover. If we look to other sources, the answers can be troubling.

John T. Molloy's perennially popular self-help manual "New Dress for Success" also tells racial minorities to cover. Molloy advises African-Americans to avoid "Afro hairstyles" and to wear "conservative pinstripe suits, preferably with vests, accompanied by all the establishment symbols, including the Ivy League tie." He urges Latinos to "avoid pencil-line mustaches," "any hair tonic that tends to give a greasy or shiny look to the hair," "any articles of clothing that have Hispanic associations" and "anything that is very sharp or precise."

Molloy is equally frank about why covering is required. The "model of success," he says, is "white, Anglo-Saxon and Protestant." Those who do not possess these traits "will elicit a negative response to some degree, regardless of whether that response is conscious or subconscious." Indeed, Molloy says racial minorities must go "somewhat overboard" to compensate for immutable differences from the white mainstream. After conducting research on African-American corporate grooming, Molloy reports that "blacks had not only to dress more conservatively but also more expensively than their white counterparts if they wanted to have an equal impact."

Molloy's basic point is supported by social-science research. The economists Marianne Bertrand and Sendhil Mullainathan recently conducted a study in which they sent out résumés that were essentially identical except for the names at the top. They discovered that résumés with white-sounding names like Emily Walsh or Greg Baker drew 50 percent more callbacks than those with African-American-sounding names like Lakisha Washington or Jamal Jones. So it seems that even when Americans have collectively set our faces against racism, we still react negatively to cultural traits—like hairstyles, clothes or names—that we associate with historically disfavored races.

We can see a similar dynamic in the termination of Robin Shahar. Michael Bowers, the state attorney general, disavowed engaging in first-generation discrimination when he said he had no problem with gay employees. This raises the question of why he fired Shahar for having a religious same-sex commitment ceremony. Unlike American Airlines, Bowers provided some answers. He argued that retaining Shahar would compromise the department's ability to deny same-sex couples marriage licenses and to enforce sodomy statutes.

Neither argument survives scrutiny. At no point did Shahar seek to marry her partner legally, nor did she agitate for the legalization of same-sex marriage. The Georgia citizenry could not fairly have assumed that Shahar's religious ceremony would entitle the couple to a civil license. Bowers's claim that Shahar's wedding would compromise her ability to enforce sodomy statutes is also off the mark. Georgia's sodomy statute (which has since been struck down) punished cross-sex as well as same-sex sodomy, meaning that any heterosexual in the department who had ever had oral sex was as compromised as Shahar.

Stripped of these rationales, Bowers's termination of Shahar looks more sinister. When she told a supervisor she was getting married, he congratulated her. When he discovered she was marrying a woman, it wasn't long before she no longer had a job. Shahar's religious ceremony was not in itself indiscreet; cross-sex couples engage in such ceremonies all the time. If Shahar was flaunting anything, it was her belief in her own equality: her belief that she, and not the state, should determine what personal bonds are worthy of celebration.

The demand to cover is anything but trivial. It is the symbolic heartland of inequality—what reassures one group of its superiority to another. When dominant groups ask subordinated groups to cover, they are asking them to be small in the world, to forgo prerogatives that the dominant group has and therefore to forgo equality. If courts make critical goods like employment dependent on covering, they are legitimizing second-class citizenship for the subordinated group. In doing so, they are failing to vindicate the promise of civil rights.

So the covering demand presents a conundrum. The courts are right to be leery of intervening in too brusque a manner here, as they cannot risk playing favorites among groups. Yet they also cannot ignore the fact that the covering demand is where many forms of inequality continue to have life. We need a paradigm that gives both these concerns their due, adapting the aspirations of the civil rights movement to an increasingly pluralistic society.

THE NEW CIVIL RIGHTS

The new civil rights begins with the observation that everyone covers. When I lecture on covering, I often encounter what I think of as the "angry straight white man" reaction. A member of the audience, almost invariably a white man, almost invariably angry, denies that covering is a civil rights issue. Why shouldn't racial minorities or women or gays have to cover? These groups should receive legal protection against discrimination for things they cannot help. But why should they receive protection for behaviors within their control—wearing cornrows, acting "feminine" or flaunting their sexuality? After all, the questioner says, I have to cover all the time. I have to mute my depression, or my obesity, or my alcoholism, or my shyness, or my working-class background or my nameless anomie. I, too, am one of the mass of men leading lives of quiet desperation. Why should legally protected groups have a right to self-expression I do not? Why should my struggle for an authentic self matter less?

I surprise these individuals when I agree. Contemporary civil rights has erred in focusing solely on traditional civil rights groups—racial minorities, women, gays, religious minorities and people with disabilities. This assumes those in the so-called mainstream—those straight white men—do not also cover. They are understood only as obstacles, as people who prevent others from expressing themselves, rather than as individuals who are themselves struggling for self-definition. No wonder they often respond to civil rights advocates with hostility. They experience us as asking for an entitlement they themselves have been refused—an expression of their full humanity.

Civil rights must rise into a new, more inclusive register. That ascent makes use of the recognition that the mainstream is a myth. With respect to any particular identity, the word "mainstream" makes sense, as in the statement that straights are more mainstream than gays. Used generically, however, the word loses meaning. Because human beings hold many identities, the mainstream is a shifting coalition, and none of us are entirely within it. It is not normal to be completely normal.

This does not mean discrimination against racial minorities is the same as discrimination against poets. American civil rights law has correctly directed its concern toward certain groups and not others. But the aspiration of civil rights—the aspiration that we be free to develop our human capacities without the impediment of witless conformity—is an aspiration that extends beyond traditional civil rights groups.

To fulfill that aspiration, we must think differently both within the law and outside it. With respect to legal remedies, we must shift away from claims that demand equality for particular groups toward claims that demand liberty for us all. This is not an exhortation that we strip protections from currently recognized groups. Rather, it is a prediction that future courts will be unable to sustain a group-based vision of civil rights when faced with the broad and irreversible trend toward demographic pluralism. In an increasingly diverse society, the courts must look to what draws us together as citizens rather than to what drives us apart.

As if in recognition of that fact, the Supreme Court has moved in recent years away from extending protections on the basis of group membership and toward doing so on the basis of liberties we all possess. In 2003, the court struck down a Texas statute that prohibited same-sex sodomy. It did not, however, frame the case as one concerning the equality rights of gays. Instead, it cast the case as one concerning the interest we all—straight, gay or otherwise—have in controlling our intimate lives. Similarly, in 2004, the court held that a state could be required by a Congressional statute to make its courthouses wheelchair accessible. Again, the court ruled in favor of the minority group without fram-

ing its analysis in group-based equality rhetoric. Rather, it held that all people—disabled or otherwise—have a "right of access to the courts," which had been denied in that instance.

In these cases, the court implicitly acknowledged the national exhaustion with group-based identity politics and quieted the anxiety about pluralism that is driving us back toward the assimilative ideal. By emphasizing the interest all individuals have in our own liberty, the court focused on what unites us rather than on what divides us. While preserving the distinction between being and doing, the court decided to protect doing in its own right.

If the Supreme Court protects individuals against covering demands in the future, I believe it will do so by invoking the universal rights of people. I predict that if the court ever recognizes the right to speak a native language, it will protect that right as a liberty to which we are all entitled, rather than as a remedial concession granted to a particular national-origin group. If the court recognizes rights to grooming, like the right to wear cornrows, I believe it will do so under something akin to the German Constitution's right to personality rather than as a right attached to racial minorities. And I hope that if the court protects the right of gays to marry, it will do so by framing it as the right we all have to marry the person we love, rather than defending "gay marriage" as if it were a separate institution.

A liberty-based approach to civil rights, of course, brings its own complications, beginning with the question of where my liberty ends and yours begins. But the ability of liberty analysis to illuminate our common humanity should not be underestimated. This virtue persuaded both Martin Luther King Jr. and Malcolm X to argue for the transition from civil rights to human rights at the ends of their lives. It is time for American law to follow suit.

While I have great hopes for this new legal paradigm, I also believe law will play a relatively small part in the new civil rights. A doctor friend told me that in his first year of medical school, his dean described how doctors were powerless to cure the vast majority of human ills. People would get better, or they would not, but it would not be doctors who would cure them. Part of becoming a doctor, the dean said, was to surrender a layperson's awe for medical authority. I wished then that someone would give an analogous lecture to law students and to Americans at large. My education in law has been in no small part an education in its limitations.

As an initial matter, many covering demands are made by actors the law does not—and in my view should not—hold accountable, like friends, family, neighbors, the "culture" or individuals themselves. When I think of the covering demands I have experienced, I can trace many of them only to my own censorious consciousness. And while I am often tempted to sue myself, I recognize this is not my healthiest impulse.

Law is also an incomplete solution to coerced assimilation because it has yet to recognize the myriad groups that are subjected to covering demands even though these groups cannot be defined by traditional classifications like race, sex, orientation, religion and disability. Whenever I speak about covering, I receive new instances of identities that can be covered. The law may someday move to protect some of these identities. But it will never protect them all.

For these and other reasons, I am troubled that Americans seem increasingly inclined to turn toward the law to do the work of civil rights precisely when they should be turning away from it. The primary solution lies in all of us as citizens, not in the tiny subset of us who are lawyers. People confronted with demands to cover should feel emboldened to seek a reason for that demand, even if the law does not reach the actors making the demand or recognize the group burdened by it. These reason-forcing conversations should happen outside courtrooms—in public squares and prayer circles, in workplaces and on playgrounds. They should occur informally and intimately, in the everyday places where tolerance is made and unmade.

What will constitute a good-enough reason to justify assimilation will obviously be controversial. We have come to some consensus that certain reasons are illegitimate—like racism, sexism or religious intolerance. Beyond that, we should expect conversations rather than foreordained results—

what reasons count, and for what purposes, will be for us all to decide by facing one another as citizens. My personal inclination is always to privilege the claims of the individual against countervailing interests like "neatness" or "workplace harmony." But we should have that conversation.

Such conversations are the best—and perhaps the only—way to give both assimilation and authenticity their due. They will help us alleviate conservative alarmists' fears of a balkanized America and radical multiculturalists' fears of a monocultural America. The aspiration of civil rights has always been to permit people to pursue their human flourishing without limitations based on bias. Focusing on law prevents us from seeing the revolutionary breadth of that aspiration. It is only when we leave the law that civil rights suddenly stops being about particular agents of oppression and particular victimized groups and starts to become a project of human flourishing in which we all have a stake.

I don't teach classes on gay rights any more. I suspect many of my students now experience me as a homosexual professional rather than as a professional homosexual, if they think of me in such terms at all. But I don't experience myself as covering. I've just moved on to other interests, in the way scholars do. So the same behavior—not teaching gay rights—has changed in meaning over time.

This just brings home to me that the only right I have wanted with any consistency is the freedom to be who I am. I'll be the first to admit that I owe much of that freedom to group-based equality movements, like the gay rights movement. But it is now time for us as a nation to shift the emphasis away from equality and toward liberty in our debates about identity politics. Only through such freedom can we live our lives as works in progress, which is to say, as the complex, changeful and contradictory creatures that we are.

DISCUSSION QUESTIONS

1. What choices does one with an outsider identity face?
2. What are the costs of mesearch?
3. What are the costs of covering versus passing?

READING 54

The Other Movement That Rosa Parks Inspired: By Sitting Down, She Made Room for the Disabled

Charles Wilson

On an unseasonably warm September day in 1984, about a dozen men and women rolled their wheelchairs in front of a city bus that was pulling onto State Street in Chicago. Then they sat there and didn't move. The group had no secret agenda, they simply wanted to make a point. Days before, the Chicago Transit Authority had announced that it was purchasing 363 new public buses—and that none of them would be equipped with wheelchair lifts to serve disabled passengers because the lifts had been deemed too expensive. This ragtag group of wheelchair riders, who were affiliated with a disability rights organization called ADAPT, or Americans Disabled for Accessible Public Transit, decided to protest that decision by obstructing a bus until the police carted them away. Every one of them wore a simple paper name tag, the sort that you would normally see at a meet-and-greet. They all said: "My name is Rosa Parks."

Rosa Parks's act of courage in Montgomery, Ala., in 1955 did more than dismantle the system of racial segregation on public transportation. Her refusal to give up her seat to a white man also created a legacy she never could have foreseen. It was through Parks's example that the disabled community transformed its own often disorganized cause into a unified disability rights movement. "Had it not been for Parks and the bus boycott, there is no question that the disability rights movement would have been light years behind, if it would have ever occurred," says Michael Auberger, a disability rights activist who was one of the first to place his

Charles Wilson, a writer who lives in New York City, has been doing research for a book about the disability rights movement.

wheelchair in front of a bus in the early 1980s. "Her genius was that she saw the bus as the great integrator. It took you to work, it took you to play, it took you to places that you were never before seen. We began to see the bus the same way, too, and it empowered a group of people who had been just as disenfranchised as African Americans."

The disability rights movement could in no sense have been called a movement when Parks refused to yield her seat. At that time, the unemployment rate for people with disabilities reached over 70 percent, and organizations that rallied for rights for people with disabilities focused on solutions that were specific to a single disorder. "The disability community was fragmented," says Bob Kafka, a quadriplegic who broke his neck in 1973 and who was an early organizer for ADAPT. "The deaf community wanted interpreters. People with mobility issues wanted curb cuts. The blind wanted more sensory communication. Everyone saw themselves as a deaf person, or a blind person, or a mental health person. We were tossed salad, not fondue."

Parks's action offered these separate communities a strategy that unified their various wishes. "Rosa Parks energized us in that she was the perfect symbol for when the meek become militant," says Kafka. "She was someone who was willing to cross the line." And the fight for accessible public transportation was to be the single issue that catalyzed disparate disability groups into a common cause.

By the 1960s and, '70s, many cities had introduced paratransit services that picked up disabled patients. The officials who controlled city budgets, though, typically stipulated that these buses could be used by an individual only a few times a month and that the buses could be used only by appointment. So, in the late '70s and early '80s, some activists began to extend the logic of Parks's silent act of defiance to their own cause: Buses that divided people into separate categories, they said, were inherently unequal. Disabled people shouldn't be limited to using paratransit buses. They deserved to ride the city buses just like everyone else.

"How could you go to school, or go on a date, or volunteer somewhere if the only trips deemed worth funding for you were medical trips?" wrote ADAPT member Stephanie Thomas in her introduction to "To Ride the Public's Buses," a collection of articles about the early bus actions that appeared in *Disability Rag*. "How could you get a job if you could only get 3 rides a week? If you were never on time?"

Parks's method of dissent—sitting still—was well suited to a community in which many people found themselves having to do that very thing all day long. Within two decades of her refusal to give up her seat, disabled people in cities across the country began staging their own "sit-ins" by parking their wheelchairs in front of ill-equipped city buses—or, alternatively, by ditching their wheelchairs and crawling onto the stairs of the bus vestibules.

Some of the sit-ins were individual acts of defiance. In Hartford, Conn., 63-year-old Edith Harris parked her wheelchair in front of 10 separate local buses on a single day after waiting nearly two hours for an accessible bus. Increasingly, though, the sit-ins were organized by ADAPT and involved many wheelchair users at a single location.

These actions began to change both how disabled people were perceived and how they perceived themselves. "Without the history of Parks and Martin Luther King, the only argument that the disability community had was the Jerry Lewis Principle," explains Auberger. "The Poor Pathetic Cripple Principle. But if you take a single disabled person and you show them that they can stop a bus, you've empowered that person. And you've made them feel they had rights."

The sit-ins also began to bring about concrete changes in the policies of urban transportation boards. In 1983, the city of Denver gave up its initial resistance and retrofitted all 250 of its buses with lifts after 45 wheelchair users blocked buses at the downtown intersection of Colfax Avenue and Broadway. Similar moves were made by Washington's Metro board in 1986 and by Chicago's transit authority in 1989. And in 1990, when the landmark Americans With Disabilities Act cleared Congress, the only provisions that went into effect immediately were those that mandated accessible public transportation.

If Rosa Parks left a lasting legacy on the disability rights movement, it is important to recog-

nize that it is a legacy that is largely unfinished. A restored version of the bus that Rosa Parks rode in Montgomery recently went on display at the Henry Ford Museum near Detroit, the city where Parks lived her last decades. . . . Detroit's mayor, Kwame Kilpatrick . . . memorialized Parks by saying that "she stood up by sitting down. I'm only standing here because of her."

Kilpatrick failed to mention a further irony, though: The Justice Department [had recently] joined a suit against his city. . . . It was initially filed in August 2004, by Richard Bernstein, a blind 31-year-old lawyer from the Detroit suburb of Farmington Hills, on behalf of four disabled inner-city clients. His plaintiffs said that they routinely waited three to four hours in severe cold for a bus with a working lift. Their complaint cited evidence that half of the lifts on the city's bus fleet were routinely broken. The complaint did not ask for compensation. It demanded only that the Motor City comply with the Americans with Disabilities Act. The city recently purchased more accessible buses, but the mayor didn't offer a plan for making sure the buses stayed in good working order. He has publicly disparaged Bernstein on radio as an example of "suburban guys coming into our community trying to raise up the concerns of people when this administration is going to the wall on this issue of disabled riders."

Mayor Kilpatrick is not going to the wall, and neither are many other mayors in this country. A 2002 federal Bureau of Transportation Statistics study found that 6 million Americans with disabilities still have trouble obtaining the transportation they need. Many civic leaders and officials at transit organizations have made arguments about the economic difficulty of installing lifts on buses and maintaining them. But they are seeing only one side of the argument: More people in the disability community would pursue jobs and pay more taxes if they could only trust that they could get to work and back safely.

Public officials who offered elaborate eulogies to Parks's memory . . . should evaluate whether they are truly living up to the power of her ideas. During a visit to Detroit . . . to speak to disabled transit riders for a project I was working on, I met Robert Harvey, who last winter hurled his wheelchair in front of a bus pulling onto Woodward Avenue after four drivers in a row had passed him by. (He was knocked to the curb.) I met Carolyn Reed, who has spina bifida and had lost a job because she could rarely find a bus that would get her to work on time. Her able bodied friends had also recently stopped inviting her to the movies. She guessed why: A few times over the past months, they had found themselves waiting late at night with her for hours to catch a bus with a working lift. "I'd say, 'Go ahead, go ahead, I'll be all right,'" she told me. "And they'd say, 'We're not leaving you out here.'" I also met Willie Cochran, a double amputee who once waited six hours in freezing temperatures for a bus that would take him home from dialysis treatment.

None of this should be happening in America. "Rosa Parks could get on the bus to protest," says Roger McCarville, a veteran in Detroit who once chained himself to a bus. "We still can't get on the bus." A true tribute to Parks would be to ensure that every American can.

DISCUSSION QUESTIONS

1. How did the lack of access to public transportation promote a disability movement?
2. Why are sit-ins an effective form of protest?
3. What message is sent when the disabled are kept waiting or are not picked up by public transportation?

LANGUAGE

READING 55

Gender Stereotyping in the English Language

Laurel Richardson

Everyone in our society, regardless of class, ethnicity, sex, age, or race, is exposed to the same language, the language of the dominant culture. Analysis of verbal language can tell us a great deal about a people's fears, prejudices, anxieties, and interests. A rich vocabulary on a particular subject indicates societal interests or obsessions (e.g., the extensive vocabulary about cars in America). And different words for the same subject (such as *freedom fighter* and *terrorist, passed away* and *croaked, make love* and *ball*) show that there is a range of attitudes and feelings in the society toward that subject.

It should not be surprising, then, to find differential attitudes and feelings about men and women

Laurel Richardson is emeritus professor of sociology at The Ohio State University.

rooted in the English language. Although the English language has not been completely analyzed, six general propositions concerning these attitudes and feelings about males and females can be made.

First, in terms of grammatical and semantic structure, women do not have a fully autonomous, independent existence; they are part of man. The language is not divided into male and female with distinct conjugations and declensions, as many other languages are. Rather, *women* are included under the generic *man*. Grammar books specify that the pronoun *he* can be used generically to mean *he* or *she*. Further, *man*, when used as an indefinite pronoun, grammatically refers to both men and women. So, for example, when we read *man* in the following phrases we are to interpret it as applying to both men and women: "man the oars," "one small step for man, one giant step for mankind," "man, that's tough," "man overboard," "man the toolmaker," "alienated man," "garbageman." Our rules of etiquette complete the grammatical presumption of inclusivity. When two persons are pronounced "man and wife," Miss Susan Jones changes her entire name to Mrs. Robert Gordon (Vanderbilt, 1972). In each of these correct usages, women are a part of man; they do not exist autonomously. The exclusion of women is well expressed in Mary Daly's ear-jarring slogan "the sisterhood of man" (1973:7–21).

However, there is some question as to whether the theory that *man* means everybody is carried out in practice (see Bendix, 1979; Martyna, 1980). For example, an eight-year-old interrupts her reading of "The Story of the Cavemen" to ask how we got here without cavewomen. A ten-year-old thinks it is dumb to have a woman post*man*. A beginning anthropology student believes (incorrectly) that all shamans ("witch doctors") are males because her textbook and professor use the referential pronoun *he*.

But beginning language learners are not the only ones who visualize males when they see the word *man*. Research has consistently demonstrated that when the generic *man* is used, people visualize men, not women (Schneider & Hacker, 1973; DeStefano, 1976; Martyna, 1978; Hamilton & Henley, 1982). DeStafano, for example, reports that college students choose silhouettes of males for sentences with the word *man* or *men* in them. Similarly, the presumably generic *he* elicits images of men rather than women. The finding is so persistent that linguists doubt whether there actually is a semantic generic in English (MacKay, 1983).

Man, then, suggests not humanity but rather male images. Moreover, over one's lifetime, an educated American will be exposed to the prescriptive *he* more than a million times (MacKay, 1983). One consequence is the exclusion of women in the visualization, imagination, and thought of males and females. Most likely this linguistic practice perpetuates in men their feelings of dominance over and responsibility for women, feelings that interfere with the development of equality in relationships.

Second, in actual practice, our pronoun usage perpetuates different personality attributes and career aspirations for men and women. Nurses, secretaries, and elementary school teachers are almost invariably referred to as *she;* doctors, engineers, electricians, and presidents as *he*. In one classroom, students referred to an unidentified child as *he* but shifted to *she* when discussing the child's parent. In a faculty discussion of the problems of acquiring new staff, all architects, engineers, security officers, faculty, and computer programmers were referred to as *he;* secretaries and file clerks were referred to as *she*. Martyna (1978) has noted that speakers consistently use *he* when the referent has a high-status occupation (e.g., doctor, lawyer, judge) but shift to *she* when the occupations have lower status (e.g., nurse, secretary).

Even our choice of sex ascription to nonhuman objects subtly reinforces different personalities for males and females. It seems as though the small (e.g., kittens), the graceful (e.g., poetry), the unpredictable (e.g., the fates), the nurturant (e.g., the church, the school), and that which is owned and/or controlled by men (e.g., boats, cars, governments, nations) represent the feminine, whereas that which is a controlling forceful power in and of itself (e.g., God, Satan, tiger) primarily represents the masculine. Even athletic teams are not immune. In one college, the men's teams are called the Bearcats and the women's teams the Bearkittens.

Some of you may wonder whether it matters that the female is linguistically included in the male. The inclusion of women under the pseudo-generic *man* and the prescriptive *he,* however, is not a trivial issue. Language has tremendous power to shape attitudes and influence behavior. Indeed, MacKay (1983) argues that the prescriptive *he* "has all the characteristics of a highly effective propaganda technique": frequent repetition, early age of acquisition (before age 6), covertness (*he* is not thought of as propaganda), use by high-prestige sources (including university texts and professors), and indirectness (presented as though it were a matter of common knowledge). As a result, the prescriptive affects females' sense of life options and feelings of well-being. For example, Adamsky (1981) found that women's sense of power and importance was enhanced when the prescriptive *he* was replaced by *she*.

Awareness of the impact of the generic *man* and prescriptive *he* has generated considerable activity to change the language. One change, approved by the Modern Language Association, is to replace the prescriptive *he* with the plural *they*—as was accepted practice before the 18th century. Another is the use of *he or she*. Although it sounds awkward at first, the *he or she* designation is increasingly being used in the media and among people who have recognized the power of the pronoun to perpetuate sex stereotyping. When a professor, for example, talks about "the lawyer" as "he or she," a speech pattern that counteracts sex stereotyping is modeled. This drive to neutralize the impact of pronouns is evidenced further in the renaming of occupations: a policeman is now a police officer, a postman is a mail carrier, a stewardess is a flight attendant.

Third, linguistic practice defines females as immature, incompetent, and incapable and males as mature, complete, and competent. Because the words *man* and *woman* tend to connote sexual and human maturity, common speech, organizational titles, public addresses, and bathroom doors frequently designate the women in question as *ladies*. Simply contrast the different connotations of *lady* and *woman* in the following common phrases:

Luck, be a lady (woman) tonight.

Barbara's a little lady (woman).

Ladies' (Women's) Air Corps.

In the first two examples, the use of *lady* desexualizes the contextual meaning of *woman*. So trivializing is the use of *lady* in the last phrase that the second is wholly anomalous. The male equivalent, *lord,* is never used; and its synonym, *gentleman,* is used infrequently. When *gentleman* is used, the assumption seems to be that certain culturally condoned aspects of masculinity (e.g., aggressivity, activity, and strength) should be set aside in the interests of maturity and order, as in the following phrases:

A gentlemen's (men's) agreement.

A duel between gentlemen (men).

He's a real gentleman (man).

Rather than feeling constrained to set aside the stereotypes associated with *man,* males frequently find the opposite process occurring. The contextual connotation of *man* places a strain on males to be continuously sexually and socially potent, as the following examples reveal:

I was not a man (gentleman) with her tonight.

This is a man's (gentleman's) job.

Be a man (gentleman).

Whether males, therefore, feel competent or anxious, valuable or worthless in particular contexts is influenced by the demands placed on them by the expectations of the language.

Not only are men infrequently labeled *gentlemen*, but they are infrequently labeled *boys*. The term *boy* is reserved for young males, bellhops, car attendants, and as a putdown to those males judged inferior. *Boy* connotes immaturity and powerlessness. Only occasionally do males "have a night out with the boys." They do not talk "boy talk" at the office. Rarely does our language legitimize carefreeness in males. Rather, they are expected, linguistically, to adopt the responsibilities of manhood.

On the other hand, women of all ages may be called *girls*. Grown females "play bridge with the girls" and indulge in "girl talk." They are encouraged to remain childlike, and the implication is that they are basically immature and without power. Men can become men, linguistically, putting aside the immaturity of childhood; indeed, for them to retain the openness and playfulness of boyhood is linguistically difficult.

Further, the presumed incompetence and immaturity of women are evidenced by the linguistic company they keep. Women are categorized with children ("women and children first"), the infirm ("the blind, the lame, the women"), and the incompetent ("women, convicts, and idiots"). The use of these categorical designations is not accidental happenstance; "rather these selectional groupings are powerful forces behind the actual expressions of language and are based on distinctions which are not regarded as trivial by the speakers of the language" (Key, 1975:82). A total language analysis of categorical groupings is not available, yet it seems likely that women tend to be included in groupings that designate incompleteness, ineptitude, and immaturity. On the other hand, it is difficult for us to conceive of the word *man* in any categorical grouping other than one that extends beyond humanity, such as "Man, apes, and angels" or "Man and Superman." That is, men do exist as an independent category capable of autonomy; women are grouped with the stigmatized, the immature, and the foolish. Moreover, when men are in human groupings, males are invariably first on the list ("men and women," "he and she," "man and wife"). This order is not accidental but was prescribed in the 16th century to honor the worthier party.

Fourth, in practice women are defined in terms of their sexual desirability (to men); men are defined in terms of their sexual prowess (over women). Most slang words in reference to women refer to their sexual desirability to men (e.g., *dog, fox, broad, ass, chick*). Slang about men refers to their sexual prowess over women (e.g., *dude, stud, hunk*). The fewer examples given for men is not an oversight. An analysis of sexual slang, for example, listed more than 1,000 words and phrases that derogate women sexually but found "nowhere near this multitude for describing men" (Kramarae, 1975:72). Farmer and Henley (cited in Schulz, 1975) list 500 synonyms for *prostitute,* for example, and only 65 for *whoremonger.* Stanley (1977) reports 220 terms for a sexually promiscuous woman and only 22 for a sexually promiscuous man. Shuster (1973) reports that the passive verb form is used in reference to women's sexual experiences (e.g., *to be laid, to be had, to be taken*), whereas the active tense is used in reference to the male's sexual experience (e.g., *lay, take, have*). Being sexually attractive to males is culturally condoned for women and being sexually powerful is approved for males. In this regard, the slang of the street is certainly not countercultural; rather it perpetuates and reinforces different expectations in females and males as sexual objects and performers.

Further, we find sexual connotations associated with neutral words applied to women. A few examples should suffice. A male academician questioned the title of a new course, asserting it was "too suggestive." The title? "The Position of Women in the Social Order." A male tramp is simply a hobo, but a female tramp is a slut. And consider the difference in connotation of the following expressions:

It's easy.

He's easy.

She's easy.

In the first, we assume something is "easy to do"; in the second, we might assume a professor is an "easy grader" or a man is "easygoing." But when we read "she's easy," the connotation is "she's an easy lay."

In the world of slang, men are defined by their sexual prowess. In the world of slang and proper speech, women are defined as sexual objects. The rule in practice seems to be: If in doubt, assume that any reference to a women has a sexual connotation. For both genders, the constant bombardment of prescribed sexuality is bound to have real consequences.

Fifth, women are defined in terms of their relations to men; men are defined in terms of their relations to the world at large. A good example is seen in the words *master* and *mistress.* Originally these words had the same meaning—"a person who holds power over servants." With the demise of the feudal system, however, these words took on different meanings. The masculine variant metaphorically refers to power over something; as in "He is the master of his trade"; the feminine variant metaphorically (although probably not in actuality) refers to power over a man sexually, as in "She is Tom's mistress." Men are defined in terms of their power in the occupational world, women in terms of their sexual power over men.

The existence of two contractions for Mistress (*Miss* and *Mrs.*) and but one for Mister (*Mr.*) underscores the cultural concern and linguistic practice: women are defined in relation to men. Even a divorced woman is defined in terms of her no-longer-existing relation to a man (she is still *Mrs. Man's Name*). But apparently the divorced state is not relevant enough to the man or to the society to require a label. A divorced woman is a *divorcee,* but what do you call a divorced man? The recent preference of many women to be called *Ms.* is an attempt to provide for women an equivalency title that is not dependent on marital status.

Sixth, a historical pattern can be seen in the meanings that come to be attached to words that originally were neutral: those that apply to women acquire obscene and/or debased connotations but no such pattern of derogation holds for neutral words referring to men. The processes of *pejoration* (the acquiring of an obscene or debased connotation) and *amelioration* (the reacquiring of a neutral or positive connotation) in the English language in regard to terms for males and females have been studied extensively by Muriel Schulz (1975).

Leveling is the least derogative form of pejoration. Through leveling, titles that originally referred to an elite class of persons come to include a wider class of persons. Such democratic leveling is more common for female designates than for males. For example, contrast the following: *lord-lady (lady); baronet-dame (dame); governor-governess (governess).*

Most frequently what happens to words designating women as they become pejorated, however, is that they come to denote or connote sexual wantonness. *Sir* and *mister,* for example, remain titles of courtesy, but at some time *madam, miss,* and *mistress* have come to designate, respectively, a brothelkeeper, a prostitute, and an unmarried sexual partner of a male (Schulz, 1975:66).

Names for domestic helpers, if they are females, are frequently derogated. *Hussy,* for example, originally meant "housewife." *Laundress, needlewoman, spinster* ("tender of the spinning wheel"), and *nurse* all referred to domestic occupations within the home, and all at some point became slang expressions for prostitute or mistress.

Even kinship terms referring to women become denigrated. During the 17th century, *mother* was used to mean "a bawd"; more recently *mother (mothuh f———)* has become a common derogatory epithet (Cameron, 1974). Probably at some point in history every kinship term for females has been derogated (Schulz, 1975:66).

Terms of endearment for women also seem to follow a downward path. Such pet names as Tart, Dolly, Kitty, Polly, Mopsy, Biddy, and Jill all eventually became sexually derogatory (Schulz, 1975:67). *Whore* comes from the same Latin root as *care* and once meant "a lover of either sex."

Indeed, even the most neutral categorical designations—*girl, female, woman, lady*—at some point in their history have been used to connote sexual immorality. *Girl* originally meant "a child of either sex"; through the process of semantic degeneration it eventually meant "a prostitute." Although *girl* has lost this meaning, *girlie* still retains sexual connotations. *Woman* connoted "a mistress" in the early 19th century; *female* was a degrading epithet in the latter part of the 19th century; and when *lady* was introduced as a euphemism, it too became deprecatory. "Even so neutral a term as *person,* when it was used as substitute for *woman,* suffered [vulgarization]" (Mencken, 1963: 350, quoted in Schulz, 1975:71).

Whether one looks at elite titles, occupational roles, kinship relationships, endearments, or age-sex categorical designations, the pattern is clear. Terms referring to females are pejorated—"become negative in the middle instances and abusive in the extremes" (Schulz, 1975:69). Such semantic derogation, however, is not evidenced for male referents. *Lord, baronet, father, brother, nephew, footman, bowman, boy, lad, fellow, gentleman, man, male,* and so on "have failed to undergo the derogation found in the history of their corresponding feminine designations" (Schulz, 1975:67). Interestingly, the male word, rather than undergoing derogation, frequently is replaced by a female referent when the speaker wants to debase a male. A weak man, for example, is referred to as a *sissy* (diminutive of sister), and an army recruit during basic training is called a *pussy.* And when one is swearing at a male, he is referred to as a *bastard* or a *son-of-a-bitch*—both appellations that impugn the dignity of a man's mother.

In summary, these verbal practices are consistent with the gender stereotypes that we encounter in everyday life. Women are thought to be a part of man, nonautonomous, dependent, relegated to roles that require few skills, characteristically incompetent and immature, sexual objects, best defined in terms of their relations to men. Males are visible, autonomous and independent, responsible for the protection and containment of women, expected to occupy positions on the basis of their high achievement or physical power, assumed to be sexually potent, and defined primarily by their relations to the world of work. The use of the language perpetuates the stereotypes for both genders and limits the options available for self-definition.

DISCUSSION QUESTIONS

1. Why is it important to be cautious about the use of language if one is trying to avoid stereotypes?
2. What new words, besides *Ms.,* have been invented to avoid stereotypes?

REFERENCES

Adamsky, C. 1981. "Changes in pronominal usage in a class-room situation." *Psychology of Women Quarterly* 5:773–79.

Bendix, J. 1979. "Linguistic models as political symbols: Gender and the generic 'he' in English." In J. Orasanu, M. Slater, and L. L. Adler, eds., *Language, sex and gender; Does la différence make a difference?* pp. 23–42. New York: New Academy of Science Annuals.

Cameron, P. 1974. "Frequency and kinds of words in various social settings, or What the hell's going on?" In M. Truzzi, ed., *Sociology for pleasure*, pp. 31–37. Englewood Cliffs, NJ: Prentice-Hall.

Daly, M. 1973. *Beyond God the father.* Boston: Beacon Press.

DeStefano, J. S. 1976. Personal communication. Columbus: Ohio State University.

Hamilton, N., & Henley, N. 1982. "Detrimental consequences of the generic masculine usage." Paper presented to the Western Psychological Association meetings, Sacramento.

Key, M. R. 1975. *Male/female language.* Metuchen, NJ: Scarecrow Press.

Kramarae, Cheris. 1975. "Woman's speech: Separate but unequal?" In Barrie Thorne and Nancy Henley, eds., *Language and sex: Difference and dominance,* pp. 43–56. Rowley, MA: Newbury House.

MacKay, D. G. 1983. "Prescriptive grammar and the pronoun problem." In B. Thorne, C. Kramarae, and N. Henley, eds., *Language, gender, and society,* pp. 38–53. Rowley, MA: Newbury House.

Martyna, W. 1978. "What does 'he' mean? Use of the generic masculine." *Journal of Communication* 28:131–38.

Martyna, W. 1980. "Beyond the 'he/man' approach: The case for nonsexist language." *Signs* 5:482–93.

Mencken, H. L. 1963. *The American language.* 4th ed. with supplements. Abr. and ed. R. I. McDavis. New York: Knopf.

Schneider, J., & Hacker, S. 1973. "Sex role imagery in the use of the generic 'man' in introductory texts: A case in the sociology of sociology." *American Sociologist* 8:12–18.

Schulz, M. R. 1975. "The semantic derogation of women." In B. Thorne and N. Henley, eds., *Language and sex: Difference and dominance,* pp. 64–75. Rowley, MA: Newbury House.

Shuster, Janet. 1973. "Grammatical forms marked for male and female in English." Unpublished paper. Chicago: University of Chicago.

Stanley, J. P. 1977. "Paradigmatic woman: The prostitute." In D. L. Shores, ed., *Papers in language variation.* Birmingham: University of Alabama Press.

Vanderbilt, A. 1972. *Amy Vanderbilt's etiquette.* Garden City, NY: Doubleday.

READING 56

Claiming Disability: Knowledge and Identity

Simi Linton

NAMING THE GROUP

. . . Across the world and throughout history various terminologies and meanings are ascribed to the types of human variations known in contemporary Westernized countries as disabilities. Over the past century the term *disabled* and others, such as *handicapped* and the less inclusive term *crippled*, have emerged as collective nouns that convey the idea that there is something that links this disparate group of people. The terms have been used to arrange people in ways that are socially and economically convenient to the society.

There are various consequences of the chosen terminology and variation in the degree of control that the named group has over the labeling process. The terms *disability* and *disabled people* are the most commonly used by disability rights

Simi Linton is a longtime disability rights scholar and a professor of psychology at Hunter College.

activists, and recently policy makers and health care professionals have begun to use these terms more consistently. Although there is some agreement on terminology, there are disagreements about what it is that unites disabled people and whether disabled people should have control over the naming of their experience.

The term *disability*, as it has been used in general parlance, appears to signify something material and concrete, a physical or psychological condition considered to have predominantly medical significance. Yet it is an arbitrary designation, used erratically both by professionals who lay claim to naming such phenomena and by confused citizens. A project of disability studies scholars and the disability rights movement has been to bring into sharp relief the processes by which *disability* has been imbued with the meaning(s) it has and to reassign a meaning that is consistent with a sociopolitical analysis of disability. Divesting it of its current meaning is no small feat. As typically used, the term *disability* is a linchpin in a complex web of social ideals, institutional structures, and government policies. As a result, many people have a vested interest in keeping a tenacious hold on the current meaning because it is consistent with the practices and policies that are central to their livelihood or their ideologies. People may not be driven as much by economic imperatives as by a personal investment in their own beliefs and practices, in metaphors they hold dear, or in their own professional roles. Further, underlying this tangled web of needs and beliefs, and central to the arguments presented [here] is an epistemological structure that both generates and reflects current interpretations.[1]

A glance through a few dictionaries will reveal definitions of disability that include incapacity, a disadvantage, deficiency, especially a physical or mental impairment that restricts normal achievement; something that hinders or incapacitates, something that incapacitates or disqualifies. Legal definitions include legal incapacity or disqualification. *Stedman's Medical Dictionary* (1976) identifies *disability* as a "medicolegal term signifying loss of function and earning power," whereas *disablement*

is a "medicolegal term signifying loss of function without loss of earning power" (400). These definitions are understood by the general public and by many in the academic community to be useful ones. *Disability* so defined is a medically derived term that assigns predominantly medical significance and meaning to certain types of human variation.

The decision to assign medical meanings to *disability* has had many and varied consequences for disabled people. One clear benefit has been the medical treatments that have increased the well-being and vitality of many disabled people, indeed have saved people's lives. Ongoing attention by the medical profession to the health and well-being of people with disabilities and to prevention of disease and impairments is critical. Yet, along with these benefits, there are enormous negative consequences that will take a large part of this [article] to list and explain. Briefly, the medicalization of disability casts human variation as deviance from the norm, as pathological condition, as deficit, and, significantly, as an individual burden and personal tragedy. Society, in agreeing to assign medical meaning to *disability*, colludes to keep the issue within the purview of the medical establishment, to keep it a personal matter and "treat" the condition and the person with the condition rather than "treating" the social processes and policies that constrict disabled people's lives. The disability studies' and disability rights movement's position is critical of the domination of the medical definition and views it as a major stumbling block to the reinterpretation of *disability* as a political category and to the social changes that could follow such a shift.

While retaining the term *disability*, despite its medical origins, a premise of most of the literature in disability studies is that *disability* is best understood as a marker of identity. As such, it has been used to build a coalition of people with significant impairments, people with behavioral or anatomical characteristics marked as deviant, and people who have or are suspected of having conditions, such as AIDS or emotional illness, that make them targets of discrimination.[2] As rendered in disability studies scholarship, disability has become a more capacious category, incorporating people with a range of physical, emotional, sensory, and cognitive conditions. Although the category is broad, the term is used to designate a specific minority group. When medical definitions of *disability* are dominant, it is logical to separate people according to biomedical condition through the use of diagnostic categories and to forefront medical perspectives on human variation. When disability is redefined as a social/political category, people with a variety of conditions are identified as *people with disabilities* or *disabled people,* a group bound by common social and political experience. These designations, as reclaimed by the community, are used to identify us as a constituency, to serve our needs for unity and identity, and to function as a basis for political activism.

The question of who "qualifies" as disabled is as answerable or as confounding as questions about any identity status. One simple response might be that you are disabled if you say you are. Although that declaration won't satisfy a worker's compensation board, it has a certain credibility with the disabled community. The degree and significance of an individual's impairment is often less of an issue than the degree to which someone identifies as disabled. Another way to answer the question is to say that disability "is mostly a social distinction . . . a marginalized status" and the status is assigned by "the majority culture tribunal" (Gill 1994, 44). But the problem gets stickier when the distinction between disabled and nondisabled is challenged by people who say, "Actually, we're all disabled in some way, aren't we?" (46). Gill says the answer is no to those whose difference "does *not* significantly affect daily life and the person does not [with some consistency] present himself/herself to the world at large as a disabled person" (46). I concur with Gill; I am not willing or interested in erasing the line between disabled and nondisabled people, as long as disabled people are devalued and discriminated against, and as long as naming the category serves to call attention to that treatment.

Over the past twenty years, disabled people have gained greater control over these definitional issues. *The disabled* or *the handicapped* was replaced in the mid-70s by *people with disabilities* to maintain disability as a characteristic of the individual, as opposed to the defining variable. At the time, some people would purposefully say *women and men with disabilities* to provide an extra dimension to the people being described and to deneuter the way *the disabled* were traditionally described. Beginning in the early 90s *disabled people* has been increasingly used in disability studies and disability rights circles when referring to the constituency group. Rather than maintaining disability as a secondary characteristic, *disabled* has become a marker of the identity that the individual and group wish to highlight and call attention to. . . . The terms *disabled* and *nondisabled* are used frequently to designate membership within or outside the community. Disabled is centered, and nondisabled is placed in the peripheral position in order to look at the world from the inside out, to expose the perspective and expertise that is silenced. Occasionally, *people with disabilities* is used as a variant of *disabled people.* The use of *nondisabled* is strategic: to center disability. . . .

NICE WORDS

Terms such as *physically challenged,* the *able disabled, handicapable,* and *special people/children* surface at different times and places. They are rarely used by disabled activists and scholars (except with palpable irony). Although they may be considered well-meaning attempts to inflate the value of people with disabilities, they convey the boosterism and do-gooder mentality endemic to the paternalistic agencies that control many disabled people's lives.

Physically challenged is the only term that seems to have caught on. Nondisabled people use it in conversation around disabled people with no hint of anxiety, suggesting that they believe it is a positive term. This phrase does not make much sense to me. To say that I am physically challenged is to state that the obstacles to my participation are physical, not social, and that the barrier is my own disability. Further, it separates those of us with mobility impairments from other disabled people, not a valid or useful partition for those interested in coalition building and social change. Various derivatives of the term *challenged* have been adopted as a description used in jokes. For instance, "vertically challenged" is considered a humorous way to say short, and "calorically challenged" to say fat. A review of the Broadway musical *Big* in the *New Yorker* said that the score is "melodically challenged."

I observed a unique use of *challenged* in the local Barnes and Nobles superstore. The children's department has a section for books on "Children with Special Needs." There are shelves labeled "epilepsy" and "Down Syndrome." A separate shelf at the bottom is labeled "Misc. Challenges," indicating that it is now used as an organizing category.

The term *able disabled* and *handicapable* have had a fairly short shelf life. They are used, it seems, to refute common stereotypes of incompetence. They are, though, defensive and reactive terms rather than terms that advance a new agenda.

An entire profession, in fact a number of professions, are built around the word *special*. A huge infrastructure rests on the idea that *special children* and *special education* are valid and useful structuring ideas. Although dictionaries insist that *special* be reserved for things that surpass what is common, are distinct among others of their kind, are peculiar to a specific person, have a limited or specific function, are arranged for a particular purpose, or are arranged for a particular occasion, experience teaches us that *special* when applied to education or to children means something different.

The naming of disabled children and the education that "is designed for students whose learning needs cannot be met by a standard school curriculum" (*American Heritage Dictionary* 1992) as *special* can be understood only as a euphemistic formulation, obscuring the reality that neither the children nor the education are considered desirable and that they are not thought to "surpass what is common."

Labeling the education and its recipients special may have been a deliberate attempt to confer legitimacy on the educational practice and to prop up a discarded group. It is also important to consider the unconscious feelings such a strategy may mask. It is my feeling that the nation in general responds to disabled people with great ambivalence. Whatever antipathy and disdain is felt is in competition with feelings of empathy, guilt, and identification. The term *special* may be evidence not of a deliberate maneuver but of a collective "reaction formation," Freud's term for the unconscious defense mechanism in which an individual adopts attitudes and behaviors that are opposite to his or her own true feelings, in order to protect the ego from the anxiety felt from experiencing the real feelings.

The ironic character of the word *special* has been captured in the routine on *Saturday Night Live,* where the character called the "Church Lady" declares when she encounters something distasteful or morally repugnant, "Isn't that special!"

NASTY WORDS

Some of the less subtle or more idiomatic terms for disabled people such as: *cripple, vegetable, dumb, deformed, retard,* and *gimp* have generally been expunged from public conversation but emerge in various types of discourse. Although they are understood to be offensive or hurtful, they are still used in jokes and in informal conversation.

Cripple as a descriptor of disabled people is considered impolite, but the word has retained its metaphoric vitality, as in "the exposé in the newspaper crippled the politician's campaign." The term is also used occasionally for its evocative power. A recent example appeared in *Lingua Franca* in a report on research on the behaviors of German academics. The article states that a professor had "documented the postwar careers of psychiatrists and geneticists involved in gassing thousands of cripples and schizophrenics" (Allen 1996, 37). *Cripple* is used rather loosely here to describe people with a broad range of disabilities. The victims of Nazi slaughter were people with mental illness, epilepsy, chronic illness, and mental retardation, as well as people with physical disabilities. Yet *cripple* is defined as "one that is partially disabled or unable to use a limb or limbs" (*American Heritage Dictionary* 1992) and is usually used only to refer to people with mobility impairments. Because *cripple* inadequately and inaccurately describes the group, the author of the report is likely to have chosen this term for its effect.

Cripple has also been revived by some in the disability community who refer to each other as "crips" or "cripples." A performance group with disabled actors call themselves the "Wry Crips." "In reclaiming 'cripple,' disabled people are taking the thing in their identity that scares the outside world the most and making it a cause to revel in with militant self-pride" (Shapiro 1993, 34).

A recent personal ad in the *Village Voice* shows how "out" the term is:

> **TWISTED CRIP:** Very sexy, full-figured disabled BiWF artist sks fearless, fun, oral BiWF for hot, no-strings nights. Wheelchair, tattoo, dom. Shaved a + N/S. No men/sleep-overs.

Cripple gimp, and *freak* as used by the disability community have transgressive potential. They are personally and politically useful as a means to comment on oppression because they assert our right to name experience.

SPEAKING ABOUT OVERCOMING AND PASSING

The popular phrase *overcoming a disability* is used most often to describe someone with a disability who seems competent and successful in some way, in a sentence something like "She has overcome her disability and is a great success." One interpretation of the phrase might be that the individual's disability no longer limits her or him, that sheer strength or willpower has brought the person to the point where the disability is no longer a hindrance. Another implication of the phrase may be that the person has risen above society's expectation for someone with those characteristics. Because it is physically impossible to *overcome* a disability, it seems that what is *overcome* is the social stigma of having a disability. This idea is reinforced by the equally confounding statement. "I never think of you as disabled." An implication of these statements is that the other members of the group from which the individual has suppos-

edly moved beyond are not as brave, strong, or extraordinary as the person who has *overcome* that designation.

The expression is similar in tone to the phrase that was once more commonly used to describe an African American who was considered exceptional in some way: "He/she is a credit to his/her race." The implication of this phrase is that the "race" is somehow discredited and needs people with extraordinary talent to give the group the credibility that it otherwise lacks. In either case, talking about the person who is African American or talking about the person with a disability, these phrases are often said with the intention of complimenting someone. The compliment has a double edge. To accept it, one must accept the implication that the group is inferior and that the individual is unlike others in that group.

The ideas imbedded in the *overcoming* rhetoric are of personal triumph over a personal condition. The idea that someone can *overcome* a disability has not been generated within the community; it is a wish fulfillment generated from the outside. It is a demand that you be plucky and resolute, and not let the obstacles get in your way. If there are no curb cuts at the corner of the street so that people who use wheelchairs can get across, then you should learn to do wheelies and jump the curbs. If there are no sign language interpreters for deaf students at the high school, then you should study harder, read lips, and stay up late copying notes from a classmate. When disabled people internalize the demand to "overcome" rather than demand social change, they shoulder the same kind of exhausting and self-defeating "Super Mom" burden that feminists have analyzed.

The phrase *overcome a disability* may also be a shorthand version of saying "someone with a disability overcame many obstacles." Tremblay (1996) uses that phrase when describing behaviors of disabled World War II veterans upon returning to the community: "[T]heir main strategies were to develop individualized strategies to overcome the obstacles they found in the community" (165). She introduces this idea as a means to describe how the vets relied on their own ingenuity to manage an inaccessible environment rather than demand that the community change to include them.

In both uses of *overcome,* the individual's responsibility for her or his own success is paramount. If we, as a society, place the onus on individuals with disabilities to work harder to "compensate" for their disabilities or to "overcome" their condition or the barriers in the environment, we have no need for civil rights legislation or affirmative action.

Lest I be misunderstood, I don't see working hard, doing well, or striving for health, fitness, and well-being as contradictory to the aims of the disability rights movement. Indeed, the movement's goal is to provide greater opportunity to pursue these activities. However, we shouldn't be impelled to do these because we have a disability, to prove to some social overseer that we can perform, but we should pursue them because they deliver their own rewards and satisfactions. . . .

NORMAL/ABNORMAL

Normal and *abnormal* are convenient but problematic terms used to describe a person or group of people. These terms are often used to distinguish between people with and without disabilities. In various academic disciplines and in common usage, *normal* and *abnormal* assume different meanings. In psychometrics, *norm* or *normal* are terms describing individuals or characteristics that fall within the center of the normal distribution on whatever variable is being measured. However, as the notion of *normal* is applied in social science contexts and certainly in general parlance, it implies its obverse—*abnormal*—and they both become value laden. Often, those who are not deemed normal are devalued and considered a burden or problem, or are highly valued and regarded as a potential resource. Two examples are the variables of height and intelligence. Short stature and low measured intelligence are devalued and labeled abnormal, and people with those characteristics are considered disabled. Tall people (particularly males) and high scores on IQ tests are valued, and,

although not normal in the statistical sense, are not labeled abnormal or considered disabled.[3]

Davis (1995) describes the historical specificity of the use of *normal* and thereby calls attention to the social structures that are dependent on its use. "[T]he very term that permeates our contemporary life—the normal—is a configuration that arises in a particular historical moment. It is part of a notion of progress of industrialization, and of ideological consolidation of the power of the bourgeoisie. The implications of the hegemony of normalcy are profound and extend into the very heart of cultural production" (49).

The use of the terms *abnormal* and *normal* also moves discourse to a high level of abstraction, thereby avoiding concrete discussion of specific characteristics and increasing ambiguity in communication. In interactions, there is an assumed agreement between speaker and audience of what is normal that sets up an aura of empathy and "us-ness." This process "enhances social unity among those who feel they are normal" (Freilich, Raybeck, and Savishinsky 1991, 22), necessarily excluding the other or abnormal group.

These dynamics often emerge in discussions about disabled people when comparisons are made, for instance, between "the normal" and "the hearing impaired," or "the normal children" and "the handicapped children." The first example contrasts two groups of people; one defined by an abstract and evaluative term (the normal), the other by a more specific, concrete, and nonevaluative term (the hearing impaired). In the second comparison, the "handicapped children" are labeled abnormal by default. Setting up these dichotomies avoids concrete discussion of the ways the two groups of children actually differ, devalues the children with disabilities, and forces an "us and them" division of the population.

The absolute categories *normal* and *abnormal* depend on each other for their existence and depend on the maintenance of the opposition for their meaning. Sedgwick (1990), in *Epistemology of the Closet,* comments on a similar pattern in the forced choice categories homosexual and heterosexual:

[C]ategories presented in a culture as symmetrical binary oppositions—heterosexual/homosexual, in this case—actually subsist in a more unsettled and dynamic tacit relation according to which, first, term B is not symmetrical with but subordinated to term A; but, second, the ontologically valorized term A actually depends for its meaning on the simultaneous subsumption and exclusion of term B; hence, third, the question of priority between the supposed central and the supposed marginal category of each dyad is irresolvably unstable, an instability caused by the fact that term B is constituted as at once internal and external to term A. (9–10)

Despite the instability and the relational nature of the designations *normal* and *abnormal*, they are used as absolute categories. They have achieved their certainty by association with empiricism, and they suffer from empiricism's reductive and simplifying tendencies. Their power and reach are enormous. They affect individuals' most private deliberations about their worth and acceptability, and they determine social position and societal response to behavior. The relationship between abnormality and disability accords to the nondisabled the legitimacy and potency denied to disabled people. And, central to our concerns here, the reification of *normal* and *abnormal* structures curriculum. Courses with titles such as "Abnormal Psychology," "Sociology of Deviance," "Special Education," and "Psychopathology" assume the internal consistency of a curriculum focused on "the abnormal" and depend on the curriculum of the "normal" being taught elsewhere. In fact, this organization of knowledge implicitly suggests that the rest of the curriculum is "normal."

Rosemarie Garland Thomson (1997) has coined the term *the normate,* which, like *nondisabled,* is useful for marking the unexamined center. "This neologism names the veiled subject position of cultural self, the figure outlined by the array of deviant others whose marked bodies shore up the normate's boundaries. The term *normate* usefully designates the social figure through which people can represent themselves as definitive human beings" (8). By meeting *normal* on some of its own terms, *normate* inflects its root, and challenges the validity, indeed the possibility, of normal. At the same time, its ironic twist gives a more flavorful reading of the idea of nomal.

PASSIVITY VERSUS CONTROL

Language that conveys passivity and victimization reinforces certain stereotypes when applied to disabled people. Some of the stereotypes that are particularly entrenched are that people with disabilities are more dependent, childlike, passive, sensitive, and miserable and are less competent than people who do not have disabilities. Much of the language used to depict disabled people relates the lack of control to the perceived incapacities, and implies that sadness and misery are the product of the disabling condition.

These deterministic and essentialist perspectives flourish in the absence of contradictory information. Historically, disabled people have had few opportunities to be active in society, and various social and political forces often undermine the capacity for self-determination. In addition, disabled people are rarely depicted on television, in films, or in fiction as being in control of their own lives—in charge or actively seeking out and obtaining what they want and need. More often, disabled people are depicted as pained by their fate or, if happy, it is through personal triumph over their adversity. The adversity is not depicted as lack of opportunity, discrimination, institutionalization, and ostracism; it is the personal burden of their own body or means of functioning.

Phrases such as *the woman is a victim of cerebral palsy* implies an active agent (cerebral palsy) perpetrating an aggressive act on a vulnerable, helpless "victim." The use of the term *victim,* a word typically used in the context of criminal acts, evokes the relationship between perpetrator and victim. Using this language attributes life, power, and intention to the condition and disempowers the person with the disability, rendering him or her helpless and passive. Instead, if there is a particular need to note what an individual's disability is, saying *the woman has cerebral palsy* describes solely the characteristic of importance to the situation, without imposing extraneous meaning.

Grover (1987) analyzes the word *victim* as used to describe people with AIDS. She notes that the term implies fatalism, and therefore "enable[s] the passive spectator or the AIDS 'spectacle' to remain passive." Use of the term may also express the unconscious wish that the people with AIDS may have been "complicit with, to have courted, their fate" (29), in which case the individual would be seen as a *victim* of her or his own drives. This is particularly apparent when the phrase *innocent victim* is used to distinguish those who acquire HIV from blood transfusions or other medical procedures from those who contract HIV from sexual contact or shared needles. This analysis is also pertinent to people with other disabilities because a number of belief systems consider disability, or some disabilities, as punishment for sin in this or a former life.

Disabled people are frequently described as *suffering from* or *afflicted with* certain conditions. Saying that someone is *suffering from* a condition implies that there is a perpetual state of suffering uninterrupted by pleasurable moments or satisfactions. *Afflicted* carries similar assumption. The verb *afflict* shares with *agonize, excruciate, rack, torment,* and *torture* the central meaning "to bring great harm or suffering to someone" (*American Heritage Dictionary* 1992, 30). Although some people may experience their disability this way, these terms are not used as descriptors of a verified experience but are projected onto disability. Rather than assume suffering in the description of the situation, it is more accurate and less histrionic to say simply that a person *has a disability*. Then, wherever it is relevant, describe the nature and extent of the difficulty experienced. My argument here isn't to eliminate descriptions of suffering but to be accurate in their appointment. It is interesting that AIDS activists intentionally use the phrase *living with AIDS* rather than *dying from AIDS*, not to deny the reality of AIDS but to emphasize that people are often actively engaged in living even in the face of a serious illness.

The ascription of passivity can be seen in language used to describe the relationship between disabled people and their wheelchairs. The phrases *wheelchair bound* or *confined to a wheelchair* are frequently seen in newspapers and magazines, and heard in conversation. A more puzzling variant was spotted in *Lingua Franca*, which described the former governor of Alabama, George Wallace, as the "slumped, wheelchair-ridden 'Guv'nah'" (Zalewski 1995, 19). The choice here was to paint the wheelchair user as *ridden*, meaning "dominated, harassed, or obsessed by" (*American Heritage Dictionary* 1992), rather than the rider in the wheelchair. The various terms imply that a wheelchair restricts the individual, holds a person prisoner. Disabled people are more likely to say that someone *uses a wheelchair*. The latter phrase not only indicates the active nature of the user and the positive way that wheelchairs increase mobility and activity but recognizes that people get in and out of wheelchairs for different activities: driving a car, going swimming, sitting on the couch, or, occasionally, for making love. . . .

MULTIPLE MEANINGS

Are *invalid*, with the emphasis on the first syllable, and *invalid*, with the emphasis on the second, synonyms or homonyms? Does the identical housing of *patient*, the adjective, and *patient*, the noun, conflate the two meanings? Did their conceptual relationship initially determine their uniform casing?

For instance, *invalid* is a designation used to identify some disabled people. The term is seen most prominently on the sides of vans used to transport people with mobility impairments. Disabled people, desperate for accessible transportation, must use vans with the dubious appellation *"Invalid Coach"* printed in bold letters on the side. Aside from this being a fertile source of jokes about the aptness of these notoriously bad transportation services being identified as "not factually or legally valid; falsely based or reasoned; faulty" (*American Heritage Dictionary* 1992), those on the inside of the bus suffer the humiliation of being written off so summarily. Both *invalids* share the Latin root *invalidus,* which means weak. It could be argued that some disabilities do result in weakening of the body, or, more likely, parts of the body, but the totalizing noun, *invalid,* does not confine the weakness to the specific bodily functions; it is more encompassing.

The homonymic *patient/patient,* is, I think, not coincidental or irrelevant. The noun *patient* is a role designation that is always relational. A patient is understood to belong to a doctor or other health care professional, or more generally to an institution. As a noun, *patient* is a neutral description of the role of "one who receives medical attention, care, or treatment" (*American Heritage Dictionary* 1992). The adjective *patient* moves beyond the noun's neutral designation to describe a person who is capable of "bearing or enduring pain, difficulty, provocation, or annoyance with calmness" as well as "tolerant . . . persevering . . . constant . . . not hasty" (*American Heritage Dictionary* 1992). The "good" patient is one who does not challenge the authority of the practitioner or institution and who complies with the regimen set out by the expert, in other words a patient patient. Disabled people, who have often spent a great deal of time as patients, discuss the ways that we have been socialized in the medical culture to be compliant, and that has often undermined our ability to challenge authority or to function autonomously. Further, the description of disabled people as patients in situations where we are not, reinforces these ideas.[4]

REFLECTIONS ON THE *DIS* IN DISABILITY

Before discussing the prefix *dis,* let's examine a similar bound morpheme that conveys meaning and significantly modifies the words it is attached to. The suffix *ette,* when appended to nouns, forms words meaning small or diminutive, as in *kitchenette:* female, as in *usberette:* or imitation or inferior kind, as in *leatherette* (*American Heritage Dictionary* 1992). These various meanings of *ette* slip around in our minds to influence how we interpret other words with the same suffix. So, for instance, although the word *leatherette* is used to tell us it is not the real thing and an inferior version of leather, *usherette* becomes, by association, not only the female version of usher but denotes a poor imitation. *Usherette* becomes, like *kitchenette,* the diminutive version. These various meanings tumble into one another, propagating new meanings, unintended and imprecise. I recently met a woman who told me that she had been a Rockette at Radio City Music Hall in Rockefeller Center for twenty years. I realized that this string of high-kicking, synchronized dancing women are perpetually cast as the smaller, imitation, inferior and female counterparts of the great male barons, the Rockefellers.

The prefix *dis,* like the suffix *ette,* has similarly unchecked impulses. Although *ette* qualifies its base and reduces it to the more diminutive and less valid version, a relationship is maintained between the base and its amended version. However, the prefix *dis* connotes separation, taking apart, sundering in two. The prefix has various meanings such as not, as in *dissimilar;* absence of, as in *disinterest;* opposite of, as in *disfavor;* undo, do the opposite of, as in *disarrange;* and deprive of, as in *disfranchise.* The Latin root *dis* means apart, asunder. Therefore, to use the verb *disable,* means, in part, to deprive of capability or effectiveness. The prefix creates a barrier, cleaving in two ability and its absence, its opposite. Disability is the "not" condition, the repudiation of ability.

Canguilhem (1991), in his explorations of the normal and the pathological, recognizes the way that prefixes signal their relationship to the words they modify. He asserts that

> the pathological phenomena found in living organisms are nothing more than quantitative variations, greater or lesser according to corresponding physiological phenomena. Semantically, the pathological is designated as departing from the normal not so much by *a-* or *dys-* as by *hyper-* or *hypo-.* . . . [T]his approach is far from considering health and sickness as qualitatively opposed, or as forces joined in battle. (42)

Ette, hyper and *hypo,* and *dis* have semantic consequences, but, moreover, each recapitulates a particular social arrangement. The suffix *ette* not only qualifies the meaning of the root word it is attached to but speaks of the unequal yet dynamic relationship between women and men, in which "woman was, as we see in the profoundly influential works of Aristotle, not the equal opposite of man but a failed version of the supposedly defining type" (Minnich 1990, 54). The medical prefixes *hyper* and *hypo* are typically attached to medical conditions that are temporary or circumscribed. People with those conditions are not socially marked and separated as are those with the more pronounced, and long standing conditions known as disabilities. With *hyper* and *hypo* conditions, there is less semantic and social disjuncture. However, the construction of *dis/ability* does not imply the continuum approach Canguilhem finds in diagnostic categories. *Dis* is the semantic reincarnation of the split between disabled and nondisabled people in society.

Yet *women and men with disabilities, disabled people,* and the *disability community* are terms of choice for the group. We have decided to reassign meaning rather than choose a new name. In retaining *disability* we run the risk of preserving the medicalized ideas attendant upon it in most people's idea of disability. What I think will help us out of the dilemma is the naming of the political category in which *disability* belongs. Women is a category of *gender,* and black or Latino/a are categories of *race/ethnicity,* and it is the recognition of those categories that has fostered understanding of the political meaning of *women* and *black.* Although *race* and *gender* are not perfect terms because they retain biological meanings in many quarters, the categories are increasingly understood as axes of oppression; axes along which power and resources are distributed. Although those of us within the disability community recognize that power is distributed along disability lines, the naming and recognition of the axis will be a significant step in gaining broader recognition of the issues. Further, it will enrich the discussion of the intersections of the axes of class, race, gender and sexual orientation, and disability.

Constructing the axis on which disabled and nondisabled fall will be a critical step in marking all points along it. Currently, there is increased attention to the privileged points on the continua of race, gender, and sexual orientation. There is growing recognition that the white, the male, and the heterosexual positions need to be noted and theorized. Similarly, it is important to examine the nondisabled position and its privilege and power. It is not the neutral, universal position from which disabled people deviate, rather, it is a category of people whose power and cultural capital keep them at the center.

In this [article], though, disabled people's perspectives are kept central and are made explicit, partly to comment on how marginal and obscure they typically are, and partly to suggest the disciplinary and intellectual transformation consequent on putting disability studies at the center.

DISCUSSION QUESTIONS

1. What is your reaction to Linton's analysis of terms like *challenged, special,* or *overcome?* Do you think these terms are disappearing?
2. What are the contradictions and tensions in the term *disability?*

NOTES

1. Various authors have discussed issues related to definitions of *disability.* See Wendell (1996), Longmore (1985, 1987), and Hahn (1987), and also the June Isaacson Kailes (1995) monograph *Language Is More Than a Trivial Concern!* which is available from the Institute on Disability Culture, 2260 Sunrise Point Road, Las Cruces, New Mexico 88011.
2. The definition of *disability* under the Americans with Disabilities Act is consistent with the sociopolitical model employed in disability studies. A person is considered to have a disability if he or she:

   - has a physical or mental impairment that substantially limits one or more of his or her major life activities;
   - has a record of such an impairment or
   - is regarded as having such an impairment.

   The last two parts of this definition acknowledge that even in the absence of a substantially limiting impairment, people can be discriminated against. For instance, this may occur because someone has a facial disfigurement or has, or is suspected of having, HIV or mental illness. The ADA recognizes that social forces, such as myths and fears regarding disability, function to substantially limit opportunity.

3. I am indebted to my colleague John O'Neill for his input on these ideas about the use of the term *normal.*

4. See June Isaacson Kailes's (1995), *Language Is More Than a Trivial Concern!* for a discussion on language use.

REFERENCES

Allen, A. 1996. Open secret: A German academic hides his past—in plain sight. *Lingua Franca* 6 (3): 28–41.

American Heritage Dictionary. 1992. 3d ed. Boston: Houghton Mifflin.

Canguilhem, G. 1991. *The normal and the pathological.* New York: Zone Books.

Davis, L. J. 1995. *Enforcing normalcy: Disability, deafness, and the body.* London: Verso.

Freilich, M., Raybeck, D., and Savishinsky, J. 1991. *Deviance: Anthropological perspectives.* New York: Bergin and Garvey.

Gill, C. J. 1994. Questioning continuum. In B. Shaw, ed., *The ragged edge: The disability experience from the pages of the first fifteen years of "The Disability Rag,"* 42–49. Louisville, Ky.: Advocado Press.

Grover, J. Z. 1987. AIDS: Keywords. In Douglas Crimp, ed., *AIDS: Cultural analysis,* 17–30. Cambridge: MIT Press.

Hahn, H. 1987. Disability and capitalism: Advertising the acceptably employable image. *Policy Studies Journal* 15 (3): 551–70.

Kailes, J. I. 1995. *Language is more than a trivial concern!* (Available from June Isaacson Kailes, Disability Policy Consultant, 6201 Ocean Front Walk, Suite 2, Playa del Rey, California 90293–7556)

Longmore, P. K. 1985. The life of Randolph Bourne and the need for a history of disabled people. *Reviews in American History* 586 (December): 581–87.

———. 1987. Uncovering the hidden history of people with disabilities. *Reviews in American History* 15 (3) (September): 355–64.

Minnich, E. K. 1990. *Transforming knowledge.* Philadelphia: Temple University Press.

Sedgwick, E. K. 1990. *Epistemology of the closet.* Berkeley: University of California Press.

Shapiro, J. P. 1993. *No pity: People with disabilities forging a new civil rights movement.* New York: Times Books.

Stedman's Medical Dictionary. 1976. 23d ed. Baltimore: Williams and Wilkins.

Thomson, R. G. 1997. *Extraordinary bodies: Figuring physical disability in American culture and literature.* New York: Columbia University Press.

Tremblay, M. 1996. Going back to civvy street: A historical account of the Everest and Jennings wheelchair for Canadian World War II veterans with spinal cord injury. *Disability and Society* 11 (2): 149–69.

Wendell, S. 1996. *The rejected body: Feminist philosophical reflections on disability.* New York: Routledge.

Zalewski, D. 1995. Unfriendly competition. *Lingua Franca* 5 (September/October): 19–21.

READING 57

Colormute: Race Talk Dilemmas in an American School

Mica Pollock

Analysts writing on race in the United States often try to remind "everyday people" of a basic paradox about our categories of racial difference: "racial" categories are fake units of human diversity (the world's "racial" groups are more genetically diverse *within* themselves than *between* themselves), yet we have, over centuries of social racializing practice, created a country of "racially" "different folks."[1] We have long lumped together diverse people into simple "racial" units in a system of social relations and differentially distributed power: as Outlaw (1990) puts it, "That 'race' is without a scientific basis in biological terms does not mean, thereby, that it is without any social value" (77–78). Race categories are inherently paradoxical, many scholars have argued, since they are simultaneously invalid *and* now "a key component of our 'taken-for-granted valid reference schema' through which we get on in the world" (58).[2] Yet while analysts struggle to articulate this complex paradox of race to the public, everyday people themselves treat racial categories this paradoxically all the time. We can see this best in places where the very idea of "race groups" is both contested daily and repeatedly imposed.

Among Columbus [High School] students, as [my research] shows, the lines delineating "race groups" were daily both fundamentally blurred and constantly redrawn. Many students across Columbus,

Mica Pollock, an anthropologist, is a professor in the Harvard Graduate School of Education.

for example, listed strings of categories to describe themselves: at Columbus, being "mixed" was an exceedingly common way of life, and even students who did not consider themselves "mixed" acknowledged that it was often quite hard to tell "what" anybody at Columbus "was." At Columbus, where many students spoke of being uninformed about what "races" they were and joked about looking like races that they were not, racial categorization was routinely put up for debate. Yet these daily negotiations over race group membership coexisted with the described simplicity of "six different groups": while racialized *identities* at Columbus were admittedly infinitely complex, racial *identification* was an accepted process of social simplification.[3] Often seemingly forgetting the widespread complications of individual "mixture," students routinely divided the student body into a basic taxonomy of six groups they called "racial"—"Latinos," "blacks," "Filipinos," "Samoans," "Chinese," and "whites."[4] I call this paradoxical treatment of race categories "race-bending," as Columbus students both defied and strategically imposed such simple "racial" labels every day—and in the process, they demonstrated that racial categories will for some time remain key social ordering devices. Indeed, . . . Columbus students demonstrated quite gracefully a basic paradox of U.S. racial practice that professional analysts of race articulate only rather clumsily: *we don't belong to simple race groups, but we do. . . .*

Student *talk* at Columbus itself demonstrated this contradiction exquisitely. Within many single interactions and even within single sentences at Columbus, student talk both struggled against racial categories and gave in to them. That is, students talked alternately as if "race" labels were a perfectly adequate summation of human diversity and as if such single labels did not accurately fit people at all. Whether they talked one way or the other depended, tautologically, on whether they were debating the very process of racial categorization or simply describing the world as racially ordered. . . . Students always wound up contesting easy accounts of race-group membership in casual and classroom discussions *about racial classification itself.* Yet throughout

these very conversations and almost always when talking with adults about other things, . . . students employed a shorthand language of simple race terms that assumed people fit easily into a simple, six-group race taxonomy. This simple language of what I call "lump-sum" racial terms dominated Columbus's daily race talk, and it was particularly fundamental to talk of school's preeminent racial anxiety: equality. When calling for students' equal "race"-group representation in the various public arenas of school life, that is, nobody contested the placement of people *into* "racial groups"—they simply asked whether each of these groups got its due attention. In keeping simple racial identifications strategically available for inequality analysis despite their startling diversity of identities, Columbus students demonstrated that racial categories are in fact always birthed in inequality contexts—and that in a nation with a legacy of simple-race logic, negotiating toward equality will accordingly require using "racial" categories strategically even as we alternately call them into question.[5]

We start, then, by listening to students talking about racial classification itself. As the following fieldnotes demonstrate, students debating the classification of specific people always made the boundaries of race categories seem negotiable rather than firm; talking *about* racial classification always exposed racialization itself as a negotiated human process of differentiating "peoples."[6] Yet throughout these very recurrent games of "guessing" one another's race group membership, students hinted that everyone in the end was somehow supposed to be racially identifiable—and in doing so, they indicated that they would accept the use of simple race categories at certain times and for certain purposes to describe complex people.

STUDENTS TALKING ABOUT RACIAL CLASSIFICATION ITSELF

I had already finished a year's tenure at Columbus as an Ethnic Literature teacher when I participated in the following conversation as a researcher hanging out in a school library study hall. The study hall teacher, a former colleague, had asked me to request that a student take his hat off. "School rule," I explained to the student, smiling; he was small, wiry, light-brown-skinned, with a pointed nose and freckles, enveloped in baggy clothes and a big black skicap. He was "allergic to Columbus," he joked as he removed his cap, taking care to add that he was "just playin'." Pointing out another student, he suddenly started a guessing game:

"Does that girl over there look Mexican to you?" he asked. "I don't know, do you think she does?" I asked. "Don't you think she looks Mexican?" he repeated. "I guess so, why?" I asked. "'Cause she's not Mexican, she's Samoan!" he said, smiling. "Samoan and white, with some black," he added. "Hey, don't be pointing!" the girl yelled over at us, smiling slightly. "I ain't no Mexican!" she added. "How do you know so much about her?" I asked him. "She's my cousin. And she's his cousin too, and he's mine!" he said, pointing to a guy sitting next to him who was somewhat bigger, with curlier hair, fewer freckles, and a wider nose. "So are you Samoan too?" I asked. "Yeah, Samoan . . . and part white, and part Chinese," he said. "So do you call yourself Samoan?" I asked [*I myself keep imposing this lump-sum categorization*]. "Yeah . . . and part white, and part Chinese!" he said, laughing.

The girl next to him said, "I'm Samoan, black, Puerto Rican, Filipino, and Indian." She was tall, freckled, with long braid extensions wrapped up into a loose knot on her head; I had met her earlier that day. "Indian from India, or Native American?" I asked, pointing at the table to mean "the U.S." "Native American," she said, mimicking my gesture. "How do you know all this about yourself?" I asked her. "My mom! My mom tells me," she replied. "What does she call herself?" I asked. "Others," she said matter-of-factly. "What?" I asked. "Others, like that's what she puts down," she said. "Oh, on forms and stuff. What do you put?" I asked. "Other," she said. "That's what I put, too," said the small guy, adding, "I don't know what to put. Or I put 'Polynesian.'"

"What'd you say you were?" called over a girl with straightened-looking hair and slightly darker skin. "Samoan, black, Puerto Rican, Filipino, and Indian," the freckled girl repeated. "Hey, you tryin' to be like ME," the other girl called back, smiling slightly. "Nobody's tryin' to be like nobody," said the small boy. [*Guessing game starts again:*] "I bet I can tell

what everybody is," he said. "Like you, you're black and Filipino, right?" he said to a guy down the table. "What?" the guy replied. "You're black and Filipino, right?" he repeated. "Yeah," this guy said, nodding slowly. "And he's part Samoan and part white," the small boy said, gesturing toward a guy with a long braid sitting two seats away. "What's your dad?" a girl asked this braided kid. "He's French," he replied, very softly. "I can always tell a Samoan," said the small guy, shaking his head and smiling. "How?" I asked. "I just can," he said.

The simple identification "Samoan" triumphed at the close of this brief exchange, despite the students' proudly announced complexity. While racial identities were being treated here as infinitely expandable—a "Samoan" could actually be "Samoan and white, with some black," or "Samoan and part white and part Chinese"—the complexity of "being" "Samoan, black, Puerto Rican, Filipino, and Indian" could easily be reduced to a one-word identification prioritizing one label on the list. Both the single-word options of "forms" requiring respondents to "put down" single identifications (even the bottomless, hypersimplified "other") and the simplifying language of one's study-hall peers enforced this simple identification process. Still, as the small boy turned to another student to continue the guessing game (momentarily replacing "race" with the sporadic synonym "nationality"), the students demonstrated that being a "full" member of any single "group" at Columbus still often seemed an exception to the normality of "mixture":

"What's your nationality?" he asked another girl, who was sitting at our table. "Full black, right?" he added. She nodded slowly, her lips pursed. "Full black?" I repeated. She nodded. "Nothing of anything else?" I asked. She shook her head slowly. "I don't think so," she said. "So you call yourself black—you don't ever use 'African-American' or whatever . . . ?" I asked. "I'm BLACK," she said, shrugging her shoulders and shaking her head. "She's full Samoan," said the smaller guy, pointing to another girl at our table.

He and the bigger guy started asking the five-ethnicity girl about Samoan words. She translated the first five or ten words they said as "shit," or some variation thereof. "Where'd you learn all *these*, your mother?!" I asked her. We laughed. Then she started translating different words they tested her with—"nose," and "pregnant woman." When she got that one they seemed surprised, and somehow convinced that she really knew her stuff. "Wow! Are you fluent in Samoan?" I asked, also surprised. She nodded. "Do you speak 'Puerto Rican'?" I asked, smiling. "No, I don't really speak Spanish," she said. "What else did you say you were?" I asked. [*I'm in the race talk groove now: one "is" a group or a combination of groups.*] She repeated her list. "Do you speak Tagalog?" I asked. She shook her head. "Did you ever live in Samoa?" I asked. Yes, she said, she lived there with her grandmother for two years when she was younger. "Do you speak Samoan at home?" I asked. She nodded.

[*Trying to join the game more explicitly, I find that the category "white" is not expected to be much fun:*] "So what do I look like?" I asked the guys. "White," said the smaller one. "No more specific than that?" I asked. "What do you mean—you're white," he said. "So you get to be Samoan, white, and Chinese and I just get to be 'white'?" I asked. He smiled. "Like what kind of things?" he asked. "I dunno," I said, shrugging. "German?" one of the guys said. I kept shrugging, and eventually said that I had grandparents from Russia. "So you're Russian," said the smaller guy. [*Simple identification triumphs—the label is a new one for me, but I accept it.*] I shrugged and nodded. "I guess so," I said.

[*Now, someone starts dividing the category "Samoan" into even smaller parts.*] "Are you from Western Samoa or American?" the small guy asked the 5-ethnicity girl. "American," she said. "Is there a difference?" I asked. "Yeah," the boys said. "Then there's Tongans, and Fijians," the small guy said. "Are Tongans different?" I asked. "Yeah—we don't eat horses!" said the bigger guy. Several people laughed. "WE eat the pig, and chicken," he continued. "Everyone eats chicken!" said the smaller guy. "And __, and __," continued the guys, naming foods in Samoan and laughing. "Who's 'we'?!" I asked. "Samoans," they answered.

Simple identification triumphed again here. Struggling throughout the conversation to understand the student's constantly shifting lines of differentiation (hence my overwhelmed "who's 'we'?!"), I myself, of course, kept fueling the quest to draw simpler classificatory lines, with questions like "Is there a difference?" and "Are Tongans dif-

ferent?"[7] Yet as the students themselves contrasted the lump-sum category "Samoan" to absent groups like "Tongans" and "Fijians," they melted their own sub-distinctions of national origin (Western vs. American Samoa) back into the simplicity of "Samoanness." Mystified by the suddenly simplified self-identification of this now-assembled group of "Samoans," I next asked who in the group had actually been to Samoa. The "5-ethnicity girl," the bigger boy, and the braided boy said they had, while the small boy who could "always tell a Samoan" said he had actually never visited. Yet whether one had actually been to Samoa, he indicated, seemed less important to claiming "Samoanness" than whether one had people around to tell stories about it:

"So you've never been to Samoa?" I asked the smaller guy. "No," he said. "How do you know this stuff?" I asked. "My mom told me," he said. "And they eat __," added the 5-ethnicity girl, still harking back to the food list with a word in Samoan. "Who's 'they'?" I asked her. "Oh, well, 'us,' I guess . . . but I don't EAT spinach," she said. "And Tongans have big noses," added the small guy. "Like some, Samoans, too, hella big!" added the bigger guy. A girl at the table raised her head from her magazine (*Ebony*) and said, "Don't be putting us down like that, I ain't no Tongan, we don't got noses nearly that big."

The "Samoan," "white," and "black" girl cousin who supposedly looked "Mexican" came nearby. "Hella heavy lipstick, man!" said one of the guys. "Hey, you better wash off that eye stuff, you look like a Mexican," said the small guy, smiling. "Is that an insult?" I asked him quizzically. "No," he replied. "Mehicano," he mused, seeming to like the way it sounded. "You guys act Mexican, cause you're from LA," the kid with a braid said to him, adding, "I never seen a Samoan that looks like you."

Group boundaries were simultaneously blurred and reinscribed here. The students had spent much of this conversation debating the very category "Samoan," but somehow through all this contestation the category "Samoan" survived. With the telling "oh, well, 'us,' I guess," the "5-ethnicity girl" indicated that a sense of one's "Samoan" *identity* could suddenly hinge precariously on whether or not one ate spinach, or whether or not one knew a Samoan word;

yet people could be simply *identified* as "Samoan" even if they were only "part" Samoan, or even if they didn't really "look" Samoan, with or without knowledge of the Samoan language or a taste for Samoan foods.[8] They could wash off temporary "Mexican" appearances or cease "Mexican"/"LA" behaviors and return to Samoanness; they could *be* Samoan having grown up in Samoa, spent two years there, or never been. A "Samoan" girl reading a magazine targeted toward "blacks," a boy who was "Samoan and part white and part Chinese," a boy who was "part Samoan and part white," and a girl who was "Samoan, black, Puerto Rican, Filipino, and Indian" all finally identified themselves as matter-of-factly "Samoan" in comparison to other matter-of-factly bounded groups ("Mexicans," "Tongans," "Fijians") said to have bigger noses, wear more makeup, or eat stranger foods. Despite the complexities of "mixture," migration, and family history, it seemed, one was strategically *still* "*Samoan*"—particularly when ranking "Samoans" in comparison to other lump-sum groups. . . .

Student life at Columbus was always inordinately complicated, and so it often seemed that placing "racial" boundaries on Columbus students was an inherently inaccurate exercise. At Columbus, a "Filipino" student speaking Tagalog to a friend at one moment might call him "homie" the next, just as a "Latino" student might switch from speaking rapid Spanish to chanting rhythmic English rap lyrics under his breath; students across Columbus dished out and responded to the adult-baffling, racialized friendship term "nigga." . . . At assemblies, speakers of all languages would address the assembled student body with the obligatory "Columbus in the house!" just as speakers of all languages greeted each other in the hallway with terms of endearment like "hey, blood." When a student hard-rock band of several Filipino-looking students and a black-looking drummer stunned the traditionally hip-hop crowd in one student assembly, one teacher called the performance a "culture shock."

Columbus, which often seemed to present a shared youth "culture," was not always carved into six simple racial groups. Yet the daily motions

of complex racial identities did not erase racial categories as crucial and strategic social ordering devices. The reality of racial practice at Columbus was the coexistence of limitless complexity and pointed simplification: the routine defiance of racial categories alternated with a continually imposed simple categorical order. There are times, of course, when "natives" themselves impose simple categories upon their own complex societies, and for Columbus students, this imposition of simplification was itself a strategic cultural act.[9] Daily, Columbus students employed the logic of racial difference even as they deconstructed it, only "partially penetrating" the racial classificatory system.[10] Every day, they knowingly sacrificed the detailed complexities of individual "identity" to a national habit of simple racial identification, as a strategic response within an inequitable country that has for generations bluntly asked us what we "are."

Some analysts have argued that contemporary U.S. youths' self-conscious announcements of "mixed" ancestry, combined with their often seemingly easy association with one another (when desegregated demographics allow), are signals that U.S. racial categories themselves are finally near their demise.[11] Indeed, some public figures are actively attacking politically the very practice of racial classification in the name of the nation's growing population of "multiracial" youth. In California, Ward Connerly, the UC regent behind the state's anti-affirmative-action Proposition 209, has explained his current "Racial Privacy" public initiative (which hopes to ban race data altogether from public school records in the state) by pleading openly with voters to let "mixed" youth have "freedom from race" and "just be Americans."[12] Yet young Americans . . . themselves employ simple "race" categories daily, in concert with the adults around them—especially in school, perhaps, and especially for the purposes of "fairness."[13] Both defying and utilizing the racial logic available for use in America, Columbus students bent racial categories rather than fully breaking them—and in doing so, they demonstrated that as racial classification itself is still a complicated part of struggles over power, creating equality will for a time longer require speaking categorically while alternately interrogating the very reality of categories themselves. . . .

DISCUSSION QUESTIONS

1. What racial labels are used in this school?
2. Why are placing racial boundaries on people an inherently inaccurate exercise?
3. Why did Columbus students bend racial categories?

NOTES

1. For more discussion of the historical process of slotting people into "race" groups often called racialization (and what Omi and Winant (1994) call "racial formation" see Roediger 1991, Espiritu 1992, Almaguer 1994, Haney Lopez 1996, Davis 1997, Sacks 1997, Saragoza et al. 1998.

2. For other useful articulations of this paradox, see also Winant 1998, Jackson 2001, and the American Anthropological Association's "Statement on 'Race'" (1998). Haney Lopez (1995) similarly argues succinctly that "race is neither an essence nor an illusion" (193).

3. Baker (2000) makes this useful distinction between "identity" and "identification" in his discussion of a late-1990s controversy over a "mixed-race" category of the U.S. census. While proponents of the "mixed-race" category demanded that the Census allow individuals to accurately record their complex *identities*, Baker suggests, opponents (like the NAACP) argued that distributing resources necessitated simpler, lump-sum racial *identification*. For further analysis of this controversy, see Cose 1997.

4. Again, that students called all six categories "racial" corroborates the findings of Rumbaut (forthcoming), who notes that in California's demographically and politically complex setting, young people called both "pan-ethnic" labels like "Latino" and "black" and "foreign national" labels like "Filipino" "races." Rumbaut noted "a substantial proportion of youths who conceived of their nationality of origin as a fixed racial category."

5. Other scholars have noted such strategic employment of simple self-categorizations within inequality contexts. Gayatri Spivak (1987) coined the phrase "strategic essentialism" to refer to the use of simple, primordial categories to reference groups for those groups' own political benefit (despite the reductive consequences of such primordialism). British sociologist Stuart Hall has been central in framing race categories as "strategic places from which to speak" when navigating inequality systems (see Sharma, 1996, 34, for further discussion). Paul Gilroy (1993) has described the strategic use of race categories to label communities bounded by historic struggles against racism and racial inequality as a tactic or "anti-anti-essentialism." Omi and Winant (1994) document many examples of purposeful racialization, or the seizing of race categories to describe selves in order to wield community and political power in the context of inequality structures. Finally, much anthropological work, such as work on indigenous rights movements, has also explored dynamics of "strategic essentialism." As Hodgson (2002) argues, many anthropologists, building also on philosopher Charles Taylor's work on "the politics of recognition" (see Taylor 1994), have argued that indigenous peoples who "demand that their rights be acknowledged must fill the places of recognition that others provide . . . [e]ven as they seek to stretch, reshape, or even invert the meanings implied" (Li 2001, cited in Hodgson 2002, p. 1041).

6. Similarly, in a recent ethnography of adults in Harlem, John Jackson (2001) argues that everyday "jostling for certainty over which particular *behaviors* are labeled black or white" (187, emphasis mine) opens up a space for contesting the very idea of racial difference. Jostling over how particular people are labeled, I would argue, similarly always demonstrates that racial difference is produced rather than "natural."

7. Throughout my research, I particularly asked students "Who's 'we'?" in the midst of our conversations in order to get them to articulate their running classifications of self and others. For another application of this fieldwork strategy of attending closely to shifting youth "we's," "they's," and "I's," see also Varenne 1982.

8. For a similar example of U.S. youth play over classification, see Bailey 2000, who demonstrates Rhode Island youth contesting racialized ("black") and national-origin ("Dominican"/"Spanish") classifications through the use of various languages in informal conversations. By switching rapidly between Standard English, African-American Vernacular English, and Spanish, Bailey writes, the youth studied used language as "the key to racial/ethnic identity, preceding phenotype." Yet even while these youth used language to *contest* racialized classifications (such that someone who "looked" "black" could prove he "was" instead "Spanish" by speaking Spanish), Bailey notes that they also used race labels to *impose* racialized "social classification[s] based on phenotype" on one another (557).

9. One predecessor's words offer some final guidance for understanding how people both defy social categoriza-

tions in daily life and employ these categorizations in order to create and navigate a predictable social structure. When anthropologist E. R. Leach began work with the Kachin in Burma in the 1950s, he found, as he wrote, that Kachin social organization seemed startlingly in flux. Like many British anthropologists of his time, Leach had been interested initially in the Kachin's social ranking system; yet among the Kachin, he quickly realized, such rankings were clear-cut "in theory" but not in practice. "Although a man's rank is in theory precisely defined by his birth." Leach (1954) explained, "there is an almost infinite flexibility in the system as actually applied" (167). Leach argued that acting *as if* things were simply ordered, however, was itself a key part of cultural practice. That is, while there might be debate over who would serve as the Kachin chief, the *category* of "chief" was a given. Delineating such simple social categories, he argued, was thus not just "an analytical device of the social anthropologist": "it also corresponds to the way that Kachins themselves apprehend their own system through the medium of the verbal categories of their own language" (ix). The "verbal categories" of Kachin talk described how Kachin people "apprehended" their social categories, not necessarily how they always lived them—but as there would always be a "chief," conceptual social schemes in the end organized lives in practice as well as in theory.

10. On the concept of working-class youth only "partially penetrating" the class system in Britain (that is, challenging the middle-class authority of schooling even while slotting themselves into working-class jobs), see Willis 1977.

11. See, e.g., Heath 1995. For a similar argument about the dwindling demographic future of U.S. "races," see Sanjek 1996.

12. As one think tank reported on a public speech by Connerly on his proposed "Racial Privacy Initiative,"

Mr. Connerly (like so many Californians) is a prime example of the absurdity of racial classification. His heritage includes Irish, African and Choctaw native American ancestors. His wife is Irish. His son married a Vietnamese girl.

"But when people find out my grandchildren are Ward Connerly's grandchildren, they often say, 'Oh, you're black,'" he told the audience. "This initiative is for the growing population of kids who don't know what box to check—and shouldn't have to decide. Please give them freedom from race and let them just be Americans." See "Editorial: Undermining Identity Politics. American Civil Rights Coalition, April 5, 2002. (http://www.acrc1.org/editorial.htm) [*sic*]

13. As Loury (2000) argues in a foreword to a study supporting affirmative-action policies, "The implicit assumption of color-blind advocates is that, if we would just stop putting people into these [administrative] boxes, they would oblige us by not thinking of themselves in these terms. But, this assumption is patently false" (Bowen and Bok 1998, xxviii).

REFERENCES

Almaguer, Tomas. 1994. *Racial Fault Lines: The Historical Origins of White Supremacy in California.* Berkeley: University of California Press.

American Anthropological Association. 1998. AAA Statement on "Race." *Anthropology Newsletter.* May 17, p. 1.

Bailey, Benjamin. 2000. Language and Negotiation of Ethnic/Racial Identity among Dominican Americans. *Language and Society* 29: 555–82.

Baker, Lee. 2000. Profit, Power, and Privilege: The Racial Politics of Ancestry. Paper presented at the Annual Meeting of the American Educational Research Association, New Orleans, LA, April 25.

Bowen, William G., and Derek Bok. 1998. *The Shape of the River: Long-Term Consequences of Considering Race in College and University Admissions.* Princeton, NJ: Princeton University Press.

Cose, Ellis. 1997. *Colorblind: Seeing beyond Race in a Race-Obsessed World.* New York: HarperCollins Publishers.

Davis, F. James. 1997. *Who Is Black? One Nation's Definition.* University Park, PA: Pennsylvania State University Press.

Espiritu, Yen Le. 1992. *Asian American Panethnicity: Bridging Institutions and Identities.* Philadelphia: Temple University Press.

Gilroy, Paul. 1993. *The Black Atlantic.* Cambridge, MA: Harvard University Press.

Haney Lopez, Ian F. 1995. The Social Construction of Race. In *Critical Race Theory: The Cutting Edge,* edited by Richard Delgado. Philadelphia: Temple University Press.

———. 1996. *White by Law: The Legal Construction of Race.* New York: New York University Press.

Heath, Shirley Brice. 1995. Race, Ethnicity, and the Defiance of Categories. In *Toward a Common Destiny: Improving Race and Ethnic Relations in America,* edited by Willis D. Hawley and Anthony W. Jackson. San Francisco: Jossey-Bass Publishers.

Hodgson, Dorothy L. 2002. Introduction: Comparative Perspectives on the Indigenous Rights Movement in Africa and the Americas. *American Anthropologist,* 104 (4), December: 1037–49.

Jackson, John L., Jr. 2001. *Harlemworld: Doing Race and Class in Contemporary Black America.* Chicago: University of Chicago Press.

Leach, Edmund. 1954. *Political Systems of Highland Burma.* London: Athlone Press.

Li, Tanya Murray. 2001. Masyarakat Adat, Difference and the Limits of Recognition in Indonesia's Forest Zone. *Modern Asia Studies* 35 (3): 645–76.

Omi, Michael, and Howard Winant. 1994. *Racial Formation in the United States: From the 1960s to the 1990s.* 2d ed. New York: Routledge.

Outlaw, Lucius. 1990. Toward a Critical Theory of "Race." In *Anatomy of Racism,* edited by David Theo Goldberg. Mineapolis: University of Minnesota Press.

Roediger, David R. 1991. *The Wages of Whiteness: Race and the Making of the American Working Class.* London: Verso.

Rumbaut, Rubén. Forthcoming. Sites of Belonging: Acculturation, Discrimination, and Ethnic Identity Among Children of Immigrants. In *Discovering Successful Pathways in Children's Development: New Methods in the Study of Childhood and Family Life,* edited by Thomas S. Weisner. Chicago: University of Chicago Press.

Sacks, Karen Brodkin. 1997. How Did Jews Become White Folks? In *Critical White Studies,* edited by Richard Delgado and Jean Stefancic. Philadelphia: Temple University Press.

Sanjek, Roger. 1996. The Enduring Inequalities of Race. In *Race,* edited by Steven Gregory and Roger Sanjek. New Brunswick, NJ: Rutgers University Press.

Saragoza, Alex M., Concepción Juarez, Abel Valenzuela, Jr., and Oscar Gonzalez. 1998. Who Counts? Title VII and the Hispanic Classification. In *The Latino/a Condition: A Critical Reader,* edited by Richard Delgado and Jean Stefancic. New York: New York University Press.

Sharma, Sanjay. 1996. Noisy Asians or "Asian Noise"? In *Dis-Orienting Rhythms: The Politics of the New Asian Dance Music,* edited by Sanjay Sharma, John Hutnyk, and Ashwani Sharma. London: Zed Books.

Spivak, Gayatri Chakravorty. 1987. Subaltern Studies: Deconstructing Historiography. In Spivak, *In Other Worlds: Essays in Cultural Politics.* New York: Routledge.

Taylor, Charles. 1994. The Politics of Recognition. In Charles Taylor et al., *Multiculturalism: Examining the Politics of Recognition,* edited and introduced by Amy Gutmann. Princeton, NJ: Princeton University Press.

Varenne, Herve. 1982. Jocks and Freaks: The Symbolic Structure of the Expression of Social Interaction among American Senior High School Students. In *Doing the Ethnography of Schooling,* edited by George Spindler. New York: Holt, Rinehart and Winston.

Willis, Paul. 1977. *Learning to Labor: How Working-Class Kids Get Working-Class Jobs.* New York: Columbia University Press.

Winant, Howard. 1998. Racial Dualism at Century's End. In *The House That Race Built,* edited by W. Lubiano. New York: Vintage Books.

BRIDGING DIFFERENCES

FRAMEWORK ESSAY

A book such as *The Meaning of Difference* runs the risk of leaving students with the feeling that there is little they can do to challenge the constructions of difference. Having recognized the power of master statuses and the significance of our conceptions of difference in everything from personal identity to world events, it is easy to feel powerless in the face of what appear to be overwhelming social forces.

But we did not embark on writing this book because we felt powerless or wanted you to feel that way. For us, the idea of looking at race, sex, social class, sexual orientation, and disability *all together* opened up new possibilities for understanding and creating alliances. When we started to talk about this book over ten years ago, comparing our teaching experiences in a highly diverse university and our personal experiences of stigma and privilege, we were amazed by the connections we saw. That impression grew as we talked with students and friends who were members of other groups. Over time, we learned that understanding the similarities *across* groups opened up new ways of thinking: experiences could be accumulated toward a big picture, rather than suffered in relative isolation; people could be different but still have had the same experience; people who never had the experience might still have ways to understand it. We believe the world is more interesting and hopeful with the realization that the experience of being in "the closet" is generally the same irrespective of which status brought you there, or that a variety of race and ethnic groups are subject to racial profiling, or that women often experience the double consciousness that W. E. B. Du Bois described for blacks. When we realized how readily people could generalize from their own experience of stigma and privilege to what others might experience, we were energized.

That energy led to this book. But what should you do with your energy and insight? Or if you are feeling beaten down and depressed, rather than energized, what might you do about that?

Let us start with the worst-case scenario—that is, the possibility that you feel powerless to bring about social change, and hopelessly insignificant in the face of overwhelming social forces. Unfortunately, this is not an uncommon outcome in higher education, nor is it distinctive to this subject matter. The emphasis in higher education is more on "understanding" than "doing." Most university course work stresses detached, value-neutral reasoning, not passionate advocacy for social change.

> In the natural sciences, it is taken for granted that the aim is to explain an external order of nature. In literature, the text is an object to be interpreted. In politics, government is a phenomenon to be analyzed. Everywhere, it is intimated that the stance of the educated person should be that of the spectator. . . . In the contemporary university, one quickly learns that certain questions are out of order. One does not ask persistently about what ought to be done, for normative questions entail what are called value judgments, and these are said to be beyond the scope of scientific analysis. (Anderson, 1993:34–35, 36)

Paradoxically, however, education is also the source of much social change. We all know this almost instinctively. Educational institutions teach us our rights and our history, sharpen our thinking and decision-making, and open us to others' lived experience. Learning *changes* us, and higher education is explicit in its intention to produce that effect. The university is, after all, "an *educational* institution. As such, it is expected to have an impact on the society of which it is a part. . . . [T]he task of the university is not only to explore, systematically, the nature of the world, but also to scrutinize the practices of everyday life to see if they can be improved" (Anderson, 1993:59).

Recognizing the paradoxical nature of higher education, that it can both empower and disempower, means, in truth, that an element of choice—your choice—is involved in whether you are discouraged or inspired at the end of a course.

There is, however, another reason you might leave this material feeling powerless. This has more to do with the nature of society than with the nature of education, but it again involves paradox and personal choice. Eminent sociologist Peter Berger called this the "Janus-faced" nature of human society. The Roman god Janus, for whom January was named, symbolized beginnings and endings, past and future, change and transition, and was depicted as having two faces looking in opposite directions. Berger used that image to convey that just as individuals are rarely wholly powerful, neither are they wholly powerless. In this analogy, Berger found a visual image for the truth that we are *both* the authors and victims—architects and prisoners—of social life. We *both* make society and are made by it. (And in our own spirit of powerfulness, we have edited out the sexism in Berger's prose below.)

> No social structure, however massive it may appear in the present, existed in this massivity from the dawn of time. Somewhere along the line each one of its salient features was concocted by human beings, whether they were charismatic visionaries, clever crooks, conquering heroes or just individuals in positions of power who hit on what seemed to them a better way of running the show. Since all social systems were created by [humans], it follows that [humans] can also change them.
>
> Every [person] who says "I have no choice" in referring to what his [or her] social role demands of him [or her] is engaged in "bad faith." . . . [People] are responsible for their actions. They are in "bad faith" when they attribute to iron necessity what they themselves are choosing to do. (Berger, 1963:128, 143–44)

While you do not have the power to change everything, you certainly have the power to change some things. Gandhi's paradox, discussed by Allan Johnson in Reading 59, captures this point: "Gandhi once said that nothing we do as individuals matters, but that it's vitally important to do it anyway."

So we urge you to move beyond your sense of being powerless and get on with the work of social change. We offer some suggestions for that process below, much of it drawn from work we have found both inspirational and practical.

We Make the Road by Walking

"We make the road by walking" was Spanish poet Antonio Machado's (1875–1939) adaptation of a proverb: "*se hace camino al andar,*" or "you make the way as you go." It is also the title of a published dialogue between two famous educator-activists, Myles Horton and Paulo Freire (Bell, Gaventa, and Peters, 1990).

Myles Horton founded the Highlander Folk School in Tennessee in 1932, when American racial segregation was still firmly in place. A unique school, Highlander offered racially integrated adult education—especially in history, government, and leadership—to the rural poor and working-class residents of the Cumberland Mountain communities. Horton's aim was to "use education as one of the instruments for bringing about a new social order" (Bell et al., 1990:xxiii). While many southern labor union leaders studied at Highlander, the school is probably best known for its contribution to the civil rights movement. Highlander taught the methods of nonviolence and started "Citizenship Schools," which taught southern blacks to read and write, so that they could pass the tests required to vote. (Literacy tests have been used in many countries to keep poor people from voting. In the United States, they were used in southern states to keep African Americans from voting, until passage of the 1965 Voting Rights Act). Probably the most famous Highlander student was Rosa Parks, who attended the school shortly before her refusal to move to the back of the bus sparked the Montgomery, Alabama, bus boycott and the civil rights movement.

Paulo Freire, author of the classic, *Pedagogy of the Oppressed,* was in charge of a Brazilian national literacy program in the 1960s, before the government was overthrown by a military coup. Like American blacks before 1965, Brazil's poor were also denied the right to vote because they were illiterate. After the coup, Freire was forced to flee from Brazil, but he went on to write and develop literacy programs elsewhere. His work was distinguished by its emphasis on teaching literacy through real community issues. His belief that education must operate as a dialogue, rooted in values and committed to transforming the world, made him one of the most influential thinkers of the last century.

Apart from the example that Myles Horton's and Paulo Freire's lives provide for the power of education to produce social change, we turn to them here for some basic lessons about transforming learning into action. First, we hope the phrase "we make the road by walking" helps you remember that *you* are the best person to know which "social interventions" will work for you. There is probably nothing more fundamental to social change than learning who you are, finding and honoring that authentic self, recognizing that it is multifaceted, complex, and *evolving*—and then making sure that the social change methods you use are consistent with that self. If you are going to pursue something as important as social change, it might as well be *you* who is doing it, not your impersonation of someone else.

"We make the road by walking" also conveys that the road has not already been built. While there are many helpful resources, you will not find a recipe book designed for all the situations you will face, nor would that necessarily be a good idea. One of Horton's experiences with a union strike committee illustrates this point:

> [Members of the committee] were getting desperate. They said: "Well, now you've had more experience than we have. You've got to tell us what to do. You're the expert." I said: "No, let's talk about it a little bit more. In the first place I don't know what to do, and if I did know what to do I wouldn't tell you, because if I had to tell you today then I'd have to tell you tomorrow, and when I'm gone you'd have to get somebody else to tell you." One guy reached in his pocket and pulled out a pistol and says, "Goddamn you, if you don't tell us I'm going to kill you." I was tempted then to become an instant expert, right on the spot! But I knew that if I did that, all would be lost and then all the rest of them would start asking me what to do. So I said: "No. Go ahead and shoot if you want to, but I'm not going to tell you." And the others calmed him down. (Bell et al., 1990:126)

So it is important to recognize that to some extent, you will need to be your *own* resource, *and* you will never have all the answers you need. Horton described two approaches to this inevitable incompleteness. First, "What I finally decided, after three or four years of reading and studying and trying to figure this thing out, was that *the way to do something was to start doing it and learn from it*" (Bell et al., 1990:40; emphasis added). And second, "*People learn from each other.* You don't need to know the answer" (Bell et al., 1990:55; emphasis added). As many of the personal accounts included in this book show, we make the road by walking.

Work on Yourself First

Challenging social constructions of difference by working on yourself first, may not seem earth shattering, but it is the unavoidable first step on the road. We think there are four main lessons on which to concentrate.

1. Increase your tolerance for making mistakes.   In his dialogue with Miles Horton, Paolo Freire remarked, "I am always in the beginning, as you"—and at that point Freire was 66 years old and Horton 82. The Reverend Jessie Jackson often reminds his listeners and himself, "The Lord is not done with me yet." Realizing how little you know about other people's life experience is a way to prepare for the absolute inevitability that, in trying to build connections across difference, *you will make mistakes.* You must increase your tolerance of your mistakes or risk giving up altogether, and you must try to focus on learning from all these attempts—good, bad, or ugly. As one of our colleagues often tells her students, when you are worried that you'll say the wrong thing, you wind up holding back, not extending yourself—and missing an opportunity for connection. Our advice is to just get used to making mistakes. There is no way around them.

2. Appreciate the statuses you occupy.   "Appreciating" your statuses—*stigmatized and privileged*—may sound odd, but it is the foundation that allows you to respond with more clarity to others' experiences of their statuses. By appreciating your own statuses, we mean honoring, valuing, and having some reasonable level of comfort about being white, black, Asian Latino; male or female; wealthy, middle class, or poor; disabled or nondisabled; straight or gay. Appreciating your status means not being ashamed of who you are.

> Is there a part of your identity of which you are not proud? Is there a part of who you are that you tend to hide from people? *One of the most profound blows to oppression is claiming legitimate delight in who we are.* . . . Notice where you struggle in claiming pride in who you are. This is the preliminary work that must be done to work against all forms of oppression.
>
> Reclaiming pride in our identities entails knowing our histories, becoming familiar not only with the side of history that causes us shame but also with the side that offers us hope. Ever mindful not to distort historical realities, it is nonetheless possible, even in the midst of the worst acts of oppression, to claim as our ancestors the few people who resisted the oppression. For example, in the present, it is useful for many people of German heritage to remember that there were heroic Germans who resisted Nazi anti-Semitism. . . . [A]long with the unfathomable devastation of the Holocaust, this minority tradition of resistance is also part of the history of the German people. (Brown and Mazza, 1997:5–6; emphasis added)

Ironically, at this juncture in American society, some level of shame seems to adhere to stigmatized *and* privileged statuses. We don't want to mislead you into thinking that getting over being ashamed of the statuses you occupy is an easy task, but recognizing the existence of shame and its dysfunction is an important first step. As Brown and Mazza suggest above, learning the *full* history of "your people"—good deeds and bad—will help you find heroes, as well as avoid false pride.

3. Learn to "sit in the fire." For those in privileged statuses, guilt seems to be the most common reaction to discussions of prejudice and discrimination. For those in stigmatized statuses, anger probably ranks at the top. Those who occupy both privileged and stigmatized statuses are "privileged" to experience both ends of this emotional continuum! Insofar as race, sex, social class, disability, and sexual orientation are *all* on the table, *everyone* will probably have the opportunity for an intense emotional experience. That's a lot of emotion, not to mention that people have varying abilities to talk about—or even experience—those feelings. Either way, bridging differences sometimes means we must be willing to "sit in the fire" (Mindell, 1995) of conflict and intense emotion.

Regarding guilt, our advice is not to succumb to it. It is both immobilizing and distracting. Focusing on how badly *you* feel means that *you* are the subject of attention, not the people whose experience you are trying to understand.

About anger, our advice is more complicated. When it's someone else's anger, listen carefully so that you can understand it. Don't stop listening because you don't like the message or the way it is packaged. Don't take an expression of anger personally unless you are told it actually is about you. Try not to let someone else's anger trigger your own, because that will distract you from listening. Recognize that you can withstand someone's anger.

When you are the one who is angry, try not to let it overwhelm you. Try to distinguish between a setting in which you are under attack, and one populated by friends, or potential friends, who are trying to learn about your experience. Try to distinguish people who are malevolent from those who are misguided, or simply awkward in their efforts to help. Try to avoid self-righteousness. Your having been injured doesn't mean that you have not also inflicted injury. Remember that "every person is important, even those who belong to majority groups that have historically oppressed other groups" (Brown and Mazza, 1997:5).

As you experience sitting in the fire, remember that *the benefits of diversity derive from engagement, not passive observation. Contact will inevitably entail periods of disagreement and conflict.* Parker Palmer is a sociologist and nationally renowned expert on higher education. We quote him at length below, because he offers such a clear picture of what both frightens and draws us to engagement across difference.

> We collaborate with the structures of separation because they promise to protect us against one of the deepest fears at the heart of being human—the fear of having a live encounter with alien "otherness," whether the other is a student, a colleague, a subject, or a self-dissenting voice within. *We fear encounters in which the other is free to be itself, to speak its own truth, to tell us what we may not wish to hear. We want those encounters on our own terms, so that we can control their outcomes, so that they will not threaten our view of world and self. . . .*

This fear of the live encounter is actually a sequence of fears that begins in the fear of diversity. As long as we inhabit a university made homogeneous by our refusal to admit otherness, we can maintain the illusion that we possess the truth about ourselves and the world—after all, there is no "other" to challenge us! But as soon as we admit pluralism, we are forced to admit that ours is not the only standpoint, the only experience, the only way, and the truths we have built our lives on begin to feel fragile. . . .

Otherness, taken seriously, always invites transformation, calling us not only to new facts and theories and values but also to new ways of living our lives—and that is the most daunting threat of all. (Palmer, 1998: 36–38; emphasis added)

But what if there appears to be no diversity in the setting in which you find yourself? The odds are that that is just the appearance of things. No matter how homogeneous a group may seem, there will be layers of significant difference beneath the appearances. "Taking the time to examine [those less visible differences] can be invaluable, not only for creating a climate that welcomes the differences already present in the group, but also for laying the groundwork for becoming more inclusive of other differences" (Brown and Mazza, 1997:13).

4. Be an ally. Appreciate your allies.   We conclude this list with what we think is the most important of the lessons: Be an ally; find allies; appreciate your allies. There is nothing complicated about the concept of an ally: an ally is simply someone from a privileged status actively committed to eliminating stigma and the ill-treatment of those in stigmatized statuses. If you remember a time when you were treated unfairly because of a status you occupy and think about what you *wish* someone had done or said on your behalf, you will then understand the critical role an ally can play, and you will have a good sense of what the role calls for. Beyond that, you can learn about being an ally by asking people what would be helpful and by educating yourself about the history and experience of those in stigmatized groups.

Many of the personal accounts in this book are about having or wishing for an ally. Indeed, if "ally" were an entry in the help-wanted section of the newspaper, the opportunities would be described as "unlimited." John Larew's article on legacy admissions (Reading 38) is an example of being an ally. The article—written while he was editor of Harvard's *Crimson Tide*—sparked an extended, national discussion on legacy admissions. Larew can take considerable credit for the attention now being paid to the underrepresentation of low-income students in colleges and universities.

While Larew's article grew out of his daily experience and the media access he had as editor of the *Tide*, other ways of being an ally are available to virtually anyone, anytime—even, for example, at lunch. We single out this meal, because it is generally a public one, in which members of stigmatized categories are likely to find themselves with limited options; eat with other members of the category, eat alone, or hide. So an ally (or potential ally) might extend an invitation to share a sandwich.

Being an ally, however, is not only about what you can do on your own. It is also about joining with others in collective action. The social movements that have historically transformed the status of stigmatized groups in America, such as the women's movement or civil rights movement, included some people from privileged statuses, just as privileged allies have joined with members of stigmatized groups in innumerable more localized ways: university chapters of Men against Sexism, community groups like Parents and Friends of Lesbians and Gays, elected officials who sponsor antidiscrimination legislation, the 1960s college students who risked their lives to register black voters in the South, the Muslims in Rwanda who helped Tutsis escape from the 1994 genocide. You might consider how you could become an ally who makes a difference.

Still, *getting* allies sometimes requires *asking for help* and even telling people what you specifically want or don't want them to do. People who are disabled do this in a powerful video on YouTube called "A Credo for Support," telling their potential allies:

> Do not see my disability as the problem. Recognize that my disability is an attribute.
>
> Do not try to fix me, because I am not broken. Support me. I can make my contribution to the community in my way.
>
> Do not see me as your client. I am your fellow citizen. See me as your neighbor. Remember, none of us can be self-sufficient.
>
> Do not try to change me. You have no right. Help me learn what I want to know.
>
> Do not try to be my friend. I deserve more than that. Get to know me. We may become friends.
>
> Do not help me, even if it does make you feel good. Ask me if I need your help.
>
> Do not admire me. A desire to live a full life does not warrant adoration. Respect me, for respect presumes equity.
>
> Do not tell, correct, and lead. Listen, support, and follow.
>
> Do not work on me. Work with me. (Kunc and Van der Klift, 2007)

While you might wish for allies who could read your mind and step in and out at exactly the right moment it is unlikely you will find people like that. The people you do find, however, will probably be ones more easily recruited to become allies with appreciation than with guilt.

> We rarely increase our effectiveness by dwelling on all of the things we still need to get right. This principle is especially important for those of us who are seeking allies. Pointing out only how the people around us have failed usually only increases their discouragement. Remembering the successes can lead to increased confidence and a greater ability to be an effective ally. (Brown and Mazza, 1997:49)

Of all potential allies, white men who are straight and nondisabled can be the most powerful. When such a person speaks on behalf of those in stigmatized statuses, he stands a good chance of being heard, if only because he appears not to be acting out of vested interest. His intervention can change the dynamic, provide a role model for others, and give those in stigmatized statuses a break from always being the ones to raise the contentious points. Once, on a panel about gender, we saw one of the men flag issues of sexism that the women panelists would otherwise have had to note. It seemed to us that they appreciated his intervention. In our own work settings, we have definitely appreciated the occasions when a white man has taken leadership on issues of sexual harassment, signed up for the "special interest" committee, or spoken up for the interests of people of color or white women.

Being an ally is also sometimes called for among one's friends and loved ones, in those more private settings where people feel freer to air and cultivate their prejudices. Like Paul Kivel in Reading 62, who suggests some ways to respond in these situations, we would also urge you to be an "ally with a heart" in these settings.

> Condemning people, shaming them, and making them feel guilty are all unproductive strategies: They all increase defensiveness rather than creating an opening for change. . . . Condemning people rarely helps them to change their behavior. Instead, think about what you honestly appreciate about the person. Also consider the ways that person has made any progress, even if it's only slight, on the issue that is of concern to you. Practice telling that person the things she is doing right. Appreciation leads to action; condemnation leads to paralysis.
>
> People are often afraid to appreciate someone whose behavior they disapprove of, for fear that the appreciation will keep the oppressive behavior unchallenged. However, only by seeing what is human in the person who acts oppressively can we hope to bring about change. All of us are more receptive to suggestions to change when we know we are liked. (Brown and Mazza, 1997:3)

A Concluding Note

We opened this essay worried that our readers felt powerless and insignificant. We close with the hope that you now understand that challenging the constructions of difference is well within *all* of our capabilities.

KEY CONCEPTS

ally Someone from a privileged status committed to eliminating stigma and the ill-treatment of those in stigmatized statuses. (page 473)

Gandhi's paradox While nothing we do as individuals matters, it is important to take action anyway. (page 469)

Janus-faced nature of society That people create society, but also that society constrains people. (page 469)

REFERENCES

Anderson, Charles W. 1993. *Prescribing the Life of the Mind: An Essay on the Purpose of the University, the Aims of Liberal Education, the Competence of Citizens, and the Cultivation of Practical Reason.* Madison: University of Wisconsin Press.

Bell, Brenda, John Gaventa, and John Peters. 1990. *We Make the Road by Walking: Conversations on Education and Social Change.* Philadelphia: Temple University Press.

Berger, Peter L. 1963. *Invitation to Sociology: A Humanistic Perspective.* New York: Anchor Books.

Brown, Cherie R., and George J. Mazza. 1997. *Healing into Action: A Leadership Guide for Creating Diverse Communities.* Washington, DC: National Coalition Building Institute.

Kunc, Norman , and Emma Van der Klift. 2007. A Credo for Support (People 1st Version). People First of San Luis Obispo. http://www.youtube.com/watch?v=wunHDfZFxXw (accessed May 2007).

Mindell, Arnold. 1995. *Sitting in the Fire: Large Group Transformation Using Conflict and Diversity.* Portland, OR: Lao Tse Press.

Palmer, Parker J. 1998. *The Courage to Teach: Exploring the Inner Landscape of a Teacher's Life.* San Francisco: Jossey-Bass.

READING 58

Influencing Public Policy

Jeanine C. Cogan

. . . Federal and state politics are commonly portrayed as open only to a few select stakeholders, as too complex to maneuver, and/or as too big for an individual to have an impact on. One goal of this [discussion] is to correct these misperceptions with information on and tools for how to successfully influence policy. This [discussion] reflects my experience as a policy advocate at the federal level. However, the basic principles and strategies described here can be applied to other levels of government and policy development. This [discussion] considers three topics: the players in policy development, the lifestyle of policy makers, and how you too can influence policy.

THE PLAYERS IN FEDERAL POLICY DEVELOPMENT

There are at least five central groups or stakeholders involved in influencing the legislative process: constituents, organizations or interest groups, coalitions, members of Congress, and congressional staffers. The role that each plays in the federal policy-making process is briefly described below.

Constituents

Anyone eligible to vote is a constituent. This probably includes you and many of the people you care about. As such, your primary mechanism for influencing the federal legislative process is through your members of Congress: senators and representatives. According to the American Psychological Association,[1] some members of Congress view their constituents as having the most influence on their

voting decisions—more than lobbying groups, their colleagues, and party pressures. Because the people in their districts vote members of Congress into office, members are motivated to attend to constituent concerns. Indeed, constituent service is one of the most important aspects of congressional life.[2]

Constituents articulate their views and concerns to members through visits, letters, e-mail, and/or phone calls. In addition, grassroots activism, such as rallies and protests, is effective in mobilizing constituents within a community and to focus members' attention on specific issues. Constituents may also be members of or become involved in organizations that work to influence policy.

Advocacy Organizations

There are numerous types of organizations and interest groups that advocate for specific policies. They cover a range of issues, including business and industry, science and technology, professional interests, labor, civil rights, public interest, and governmental interests.[3] Organizations often have a person or office responsible for advocating on behalf of their members' interests and concerns. Advocating on behalf of a large number of people across the nation can offer more political weight to a message than simply advocating on behalf of one's own interests as a constituent.[4]

Congressional staff often work closely with advocacy groups.[5] In order to move a bill forward, staffers may work with advocacy groups to identify members in key congressional districts who need to be contacted directly by their local constituents. Such grassroots support for a bill may help it gain active congressional consideration and increase its priority as an issue on the legislative agenda.

. . . To be able to exert more significant influence, advocacy groups may coordinate efforts and work together through coalitions.

Coalitions

Coalitions typically are composed of clusters of advocacy organizations that share common interests or political positions with the aim of developing strength

Jeanine C. Cogan is assistant director of the Other 3Rs Project at the Center for Psychology in Schools and Education at the American Psychological Association.

in numbers in order to influence policy. The coalition is designed to bring diverse organizations together to lobby on national policies, promote grassroots activism, and educate the public.[6] Members of a coalition may establish personal relationships with staff and members of Congress, which can contribute to the success of a bill or other policy initiative. Coalitions vary significantly in their membership, structure, and missions. Their constituencies and agendas may shift and adapt according to the changing policy environment and legislative focus. Membership within a coalition is typically on a group, rather than individual, basis. Coalition activities include regular meetings, federal and local outreach efforts, the sharing of knowledge and resources, and strategizing about how to optimize their influence. Working in coalitions maximizes the likelihood of successfully influencing the legislative process by allowing a large number of people to express their opinion on an issue in a short period of time.

Members of Congress

Certainly, a legislator's colleagues, the other policy makers, are another important influence. Numerous factors contribute to the decisions legislators make.[7] Three primary considerations are key in members' political decisions: (1) to satisfy constituents, (2) to enhance their personal reputations within the political world, and (3) to create good policy. All three can be accomplished when members have the skill to successfully work with and influence one another.[8] Members influence each other through direct one-on-one interaction, legislation, briefings, hearings, speeches, and the press. The well-known "Dear Colleague" letter on Capitol Hill, in which members explain legislation to their colleagues and urge them either to become cosponsors or to vote along similar lines, is a primary strategy for influencing other members.

Members also influence each other through party affiliation and loyalty. Party politics plays a significant role in members' policy decisions.[9] Party leadership may urge members to vote in a certain way on specific legislation. Partisan politics are most apparent in party "whipping." Whipping occurs when party leadership strongly encourages members to

vote in a particular way with the implied assumption that doing so will result in rewards. For voting along party lines, members can be rewarded with positions on more powerful committees, among other things that give them more power and clout with colleagues. This influence with colleagues may translate into a greater likelihood of successfully addressing constituent concerns, thereby improving reelection possibilities.

Congressional Staff

Until the 1950s, the U.S. Congress was a part-time institution that worked for 9 of the 24 months of a congressional session. The congressional workload has doubled in the last 30 years.[10] Currently, members work 18 months per session. The increased workload resulted from a series of decisions that enlarged congressional staff assistance, beginning in 1946 with the Legislative Reorganization Act.[11] For example, in 1967 members of the House of Representatives employed 4,000 people as personal staff. By 1990 that number had doubled. Interestingly, some scholars have argued that the increase of staff has resulted in expanded staff autonomy. With larger staffs, members are able to take on more issues and expand their workload. In turn, members need to rely more on and increasingly delegate independent authority to their staff.

Consequently, staff play a critical role in determining policy. Members rely on staff to track specific issues, write speeches, educate them on a range of topics, advise them on legislation and policy decisions, and write legislation. The autonomy and influence of a staffer depends on a range of factors including their individual personalities, the structure of the office, and the members' style.[12]

THE LIFESTYLE OF A POLICY MAKER

"To best understand the way in which federal policy is formulated, it helps to think of Capitol Hill as a community, or culture, with its own inhabitants, rules, norms, and social processes."[13] Only by understanding the culture of politicians can

BOX 1

Write an Effective Briefing Sheet or Talking Points

1. *First identify the goal and state it clearly.* Why are you lobbying the member? What is the reason for meeting with the staffer?
2. *Summarize the research and main arguments using bullet points.*
3. *Stay focused on one topic.* If you wish to discuss more than one topic, prepare separate briefing memos (one per topic).
4. *Be concise.* Keep briefing memos to one page, if possible. If the message cannot be conveyed in a page or two, you will likely lose the opportunity to influence the staff.
5. *Make the briefing memo easy to read and visually appealing.*

scientists, lobbyists, activists, or anyone else hope to influence the federal process and shape public policy.[14] Four central characteristics of congressional offices are the rapid pace, the large workload, the valuing of direct experience over other data, and the need to compromise.

Political life is typically a lifestyle of unanticipated, urgent deadlines. Given these tight timelines, it is not uncommon for staffers to become "experts" on a specific topic in a few days or mere hours. Therefore, as they are searching for facts on a topic, staffers must rely on easily accessible, digestible resources—typically the Internet or talking points provided by advocates. The outcome of such quick research is often a blend of substantive and political information. Also, with the expanded congressional workload, staffers are typically stretched so thin that reading one-page summaries is all they have time to do. Extensive reports are often useless unless there is a one- or two-page summary (called talking points or briefing memo).[15] Boxes 1 and 2 explain how to prepare such documents.

Although some policy makers appreciate the importance and usefulness of considering scientific data in their decision-making process, they tend to place greater value on precedent and anecdotal evidence. It is not unusual for legislation to remain stagnant until

BOX 2

An Effective Briefing Memo

GOAL: WE URGE YOUR BOSS TO SUPPORT THE HATE CRIMES PREVENTION ACT (HCPA)

WHY WE NEED THE HCPA

- According to community surveys, violence against individuals on the basis of their real or perceived race, ethnicity, religion, sexual orientation, gender, disability, and other social groupings is a fact of life in the United States.
- A civil rights statute, Section 245 of Title 18 U.S.C., gives federal prosecutors the authority to investigate allegations of hate violence based on race, religion, and national origin. This avenue for federal involvement is necessary in order to address cases where state and local authorities fail to properly respond to victims' allegations. Currently such federal investigations are minimal, with typically less than 10 prosecutions annually.
- This statute is critical for responding to the problem of hate violence, yet it does not include a broad definition of hate crimes in line with more recent legislation. In 1994 Congress passed the Hate Crimes Sentencing Enhancement Act as part of the Violent Crime Control and Law Enforcement Act of 1994. In this law, hate crimes were defined broadly as a crime committed against the person:

  > "because of the actual or perceived race, color, religion, national origin, ethnicity, gender, disability, or sexual orientation of that person."

PURPOSE OF THE HCPA

- The main purpose of the HCPA is to bring Section 245 of Title 18 U.S.C. in line with this recent hate crimes definition so that federal officials can investigate and prosecute crimes motivated by hate based on the victim's real or perceived gender, disability, or sexual orientation.
- The Department of Justice (DOJ) receives inquiries from families of gay victims asking for their involvement when local authorities have failed to respond. Unfortunately, the DOJ does not have the authority to investigate such cases. The DOJ considers this bill an important measure in assisting them to properly respond to victims' concerns.

I wrote this example of a briefing memo specifically for the purposes of this [discussion]. The material is based on my advocacy work in the Public Policy Office at the American Psychological Association.

an event occurs to galvanize members of Congress. For example, in 1998 the Hate Crimes Prevention Act received attention, with hearings in both the House and Senate, only after an African American man was brutally murdered in Jasper, Texas. Similarly, critical gun control legislation that had been introduced each session of Congress for a number of years was not seriously considered until after the Columbine High School shooting in Littleton, Colorado, in 1999. The palpable role of real-life stories in members' policy decisions may in part reflect that they are primarily motivated to address the needs of their constituents and do so after hearing of their concerns and hardships. Additionally, research on persuasion shows that, depending on the audience, appealing to one's emotions, especially with fear-arousing messages, can be a powerful method of communication.[16] This lesson has not gone unnoticed by policy makers.

Given the nature of our two-party system of government, members must work with individuals who may have very different opinions and perspectives on an issue. As a consequence, to move a policy initiative forward one must have enough support, which often requires negotiation and compromise. This tendency to compromise may collide with the desires and expectations of constituents and advocacy groups.

Understanding the unique culture of policy makers allows you to be more effective in influencing federal policy. Given the rapid pace and heavy workloads, you can increase your effectiveness in working with congressional offices by interacting with staff in a way that shows respect for staffers' time and efforts. Additionally, when working with staff it is useful to offer both data and personal stories of affected individuals. Finally, you may be more successful working with staff if you have an understanding of the limitations of members of Congress due to the institutional tendency toward compromise.

INFLUENCING PUBLIC POLICY

There are two basic avenues by which you can shape policy. In some cases, you will want to influence legislators on issues that are already on the public agenda. In others, you will want to create legislative support for an unknown or invisible issue.

Influencing Legislators on Existing Issues

As you already know, voting constituents are greatly valued in legislative offices. A constituent communicating concerns to members of Congress can play an influential role in the legislative process. The most common way in which individuals can influence policy is to register opinions on already existing bills. Interested constituents can communicate with members of Congress or work in coalitions to promote or prevent the passage of particular legislation.

Contacting Members of Congress The first step in effective communication with Congress is to determine the best person to contact. Usually, contacting your own legislator—the person who represents your congressional district—is most effective. As your elected official, this is the person who represents you and therefore must be sensitive to your views and concerns. Occasionally, however, in order to achieve a certain goal it will be more appropriate to contact other members of Congress. For example, if a member is recognized as a leader on an issue in which you have expertise or interest, then contacting that member is appropriate, even if he or she does not represent your congressional district or state.

Constituents can contact members of Congress through phone calls, letter writing, e-mail, or a visit (see Boxes 3 and 4). The purpose of the communication often determines which mode of communication to use. For example, is the communication meant to register an opinion or to educate members of Congress on a particular issue? Is it designed to establish a relationship with the congressional office? Is an immediate response and action needed?

If a bill is currently being debated, it is controversial, and/or there are other time pressures, you may be more successful communicating with members by phone. Members of Congress may inquire from staff what their constituents are expressing and consider this when making policy decisions. Constituents interested in calling members should call the U.S. Capitol Switchboard at 202-224-3121 and ask for their representative and/or senator.

BOX 3

Contact Your Legislators

FEDERAL LEVEL

When writing a letter to your member of Congress use the following congressional addresses:

(Your Congressperson) The Honorable First, Last Name
U.S. House of Representatives
Washington, DC 20515

(Your Senator) The Honorable First, Last Name
U.S. Senate
Washington, DC 20510

When calling your member of Congress, use the U.S. Capitol Switchboard at 202-224-3121. Constituents should ask for their representative and/or senator.

STATE AND LOCAL LEVEL

Use GovSpot at *www.govspot.com* to identify and contact your state and local leaders. GovSpot.com is a nonpartisan government information portal designed to simplify the search for relevant government information online. This resource offers a collection of top government and civic resources such as government websites and documents, facts and figures, news, political information, and how to locate state and local policy makers.

If you are interested in receiving a response to an inquiry or educating members of Congress, then writing a letter or setting up a visit are preferable. (For help organizing and conducting visits to congressional offices, refer to Box 4.) The most effective letters are those that are concise and focused on one issue. (An example of a sample letter is shown in Box 5.) To write an effective letter, you should follow these three steps:

1. *State the purpose.* The first paragraph should include who you are and why you are writing this particular member of Congress. For example, "I am writing you as a constituent in your district." This is followed by the purpose of the letter. Bill names and/or numbers should be used if possible and applicable; for example, "I am writing to urge you to vote for the Hate Crimes Prevention Act."

2. *State the evidence/argument.* The purpose is followed by a rationale for the requested action. For example, "Given that so many states currently do not have laws that allow crimes to be investigated as hate crimes, the passage of this bill is necessary." Personal experiences that support the stated position can be concisely summarized as well. If you would like to make a research-based argument, then a short summary of the research or the presentation of some data can be effective.

3. *Ask for a response.* To optimize the impact of a correspondence, you should conclude by specifically asking members to reply. Responding to constituent mail is a vital role of congressional offices. The last paragraph should reiterate your concern and request a response.[17]

Effective Advocacy   When interacting with policy makers, advocates may err by being overly critical without offering specific suggestions or alternatives. Making this mistake will limit your effectiveness. Most legislators and their staff want to write the best bills possible and implement effective policies. For this reason, you should view the staffer as a friend, not a foe. Many staffers will be open to your expertise and ideas (though they may not always implement them). Therefore, when possible, it is useful to offer particular strategies for implementing the goals or ideas you want to promote.

For example, if you support the overall purpose of a bill but think it has flaws, prepare talking points that outline the concerns and offer alternatives. When I served as a legislative assistant for Congresswoman DeGette, I wrote a bill that health consumers supported but health providers opposed. After introducing the bill, many provider groups were critical and some raised legitimate concerns. The groups who were most effective were those that offered alternative language for the bill. Even if they agree with your perspective, legislative staffers may not have the time or expertise to find a solution for your concern. However, you can play a unique role in the legislative process by offering specific solutions and assistance to the congressional staff.

BOX 4

Organize Visits with Elected Officials

One of the best avenues to equality for LGB Americans is through establishing a personal relationship with your elected officials. Like any relationship, these relationships require cultivation over time and will involve developing ties to the elected official as well as members of their staff. A personal visit can be key to this kind of interaction. For state and local officials, this may not be difficult. If a visit to Washington, D.C., is difficult, you can arrange to visit your members of Congress when they return to their district office.

When you schedule such a visit, it may be helpful to organize a small group of like-minded voters. Taking a delegation of interested persons with you will enhance your visit. If this is not possible, bring at least one other person with you for support.

Your meeting will be most effective by doing the following:

- Identify the "visit team" (no more than six individuals) from your state or district who are interested in LGB issues.
- If you are from a big state and you are meeting with your senator, you may want to include individuals from several points around the state. The same is true for congressional districts and for state and local officials.
- The official's political party doesn't really matter. However, it helps if you can get someone on your team who is politically well connected or has a good sense of the local political dynamic.
- Make sure members of your team are comfortable with the process. If they are truly uncomfortable, they may detract from the overall impression you want to leave with your elected official.
- Arrange the date, time, and place for a premeeting of the visit team. Use this meeting (or at least a conference call) to make sure everyone is on board. You do not want questions or disagreements within your group during the visit.
- Arrange the date, time, and place for a meeting by contacting the state, district, or local office of the elected official you wish to meet.
- Coordinate the participants in the meeting to make sure that the visit team "sings with one voice" in making points with the elected official.
- Use the material in *Everyday Activism* to arm the team with the facts. In addition, do some research on the local situation so that you can personalize your arguments.
- Visit-team leaders should be prepared to guide and direct the meeting. After assembling at the office, team members should introduce themselves and identify the organization or institution with which they are affiliated.
- The visit-team leader should then lay out the problem and briefly outline the impact of the issue on the official's constituency.
- An open discussion should follow, with each team member providing his or her input while maintaining as much of a conversational tone as possible.
- Above all **listen.** Try to ascertain where your official is coming from. Employ active listening techniques to show her or him that you understand the concerns being raised. Try to answer objections and concerns as appropriate but don't get into a fight. Be firm and assertive but **not** combative.
- Be sure that the elected official is asked at some point to take a certain action, to support a policy initiative, or vote in a particular way on current legislation. For example:

  "Will you please assist our efforts to overturn the ban on lesbian and gay men in the military? Specifically, we would like for you to sponsor legislation to repeal the ban."
  "Will you support efforts to end workplace discrimination against lesbian and gay men? Specifically, we would like for you to co-sponsor ENDA."

- If the official expresses uncertainty about the facts, offer to provide further information to document the facts. . . .
- After the visit, send a follow-up letter thanking the official for his or her time and consideration. Include the information you offered to provide (e.g., a copy of the relevant policy brief) with your letter.

Adapted from unpublished materials originally drafted by William Baily, American Psychological Association.

BOX 5

An Effective Constituent Letter

The Honorable John Doe
U.S. House of Representatives
Washington, DC 20515

Dear Representative John Doe:

   I am a constituent and am writing to ask you to oppose the proposed amendment by Congressman Todd Tiahrt (R-Kan.) to the D.C. appropriations bill that would prevent unmarried couples from adopting children in Washington, D.C. This current bill is ill-conceived and based on a number of inaccurate beliefs about lesbians and gay men as parents.

   As a lesbian mother, I live in constant fear of losing custody of my child even though I am a nurturing, committed parent. I participate actively in the school board and related activities. My ability to be a caring and effective parent has nothing to do with my sexual orientation. This current amendment further threatens my daily existence as a parent.

   According to the American Psychological Association, research shows that lesbians and gay men are fit parents. Contrary to the belief that gay parents may have a negative influence on their children, when compared with children of heterosexual parents, children of gay men or lesbians show no marked difference in their intelligence, psychological adjustment, social adjustment, popularity with friends, development of sex role identity, or development of sexual orientation. Overall, the belief that children of gay and lesbian parents suffer deficits in personal development has no empirical foundation.

   In sum, the characterization of homosexual parents as being a threat to children is inaccurate, therefore calling into question policy decisions based on this belief. I urge you to oppose this amendment. I look forward to hearing your perspective.

Respectfully,
Jane Smith

I wrote this as an example of a good constituent letter. The Tiahrt amendment was introduced to the D.C. appropriations bill in 1997. Although it was eliminated, a similar amendment had been introduced every year since.

Creating Congressional Support for an Unknown Issue

In addition to influencing important policy decisions about existing legislation and visible issues, you can also help set the legislative agenda. For example, hate crimes legislation grew out of a national coordinated movement that promoted this issue as an important policy priority. Individuals and organizations met with members of Congress urging them to recognize and address this growing problem.

Finding Members to Support and Promote an Issue Members of Congress become known for their leadership in particular areas. You should research which member is likely to support and promote your issue. Given the continuing hostile environment toward LGBs, most members, even leaders on LGB-positive policies, will not showcase their work on LGB rights. So while information about members' policy priorities and accomplishments is available on their websites, you may have to look beyond their bios or issues of interest. For example, Rep. Christopher Shays (R-Conn.) has been a leading advocate for [the Employment Nondiscrimination Act]. However, his endless support for LGB protections against workplace discrimination is not obvious from his website under the heading "issues." Instead, you have to look under "press releases." Keep this in mind as you explore members' homepages and other information. The Internet address for members' homepages for the House of Representatives is www.house.gov. For the Senate, it is www.senate.gov. Members' biographies are also available by accessing the website on biographical directories of members of Congress at bioguide.congress.gov. An excellent book, titled *Politics in America,* provides descriptions of the members of Congress and is published each year by the *Congressional Quarterly.*

   Another useful avenue for learning the legislative priorities of members is to see what bills they introduced or co-sponsored through accessing the Thomas website at thomas.loc.gov. This site provides information about the bills members have introduced and/or co-sponsored, as well as the text of legislation, congressional records, committee information, and bill status and summaries.

Establishing Relationships with Congressional Staff

As you have learned already, congressional staff are critical in policy development and their influence can be substantial. Staffers serve as gatekeepers to members of Congress by deciding who receives entrée into the office. If staff advise the member of Congress to meet with a particular advocacy group, the member is likely to do so. Given this influence, advocates interested in making contact with their representatives should establish rapport with the legislative staff. To this end, you can seek an appointment by calling the legislative assistant currently working on the issue of interest. In order to increase the chances of success, you should offer an explanation for choosing this particular member and state the purpose of the proposed meeting. For example, "I am calling you because your boss is a leader on employment issues. I know she led the fight to save small businesses last year. I would like to schedule an appointment with you to discuss another important employment issue: the need for legislation to prevent work-related discrimination based on sexual orientation."

Educating Staff The primary goal of working with congressional members is to increase their knowledge and understanding of a particular topic that can lead to congressional interest and action. Because advocates tend to hold detailed knowledge on a specific topic while staffers have a little information about many topics, staffers typically welcome information. Due to the workload constraints, you should present concise summaries and clearly outlined points and goals. To facilitate this process, prepare handouts for congressional staff with talking points or briefing memos that summarize the topic. . . . As you have already seen, Box 1 provides guidelines for writing an effective policy brief and Box 2 contains an example.

Addressing Inaccurate Perceptions and Reaching a Broader Audience Given that there is so much misinformation about the lives of LGBs, one of the most important roles you can play is to correct myths and stereotypes. This is where research is particularly helpful. The American Psychological Association (APA) has created many documents based on solid social science evidence. Summaries of research that clarify the truth about LGBs' lives and experiences are readily available by accessing the American Psychological Association Lesbian, Gay, and Bisexual Concerns Office website at www.apa.org/pi/lgbc/publications/pubsreports.html.

In addition to educating the major players in the policy process, you may need to reach broader audiences with your efforts to raise awareness and correct misinformation. Writing letters to the editor of local, regional, and national publications is one way to do this. Most policy makers pay close attention to the media in their districts, so such letters can also have an impact on policy making. In addition, many newspapers welcome well-written op-ed columns on issues of concern to their readers. The guidance provided in Boxes 6 and 7 may help you get your ideas into print.

CONCLUSION

Every day, thousands of people are actively lobbying members of Congress in an effort to influence policy. In order to defend against anti-LGB policies and to advocate for policies that are proactive in improving the lives of lesbian, gay, and bisexual people, we must remain active participants in the legislative process. From writing letters to establishing more enduring relationships with congressional staffers, we all can and do influence policy.

To some this process may seem cumbersome and complicated. However, please remember that help is always available. If you have questions about the federal government, trained staff at the Federal Consumer Information Center will answer your questions about federal programs, benefits, or services. You can call their toll-free hotline at 800-688-9889 (TTY 800-326-2996) between 9 A.M. and 8 P.M. Eastern time or use their website (www.info.gov).

BOX 6

Write a Letter to the Editor

- Make one point (or at most two) in your letter or fax. State the point clearly, ideally in the first sentence.
- Make your letter timely. If you are not addressing a specific article, editorial, or letter that recently appeared in the paper you are writing to, then tie your issue to a recent event.
- Familiarize yourself with the coverage and editorial position of the paper to which you are writing. Refute or support specific statements, address relevant facts that are ignored, but avoid blanket attacks on the media in general or the newspaper in particular.
- Check the letter specifications of the newspaper to which you are writing. Length and format requirements vary from paper to paper. (Generally, roughly two short paragraphs are ideal.) You also must include your name, signature, address, and phone number.
- Look at the letters that appear in your paper. Are the letters printed usually of a certain type?
- Support your facts. If the topic you address is controversial, consider sending documentation along with your letter. But don't overload the editors with too much information.
- Keep your letter brief. Type it.
- Find others to write letters when possible. This will show that other individuals in the community are concerned about the issue. If your letter doesn't get published, perhaps someone else's on the same topic will.
- Monitor the paper for your letter. If your letter has not appeared within a week or two, follow up with a call to the editorial department of the newspaper.
- Write to different sections of the paper when appropriate. Sometimes the issue you want to address is relevant to the lifestyle, book review, or other section of the paper.

Text adapted from Fairness and Accuracy in Reporting (FAIR) at www.fair.org.

BOX 7

Write an Op-Ed

An op-ed gets its name because of its placement opposite the editorial page. It is longer than a letter to the editor—usually 500–800 words. Also often referred to as an opinion editorial, these are more difficult to get printed than a letter to the editor but can be very effective.

Getting It in Print

- *Pick the right author.* Many papers will only print an op-ed from a representative of an organization or from a noted authority. A meeting with the editor can also help to establish the author as credible. Using a local spokesperson increases the local perspective or interest, especially on issues with national significance.
- *Pitch the article ahead of time.* Ideally, pitch your idea to the editor about 2 weeks before you want it to run. If you are responding to an op-ed that has just been published, contact the op-ed page editor right away to ask about a response. Even if they don't ask, offer to send a draft for their consideration.
- *Follow the guidelines.* Call your paper to find out the preferred length for an op-ed, deadlines, and any other requirements. Unless guidelines say otherwise, submit the piece typed and double-spaced on white paper with 1-inch margins. Ideally, the first page should be on your letterhead. Have a header at the top of each additional page with your name, the date, and the page number. Fax, mail, e-mail, or hand deliver the piece to the op-ed page editor.
- *Have a specific point of view and something fresh to offer.* Try to be ahead of the curve in public discussion of an issue. Let friends and peers review the piece and offer comments.
- *Follow up.* Follow the mailing with a phone call to the op-ed page editor. Be polite and respectful of his or her schedule, but try to emphasize again, as feels appropriate, why the paper should run the piece. Remember—there is a lot of competition for space on the op-ed page. If you are not successful on your first try, don't give up.

Text adapted from PFLAG at www.pflag.org.

Although this [discussion] has focused on advocacy at the federal level, the same basic principles and processes can be applied at any level. Whether you want to push for LGB-affirming legislation on Capitol Hill, in your state legislature, or with local elected officials, you will be most effective when you educate yourself and share that knowledge with those you wish to influence. Developing relationship networks can be an effective strategy for educating officials and members of their staffs regardless of the level of government. Well-crafted letters to the editor and op-ed columns can raise awareness of the issues locally, regionally, and nationally. . . . Use the lessons you have learned from this discussion and make a difference.

DISCUSSION QUESTIONS

1. Does Cogan's description of "Capitol Hill culture" fit with your assumptions about how government works? What surprised you in her description? What didn't?

2. Does the information in Cogan's article make you feel any more comfortable about pursuing "everyday activism" on issues important to you? Why or why not?

NOTES

1. American Psychological Association. (1995). *Advancing psychology in the public interest: A psychologist's guide to participation in federal policy making.* Washington, DC: Author.

2. Wells, W. G. (1996). *Working with Congress: A practical guide for scientists and engineers.* Washington, DC: American Association for the Advancement of Science.

3. Lorion, R. P., & Iscoe, I. (1996). Reshaping our views of our field. In R. P. Lorion, I. Iscoe, P. H. DeLeon, & G. R. VandenBos (Eds.), *Psychology and public policy* (pp. 1–19). Washington, DC: American Psychological Association. Truman, D. B. (1987). The nature and functions of interest groups: The governmental process. In P. Woll (Ed.), *American government: Readings and cases* (pp. 255–262). Boston: Little, Brown.

4. Ceaser, J. W., Bessette, J. M., O'Toole, L. J., & Thurow, G. (1995). *American government: Origins, institutions, and public policy* (4th ed.). Dubuque, IA: Kendall/Hunt.

5. Nickels, I. B. (1994). *Guiding a bill through the legislative process* (Congressional Research Service Report for Congress, 94-322 GOV). Washington, DC: Library of Congress.

6. Key, V. O. (1987). The nature and functions of interest groups: Pressure groups. In P. Woll (Ed.), *American government: Readings and cases* (pp. 266–273). Boston: Little, Brown.

7. American Psychological Association, 1995 (see note 1). Wells, 1996 (see note 2).

8. Drew, E. (1987). A day in the life of a United States Senator. In P. Woll (Ed.), *American government: Readings and cases* (pp. 487–497). Boston: Little, Brown. Vincent, T. A. (1990). A view from the Hill: The human element in policy making on Capitol Hill. American Psychologist, 45(1), 61–64.

9. American Psychological Association, 1995.

10. Wells, 1996.

11. Rundquist, P. S., Schneider, J., & Pauls, F. H. (1992). *Congressional staff: An analysis of their roles, functions, and impacts* (Congressional Research Service Report for Congress, 92-90S). Washington, DC: Library of Congress.

12. Redman, E. (1987). Congressional staff: The surrogates of power. In P. Woll (Ed.), *American government: Readings and cases* (pp. 452–461). Boston: Little, Brown. Rundquist, Scheider, & Pauls, 1992.

13. Vincent, T. A., 1990, p. 61 (see note 8).

14. Bevan, W. (1996). On getting in bed with a lion. In R. P. Lorion, I. Iscoe, P. H. DeLeon, & G. R. VandenBos (Eds.), *Psychology and public policy* (pp. 145–163). Washington, DC: American Psychological Association. Nissim-Sabat, D. (1997). Psychologists, Congress, and public policy. Professional Psychology: Research and Practice, 28(3). 275–280. Wells, 1996 (see note 2).

15. This is the rationale for including briefing memos throughout this [discussion].

16. For example, Wilson, D. K., Purdon, S. E., & Wallston, A. (1988). Compliance to health recommendations: A theoretical overview of message framing. Health Education Research, 3, 161–171.

17. American Psychological Association, 1995 (see note 1). For more information on how to write an effective letter, the reader is referred to the information brochure written by the APA titled: Calkins, B. J. (1995). *Psychology in the public interest: A psychologist's guide to participation in federal policy making.* Washington, DC: APA. Available at www.apa.org/ppo/grassroots/sadguide.html.

READING 59

What Can We Do? Becoming Part of the Solution

Allan G. Johnson

The challenge we face is to change patterns of exclusion, rejection, privilege, harassment, discrimination, and violence that are everywhere in this society and have existed for hundreds (or, in the case of gender, thousands) of years. We have to begin by thinking about the trouble and the challenge in new and more productive ways. . . .

Allan G. Johnson is a professor of sociology at Hartford College for Women.

Large numbers of people have sat on the sidelines and seen themselves as neither part of the problem nor the solution. Beyond this shared trait, however, they are far from homogeneous. Everyone is aware of the whites, heterosexuals, and men who intentionally act out in oppressive ways. But there is less attention to the millions of people who know inequities exist and want to be part of the solution. Their silence and invisibility allow the trouble to continue. Removing what silences them and stands in their way can tap an enormous potential of energy for change. . . .

MYTH 1: "IT'S ALWAYS BEEN THIS WAY, AND IT ALWAYS WILL"

If you don't make a point of studying history, it's easy to slide into the belief that things have always been the way we've known them to be. But if you look back a bit further, you find racial oppression has been a feature of human life for only a matter of centuries, and there is abundant evidence that male dominance has been around for only seven thousand years or so, which isn't very long when you consider that human beings have been on the earth for hundreds of thousands of years.[1] So when it comes to human social life, the smart money should be on the idea that *nothing* has always been this way or any other.

This idea should suggest that nothing *will* always be this way or any other, contrary to the notion that privilege and oppression are here to stay. If the only thing we can count on is change, then it's hard to see why we should believe for a minute that *any* kind of social system is permanent. Reality is always in motion. Things may appear to stand still, but that's only because humans have a short attention span, dictated perhaps by the shortness of our lives. If we take the long view—the *really* long view—we can see that everything is in process all the time.

Some would argue that everything *is* process, the space between one point and another, the movement from one thing toward another. What we may see as permanent end points—world capitalism,

Western civilization, advanced technology, and so on—are actually temporary states on the way to other temporary states. Even ecologists, who used to talk about ecological balance, now speak of ecosystems as inherently unstable. Instead of always returning to some steady state after a period of disruption, ecosystems are, by nature, a continuing process of change from one arrangement to another. They never go back to just where they were.

Social systems are also fluid. A society isn't some hulking *thing* that sits there forever as it is. Because a system happens only as people participate in it, it can't help being a dynamic process of creation and re-creation from one moment to the next. In something as simple as a man following the path of least resistance toward controlling conversations (and a woman letting him do it), the reality of male privilege in that moment comes into being. This is how we *do* male privilege, bit by bit, moment by moment. This is also how individuals can contribute to change: by choosing paths of *greater* resistance, as when men don't take control and women refuse their own subordination.

Since people can always choose paths of greater resistance or create new ones entirely, systems can only be as stable as the flow of human choice and creativity, which certainly isn't a recipe for permanence. In the short run, systems of privilege may look unchangeable. But the relentless process of social life never produces the exact same result twice in a row, because it's impossible for everyone to participate in any system in an unvarying and uniform way. Added to this are the dynamic interactions that go on among systems—between capitalism and the state, for example, or between families and the economy—that also produce powerful and unavoidable tensions, contradictions, and other currents of change. Ultimately, systems can't help changing.

Oppressive systems often *seem* stable because they limit people's lives and imaginations so much that they can't see beyond them. But this masks a fundamental long-term instability caused by the dynamics of oppression itself. Any system organized around one group's efforts to control and exploit another is a losing proposition, because it contradicts the essentially uncontrollable nature of reality and does violence to basic human needs and values. For example, as the last two centuries of feminist thought and action have begun to challenge the violence and break down the denial, patriarchy has become increasingly vulnerable. This is one reason male resistance, backlash, and defensiveness are now so intense. Many men complain about their lot, especially their inability to realize ideals of control in relation to their own lives,[2] women, and other men. Fear of and resentment toward women are pervasive, from worrying about being accused of sexual harassment to railing against affirmative action.

No social system lasts forever, but this is especially true of oppressive systems of privilege. We can't know what will replace them, but we can be confident that they will go, that they *are* going at every moment. It's only a matter of how quickly, by what means, and toward what alternatives, and whether each of us will do our part to make it happen sooner rather than later and with less rather than more human suffering in the process.

MYTH 2: GANDHI'S PARADOX AND THE MYTH OF NO EFFECT

Whether we help change oppressive systems depends on how we handle the belief that nothing we do can make a difference, that the system is too big and powerful for us to affect it. The complaint is valid if we look at society as a whole: it's true that we aren't going to change it in our lifetime. But if changing the entire system through our own efforts is the standard against which we measure the ability to do something, then we've set ourselves up to feel powerless. It's not unreasonable to want to make a difference, but if we have to *see* the final result of what we do, then we can't be part of change that's too gradual and long term to allow that. We also can't be part of change that's so complex that we can't sort out our contribution from countless others that combine in ways we can never grasp. The problem of privilege and oppression requires complex and long-term change coupled

with short-term work to soften some of its worst consequences. This means that if we're going to be part of the solution, we have to let go of the idea that change doesn't happen unless we're around to see it happen.

To shake off the paralyzing myth that we cannot, individually, be effective, we have to alter how we see ourselves in relation to a long-term, complex process of change. This begins by altering how we relate to time. Many changes can come about quickly enough for us to see them happen. When I was in college, for example, there was little talk about gender inequality as a social problem, whereas now there are more than five hundred women's studies programs in the United States. But a goal like ending oppression takes more than this and far more time than our short lives can encompass. If we're going to see ourselves as part of that kind of change, we can't use the human life span as a significant standard against which to measure progress.

To see our choices in relation to long-term change, we have to develop what might be called "time constancy," analogous to what psychologists call "object constancy." If you hold a cookie in front of very young children and then put it behind your back while they watch, they can't find the cookie because they apparently can't hold on to the image of it and where it went. They lack object constancy. In other words, if they can't see it, it might as well not even exist. After a while, children develop the mental ability to know that objects or people exist even when they're out of sight. In thinking about change and our relation to it, we need to develop a similar ability in relation to time that enables us to carry within us the knowledge, the faith, that significant change happens even though we aren't around to see it.

Along with time constancy, we need to clarify for ourselves how our choices matter and how they don't. Gandhi once said nothing we do as individuals matters, but that it's vitally important to do it anyway. This touches on a powerful paradox in the relationship between society and individuals. Imagine, for example, that social systems are trees and we are the leaves. No individual leaf on the tree matters; whether it lives or dies has no effect on much of anything. But collectively, the leaves are essential to the whole tree because they photosynthesize the sugar that feeds it. Without leaves, the tree dies.

So leaves matter and they don't, just as we matter and we don't. What each of us does may not seem like much, because in important ways, it *isn't* much. But when many people do this work together, they can form a critical mass that is anything but insignificant, especially in the long run. If we're going to be part of a larger change process, we have to learn to live with this sometimes uncomfortable paradox.

A related paradox is that we have to be willing to travel without knowing where we're going. We need faith to do what seems right without necessarily being sure of the effect that will have. We have to think like pioneers who may know the direction they want to move in or what they would like to find, without knowing where they will wind up. Because they are going where they've never been before, they can't know whether they will ever arrive at anything they might consider a destination, much less the kind of place they had in mind when they first set out. If pioneers had to know their destination from the beginning, they would never go anywhere or discover anything.

In similar ways, to seek out alternatives to systems of privilege it has to be enough to move away from social life organized around privilege and oppression and to move toward the certainty that alternatives are possible, even though we may not have a clear idea of what those are or ever experience them ourselves. It has to be enough to question how we see ourselves as people of a certain race, gender, class, and sexual orientation, for example, or examine how we see capitalism and the scarcity and competition it produces in relation to our personal striving to better our own lives, or how oppression works and how we participate in it. Then we can open ourselves to experience what happens next.

When we dare ask core questions about who we are and how the world works, things happen that we can't foresee; they don't happen unless we *move*, if only in our minds. As pioneers, we discover what's possible only by first putting ourselves in motion, because we have to move in order to change our position—and hence put perspective—on where we are, where we've been, and where we might go. This is how alternatives begin to appear.

The myth of no effect obscures the role we can play in the long-term transformation of society. But the myth also blinds us to our own power in relation to other people. We may cling to the belief that there is nothing we can do precisely because we subconsciously know how much power we *do* have and are afraid to use it because people may not like it. If we deny our power to affect people, then we don't have to worry about taking responsibility for how we use it or, more significant, how we don't.

This reluctance to acknowledge and use power comes up in the simplest everyday situations, as when a group of friends starts laughing at a racist, sexist, or homophobic joke and we have to decide whether to go along. It's just a moment among countless such moments that constitute the fabric of all kinds of oppressive systems. But it's a crucial moment, because the group's seamless response to the joke affirms the normalcy and unproblematic nature of it in a system of privilege. It takes only one person to tear the fabric of collusion and apparent consensus. On some level, we each know we have this potential, and this knowledge can empower us or scare us into silence. We can change the course of the moment with something as simple as visibly not joining in the laughter, or saying "I don't think that's funny." We know how uncomfortable this can make the group feel and how they may ward off their discomfort by dismissing, excluding, or even attacking us as bearers of bad news. Our silence, then, isn't because nothing we do will matter, our silence is our not *daring* to matter.

Our power to affect other people isn't simply the power to make them feel uncomfortable. Systems shape the choices people make primarily by providing paths of least resistance. Whenever we openly choose a different path, however, we make it possible for others to see both the path of least resistance they're following and the possibility of choosing something else.

If we choose different paths, we usually won't know if we're affecting other people, but it's safe to assume that we are. When people know that alternatives exist and witness other people choosing them, things become possible that weren't before. When we openly pass up a path of least resistance, we increase resistance for other people around that path, because now they must reconcile their choice with what they've seen us do, something they didn't have to deal with before. There's no way to predict how this will play out in the long run, but there's certainly no good reason to think it won't make a difference.

The simple fact is that we affect one another all the time without knowing it. When my family moved to our house in the woods of northwestern Connecticut, one of my first pleasures was blazing walking trails through the woods. Some time later I noticed deer scat and hoofprints along the trails, and it pleased me to think they had adopted the trail I'd laid down. But then I wondered if perhaps I had followed a trail laid down by others when I cleared "my" trail. I realized that there is no way to know that anything begins or ends with me and the choices I make. It's more likely that the paths others have chosen influence the paths I choose.

This suggests that the simplest way to help others make different choices is to make them myself, and to do it openly. As I shift the patterns of my own participation in systems of privilege, I make it easier for others to do so as well, and harder for them not to. Simply by setting an example—rather than trying to change them—I create the possibility of their participating in change in their own time and in their own way. In this way I can widen the circle of change without provoking the kind of defensiveness that perpetuates paths of least resistance and the oppressive systems they serve.

It's important to see that in doing this kind of work, we don't have to go after people to change their minds. In fact, changing people's minds may play a relatively small part in changing societies. We won't succeed in turning diehard misogynists into practicing feminists, for example, or racists into civil rights activists. At most, we can shift the odds in favor of new paths that contradict the core values that systems of privilege depend on. We can introduce so many exceptions to the paths that support privilege that the children or grandchildren of diehard racists and misogynists will start to change their perception of which paths offer the least resistance. Research on men's changing attitudes toward the male provider role, for example, shows that most of the shift occurs *between* generations, not within them.[3] This suggests that rather than trying to change people, the most important thing we can do is contribute to the slow evolution of entire cultures so that forms and values which support privilege begin to lose their "obvious" legitimacy and normalcy and new forms emerge to challenge their privileged place in social life.

In science, this is how one paradigm replaces another.[4] For hundreds of years, for example, Europeans believed that the stars, planets, and sun revolved around Earth. But scientists such as Copernicus and Galileo found that too many of their astronomical observations were anomalies that didn't fit the prevailing paradigm: if the sun and planets revolved around the Earth, then they wouldn't move as they did. As such observations accumulated, they made it increasingly difficult to hang on to an Earth-centered paradigm. Eventually the anomalies became so numerous that Copernicus offered a new paradigm, which he declined to publish for fear of persecution as a heretic, a fate that eventually befell Galileo when he took up the cause a century later. Eventually, however, the evidence was so overwhelming that a new paradigm replaced the old one.

In similar ways, we can see how systems of privilege are based on paradigms that shape how we think about difference and how we organize social life in relation to it. We can openly challenge those paradigms with evidence that they don't work and produce unacceptable consequences for everyone. We can help weaken them by openly choosing alternative paths in our everyday lives and thereby provide living anomalies that don't fit the prevailing paradigm. By

PERSONAL ACCOUNT

Parents' Underestimated Love

"Coming out of the closet" to my parents has been the most liberating thing that I have done in my life because having my homosexuality discovered by my parents was my biggest fear. Although I didn't grow up in a particularly homophobic environment, innately I knew that homosexuality was different and wasn't accepted because of rigid social norms and religious doctrines. I lived in anguish of being exposed and of the consequences that would come with being the queer one.

Keeping the secret from my traditional Salvadoran parents created a wedge that made it difficult for me to bond with my parents and have them participate fully in my life. I became a recluse and avoided much parental interaction to avoid questions about girlfriends. During my teenage years, girlfriends were expected from a "good and healthy" boy such as myself. I felt that my lack of interest in girls would have led to probes from my parents, and plus, I wasn't the typical macho boy who was into sports, cars, etc. . . . I was the "sensitive type." To avoid any suspicion, I limited my interaction with my

parents. I felt that if I opened up to them, my sexuality would be questioned and questions like "Are you gay?" would follow. Being an academic overachiever in high school made things easier for me. Whenever the question was asked of why I didn't have a girlfriend, I had the perfect excuse, "I'm too busy with school to focus on girls . . . do you want a *Playboy* or an honor student?"

During my sophomore year in college I took a bold step and moved out of my parents' house. My move facilitated my "coming out" to my parents because the possibility of being kicked out of the house when I told them I was gay wouldn't loom over me. I didn't know if my parents would kick me out, but I couldn't run the risk of finding out. One year after moving out, I "came out." Ironically it didn't come as a surprise to my parents, and frankly it wasn't a big deal! After years of living in fear of rejection and shame, my parents accepted and reaffirmed their love and support. I underestimated the power of my parents' love.

Octavio N. Espinal

our example, we can contradict basic assumptions and their legitimacy over and over again. We can add our choices and our lives to tip the scales toward new paradigms that don't revolve around privilege and oppression. We can't tip the scales overnight or by ourselves, and in that sense we don't amount to much. But on the other side of Gandhi's paradox, it is crucial where we choose to place what poet Bonaro Overstreet called "the stubborn ounces of my weight":

STUBBORN OUNCES

(To One Who Doubts the Worth of Doing Anything If You Can't Do Everything)

You say the little efforts that I make
will do no good; they will never prevail
to tip the hovering scale
where Justice hangs in balance.
I don't think

I ever thought they would.
But I am prejudiced beyond debate
In favor of my right to choose which side
shall feel the stubborn ounces of my weight.[5]

It is in such small and humble choices that oppression and the movement toward something better actually happen.

DISCUSSION QUESTIONS

1. In a sense, Allan Johnson's discussion highlights the paradoxes inherent in the efforts to create social change. What are those paradoxes, and how does Johnson resolve them?

2. What would Johnson's advice be to someone who wants to make a difference in society? Can it be summarized in a sentence or two?

NOTES

1. See Elizabeth Fisher, *Woman's Creation: Sexual Evolution and the Shaping of Society* (New York: McGraw-Hill, 1979); Gerda Lerner, *The Creation of Patriarchy* (New York: Oxford University Press, 1986).
2. This is what Warren Farrell means when he describes male power as mythical. In this case, he's right. See *The Myth of Male Power* (New York: Berkley Books, 1993).
3. J. R. Wilkie, "Changes in U.S. Men's Attitudes towards the Family Provider Role, 1972–1989," *Gender and Society* 7, no. 2 (1993): 261–79.
4. The classic statement of how this happens is by Thomas S. Kuhn, *The Structure of Scientific Revolutions* (Chicago: University of Chicago Press, 1970).
5. Bonaro W. Overstreet, *Hands Laid Upon the Wind* (New York: Norton, 1955), p. 15.

READING 60

Racetalk: Bridging Boundaries

Kristen A. Myers

. . . People who challenge racial boundaries [are] sanctioned in many ways. However, actors are not helplessly constrained by the structure of domination. Actors can act. They can take counterhegemonic action by crossing boundaries, although crossing may be costly to some. . . .

NOT SO CLEAR-CUT: THE BLURRINESS OF BOUNDARIES

How do we know that boundaries are not fixed and impenetrable? Why do people attempt to cross at all, given the power of policing orthodoxy? One reason that people attempt to cross is that their everyday realities provide social opportunities to do so. People recognize the tractability of the boundaries themselves. For example, Harley (white) eavesdropped on two black men while waiting in line in the cafeteria:

Kristen A. Myers is a professor of sociology at Northern Illinois University.

At lunch today, two black guys were standing with me in the lunch line—one in front, and one behind. They were talking over me about how they only care about the history of their people, and that's all that should be taught. I didn't flinch or say anything; I just listened. Then, when the guy ahead of me picked up a plate, he handed it to me before he took one for himself. I was confused.

Harley had assumed—due to the politics of this conversation and the pervasive trope of blackness in society—that these men were black militants who hated whites. She was, therefore, confused when one of the men treated her like a peer and passed her a plate. He did so even before taking one for himself. In this instance, the previously stark outlines of the habitus blurred. The boundaries blurred as well.

Elizabeth (black) observed the boundaries melt away in a most unusual way. She went to a casino. She left her ID at home, so she could not get in. She was waiting around for her friends in the lobby area:

This white lady came up to me and asked if I wanted to join her family for dinner. Well I was shocked—me eat dinner with these white strangers? She said the casino gave them four buffet tickets and there were only three of them. So I went. I can truly say that as I walked with them to our table, I felt all eyes on us. So I just smiled and walked like we were family—me being adopted of course—ha ha. Well to make a long story short, we ate and conversed and it was like being with my own family.

Elizabeth was amazed by this experience. She shared it with a black friend, who disabused her of her boundary-free vision:

Whoa did he make a big deal of it. He said, "I can't believe you ate with them, I could never do that." I said, "Why not? Them people [are] like me and you, and the food was free." He said I was crazy and he just couldn't see himself eating with white folks. I said that I used to feel that way, but I've had several occasions that changed my mind. I remember when I had dinner with the faculty in the sociology department. I was so nervous, not just because they were white but they were all educated. I was afraid I would do something silly. But they all were great and ate dinner just like black folks, somewhat (smile).

For Elizabeth, the boundaries were not clear-cut. She saw wiggle room that empowered her to take boundary-crossing risks. Real life does not always conform with racist orthodoxy. There are seeds of heterodoxy laying around. The willing and able collect them and use them in order to breach boundaries. . . .

NAMING THE ELEPHANT IN THE ROOM

In interracial social situations, difference loomed large like an elephant in the room that everyone pretended not to notice, even while they maneuvered around it awkwardly. Occasionally, people used racetalk to name the elephant—call race for what it was—in order to move on. Take, for example, this incident recorded by Jonathan (white):

> I was delivering with another co-worker, Tyrone. He is black and he was listening to the stereotypical "black" music. He asked me if I like this kind of music. I said it was alright to listen to. He then asked if I would fuck a black girl. I laughed in shock, but Tyrone said, "Seriously, it's all the same on the inside." I didn't say anything. He then said he just likes to fuck with all the white boys. I didn't feel threatened; it was funny.

Tyrone sensed racial tension and sought to diffuse it. He did so (a) by naming the elephant: race. And (b) he invoked their commonalities as straight men: having sex with women. He seemed to be testing Jonathan, shocking him to see how he would react. Could Jonathan handle this relationship? Apparently so. Although this moment was strained, it seemed to relax their future interactions. Lavinia (white) recorded a similar incident:

> Mel (white) said that during his first semester as a freshman, he went to his first class and sat in the back of the room. Then this black guy sat down next to him, turned and said, "So it looks like we're the only two black guys in this class." The black guy cracked up, since Mel is obviously not African American. They've been friends ever since.

Black students often face the experience of being in the numerical minority in college classrooms, which is a source of discomfort. However, this student turned the situation on its ear and brought Mel into the joke, even though he was ostensibly an outsider. Mel breached the racial boundary in a lasting way.

Other people dealt with the elephant by minimizing it. For example, Joan's (white) friends trivialized their racial/ethnic differences:

> My Indian boyfriend told me about the names that he and his friends call each other. For instance, he is the "brown boy," because he is Indian. They call another guy "black boy," and another, "yellow boy." They also refer to each other as kinds of chocolate: milk, dark, and white. Ever since he told me that, I call him "brown boy" and he calls me "his little white girl."

While this strategy worked within the group—in which they agreed upon their use of terms—it often looked strange to outsiders:

> My boyfriend was playing video games with his friends and the characters on the screen were colors. As they played, they yelled out things like "Kill the black boy!", referring to the character on the screen, as opposed to the green one and the purple one. People walked past their room and stared at them because they were screaming this out. They stopped yelling after that.

Joan's friends minimized the power of racial and ethnic differences within their group by decontextualizing them from their historical legacies. This strategy sufficed for them, even though it did not work in mixed company. They moved beyond the elephant in the room in order to build more complex relationships.

SHARING STORIES: EDUCATING ONE ANOTHER

Once people no longer viewed racial difference as an obstacle, they often began to share personal stories and standpoints. These were the kinds of conversations people have when they get to know each other—they shared their backgrounds in the hopes of strengthening their blossoming relationships. For example, Blueangel (black) talked to a Greek friend of hers: "He told me how his grandma came off the boat so she did not know much English.

They just spoke Greek at him." This was a simple, nonjudgmental conversation about language. In another conversation, Blueangel (black) talked to a white guy on her hall about tanning:

> He explained to me that he was Swedish and that in the sun he does not tan; he burns. I said that I understood, because I got extremely dark in the summer time. He said that when the Vikings came over, they saw the sun and turned back around to their homeland of snow and little sun.

Here Blueangel and her friends merely shared information about the differences they experienced due to their race.

Other conversations were more pointed, geared toward clearing up misinformation that one group might have learned about the other. For example, Anastasia's (black) brother Wendal (black) talked with a friend, Mark (white):

> Mark said the only reason white women want black men was because of sex and money. He said that black men have always wanted white women. Wendal said, "No, that is a myth. Blacks were afraid to go with white women because they would be lynched. Also, white women were seen as tarnished. Rather, it was white men who have always wanted black women, because they raped them during slavery."

Wendal used the trust of their friendship to correct Mark's misinformation, and because of their trust, Mark was able to hear the information and not react defensively. Building trusting relationships was therefore an important element in challenging the structure of domination.

FINDING THE CONNECTION

Merely sharing background information was not enough to forge a bond between people across color lines, although it was a useful tool in getting to that point. To connect on a deeper level, people sought commonalities between them despite their obvious racial/ethnic differences. For example, Joan (white) recorded this incident:

> My friend Carol (white) told me about her job. She is the only woman and the only white person. When the guys at work found out that she spoke Spanish, they became more accepting of her.

Carol's coworkers saw her language skills as a point of connection, despite her gender and racial difference from them. Carter (black) and Mitch (white) made a similar connection in this conversation about a band they liked:

> Mitch: I've seen them play, man. They get down!
> Carter: Really? Are they a funk band?
> Mitch: Yeah, they're diverse too.
> Carter: Is the drummer black or white?
> Mitch: He's black. I've never seen a white drummer that could blast a funky groove.
> Carter: You know, come to think of it, I haven't either. At least, I can't think of any right now.

Mitch and Carter did not shy away from race as a topic—indeed it strengthened their musical connection.

A connection did not have to be grounded in reality in order for it to work. For example, Maggie (Latina) joked with Cary (white) over dinner:

> Maggie: Are you going to eat that? It's so gross.
> Cary: I felt like spicy Mexican food today. You know to fulfill my Mexican blood.
> Maggie: What are you talking about? You have no Mexican blood. You are related to your cousins that are half Mexican, but not your half. That does not make you Mexican.
> Cary: Yeah, well, the blond hair and white skin doesn't mean anything. I know there is some Mexican in me, so I'm going to feed it. Hahahah.

Cary fabricated a connection to Maggie—and she knew it—but it was successful. Precious (black) recorded an incident also grounded in myth:

> I overheard Johnson (black) and Luke (white) talking about how Luke was up all night getting it on with his wife. While Luke walked away, Johnson said, "He's a black man trapped in a white man's body."

To connect with Luke, Johnson invoked the trope of the black buck. However, he used it as a term of endearment rather than as a means to reify this racist image. Underscoring this connection, Precious handwrote in her field notes, "This is how we identify with them." In another incident, Precious wrote:

I told Penelope and Johnson that I saw an Asian with an afro earlier that day. Penelope said, "Japanese get their hair permed to be kinky like ours. They love hip hop in their culture."

Whether or not this is true, Penelope appreciated what she saw as an attempt to bridge boundaries.

In some racetalk, finding a connection led to warm interchanges that boded well for future boundary spanning, as in this conversation between good friends Carter (black) and Jerry (white). They discussed Carter's girlfriend (white):

> Jerry: I can tell you like her.
> Carter: Why do you say that?
> Jerry: Just look at yourself! You get all googly whenever you see her! I can see you blush even!
> Carter: No, you can't!
> Jerry: Yeah! I mean, you're not even white and your face gets red!

Jerry thought that it was sweet that Carter blushed—just as a white guy like Jerry might do. The good will in this interchange itself was noteworthy given that they discussed an interracial relationship, which would typically be sanctioned by policing orthodoxy. Instead, Jerry and Carter's connection helped them overcome "typical" orthodoxy, and they celebrated the breaching of racist boundaries.

Once a connection was formed, an alliance could be formed, as in this incident recorded by Rachel (white):

> I was walking out of African American history class the other day and this black guy from class, Bertrand, stopped me. He said, "Hey, does this class bother you? You know, being one of the only white people? Definitely the only white girl that says anything, you know?" I said it only bothered me when I have to hear black people in the class or the black teacher talking about "I know none of you wanna deal with white folks, but you better learn how cuz you're gonna have to deal with 'em the rest of your life whether you like it or not." Bertrand agreed that he didn't think that was fair, and he was offended by those kinds of comments too. He told me that if I want to comment on anything he would support me. He said, "Now you know if you gonna say anything defendin' anything, you better get an intelligent brother like me to get your back. Don't go around saying nothing and then look around for somebody because they not gonna be there for you [without my help]." It was a relief that Bertrand talked to me when he did. I was feeling pretty uncomfortable.

Rachel was a getting a minor in Black Studies, and she was one of the few whites who routinely took such courses. She had slowly earned the trust of Bertrand, who recognized her to be an ally.

Sometimes the commonality was not mutually agreed upon. One person might assume a stronger bond than the other. In such instances, it could be used to take dominants down a peg or two, as in this incident recorded by Missy (white):

> My friend's Mexican husband, Jesus, asked what nationality I am. I told him that one of my nationality is Polish. He asked me how and when my family came here [to the United States]. I told him that my great grandparents took a boat over here. He said, "So you're a wetback?"

Jesus used racetalk to point out a connection between her life and his—they both were members of devalued immigrant groups. However, he did so sardonically. Jesus went on to deride Polish as "Polacks, poor, dirty people who don't shower every day and wear the same shirt every day." Instead of using their connection as a means to strengthen their relationship, he seemed to be putting her in her place, using irony to imply, "You are not better than Mexicans just because you are white: our ethnic stereotypes are the same." Perhaps after some reflection Missy could see this racetalk as a tool to strengthen her interracial friendships. But when she recorded the incident, she was offended.

BONDING THROUGH CONTRAST

In the racetalk, people tended to focus on differences rather than commonalities. They contrasted their group to the others. However, contrast could be a tool to bring the groups together. As such, people made jokes about the difference. They connected as people *in spite* of their differences. For example, Jaime (white) wrote:

I was sitting at breakfast with Roy (black) and we observed the windy, cold-looking weather outside. We observed that crazy people only wore sweatshirts when it looked like it was freezing outside. Roy joked that when it's cold out you see white folks with shorts and a T-shirt when black folks are wearing winter coats. And when black folks are wearing scarves, white folks think it's nothing. All of us just laughed.

Similarly, Roger (white) eavesdropped on a conversation between two white and one black men:

> The African American said, "I don't know how you do it. Brothers hate the cold. And you all be skiing and playing hockey. It's crazy!" The white guys chuckled and they all began talking about how they were going out drinking this weekend.

Understanding and bridging boundaries meant dealing with perceptions of how "we" do things versus how "they" do things. Precious (black) listened to a conversation between Johnson (black), Luke (white), and Murray (black) while they all smoked pot. Johnson said of Luke, "He's a white boy used to smoking two hits per joint and then passin' it."

Carter (black) recorded another conversation contrasting white and black styles of worship. He was talking with his white friend Bev:

> Carter: So how's church going for you?
> Bev: Really good! Hey, I'm not trying to be racist or anything, but I'm going to a black people's church this Sunday.
> Carter: Oh, cool!
> Bev: Yeah, I wanna check it out. I'm interested in how their service may be different from the ones I usually go to.

Carter and Bev already had something in common: she dated a black man, and he dated a white woman. Yet even though they had a trusting bond—he knew where she was coming from—Bev still felt the need to assure Carter that she was not being racist. Indeed, he was very supportive of her plans. In many circumstances, then, contrasting the racialized experiences of different groups was a way of breaching boundaries in a successful manner.

Contrast with an Edge

In much of the racetalk, when people contrasted their group with another there was an edgy subtext. In these circumstances, racetalk critiqued the underlying racism in society, even while attempting to overcome it through an interracial/ethnic connection. For example, John (white) recorded this incident:

> My roommate (white) and I had people over for dinner: two African American women, one Mexican woman, and my roommate's white boyfriend. All of these people were my friends. In a conversation about movies, the Mexican woman referred to me as a "cool white boy."

This women contrasted John with other "white boys," implying that he was better than the rest of them. In other words, John was an exceptional white boy. This remark made him feel good. He felt accepted in spite of his whiteness, which might ordinarily be a handicap in an interracial friendship. Cheyenne's (white) friend Mary (black) was less subtle:

> We were out at a bar. After being hit on several times, Mary said, "Man, white boys are some stupid mother fuckers." I said, "Hey, I'm white!" Mary said, "Yeah, but you're not white to me. You're different."

As in the incident with John above. Mary contrasted blacks with whites but made an exception for Cheyenne.

Other messages lurked in the contrasts as well. For example, Cheyenne had a conversation with Lena (Latina), her sister-in-law, and Wade (white) her brother. Lena and Wade worked together:

> Wade told a crazy story about him and another guy from work. Lena said, "What a bunch of crazy white boys." My brother replied, "Yeah, well if it ain't white, it ain't right."

Lena implicitly contrasted whites (crazy) with Latinos (sane). In response, Wade invoked an old rhyme that was historically used to glorify whiteness. He used it as a tongue-in-cheek critique of whiteness.

Guido (Latino) recorded another edgy critique: "I called my roommate Skippy a 'dumb honky' today because he microwaved his salad and then didn't like how it tasted." Skippy and his friends constantly called Guido a "spic." Guido played on that here in this racetalk. The subtext here was that only a dumb white guy would think that a salad could or should be microwaved—and it took a "spic" to point that out. In another incident, Cheyenne went to a party with Mexican Americans:

> Someone told a sexual joke and someone didn't "get it." My friend Virginia said, "Why don't you go ask Cheyenne—she's one of them crazy white girls!" Of course I laughed and responded, "Yeah that's why everybody wants a white girl!"

Quick-witted Cheyenne recognized that Virginia was lumping her into the stereotype that white girls are oversexed, and she quickly rebounded with some oppositional identity work—"Yeah, that's why everybody wants me."

In all of these incidents, racetalk contrasted racial/ethnic groups, but with a critical edge. This talk reinforced interracial connections, but—because of the edge—the interactions could have gone another way. People could have been offended and challenged the racetalker, thereby damaging the bond. In order for the edgy contrast to be successful, the participants required a bond of trust based on a shared background: the bonds of family members, old friends, and roommates. This talk builds a bond because there is already a trusting connection. It is not for the fledgling relationship. As we shall see below, without a foundation of trust, the positive effect of an anti-racist critique could easily be lost in translation, and sardonic racial critiques could backfire.

The Double Edge of Contrast: Reifying Tropes

In some racetalk, contrasting differences had a *double edge* to it. The first edge was embedded in the content of the talk, as in the racetalk just discussed. The second edge was in the way that the talk was used and received. If used successfully, then people walked away feeling closer, as if they stood on a level playing field. Yet, the contrast could exacerbate and legitimate differences instead of operating as a unifying critique. In this case, the participants did not feel closer. Instead they felt offended or violated. The contrast backfired. This was especially likely when the talk contained an old trope or slur. For example, Katie (white) wrote:

> When I went to a party at my roommate Tim's (Latino) fraternity house, he warned me that I was a white girl in a brown house and I was going to get hit on a lot because browns and blacks have a thing for white girls. This was true too.

Tim's warning reified the buck image, and Katie bought into it. As such, she and Tim were further divided rather than unified.

In another example, Lavinia (white) worked as a night security officer in the dorm. Her main job was to check IDs before letting people in. One night, a white male and an Asian male approached the window. They appeared to be friends. As the Asian produced his ID, the white man joked, "Look at that Asians have such stubby fingers, he can't even get his ID out. Come on you stupid chink!" Then he asked, "Are minorities allowed in the dorms tonight? This white guy humiliated his "friend" in front of a complete stranger. Guido (Latino) recorded numerous such incidents, uncovering a theme in his relationship with his white fraternity brothers. In one incident, Guido recorded this: "My white roommate Skippy said that I did a 'spic-tacular' job on the dishes. I told him that he was really 'honk-tacular." In another incident, Guido's white fraternity brothers talked about where to go out one night. Guido was joking around, saying "yes" to every suggestion:

> Skippy said that I was once again spic-tacular, and Burt said that the minority vote didn't count, referring to me because I was Mexican. Later, Skippy's girlfriend asked if she could throw out the beans on the table. She then said, "Don't worry, Guido. I'm not talking about you."

Until logging field notes for this project, Guido did not even recognize how often his ethnicity was invoked in a pejorative manner by his closest friends. His feelings were hurt, and he began to realize that these men rarely interacted with him without centralizing his ethnicity. The elephant was always in the room, and his friends used it as a weapon rather than moving beyond it once and for all. . . . Guido slowly problematized his friendships as demeaning and eventually confronted them. . . .

It appears, based on the racetalk in this study, that people of color run emotional risks when they befriend whites. Whites use double-edged contrast in ways that are funny to them, but that inadvertently[1] harm their "friends." In these cases, whites thought that they could invoke racetalk with impunity under the auspices of friendship. But in so doing, they undermined the core of the friendship itself. . . .

EMPATHY

Joe Feagin, Hernan Vera, and Pinar Batur (2001) assert that a lack of empathy is one of the most compelling reasons that racism endures. Empathy is different from sympathy, which means to feel sorry for someone. In contrast, "empathy involves identifying strongly with the circumstances and pain of another human being" (229). According to Vera (2003), human society is impossible without empathy. At the same time, we must temper our empathy. We cannot be moved by every injustice, or we will never stop weeping. Total empathy would be disastrous. However, in steeling ourselves against the anguish of routine injustice, we have gone too far. We have shut out other people's suffering so effectively that we have lost the ability to take the role of the other, to feel and to see the world as others do. Vera and his colleagues argue that racism—through overt and symbolic violence—quashes empathy by desensitizing us to others' suffering. . . . Thus, a key to ending racism is to nurture empathy. We should attempt to truly hear and feel the world as others do. As Feagin, Vera, and Batur (2001, 229–30) argue, "an act of daring and the courage to cross often forbidden social borders are necessary to exercise human empathy of this character."

Interracial/ethnic empathy can be fostered by crossing social borders. For example, in this incident, Hedwig (white) and Chuck (black) attended a party for a Mexican coworker, Carla. A lot of the guests were Mexican. Hedwig and Chuck talked about him being the only black man at work.[2] He said,

> Yeah, I really feel comfortable now at work. I didn't always feel that way though, being a brother in the suburbs. Sometimes people look at you funny. But yeah, I can really say I feel comfortable with everyone now and I'm glad of it.

Later, the guests encouraged Hedwig and Chuck to dance. He resisted so Carla dragged Hedwig onto the floor:

> She took me out and I commented on how I felt stupid that I was the only white person dancing. A couple of times I said, "I feel so white!" Later, I tried to get Chuck to dance again. I said, "Come on it's fun! You don't think I feel silly dancing out there? I'm the only white girl here!" He said, "Well look at me. I'm the only brother. You think I don't stand out?"

Hedwig had a slight glimpse into the experiences that Chuck faced every day, and she empathized with him.

For others, the journey to empathy was longer and more painful, as in this incident recorded by Jean (white):

> This summer I was a camp counselor. I started orientation later than everyone else because I was hired to fill a spot that a girl had backed out on. I arrived at camp nervous to join this already formed group and worried about the summer to come (7 weeks). Four of the counselors were Hispanic. I became really good friends with two of them. We hung out and had very open, honest conversations. They told me that I was racist, which I vehemently denied. They argued that if I had been walking down the street, I wouldn't have given them a second look. I replied that that may be true, but it would be because I didn't know them. They then said that if a group of my friends and I were at a party and they approached me, I wouldn't take the chance to get to know them. I was baffled. How could they say these things about me?

Jean was slowly affected by her new friends' assertions:

> I then realized that I was in a unique situation. I was forced during one week of staff orientation to get to know everyone on a deep personal level or else the

summer wouldn't go well. We weren't in a normal society where people were judged on the basis of skin color. We sang songs and played games all day in our sweet little community. I realized that what my new friends were saying about the real world might be true. Maybe if I had met them on the street, I wouldn't have been as accepting. This camp experience opened my eyes. I learned a lot about myself and society as a whole.

Jean came to empathize with their feelings as outsiders, transforming their relationship from being antagonistic to being mutually beneficial and rewarding. They became allies.

Sophia (white) recorded another moving epiphany:

> One of my oldest and closest friends is Hispanic. She is second generation to this country. We have been friends since fourth grade. I remember being in her house and marveling at the cultural differences between the two of us. I learned how to make homemade tortillas, enchiladas, and stuff. I also remember my friend being very embarrassed of her own culture. She never wanted to talk about it in front of other people, besides me. She used to be teased by her other relatives. They would tell her that she was a "white girl." The part that I don't want to admit . . . but for the sake of this project . . . I remember us teasing each other. She used to call me things like Polack and Polish princess. And I used to call her things like bean and even spic. We never seemed to mind when it was each other calling ourselves that. But once one of our other friends said something like that to her, and she really cried hard! I think that is when I stopped saying things like that to her.

When Sophia recognized the power of slurs to inflict pain, she empathized and reformed. . . .

Achieving empathy was not a simple matter. In order to truly hear another person's perspective, people had to suspend their own self-interest. They had to take the other person's stories as real to her/him, even if they did not jive with their own experiences.

Failed Empathy

Empathy can, of course, fail. People might listen to others and try to identify. But if they cannot

go beyond their own experiences as the reference point for judging another's suffering, then true empathy cannot occur. I have seen many dialogues between white, brown, and black women fall apart when empathy fails. For example, I belonged to an interracial group of women that met monthly to discuss racism. One of the goals of the group was to form interracial bonds and alliances on campus. In these meetings, black and brown women shared their experiences of discrimination, pain, and isolation with white women, who genuinely wanted to listen and connect. In their efforts at empathy, however, white women encountered a pitfall. In attempting to bond through commonalities, many white women made the analytical leap between racial oppression and gender oppression. They offered counterexamples of their suffering as [white] women in a sexist society. These women meant well. The pitfall occurred because they did not recognize the differences in gender versus racial regimes. Yes, these white women had experienced myriad obstacles due to gender. But they still maintained white privilege, which the black and brown women did not possess. As African American poet Pat Parker (1978) once wrote of her white peers in the women's movement, "Sister! Your foot's smaller but it's still on my neck!" The white women in my group—in their effort to place themselves in the black and brown women's shoes—did so without being able to abandon their white privilege. Indeed, when women of color pointed this out to them, white women often became defensive, and many even cried. In crying, the white women had fully succeeded in silencing the black and brown women's issues, recentering their own victim status. Empathy failed. . . .

Reflexivity and Renewed Efforts

I end this section with a caveat: even though these attempts failed, they were genuine attempts. Without making such efforts, the walls and borders remain unbreached. We must make these challenges, learn from them when we fail, and attempt again with this new information. . . . There is ample evidence that by approaching racial boundaries reflexively, learning from our mistakes, and reapproaching them, we can indeed breach them in meaningful ways. Vera (2003) argues that racism is a skill that must be learned. As such, racism can be undermined by nurturing the lost skills of empathy. Mastery of these new skills requires time and effort, trial and error. . . .

TRULY CROSSING OVER: DECONSTRUCTING THE BOUNDARY

Truly crossing over from one side to the other of a racial/ethnic barrier was rare and difficult for subjects in this study, despite various attempts. Some strategies—like empathy and finding commonalities—were more effective than others—like using double-edged racetalk. Barrie Thorne (1993) studied crossing of gender boundaries among school kids[3] in her book, *Gender Play*. Like racial boundaries, gender boundaries are entrenched, reified, and policed in serious ways. Thorne's site of inquiry was elementary school playgrounds and classrooms. She found that most kids do not try to cross the gender boundaries. Even the teachers themselves use boundaries to control the children. For example, teachers encourage kids to sit boy-girl, or they pit boys against the girls in spelling bees. These strategies highlight a boundary, and they discourage the kids from intentionally breaching them.

Nevertheless, crossing did occur. Thorne proposed three criteria for successful crossing: (1) The child must be sincere in her/his desire to cross. (2) The child must be willing to try repeatedly to cross, until s/he is finally accepted. (3) The child must possess skills that are appropriate for activities on the "other side." The status of the crosser mattered too: popular kids could cross back and forth with no penalty to their identity, while "average" kids had to struggle according to these rules.

Crossing completely over *racial* boundaries required similar criteria. As shown above, many people failed to meet one or more of the criteria. Perhaps they were insincere or they gave up after one failed attempt. Yet, some people persevered and completely crossed. For example, Rachel (white) crossed as a Black Studies minor, becoming accepted as a peer by black students like Bertrand. Rachel earned acceptance across the boundary by (1) showing authentic, sincere respect to her black peers and the course material; (2) making repeated efforts at crossing; and (3) demonstrating in class discussion that she had the skills required to truly belong as a Black Studies student. . . . Rachel did not co-opt slang and try to pass as "black"— instead she tried to succeed as a *white* Black Studies minor. . . .

CONCLUSION

. . . People can and do cross the boundaries. Crossing costs, though. Some cross more successfully than others, weakening and/or reifying racial boundaries as they scale the walls. . . . In order to break down the system of racism, people must attempt to cross boundaries. They should do so reflexively, taking note of the effect they are having on people as they cross. People should cross sincerely, being as authentic as they can be so as to avoid reproducing damaging tropes. By successfully crossing, we nurture empathy. Only by crossing these boundaries can we dismantle the power of policing orthodoxy, which keeps people "in their place."

DISCUSSION QUESTIONS

1. Do you have a bridging story like those described by Kristen Myers?
2. Is it a surprise that naming the elephant in the room—whether it is race, sex, sexual orientation, disability, or social class—could build connections between people? If so, why do you think this comes as a surprise?
3. If you are trying to bridge boundaries, what are the key lessons you take away from Myers's analysis?

NOTES

1. I am giving whites the benefit of the double here. There is little evidence in the data that these whites wanted to cause harm. They were simply unreflective and over-entitled.
2. Most of their other coworkers were white, and they were not at the party.
3. Thorne calls her subjects "kids" rather than "children" in an attempt to use their own language for defining themselves.

REFERENCES

Feagin, Joe R., Hernan Vera, and Pinar Batur. 2001. *White Racism: The Basics*. New York: Routledge.

Parker, Pat. 1978. *Movement in Black*. Oakland, CA: Diana Press.

Thorne, Barrie. 1993. *Gender Play*. New Brunswick, NJ: Rutgers University Press.

Vera, Hernan. 2003. "Racism and the Aim of Society." Paper presented in the session, *Social Theory: Race and Equality*, American Sociological Association. August 2003, Chicago, IL.

READING 61

In Defense of Rich Kids

William Upski Wimsatt

My family never talked much about money, except to say that we were "middle-class . . . well maybe upper-middle-class." A few years ago, it became clear that both my parents and my grandmother had a lot more money than I realized. As an only child, I stood to inherit a nice chunk of it. I didn't know how much and I didn't know when. They did not want me to become spoiled or think I didn't have to work.

A lot of people will use this information to write me off. Oh, he's a rich kid. No wonder he could publish a book, probably with his parents' money. And why's he going around bragging about it?

William Upski Wimsatt is an award-winning reporter, essayist, and trend spotter. Author of *Bomb the Suburbs*, he has also written for the *Chicago Tribune* and *Vibe*.

What is he, stupid? Some of us have to work for a living, etc.

You can hate me if you want to. I am the beneficiary of a very unfair system. The system gives me tons of free money for doing nothing, yet it forces you to work two and three jobs just to get out of debt.

On top of that, I have the nerve to sit up here and talk about it and—for some it will seem—to rub it in. Most rich people are considerate enough to shut their mouths and pretend they're struggling too. To get on TV talking about, "I got this on sale."

I didn't really have anyone to talk about it with. I knew a lot of the kids I had gone to school with were in a similar situation but we never discussed our family money, except in really strange ways like how broke we were and how those other rich people were so spoiled/lucky. Our judgments of them betrayed our own underlying shame.

And let's talk right now about motives. As soon as you bring up philanthropy, people want to talk about motives. "Is he doing this for the right reasons or is he just doing this to make himself feel good?" Well, let me tell you, I am definitely doing this to make myself feel good and—call me crazy—I believe doing what you feel good about is one of the right reasons.

Yes, I have the luxury to give my money away because I know I'm going to inherit more later in life. But don't come to me with this bullshit, "Oh, it's easy for you to give away your money because you're gonna inherit more later." If it's so easy, how come more rich people aren't doing it? How come Americans only give 2% to charity across the board, whether they are rich, poor, or middle-class? I usually give away 20–30% of my income every year. But I just got my first steady job, so this year, if you throw in the book, I'll probably be giving away more like 50%.

Hell no, I'm not some kind of saint who has taken a vow of poverty and is now sitting in judgment of you or anyone else's money decisions. But be aware, it's easy to criticize my actions when you don't have much money. If you were in my situation, who's to say you'd be any different from 99% of other rich people who keep it all for themselves. Or if they do give it away, it's to big colleges, big arts, big religion, or big service, supporting bureaucratic institutions that maintain systemic problems by treating symptoms and obscuring root causes.

Which brings me to the next very selfish reason for my philanthropy. I have a political agenda and my philanthropic "generosity" plus my sense of strategy gives me more philanthropic power to change the world than people with 50 times my income.

The deeper reason why I give away my money is because I love the world. Because I'm grateful to be alive at all. Because I'm scared about where we're headed. Because we owe it to our great-grandchildren. Because we owe it to the millions of years of evolution it took to get us here. And to everyone before us who fought to change history and make things as good as they are now. Because I know how to change history and I know it takes money. Because I get more joy out of making things better for everyone than I get out of making things materially better for myself. Because I know how to make and spend money on myself. It's boring. There's no challenge in it. And no love in it. I love helping good things happen, and supporting people I believe in. Especially people and organizations that have NO money put into them by traditional foundations and charities. I'm not talking about your everyday charities like diabetes or your college(s) that already have multi-million dollar budgets set up to fight for them.

They're new.

They don't exist yet.

They're like diabetes in 1921, the year before they extracted insulin.

They're like your college the year before it was founded.

Don't get me wrong. My father has juvenile diabetes. And I love my college too. But the money supporting the Juvenile Diabetes Foundation, and my college is already so big, their fundraising operations so effective, that giving my money to them is a drop in the bucket.

For the organizing efforts I want to support, every dollar is like a seed, helping not only to create a new kind of organization, but an organization that will be copied and that decades from now will establish new fields of work. It is the most strategic way possible to change the course of history, and the most unpopular because it's so high-risk. . . .

THE MOST EFFECTIVE THING YOU EVER DO

. . . What if we could double the number of cool rich people who are funding social change from say five hundred to a thousand? Then we could double the number of organizers on the street, lawyers in the court rooms, lobbyists in Congress. Double the number of investigative reporters. There are so many people who want to do progressive work who can't because there aren't enough activist jobs. People come out of law school to become environmental lawyers and they end up having to defend corporations because they have to pay off their student loans. Environmental groups can't afford to hire them. The same goes for radical artists and journalists, forced to get jobs in advertising and public relations.

Five hundred more cool rich people could change all that.

Five hundred cool rich people could change the political landscape of this country.

Now don't get me wrong. I'm not saying philanthropy will solve all our problems, especially not the way 99% of it is done now. I'm not saying cool rich people are any more important or worthy than any other people. Poor people are made to feel like they aren't worth anything and that's wrong. I don't want to feed into that by focusing on rich people for a while. We need billions of people from billions of backgrounds trying billions of strategies to save this planet. It's just that every serious effort to change things takes people with money who understand how to support a movement. All these naive college or punk or hip-hop revolutionaries talking about, "Fuck that. I don't know any rich people and if I do they're assholes and anyway, I don't need their money." I only have one thing to say. Wait until your community center gets shut down. Wait until your broke grassroots genius friends start burning out because they have to do menial shit all day because they don't have the time or capital to make their dreams come true.

Consider these statistics. There are about five million millionaire households in the U.S. That's approximately one out of every 50 people. So, if you are a social person (not a hermit) and you are not currently serving a life sentence in prison, then chances are you will have the opportunity at some point in your life to get to know a number of people who are, at the very least, millionaires. Most of the time you will not know they are millionaires. Half of the time, millionaires don't even realize they are millionaires. My parents didn't realize they were. People usually have their assets tied up in many different forms such as houses, trusts, mutual funds, stocks, bonds and retirement accounts.

Less than 1% of all charitable giving ends up in the hands of people who are working to change the system. As Teresa Odendahl has pointed out in her ironically titled book *Charity Begins at Home,* contrary to popular belief, most charity money does not go to help poor children help themselves. The vast majority of money goes to big churches, big colleges, big hospitals, big arts and social service organizations which either directly cater to privileged people, or which treat the symptoms of social ills without ever addressing the root causes. . . .

Over the next 50 years, the upper-classes of my generation stand to inherit or earn the greatest personal fortune in history, while the lower classes both here and internationally will continue slipping deeper into poverty and debt.

That's where the Cool Rich Kids Movement comes in. Actually there isn't much of a "Cool Rich Kids Movement." That's just what I call the loose-knit network of maybe 100 of us young people with wealth who are in conversation with each other, and who support each other in taking small but significant actions. We are asking our parents to teach us about money. We are helping our families make responsible decisions about investments. Some of us are getting on the boards of family foundations or helping our families to start them. We introduce each other to amazing grassroots people to break

the isolation of wealth. We are just in the process of getting organized. We had our first conference last spring, sponsored by the Third Wave Foundation in New York. More are planned.

My goal is to get more young people with wealth in on the conversation. With five million millionaires in the U.S., even if we only spoke to the coolest 1% of all millionaire kids, that's still 50,000 people!

One half of the money I give away every year goes directly to grassroots youth activist organizations that I have a relationship with. (No, I don't make them kiss up to me. I just give it to them, thank them for their hard work and if they feel funny about it, I remind them that the only reason I have the money in the first place is because I've been so privileged and so many people have helped me. So it wasn't really "my" money to begin with. Oftentimes I have to *insist* that people take my money. We've all had so many bad experiences.)

The other half of my money I donate to organizing people with wealth.

That may seem strange at first.

Why give money to people who already have wealth?

From all my experience with grassroots organizations, I believe that organizing people with wealth is the most powerful work I do. And paradoxically, it is some of the hardest work to fundraise for because everybody including rich people thinks, "Why give rich people more money?" And that's why only a few dozen people in America have the job of helping rich people figure out how to come to terms with and do cool things with their money.

I think we need more of those people in the world.

So recently, I've changed my focus in a big way.

I joined the board of More Than Money. I am helping to start the Active Element Foundation, which is the first foundation that will specifically work with young donors on funding grassroots youth activism. And I'm also helping to start the Self-Education Foundation, which will tap successful people who either didn't like school or who dropped out to fund self-education resource centers which will support poor kids to take learning into their own hands. I am helping to organize a series of conferences around the country for young people with wealth, put on by The Third Wave Foundation and the Comfort Zone. . . .

I believe the most effective thing I do for the world every year is to buy gift subscriptions of *More Than Money Journal* for my privileged friends and to keep a ready supply of *Money Talks. So Can We.* for every cool young person I meet who has money. This is the most effective action I do. Any other possible action I could do, one cool rich person could hire ten more people to take my place.

But there's very little room in our culture to talk about having money and funding renegade work. Most rich people be like, "See you later." And most grassroots people be like, "It's easy for you because you're rich." There's resentment either way. People who aren't rich can play a huge role supporting us. So many of my friends who aren't wealthy act like, "Ha ha ha, going to your rich kids conference." That's not going to make me want to talk to you. If you are truly down to change the world, don't try to score points by alienating your rich friends with snide remarks. If you take the time to truly understand us and support us as people, more than likely, we will do the same for you. Rich people don't choose to be born rich any more than poor people choose to be born poor. The sickness of our society damages us each in different and complicated ways, and we sometimes forget that rich people get damaged too. Not just in a mocking way, like, "Oh, they're so spoiled." But in a real way. One of the most common ways privileged people get damaged is that we are taught not to talk about money. We put a wall around ourselves, and then it is hard for us to be honest with people who aren't rich. This makes us cold and creates a vicious cycle of not trusting and not sharing ourselves or our money.

There are only a few of us out here doing this work, which is why I have been thrust into the spotlight. It's a little ridiculous actually that I am speaking for rich kids when I haven't even inherited my money yet. But there was a deafening silence and someone needed to come out here and give us a bold public voice. Do you have any cool rich friends who may be looking for people in similar situations to talk to?

Hint: You do.

Please please please pass this along to them.

It just might be the most effective thing you ever do.

DISCUSSION QUESTIONS

1. Would you rather have money or a large number of supporters if you were seeking to create social change?
2. How much money would you want to have before you considered giving away some of it to create social change?

READING 62

Uprooting Racism: How White People Can Work for Racial Justice

Paul Kivel

"THANK YOU FOR BEING ANGRY"

A person of color who is angry about discrimination or harassment is doing us a service. That person is pointing out something wrong, something that contradicts the ideals of equality set forth in our Declaration of Independence and Bill of Rights. That person is bringing our attention to a problem that needs solving, a wrong that needs righting. We could convey our appreciation by saying, "Thank you, your anger has helped me see what's not right here." What keeps us from responding in this way?

Paul Kivel is a teacher, trainer, consultant, writer, and community educator on men's lives and violence, family and dating abuse, youth violence, racism, homophobia, and raising boys.

Anger is a scary emotion in our society. In mainstream white culture we are taught to be polite, never to raise our voices, to be reasonable and to keep calm. People who are demonstrative of their feelings are discounted and ridiculed. We are told by parents just to obey "because I said so." We are told by bosses, religious leaders and professional authorities not to challenge what they say, "or else" (or else you'll be fired, go to hell, be treated as "crazy"). When we do get angry we learn to stuff it, mutter under our breath and go away. We are taught to turn our anger inward in self-destructive behaviors. If we are men we are taught to take out our frustrations on someone weaker and smaller than we are.

When we have seen someone expressing anger, it has often been a person with power who was abusing us or someone else physically, verbally or emotionally. We were hurt, scared or possibly confused. Most of us can remember a time from our youth when a parent, teacher, coach, boss or other adult was yelling at us abusively. It made us afraid when those around us became angry. It made us afraid of our own anger.

A similar response is triggered when a person of color gets angry at us about racism. We become scared, guilty, embarrassed, confused and we fear everything is falling apart and we might get hurt. If the angry person would just calm down, or go away, we could get back to the big, happy family feeling.

Relationships between people of color and whites often begin as friendly and polite. We may be pleased that we know and like a person from another cultural group. We may be pleased that they like us. We are encouraged because despite our fears, it seems that it may be possible for people from different cultures to get along together. The friendships may confirm our feelings that we are different from other white people.

But then the person of color gets angry. Perhaps they are angry about something we do or say. Perhaps they are angry about a comment or action by someone else, or about racism in general. We may back off in response, fearing that the relationship is falling apart. We aren't liked anymore. We've been found out to be racist. For a person of color, this may be a time of hope that the relationship can become more intimate and honest. The anger may be an attempt to test the depths and possibilities of the friendship. They may be open about their feelings, to see how safe we are, hoping that we will not desert them. Or the anger may be a more assertive attempt to break through our complacency to address some core assumptions, beliefs or actions.

Many white people have been taught to see anger and conflict as a sign of failure. They may instead be signs that we're becoming more honest, dealing with the real differences and problems in our lives. If it is not safe enough to argue, disagree, express anger and struggle with each other what kind of relationship can it be?

We could say, "Thank you for pointing out the racism because I want to know whenever it is occurring." Or, "I appreciate your honesty. Let's see what we can do about this situation." More likely we get scared and disappear, or become defensive and counterattack. In any case, we don't focus on the root of the problem, and the racism goes unattended.

When people of color are angry about racism it is legitimate anger. It is not their oversensitivity, but our lack of sensitivity, that causes this communication gap. They are vulnerable to the abuse of racism every day. They are experts on it. White society, and most of us individually, rarely notice racism.

It is the anger and actions of people of color that call our attention to the injustice of racism. Sometimes that anger is from an individual person of color who is talking to us. At other times it is the rage of an entire community protesting, bringing legal action or burning down buildings. Such anger and action is almost always a last resort, a desperate attempt to get our attention when all else fails.

It is tremendously draining, costly and personally devastating for people of color to have to rage about racism. They often end up losing their friends, their livelihoods, even their lives. Rather than attacking them for their anger, we need to ask ourselves how many layers of complacency, ignorance, collusion, privilege and misinformation have we put into place for it to take so much outrage to get our attention?

The 1965 riots in Watts, as never before, brought our attention to the ravages of racism on the African-American population living there. In 1968 a national report by the Kerner Commission warned us of the dangers of not addressing racial problems. Yet in 1992, when there were new uprisings in Los Angeles, we focused again on the anger of African Americans, on containing that anger, protecting property and controlling the community, rather than on solving the problems that cause poverty, unemployment, crime and high drop-out rates. As soon as the anger was contained, we turned our attention elsewhere and left the underlying problems unaddressed. The only way to break this cycle of rage is for us to seriously address the sources of the anger, the causes of the problems. And in order to do that, we need to talk about racism directly with each other.

BEING A STRONG WHITE ALLY

What kind of active support does a strong white ally provide? People of color that I have talked with over the years have been remarkably consistent in describing the kinds of support they need from white allies. The following list is compiled from their statements at workshops I have facilitated. The focus here is on personal qualities and interpersonal relationships. More active interventions are discussed in the next part of [this discussion].

What people of color want from white allies:

"Respect"
"Find out about us"
"Don't take over"
"Provide information"
"Resources"
"Money"
"Take risks"
"Don't take it personally"
"Understanding"
"Teach your children about racism"
"Speak up"
"Don't be scared by my anger"
"Support"
"Listen"
"Don't make assumptions"
"Stand by my side"
"Don't assume you know what's best for me"
"Your body on the line"
"Make mistakes"
"Honesty"
"Talk to other white people"
"Interrupt jokes and comments"
"Don't ask me to speak for my people"

BASIC TACTICS

Every situation is different and calls for critical thinking about how to make a difference. Taking the statements above into account, I have compiled some general guidelines.

1. *Assume racism is everywhere, every day.* Just as economics influences everything we do, just as our gender and gender politics influence everything we do, assume that racism is affecting whatever is going on. We assume this because it's true, and because one of the privileges of being white is not having to see or deal with racism all the time. We have to learn to see the effect that racism has. Notice who speaks, what is said, how things are done and described. Notice who isn't present. Notice code words for race, and the implications of the policies, patterns and comments that are being expressed. You already notice the skin color of everyone you meet and interact with—now notice what difference it makes.

2. *Notice who is the center of attention and who is the center of power.* Racism works by directing violence and blame toward people of color and consolidating power and privilege for white people.

3. *Notice how racism is denied, minimized and justified.*

4. *Understand and learn from the history of whiteness and racism.* Notice how racism has changed over time and how it has subverted or resisted challenges. Study the tactics that have worked effectively against it.

5. *Understand the connections between racism, economic issues, sexism and other forms of injustice.*

6. *Take a stand against injustice.* Take risks. It is scary, difficult, risky and may bring up many feelings, but ultimately it is the only healthy and moral human thing to do. Intervene in situations where racism is being passed on.

7. *Be strategic.* Decide what is important to challenge and what's not. Think about strategy in particular situations. Attack the source of power.

8. *Don't confuse a battle with the war.* Behind particular incidents and interactions are larger patterns. Racism is flexible and adaptable. There will be gains and losses in the struggle for justice and equality.

9. *Don't call names or be personally abusive.* Since power is often defined as power over others—the ability to abuse or control people—it is easy to become abusive ourselves. However, we usually end up abusing people who have less power than we do because it is less dangerous. Attacking people doesn't address the systemic nature of racism and inequality.

10. *Support the leadership of people of color.* Do this consistently, but not uncritically.

11. *Don't do it alone.* You will not end racism by yourself. We can do it if we work together. Build support, establish networks, work with already established groups.

12. *Talk with your children and other young people about racism.*

IT'S NOT JUST A JOKE

"Let me tell you about the Chinaman who . . . " What do you do when someone starts to tell a joke which you think is likely to be a racial putdown? What do you do if the racial nature of the joke is only apparent at the punchline? How do you respond to a comment which contains a racial stereotype?

Interrupting racist comments can be scary because we risk turning the attack or anger toward us. We are sometimes accused of dampening the mood, being too serious or too sensitive. We may be ridiculed for being friends of the _____. People may think we're arrogant or trying to be politically correct. They may try to get back at us for embarrassing them. If you're in an environment where any of this could happen, then you know that it is not only not safe for you, it's even more unsafe for people of color.

People tell jokes and make comments sometimes out of ignorance, but usually knowing at some level that the comment puts down someone else and creates a collusion between the speaker and the listener. The joketeller is claiming that we're normal, intelligent and sane, and others are not. The effect is to exclude someone or some group of people from the group, to make it a little (or a lot) more unsafe for them to be there. Furthermore, by objectifying someone, it makes it that much easier for the next person to tell a joke, make a comment or take stronger action against any member of the objectified group.

The reverse is also true. Interrupting such behavior makes it less safe to harass or discriminate, and more safe for the intended targets of the abuse. Doing nothing is tacit approval and collusion with the abuse. There is no neutral stance. If someone is being attacked, even by a joke or teasing, there are no innocent bystanders.

As a white person you can play a powerful role in such a situation. When a person of color protests against being put down in an atmosphere where they are already disrespected, they are often discounted as well. You, as a white person interrupting verbal abuse, may be listened to and heeded because it breaks the collusion from other white people that was expected by the abuser. If a person of color speaks up first then you can support them by stating why you think it is right to challenge the comments. In either case, your intervention as a white person challenging racist comments is important and often effective.

What can you actually say in the presence of derogatory comments? There are no right or wrong answers. The more you do it the better you get. Even if it doesn't come off as you intended, you will influence others to be more sensitive and you will model the courage and integrity to interrupt verbal abuse. Following are suggestions for where to start.

If you can tell at the beginning that a joke is likely to be offensive or involves stereotypes and putdowns, you can say something like, "I don't want to hear a joke or story that reinforces stereotypes or puts down a group of people." Or, "Please stop right there. It sounds like your story is going to make fun of a group of people and I don't want to hear about it." Or, "I don't like humor that makes it unsafe for people here." Or, "I don't want to hear a joke that asks us to laugh at someone else's expense." There are many ways to say something appropriate without attacking or being offensive yourself.

Using "I" statements should be an important part of your strategy. Rather than attacking someone, it is stronger to state how you feel, what you want. Other people may still become defensive, but there is more opportunity for them to hear what you have to say if you word it as an "I" statement.

Often you don't know the story is offensive until the punchline. Or you just are not sure what you're hearing, but it makes you uncomfortable. It is appropriate to say afterwards that the joke was inappropriate because . . . , or the story was offensive because . . . , or it made you feel uncomfortable because . . . Trust your feelings about it!

In any of these interactions you may need to explain further why stories based on stereotypes reinforce abuse, and why jokes and comments that put people down are offensive. Rather than calling someone racist, or writing someone off, interrupting abuse is a way to do public education. It is a way to put what you know about racial stereotypes and abuse into action to stop them.

Often a person telling a racial joke is defensive about being called on the racism and may argue or defend themselves. You don't have to prove anything, although a good discussion of the issues is a great way to do more education. It's now up to the other person to think about your comments and to decide what to do. Everyone nearby will have heard you make a clear, direct statement challenging verbal abuse. Calling people's attention to something they assumed was innocent makes them more sensitive in the future and encourages them to stop and think about what they say about others.

Some of the other kinds of reactions you can expect are:

"It's only a joke." "It may 'only' be a joke but it is at someone's expense. It creates an environment that is less safe for the person or group being joked about. Abuse is not a joke."

"I didn't mean any harm." "I'm sure you didn't. But you should understand the harm that results even if you didn't mean it, and change what you say."

"Is this some kind of thought patrol?" "No, people can think whatever they want to. But we are responsible for what we say in public. A verbal attack is like any other kind of attack, it hurts the person attacked. Unless you intentionally want to hurt someone, you should not tell jokes or stories like this."

"This joke was told to me by a member of that group." "It really makes no difference who tells it. If it is offensive then it shouldn't be told. It is sad but true that some of us put down our own racial or ethnic group. That doesn't make it okay or less hurtful."

Sometimes the speaker will try to isolate you by saying that everyone else likes the story, everyone else laughed at the joke. At that point you might want to turn to the others and ask them if they like hearing jokes that are derogatory, do they like stories that attack people?

Sometimes the joke or derogatory comment will be made by a member of the racial group the comment is about. They may believe negative stereotypes about their racial group, they may want to separate themselves from others like themselves, or they may have accepted the racial norms of white peers in order to be accepted. In this situation it is more appropriate, and probably more effective, to talk to that person separately and express your concerns about how comments reinforce stereotypes and make the environment unsafe.

PERSONAL ACCOUNT

Where Are You From?

As a freshman at a predominantly white private college, I was confronted with a number of unusual situations. I was extremely young for a college freshman (I was sixteen), I was African American, and I was placed in upper-division courses, because of my academic background. So being accepted and fitting in were crucial to me.

I was enrolled in a course, political thought, with approximately thirty other students, mostly juniors and seniors who had taken courses with this professor before. I was the only African American in the class. During introductions for the first class, he never got around to letting me speak, even though he went alphabetically on the list (my last name begins with a "C"). Later, I began to be aware of his exclusion of me from class discussion.

By the third class, I guess he felt there was no longer any way he could avoid speaking to me. He asked me a few questions about myself—where I was from, what high school had I attended, and what was my major. His questions began to seem like a personal attack, and then finally he asked, "Why are you here?" "Where are you from?" I was quite taken aback by his line of questioning, when one of the upperclassmen (a white man) responded for me. "She's a freshman, Dr. B. Any more questions?" That guy became one of my closest friends. We have maintained contact ever since college. His response to Dr. B. totally changed the professor's way of treating me.

C.C.

Speaking out makes a difference. Even a defensive speaker will think about what you said and probably speak more carefully in the future. I have found that when I respond to jokes or comments, other people come up to me afterwards and say they are glad I said something because the comments bothered them too but they didn't know what to say. Many of us stand around, uneasy but hesitant to intervene. By speaking out we model effective intervention and encourage other people to do the same. We set a tone for being active rather than passive, challenging racism rather than colluding with it.

The response to your intervention also lets you know whether the abusive comments are intentional or unintentional, malicious or not. It will give you information about whether the speaker is willing to take responsibility for the effects words have on others. We all have a lot to learn about how racism hurts people. We need to move on from our mistakes, wiser from the process. No one should be trashed.

If the speaker persists in making racially abusive jokes or comments, then further challenge will only result in arguments and fights. People around them need to take the steps necessary to protect themselves

from abuse. You may need to think of other tactics to create a safe and respectful environment, including talking with peers to develop a plan for dealing with this person, or talking with a supervisor.

If you are in a climate where people are being put down, teased or made the butt of jokes based on their race, gender, sexual orientation, age or any other factor, you should investigate whether other forms of abuse such as sexual harassment or racial discrimination are occurring as well. Jokes and verbal abuse are obviously not the most important forms that racism takes. However, we all have the right to live, work and socialize in environments free from verbal and emotional harassment. In order to create contexts where white people and people of color can work together to challenge more fundamental forms of racism, we need to be able to talk to each other about the ways that we talk to each other.

DISCUSSION QUESTIONS

1. When is anger about racism appropriate?
2. What are some of the contradictions between the American ideals of equality and reality?

CREDITS

Gillian Carroll, "An Opportunity to Get Even"

Tara S. Ellison, "Living Invisibly"

Octavio N. Espinal, "Parents' Underestimated Love"

Ruth C. Feldsberg, "What's in a Name?"

Francisco Hernandez, "Just Something You Did as a Man"

Sarah Herschler, "My Secret"

Eric Jackson, "My Strategies"

Sandra Pamela Maida, "How I Learned to Appreciate Printers"

Anthony McNeill, "Just Like My Mama Said"

Isabelle Nguyen, "Let Me Work for It!"

Tim Norton, "He Hit Her"

LeiLani Page, "Lucky Americans"

Rose B. Pascarell, "That Moment of Visibility"

Mindy Peral, "The Best of Both Worlds"

Sherri H. Pereira, "I Thought My Race Was Invisible"

Hoorie I. Siddique, "I Am a Pakistani Woman"

Photo Credits:

page 1, Photodisc

page 193, © Bob Daemmrich/The Image Works

page 250, (top) AP Photo/Dave Martin, (bottom) Chris Graythen/Getty Images

page 333, Hisham F. Ibrahim/Getty Images

page 467, David Young-Wolff/PhotoEdit

INDEX

A page number followed by *b* indicates a box; one followed by *fig* indicates an illustrated figure; one followed by *n* indicates a note; one followed by *t* indicates a table.